ASCENT

CENTER FOR TECHNICAL KNOWLEDGE

Autodesk® Inventor® 2021 Introduction to Solid Modeling Part 2

Learning Guide

Mixed Units - 1st Edition

AUTODESK.

Authorized Publisher

ASCENT - Center for Technical Knowledge®
Autodesk® Inventor® 2021
Introduction to Solid Modeling - Part 2
Mixed Units - 1st Edition

Prepared and produced by:

ASCENT Center for Technical Knowledge
630 Peter Jefferson Parkway, Suite 175
Charlottesville, VA 22911

866-527-2368
www.ASCENTed.com

Lead Contributor: Jennifer MacMillan

ASCENT - Center for Technical Knowledge (a division of Rand Worldwide Inc.) is a leading developer of professional learning materials and knowledge products for engineering software applications. ASCENT specializes in designing targeted content that facilitates application-based learning with hands-on software experience. For over 25 years, ASCENT has helped users become more productive through tailored custom learning solutions.

We welcome any comments you may have regarding this guide, or any of our products. To contact us please email: feedback@ASCENTed.com.

AS-INV2101-ISM1MU-SG2 // IS-INV2101-ISM1MU-SG2

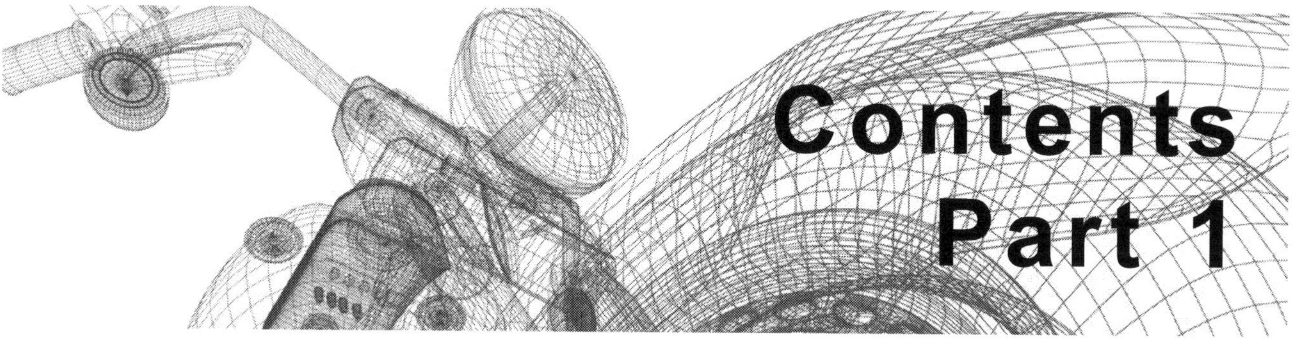

Contents Part 1

Preface .... **xvii**

In This Guide .... **xxi**

Practice Files .... **xxiii**

Chapter 1: Introduction to Autodesk Inventor **1-1**

1.1 Introduction **1-2**

1.2 Autodesk Inventor Fundamentals **1-4**
- Feature-Based Modeling 1-4
- Parametric Features 1-6
- Associative 1-7
- Assembly Management 1-7
- Model Documentation 1-7

1.3 Getting Started **1-8**
- My Home 1-8
- Project Files 1-10
- Opening Files 1-11

1.4 Autodesk Inventor Interface **1-12**
- Interface 1-12
- Modeling Tools 1-17
- Accessing Help 1-20

1.5 Model Manipulation **1-22**
- Model Orientation 1-22
- Model Display 1-27
- Object Selection 1-28
- Entity Selection 1-30

Practice 1a Open and Manipulate a Part **1-32**

Chapter Review Questions **1-50**

Command Summary **1-53**

Chapter 2: Creating the Base Feature **2-1**

2.1 Creating a New Part File **2-2**
Using the Default Template 2-2
Selecting a Template 2-3
Origin Features 2-5

2.2 Sketched Base Features **2-6**
Setting an Origin Plane as Default 2-8
Grid and Axis Display 2-9
Sketch Entities 2-10
Sketching Revolved Sections 2-11
Dynamic Input & Dimensioning for Sketching 2-12
Dimensioning 2-12
Constraining 2-16
Depth 2-20
Direction 2-20

2.3 Editing Sketched Features **2-23**
Show Dimensions 2-23
Sketch Visibility 2-24
Edit Sketch 2-24
Edit Feature 2-25
Show Input 2-25
Change the Sketch Plane 2-25

Practice 2a Extruded Base Features I **2-26**

Practice 2b Extruded Base Features II **2-38**

Practice 2c Revolved Base Feature **2-44**

Practice 2d Additional Parts **2-49**

Chapter Review Questions **2-50**

Command Summary **2-54**

Chapter 3: Additional Sketching Tools **3-1**

3.1 Additional Entity Types **3-2**
Tangent Arc Using a Line 3-5
Tangent Line Between Two Circles/Arcs 3-5
Fillets and Chamfers 3-6
Point Snaps 3-8
Construction Entities 3-8

3.2 Basic Editing Tools **3-10**
Trim 3-10
Extend 3-10
Mirror 3-11

3.3 Additional Constraint Tools 3-12
Reviewing Existing Constraints 3-12
Reviewing Degrees of Freedom 3-12
Assigning Constraints 3-13
Over Constraining Entities 3-18
Constraint Settings 3-19
Deleting Constraints 3-22
Relax Mode 3-22

3.4 Additional Dimension Tools 3-24
Center Dimensions 3-24
Radius/ Diameter Dimensions 3-24
Angular Dimensions 3-25
Tangent Dimensions 3-25
Revolved Sketch Dimensions 3-26
Arc Length Dimensions 3-26
Dimension Types 3-27
Over Dimensioned Entities 3-27

Practice 3a Apply Constraints 3-28

Practice 3b Create Sketched Geometry I 3-33

Practice 3c Create Sketched Geometry II 3-40

Practice 3d Create Sketched Geometry III 3-46

Practice 3e (Optional) Manipulating Entities 3-51

Chapter Review Questions 3-52

Command Summary 3-56

Chapter 4: Sketch Editing Tools 4-1

4.1 Advanced Editing Tools 4-2
Move, Copy, Rotate, Scale, and Stretch 4-2
Split 4-5
Copy and Paste 4-5

4.2 Rectangular Sketch Patterns 4-6

4.3 Circular Sketch Patterns 4-8

4.4 Sketch Preferences 4-10
Application Options 4-10
Document Settings 4-11

Practice 4a Sketch Editing Tools 4-12

Practice 4b Copy and Paste a Sketch 4-17

Practice 4c Pattern Sketched Entities 4-21

Chapter Review Questions 4-26

Command Summary 4-28

Chapter 5: Sketched Secondary Features 5-1

5.1 Sketched Secondary Features 5-2

5.2 Using Existing Geometry 5-7
Offset 5-7
Projected Geometry 5-8
Share Sketch 5-9
Using AutoCAD Data in Inventor 5-10

5.3 Sketching Tips 5-12
Dynamic Input & Dimensioning for Sketching 5-12
Precise Input 5-12

Practice 5a Create a Sketched Revolve 5-15

Practice 5b Create Sketched Extrusions 5-19

Practice 5c Share Sketch 5-26

Practice 5d (Optional) Create a Sketch Using Precise Coordinates 5-29

Chapter Review Questions 5-37

Command Summary 5-41

Chapter 6: Creating Pick and Place Features 6-1

6.1 Edge Chamfer 6-2

6.2 Constant Fillets 6-7
Continuity 6-10
Additional Fillet Options 6-11

6.3 Variable Fillets 6-14

6.4 Face Fillets 6-18

6.5 Full Round Fillets 6-20

6.6 Holes 6-22
Linear Placement 6-29
Concentric Placement 6-31
Placing Multiple Holes 6-32
Hole Presets 6-32

6.7 Threads 6-34

6.8 Editing Pick and Place Features 6-36

6.9 Creation Sequence 6-37

Practice 6a Add Pick and Place Features 6-38

Practice 6b Create a Coaxial Hole 6-48

Practice 6c Add Fillets 6-52

Practice 6d (Optional) Adding Pick and Place Features 6-58
Chapter Review Questions 6-59
Command Summary 6-62

Chapter 7: Work Features 7-1
7.1 Work Planes 7-2
7.2 Work Axes 7-7
7.3 Work Points 7-10
Practice 7a Using Work Features to Create Geometry I 7-13
Practice 7b Using Work Features to Create Geometry II 7-17
Practice 7c (Optional) Using Work Features to Create Geometry III 7-23
Chapter Review Questions 7-31
Command Summary 7-33

Chapter 8: Equations 8-1
8.1 Equations 8-2
8.2 Parameters 8-8
Model Parameters 8-8
User Parameters 8-9
Practice 8a Add Equations 8-13
Practice 8b Add Parameters 8-17
Practice 8c Working with Parameters 8-23
Chapter Review Questions 8-33
Command Summary 8-36

Chapter 9: Additional Features 9-1
9.1 Face Draft 9-2
9.2 Splitting a Face or Solid 9-12
9.3 Shells 9-15
9.4 Ribs 9-19
Practice 9a Create Shell and Ribs 9-25
Practice 9b Create Ribs with Bosses 9-29
Practice 9c Splitting a Face 9-34
Chapter Review Questions 9-39
Command Summary 9-41

Chapter 10: Model and Display Manipulation 10-1

10.1 Reordering Features 10-2

10.2 Inserting Features 10-3

10.3 Suppressing Features 10-4

10.4 Section Views 10-6

10.5 Design Views 10-8

Practice 10a Section and Design Views 10-9

Practice 10b Feature Order 10-15

Chapter Review Questions 10-23

Command Summary 10-26

Chapter 11: Fixing Problems 11-1

11.1 Sketch Failure 11-2

11.2 Feature Failure 11-4
Sketch Doctor 11-4
Design Doctor 11-6

Practice 11a Resolve Sketch Problems 11-9

Practice 11b Resolve Feature Failure 11-13

Chapter Review Questions 11-16

Command Summary 11-18

Chapter 12: Sweep Features 12-1

12.1 Sweep Features 12-2

Practice 12a Creating Swept Geometry I 12-7

Practice 12b Creating Swept Geometry II 12-12

Practice 12c (Optional) Additional Swept Geometry 12-16

Chapter Review Questions 12-17

Command Summary 12-19

Chapter 13: Loft Features 13-1

13.1 Rail and Center Line Lofts 13-2

13.2 Advanced Loft Options 13-6
Conditions Tab 13-6
Transition Tab 13-11

Practice 13a Rail Lofts 13-12

Practice 13b Center Line Loft 13-15

Practice 13c Loft Creation I 13-17

Practice 13d (Optional) Loft Creation II **13-24**
Chapter Review Questions **13-28**
Command Summary **13-30**

Chapter 14: Duplication Tools **14-1**
14.1 Rectangular Feature Patterns **14-2**
14.2 Circular Feature Patterns **14-9**
14.3 Sketched Driven Patterns **14-14**
14.4 Mirror Parts or Features **14-17**
14.5 Manipulate Patterns and Mirror Features **14-19**
Suppress Patterns 14-19
Edit Pattern 14-19
Delete Patterns 14-19
Practice 14a Pattern Features **14-20**
Practice 14b Mirror a Model **14-27**
Practice 14c Mirror Features **14-29**
Chapter Review Questions **14-32**
Command Summary **14-35**

Chapter 15: Feature Relationships **15-1**
15.1 Establishing Relationships **15-2**
Pick and Place Features 15-2
Sketched Features 15-3
15.2 Controlling Relationships **15-7**
15.3 Investigating Relationships **15-8**
Model Browser 15-8
Equations 15-9
15.4 Changing Relationships **15-10**
Practice 15a Change Feature Relationships **15-12**
Practice 15b Delete a Sketch Plane **15-15**
Chapter Review Questions **15-17**

Appendix A: Sketching Options **A-1**
A.1 Sketch Geometry Creation Options **A-2**
A.2 Sketch Editing Options **A-5**
A.3 Sketch Constraint Options **A-6**
A.4 Dimension Type Options **A-7**

Appendix B: Primitive Base Features B-1

B.1 Primitive Base Features B-2

Practice B1 Creating a Primitive B-6

Appendix C: Additional Practices I C-1

Practice C1 Part Creation C-2

Practice C2 Creating a Sweep and Loft... C-11

Index Index-1

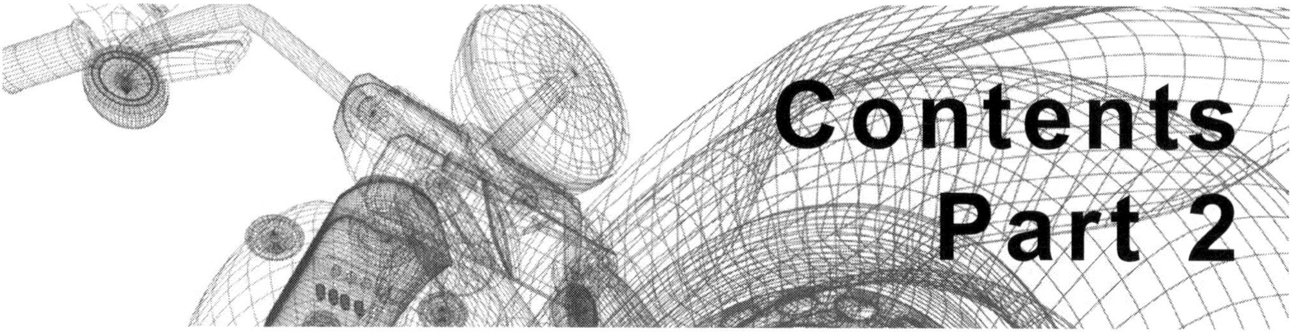

Contents Part 2

Preface .... **xvii**

In This Guide .... **xxi**

Practice Files .... **xxiii**

Chapter 16: Assembly Environment **16-1**

- **16.1 Assembling Components Using Constraints** **16-2**
  - Assembly Examples 16-12
- **16.2 Assemble Mini-Toolbar** **16-16**
- **16.3 Content Center** **16-19**
  - Searching the Content Center 16-20
- **16.4 Assembly Browser** **16-21**
- **16.5 Saving Files** **16-23**
- **Practice 16a Assembly Basics I (Constraints)** **16-24**
- **Chapter Review Questions** **16-44**
- **Command Summary** **16-50**

Chapter 17: Joint Connections **17-1**

- **17.1 Assembling Components Using Joints** **17-2**
- **Practice 17a Assembly Basics II (Joints)** **17-14**
- **Practice 17b Assembly Basics III** **17-27**
- **Chapter Review Questions** **17-31**
- **Command Summary** **17-34**

Chapter 18: Manipulating Assembly Display **18-1**

- **18.1 Moving and Rotating Assembly Components** **18-2**
  - Moving Components 18-2
  - Rotating Components 18-3
  - Updating the Assembly 18-4

18.2 Suppressing Constraints 18-5

18.3 Component Display 18-6
Visible Components 18-6
Enabling Components 18-6
Isolating Components 18-7
Transparent Components 18-8
Section Views 18-8
Design Views 18-10

18.4 Selection Options in Assemblies 18-14

Practice 18a Assemble Components 18-16

Chapter Review Questions 18-25

Command Summary 18-29

Chapter 19: Model Information 19-1

19.1 Measurement Tools 19-2
Measuring Entities and Points 19-3
Measure the Distance Between Components 19-4
Measuring an Angle 19-5
Measuring Planar Faces 19-6
Measuring Cylindrical Faces 19-6
Restart a Measurement 19-7
Add to Accumulate 19-7
Context Sensitive Measurements 19-8
Using Measure When Entering Required Values 19-8
Region Properties 19-9

19.2 Model Properties 19-10
iProperties 19-10
Model Color 19-12

Practice 19a Properties and Measurements 19-13

Practice 19b (Optional) Model Measurements 19-19

Chapter Review Questions 19-21

Command Summary 19-23

Chapter 20: Presentation Files 20-1

20.1 Creating Presentations 20-2

20.2 Storyboards 20-5
Animations 20-6
Actions 20-14
Playing a Storyboard 20-18

20.3 Snapshot Views 20-19
Creating Snapshots from a Storyboard 20-19
Creating Independent Snapshots 20-20

Editing a Snapshot View 20-21
Creating a Drawing View from a Snapshot View 20-22

20.4 Publishing a Presentation File 20-24

Practice 20a Create an Animation 20-27

Practice 20b Create Snapshots 20-39

Chapter Review Questions 20-45

Command Summary 20-47

Chapter 21: Assembly Tools 21-1

21.1 Replacing Components 21-2
Replace Components 21-2
Save and Replace Components 21-2

21.2 Duplicating Components 21-3
Mirror 21-3
Copy 21-4
Pattern 21-5

21.3 Restructuring Components 21-6
Promote 21-7
Demote 21-7
Assembly Folders 21-8

21.4 Driving Constraints 21-9

21.5 Contact Solver 21-11

21.6 Interference 21-13

21.7 Error Recovery 21-16

Practice 21a Using Assembly Tools 21-17

Practice 21b Replacing Components 21-22

Practice 21c Restructuring the Assembly 21-26

Practice 21d Controlling Assembly Motion 21-29

Chapter Review Questions 21-35

Command Summary 21-38

Chapter 22: Assembly Parts and Features 22-1

22.1 Assembly Parts 22-2

22.2 Assembly Features 22-5
Participant Parts 22-5

Practice 22a Creating Parts and Features in an Assembly 22-7

Chapter Review Questions 22-18

Command Summary 22-20

Chapter 23: Assembly Bill of Materials 23-1

23.1 Create Virtual Components 23-2

23.2 Create Bill of Materials 23-4
BOM Structure 23-7
Quantity 23-9
Equivalent Components 23-9
Material 23-9
Column and Row Organization 23-10
Item Numbering 23-10
Part Number Merge Settings 23-13

Practice 23a Bill of Materials 23-15

Chapter Review Questions 23-23

Command Summary 23-25

Chapter 24: Working with Projects 24-1

24.1 Project Files 24-2
Activating a Project File 24-3
Loading a Project File 24-3
Creating a New Project File 24-3
Project Tree Customization 24-5
Search Sequence 24-7

24.2 Resolving Links 24-9

Practice 24a Creating a Project File 24-12

Chapter Review Questions 24-18

Command Summary 24-20

Chapter 25: Drawing Basics 25-1

25.1 Creating a New Drawing 25-2

25.2 Base and Projected Views 25-4
Base Views 25-4
Projected Views 25-7
Raster Views 25-8

25.3 Additional Drawing Views 25-10
Auxiliary Views 25-10
Section Views 25-11
Detailed Views 25-13
Overlay Views 25-14
Draft Views 25-16
Break Views 25-17
Break Out Views 25-18
Slice Views 25-19
Crop Views 25-20

25.4 Manipulating Views 25-22
Delete Views 25-22
Suppress Views 25-22
Move Views 25-23
View Orientation 25-23
Transparent Components 25-23
View Alignment 25-23
Change View Scale 25-24
Editing View Labels 25-24
Replace Models 25-25
View Properties 25-26
Editing Sheets 25-26

Practice 25a Create a Drawing I 25-27

Practice 25b Create a Drawing II 25-38

Practice 25c Create a Drawing III 25-42

Chapter Review Questions 25-45

Command Summary 25-49

Chapter 26: Detailing Drawings 26-1

26.1 Dimensions 26-2
Model Dimensions 26-2
Drawing Dimensions 26-4
Editing Drawing Dimensions 26-10
Dimension Styles 26-12

26.2 Drawing Sheets 26-14

26.3 Parts List 26-16
Creating the Parts List 26-16
Editing the Parts List 26-18

26.4 Balloons 26-22
Placing Balloons Individually 26-22
Placing Balloons Globally 26-23
Manipulating Balloons 26-23

26.5 Styles and Standards 26-25
Standards 26-26
Styles 26-27

26.6 Hatching 26-29

Practice 26a Detailing a Drawing I 26-31

Practice 26b Detailing a Drawing II 26-42

Practice 26c (Optional) Create a Drawing 26-49

Chapter Review Questions 26-50

Command Summary 26-54

Chapter 27: Drawing Annotations **27-1**

27.1 Text **27-2**
Modifying Text 27-3
Adding Model or User Parameters as Text 27-4
Adding Properties as Text 27-5

27.2 Symbols **27-6**

27.3 Hole and Thread Notes **27-8**
Creating a Hole or Thread Note 27-8
Adding Text to a Hole Note 27-8
Editing a Hole Note 27-9
Hole Quantity in Notes 27-9
Hiding Hole or Thread Note Values 27-10

27.4 Chamfer Notes **27-11**
Creating Chamfer Notes 27-11
Editing Chamfer Notes 27-11

27.5 Center Marks and Center Lines **27-13**
Center Marks 27-13
Center Line 27-13
Center Line Bisector 27-14
Centered Pattern 27-14

27.6 Hole Tables **27-15**
Editing Hole Tables or Tags 27-17

27.7 Revision Tables and Tags **27-18**
Editing the Revision Table Format 27-18
Revision Tags 27-20

Practice 27a Adding Text and Symbols **27-21**

Practice 27b Notes, Center Marks, and Center Lines **27-29**

Practice 27c Adding a Revision Table and Tags **27-35**

Practice 27d Adding Hole Tables **27-40**

Chapter Review Questions **27-44**

Command Summary **27-46**

Chapter 28: Customizing Autodesk Inventor **28-1**

28.1 Application Options **28-2**
General Tab 28-2
File Tab 28-2
Colors Tab 28-3
Display Tab 28-3
Drawing Tab 28-3
Prompts Tab 28-4
Sketch Tab 28-4
Part Tab 28-5
Assembly Tab 28-6

28.2 Document Settings 28-7
Standard Tab 28-7
Units Tab 28-7
Sketch Tab 28-8
Modeling Tab 28-9
Bill of Materials Tab 28-10
Default Tolerance Tab 28-10
Drawing Tab 28-11
Sheet Tab 28-11

28.3 File Properties 28-12

28.4 Changing Part Units 28-14

28.5 Command Customization 28-15
Ribbon 28-15
Keyboard 28-17
Marking Menu 28-19

Practice 28a Customizing File Properties 28-21

Chapter Review Questions 28-25

Command Summary 28-28

Appendix D: Effective Modeling Final Review D-1

D.1 Design Considerations D-2
Part Design Considerations D-2
Assembly Design Considerations D-2

D.2 Modeling Tips and Techniques D-3
Capturing Design Intent D-3
Features D-3
Face Drafts and Fillets D-5

D.3 Model Investigation D-7
Model Browser D-7
Equations D-8
Measuring Options D-8

Appendix E: Additional Practices II E-1

Practice E1 Assembling with Joints E-2

Practice E2 Turntable Assembly E-23

Practice E3 Assembly Parts and Features E-29

Practice E4 Drawing Creation I E-36

Practice E5 Drawing Creation II E-37

Practice E6 Drawing Creation III E-39

Index Index-1

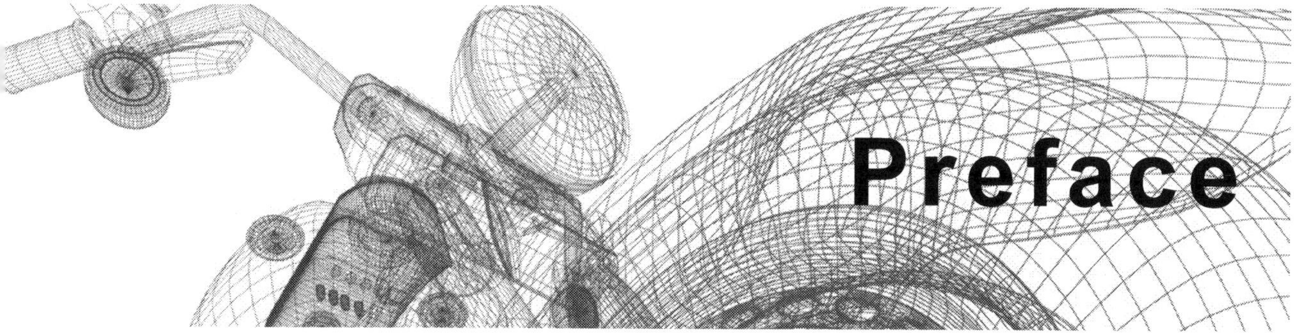

Preface

The *Autodesk® Inventor® 2021: Introduction to Solid Modeling* guide provides you with an understanding of the parametric design philosophy through a hands-on, practice-intensive curriculum. You will learn the key skills and knowledge required to design models using Autodesk Inventor, starting with conceptual sketching, through to solid modeling, assembly design, and drawing production.

Topics Covered

- Understanding the Autodesk Inventor software interface
- Creating, constraining, and dimensioning 2D sketches
- Creating and editing the solid base 3D feature from a sketch
- Creating and editing secondary solid features that are sketched and placed
- Creating equations and working with parameters
- Manipulating the display of the model
- Resolving feature failures
- Duplicating geometry in the model
- Placing and constraining/connecting parts in assemblies
- Manipulating the display of components in an assembly
- Obtaining model measurements and property information
- Creating Presentation files (Exploded views)
- Modifying and analyzing the components in an assembly
- Simulating motion in an assembly
- Creating parts and features in assemblies
- Creating and editing an assembly Bill of Materials
- Working with projects
- Creating and annotating drawings and views
- Customizing the Autodesk Inventor environment

Prerequisites

- Access to the 2021.0 version of the software, to ensure compatibility with this guide. Future software updates that are released by Autodesk may include changes that are not reflected in this guide. The practices and files included with this guide are not compatible with prior versions (i.e., 2020).
- As an introductory guide, *Autodesk® Inventor® 2021: Introduction to Solid Modeling* does not assume prior knowledge of any 3D modeling or CAD software. You need to be experienced with the Windows operating system, and having a background in drafting of 3D parts is recommended.

Note on Software Setup

This guide assumes a standard installation of the software using the default preferences during installation. Lectures and practices use the standard software templates and default options for the Content Libraries.

Students and Educators Can Access Free Autodesk Software and Resources

Autodesk challenges you to get started with free educational licenses for professional software and creativity apps used by millions of architects, engineers, designers, and hobbyists today. Bring Autodesk software into your classroom, studio, or workshop to learn, teach, and explore real-world design challenges the way professionals do.

Get started today - register at the Autodesk Education Community and download one of the many Autodesk software applications available.

Visit www.autodesk.com/education/home/

Note: Free products are subject to the terms and conditions of the end-user license and services agreement that accompanies the software. The software is for personal use for education purposes and is not intended for classroom or lab use.

Lead Contributor: Jennifer MacMillan

With a dedication for engineering and education, Jennifer has spent over 20 years at ASCENT managing courseware development for various CAD products. Trained in Instructional Design, Jennifer uses her skills to develop instructor-led and web-based training products as well as knowledge profiling tools.

Jennifer has achieved the Autodesk Certified Professional certification for Inventor and is also recognized as an Autodesk Certified Instructor (ACI). She enjoys teaching the training courses that she authors and is also very skilled in providing technical support to end-users.

Jennifer holds a Bachelor of Engineering Degree as well as a Bachelor of Science in Mathematics from Dalhousie University, Nova Scotia, Canada.

Jennifer MacMillan has been the Lead Contributor for *Autodesk Inventor: Introduction to Solid Modeling* since 2007.

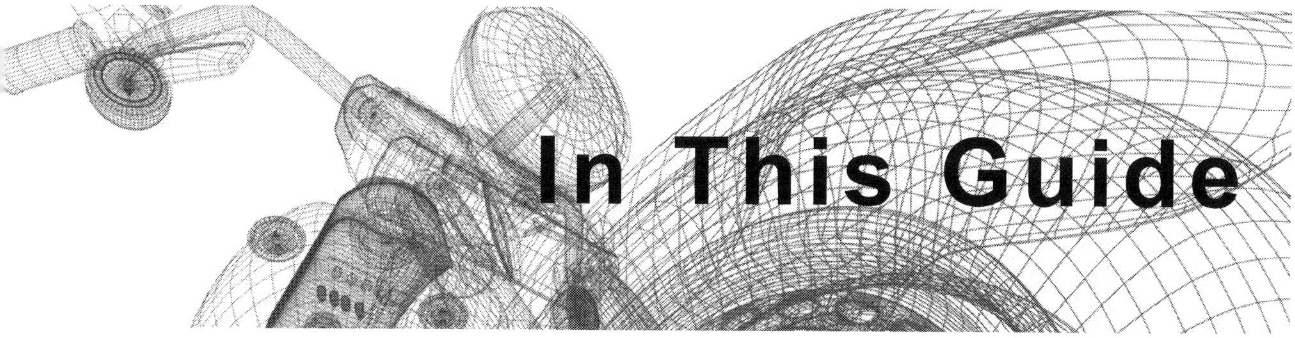

In This Guide

The following highlights the key features of this guide.

Feature	Description
Practice Files	The Practice Files page includes a link to the practice files and instructions on how to download and install them. The practice files are required to complete the practices in this guide.
Chapters	A chapter consists of the following - Learning Objectives, Instructional Content, Practices, Chapter Review Questions, and Command Summary. • **Learning Objectives** define the skills you can acquire by learning the content provided in the chapter. • **Instructional Content**, which begins right after Learning Objectives, refers to the descriptive and procedural information related to various topics. Each main topic introduces a product feature, discusses various aspects of that feature, and provides step-by-step procedures on how to use that feature. Where relevant, examples, figures, helpful hints, and notes are provided. • **Practice** for a topic follows the instructional content. Practices enable you to use the software to perform a hands-on review of a topic. It is required that you download the practice files (using the link found on the Practice Files page) prior to starting the first practice. • **Chapter Review Questions**, located close to the end of a chapter, enable you to test your knowledge of the key concepts discussed in the chapter. • **Command Summary** concludes a chapter. It contains a list of the software commands that are used throughout the chapter and provides information on where the command can be found in the software.
Appendices	Appendices provide additional information to the main course content. It could be in the form of instructional content, practices, tables, projects, or skills assessment.

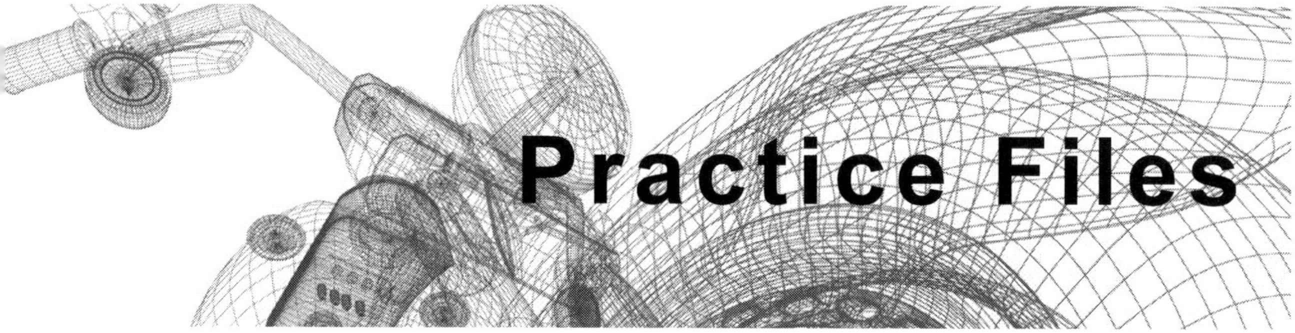

Practice Files

To download the practice files for this guide, use the following steps:

1. Type the URL ***exactly as shown below*** into the address bar of your Internet browser, to access the Course File Download page.

   Note: If you are using the ebook, you do not have to type the URL. Instead, you can access the page simply by clicking the URL below.

   https://www.ascented.com/getfile/id/maculinea

2. On the Course File Download page, click the **DOWNLOAD NOW** button, as shown below, to download the .ZIP file that contains the practice files.

3. Once the download is complete, unzip the file and extract its contents.

   The recommended practice files folder location is:
   C:\Autodesk Inventor 2021 Intro Practice Files

   Note: It is recommended that you do not change the location of the practice files folder. Doing so may cause errors when completing the practices.

Stay Informed!

To receive information about upcoming events, promotional offers, and complimentary webcasts, visit:

www.ASCENTed.com/updates

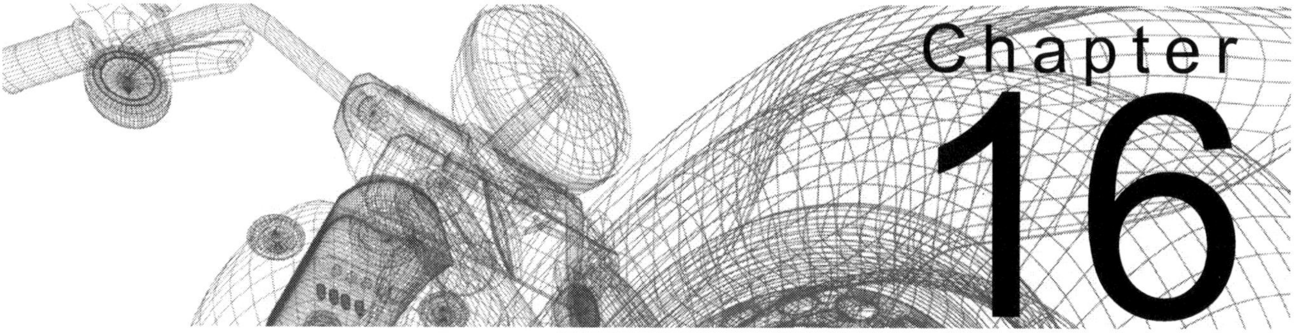

Assembly Environment

An assembly file in Autodesk® Inventor® enables you to combine the components that have been modeled to create a top-level assembly that communicates how all the components are combined. Both parts and other assemblies, referred to as subassemblies, can be referenced in an assembly.

Learning Objectives in This Chapter

- Create a new assembly file using a standard template.
- Place, constrain, and edit components in an assembly file.
- Place a selected family member from the Content Center into an assembly.
- Use the Model browser to find items, filter information, and switch between the Modeling and Assembly views for an assembly.
- Save new and existing assembly files.

16.1 Assembling Components Using Constraints

You place and constrain components to create an assembly. Constraints are specified to locate components parametrically with respect to other components. Similar to the dependencies between features in a part, relationships also exist in an assembly when components are assembled relative to one another.

General Steps

Use the following general steps to create an assembly and place components:

1. Create an assembly file.
2. Place components in the assembly file.
3. Drag parts and display degrees of freedom.
4. Select a constraint type.
5. Select references on the components.
6. Assign an offset value, as required.
7. Repeat Step 4 to Step 6 until the components are fully constrained.
8. Complete the component placement.
9. Edit the component placement, as required.

Step 1 - Create an assembly file.

*You can also open the New File dialog box by clicking (New) in the Quick Access Toolbar or in the **File** menu.*

The first step in creating an assembly is to start a new file based on an assembly template. This can be done using the *My Home* tab in the graphics window and by clicking **Assembly** to create an assembly with the default template. Alternatively, in the *Get Started* tab>Launch panel, click (New), select an .IAM template in the Create New File dialog box, and click **Create**.

Step 2 - Place components in the assembly file.

To add a component to the assembly, in the *Assemble* tab>Component panel, click (Place). In the Place Component dialog box, select the component to add and click **Open**. It is possible to select multiple components by holding <Ctrl> or <Shift> while selecting.

Components that can be added to an assembly include parts (.IPT), library components, and other assembly models called subassemblies (.IAM). Subassemblies act as single components.

To locate the first component, you can freely place it in the assembly or ground it to the assembly coordinate system (0,0,0).

- To freely locate the component in the assembly, click in the graphics window with the left mouse button to place it.
- To ground the component, right-click and select **Place Grounded at Origin** in the marking menu as shown in Figure 16–1.

*Before locating a component in the assembly you can use **Rotate X 90**, **Rotate Y 90**, or **Rotate Z 90** to reorient the model before placement.*

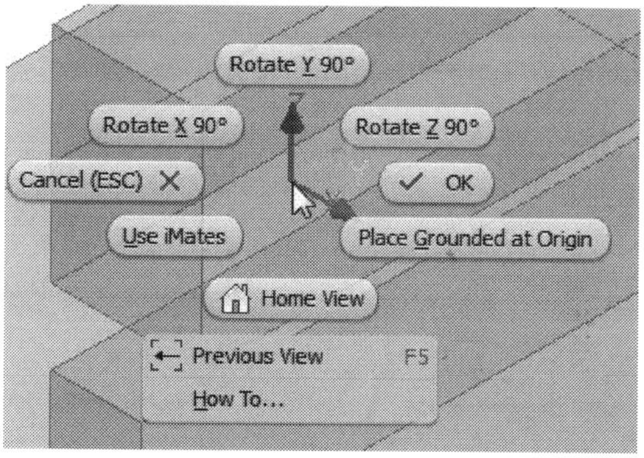

Figure 16–1

Once placed freely or grounded, a second instance of the component is immediately available for further placement. To complete the operation without assembling any additional instances of the same component, right-click and select **Cancel [Esc]** or **OK**. Alternatively, you can press <Esc>.

It is good practice to ground at least one component. This component serves as the base on which the rest of the assembly is built. To automatically ground the first assembled component, set the ***Place and ground first component at origin*** *option in the Assembly tab in the Application Options dialog box.*

In the *Assemble* tab>Component panel, click (Place) to add additional components to the assembly. Any secondary component can also be grounded, if required by right-clicking and selecting **Place Grounded at Origin** in the marking menu.

- Grounded parts are indicated by the pushpin symbol in the Model browser and by at the cursor when the model is highlighted, as shown in Figure 16–2.

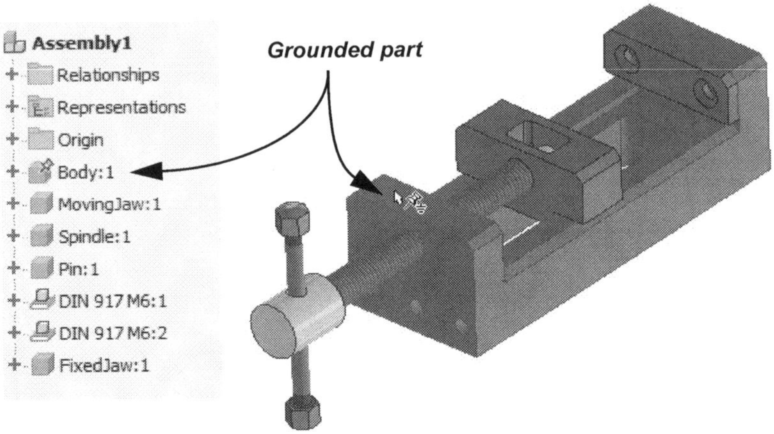

Figure 16–2

- To unground the first part, or to ground another assembly component, right-click on it in the assembly window or Model browser and clear the **Grounded** option.

Repeat these steps to add all of the required components.

Step 3 - Drag parts and display degrees of freedom.

Once components are placed in the assembly, you can begin constraining any non-grounded components. To prepare for constraining you might want to move them. This can be done using any of the following methods:

- To drag a part, select it and drag it to a new location in the assembly window (hold the left mouse button while dragging). Alternatively, you can use (Free Move) in the *Assemble* tab>Position panel.

- To rotate a single component in the assembly, in the *Assemble* tab>Position panel, click (Free Rotate) and select the component. Similar to globally rotating the assembly, hold the left mouse button while dragging to rotate only the selected component.

An unconstrained component has six degrees of freedom. It can translate in three directions (X, Y, and Z) and rotate about three axes (X, Y, and Z), as shown in Figure 16–3.

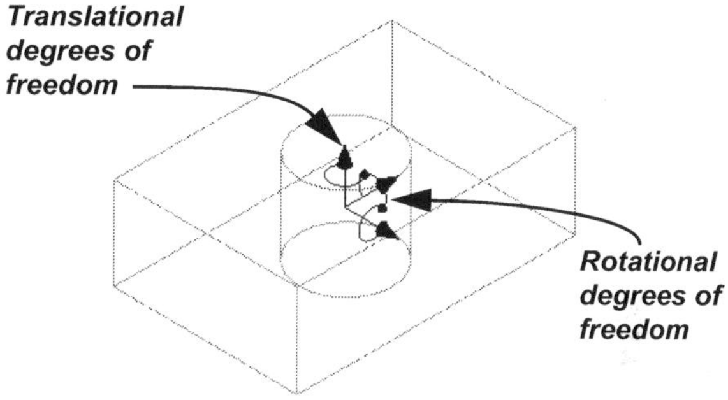

Figure 16–3

Degrees of freedom symbols do not display on a grounded part because the part does not have any degrees of freedom.

- To display the degrees of freedom for components, in the *View* tab>Visibility panel, click (Degrees of Freedom). By default, they are not displayed.

> **Hint: Degree of Freedom Analysis**
>
> The **Degree of Freedom Analysis** command provides a summary of the degrees of freedom remaining in all of the components in the assembly.
>
> To open the Degree of Freedom Analysis dialog box, in the *Assemble* tab>Productivity panel, click (Degree of Freedom Analysis). This dialog box lists all assembly components and lists the translational and rotational degrees of freedom remaining for each component.
>
> - To graphically display the remaining degrees of freedom in the graphics window, select a component name in the dialog box.
> - To visually animate the degrees of freedom remaining, select **Animate Freedom** in the dialog box and select a component name.

Step 4 - Select a constraint type.

In the *Assemble* tab>Relationships panel, click (Constrain) to open the Place Constraint dialog box. In this dialog box, you select the constraint type in the *Type* area and define how the components are oriented relative to one another in the *Solution* area. Depending on the type of constraint being created, the dialog box updates appropriately to provide the required options. The available constraint types are described as follows:

Mate

The Mate constraint ( ) positions two components adjacent to each other. It can be assigned between two planes, edges, center points, or work points. The Plane-Plane Mate constraint removes one translational and two rotational degrees of freedom. When planes or the center point of a circular edge are selected, the Mate orientation solutions are shown in Figure 16–4.

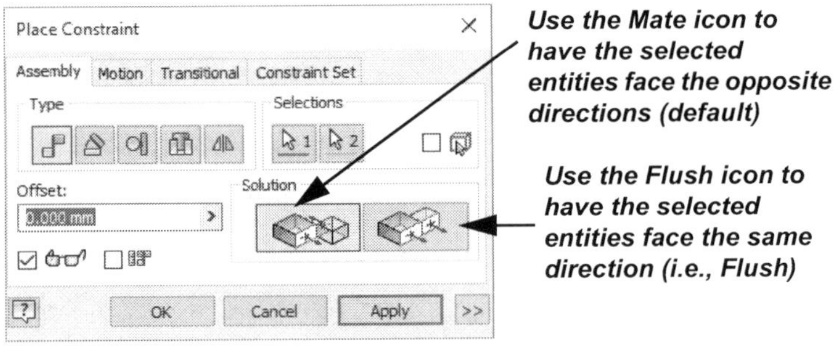

Figure 16–4

When linear edges or axes selected, the Mate orientation solutions are shown in Figure 16–5.

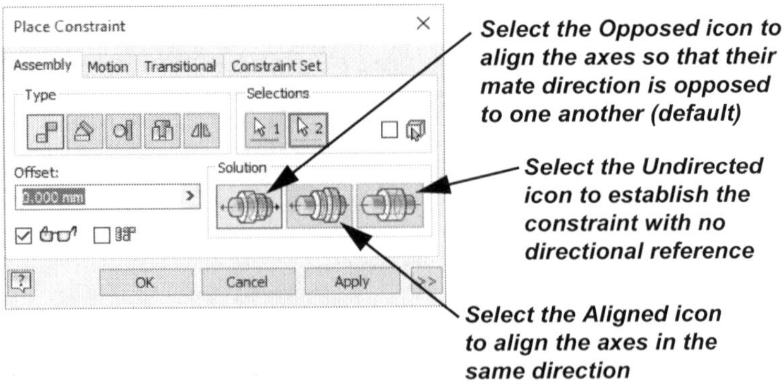

Figure 16–5

Angle

The Angle constraint ( ) specifies the angle between two edges, two planes, or an edge and a plane of the components. This constraint removes only two rotational degrees of freedom. The available Angle orientation solutions are shown in Figure 16–6.

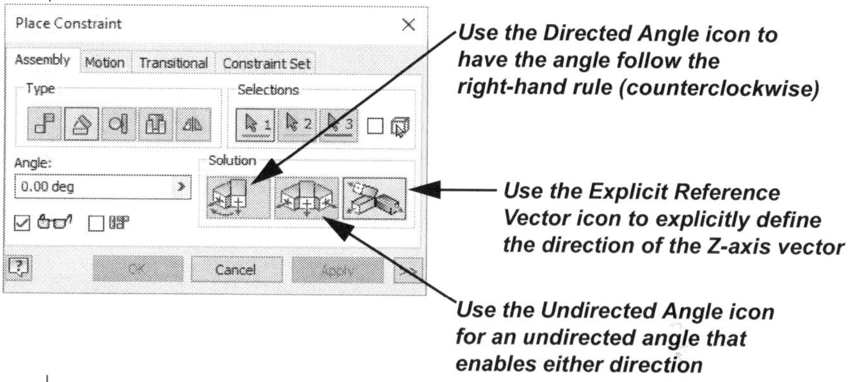

Figure 16–6

Tangent

The Tangent constraint ( ) positions two components tangent to each other. This constraint only removes one translational degree of freedom. The available Tangent orientation solutions are shown in Figure 16–7.

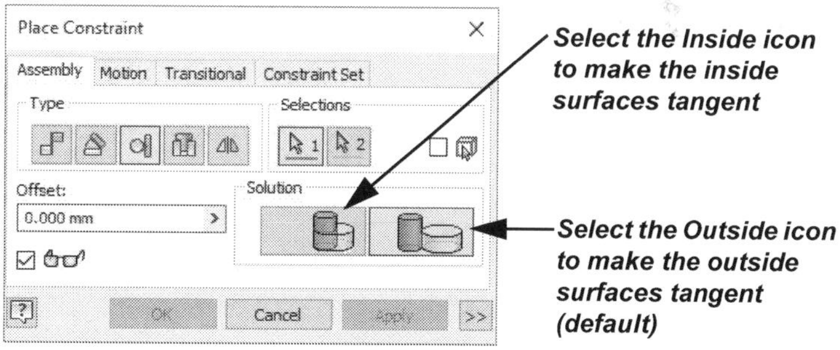

Figure 16–7

Insert

The Insert constraint ( ) enables you to position two components to fit into each other. This constraint removes three translational and two rotational degrees of freedom by mating the axis of two components, as well as applying a Mate constraint between two planar faces. To remove the final rotation degree of freedom, enable (Lock Rotation). The available Insert orientation solutions are shown in Figure 16–8.

*The Model browser icon used to identify an Insert constraint varies depending on whether **Lock Rotation** has been set. The icon indicates constaints where a rotational degree of freedom is still available and the icon indicates constraints where it has been locked.*

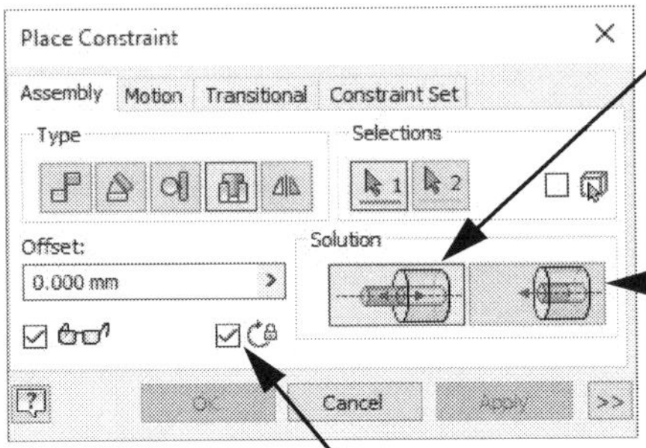

Figure 16–8

Symmetry

The Symmetry constraint ( ) enables you to position two components symmetrically about a plane or planar face. This constraint removes one translational and two rotational degrees of freedom by creating symmetry between reference planes or edges. When you place a Symmetry constraint, the dialog box opens as shown in Figure 16–9.

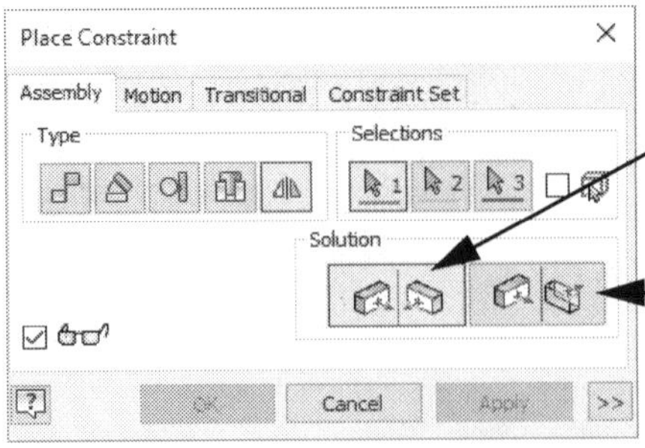

Figure 16–9

UCS

A UCS constraint enables you to position two components so that the UCS in each component is selected to be constrained to the other. This constraint removes three translational and three rotational degrees of freedom. It can be assigned on the *Constraint Set* tab in the Place Constraint dialog box, or using the **UCS to UCS** assemble option, as shown in Figure 16–10.

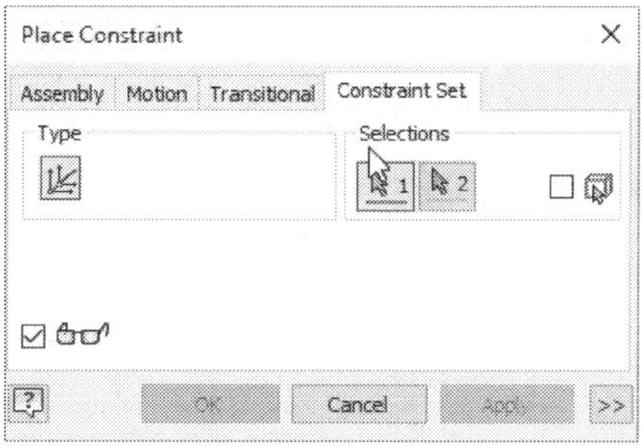

Figure 16–10

Step 5 - Select references on the components.

Reference selection on both components is required to fully define each constraint. Depending on the type of constraint being defined, you can select any of the following geometry types to define the reference:

- Faces
- Planes
- Lines (edges, curves, or axes)
- Points (work points, center points, or vertices)

When selecting references, you can select faces through parts by hovering the cursor over the face and selecting it in the Select Other drop-down list.

How To: Assign References

1. Ensure the  (First Selection) field is active.
2. Select the geometry reference on the first component that is appropriate for the constraint type.
3. Ensure the  (Second Selection) field is active.
4. Select the geometry reference on the second component that is appropriate for the constraint type.

To preview the effect of the added constraint in the assembly, click (Show Preview).

Hint: Isolating Components During Reference Selection.

To isolate a component so that you can only select specific reference geometry on that component, click (Pick part first) in the Place Constraint dialog box and then select the component to isolate. This option is valuable during reference selection when components are close to each other or when one component obscures another.

Step 6 - Assign an offset value, as required.

You can assign an offset value between selected references in the Place Constraint dialog box.

is only available for the Mate and Angle constraints.

- If the (Predict Offset and Orientation) option is enabled when you select two component references, the current distance (offset value or angle) between them automatically displays in the *Offset* field in the dialog box.

Step 7 - Repeat Step 4 to Step 6 until the components are fully constrained.

When components are copied and pasted, their constraints are only copied with them if both of the components used in defining the constraint are copied.

Once references and any offset value has been selected, click **Apply** to complete the constraint definition. Continue adding constraints between components until all required degrees of freedom are removed.

Step 8 - Complete the component placement.

Once the components have been fully constrained, click **Cancel** to close the Place Constraint dialog box. Alternatively, right-click in the graphics window and select **Cancel (ESC)**.

- The default naming convention for a constraint includes the constraint type and a sequential numerical number. To rename a constraint, double-click on the constraint name in the Model browser and enter a new name.

- The assembly file stores links to and constraint information for the components used in the assembly. The geometry of the components is still defined in the individual .IPT (part) files.

Hint: Showing Constraints in the Graphics Window.

To show glyphs in the model that indicate an assigned constraint, click (Show) in the Relationships panel and select a component. Preselecting all of the components and selecting this option displays all of the glyphs. Use (Hide All) to clear them from the display.

Step 9 - Edit the component placement, as required.

Constraints are listed in the Model browser under the component(s) to which they are applied. Expand the component in the Model browser to display all of its constraints. Additionally, all of the constraints are listed in the **Relationships** node at the top of the Model browser. Consider the following:

By double-clicking on a component you display the 3D Model tab, enabling you to edit the part while remaining in the assembly.

- To modify an offset value, select the constraint in the Model browser and enter a new offset value in the field that displays at the bottom of the Model browser.
- To edit a constraint, right-click on the constraint in the Model browser and select **Edit**. The original Edit Constraint dialog box opens and you can change any of the elements.
- To review failed (sick) constraints, click (Show Sick) in the Relationships panel. Edit the references as required to resolve the issues.
- To delete a sick constraint, right-click on its glyph and select **Delete** or delete it in the Model browser.

Assembly Examples

The following examples use different combinations of Mate constraint references to create fully constrained assemblies. The components to be placed are shown in Figure 16–11.

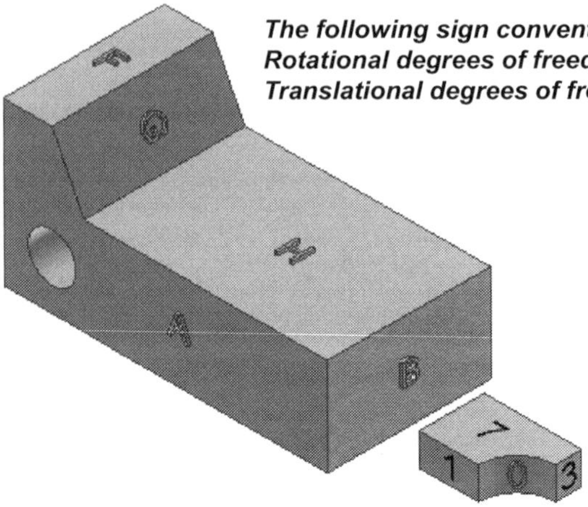

The following sign conventions are used:
Rotational degrees of freedom = R
Translational degrees of freedom = T

Figure 16–11

Example 1: Mate (Plane-Plane)

The combination of constraints and references shown in Figure 16–12 is used to create the fully constrained assembly.

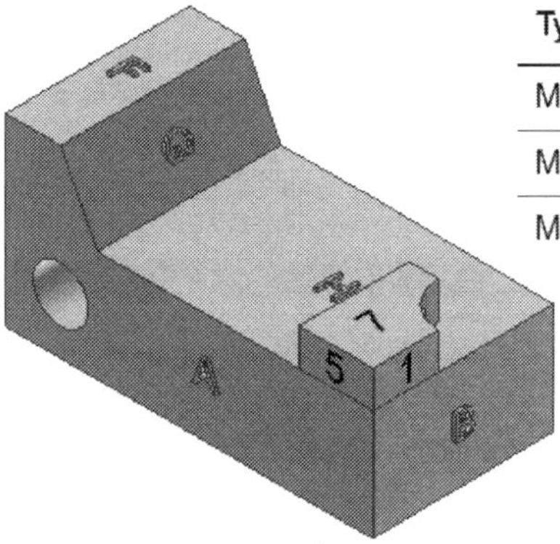

Type	References	Offset	DOF removed
Mate	Faces 6 and H	0.00mm	Two **R** and one **T**
Mate (Flush)	Faces 5 and A	0.00mm	One **R** and one **T**
Mate (Flush)	Faces 1 and B	0.00mm	One **T**

Figure 16–12

Hint: Mate constraints orient components so that surface normals are facing one another. This can sometimes make reference selection difficult, as it can hide references. Alternatively, consider using the Mate - Flush constraint until all of the references have been selected and then switch back to the Mate constraint.

Example 2: Mate (Line - Plane)

The combination of constraints and references shown in Figure 16–13 is used to create the fully constrained assembly.

Type	References	Offset	DOF removed
Mate	Faces 6 and H	0.00mm	Two **R** and one **T**
Mate	Face 1 and Face A edge	0.00mm	One **R** and one **T**
Mate	Face 3 and Face B edge	0.00mm	One **T**

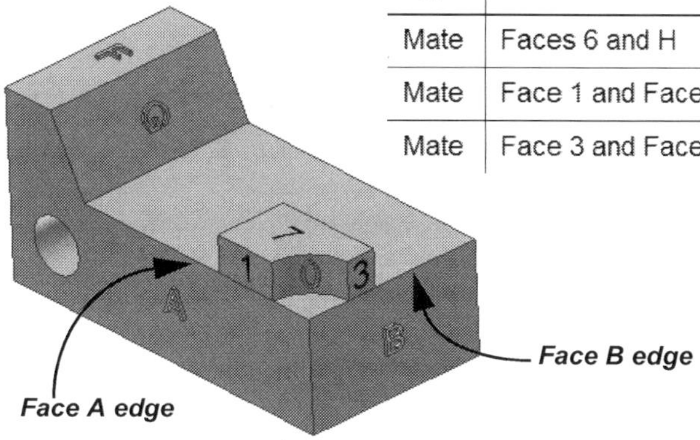

The Line-Plane Mate constraint type removes one translational and one rotational degree of freedom

Figure 16–13

Example 3: Mate (Line - Line)

The combination of constraints and references shown in Figure 16–14 is used to create the fully constrained assembly.

Type	References	Offset	DOF removed
Mate	Face F and Face 6	0.00mm	One **T**
Mate	Face 1 edge and face A edge	0.00mm	Two **R** and two **T**
Mate	Face 3 edge and face F edge	0.00mm	One **R** and one **T**

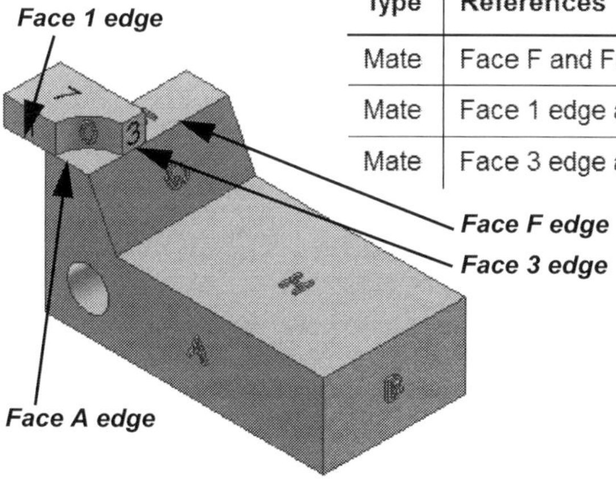

The Line-Line Mate constraint type removes two translational and two rotational degrees of freedom

Figure 16–14

Example 4: Mate (Work Point - Work Point)

The combination of constraints and references shown in Figure 16–15 is used to create the fully constrained assembly.

Type	References	Offset	DOF removed
Mate	Point from each part	0.00mm	Three **T**
Flush	Faces 1 and A	0.00mm	Two **R**
Mate	Faces 6 and H	0.00mm	One **R**

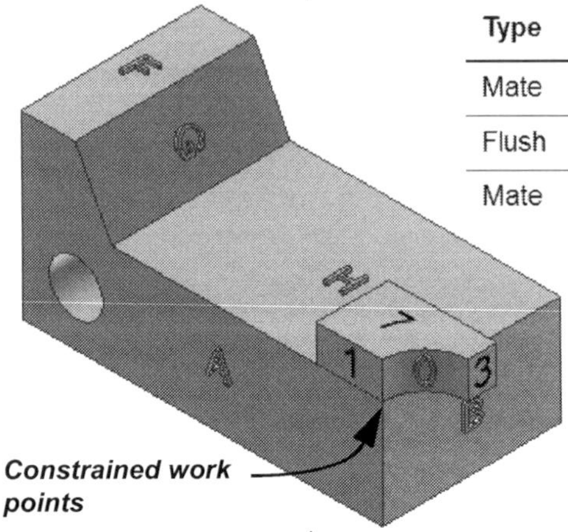

Constrained work points

The Mate constraint type between work points removes three translational degrees of freedom

Figure 16–15

Example 5: Tangent and Angle

The combination of constraints and references shown in Figure 16–16 is used to create the fully constrained assembly.

Type	References	Offset	DOF removed
Tangent	Faces H and 4	0.00mm	One **R** and one **T**
Flush	Faces 1 and A	0.00mm	One **R** and one **T**
Tangent	Faces G and 4	0.00mm	One **T**
Angle	Faces F and 5	25deg	One **R**

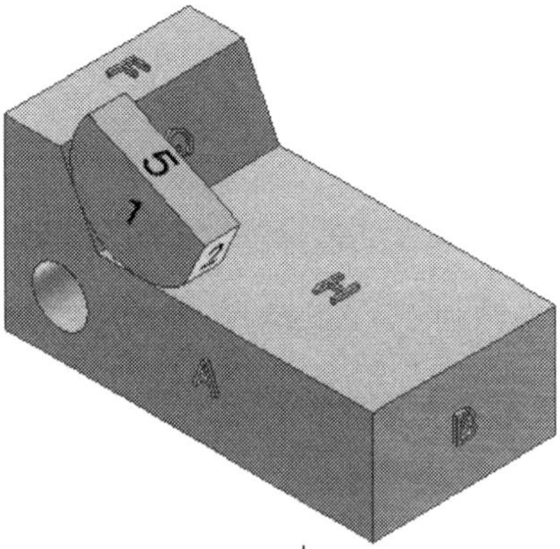

Figure 16–16

Example 6: Insert and Mate

This example uses different combinations of constraints to create the fully constrained assembly. You can create this assembly with only one constraint (Insert). However, if you want to orient the bolt in a certain direction, add an additional Mate constraint (Flush) or an Angle constraint. The components to be placed are shown in Figure 16–17.

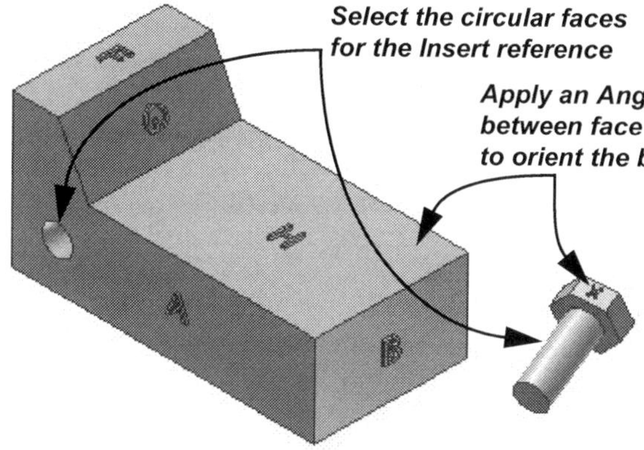

Figure 16–17

The combination of constraints and references shown in Figure 16–18 are used to create the fully constrained assembly.

Type	References	Offset	DOF removed
Insert Opposed	The circular faces	0.00mm	Two **R** and Three **T**
Angle	Face H and X	0.00deg	One **R**

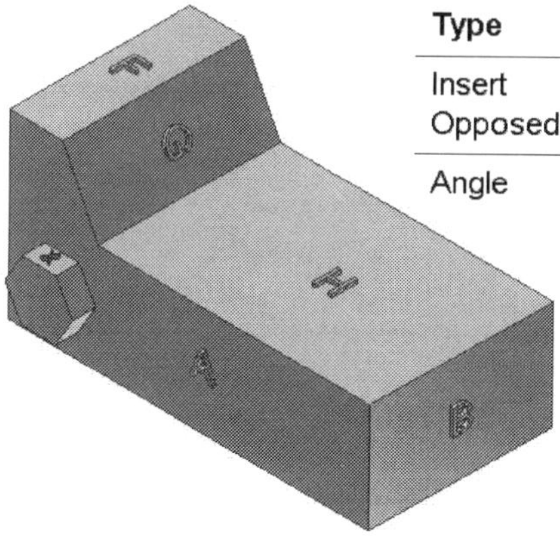

Figure 16–18

16.2 Assemble Mini-Toolbar

The Assemble mini-toolbar provides an alternative to using the Place Constraint dialog box when assigning constraints. This tool eliminates the need to interact with a dialog box and enables you to work directly with the model to assign constraints.

You can access this interface using either of the following methods:

- Once a component is initially placed, and prior to right-clicking and selecting **OK**, select a reference entity on the new component to begin assigning a constraint.
- In the *Assemble* tab>expanded Relationships panel, click  (Assemble) to activate the mini-toolbar interface.

By default, when the mini-toolbar is activated, the  (Automatic) constraint is selected in the mini-toolbar. Based on the selected model references, the software decides which constraint to assign. Alternatively, you can manually select the constraint type in the drop-down list, as shown in Figure 16–19. Each constraint type is listed with multiple orientation options, if available.

Automatic is the default option and enables the software to assume the constraint based on reference selection

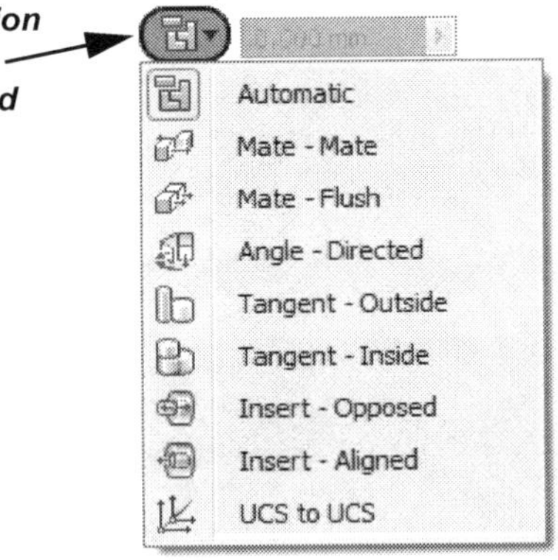

Figure 16–19

As references are selected, the components are immediately previewed in their new position, as shown in Figure 16–20. Click to apply the constraint.

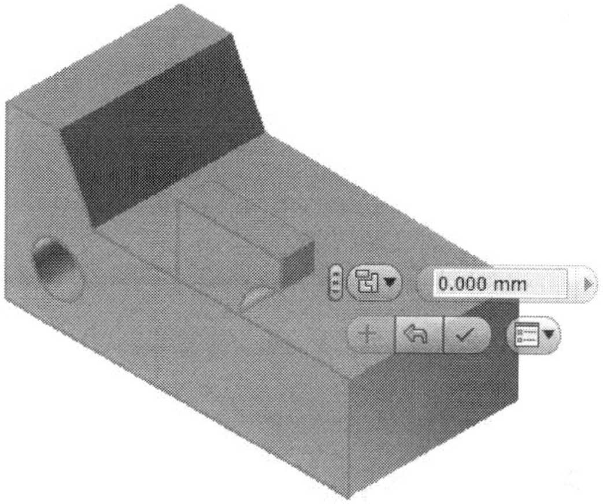

Figure 16–20

- As references are selected, the drop-down list in the mini-toolbar refines the list of possible constraint options. If required, you can switch from (Automatic) to a more specific constraint type. Continue to select references and assign them until the component is fully located in the assembly.
- Click to apply the constraint and close the Assemble mini-toolbar.
- If you initiated the Assemble mini-toolbar during component placement, a duplicate of the assembled component will display in the graphics window. You can continue to assemble another copy, or right-click and select **OK** to cancel placement.

Constrain vs. Assemble

The following are some differences between the **Constrain** option and the Assemble mini-toolbar when used to constrain components:

- When using the Assemble mini-toolbar, you can focus on the reference selection first. Once references have been selected, you can refine the constraint type.

- When using the Assemble mini-toolbar, each constraint is added independently and is not compared to existing constraints. This means that conflicting constraints are not recognized until you click to complete the command. At this point, any conflicting constraints are reported and must be fixed.
- When using the **Constrain** option, you can permit the software to interpret an offset value. This is not possible with the Assemble mini-toolbar.

16.3 Content Center

The Autodesk Inventor software has a standard library (Content Center) that contains a variety of commonly used parts (e.g., nuts, bolts, and screws) that can be used instead of creating a new part. To open the Content Center, use one of the following methods:

- In the **File** Menu, select **Open>Open from Content Center**.
- In the *Assemble* tab>Component panel, click (Place from Content Center) in the expanded Place drop-down list.
- Switch to the Favorites browser when a part or assembly is open. To open this browser, click in the Model browser header and select **Favorites** from the drop-down list.

How To: Add a Library Part to an Assembly

1. Select the type in the Category View panel, as shown in Figure 16–21. All of the families for that type are listed in the List View panel.
2. Click on a family in the List View panel, as shown in Figure 16–21. All of the parts available from that family are listed in the Table View panel.

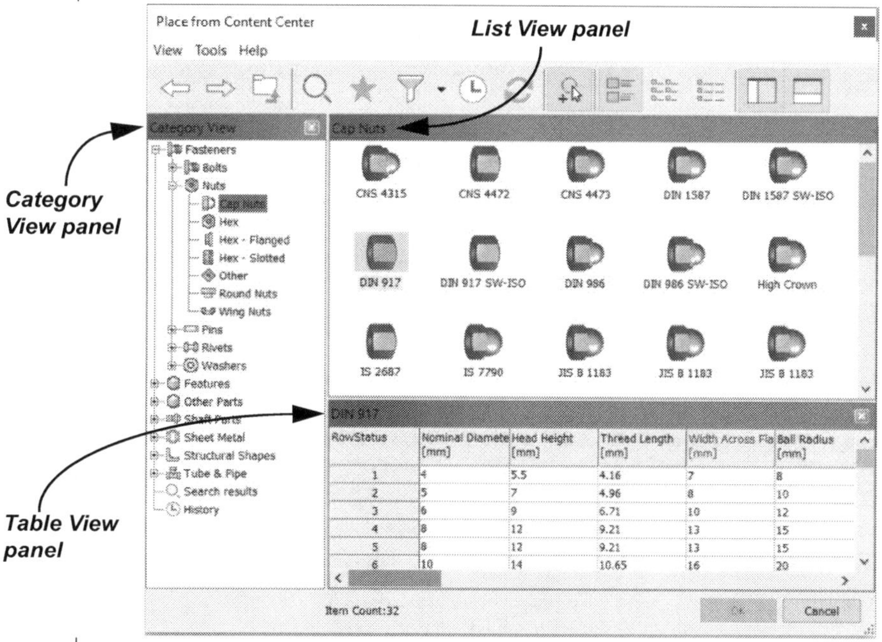

Figure 16–21

The (Autodrop) command is available in the Content Center toolbar. You can also hold <Alt> while double-clicking on the part or feature in the Content Center to toggle the AutoDrop status.

3. Use any of the following to add the library part.
   - With (Autodrop) enabled, double-click on the required family type in the List View panel. Select references in the assembly to place the new component. Once references are selected, the part is automatically generated to fit the selected references. Use the options in the AutoDrop dialog box to change the size ( ), place the part and add another ( ), or place a single instance of the part ( ). Constraints are automatically assigned based on the selected references.
   - With (Autodrop) disabled, double-click on the required family type in the List View panel. Select a size from the sizing dialog box that opens, Click **OK**, and then place and constrain the new part.
   - Double-click on the required family member in the Table View panel. The part is generated and attaches itself to the cursor to be placed and constrained in the assembly. When selecting directly in the Table View panel, the Autodrop setting does not have any impact.

Searching the Content Center

A significant number of features are stored in the Content Center. To use the search environment, click (Search) or select **Tools>Search** to open the **Quick Search** tool at the top of the Content Center dialog box.

> **Hint: Content Center Features**
>
> The Content Center not only provides access to a library of part files, it also contains commonly used and sized features that can be added to a model. The Content Center contains both parts and features when working in an assembly model, but only contains features when working in a part model.

16.4 Assembly Browser

The Model browser lists all of the parts, subassemblies, and design views that make up an assembly. The following can be done using the Model browser.

- You can manipulate parts in the Model browser. To open a component, right-click on the component in the Model browser and select **Open**. The part or subassembly opens in a separate window.
- You can open a drawing directly from the Model browser by right-clicking the assembly name and selecting **Component>Open Drawing**. If a drawing with the same name as the assembly exists, it automatically opens. If not, the Open dialog box opens for you to select the filename.
- You can create a drawing file directly from the Model browser by right-clicking on the assembly name and selecting **Create Drawing View**. You are immediately prompted to select a template. You can then begin the placement of the base view and any of its dependent projected views. Similarly, you can create a Presentation file by right-clicking and selecting **Create Presentation**.
- You can change the Model browser's display style. Select **Modeling** at the top of the Model browser to display component features and select **Assembly** to display the constraints, as shown in Figure 16–22.

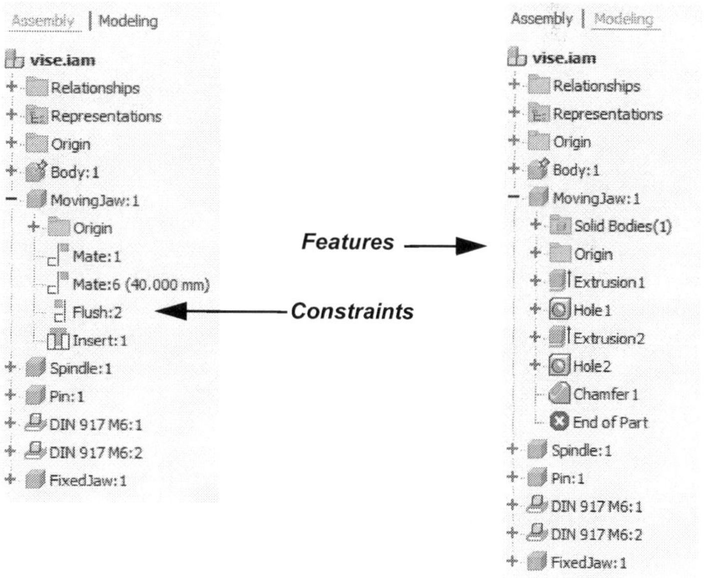

Figure 16–22

- You can manipulate the display of the Model browser using the **Display Preference** options shown in Figure 16–23. This enables you to hide work planes, notes, documents, and warnings. Using the **Show Children Only** option, you can list only first-level components in the Model browser (components in sub-assemblies are not listed).

- Use **Find** in the drop-down menu (shown in Figure 16–23) to search for objects, such as components, features, constraints, and sketches. This icon opens the same dialog box and options as when you click  (Find Component) in the *Tools* tab>Find panel.

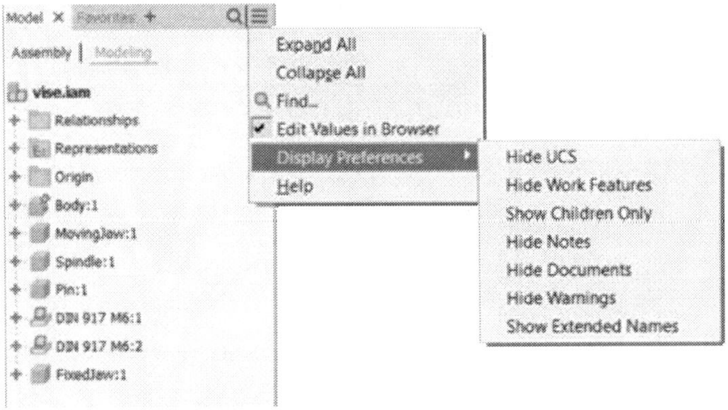

Figure 16–23

16.5 Saving Files

*Alternatively, click **Save** in the **File** menu.*

To save an assembly file, click (Save) in the Quick Access Toolbar. If the assembly has not been saved before, the Save As dialog box opens. Enter a name for the assembly and click **Save**. If the assembly has been saved before, the Save dialog box opens as shown in Figure 16–24.

The Save dialog box lists the components that require saving, their checkout status (if a Vault project is active), and enables you to set whether or not to save each file.

*By default, all of the modified files are marked to be saved. Clicking **Yes to All** saves all files, regardless, if they changes were made. Additionally, if you are working with the Autodesk Vault software, all of the saved files receive new versions based on the save date, not based on whether the physical model was actually changed.*

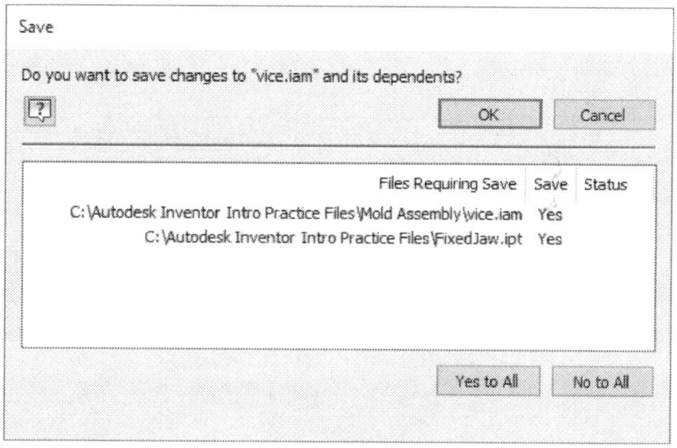

Figure 16–24

- If you do not want to save a particular file, change the **Yes** to **No** by clicking on it in the *Save* column.
- Files available for checkout (which you have edited without checking out) are marked **Yes** for saving and the file is saved and available for check out. If you select **Yes** to change it to **No**, the file is not saved.

Once you have decided which files to save, click **OK** to save the selected files.

Practice 16a Assembly Basics I (Constraints)

Practice Objectives

- Place and constrain components in an assembly.
- Place a Content Center component in an assembly.
- Modify assembly dimensions to change the position of components relative to one another.
- Edit existing component placement references.

In this practice, you will create a new assembly and assemble the components, as shown in Figure 16–25. In addition, you will redefine the original constraints and references, and make modifications. You will use both the **Constrain** and **Assemble** commands to assemble components.

Figure 16–25

Task 1 - Create an assembly and assemble the first component.

1. Use the *My Home* tab in the graphics window to create a new assembly file using the standard metric (mm) template.

> **Hint: Verifying the My Home Templates**
>
> To verify which Template is assigned to be used with the **Assembly** option, in the *New* area in the *My Home* tab, click ⚙. Using the Configure Default Template dialog box, verify the measurement units and change it if required. Alternatively, you can start the file using the **New** option and select the template.

2. In the *Assemble* tab>Component panel, click (Place). You might need to expand the Placement drop-down list to access this option.

3. Select **Body.ipt** in the Place Component dialog box and click **Open**. The component is added to the assembly.

Consider using the ***Rotate X 90****,* ***Rotate Y 90****, or* ***Rotate Z 90*** *options in the marking menu if the orientation is not correct.*

4. If the component displays in a 2D orientation, return the model to its default Home View using the ViewCube. Right-click on the model and select **Place Grounded at Origin** to ground the component.

5. Right-click and select **OK** to assemble a single instance of the component into the assembly. If you select again an additional **Body** component is added.

6. Review the Model browser. Note that the base part has been added to the browser with  (Pushpin) next to it, as shown in Figure 16–26. Hover the cursor over the **Body.ipt** component in the graphics window and note that the cursor symbol has changed to  indicating that it is grounded.

A grounded part is fixed to a location in the assembly and is not dependent on other parts.

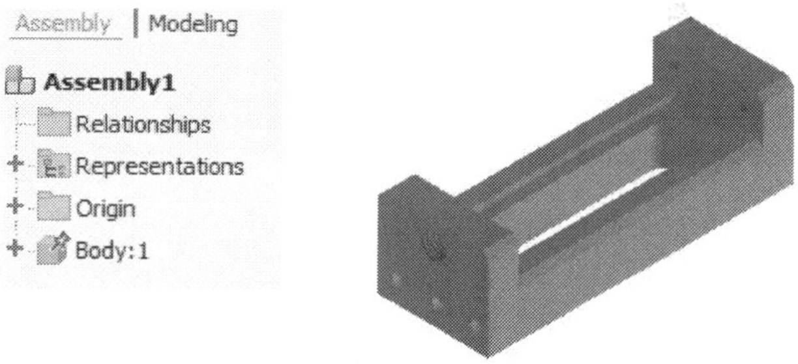

Figure 16–26

Task 2 - Add another part and apply the first constraint.

In this task, you will add and apply the first constraint to place the **MovingJaw** component in the assembly. The final placement of the component in the assembly is shown in Figure 16–27.

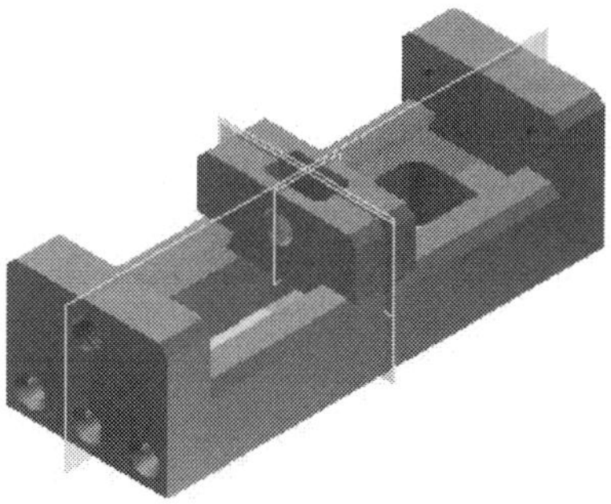

Figure 16–27

1. In the Component panel, click (Place).
2. Select **MovingJaw.ipt** in the Place Component dialog box and click **Open**.
3. Right-click on the model and select **Rotate X 90**. Continue to right-click and select **Rotate X 90** to rotate the component into a more convenient orientation for constraining, as shown in Figure 16–28.
4. Position **MovingJaw.ipt** as shown in Figure 16–28, and click the left mouse button to place it.
5. Right-click and select **OK** to place a single instance of the component in the assembly.
6. Select the *View* tab. In the Visibility panel, click (Degrees of Freedom). Note that there are six degrees of freedom for **MovingJaw.ipt** as indicated by the symbol that displays on the model.

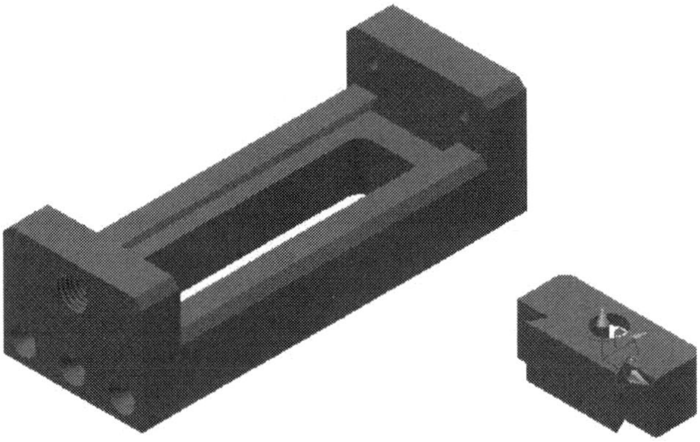

Figure 16–28

7. In the *Assemble* tab>Relationships panel, click (Constrain). The Place Constraint dialog box opens.

When selecting references, you can select faces through parts by hovering the cursor over the face and selecting it in the Select Other drop-down list.

8. Leave  (Mate) selected. Select the face of the **MovingJaw** and the face of the base, as shown in Figure 16–29. Note how the references remain highlighted once selected.

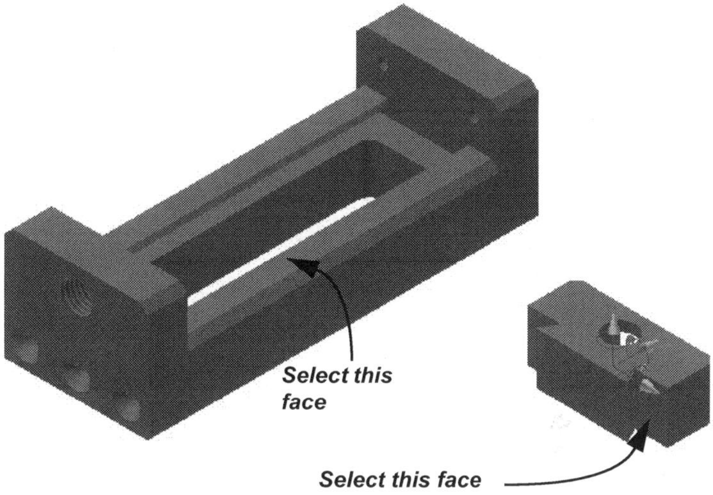

Figure 16–29

9. Click **Apply** to apply the constraint. The assembly displays similar to that shown in Figure 16–30. Once applied, the references are no longer highlighted. Note that the component can still rotate and translate.

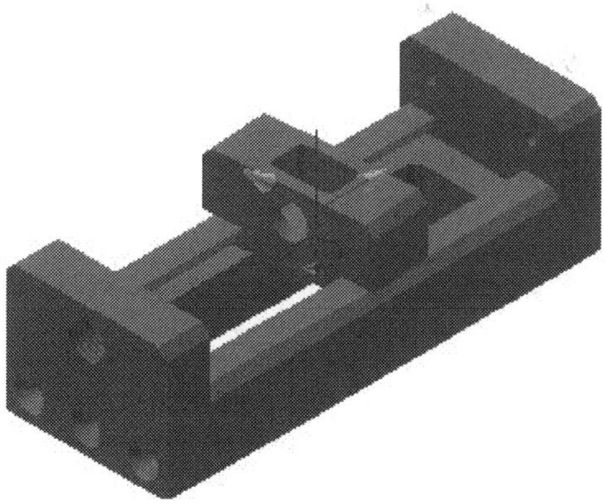

Figure 16–30

Task 3 - Apply a second constraint.

The second constraint flushes the XZ origin planes of the two components with a zero offset. Where possible, assembling to origin features is preferable as these features are never deleted or modified.

1. The  (Mate) constraint type is selected by default in the Place Constraint dialog box.
2. Click  (Flush) in the *Solution* area in the dialog box.
3. Select the XZ origin planes in each of the components. The planes can be selected in the model (if displayed) or in the Model browser.
4. Enter **0.00** in the *Offset* field.
5. Apply the constraint. The assembly displays as shown in Figure 16–31. Note that one degree of freedom still exists in the model.

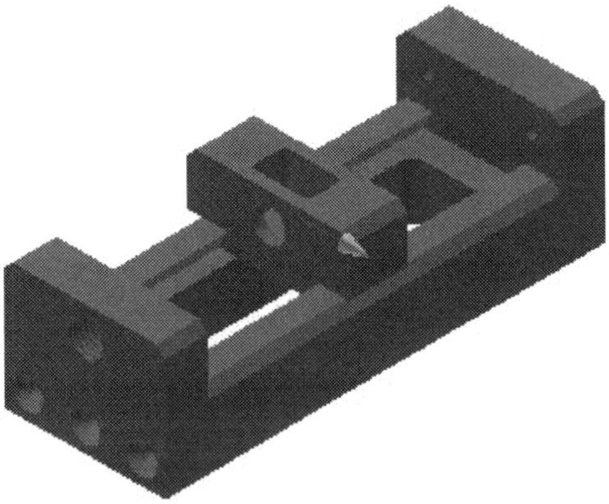

Figure 16–31

Task 4 - Apply a third constraint.

The third constraint flushes the YZ origin planes of the two components with a zero offset.

1. Select the YZ origin plane from the **Body** and **MovingJaw** parts ( (Mate) and  (Flush) are still active) to constrain the final degree of freedom.

2. Enter **0.00** in the *Offset* field.

3. Apply the constraint. The assembly displays as shown in Figure 16–32. Note that the degrees of freedom are completely removed, which means that **MovingJaw.ipt** is fully constrained.

Figure 16–32

4. Click **Cancel** to close the Place Constraint dialog box.

*Constraints are only listed in the component nodes if the Assembly View of the Model browser is active. The **Relationships** node is available in either the Assembly or Modeling View.*

5. Expand the two component's nodes in the Model browser and note that the constraints are listed. Expand the **Relationships** node at the top of the Model browser and note that the constraints are also listed in this node.

Task 5 - Add and constrain the spindle part.

In this task, you will add and constrain **Spindle.ipt** into the assembly. The final placement of the **Spindle** part in the assembly is shown in Figure 16–33.

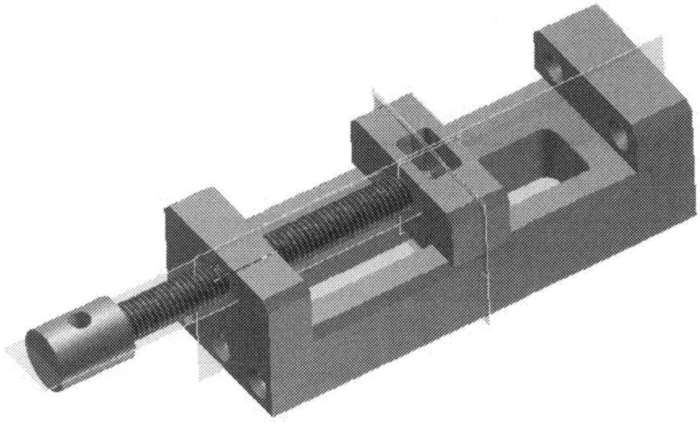

Figure 16–33

1. Toggle on the display of the origin planes in the models, if they have been toggled off.

2. In the Component panel, click  (Place).

3. Select **Spindle.ipt** in the Place Component dialog box and click **Open**.

4. Position **Spindle.ipt** as shown in Figure 16–34 and click the left mouse button to place it.

5. Right-click and select **OK** to assemble a single instance of the component in the assembly.

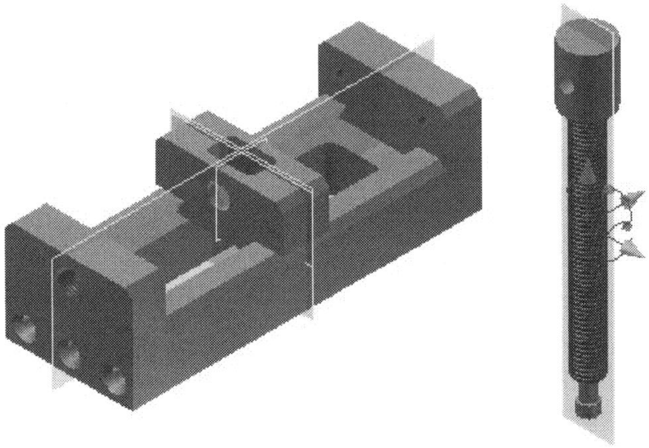

Figure 16–34

6. In the Relationships panel, click  (Constrain). The Place Constraint dialog box opens.

7. Click  (Insert) in the Place Constraint dialog box.

8. Ensure that 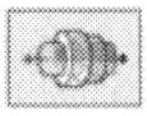 (Opposed) is selected in the *Solution* area in the dialog box.

9. Hover the cursor over the hole in the **MovingJaw**, as shown in Figure 16–35. When the edge of the hole and the axis highlight, click to select them.

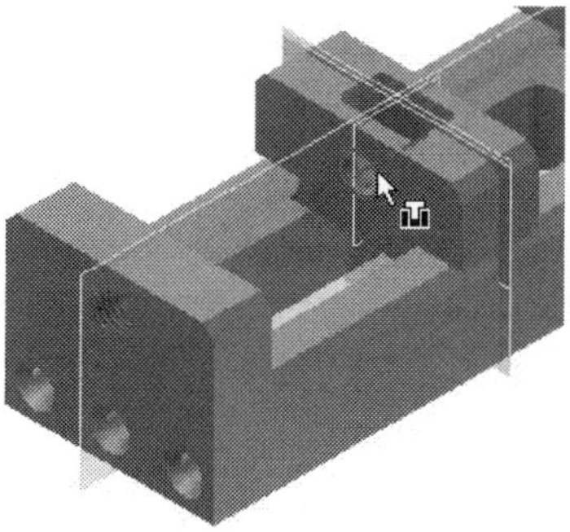

Figure 16–35

*Activating the **Free Rotate** command to rotate a component independent of another in the assembly cancels the current command. To spin during component placement, use the global **Orbit** command to rotate the entire assembly.*

10. Hover the cursor over the area shown in Figure 16–36. When the edge and axis highlight, click to select them. An Insert constraint is applied between the two highlighted axes.

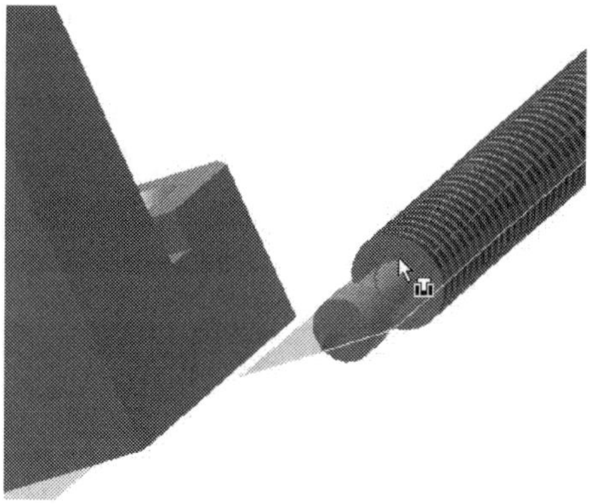

Figure 16–36

11. Click **OK** to apply the constraint and close the dialog box. The assembly displays similar to that shown in Figure 16–37.

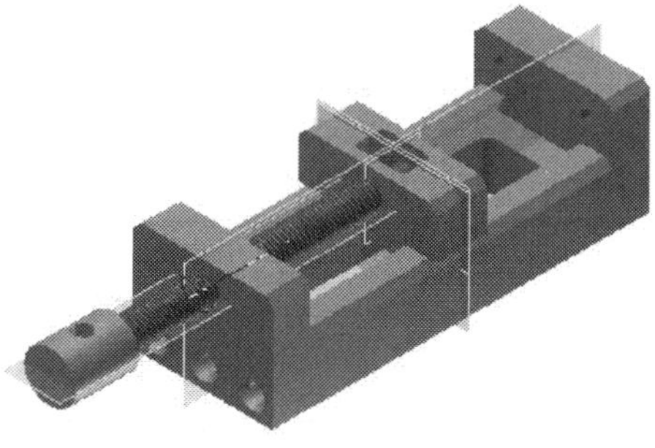

Figure 16–37

A rotational degree of freedom remains. This degree of freedom will not be removed, and the spindle will be allowed to rotate about its axis.

Task 6 - Add and constrain the pin part.

In this task, you will add and constrain **Pin.ipt** into the assembly. Its final placement is shown in Figure 16–38.

Figure 16–38

1. Place one instance of **Pin.ipt** into the assembly, as shown in Figure 16–39.

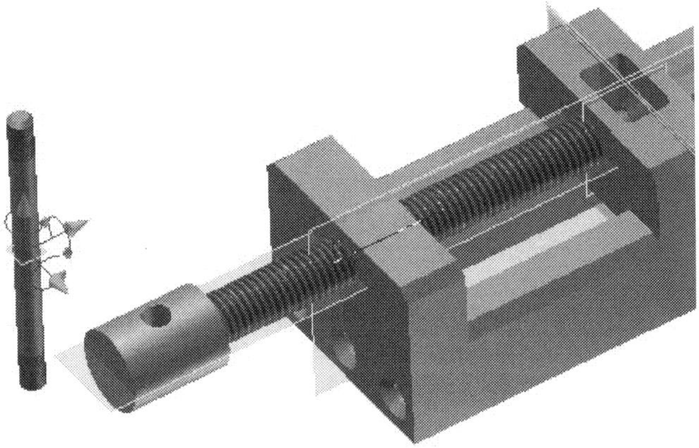

Figure 16–39

2. In the Relationships panel, click (Constrain).
3. In the Place Constraint dialog box, ensure that (Mate) is selected.
4. Select the axis of the pin and spindle, as shown in Figure 16–40. In the *Solution* area, also ensure that (Opposed) is selected.

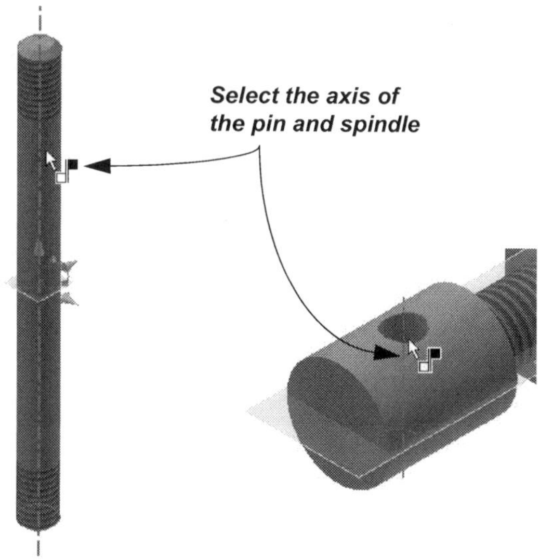

Figure 16–40

5. Click **Apply** to apply the constraint.

6. Leave 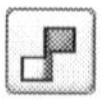 (Mate) selected in the Place Constraint dialog box and select the XZ origin plane of the spindle and the XY origin plane of the pin, as shown in Figure 16–41.

Figure 16–41

7. Click **Apply** to apply the constraint

8. A rotational degree of freedom remains. This degree of freedom will not be removed, and the pin will be allowed to rotate about its axis. Click **Cancel** to close the Place Constraint dialog box.

Task 7 - Assemble a cap nut from the Content Center.

1. In the Component panel, expand the Place drop-down list and click (Place from Content Center). The Place from Content Center dialog box opens, as shown in Figure 16–42.

*The Welcome dialog box might open if your system has not previously logged into the Content Center. If required, click **Log In**, select the **Content Center library read only user** option, and click **OK**.*

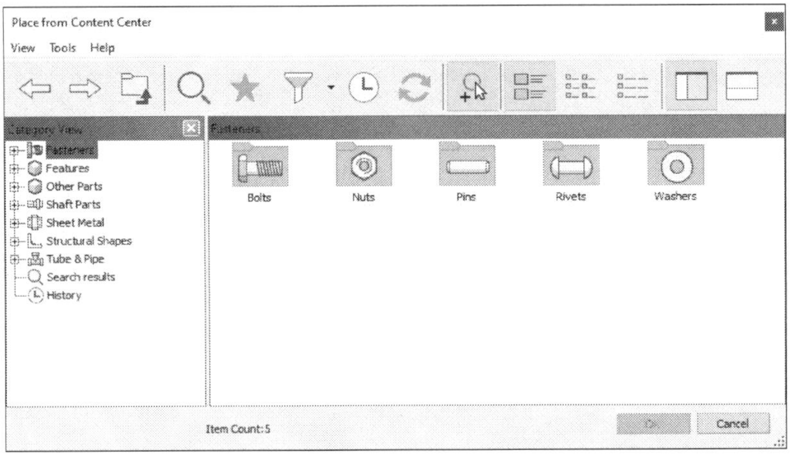

Figure 16–42

2. Toggle on (Table View) to display the Table View panel, if it is not already displayed.

3. Verify that (Autodrop) is toggled on.

4. In the Category View panel, click **Fasteners**.

5. In the List View panel, double-click on **Nuts** and then double-click on **Cap Nuts**.

6. Select **DIN 917**. The dialog box displays as shown in Figure 16–43.

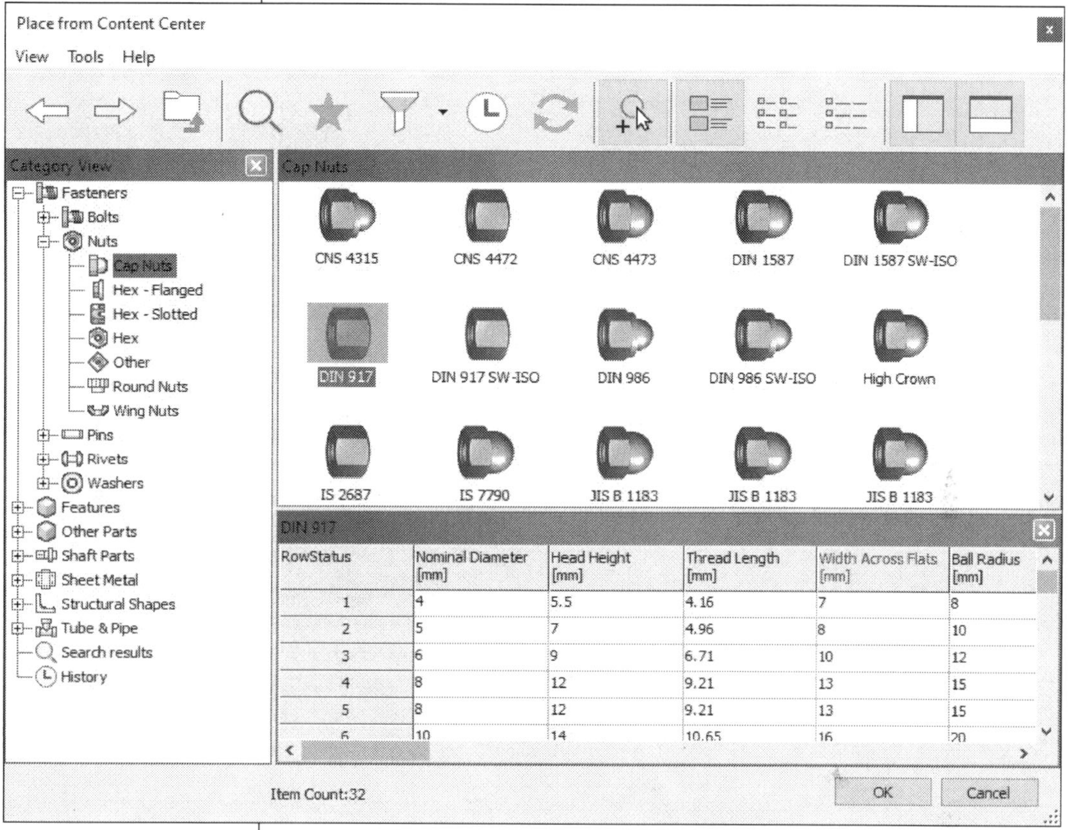

Figure 16–43

7. The diameter of the pin is 6mm. Verify that there is a cap nut with a diameter of 6mm by reviewing the Table View panel.

*The functionality that automatically resizes and places the component based on target geometry is called **AutoDrop**.*

8. A nut with the required dimensions does exist in Row 3. To insert the nut, double-click on **DIN 917** in the List View panel. Do not left-click yet; hover the cursor over the outer surface of the pin. The nut is automatically resized and snapped in position. Click to place the nut using **AutoDrop** when the outer surface of the pin highlights.

9. Move the mouse. Note that the nut can still move along the pin. A second Mate constraint needs to be applied.

10. Select the edge, as shown in Figure 16–44. The Autodrop toolbar displays.

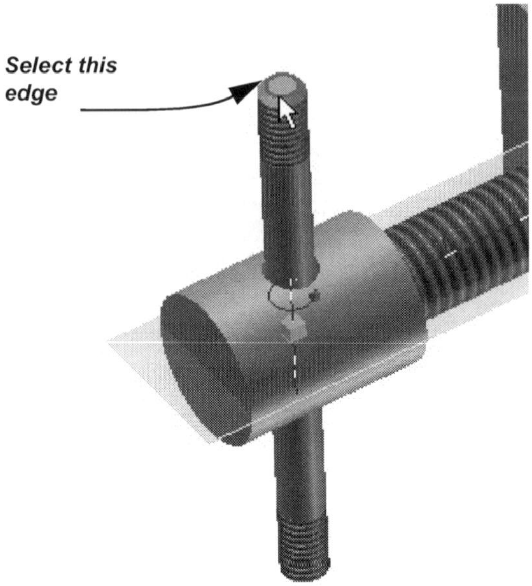

Figure 16–44

If you had to change the size of the nut, you do not need to place the component. It will be done automatically.

11. Click  (Place) to insert the component and finish the command. The model displays as shown in Figure 16–45. A rotational degree of freedom remains. This degree of freedom will not be removed and the nut can be rotated about its axis.

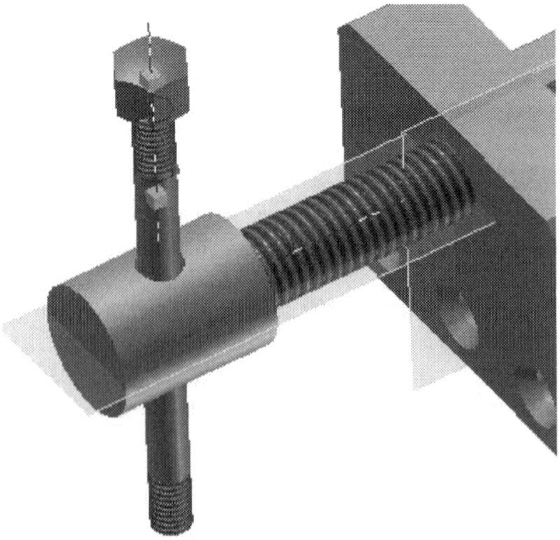

Figure 16–45

Task 8 - Modify the offset value.

The nut is not in the correct position on the pin. It needs to be offset from the selected pin surface.

1. Expand **DIN 917 M6:1** in the Model browser.

2. Highlight the last Mate constraint. The offset value displays beside it in the Model browser, as shown in Figure 16–46.

3. Change the *Offset* to **-6.5**. The Model browser displays as shown in Figure 16–46. Press <Enter>.

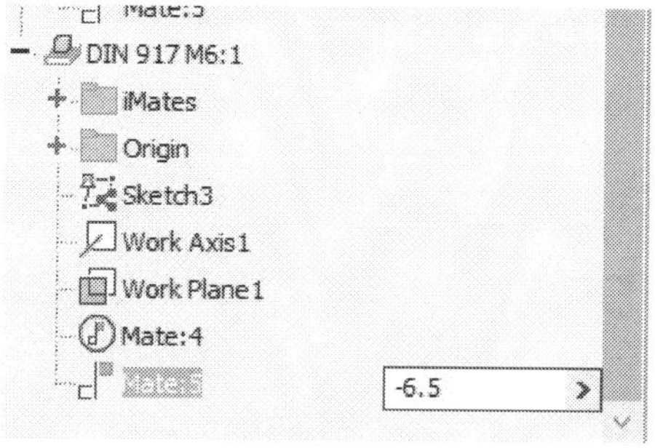

Figure 16–46

Task 9 - Assemble an additional instance of the cap nut.

In this task, you will copy and assemble a second cap nut.

1. Create a copy of the **DIN 917** component. Select **DIN 917 M6:1** in the Model browser, right-click and select **Copy**.

2. Place the cursor anywhere in the graphics window, right-click and select **Paste** to create a copy of the nut. Alternatively, you could also have dragged **DIN 917 M6:1** in the Model browser into the model to create a copy.

3. In the Relationships panel, click  (Constrain).

4. In the Place Constraint dialog box that opens, click  (Insert).

5. Ensure that 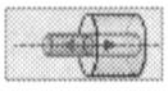 (Opposed) is selected in the *Solution* area in the dialog box.

6. Hover the cursor over the hole in the nut, as shown in Figure 16–47. When the edge of the hole and the axis highlights, click to select it.

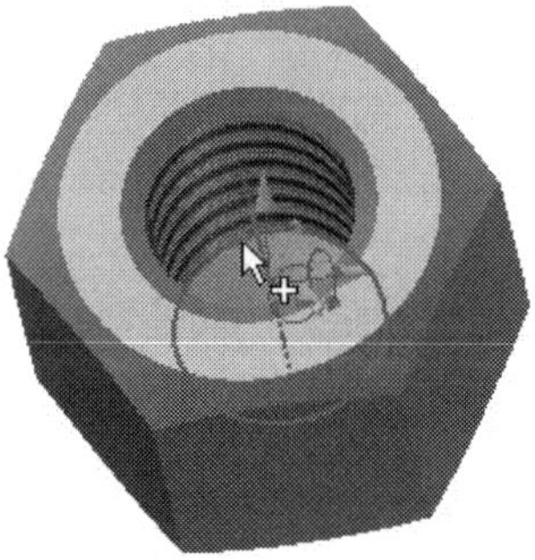

Figure 16–47

7. Hover the cursor over the area shown in Figure 16–48. When the edge and axis highlight, click to select them. An Insert constraint is applied between the two highlighted edges.

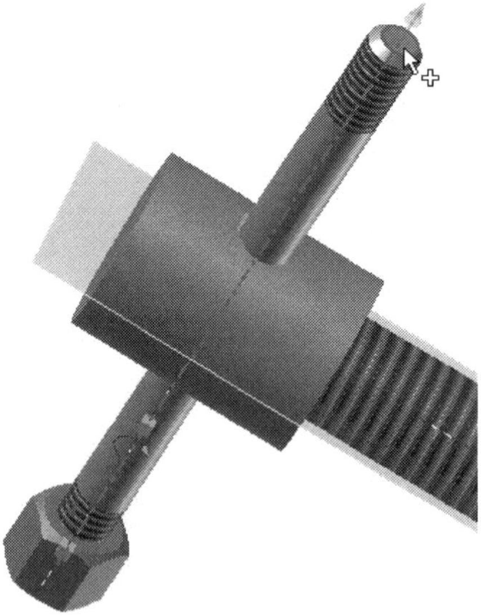

Figure 16–48

8. Apply the constraint and close the Place Constraint dialog box. The assembly displays as shown in Figure 16–49.

Figure 16–49

Task 10 - Assemble and constrain the fixed jaw.

The Assemble mini-toolbar provides an alternative to using the Place Constraint dialog box to constrain components. It enables you to quickly select references in components without activating any constraint tool. On placement, you begin selecting references and a constraint is assigned based on the references that are selected. If the assumed constraint is incorrect, you can select the appropriate option in the drop-down list. Depending on the user preference, you can use the Assemble mini-toolbar or **Constrain** option. However, once you become more familiar with assembling components, the Assemble mini-toolbar can be more efficient.

1. Place one instance of **FixedJaw.ipt** in the assembly. A second component remains attached to the cursor. Do Not right-click and select **OK**.

2. Rotate the model as shown in Figure 16–50.
3. Only the newly placed component is active for reference selection. Hover the cursor over the first circular edge reference, shown on **FixedJaw.ipt** in Figure 16–50 and select it.
4. The Assemble mini-toolbar opens immediately. Select the second circular edge reference on the **Body.ipt** component.

   as shown in Figure 16–50. The (Insert) constraint is assumed and displays in the Assemble mini-toolbar.

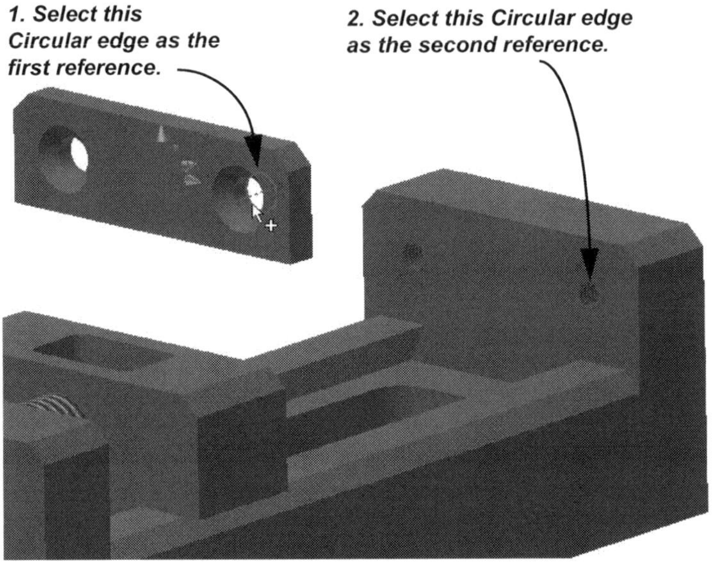

Figure 16–50

5. Click to apply the constraint.
6. Select the equivalent edges on the **FixedJaw** and **Body** parts for the left-hand hole.
7. Click to apply the constraint.

8. Click [icon] to apply the constraint and close the Assemble mini-toolbar.

9. The component is now fully located in the assembly. Because the constraints were assigned immediately on component placement, you can continue to place a second instance of **FixedJaw.ipt**. Right-click and select **OK** to end component placement. Activating and using the Assemble mini-toolbar in this way is excellent if repeating the assembly of the same component multiple times or to quickly constrain components without having to interact with the assembly commands in the ribbon.

Task 11 - Modify the constraint references.

In this task, you will modify the constraint references between the **MovingJaw** and the **Body** components. The **MovingJaw** will be able to move along the **Body** in the Y-direction. In this task, you will modify the references so that a zero offset will place the **MovingJaw** against the front wall of the **Body** component. Entering positive offset values will simulate its motion in the Y-direction.

1. For clarity, hide all of the visible work planes and the *Degrees of Freedom*. Select the *View* tab. In the Visibility panel, expand [icon] (Object Visibility) and clear the **Origin Planes** option. Click [icon] (Degrees of Freedom) to remove the degrees of freedom from display.

2. Expand the **MovingJaw** branch in the Model browser and select **Flush:1** to verify that this is the constraint that is to be edited. (Your constraint might be labeled differently. Locate the constraint that flushed the XZ origin planes of the **Body** and the **MovingJaw**.)

3. In the Model browser, double-click on **Flush:1** to open the *Edit Dimension* field. To display the components (as shown in Figure 16–51), set the offset value to **20** and press <Enter>. Depending on the order of reference selection you might need to enter **-20**.

4. Right-click on **Flush:1** in the Model browser and select **Edit**. The Edit Constraint dialog box opens with the constraint references highlighted on the model, as shown in Figure 16–51. The constraint selections are color-coded to indicate the selection numbers that correspond in the model.

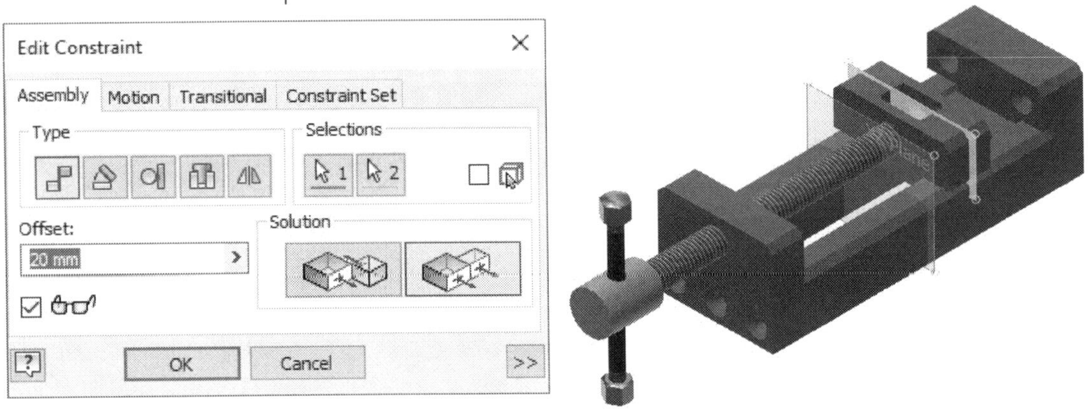

Figure 16–51

5. In the *Solution* area, click  (Mate).

6. In the *Selections* area, click the icon associated to the XZ origin plane on the **MovingJaw**. Select the face on the **MovingJaw**, as shown in Figure 16–52.

7. In the *Selection* area, click the icon associated with the XZ origin plane on the base. Select the face on the base as shown in Figure 16–52.

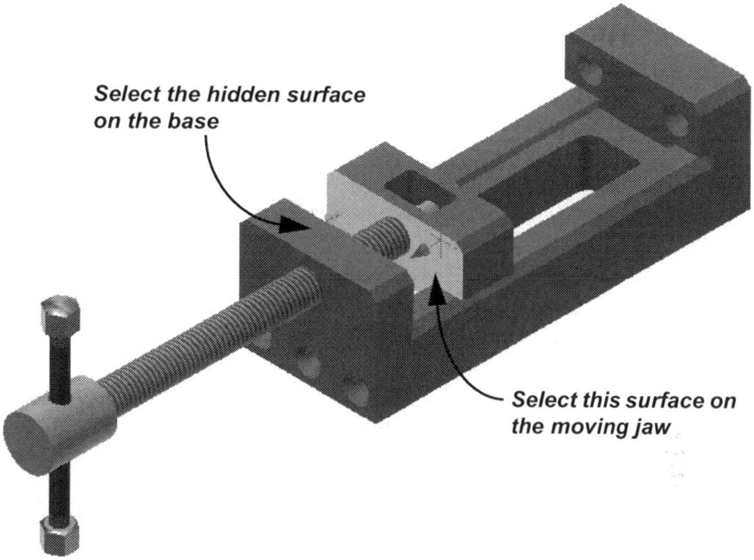

Figure 16–52

8. Click **OK**.

9. Modify the offset value of the new Mate constraint to view the motion of the **MovingJaw** along the **Body**.

10. Save the assembly. Enter **Vise** as the filename.

11. Close the window.

Chapter Review Questions

1. You cannot assemble components so that two parts occupy the same space at the same time.
   a. True
   b. False
2. In the Assembly browser, shown in Figure 16–53, what does the Pushpin icon next to the **Base_vise** part indicate?

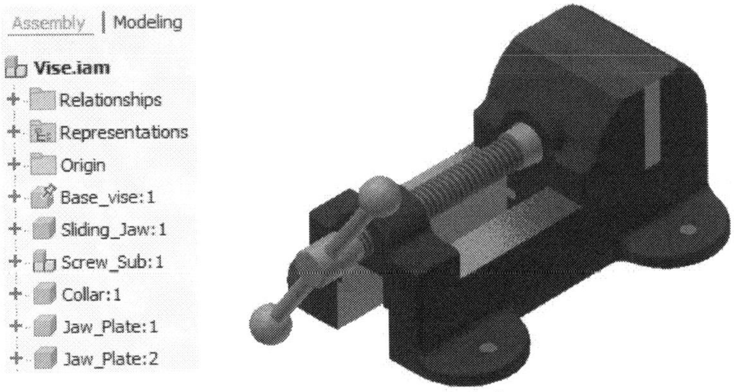

Figure 16–53

   a. The component requires additional constraints.
   b. The component is adaptive (size adjusts to fit constraints).
   c. The component was imported in SAT format (not parametric).
   d. The component is grounded (does not move).
3. How many rotational degrees of freedom (R) and translational degrees of freedom (T) does an unconstrained part or subassembly have?
   a. 1 R and 3 T
   b. 3 R and 3 T
   c. 2 R and 2 T
   d. 3 R and 1 T

4. In the Place Constraint dialog box, four areas are circled, as shown in Figure 16–54. Which area enables you to assign a constraint between two parallel surfaces as **Flush**?

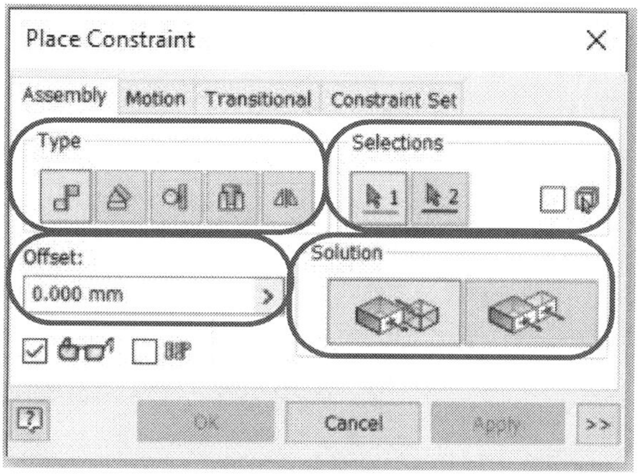

Figure 16–54

   a. *Type*
   b. *Solution*
   c. *Offset*
   d. *Selections*

5. Which of the following constraint types is highlighted in the Place Constraint dialog box, as shown in Figure 16–55?

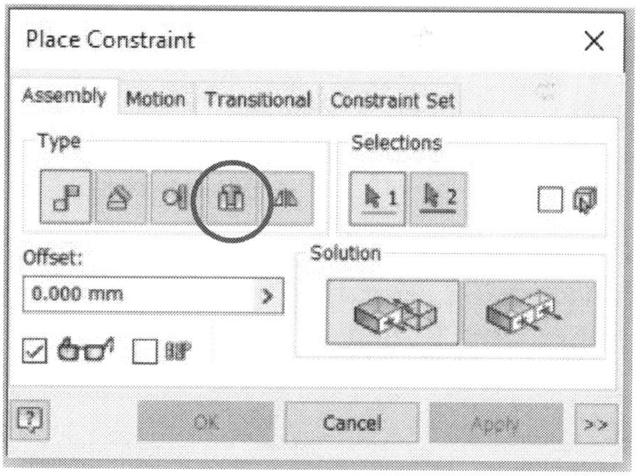

Figure 16–55

   a. Pin
   b. Flush
   c. Insert
   d. Mate

6. How would you determine how many degrees of freedom exist on a partially constrained part?

    a. All degrees of freedom are automatically displayed in the model when the Place Constraint dialog box is open.

    b. Right-click in the graphics window and select **Degree of Freedom** in the marking menu.

    c. In the *Assemble* tab>Productivity panel, expand the commands and click  (Degree of Freedom Analysis).

    d. Degrees of Freedom can only be reviewed in a sketch, not in an assembly.

7. Which of the following constraint combinations can be used to create the assembly shown on the right in Figure 16–56?

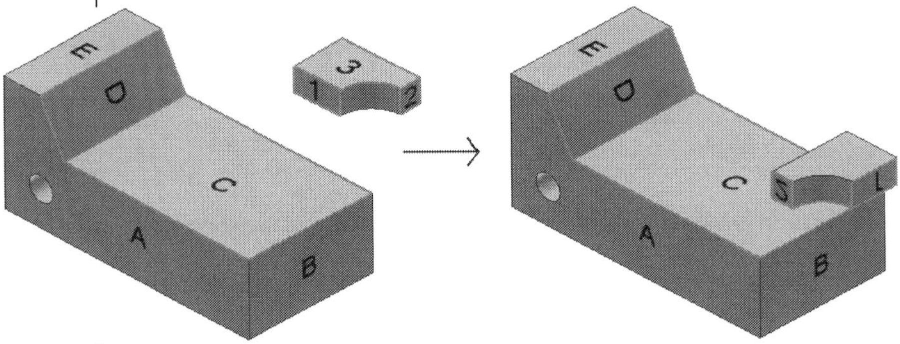

Figure 16–56

    a. Flush 1 and B, Flush Offset A and 2, Flush C and 3.

    b. Mate 1 and B, Mate Offset A and 2, Flush C and 3.

    c. Flush 1 and B, Flush Offset A and 2, Mate C and 3.

    d. Flush 1 and B, Flush Offset A and 2, Insert C and 3.

    e. Mate 1 and B, Mate Offset A and 2, Insert C and 3.

    f. Mate 1 and B, Mate Offset A and 2, Mate C and 3.

8. The pin is constrained in the holes on the part, as shown in Figure 16–57. How would you precisely control the distance between the pin heads and the sides of the part?

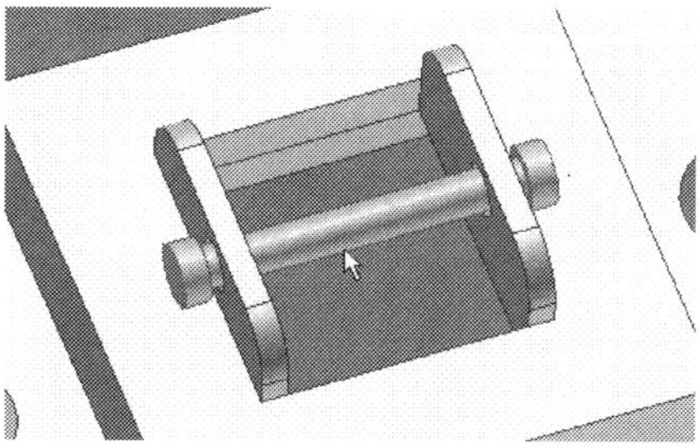

Figure 16–57

   a. Set the offset value for the constraint.
   b. Use **Move Component**.
   c. Use **Tweak Component**.
   d. Apply a dimension.

9. Which of the following statements are true of subassemblies? (Select all that apply.)
   a. They are always grounded in the assembly.
   b. They can contain other subassemblies.
   c. They are always stored as .IAM files.
   d. They act like a single component in the assembly.

10. What happens when you use the **Place** command to place an assembly file?
   a. It becomes a subassembly in the assembly.
   b. The parts of the assembly are placed as individual components at the top level of the assembly.
   c. It becomes a grounded component in the assembly no matter how many components have been assembled before it.
   d. The parts of the assembly are placed but are not enabled.

11. Which constraint type creates a Flush constraint, as shown in Figure 16–58?

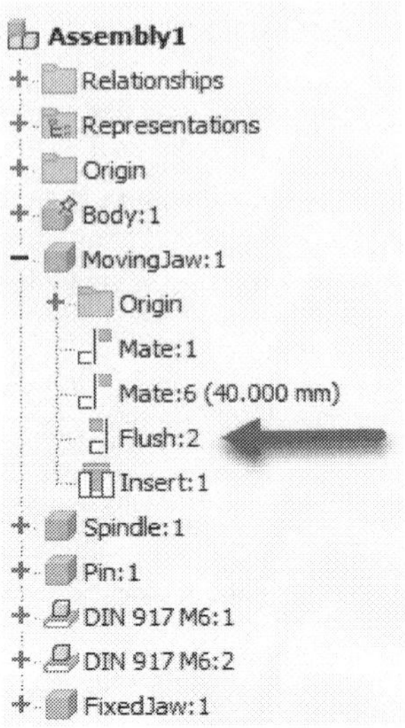

Figure 16–58

a. Insert
b. Tangent
c. Mate
d. Angle

12. What type of entities can be constrained with the Insert constraint?

a. Cylindrical entities
b. Linear entities
c. Flat entities
d. Points

13. When you set the Model browser to **Assembly View**, which of the following are listed in the Model browser display? (Select all that apply.)

a. Origin features
b. Assembly constraints
c. Assembly features
d. Part features

14. For the software to automatically set the size of a Content Center model, the **AutoDrop** option must be toggled off.
    a. True
    b. False

Command Summary

Button	Command	Location
	**Assemble**	• **Ribbon:** *Assemble* tab>Relationships panel
	**Constrain**	• **Ribbon:** *Assemble* tab>Relationships panel
	**Degrees of Freedom**	• **Ribbon:** *View* tab>Visibility panel
	**Degrees of Freedom Analysis**	• **Ribbon:** *Assemble* tab>Productivity panel
	**Free Move**	• **Ribbon:** *Assemble* tab>Position panel
	**Free Rotate**	• **Ribbon:** *Assemble* tab>Position panel
	**Hide All**	• **Ribbon:** *Assemble* tab>Relationships panel
	**Place**	• **Ribbon:** *Assemble* tab>Component panel
	**Place from Content Center**	• **Ribbon:** *Assemble* tab>Component panel • **File Menu:** Open>Open from Content Center • **Favorites Browser** (*with Part or Assembly open*)
	**Show**	• **Ribbon:** *Assemble* tab>Relationships panel
	**Show Sick**	• **Ribbon:** *Assemble* tab>Relationships panel

Joint Connections

The use of Joint connections to join components in an assembly is an alternative technique to assigning constraints. Depending on the Joint type selected, the assigned connections remove multiple degrees of freedom at once and enable you to test the movement between components based on the references you select.

Learning Objectives in This Chapter

- Use the Joint command to connect components in an assembly while maintaining the defined degree of freedom.
- Edit a joint connection so that the type, its references, or its values can be changed.

17.1 Assembling Components Using Joints

*Using the **Constrain** and **Assemble** commands, you add individual constraints between components to remove all required degrees of freedom.*

The **Joint** command offers an alternative to using the **Constrain** and **Assemble** commands. Joints enable you to define the allowable movement of a component by selecting a joint connection type. Based on the allowable movement for the selected type, all of the required degrees of freedom are removed at the same time.

General Steps

Use the following general steps to join components:

1. Launch the **Joint** command.
2. Select a joint type.
3. Select references on the components.
4. Assign a gap value, as required.
5. Assign limits, as required.
6. Complete the joint.
7. Edit the joint, as required.

Step 1 - Launch the Joint command.

To join components using the **Joint** command, in the *Assemble* tab>Relationships panel, click (Joint). The Place Joint dialog box and the mini-toolbar interface open, as shown in Figure 17–1.

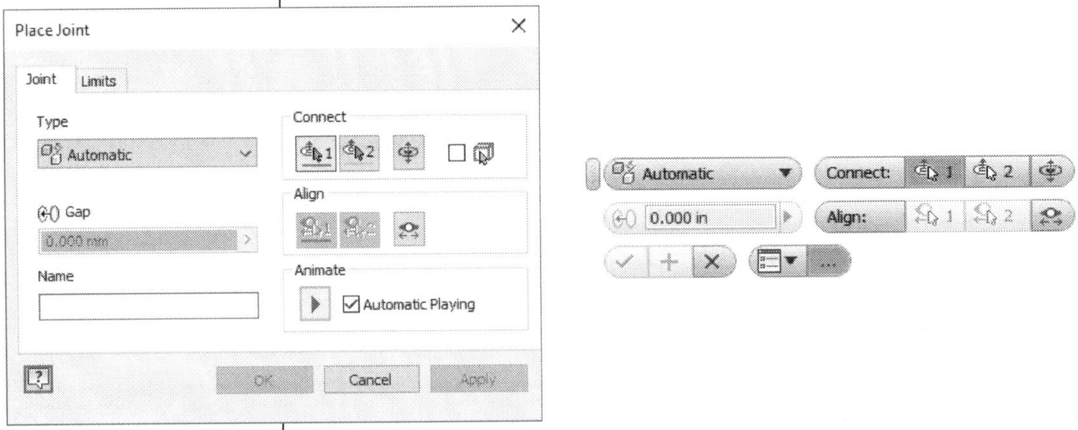

Figure 17–1

Click  in the mini-toolbar to toggle the display of the Place Joint dialog box.

The Place Joint dialog box contains the same options as the mini-toolbar as well as the following options that can't be accomplished in the mini-toolbar:

- You can toggle the visual animation when components are joined (**Automatic Playing**).
- You can assign a name to a Joint.
- The *Limits* tab enables you to specify a limit on the range of motion for a specific connection.

Step 2 - Select a joint type.

The  (Automatic) joint type is used by default. Alternatively, you can manually select a joint type in the drop-down lists, as shown in Figure 17–2.

Figure 17–2

Each joint type connection removes various Degrees of Freedom (DOF). The degrees of freedom that remain permit the type of movement indicated by the joint type. The Automatic () joint type enables the software to assume the joint type based on the selected references. Once assumed, the type can be changed if the software's assumption is incorrect.

The available joint types are listed as follows:

Joint Type	Icon	Remaining DOF
Rigid		0 Translational, 0 Rotational
Rotational		0 Translational, 1 Rotational
Slider		1 Translational, 0 Rotational
Cylindrical		1 Translational, 1 Rotational
Planar		2 Translational, 1 Rotational
Ball		0 Translational, 3 Rotational

Step 3 - Select references on the components.

References are required to fully define a joint type. Based on the selected references, the components are joined to one another and the selected joint type defines the allowable movement between the components. All of the references required for the joint types are assigned in the *Connect* and *Align* areas, as shown in Figure 17–3.

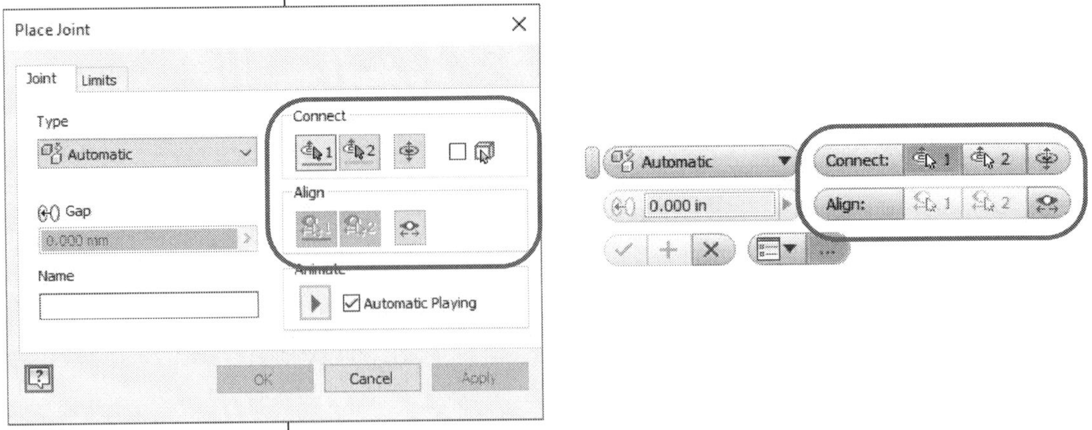

Figure 17–3

When selecting references, you can select faces through parts by hovering the cursor over the face and selecting it in the Select Other drop-down list.

By default, once a joint type is selected, the reference selection fields are automatically active. The first reference selected is assigned to the (*First Origin*) field and the second to the (*Second Origin*) field.

Before selecting a reference, it is important to note the active green dot on the highlighted entity. This point represents the Joint origin and is the point to which the joint is assigned. The location of the cursor on the entity controls which point is active. If the required point is not active, move the cursor closer to the required point to activate it. The entity on which it resides plays a secondary role in defining the orientation or alignment.

The selectable entity types are described as follows:

Entity Type	Description
Face	For a rectangular face, the active point can be on: • A corner, • The midpoint of an edge (as shown on the right), or • At the center point of the face (as shown on the left). The location of the cursor when selecting defines which point is assigned. 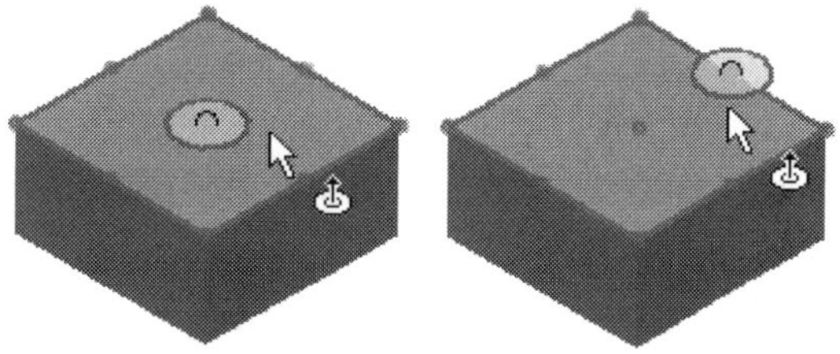
Edge (linear)	For a straight edge, the active point can be: • At either end (as shown on the right), or • At the center point of the edge (as shown on the left). The location of the cursor when selecting defines which point is assigned. 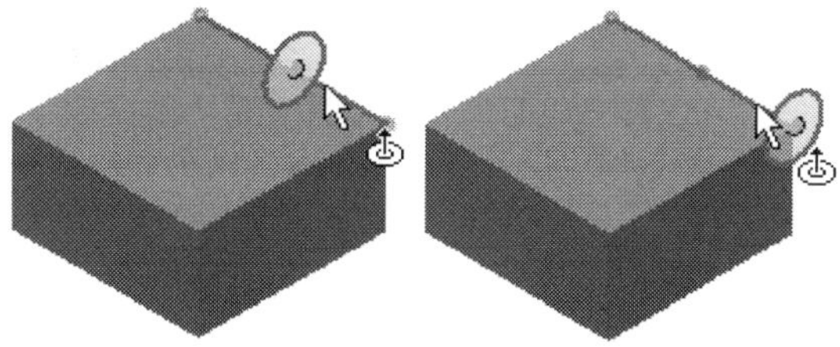

Edge (circular)	For a circular edge or face, the active point is always at the center of the edge. 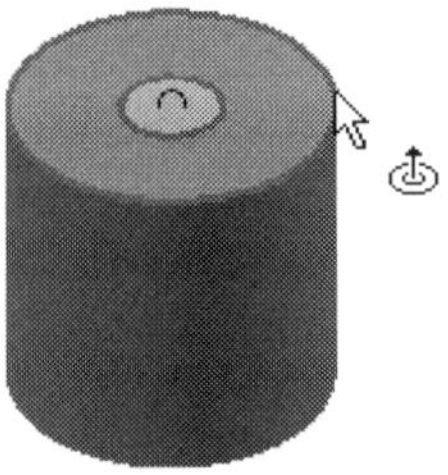
Spherical	For spherical geometry, the active point can be: • At the center of the geometry (as shown on the left), or • At points where geometry intersects with the surface of the sphere (as shown right). The location of the cursor when selecting defines which point is assigned. 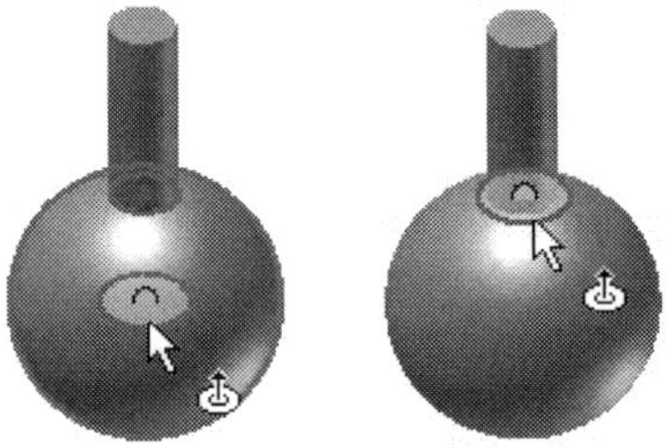

Hint: Working with Joint Origins

A new Joint Origin can be created by right-clicking and selecting **Between Two Faces**. Once active, select two faces to create the Joint Origin between them.

Alternatively, you can right-click and select **Offset Origin** and then enter offset values to locate a Joint Origin. These two options are only available as you hover over the reference and right-click, as shown in Figure 17–4. By default, the **Infer Origin** option infers the origin based on the existing geometry.

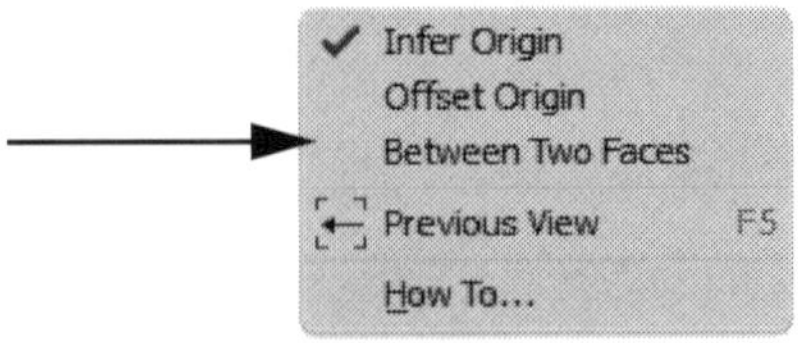

Figure 17–4

Isolating is valuable when components are close to each other, or when one component obscures another.

- Use (Pick part first) to isolate a component so that you can ensure that the correct references on the isolated component are selected.
- When selecting references, the first component you select is the component that is going to move. If it is a grounded component, you are prompted that a grounded component has been selected to be moved. You can accept this and the component remains grounded, but doing so changes the orientation of the grounded component.

To toggle off the animation preview when references are selected, clear the ***Automatic Playing*** *option in the Animate area in the Place Joint dialog box.*

Click to play the animation at any time.

Once the First and Second Origin references have been defined the alignment is automatically assumed based on the selected references, and the components automatically move into position. A short animation is played indicating the type of motion that remains between the components.

If the component is assembled in the wrong direction, consider the following:

- Click (Flip Component) in the *Connect* area to flip the component's orientation.
- Click (Invert Alignment) in the *Align* area to try inverting the alignment.
- In the Align area, select (First Alignment) or (Second Alignment) and select new references (e.g., faces, edges, or work geometry), similar to that shown in Figure 17–5.

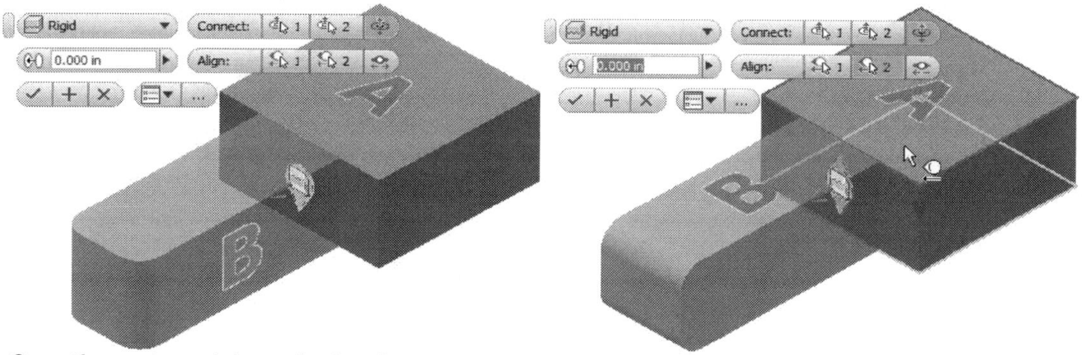

Once the center points on the two faces were selected as references, a Rigid joint was added and the components were automatically aligned.

To reorient component B relative to A, the alignment references were edited and both the A and B faces were selected.

Figure 17–5

Once a joint has been assigned you can use  *(Degrees of Freedom) to graphically display the remaining degrees of freedom to help with visualization.*

The following examples explain how components were joined using the various joint types.

Rigid

The  (Rigid) joint type removes all of the degrees of freedom, eliminating any relative motion between it and its referenced component. Welded or bolted connections are examples of the **Rigid** joint type, similar to that shown in Figure 17–6.

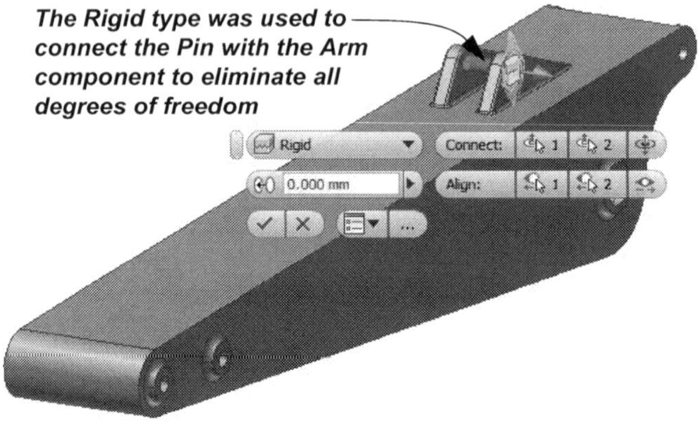

Figure 17–6

Rotational

The  (Rotational) joint type allows for rotation about an axis, similar to that shown in Figure 17–7. This joint type removes five degrees of freedom.

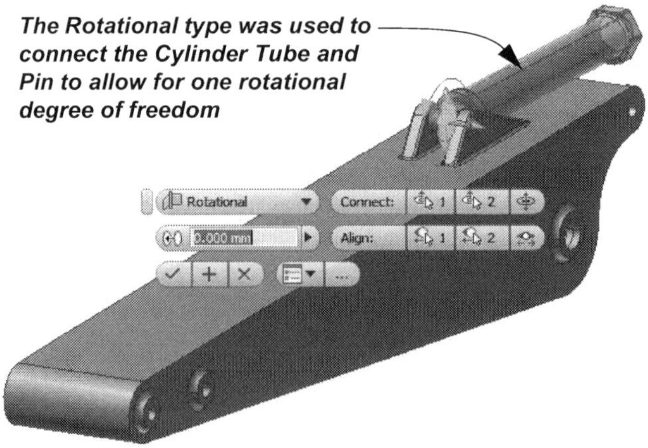

Figure 17–7

Slider

The (Slider) joint type allows for translational movement along an axis, as shown in Figure 17–8. This joint type removes five degrees of freedom.

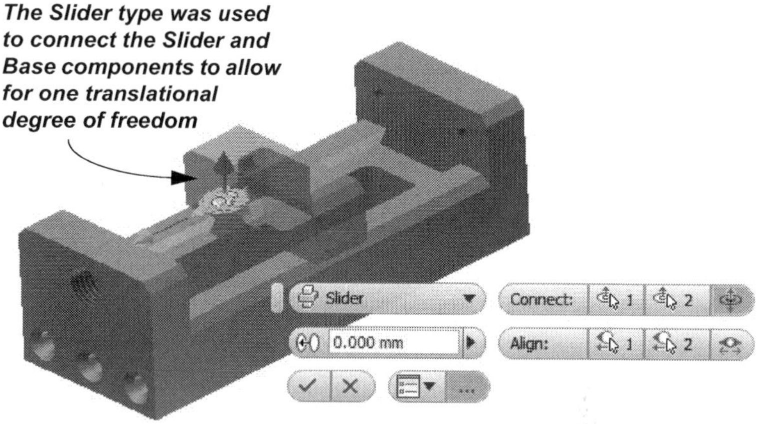

Figure 17–8

Cylindrical

The (Cylindrical) joint type enables a component to translate and rotate about a specific axis leaving two degrees of freedom available, as shown in Figure 17–9.

The preview for a new joint type does not maintain previous connections. Once assigned the relationships between all of the joint connections displays.

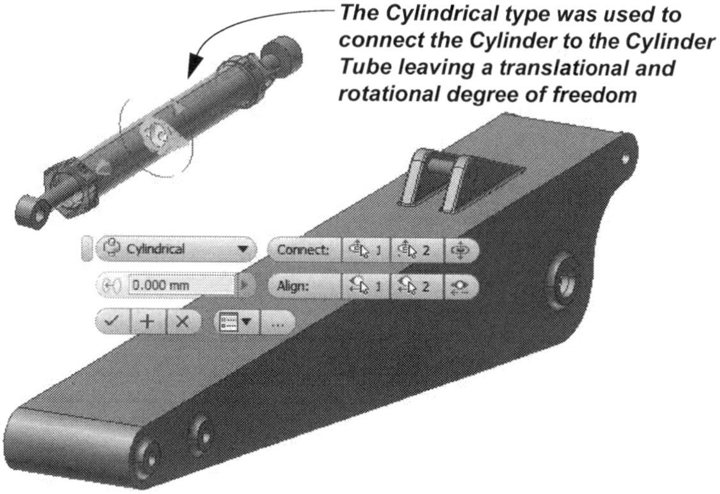

Figure 17–9

Planar

The (Planar) joint type enables a component to move in a plane, as shown in Figure 17–10. Two translational and one rotational degree of freedom remain with the component.

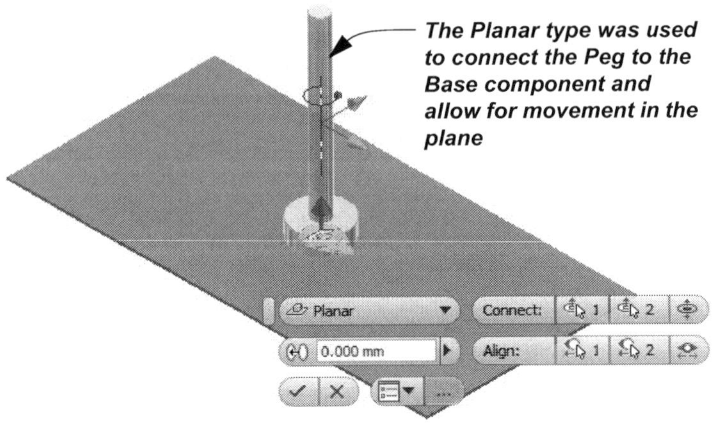

Figure 17–10

Ball

The (Ball) joint type enables a component to rotate in any direction about the origin joint, as shown in Figure 17–11. All translational degrees for freedom are removed.

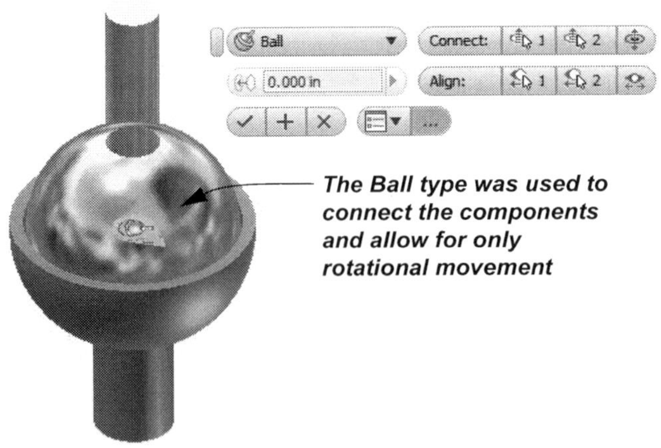

Figure 17–11

Step 4 - Assign a gap value, as required.

You can assign an gap value between selected references in the Place Joint dialog box or in the mini-toolbar. Entering a *Gap* value provides you with the flexibility of joining Origins that are at locations other than the end and center points.

Step 5 - Assign limits, as required.

Limits can only be assigned in the Place Joint dialog box. You cannot set limits in the mini-toolbar.

Limits cannot be specified for any option that is disabled, because the degree of freedom does not exist in the model.

To further control the motion that is permitted by a joint, you can define a specific range of motion. This is done by selecting the *Limits* tab in the Place Joint dialog box and entering values in the *Angular* and *Linear* areas, as shown in Figure 17–12.

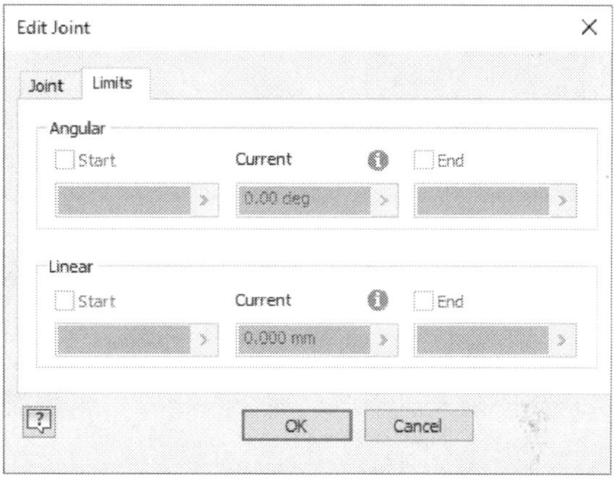

Figure 17–12

To specify a range, select **Start** or **End** and enter values to define a limit on the range of motion. For example, the angular range for a Rotational joint type can be controlled and a linear range can be specified for a Slider joint type. The *Current* value listed in each area defines the current position of the component in the assembly.

Step 6 - Complete the joint.

Click **OK** in the Place Joint dialog box or click  in the mini-toolbar to complete the joint. Alternatively, you can right-click in the graphics window and select **OK (Enter)** or press <Enter> to complete the joint.

- The default naming structure for a Joint is its type, followed by a number that indicates the number of joints of that type that have been assigned. Double-click on a joint's name in the Model browser to rename it. Alternatively, it can be renamed in the *Name* field of the dialog box.
- Use the **Lock** option (shown in Figure 17–13) to maintain the current position of the component without disabling the degrees of freedom that have been set in the component. A locked component cannot be selected to be moved. However, it updates if the connected components are moved, as opposed to grounding a component, which would lock the component in place regardless of any changes made.

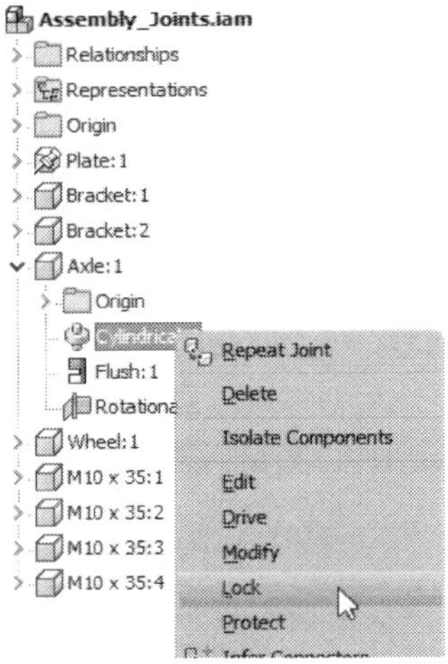

Figure 17–13

*The **Lock** and **Protect** options are only available for joints, not for constraints.*

The **Protect** option in the shortcut menu enables you to be prompted if relationships violate the degrees of freedom that have been assigned to the component with the use of a joint.

> **Hint: Combine Joints with Constraints**
>
> You can use the **Constrain** or **Assemble** commands to add additional constraints between components to further constrain any open degrees of freedom.

Step 7 - Edit the joint, as required.

Joints are listed in the Model browser under the component(s) to which they have been applied, as well as in the **Relationships** node at the top of the Model browser. Consider the following to edit a joint:

- To modify any value associated with a joint, double-click on the joint's name in the Model browser or right-click and select **Modify**. A mini-toolbar displays that enables you to enter the new values for linear or gap values.

- To change references used for a joint, right-click on the joint name in the Model browser and select **Edit**. The Edit Joint dialog box opens and you can change any of original references.

*Joint types can also be deleted by right-clicking the joint name in the Model browser and selecting **Delete**.*

- To review the relationships between components, click (Free Move) and drag a component. The connections are indicated by connecting lines and glyphs indicate the type of joints that were used as shown in Figure 17–14. You can right-click on the icons to suppress or delete a joint type.

Use (Show) in the Relationships panel to display the glyphs for any selected components. Preselecting all of the components and selecting this option displays all of the glyphs. Use (Hide All) to clear them from the display.

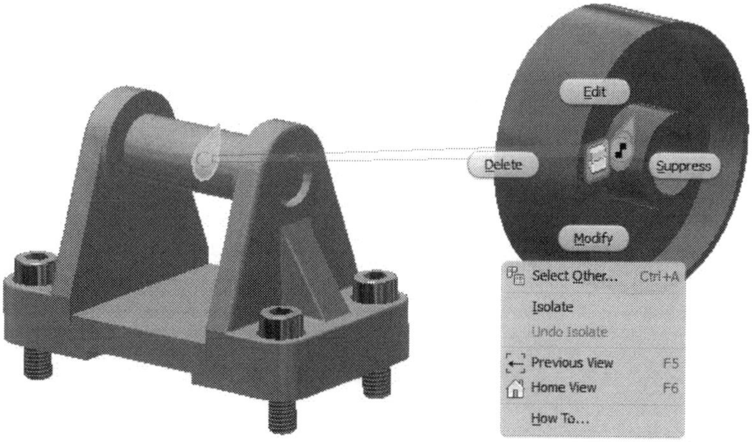

Figure 17–14

- If any of the joints are failing you can use (Show Sick) in the Relationships panel to review them. This command is only available if there are sick joints in the assembly. Edit the references as required to resolve the issues or delete the Joint.

Practice 17a Assembly Basics II (Joints)

Practice Objectives

- Use the **Joint** command to fully connect components in an assembly.
- Drag components to verify the movement in the assembly.

In this practice, you will create a new assembly and assemble the components as shown in Figure 17–15. To assemble the components you will use the **Joint** command, which will connect components relative to one another so that the assembly can easily be tested for movement.

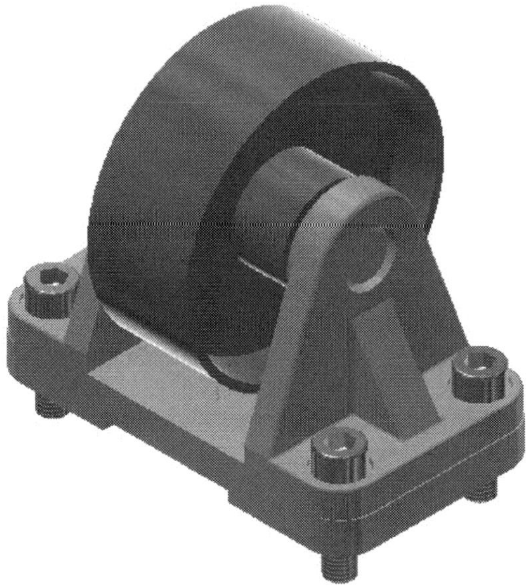

Figure 17–15

Task 1 - Create a new assembly and assemble the first component.

1. Create a new assembly file using the **Standard(mm).iam** template file.

2. In the Component panel, click  (Place).

3. Select **Plate.ipt** in the Place Component dialog box and click **Open**. The component is added to the assembly.

4. If the component displays in a 2D orientation, return the model to its default Home View using the ViewCube.

5. Right-click on the model and select **Place Grounded at Origin** to ground the component. The model displays as shown in Figure 17–16.

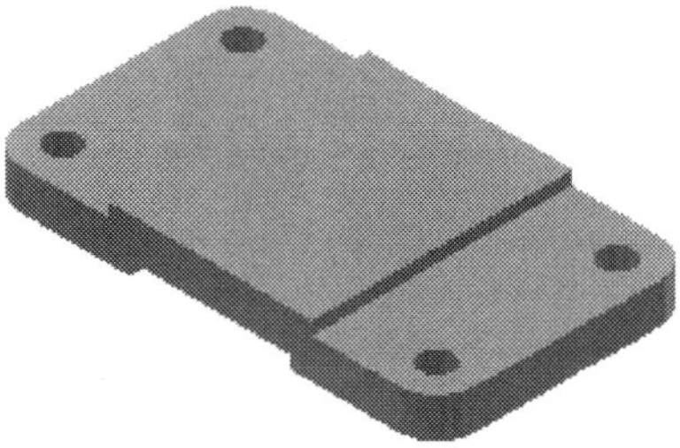

Figure 17–16

6. Right-click and select **OK** to assemble a single instance of the component into the assembly.

7. Review the Model browser and note the pushpin ( ) symbol next to the **Plate**, as shown in Figure 17–17. Hover the cursor over the **Plate.ipt** component in the graphics window. The cursor symbol indicates that it is grounded.

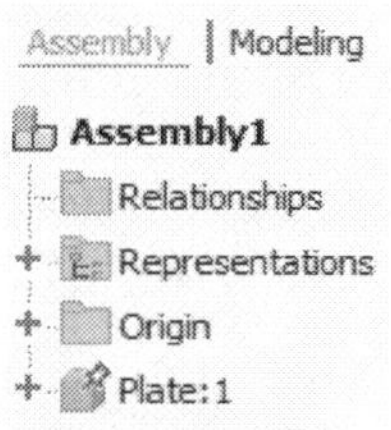

Figure 17–17

Task 2 - Assemble the Bracket component.

---

1. In the Component panel, click (Place).

2. Select **Bracket.ipt** in the Place Component dialog box and click **Open**. The component is added to the assembly.

3. Right-click on the model and select **Rotate Z 90** to rotate the component into a more convenient orientation.

4. Use the left mouse button to locate the component next to the Plate component, as shown in Figure 17–18. Right-click and select **OK** to place a single instance.

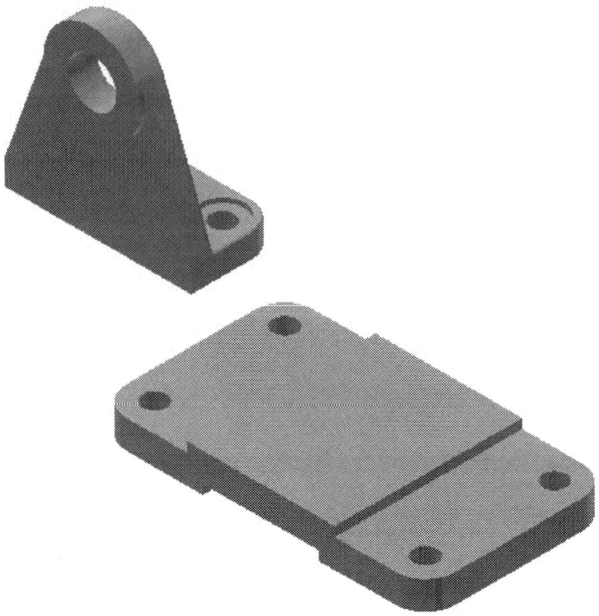

Figure 17–18

5. In the *Assemble* tab>Relationships panel, click (Joint). The Place Joint dialog box and mini-toolbar open. If the mini-toolbar is not displayed, enable it in the *View* tab> Windows panel in the User Interface list.

Once the Place Joint dialog box is toggled off, it must be enabled again to open it.

6. In the mini-toolbar, click to toggle off the display of the Place Joint dialog box. You will use the mini-toolbar to join components.
7. In the Type drop-down list in the mini-toolbar, select **Rigid**.
8. Rotate the assembly as shown in Figure 17–19.
9. On the **Bracket** component (first reference), hover the cursor over the edge shown in Figure 17–19. It will display in red with a green dot at the midpoint of the edge. Use the left mouse button to select the reference.

10. On the **Plate** component (second reference), hover the cursor over the edge shown in Figure 17–19. It will display in red with a green dot at the midpoint of the edge. Use the left mouse button to select the reference.

*Figure 17–19 shows the reference on **Bracket** already selected and the reference on **Plate** highlighted. The images displaying the reference selection in this practice will be shown in this way for the remainder of the practice. The images may also be reoriented for clarity. You can spin the model, as required, to select the required references.*

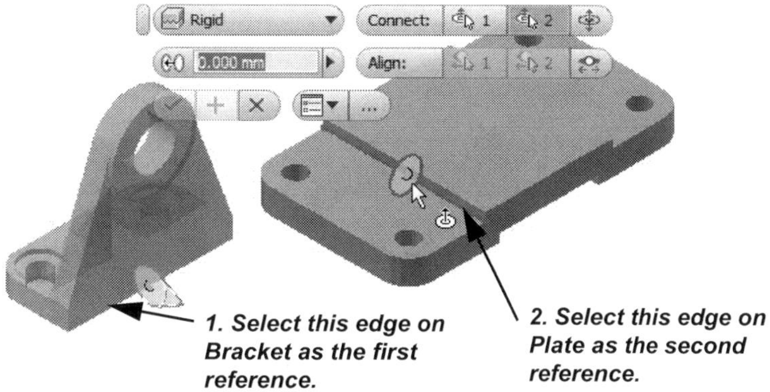

Figure 17–19

- The **Bracket** component (reference 1) moves into position and displays animated movement indicating its allowable degrees of freedom. In this case it is a rigid joint and because no movement is permitted, the animated movement is very small.

Note that you did not have to activate any of the fields in the mini-toolbar. The first reference field is immediately active and the second is activated once the first reference has been selected. Selecting the reference fields in the *Connect* field is only required when redefining a reference.

11. The components assemble in the wrong orientation. In the *Connect* area in the mini-toolbar, click  (Flip Component) to flip the component.

12. Note that while the **Bracket** component has been flipped, the alignment must also be inverted to correct the orientation. In the *Align* area in the mini-toolbar, click 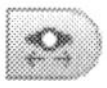 (Invert Component) to invert the component.

13. Click  (Flip Component) again to locate the component, if required.

14. Click (✓) in the mini-toolbar to complete the joint. The assembly displays as shown in Figure 17–20.

Figure 17–20

15. Expand the **Relationships** node and note that the **Rigid** joint has been added. A **Rigid** joint is also listed in the nodes for the two components.

Task 3 - Assemble a second instance of the Bracket component.

1. In the Component panel, click (Place).
2. Select **Bracket.ipt** in the Place Component dialog box and click **Open**. The component is added to the assembly.
3. Right-click on the model and select **Rotate Z 90** and **Rotate Y 90** to rotate the component into a more convenient orientation, similar to that shown in Figure 17–21.
4. Use the left mouse button to locate the component next to the Plate component, as shown in Figure 17–21. Right-click and select **OK** to place a single instance.

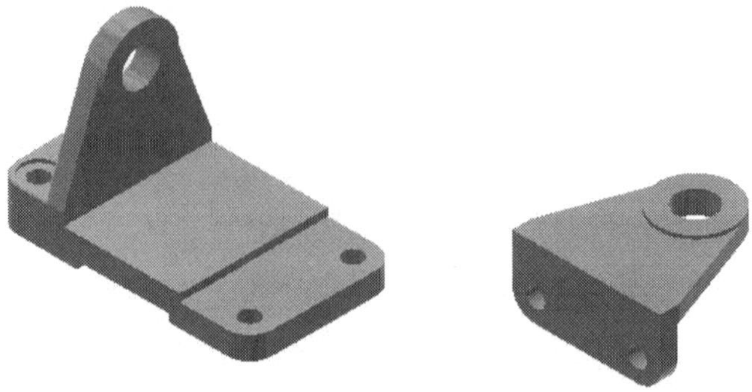

Figure 17–21

5. In the *Assemble* tab>Relationships panel, click (Joint).
6. In the Type drop-down list in the mini-toolbar, select **Rigid**.

   Previously, the two components were joined using reference edges, but for this component, faces will be used. Faces are generally the more stable selection reference.

7. On the **Bracket** component (first reference), hover the cursor over the surface shown in Figure 17–22. It will display in red. Continue to move the cursor so that the green dot displays at the midpoint of the top edge. Use the left mouse button to select the reference.
8. On the **Plate** component (second reference), hover over the face shown in Figure 17–22. It will display in red. Continue to move the cursor so that the green dot displays at the midpoint of the long edge. Use the left mouse button to select the reference.

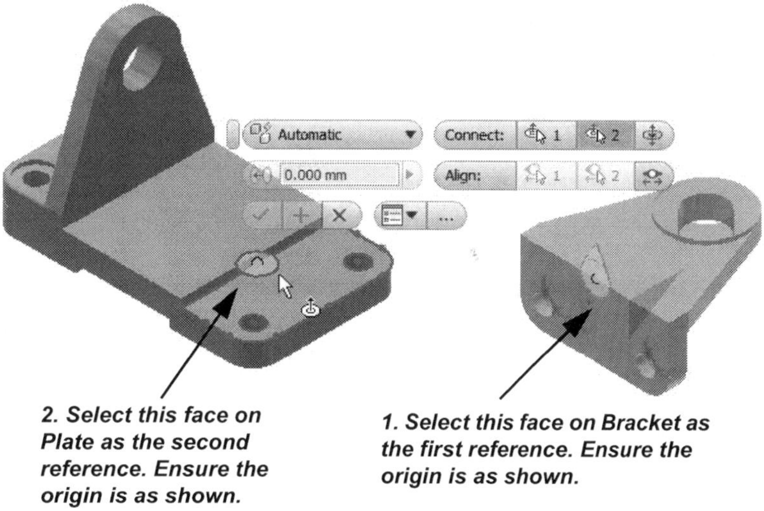

Figure 17–22

9. The **Bracket** component (reference 1) moves into position. If the components assemble in the wrong orientation, use the (Flip Component) and (Invert Component) options to reposition the component, as required.

10. Click [icon] in the mini-toolbar to complete the joint. The assembly displays as shown in Figure 17–23.

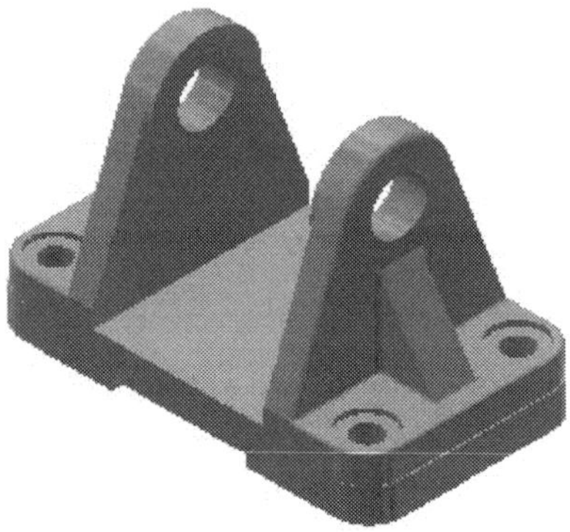

Figure 17–23

Task 4 - Assemble the Axle component.

1. In the Component panel, click [icon] (Place).
2. Select **Axle.ipt** in the Place Component dialog box and click **Open**. The component is added to the assembly.
3. Use the shortcut menu options to rotate the component into a more convenient orientation.
4. Use the left mouse button to locate the component next to the assembly, as shown in Figure 17–24. Right-click and select **OK** to place a single instance.

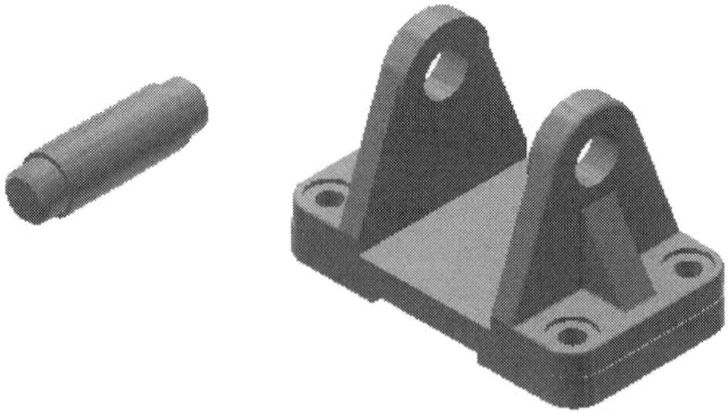

Figure 17–24

5. In the *Assemble* tab>Relationships panel, click (Joint).

   Ideally, the **Axle** component should join the midpoint of its central axis to a point midway between the two **Bracket** components. Joint references must be selected in a single component. To join the **Axle** you will be required to use both a **Joint** and **Constraint** option.

6. In the Type drop-down list in the mini-toolbar, select **Cylindrical**. This type allows for 1 translational and 1 rotational degree of freedom. The translational degree of freedom will be removed in a later step using a Mate constraint.

7. On the **Axle** component (first reference), hover the cursor over the midpoint of the cylindrical surface, shown in Figure 17–25. It will display in red with a green dot at the centerpoint of the central axis. Use the left mouse button to select the reference.

8. On the **Bracket** component (second reference), hover over the edge shown in Figure 17–25. It will display in red with a green dot at the midpoint of the edge. Use the left mouse button to select the reference.

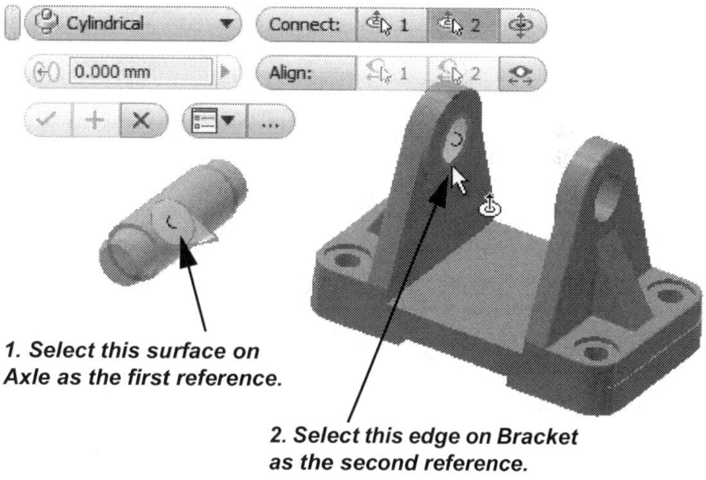

Figure 17–25

9. Click  in the mini-toolbar to complete the joint. The assembly displays as shown in Figure 17–26.

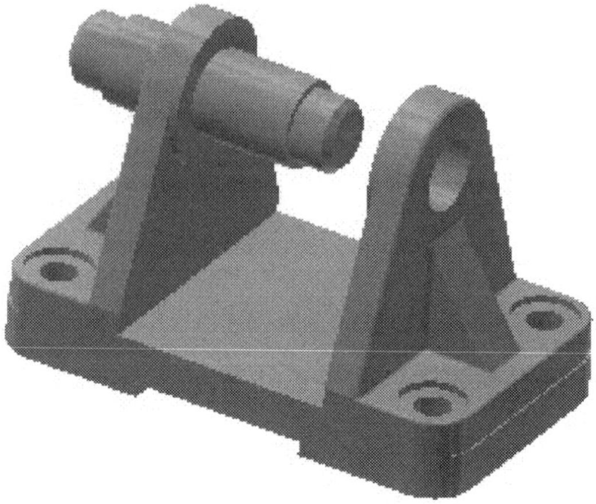

Figure 17–26

10. Drag the **Axle** and note how it moves. It can rotate in the hole and translate along the axis of the hole.

11. In the *Assemble* tab>Relationships panel, click  (Constrain). Constraints can be used to remove any unwanted degrees of freedom that result from a joint connection. In this case, you will remove the translational degree of freedom in the Axle component.

12. Assign a Mate (Flush) constraint that aligns the XY Plane in the **Axle** with the YZ Plane of the assembly.

13. Click **OK** to complete the constraint definition. Drag the Axle and note that only one rotational degree of freedom remains. To visually identify the remaining rotational degree of freedom, in the View tab>Visibility panel, click  (Degrees of Freedom). The assembly displays as shown in Figure 17–27.

Figure 17–27

14. To further remove any degrees of freedom from the assembly you can Lock joint connections. Right-click on the Cylindrical joint connection and select **Lock**. This removes the remaining rotational degree of freedom.

15. Expand the **Relationships** node and note that the Cylindrical joint and Flush constraint have been added.

Alternatively, you can use a **Rigid** joint to determine the correct offset value to locate the Axle.

Task 5 - Assemble the Wheel component.

1. Place one instance of the Wheel component, similar to the orientation shown in Figure 17–28.

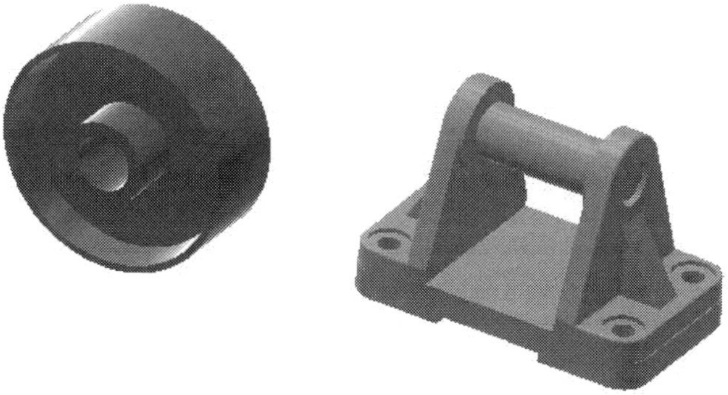

Figure 17–28

2. In the *Assemble* tab>Relationships panel, click (Joint).

3. In the Type drop-down list in the mini-toolbar, leave **Automatic** as the joint type.

To ensure that you are snapping to the proper reference, once you hover over the required surface (inner cylindrical face), press and hold <Ctrl> to maintain surface selection. You are now able to move between the origin references while remaining on the original surface.

4. On the **Wheel** component (first reference), select the midpoint of the inner cylindrical surface, shown in Figure 17–29, as the origin reference.

5. On the **Axle** component (second reference), select the midpoint of the cylindrical surface shown in Figure 17–29, as the origin reference.

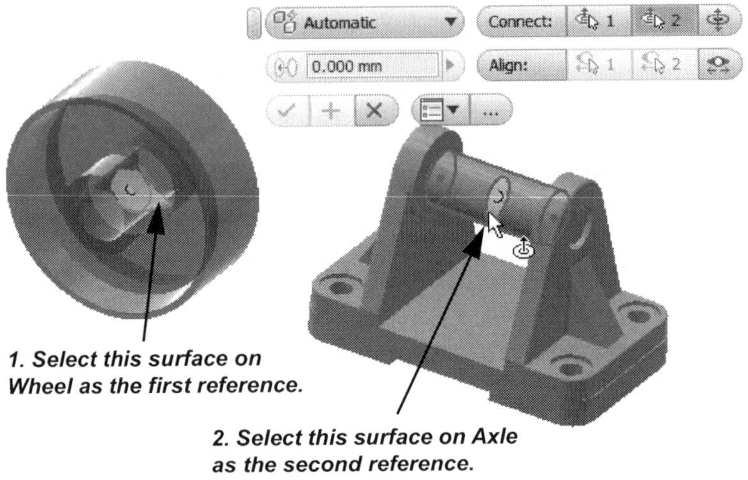

Figure 17–29

The **Wheel** component (reference 1) moves into position and displays animated movement indicating its allowable degrees of freedom. Note that the system assumed a Cylindrical joint type. A Rotational joint is required.

6. In the Type drop-down list in the mini-toolbar, select **Rotational**.

7. Click ✓ in the mini-toolbar to complete the joint. The assembly displays as shown in Figure 17–30.

Figure 17–30

Task 6 - Assemble the Screw components.

1. Place one instance of the **M10 x35** component.

2. Begin the creation of a new joint. In the Type drop-down list in the mini-toolbar, select **Rotational**.

3. On the **M10 x35** component (first reference), hover the cursor over the bottom face of the screw head so that the origin reference is shown as in Figure 17–31. Select to assign the reference.

4. On the **Bracket** component (second reference), hover the cursor over the bottom face of the counterbore hole so that the origin reference is shown as in Figure 17–31. Select to assign the reference.

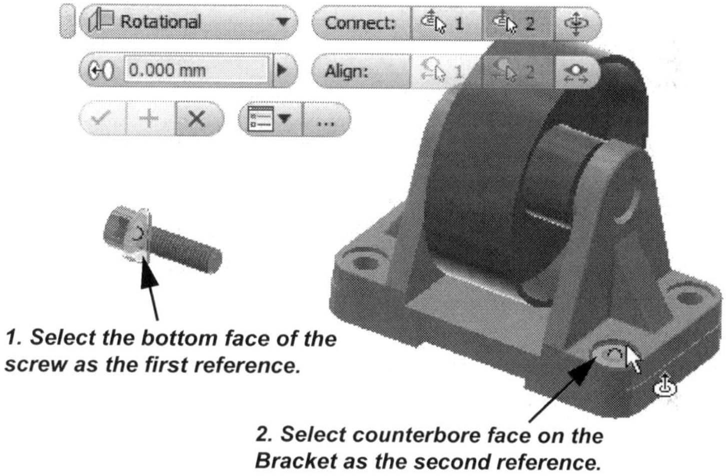

Figure 17–31

The component moves into position and displays its remaining rotational degree of freedom.

5. Complete the joint. The assembly displays as shown in Figure 17–32.

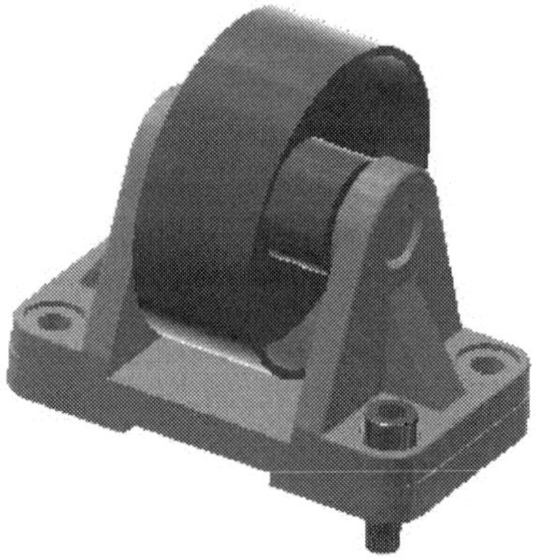

Figure 17–32

In general, it is recommended to remove degrees of freedom to eliminate the possibility to unexpected changes and so that Inventor is not forced to calculate the open movement after each update.

6. Right-click on the Rotational joint in the Model browser. Then, right-click and select **Lock** to remove its rotational degree of freedom.

7. Place a second instance of the **M10 x35** component. Instead of using a Rotational joint, assign a Rigid joint connection to remove all degrees of freedom with a single constraint.

8. Add and join the remaining screw components, as shown in Figure 17–33. Ensure all degrees of freedom are removed from the model using either of the two methods.

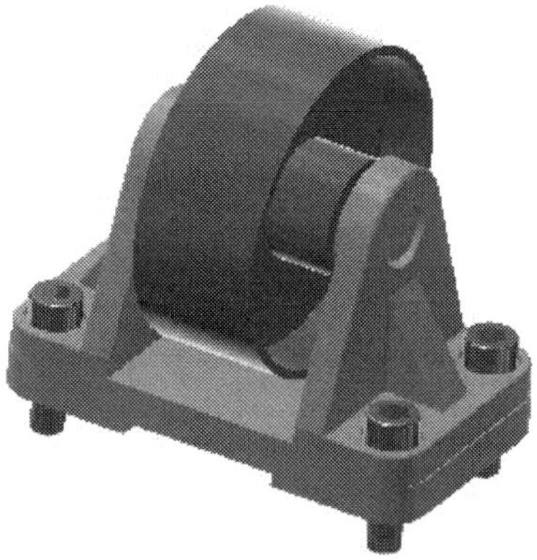

Figure 17–33

For additional practice creating joints, refer to the Appendix chapter for an additional practice.

9. Save the assembly as **Assembly_Joints.iam**.

Practice 17b Assembly Basics III

Practice Objective

- Constrain components in an assembly to maintain a single degree of freedom for translation or rotation.

In this practice, you will open an existing assembly and add joints and constraints to components. The final assembly displays as shown in Figure 17–34.

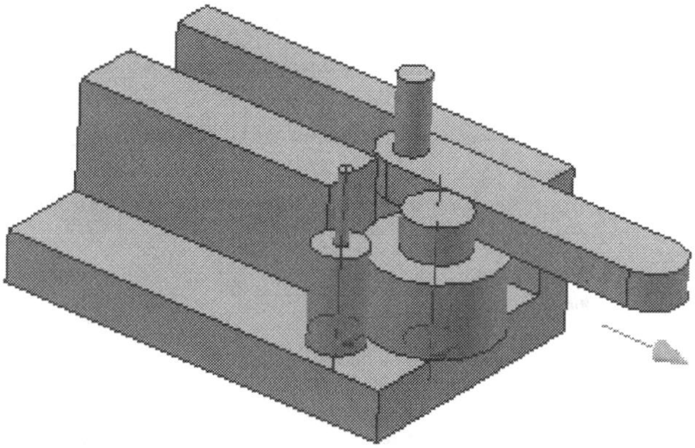

Figure 17–34

Task 1 - Open an assembly file.

1. Open **constraints.iam**. The **base** component is grounded and the other three components are not constrained.
2. Display the symbols for the degrees of freedom on the parts.

Task 2 - Apply Rotational joint connections to the rotating components.

1. Apply a Rotational joint connection between **Roll1** and **Base**. Place the shorter end of **Roll1** into the hole closest to the corner of the base, as shown in Figure 17–35. Only a single rotational degree of freedom remains.

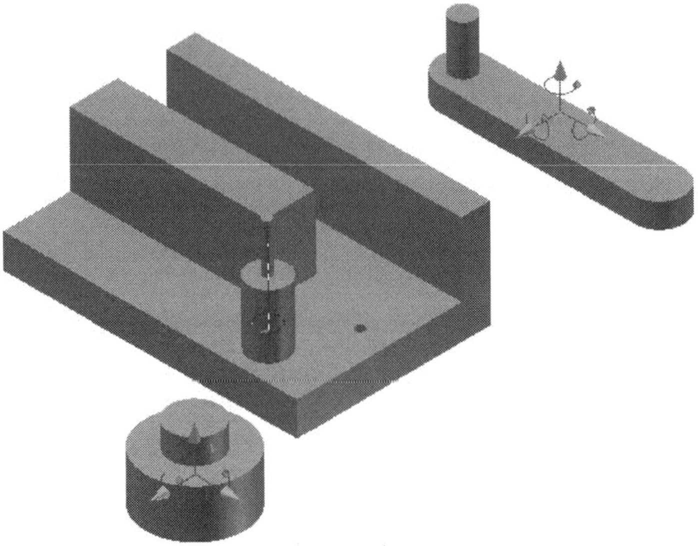

Figure 17–35

2. Apply a Rotational joint connection between **Roll2** and **Base**, as shown in Figure 17–36. Only a single rotational degree of freedom remains.

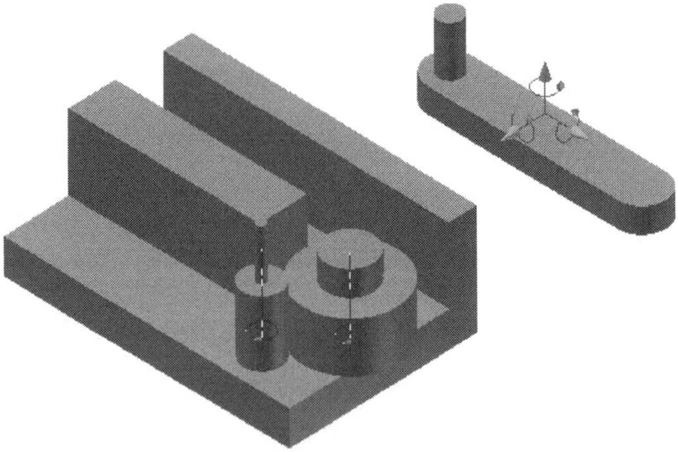

Figure 17–36

Task 3 - Apply a joint and constraint to the Sliderarm to allow for sliding movement.

1. Apply a Planar joint between the large flat face of the **Sliderarm** and the large circular face of **Roll2**, as shown in Figure 17–37.

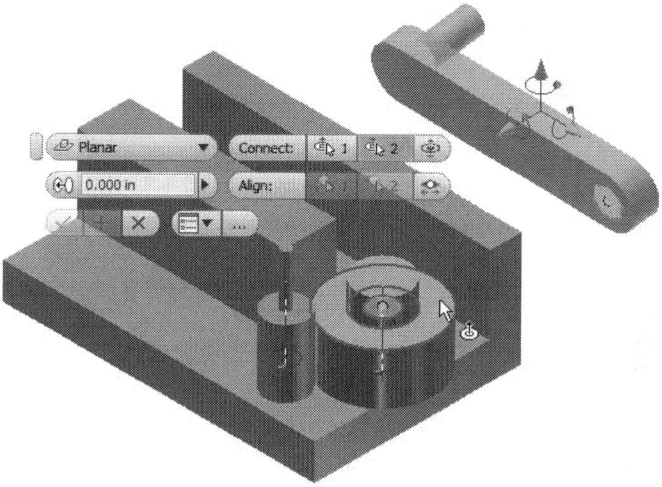

Figure 17–37

2. Apply a Tangent constraint between the rectangular side of the **Sliderarm** and the cylindrical surface on **Roll2**, as shown in Figure 17–38.

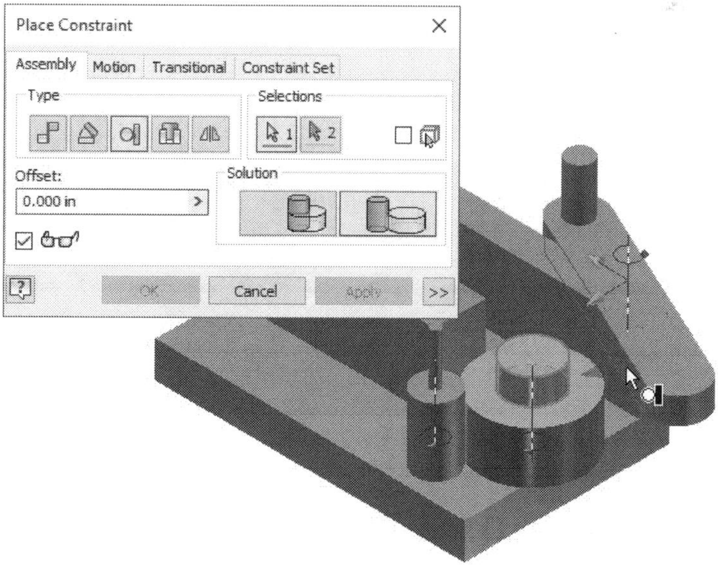

Figure 17–38

3. Apply a Mate constraint between the rectangular side of the **Sliderarm** and the rectangular side of the **Base**, as shown in Figure 17–39.

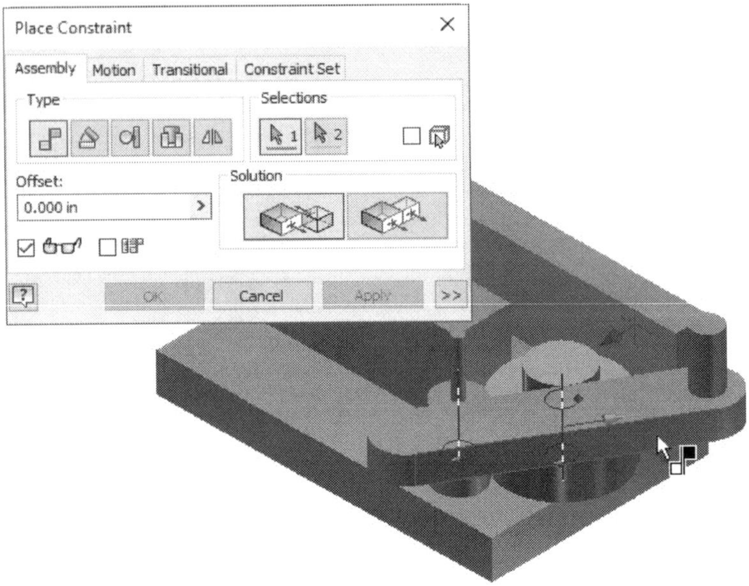

Figure 17–39

4. Select the **Sliderarm** and drag it. Note that it only moves as permitted by its one remaining degree of freedom, as shown in Figure 17–40. You can also rotate the two cylindrical parts. Work Points are provided on the edges of the cylinders to help visualize the movement.

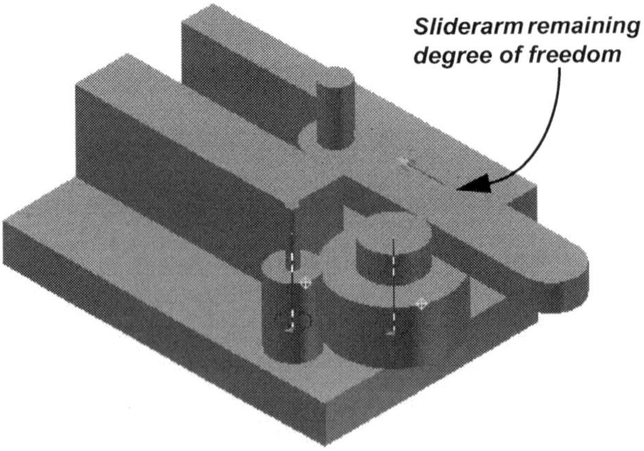

Figure 17–40

5. Save the assembly and close the window.

Chapter Review Questions

1. Once a Joint connection type has been added between components in an assembly, additional constraints can be used to further eliminate any degrees of freedom.
   a. True
   b. False

2. Match the joint type in the column on the left with its icon.

	Icon	Answer
a. Rigid		________
b. Rotational		________
c. Slider		________
d. Cylindrical		________
e. Planar		________
f. Ball		________

3. Which of the following cannot be accomplished using the mini-toolbar shown in Figure 17–41? (Select all that apply.)

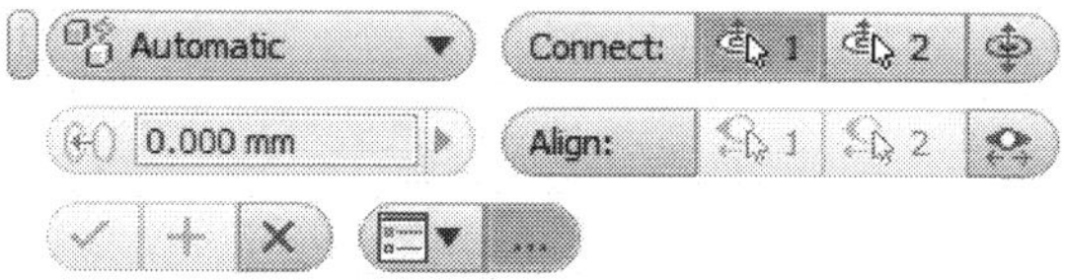

Figure 17–41

   a. Define a gap value for offsetting references.
   b. Define a limit value for range of motion.
   c. Flip components.
   d. Control whether an animation displays when components are joined.
   e. Assign a name for the joint.

4. Match the joint type in the column on the left with the degrees of freedom that remain in the assembled component after it has been assigned.

	Degrees of Freedom	Answer
a. Rigid	1 Translational, 1 Rotational	_______
b. Rotational	2 Translational, 1 Rotational	_______
c. Slider	0 Translational, 0 Rotational	_______
d. Cylindrical	0 Translational, 3 Rotational	_______
e. Planar	1 Translational, 0 Rotational	_______
f. Ball	0 Translational, 1 Rotational	_______

5. The Automatic joint type assumes the joint type without requiring you to select references on the two components being joined.
   a. True
   b. False

6. The alignment references between two components are defined by default based on the selected references. Which of the following buttons in the mini-toolbar enables you to invert the default alignment?
   a. 

   b. 

   c. 
   d. 

7. Which of the following entity types can be selected as references for joint connections? (Select all that apply.)
   a. Work Points
   b. Work Planes
   c. Work Axes
   d. Faces
   e. Edges
   f. Spherical Geometry

8. The first component reference selected to define the placement of a joint connection represents the component that is going to remain stationary when joined.
   a. True
   b. False

9. Which of the following best describes the **Lock** option when used to lock a joint?
   a. A locked component cannot be selected to be moved, but it updates if connected components are moved.
   b. A locked component is similar to a grounded component. It is locked in place regardless of changes made to connected components.

10. Which of the following options enables you to redefine the alignment references that were assigned when a joint connection was assigned?
    a. **Modify**
    b. **Edit**
    c. **Free Move**
    d. **Show Sick**

Command Summary

Button	Command	Location
	**Degrees of Freedom**	• **Ribbon:** *View* tab>Visibility panel
	**Joint**	• **Ribbon:** *Assemble* tab>Relationships panel
	**Place**	• **Ribbon:** *Assemble* tab>Component panel

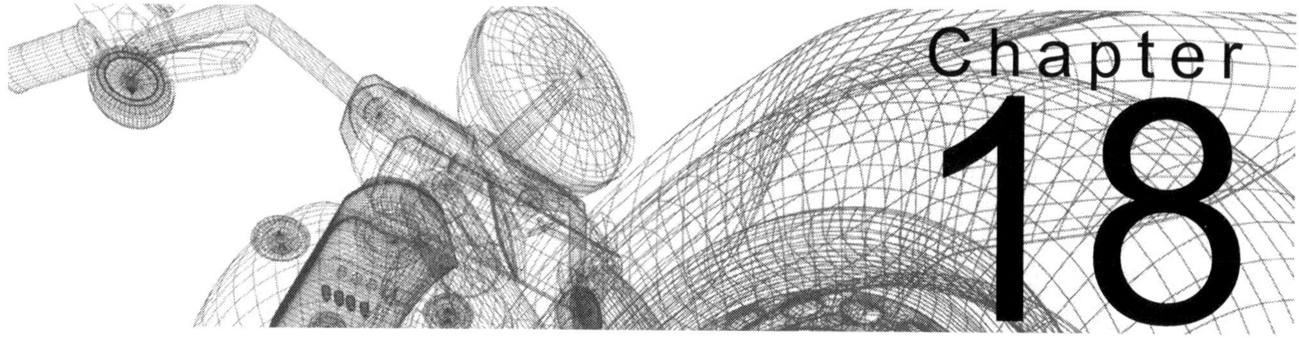

Manipulating Assembly Display

You have learned that components are constrained to one another to form assemblies. The constraints that you use result in feature relationships between the components. You now learn how to use a number of other tools in Assembly mode to evaluate and review an entire assembly.

Learning Objectives in This Chapter

- Temporarily relocate a constrained component to a new location in an assembly by moving or rotating it.
- Suppress constraints in an assembly.
- Control component display in an assembly.
- Create Section Views in an assembly that display portions of an overall assembly based on selected planes.
- Create Design View representations that store assembly display configurations.
- Use appropriate selection priority options to efficiently make selections in an assembly.

18.1 Moving and Rotating Assembly Components

Viewing or selecting references in components of a large assemblies can be challenging. Moving and rotating components is a simple way of temporarily relocating assembly components.

Moving Components

To move components in an assembly, click (Free Move) in the *Assemble* tab>Position panel, and select the component to move in the graphics window. Alternatively, you can select the component in the graphics window, right-click and select **Free Move**. Hold the left mouse button, and drag the component to a new location. Once you have moved the component, release the mouse button to drop the component.

When moving components, you can only select one component to move at a time and grounded components cannot be moved.

- If the component being moved is constrained, the **Free Move** command displays relationships as elastic bands between the constraint references. Icons indicate the original constraint type, as shown in Figure 18–1.
- Relationships are not displayed between unconstrained components.

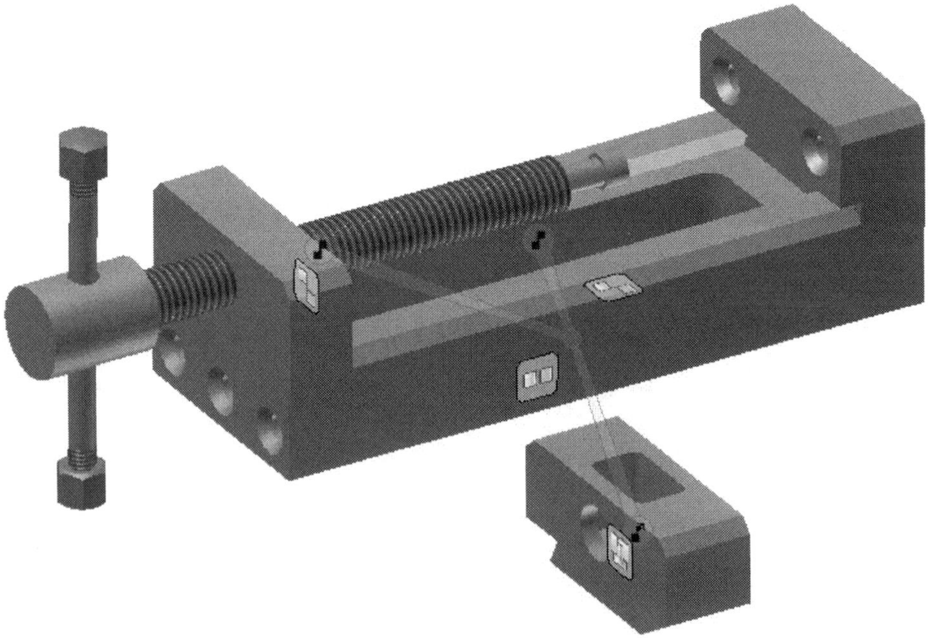

Figure 18–1

Select any of the constraint icons once a moved component has been placed and right-click to display the marking menu, as shown in Figure 18–2. The commands in the marking menu enable you to **Edit**, **Suppress**, **Delete**, or **Modify** (offset value) the selected constraint.

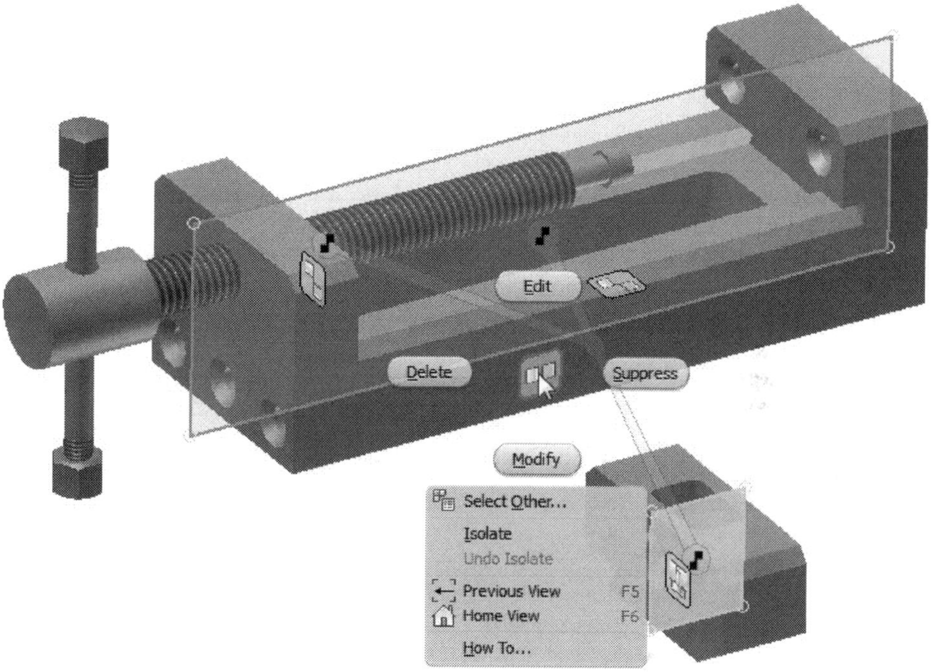

Figure 18–2

- To clear the relationship display from the model, press <Esc>, or right-click and select **OK**.

Rotating Components

Rotating components enables you to manipulate the orientation of selected assembly components independent of the overall assembly and can help with constraint selection. Grounded components cannot be rotated.

*Unlike the **Free Move** command, the **Free Rotate** command does not function differently for constrained and unconstrained components.*

To rotate assembly components, click (Free Rotate) in the *Assemble* tab>Position panel and select the component to rotate in the graphics window. Alternatively, you can select the component in the graphics window, right-click and select **Free Rotate**. A rotation circle displays in the assembly window, as it does when using the **Orbit** command.

Use the following methods to rotate (hold the left mouse button while dragging the mouse):

- Click inside the circle to rotate freely.
- Use the left or right handles to rotate about the Y-axis.
- Use the top or bottom handles to rotate about the X-axis.
- Click outside the circle to rotate about the Z-axis.

When you have finished rotating the component(s), press <Esc> or right-click and select **OK**.

Updating the Assembly

To return the parts to their constrained positions after moving or rotating them, click (Local Update) in the Quick Access Toolbar. The update options for assemblies are shown in Figure 18–3.

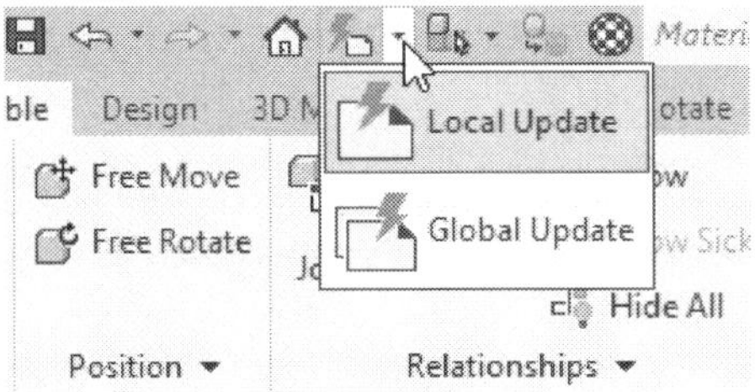

Figure 18–3

- Select (Local Update) to update an individual part or subassembly. This option is useful for large assemblies with long update times.
- Select (Global Update) to update the entire assembly. All subassemblies including the top-level assembly are updated.

18.2 Suppressing Constraints

In complex assemblies, suppressing constraints is useful for easing the assembly of other components. To suppress a constraint, right-click on the constraint in the Model browser and select **Suppress**. Repeat the process to reactivate the constraint. A suppressed constraint displays in the Model browser as a grayed symbol.

Consider the assembly shown on the right in Figure 18–4. Another component must be constrained to the component, which is inside the assembly. Constraints are suppressed between the components (shown on the left in Figure 18–4) so that you can move the lock components outside the assembly and constrain another component to them without the lock components snapping back to their constrained positions.

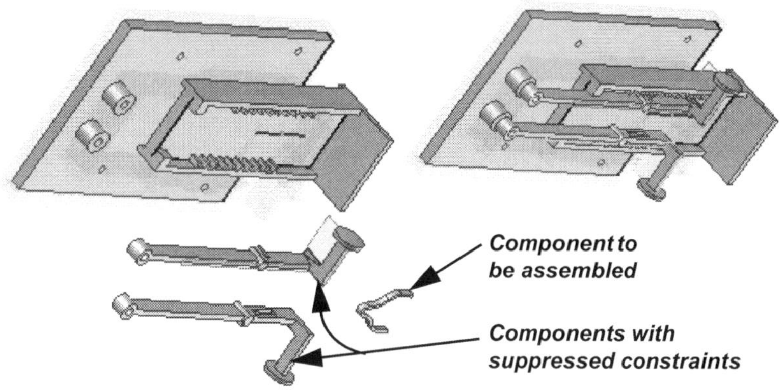

Figure 18–4

- If you have suppressed any constraints, you must reactivate them if you want them to update.

18.3 Component Display

When you add components to an assembly, they are visible and enabled by default. The following tools are available to simplify the display of assembly components:

Visible Components

You can toggle off the visibility of a component to more easily modify components, as shown in Figure 18–5. To toggle off the visibility of a component, right-click on a component in the Model browser and select **Visibility** so that it is toggled off. Alternatively, you can right-click on the component in the graphics window and select **Visibility**. The component symbol in the Model browser displays in gray and the model is no longer displayed in the graphics window, as shown in Figure 18–5. To display the component again, right-click on it in the Model browser and select **Visibility** so that it is toggled on.

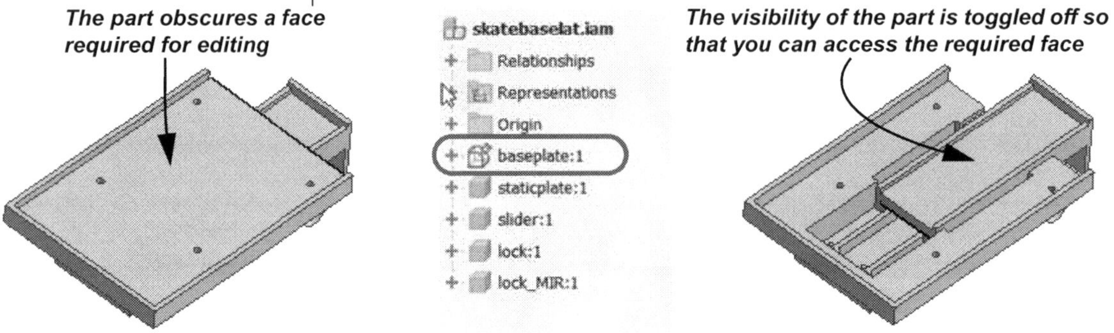

Figure 18–5

Enabling Components

You can restrict a component from being selected by disabling it, as shown in Figure 18–6. To disable a component, right-click on the component in the Model browser or in the graphics window and select **Enabled** so that it is toggled off. The component symbol in the Model browser displays in green and the model displays in a lighter shading, as shown in Figure 18–6. To re-enable the component, right-click on the component in the Model browser and select **Enabled** so that it is toggled on.

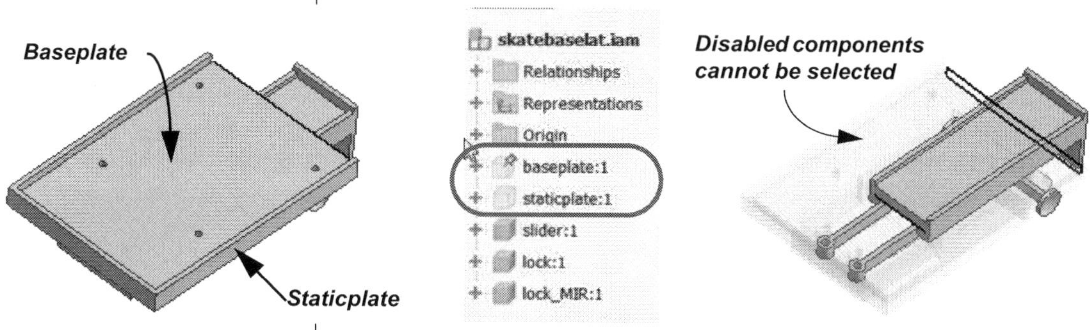

Figure 18–6

> **Hint: Advantages of the Visibility and Enabling Options**
>
> - Helps easily edit components inside or behind others.
> - Helps in selecting geometry that might be obscured.
> - Simplifies the display of the assembly.
> - Enables faster opening and updating of assembly files, because components that are not required until later in the design process are toggled off.
> - Enables you to make non-solid geometry (e.g., planes or axes) visible for constraining or referencing.

Isolating Components

Consider using a Design View if you isolate the same components routinely to create a working view.

The **Isolate** command enables you to toggle off the visibility of all of the components except the ones you need. To use the **Isolate** command, select the components in the Model browser or in the graphics window, right-click and select **Isolate**. This is useful in a large assembly to easily select references to create constraints.

To undo the **Isolate** command, right-click anywhere in the window and select **Undo Isolate**. You can only use this option once.

Transparent Components

The **Transparent** command enables you to set the visibility of an assembly component as transparent in an assembly view. Once set, the component cannot be selected; however, it remains visible in a transparent display style. To set a component to transparent, use one of the following methods:

- Right-click on the component name in the Model browser or in the graphics window and select **Transparent**.
- In the component's iProperties dialog box, on the *Occurrence* tab, select **Transparent**.

To undo the **Transparent** command, reselect the component and clear the option.

Section Views

Creating a Section View enables you to work inside assemblies while still keeping the required components visible and enabled. Section views display portions of the assembly that lie on one side or between reference planes. The three section views shown in Figure 18–7 can be created.

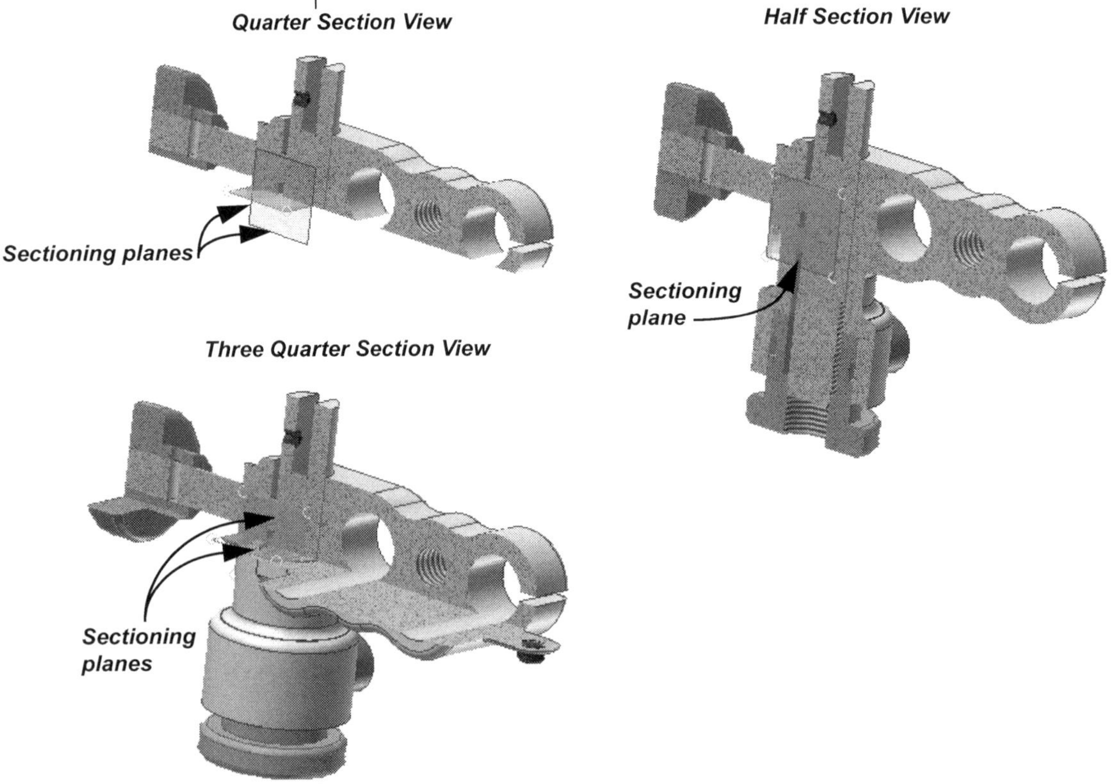

Figure 18–7

How To: Section a View

1. In the *View* tab>Appearance panel, select the type of section view in the drop-down list as shown in Figure 18–8.

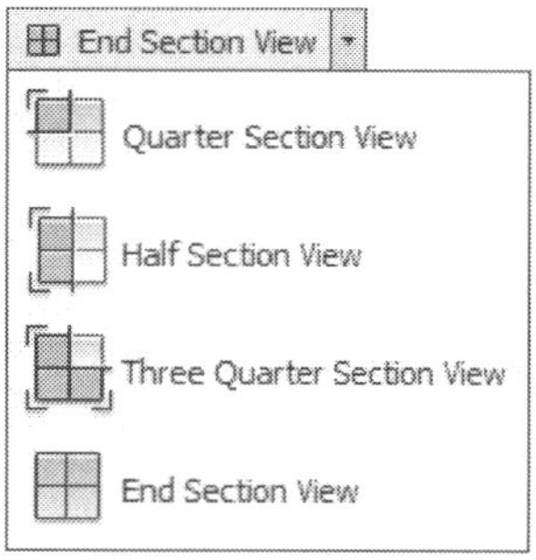

Figure 18–8

Instead of entering an offset value, you can dynamically section the model by clicking the left mouse button and dragging the cursor.

2. Select the plane to section about and if required, enter an offset value from the selected plane. Click the arrow button to continue if creating a quarter or three quarter section view.
3. For quarter and three quarter section views, select an additional plane to section about. Select the second plane, and if required, enter an offset value from the selected plane.
4. If required, flip the section by right-clicking and selecting **Flip Section**.
5. To modify the offset from a selected plane, drag the direction arrow or enter a value in the mini-toolbar field. If multiple planes were selected to define the Section View (i.e., Quarter and Three-Quarter Section Views), right-click in the graphics window and select **Virtual Movement>Section Plane #** (where # is the section plane that you want to modify, 1 or 2) to switch the active plane. Use one of the techniques to move the plane, as required.

To change the scroll increments when modifying section plane placement using the scroll wheel in the mini-toolbar field, right-click and select ***Scroll Step Size****, enter an increment value, and click the check mark icon.*

6. Right-click and select **OK** to complete the view or click the check mark icon.

- Once in a section view, you can select references on cut components. Note that edges that are generated by the cut are not selectable as they are not physical edges in the model.
- Once created, a section view cannot be redefined, you would have to recreate it to make changes.
- To return to a view of the entire part, click the End Section View icon (End Section View) in the Section View drop-down list. Section views are temporary unless used in conjunction with design views.

Design Views

A Design View enables you to save a configuration of an assembly view that can easily be recalled for future use. Design Views can store the following:

- Visibility/Isolation settings
- Enabled/disabled component settings
- Color override of components
- Assembly orientation

Saving Design Views has the following advantages:

- Saves a configuration where components are toggled on and off for ease of viewing or to ease selection.
- Creates different displays of your assembly for various purposes or different users.
- Reduces the loading or updating time of assemblies by displaying only the required components.

Figure 18–9 shows two saved Design Views of an assembly.

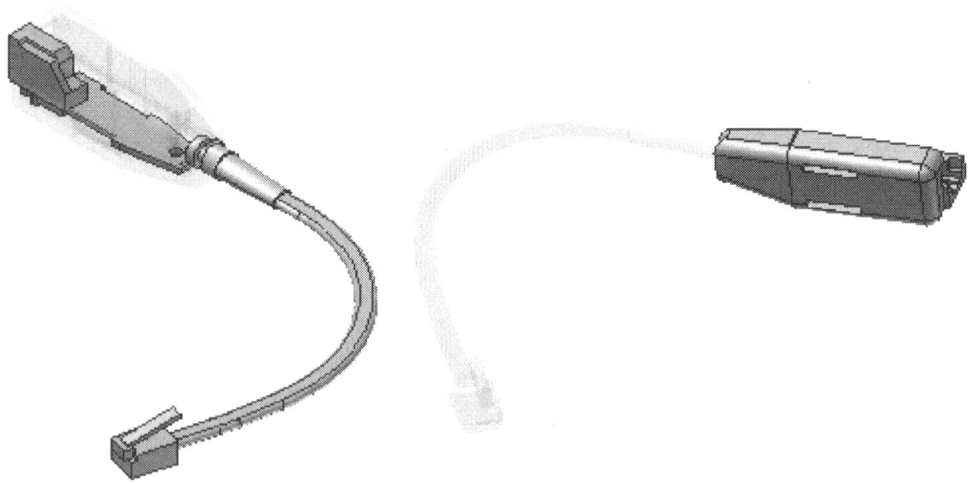

Figure 18–9

How To: Save a Design View

1. Expand the **Representations** node in the Model browser, as shown in Figure 18–10. Right-click on the **View: Default** node and select **New**.

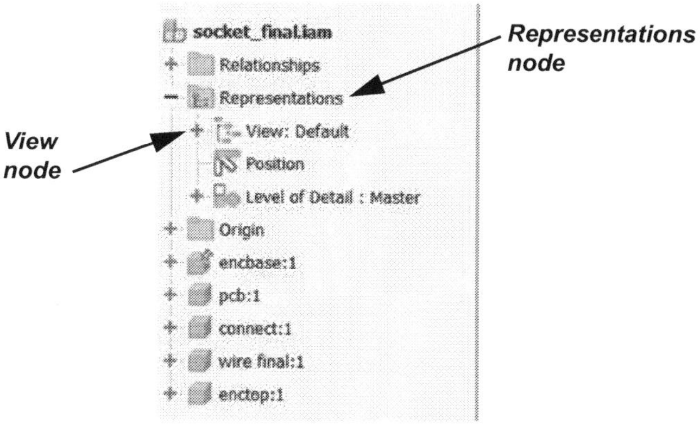

Figure 18–10

Remember to always give your design view a descriptive name to help you remember its content.

2. Configure the view display for the assembly.
3. Select the new view, left-click again (do not double-click) and enter a descriptive name (typically the same name as the assembly file) for the view.
4. To lock the design view, right-click on the view in the Model browser and select **Lock**. This restricts you or others from making changes to the design view representation at a later time and prevent newly assembled components from being included in the Design View.

The newly created design view is automatically made active. To display a different design view, right-click on an existing design view in the Model browser and select **Activate**, as shown in Figure 18–11, or double-click on another view name.

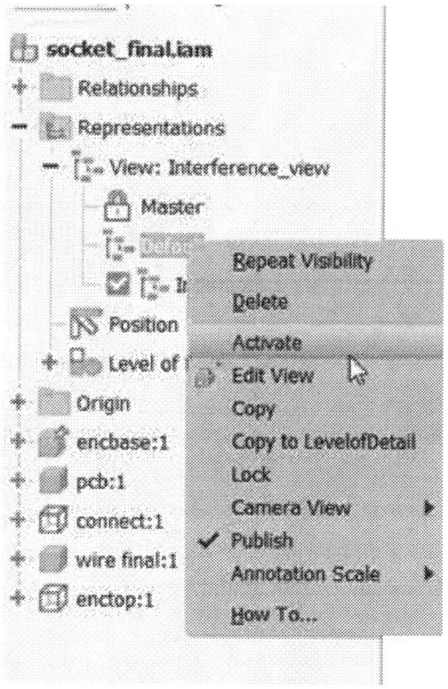

Figure 18–11

Modifying Design Views

To modify an existing Design View in a model it must be unlocked. To unlock, right-click on the Design View name in the Model browser and select **Unlock**. Once unlocked you can modify the Design View as follows:

- Change the visibility of the components in the Design View.
- Use the **Undo Isolate** command if the components were previously isolated in the Design View.
- Change which components are disabled or enabled.
- Override the appearance color of components.
- Change the assembly orientation.

As an alternative to using the **Visibility**, **Enable**, and **Undo-Isolate** commands to return components to the display in a Design View, you can also edit the included components by right-clicking on the Design View name in the Model browser and selecting **Edit View**. Once selected the mini-toolbar opens, as shown in Figure 18–12.

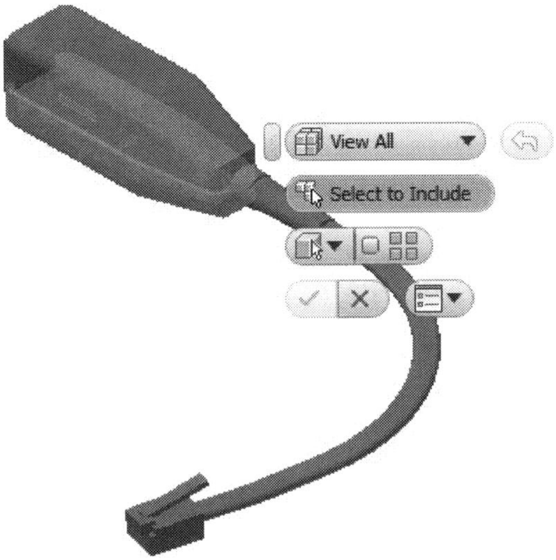

Figure 18–12

Click View Excluded in the drop-down list to filter the display so that only those previously excluded display.

- To add additional components to the Design View, ensure **View All** and **Select to Include** are active. The components highlighted in blue indicate the current components that display in the Design View. Select additional components, as required, to add components to the Design View.
- To remove previously included components to the Design View, ensure that **View Included** and **Select to Exclude** are active. Select components in the assembly to clear them from the Design View.
- Click to complete the modification.

Hint: Camera Views

Right-click and use **Camera View** for the new view to control how a custom orientation is saved with the view. The options enable you to automatically save the view orientation when the Design View is active (**Autosave Camera**). You can also clear this option and save the required orientations for the view. By default, the **Autosave Camera** option is enabled.

18.4 Selection Options in Assemblies

The assembly selection options can also be accessed by pressing and holding <Shift> as you right-click in an assembly.

Assembly selection priority options are located in the Quick Access toolbar ( ), as shown in Figure 18–13.

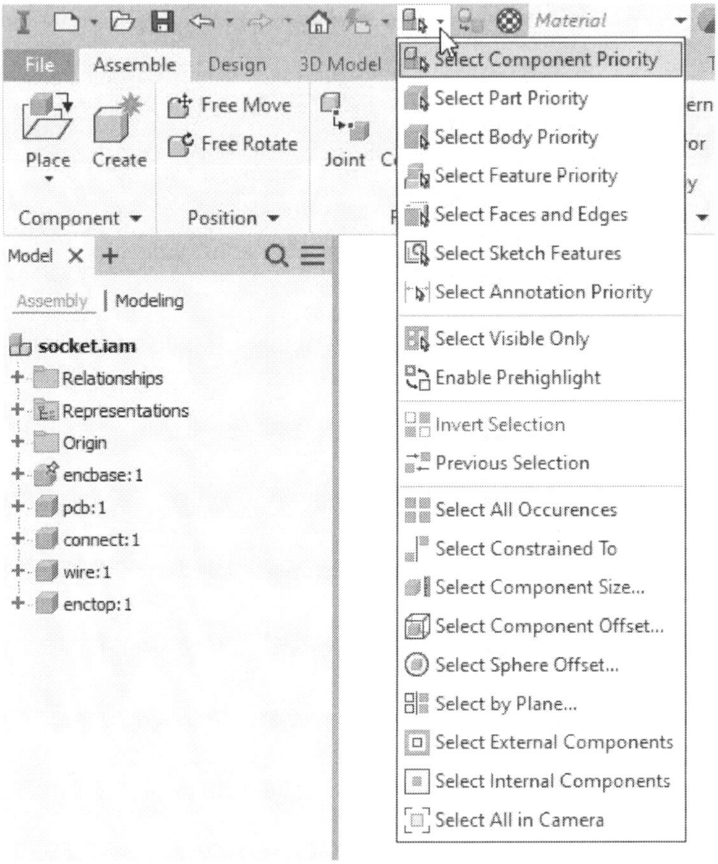

Figure 18–13

When making selections in an assembly consider enabling any one of these options to ease selection. The available options are as follows:

Option	Description
Select Component Priority	Selects an entire component, a part, or a subassembly.
Select Part Priority	Selects a part (the *leaves* in the Model browser).

Select Body Priority	Selects a Body.
Select Feature Priority	Selects a feature.
Select Faces and Edges	Selects a face or part edge.
Select Sketch Features	Selects lines, arcs, circles, splines, or other features in a sketch.
Select Annotation Priority	Selects 3D annotations.
Select Visible Only	Excludes invisible parts from the selection set.
Select Prehighlight	Enables prehighlighting when you hover the cursor over an object. The option is activated by default. Toggle this off in large assemblies to improve performance.
Invert Selection	Selects all currently deselected components.
Previous Selection	Restores the previous selection set.
Select All Occurrences	Enables you to select a component and have all of its occurrences automatically selected.
Select Constrained To	Selects components constrained to the selected component.
Select Component Size	Selects components that are larger or smaller than a selected component or a specified size.
Select Component Offset	Selects components in a bounding box, based on their distance from a selected component.
Select Sphere Offset	Selects components in a sphere, based on their distance from a selected component.
Select by Plane	Selects components based on one side of a work plane or a planar face.
Select External Components	Selects external assembly components based on a set tolerance value. 100% returns all visible components and 0% returns only the most visible component.
Select Internal Components	Selects internal assembly components based on a set tolerance value. 100% returns all components that are not visible and 1% returns all the components except for the most visible.
Select All in Camera	Selects the components in the camera view.

Practice 18a Assemble Components

Practice Objectives

- Constrain components in an assembly so that all degrees of freedom are removed.
- Create a half section view to display geometry through a selected work plane.
- Add a new view representation to an assembly such that it does not include any additional components that are added to the model.
- Use the Visibility, Enabled, and Isolate tools to control whether components are displayed and available for selection in an assembly.

In this practice, you will assemble five components to create the assembly shown in Figure 18–14. During assembly, you will manipulate the display of assembly components.

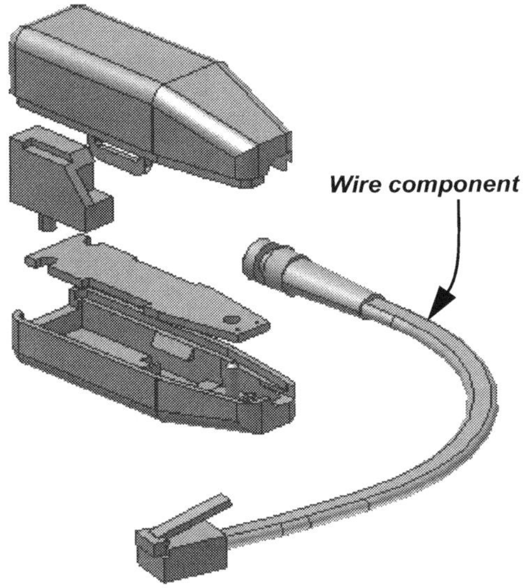

Figure 18–14

Task 1 - Create a new assembly.

1. Create a new assembly file with the standard Metric assembly template. The *Assemble* tab is the active tab.
2. Add one instance of **encbase.ipt**.

*Consider using the **Rotate X 90**, **Rotate Y 90**, or **Rotate Z 90** options in the marking menu if the orientation is not correct.*

3. If the component displays in a 2D orientation, return the model to its default Home View using the ViewCube. Right-click on the model and select **Place Grounded at Origin** to ground the component.

4. Right-click and select **OK**. The assembly displays as shown in Figure 18–15.

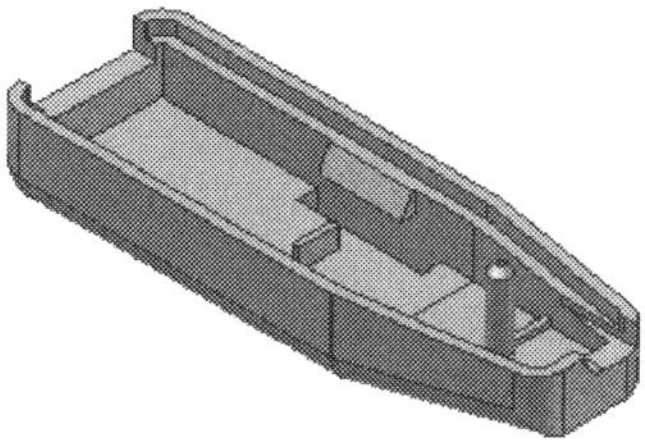

Figure 18–15

Task 2 - Add the part called pcb.ipt.

1. Add one instance of **pcb.ipt**.

2. Display the degrees of freedom symbols.

3. Constrain the **pcb** part to the **encbase** part with one Insert and one Angle constraint type. The references, offset value, and angular value for the constraints are shown in Figure 18–16.

Step 2 uses the least number of constraints that will fully constrain the part, according to the design intent.

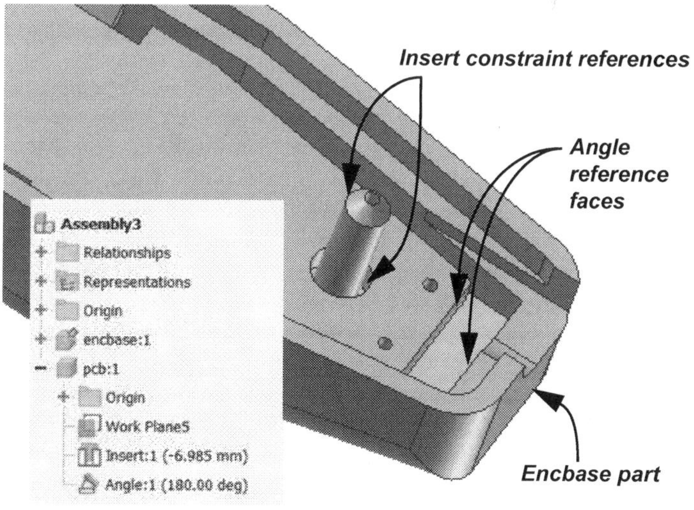

Figure 18–16

4. Save the assembly and name it **socket**.

Task 3 - Section a view and save a design view.

One flat side of the **pcb** part rests on the raised face inside the **encbase** part. In this task, you will section the assembly to display how the flat side of the **pcb** part sits on the raised face.

1. Select the *View* tab. In the Appearance panel, click (Half Section View). You might need to expand the Section View drop-down list to access this command.

2. Expand the **pcb** part in the Model browser, select **Work Plane5**. The assembly displays as shown in Figure 18–17.

3. If the other half of the section view displays, right-click in the graphics window and select **Flip Section**. Click .

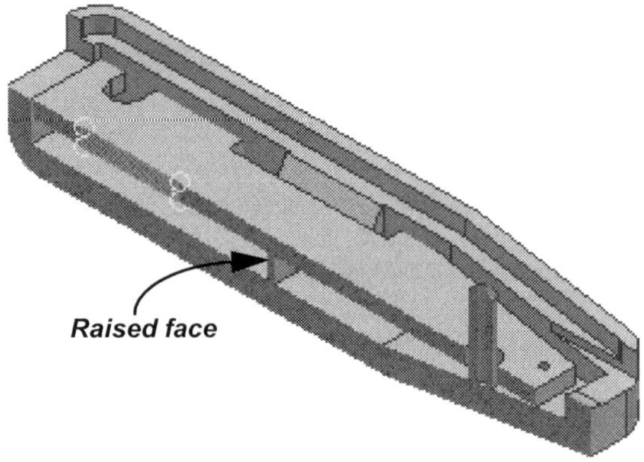

Figure 18–17

4. Reorient the model, as shown in Figure 18–18, to display the flat side of the **pcb** part on the raised face.

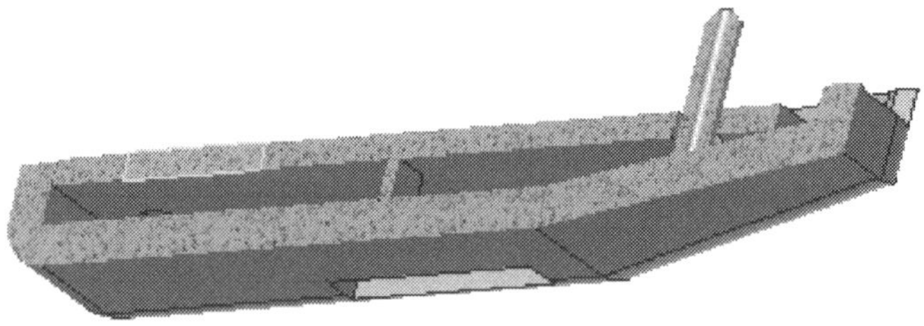

Figure 18–18

5. In the Appearance panel, click (End Section View) to display the entire assembly.

6. Reorient the model to its isometric Home view, as shown in Figure 18–19.

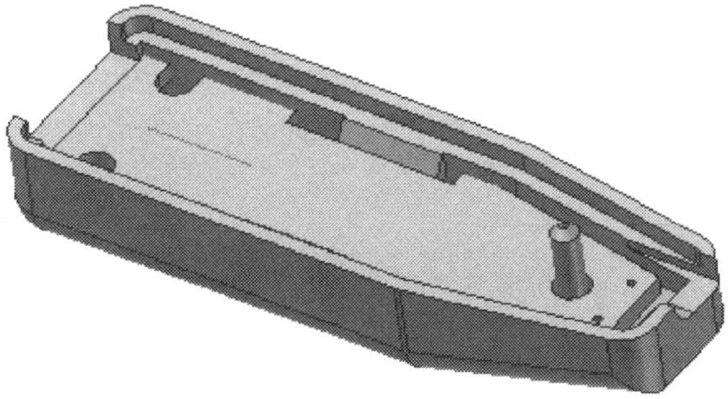

Figure 18–19

7. Create a Design View representation. Expand the **Representations** and **View** nodes in the Model browser. The Model browser displays as shown in Figure 18–20.

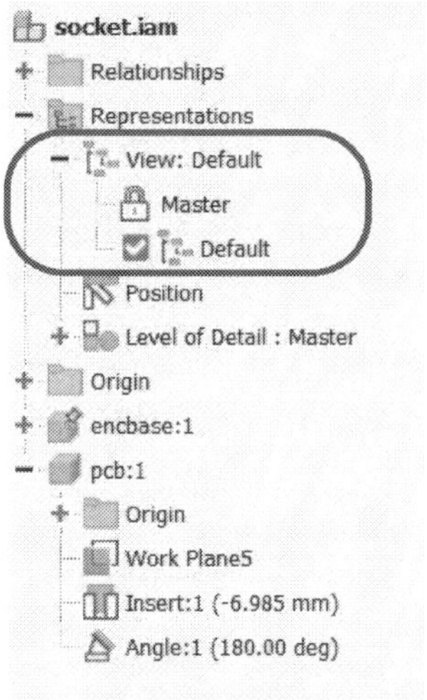

Figure 18–20

8. Right-click on **View: Default** in the Model browser and select **New**.

9. Select **View1** in the Model browser. Select it again (do not double-click) and rename the view as **Interference_view**.

10. To lock the design view, right-click on **Interference_view** in the Model browser and select **Lock**. This restricts you or others from adding components to the **Interference_view** design view representation at a later time.

11. Double-click on **Default** to make it the active Design View.

Task 4 - Add the part called connect.ipt.

1. Select the *Assemble* tab. Add one instance of **connect.ipt** to the assembly. The model displays as shown in Figure 18–21.

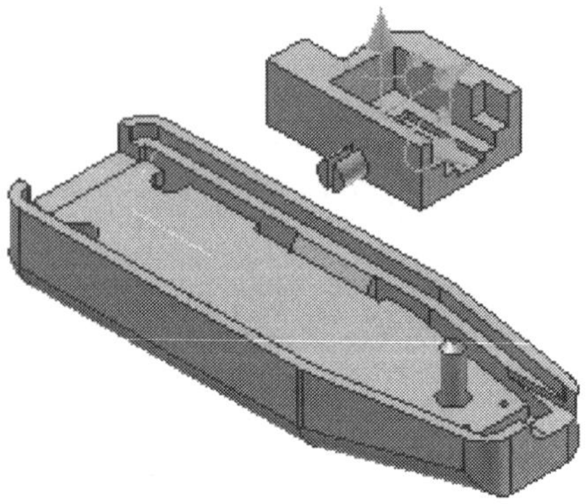

Figure 18–21

2. Right-click on **encbase:1** in the Model browser and select **Visibility**. **Encbase:1** disappears from the graphics window.

3. In the Position panel, click (Free Rotate), select the **connect.ipt** component and rotate the **connect** part, as shown in Figure 18–22. Press <Esc> to end the **Free Rotate** command.

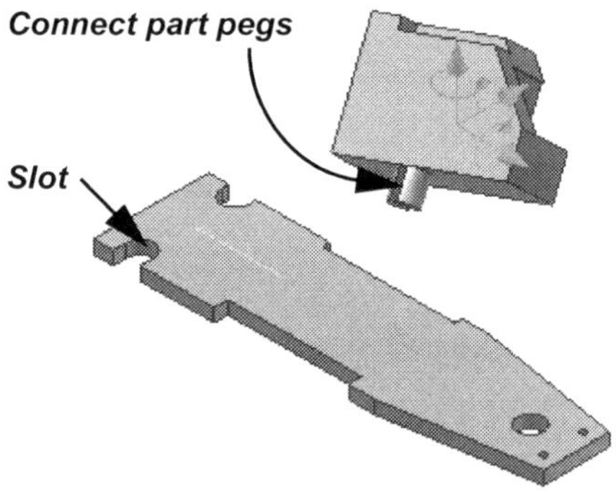

Figure 18–22

4. Add Angle and Insert constraints between the **connect** part and the **pcb** part so that the model displays as shown in Figure 18–23.

Task 7 - Modify the existing Design View.

1. Activate the locked **Interference_view**. Only the original components that were displayed when the view was created display.

2. Right-click on the **Interference_view** Design View in the Model browser, and select **Edit View**. A dialog box opens indicating that the view is locked. Click **OK**.

3. Right-click on the **Interference_view** Design View in the Model browser, and select **Unlock**.

4. Right-click on the **Interference_view** Design View in the Model browser, and select **Edit View**. The mini-toolbar and model display as shown in Figure 18–27.

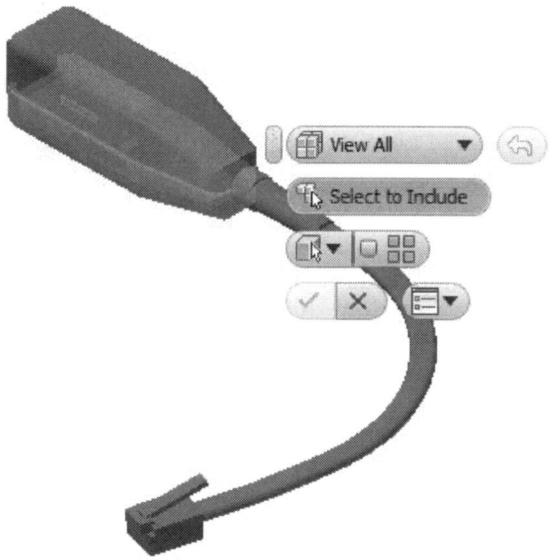

Figure 18–27

5. Click **View All** in the drop-down list if it is not already active. Note that the components that are currently included are highlighted in blue.

6. Select **enctop.ipt** and **wire.ipt** in the Model browser or directly in the graphics window to add them to the Design View. All of the visible components are now highlighted in blue, indicating that they will be visible in the Design View.

7. Click **View Included** in the drop-down list. Note that **Select to Exclude** is now active.

8. Select **enctop.ipt** in the Model browser or directly in the graphics window to remove it from the Design View.

9. Click  to complete the modification.

10. Activate the **Default** Design View. Note that all of the components are still visible.

11. Activate the **Interference_view** Design View. Note that the **wire.ipt** component has been added.

12. Activate the **Default** Design View.

13. Save the assembly. Close the model.

Chapter Review Questions

1. Which of the following statements are true about moving components in an assembly? (Select all that apply.)
   a. Components that are partially constrained can be moved by selecting and dragging them.
   b. Components that are fully constrained can be moved using the **Free Move** command.
   c. Components that are partially constrained can be moved using the **Free Move** command.
   d. Components that are fully constrained can be moved by selecting and dragging them.
2. If you move constrained components apart (as shown in Figure 18–28), how can you display them in their constrained positions again?

Figure 18–28

   a. Use **Update**.
   b. Use **Degrees of Freedom** in the *View* tab.
   c. Use **Zoom All**.
   d. Reapply the constraints.

3. Which of the following statements about (Free Rotate) is true?
    a. You can rotate multiple components at the same time.
    b. Only unconstrained components can be rotated.
    c. Grounded components cannot be rotated.
    d. When you rotate a component that is constrained, the constraints change based on a new component position.

4. Which of the following statements is true regarding suppressing constraints, as shown in Figure 18–29?

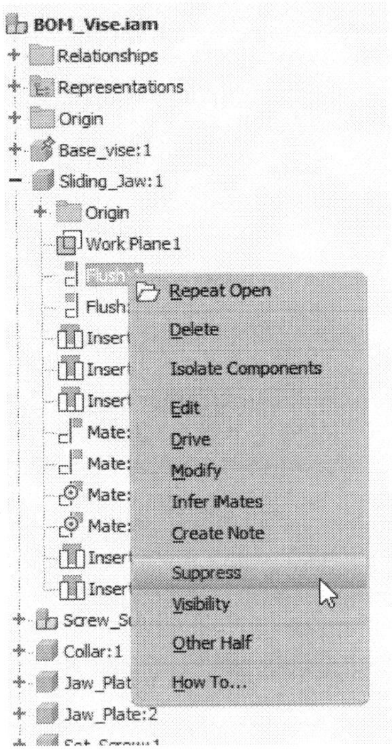

Figure 18–29

    a. Suppressing a constraint removes both components referenced in the constraint from the display.
    b. Suppressing a constraint locks the constraint references such that they cannot be edited.
    c. Suppressing a constraint removes its associated component from the display.
    d. Suppressing a constraint enables you to ignore the constraint restrictions and drag the component as required in the assembly.

5. What is the purpose of a Section View?
    a. To simplify the display of an assembly.
    b. To update an assembly more quickly.
    c. To create an exploded view of an assembly.
    d. To work inside an assembly while keeping the required components visible.
6. What is the purpose of a Design View? (Select all that apply.)
    a. To simplify the display of an assembly.
    b. To update an assembly more quickly.
    c. To return to a specific view of an assembly.
    d. To rotate assembly components.
7. Which of the following filter options is used in the Edit View mini-toolbar to remove components from an existing Design View?
    a. **View All**
    b. **View Included**
    c. **View Excluded**
8. When a Section View is active (as shown in the Three Quarter Section View in Figure 18–30), you cannot select components or reference entities.

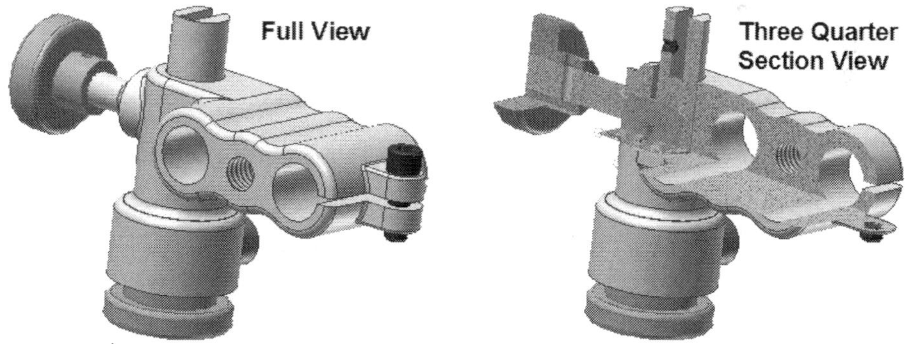

Figure 18–30

    a. True
    b. False

9. What is the difference between toggling off the visibility of a component and isolating that same component?
    a. When the visibility of a component is off, it is not displayed. However, when isolated, the visibility of all of the other components is toggled off and only the selected component is visible.
    b. No difference. Either option can be used to remove the component from the display.
    c. When the visibility of a component is off, it is not displayed; however, when isolated, the component is activated for editing.

10. Which of the following statements are true for the Model browser and assembly shown in Figure 18–31? (Select all that apply.)

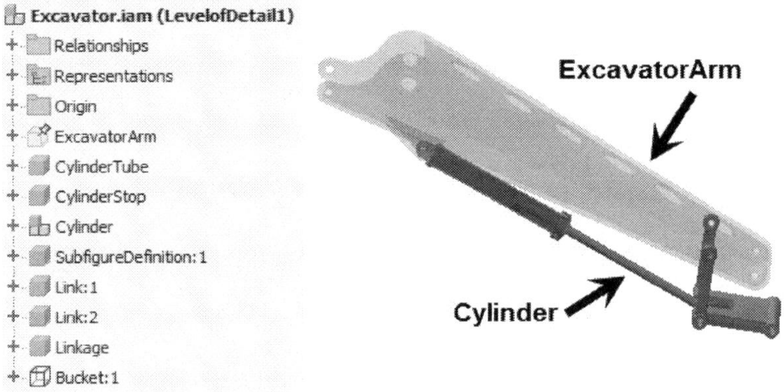

Figure 18–31

    a. **Bucket's** visibility has been cleared.
    b. **Excavator Arm** and **Cylinder** have been enabled.
    c. **Excavator Arm** is a grounded component.
    d. **Excavator Arm** has been isolated.

11. Which of the following statements is true of a part that is disabled (i.e., the **Enabled** option is cleared) in an assembly?
    a. It is completely invisible.
    b. It is completely visible but not editable.
    c. It is displayed as transparent and is not selectable.
    d. It is not subjected to constraints.

Command Summary

Button	Command	Location
N/A	**Edit View**	• **Context Menu:** In Model browser with a Design View selected
N/A	**Enable (component visibility control)**	• **Context Menu:** In Model browser with a component selected • **Context Menu:** In the graphics window with a component selected
	**Free Move (component)**	• **Ribbon:** *Assemble* tab>Position panel • **Context Menu:** In Model browser with a component selected • **Context Menu:** In the graphics window with a component selected
	**Free Rotate (component)**	• **Ribbon:** *Assemble* tab>Position panel • **Context Menu:** In Model browser with a component selected • **Context Menu:** In the graphics window with a component selected
	**Global Update (update individual part or subassembly)**	• **Quick Access Toolbar**
N/A	**Isolate (component visibility control)**	• **Context Menu:** In Model browser with a component selected • **Context Menu:** In the graphics window with a component selected
	**Local Update (update individual part or subassembly)**	• **Quick Access Toolbar**
	**Object Visibility (work features)**	• **Ribbon:** *View* tab>Visibility panel
N/A	**Suppress (constraint)**	• **Context Menu:** In Model browser with a component selected • **Context Menu:** In the graphics window with a component selected
N/A	**Undo Isolate (component visibility control)**	• **Context Menu:** In Model browser with a component selected • **Context Menu:** In the graphics window with a component selected
N/A	**Visibility (component)**	• **Context Menu:** In Model browser with a component selected • **Context Menu:** In the graphics window with a component selected

Model Information

Obtaining measurements on your model is often required for entities to which explicit dimensions have not been assigned. To accomplish this, the Autodesk® Inventor® software provides a measure tool. In addition, tools are available to assign and work with model properties to capture additional information in your model.

Learning Objectives in This Chapter

- Use the Measure command to conduct measurements in part and assembly models.
- Calculate the area of a selected closed sketch.
- Set the physical properties for a model.
- Set material appearances and overrides.

19.1 Measurement Tools

The Autodesk Inventor software enables you to measure the distance, angle, perimeter, or area for entities in part and assembly models. To conduct a measurement, use the **Measure** command using any of the following methods.

- In the *Inspect* tab>Measure panel, click (Measure).
- In the *Tools* tab>Measure panel, click (Measure).
- Right-click in the graphics window and select **Measure** in the Marking menu.

Once the command is selected, the Measure palettes display, as shown in Figure 19–1. All of the results display in this palette as you select reference entities and take measurements.

The Measure palette can be merged with the Model browser by dragging it into the Model browser area so that it is docked.

Measure Palette for Part Models

Measure Palette for Assembly Models

Figure 19–1

- For assembly models, the selection priority buttons located at the top of the palette enable you to set whether components, parts, or faces and edges are to be selected. By default, faces and edges are set. The selection priority buttons are not available for part models.
- The expandable *Advanced Setting* area enables you to define the precision for the results and whether to display the result in multiple unit formats when the measurement displays.

Measuring Entities and Points

The references that are selected for measuring are assigned colors for easy identification. The first selection is blue and the second is green.

*In some cases, you might need to hover the cursor until the **Select Other** tool displays to select the correct reference, or right-click on the reference and select **Select Other**.*

*To copy a result or all results to the clip board, right-click on the value and select **Copy** or **Copy All**.*

To measure linear and circular entities and points, the (Select Faces and Edges) option must be active for assembly models. Depending on the type or number of entities selected, the displayed results vary as follows:

- Select an edge to measure its length and select a second edge to measure the distance between them, as shown in Figure 19–2.

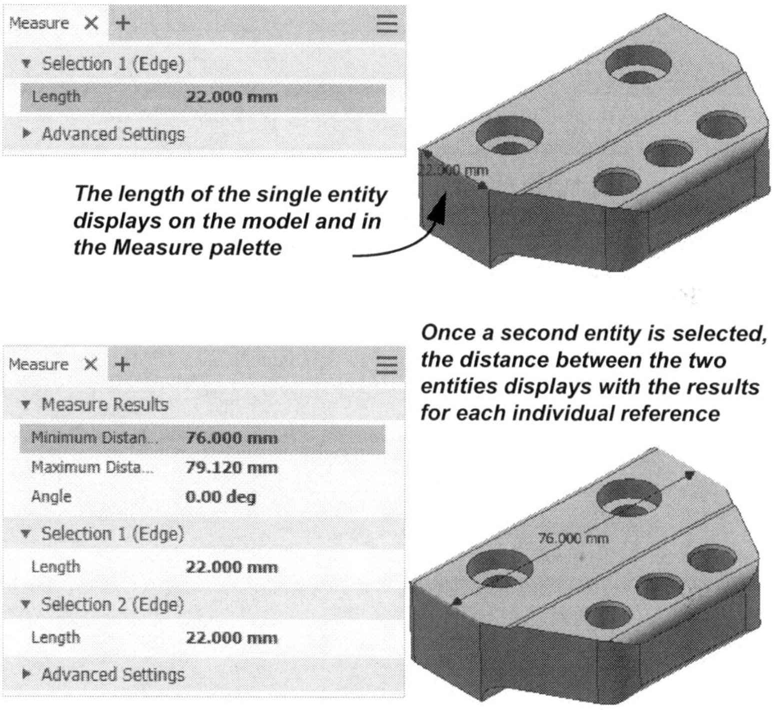

Figure 19–2

- Select a circular edge to measure its diameter, radius, length, and angle, as shown in Figure 19–3.

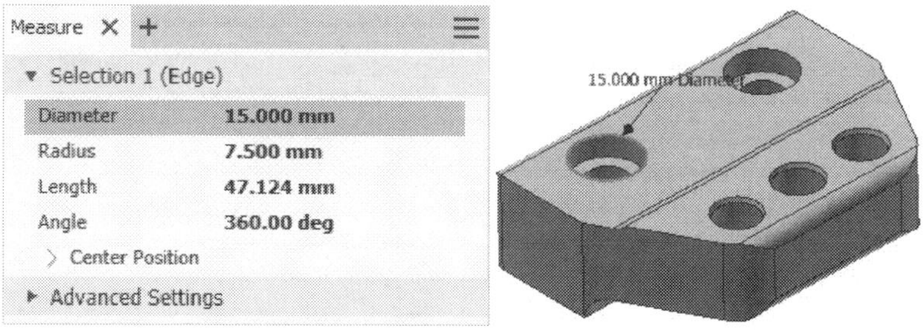

Figure 19–3

- Select a point to measure its location (X, Y, and Z) relative to the active coordinate system, as shown in Figure 19–4. Select a second point to measure the distance between them. Individual position values are also measured. The midpoints of entities can also be selected as measurement references.

*To select a center point on a circular entity, hover the cursor over the entity and use the **Select Other** tool to select the center point.*

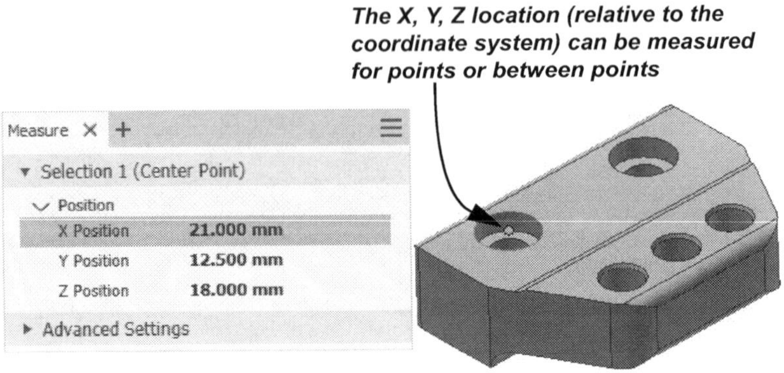

Figure 19–4

Measure the Distance Between Components

To measure the minimum distance between components, change the filter option to (Part Priority) or (Component Priority) and then select two components in the model. The Measure palette displays similar to that shown in Figure 19–5.

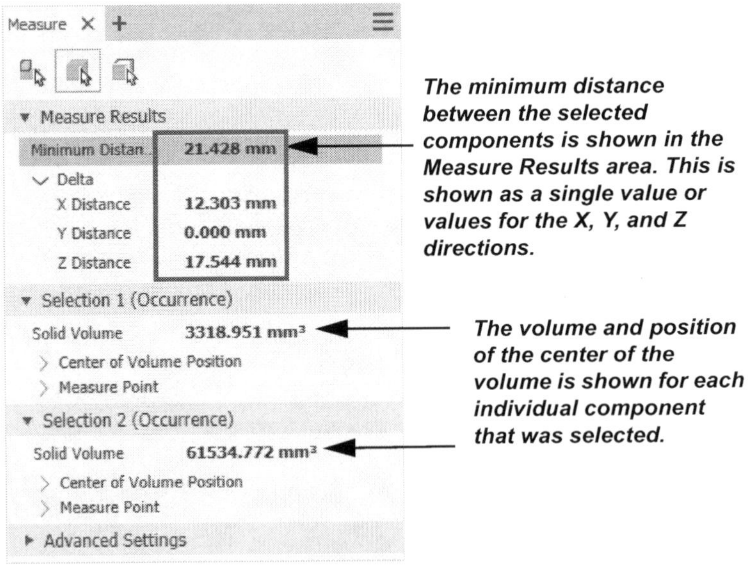

Figure 19–5

Measuring an Angle

To measure an angular value, the  (Select Faces and Edges) option must be active in an assembly. You can select references as follows:

- To measure the angle between two lines or faces, select the two lines or faces. Axes can also be selected. Angular measurements are shown in Figure 19–6.
- The measurement value that is highlighted in orange in the Measure palette is the value that displays on the model. To display another value, simply select it in the palette.

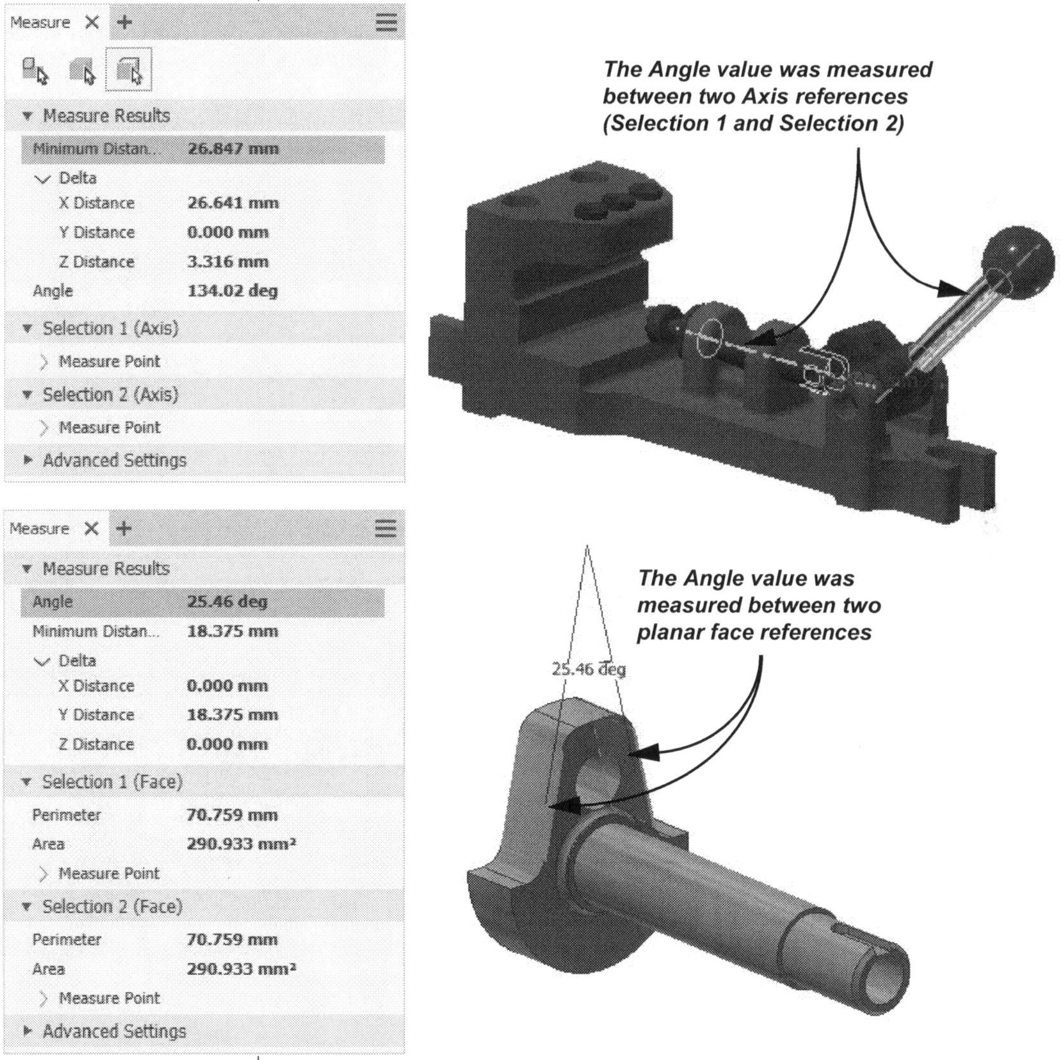

Figure 19–6

- To measure the angle created by three points, select the first two points that define a line, then hold <Shift> and select the third point that defines the angle.

- To measure the angular extent around a circular edge or arc, select it.

Measuring Planar Faces

To select a planar face for measurement, the  (Select Faces and Edges) option must be active in an assembly. Once the reference is selected, the outside perimeter, the total loop perimeter (all edges that lie on the face), and the area of the face display as shown in Figure 19–7.

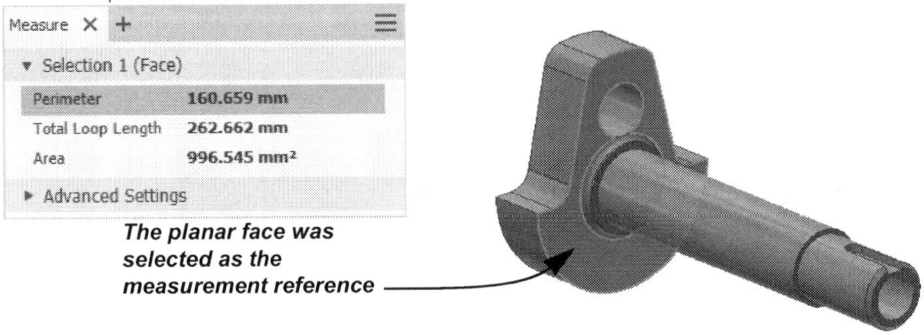

Figure 19–7

Measuring Cylindrical Faces

To select a cylindrical face for measurement, the  (Select Faces and Edges) option must be active in an assembly. Once the reference is selected, the radius, diameter, total loop perimeter (all edges that lie on the face), and the area of the face are reported, as shown in Figure 19–8.

Figure 19–8

Restart a Measurement

To take a new measurement, left-click in the graphics window to clear the reference selection. Alternatively, you can right-click and select **Restart** from the drop-down list.

Add to Accumulate

The sum of multiple linear measurements, as well as area, volume, and angular measurements can be determined using the **Add to Accumulate** option in the Measure palette.

How To: Use the accumulate function

1. Once the initial measurement is made, click **Add to Accumulate**, as shown on the left in Figure 19–9. Once selected, the *Accumulated Properties* area displays at the top of the palette, as shown on the right.

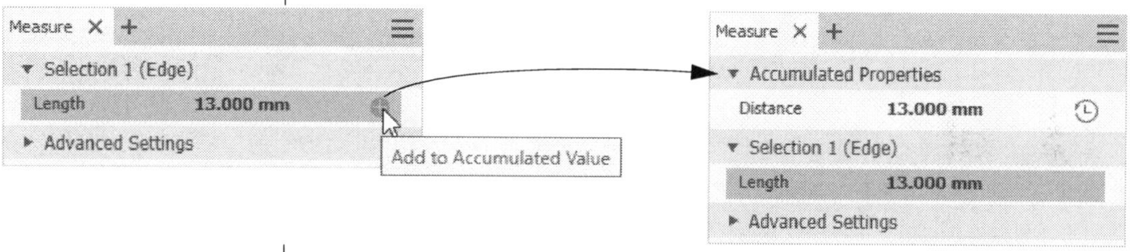

Figure 19–9

2. Select an additional entity in the graphics window. The Measure palette updates listing its values. The *Accumulated Properties* area remains at the top of the palette.
3. In the *Selection 2* area, click **Add to Accumulated Value**, as shown on the left in Figure 19–10, to add the new value to the previous one. The value updates in the *Accumulated Properties* area as shown on the right.

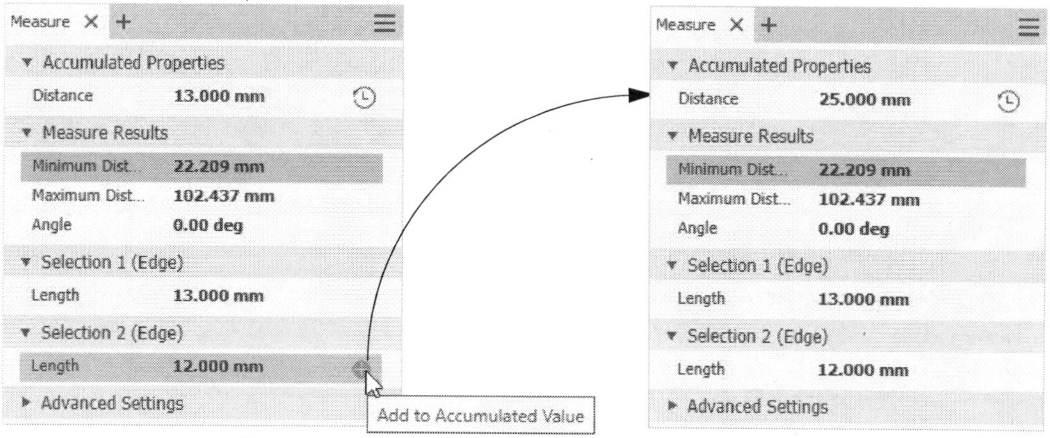

Figure 19–10

4. Continue to measure and add accumulated values as required.

Consider the following when working with accumulate values:

- To display the full list of the accumulated values, select the (History) icon.
- To clear a single value in the accumulate history list, hover over it and select (Delete) to remove it from the total.
- To clear a total accumulated value, hover over it and select (Delete) to clear it.

Context Sensitive Measurements

If an object is preselected, you can right-click and select **Measure** in the marking menu, or in the expanded **Measure** options in the shortcut menu, as shown in Figure 19–11. If the preselected objects can provide a measured value, the results are displayed.

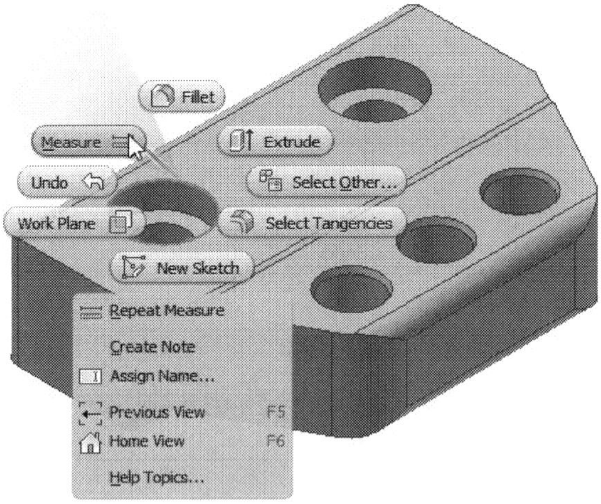

Figure 19–11

Using Measure When Entering Required Values

In most cases, if you are required to enter a value, you can use the **Measure** option (shown in Figure 19–12). This accesses the measuring tool to conduct a measurement on the model that is automatically populated into the value field.

*The **Measure** option is also available in feature dialog boxes and palettes associated with value fields.*

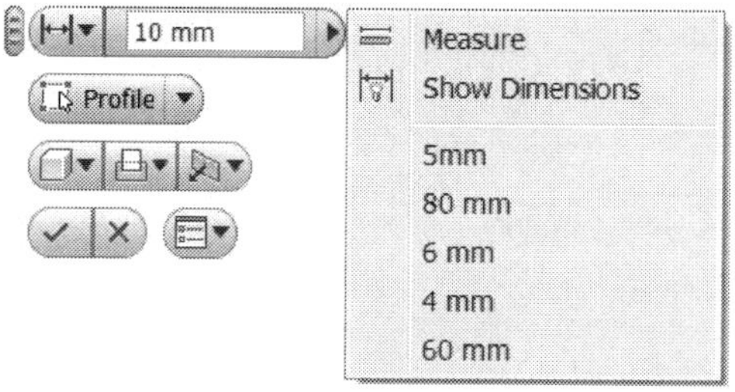

Figure 19–12

Region Properties

The **Region Properties** command calculates properties for a closed sketched area. You must be in the Sketch environment to use this command. To activate the tool, select the *Inspect* tab> Measure panel and click  (Region Properties). In the Region Properties dialog box, select **Click to Add** in the *Selections* area, select a section and click **Calculate**. The calculations are completed based on the sketch coordinate system. In Figure 19–13, the results for the sketched oblong section are shown on the right.

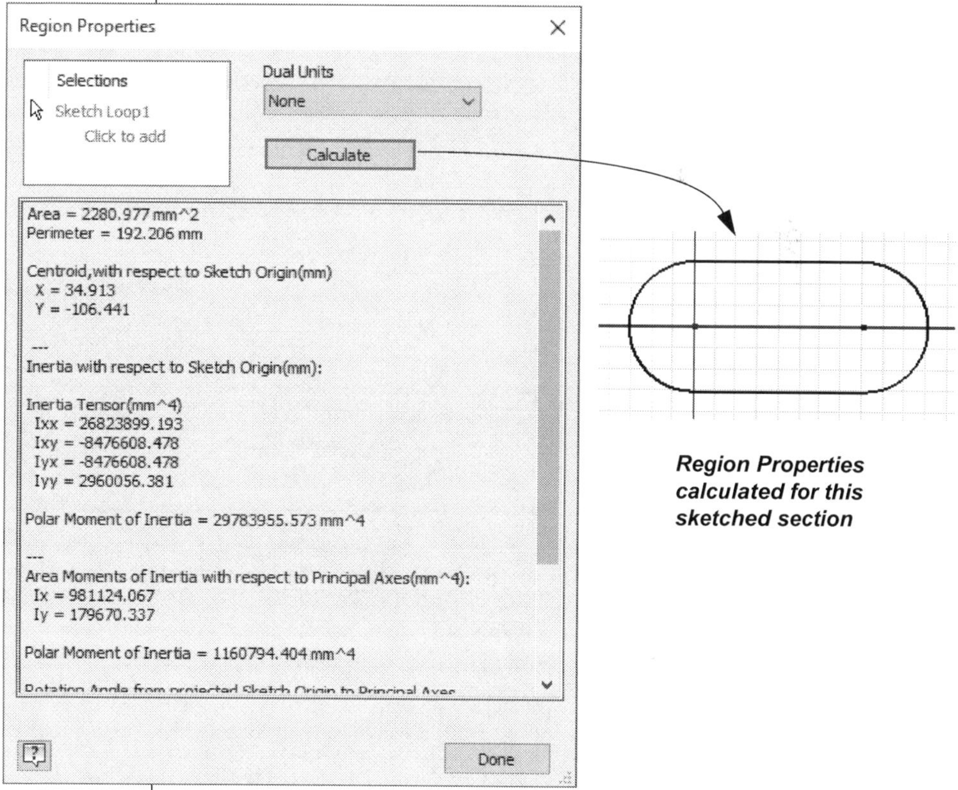

Figure 19–13

19.2 Model Properties

iProperties

By assigning a specific material to a model, you can calculate the physical properties (e.g., volume, mass, center of gravity, etc.) of the model based on that material. The physical properties of a model are listed in the model's iProperties dialog box. To access this, right-click on the model name in the Model browser, select **iProperties**, and select the *Physical* tab. To assign material, select a type in the Material drop-down list, as shown in Figure 19–14. The values in the dialog box are automatically calculated based on the material selected.

Alternatively, you can expand the ***File*** *menu and select* ***iProperties*** *to open the iProperties dialog box.*

The physical properties are not available in iFeature, presentation, or drawing files. In an assembly file, the material cannot be changed.

Select the Material type from the Material drop-down list

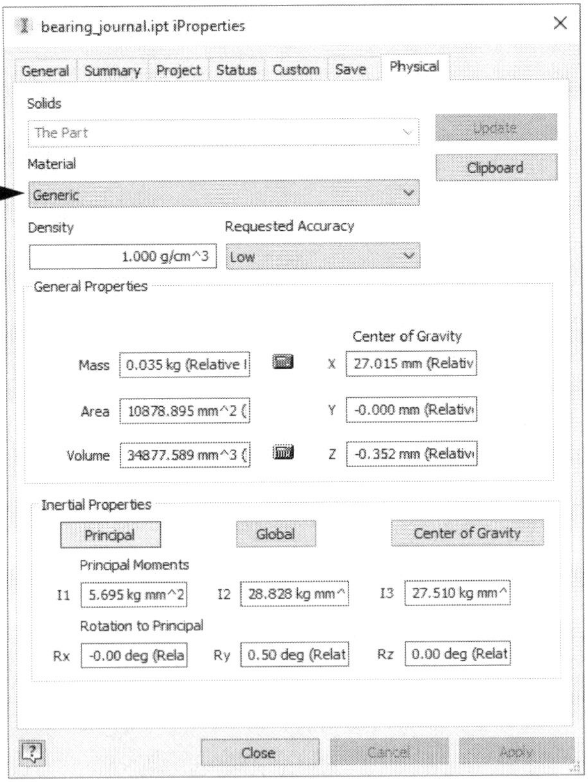

Figure 19–14

Low accuracy takes less time to calculate but is less accurate.

- The *Requested Accuracy* field sets the degree of accuracy for calculations.
- Click **Update** to recalculate the physical properties of changes to part features, or to recalculate the physical properties of an assembly after changes are made to it.
- Click **Clipboard** to copy the physical property information to the Windows clipboard for pasting into a text editor.

If the mass or volume properties are overridden, the other properties in the dialog box do not update to reflect the new value(s).

- Mass and volume properties can be overridden by entering new values directly in their fields and clicking **Apply**. Once overridden they are shown with the hand symbol, as shown in Figure 19–15. To remove the override, delete the contents of the field(s) and click **Apply**.

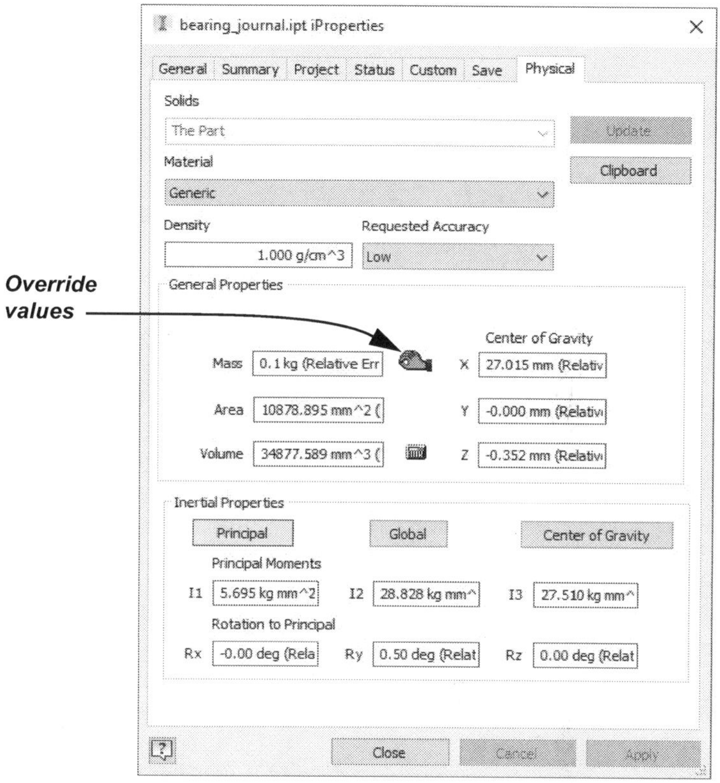

Figure 19–15

- If the material has been changed in the iProperties dialog box, the Materials drop-down list updates to reflect the change, as shown in Figure 19–16. You can use the Materials drop-down list as an alternative to changing the material in the iProperties dialog box.

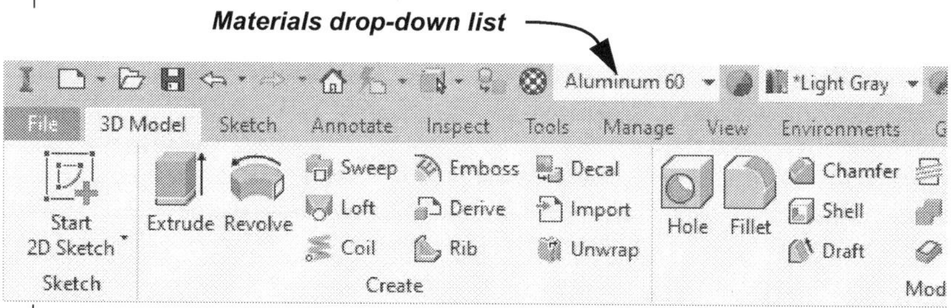

Figure 19–16

Model Color

By default, the materials listed in the Materials drop-down list are those from the Inventor Material Library. To switch to the Autodesk Material Library, select it at the bottom of the Materials drop-down list.

By default, the color of a model is based on the assigned material's color. To assign a different appearance to the model while maintaining the iProperty data for the material, you can select an alternate appearance in the Appearance Override drop-down list, as shown in Figure 19–17.

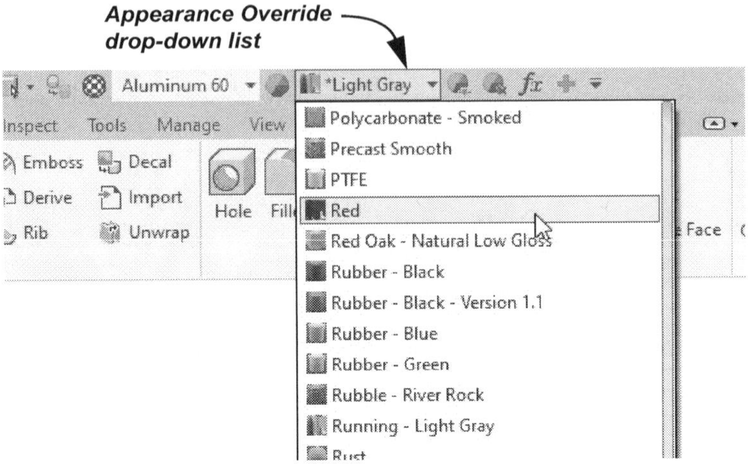

Figure 19–17

To assign an override color on specific features in the model, select the features, right-click, and select **Properties**. In the Feature Properties dialog box, select a feature appearance from the Feature Appearance drop-down list.

- Any overriden feature appearances are maintained regardless of a change to the Appearance Override.
- To clear a feature or model appearance override, in the *Tools* tab>Material and Appearance panel, click (Clear) and select the features to clear. This option is also available in the Quick Access toolbar.

Practice 19a Properties and Measurements

Practice Objectives

- Use the iProperties dialog box to change the material that is assigned to a component in an assembly.
- Use the **Measure** command to conduct measurements in a model.

In this practice, you will apply material to components in the Bore Device assembly. You will then practice taking measurements of elements in the assembly.

Task 1 - Open an assembly file.

1. Open **BoreDevice_3.iam**. The assembly displays as shown in Figure 19–18.

Figure 19–18

Task 2 - Obtain and assign model properties.

1. Double-click on the **Ball Lever** component in the Model browser to activate it.

*Alternatively, you can expand the **File** menu and select **iProperties** to open the iProperties dialog box.*

2. Right-click on **Ball Lever** in the Model browser and select **iProperties**. Select the *Physical* tab to display the physical properties of the part, as shown in Figure 19–19. Click **Update** to update the values, if required.

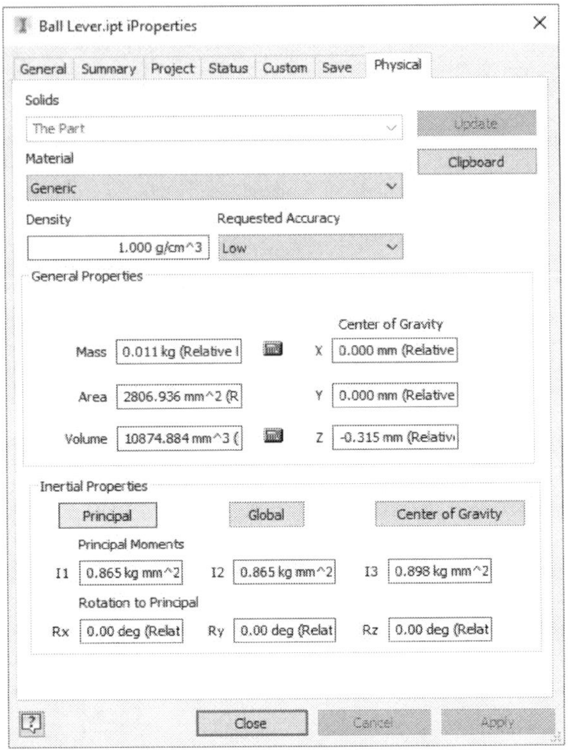

Figure 19–19

3. Select **ABS Plastic** in the Material drop-down list. The values in the dialog box update.
4. Click **Apply** and click **Close**. In the Quick Access Toolbar, note that the *Material* is set to **ABS Plastic** and the *Appearance Override* is set to **Smooth-White**.
5. In the Appearance Override drop-down list, select **Red**. The color of the model updates in the graphics window.
6. Double-click **Pin Seized** in the Model browser to activate it.
7. As an alternative to using the iProperties dialog box to assign the material, select **Aluminum-6061** in the Materials drop-down list.
8. Double-click **BoreDevice_3.iam** in the Model browser to activate the top-level assembly again.
9. Right-click **Pin Seized** in the Model browser and select **iProperties**.

10. Select the *Physical* tab when the dialog box opens. Note that the **Aluminum-6061** material has been assigned. Click **Update** to update the values, if required.
11. Close the iProperties dialog box.

Task 3 - Take a series of measurements in the model.

1. In the *Inspect* tab>Measure panel, click  (Measure). The Measure palette opens, as shown in Figure 19–20.
   - The selection priority buttons enable you to set whether components, parts, or faces and edges are to be selected. By default, faces and edges are set. Leave this selection.

Figure 19–20

   - Expand the *Advanced Setting* area of the Measure palette. This area enables you to define the precision and dual unit settings for the measurement. Leave these values at their defaults and compress this area.

2. Rotate the model as shown. Select the cylindrical surface shown in Figure 19–21. The Measure palette displays the measurement values for the *Radius*, *Diameter*, *Perimeter*, and *Area* of the selected surface.

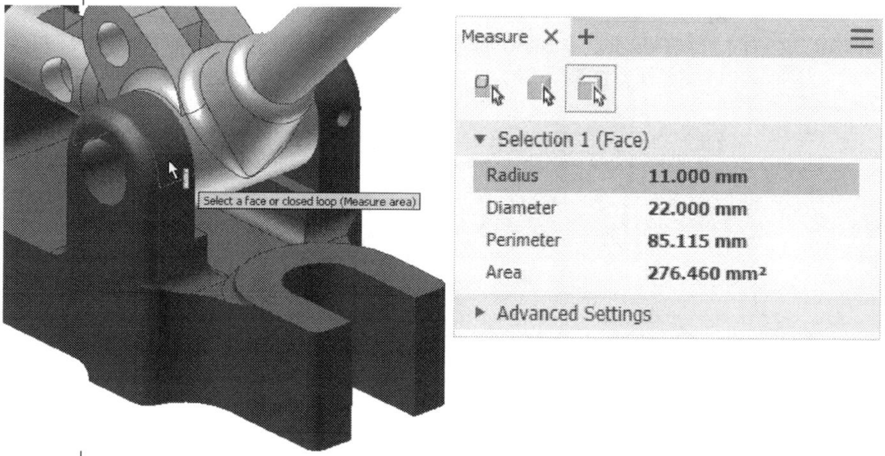

Figure 19–21

*Alternatively, you can right-click in the graphics window and select **Restart** to clear the Measure palette.*

3. Left-click in the graphics window to clear the measurements.
4. Select the top edge of the model shown in Figure 19–22. The length displays in the Measure palette.
5. Select the bottom edge of the model shown in Figure 19–22. The distance between the two edges displays in the *Measure Results* area of the Measure palette. The lengths of the individual edges also display.

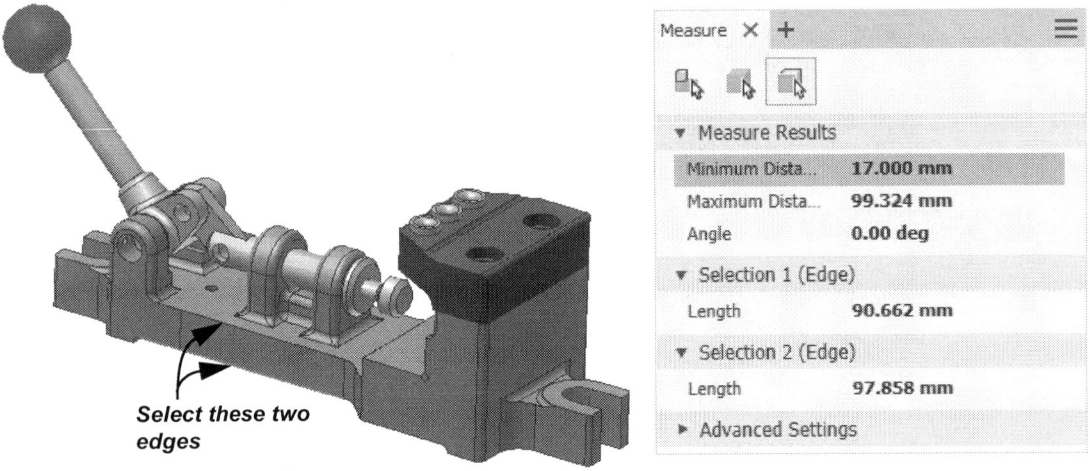

Figure 19–22

6. Left-click in the graphics window to clear the measurements.
7. Select the two circular edges shown in Figure 19–23 to measure the distance between the two holes in the **Fixture Drill** component. The Measure palette displays the distance between the centers of these edges as **40 mm**. Additional measurements are also shown.

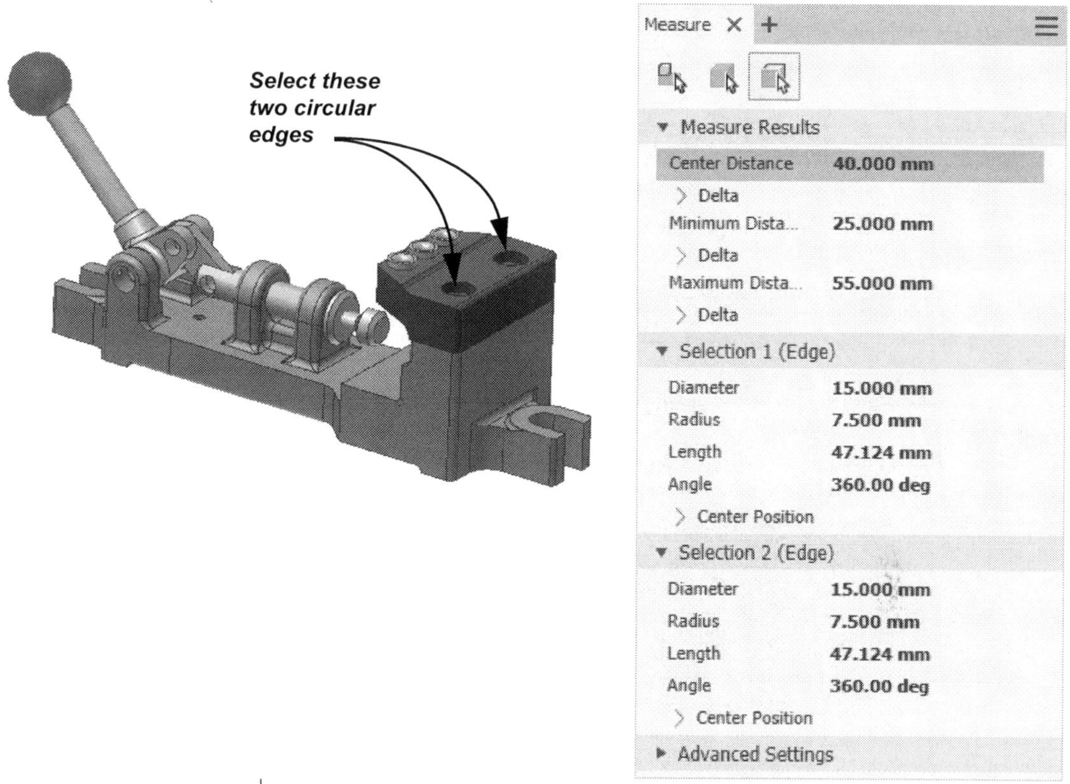

Figure 19–23

8. Left-click in the graphics window to clear the measurements.

9. Measure the distance between the surface and hole of the components shown in Figure 19–24 by first selecting the face and then selecting the circular edge. Note that the reported distance is the minimum distance to the hole. Clear the measurement.

10. Select the face first and then hover the cursor over the edge of the hole. Right-click and select **Select Other** (or hover the cursor over the edge of the hole until the Select Other list displays). In the Select Other drop-down list, select the axis of the hole. The Measure palette should display a distance of **119.562 mm**.

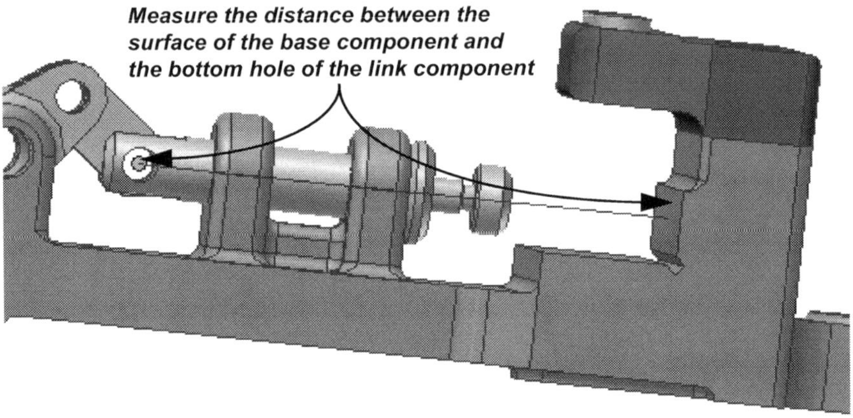

Figure 19–24

11. Practice taking additional measurements.

12. Save and close the model.

Practice 19b (Optional) Model Measurements

Practice Objective

- Select and use the correct measurement tools to obtain values for a list of required measurements.

In this practice, you are provided with a list of required measurements. You will need to select and use any of the various measurement tools to fill in a table.

Task 1 - Open a part file.

1. Open **bearing_journal.ipt**. The model displays as shown in Figure 19–25.

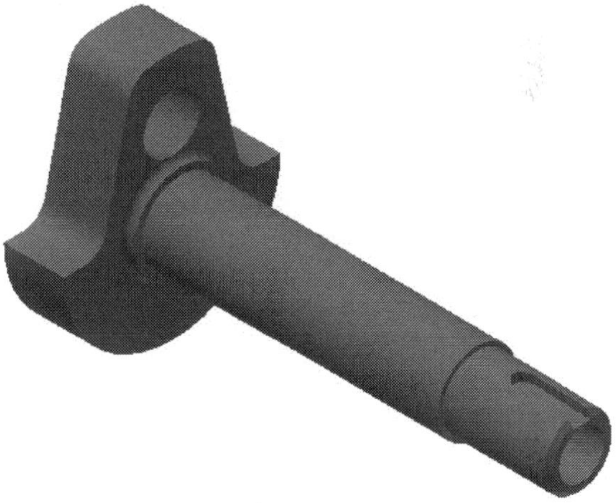

Figure 19–25

Task 2 - Take a variety of measurements.

1. Use the measuring options on the *Inspect* or *Tools* tabs to take the measurements shown in Figure 19–26. Compare your results to those listed in the table to ensure that the measurement has been taken correctly.

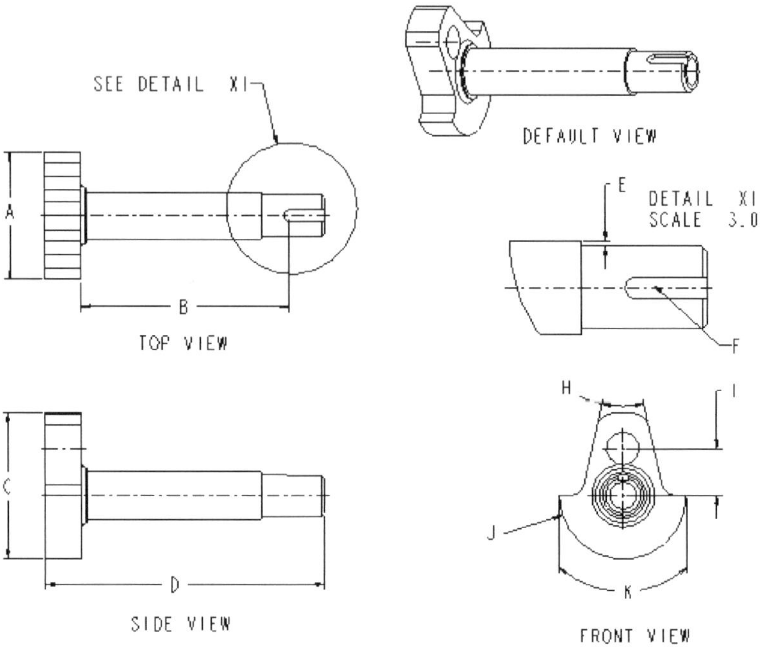

Figure 19–26

Consider creating work planes tangent to surfaces and parallel to existing work planes to determine the distances between curved surfaces.

The use of the Select Other drop-down list can help with selecting the correct references while measuring.

Dimension	Description	Value
A	Overall width of model	46.00
B	From face to center of arc on slot	75.00
C	Overall height of model	53.00
D	Overall length of model	101.00
E	Height of step	1.00
F	Surface area of slot	58.28
H	Angle	25.46
I	Center to center between shaft and hole	17.00
J	Diameter	46.00
K	Arc length	72.26

Chapter Review Questions

1. Which of the following measurements can be generated using the **Measure** option? (Select all that apply.)
   a. Edge Length
   b. Diameter
   c. Angle
   d. Distance between points
   e. Distance between edges
   f. Area of a sketch
2. Which of the following best describes how to use the **Measure** command to enter a required value in a dialog box/palette or mini-toolbar?
   a. With the dialog box/palette or mini-toolbar open, in the *Inspect* tab>Measure panel, select **Measure**. Select the geometrical references to perform the required measure. This value is automatically used in the value field.
   b. In the dialog box/palette or mini-toolbar, click the arrow next to the value field you want to change and select **Measure** in the drop-down list. Select the geometrical references to perform the required measure. This value is automatically used in the value field.
   c. In the *Inspect* tab>Measure panel, select **Measure**. Select the geometrical references to perform the required measure. Create the feature and in the expanded menu for the required dimension value, select the value that was just measured.
3. The iProperties dialog box provides you with information about which physical properties of a part? (Select all that apply.)
   a. Mass
   b. Center of Gravity
   c. Area
   d. Volume
4. In an assembly file, the material cannot be changed using the iProperties dialog box.
   a. True
   b. False

5. Where do you find information such as the mass and volume of a part, as shown in Figure 19–27?

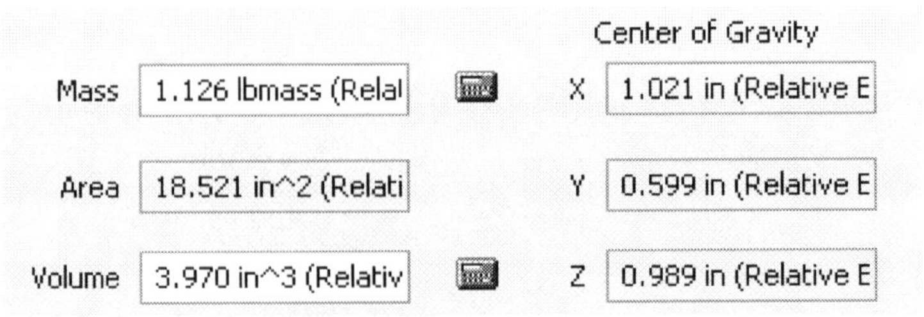

Figure 19–27

a. Analysis Tools (*Inspect* tab>Measure panel)

b. iProperties dialog box (**File** menu>**iProperties**)

c. Parameters dialog box (*Manage* tab>**Parameters**)

d. Document Settings dialog box (*Tools* tab>**Document Settings**)

6. Which of the following best describes how to change the color of a specific feature in the model?

a. Select the feature and select a material that uses the appropriate color in the Materials drop-down list.

b. Select the feature and select a material that uses the appropriate color in the *Physical* tab in the iProperties dialog box.

c. Select the feature and select a color in the Appearance Override drop-down list.

d. Select the feature and select a color in the Properties dialog box.

Command Summary

Button	Command	Location
N/A	**iProperties**	• **Context Menu:** (*from Model browser with Component name selected*) • **File Menu**
	**Measure**	• **Ribbon:** *Inspect* tab>Measure panel • **Ribbon:** *Tools* tab>Measure panel • **Context Menu:** In the graphics window with an entity selected>Measure
	**Region Properties**	• **Ribbon:** *Inspect* tab>Measure panel

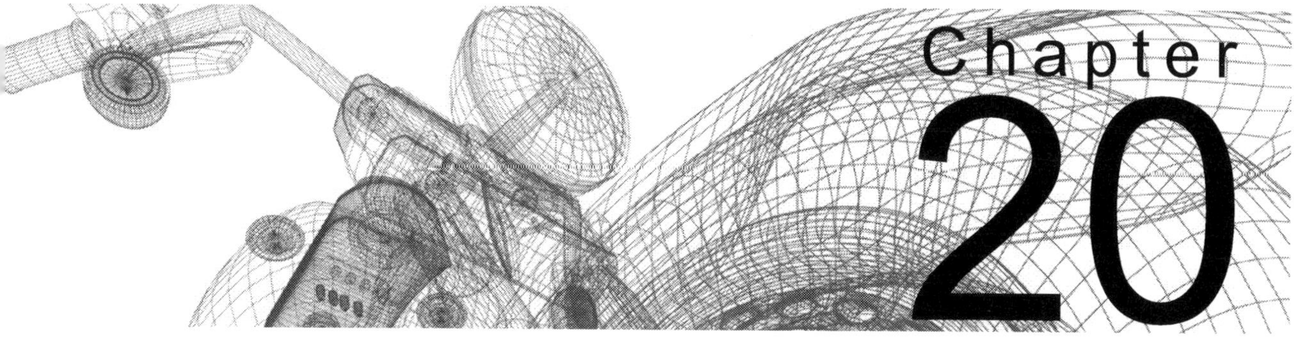

Chapter 20

Presentation Files

The presentation tools available in the Autodesk® Inventor® software enable you to create Snapshot views and animations to help document an assembly. A presentation file can be used to indicate how parts relate to each other and create an exploded view for a drawing. Animating the exploded view of the assembly enables you to further show how components fit together in the assembly.

Learning Objectives in This Chapter

- Understand how presentation files can be used to document an assembly model.
- Create a presentation file with an animation of how an assembly is to be assembled.
- Create a presentation file with Snapshot views that can be used in drawing views.
- Publish a presentation file to create images and videos.

20.1 Creating Presentations

If a component dimension is modified or if a component is removed or added in the assembly, the presentation file updates to incorporate the changes.

To create an exploded view of an assembly, you must use a presentation file. In a presentation file, you can move or rotate the components relative to one another and add trails to indicate how they relate in the assembly. This can be stored as an animation or as static images. An exploded view of an assembly is shown in Figure 20–1.

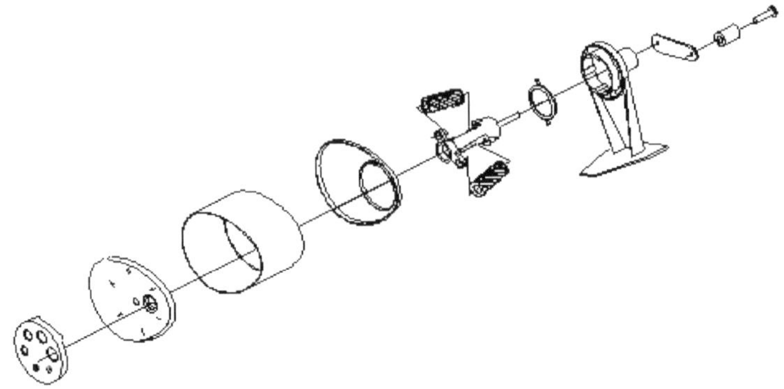

Figure 20–1

The first step in creating a presentation file is to start a new file based on a Presentation template (.IPN). To access the presentation templates, you can use any of the following:

- Click (New) in the Launch panel, the Quick Access toolbar, or in the **File** menu. Select an *.IPN template in the Create New File dialog box and click **Create**. You might need to scroll down in the list to locate this template.

To verify the default presentation template in the My Home tab, click (Configure Default Templates) and review the settings in the Configure Default Template dialog box.

- Click (Presentation) in the *My Home* tab to create a new file with the default template.
- In an open assembly model, right-click on the assembly name at the top of the Model Browser and select **Create Presentation**. Once selected, you will be prompted for the template to be used.

Once the presentation file is created, the Presentation environment displays and you are immediately prompted to select a model for the first scene. Using the Insert dialog box, you can navigate to and open the model that will be used in the presentation. The *Presentation* tab becomes the active tab and the interface includes a Model Browser, Snapshot Views browser, and the Storyboard panel, as shown in Figure 20–2.

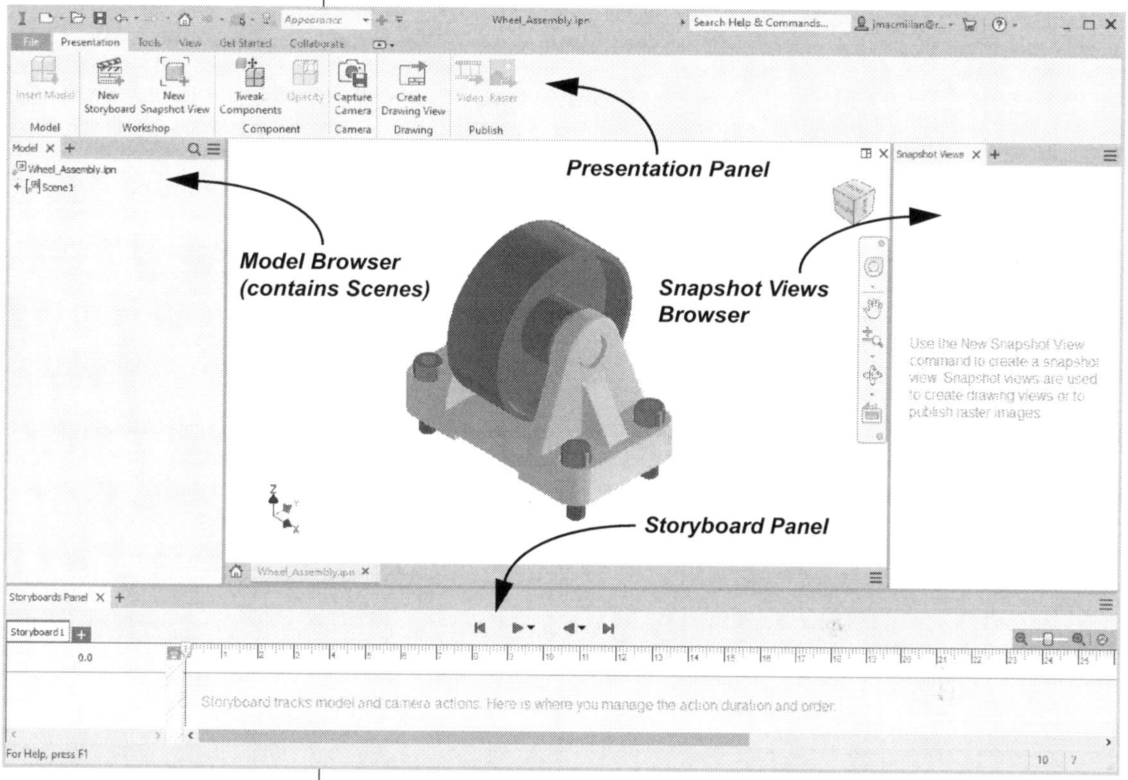

Figure 20–2

A presentation file is automatically created with an initial scene called **Scene1**.

- A file can consist of multiple scenes, all of which are independent and can reference different source models. To create additional scenes, right-click at the top of the Model Browser and select **Create Scene**.
- The model inserted in the last scene is listed at the top of the Model Browser; however, each scene contains the model that was initially assigned to it.
- Each scene can contain Snapshot views and storyboards.

Hint: Inserting Models

When selecting the model to be inserted into a scene, you can click **Options** to open the File Open Options dialog box, which enables you to:

- Insert an associative or non-associative version of a Design View Representation. If the **Associative** option is disabled on insertion, any changes in the selected Design View Representation will not update in the presentation file.
- Insert a specific Positional Representation of the model.
- Insert a specific Level of Detail Representation of the model.

If the representation of the model needs to be changed after it has been added to the scene, right-click the **Scene** node in the Model Browser and select **Representations**. You will be presented with the same File Open Options dialog box and can change the representation that is used.

20.2 Storyboards

Snapshot views can be created at specific points along the timeline. This is discussed further in the next topic.

The Storyboard panel at the bottom of the graphics window contains the list of storyboards that exist in a Presentation file. Each storyboard is included on its own tab. A storyboard can be used for the following:

- Creating an animation of the model that records component movements (i.e., assembly/disassembly).
- Creating actions to represent changes in component visibility and opacity at specific times in an animation.
- Capturing changes in camera position at specific times in an animation.

Figure 20–3 shows the components of the Storyboard panel used to create and play animations.

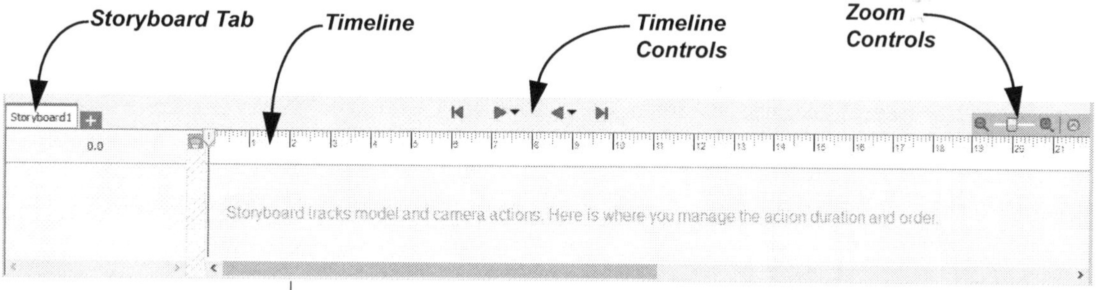

Figure 20–3

When a presentation file is created, a single storyboard is included. Additional storyboards can be included, as required. Storyboards can be independent of one another or they can work in combination with one another.

How To: Create a Storyboard

1. Activate the scene to which the storyboard will be added by double-clicking the scene name in the Model Browser.
2. In the Presentation tab>Workshop panel, click (New Storyboard). Alternatively, in the Storyboard panel at the bottom of the graphics window, click adjacent to the Storyboard tabs.

3. Select the *Storyboard Type* in the New Storyboard dialog box, as shown in Figure 20–4.

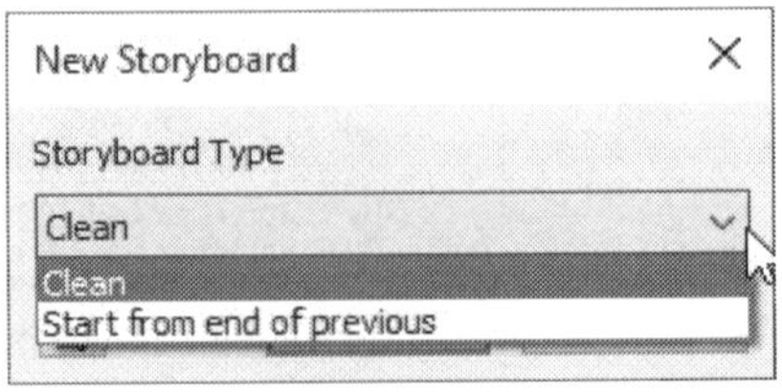

Figure 20–4

- **Clean:** Creates a new storyboard that uses the default appearance and camera settings for the active scene.
- **Start from end of previous:** Creates a new storyboard that is started from the end of another storyboard. The component positions, visibility, opacity, and camera settings from the previous storyboard is used as the starting point for the new one.

4. Click **OK**.

Hint: Storyboard Panel Customization

The Storyboard panel can be customized as follows:

- Click or in the panel to expand or compress it.
- Click and drag the panel titlebar to undock it. To redock it, drag its titlebar back into position at the bottom of the graphics window.
- Use to zoom in or out on the timeline's scale.

Animations

An animation consists of movements that are applied to selected components in the assembly. The movements are called *Tweaks* and can be linear and rotational and are set to run over a timed period (duration).

How To: Add a Tweak

1. Drag the playhead ( ) for the timeline to the required location.
2. In the *Presentation* tab>Component panel, click (Tweak Components). Alternatively, right-click and select **Tweak Components**. The mini-toolbar opens.

3. In the Model Type drop-down list (shown in Figure 20–5), select whether a **Part** or **Component** will be tweaked. Use **Components** to select subassemblies.

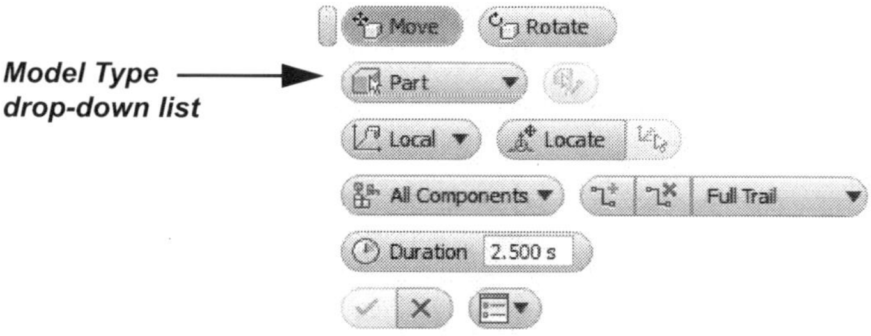

Figure 20–5

4. Select a component or multiple components to be tweaked.
    - Press and hold <Ctrl> and select components in the graphics window or from the expanded model list in the **Scene** node of the Model Browser to select multiple components.
    - Press and hold <Shift> to select a range of components in the Model Browser.
    - Select individual components or use a window selection technique to select components in the graphics window.
    - To clear a selected component, press and hold <Ctrl> and select it a second time.
    - All selected components are highlighted in blue.
5. Select the type of tweak. A triad will display on a face of the first selected component, similar to that shown in Figure 20–6 for a Move Tweak.
    - Click **Move** in the mini-toolbar to move the selected component linearly in the X, Y, or Z directions.
    - Click **Rotate** in the mini-toolbar to rotate the selected components in the XY, YZ, or XZ planes.

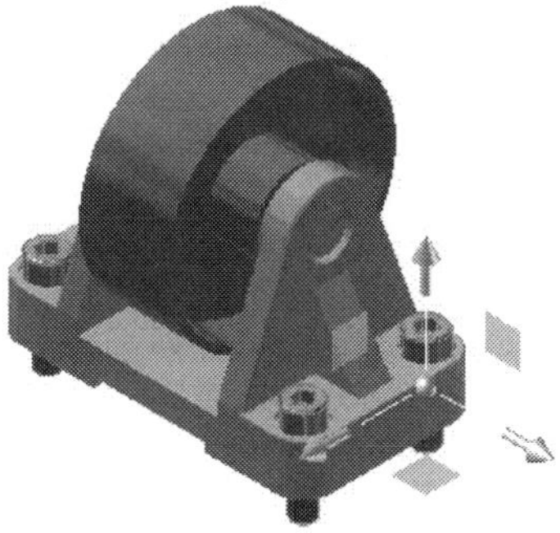

Figure 20–6

If multiple components have been selected for a Tweak, the triad displays on the first object that was selected.

6. (Optional) Reposition the triad if it does not meet the orientation requirements for the tweak.
   - Click **Locate** in the mini-toolbar. Hover the cursor over a new face reference and once the required control point on the face highlights, click to relocate the triad.
   - Use **Local** or **World** in the mini-toolbar to orient the triad relative to the component's coordinate system or the assembly coordinate system, respectively.

The default direction on the triad is gold.

7. Select the control handle on a triad and drag it to define the tweak, as shown in Figure 20–7. Alternatively, enter a specific value tweak's entry field.
   - Select an X, Y, or Z arrowhead to move linearly.
   - Select a XY, YZ, or XZ plane to move in a plane.
   - Select a rotation handle to rotate about the X, Y, or Z.

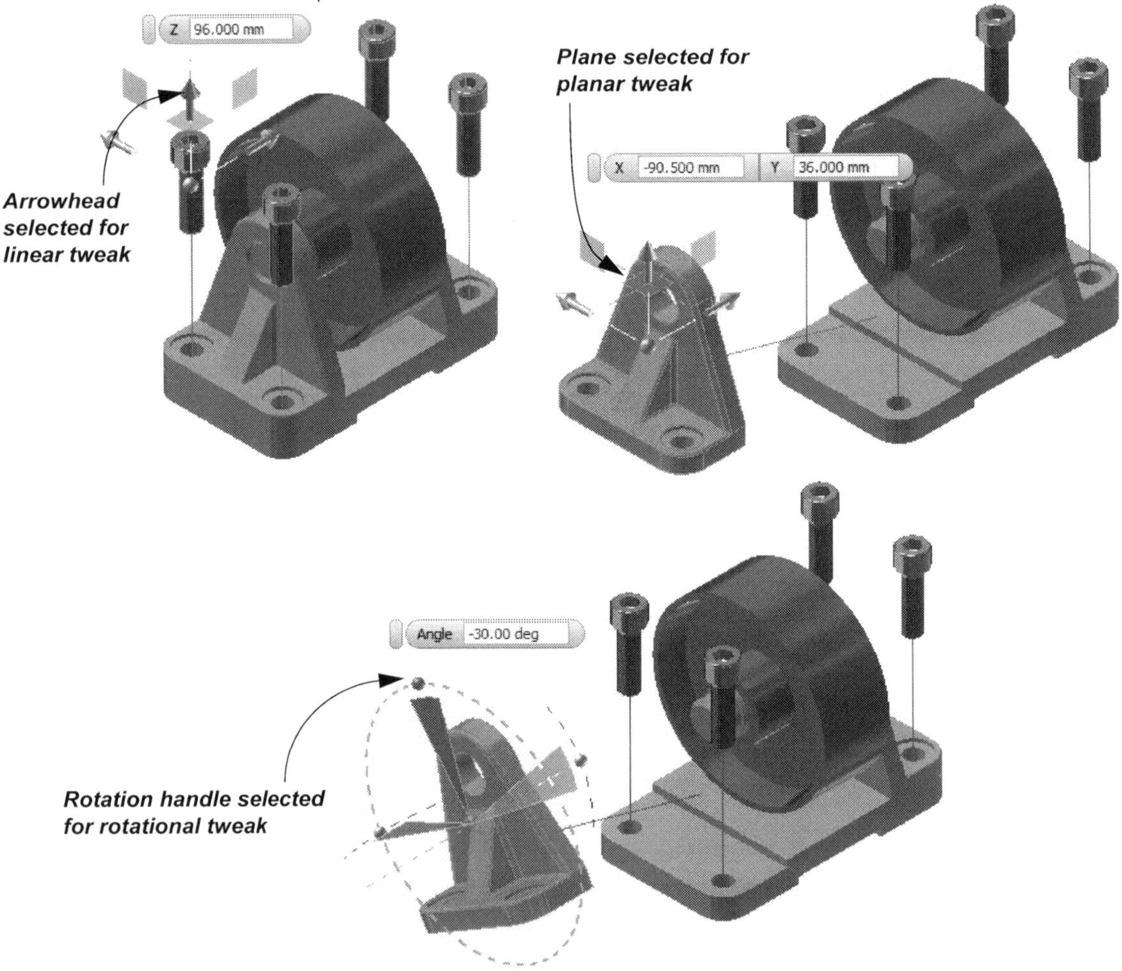

Figure 20–7

8. (Optional) Use the options in the *Trail* area of the mini-toolbar (shown in Figure 20–8) to control how the trail will be created.

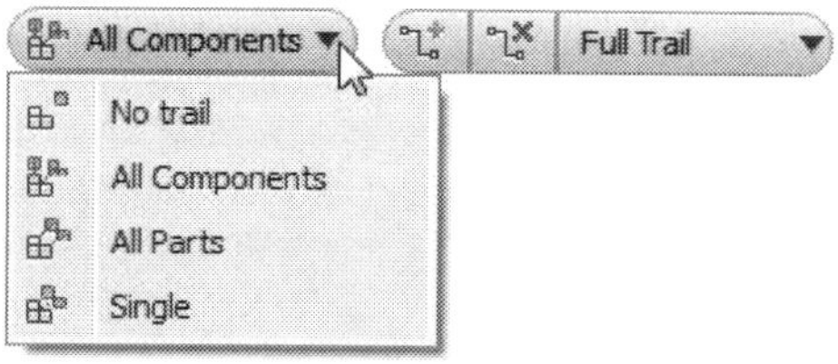

Figure 20–8

- In the drop-down list, select an option to add trails to all components in an assembly or subassembly (**All Components**) and all parts and a single trail for subassemblies (**All Parts**), a single trail for each group of selected components (**Single**), or no trail at all (**No Trails**).
- Select **Full Trail** to selectively remove or keep an entire trial or select **Trail Segment** to manipulate segments of the trail.

9. Continue to select additional triad handles to fully define the tweak or select additional components. Multiple combinations of handles and tweak types can be included.
10. Enter the **Duration** value for the tweak. The tweak will begin where the playhead was positioned and will run for the duration.
11. Complete the tweak operation:

- Click  to complete the tweak.
- Click  to cancel the operation.

Tweaks are listed in the Storyboard panel and Model Browser as shown in Figure 20–9. In this example, multiple tweaks with trails were created.

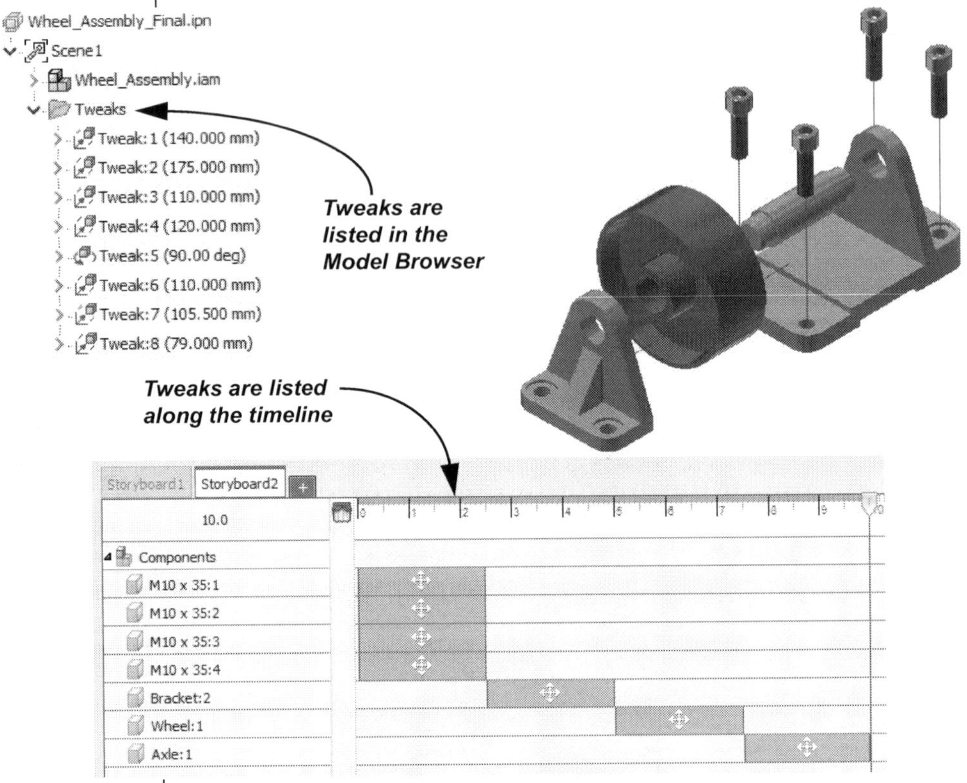

Figure 20–9

- In the Model Browser, the icons show whether the tweak is linear ( ) or rotational ( ).
- In the Storyboard panel, the symbols used to identify the duration of the tweak indicates if it is linear or planar ( ), rotational ( ),or a combination of both ( ).

Repositioning/Moving Tweaks

A tweak's timeline entry can be dragged to reposition it on the timeline. To move multiple tweaks at once, press and hold <Ctrl> to select them prior to moving. The *Duration* of the tweaks can be changed by dragging its endline to the appropriate time.

Editing Tweaks

An existing tweak can be modified in any of the following ways:

New translational or rotational movements cannot be added to an existing tweak. A new tweak must be added.

- Change the translational or rotational values initially assigned to the tweak.
- Change the duration of the tweak.
- Control the visibility of the trail lines for a tweak.

How To: Edit a Tweak's values

The Tweaks listed in the Model Browser are context sensitive. When in an animation storyboard, the tweaks belonging to the storyboard display. When editing a Snapshot View, only its tweaks display.

1. Activate the **Edit Tweak** command.
    - In the timeline, right-click a tweak's symbol and select **Edit Tweak**.
    - In the graphic window, right-click a trail line that belongs to the tweak and select **Edit Tweak**.
    - In the Model Browser, expand the *Tweaks* folder, right-click a tweak, and select **Edit Tweak**.
    - In the Model Browser, expand the *Tweaks* folder, select a tweak, and enter a new tweak value in the entry field.
    - Alternatively, double-click on the Tweak name or trail line to edit it.
2. Use the Tweak mini-toolbar to change the properties of the tweak.
    - Enter new values for the defined movements.
    - Press and hold <Ctrl> to add or remove components participating in the tweak.
    - Use the **Trail Line** options on the mini-toolbar to edit them.
    - Note that the duration cannot be edited using **Edit Tweak**.
3. Complete the edit:
    - Click  to complete the edit.
    - Click  to cancel the operation.

How To: Edit the Duration of a Tweak

1. In the timeline, right-click a tweak's symbol and select **Edit Time**. Alternatively, double-click on the Tweak symbol in the timeline.
2. Enter a new *Start*, *End* time, or *Duration* for the tweak in the mini-toolbar, as shown in Figure 20–10.

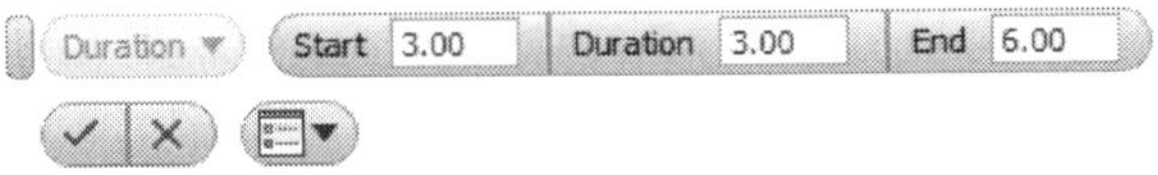

Figure 20–10

You can select multiple tweaks and edit their duration at the same time.

3. Complete the edit:
   - Click  to complete the edit.
   - Click  to cancel the operation.

Trail Visibility

Tweaks that contain trail lines can be manipulated once they are created to clear their visibility.

It is a recommended best practice to add trail lines during tweak creation and hide them, as required, after the fact.

- In the graphic window, right-click a trail line and select **Hide Trail Segment**, as shown in Figure 20–11. Using this method you can clear the trail segment for the individually selected trail line using the **Current** option or clear all trail lines in the group using the **Group** option.

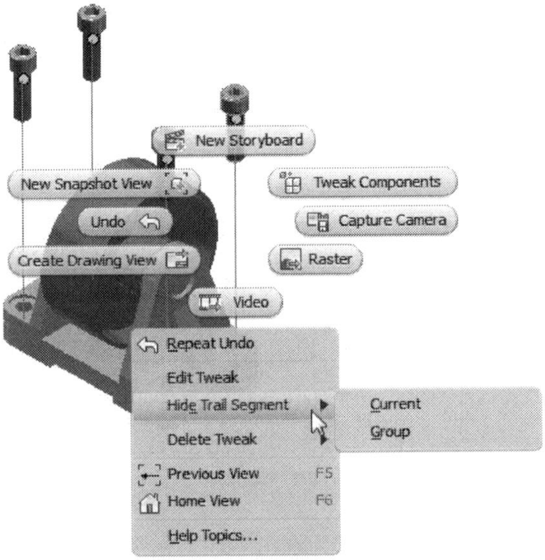

Figure 20–11

- In the Model Browser, expand the *Tweaks* folder, right-click a tweak or its component and select **Hide Trails** or **Hide Trail Segment**, as shown in Figure 20–12. By accessing the command at the Tweak level, you control all trails in the group. By accessing it at the component level you can specify it the trail for the current component (**Current**) or all components in the group are to be cleared (**Group**).

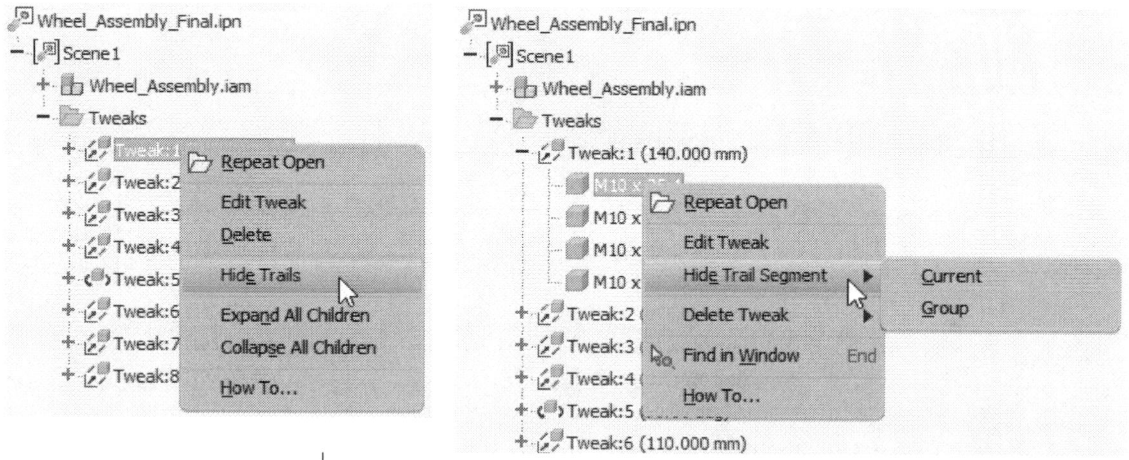

Figure 20–12

- Repeat the process using the Model Browser and use **Show Trail Segment** to return the display of trail lines to the model.

Deleting Tweaks

Similar to controlling the visibility of the trail lines in a tweak, you have multiple methods that can be used to delete individual and groups of tweaks from a presentation.

- In the graphic window, right-click a trail line and select **Delete Tweak**. Using this method, you can delete the tweak for the selected trail line using the **Current** option or delete all tweaks in the group using the **Group** option.
- In the Model Browser, expand the *Tweaks* folder, right-click a tweak and select **Delete**. All tweaks in the group are deleted.
- In the Model Browser, expand the *Tweaks* folder and **Tweak** node, right-click a component and select **Delete Tweak**.

- In the timeline, right-click on the tweak symbol and select **Delete**. You can specify it the Tweak for the current component (**Current**) or all components in the group are to be deleted (**Group**).

> **Hint: Aligning Start/End Time**
>
> To quickly align two Tweaks to either start or end at the same time, select them using <Ctrl>, right-click, and select **Align Start Time** or **Align End Time**.

Actions

Actions can be added to the timeline of a storyboard to control the appearance of components throughout an animation, or a camera position.

Model Appearance

To begin, place the timeliner playhead at the location that the action will be assigned. Actions that customize the model's appearance (visibility and opacity) can be added as follows:

*If a component was set as **Transparent** in the source assembly, that setting is visible if used in a presentation.*

- To change component opacity, select the component, and in the Component panel, click (Opacity). Use the Opacity mini-toolbar (shown in Figure 20–13) to specify the opacity value. You can use the slider or enter a value in the entry field. Click to complete the modification. Opacity actions are identified with the symbol in the timeline and are initially set as instant actions.

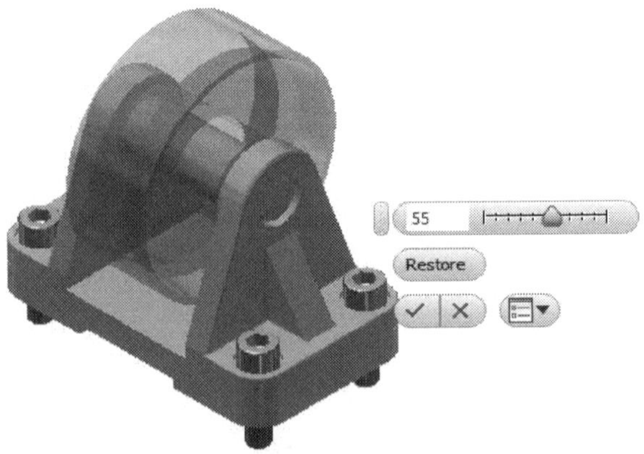

Figure 20–13

- To clear the visibility of a component, select the component in the graphic window or Model Browser, right-click and select **Visibility**. This removes the component from display in the animation at the point where the playhead was located.

  Visibility actions are identified with the symbol in the timeline and can only be instantaneous.

*Multiple Opacity settings can be modified at once by preselecting them prior to selecting **Edit Opacity**.*

- To modify a Visibility or Opacity action, move the playhead to its location on the timeline, select the component, and use the **Opacity** and **Visibility** options a second time.

*The **Edit Time** option for a Visibility action only enables you to change the time to an exact value. You cannot set a Visibility action for a duration. If the visibility is to be returned, move the playhead to the time, and toggle on the component's visibility.*

- By default, an Opacity action is set to be instantaneous; however, it can be modified to run over a specified duration.

  To edit the action, right-click the symbol in the timeline and select **Edit Time**. In the drop-down list, change the action type to **Duration**, as shown in Figure 20–14.

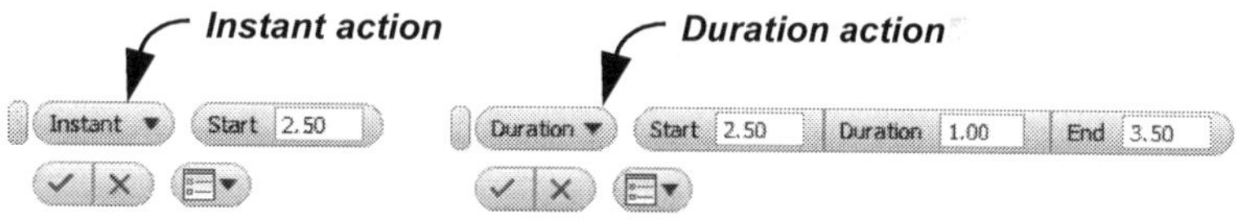

Figure 20–14

- Select and drag a Visibility or Opacity action along the timeline to relocate them.

- To delete a Visibility or Opacity action, select it in the timeline, right-click, and select **Delete**.

Camera Position

An action that changes the camera position can be set to run over a specified duration. To begin, place the timeliner playhead at the location that the action will be assigned.

How To: Customize the Model's Camera Position

1. To change position of the camera, use the ViewCube or other navigation tools to change the model orientation (camera).
2. In the Camera panel, click  (Capture Camera).
   - The action is added to the top of the timeline at the point where the playhead was positioned, as shown in Figure 20–15. It is created to run for 3 seconds.

The Camera Position action may look compressed at the top of the timeline if the timeline is not large enough and is showing the scroll bar.

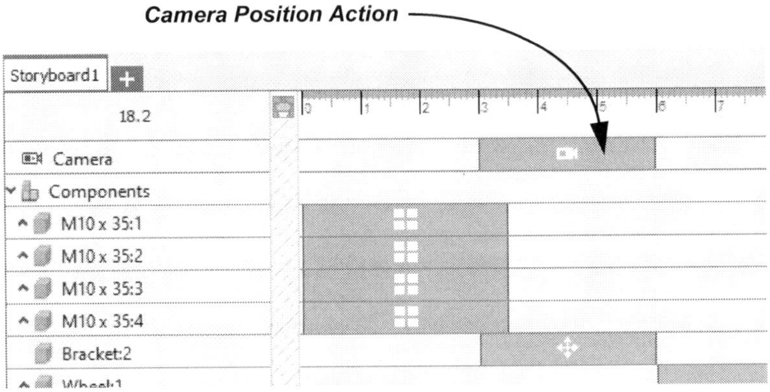

Figure 20–15

Alternatively, you can right-click on a Camera Position action in the timeline and select ***Edit Time*** *to open the mini-toolbar.*

- By default, the action is added as a Duration action. To make a change to the default duration (2.5 seconds) or change it to an Instant action, double-click the camera action on the timeline. Using the mini-toolbar (shown in Figure 20–16), you can change the type of action and its *Start*, *End,* or *Duration* times.

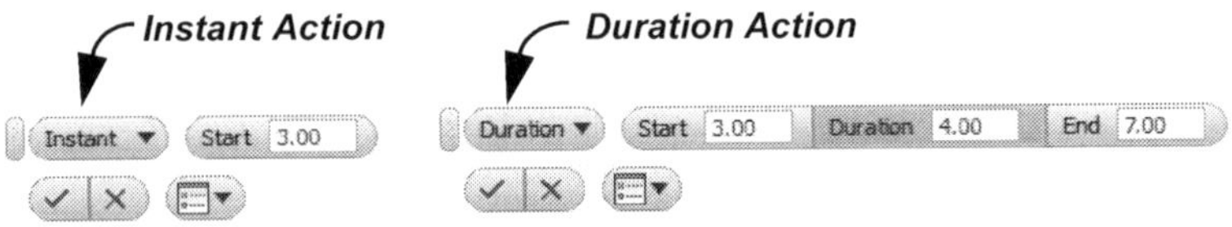

Figure 20–16

- Select and drag a Camera Position action to move it along the timeline.
- To delete a Camera Position action, select it in the timeline, right-click, and select **Delete**.

Hint: Scratch Zone

The area on the timeline that displays prior to the start of the timeline is called the *Scratch Zone*. It is identified with the symbol, as shown in Figure 20–17. The *Scratch Zone* enables you to set the initial view settings, visibility, opacity, and camera position for the assembly. When the settings are made in the *Scratch Zone*, they are not included in the animation. It simply defines how the assembly displays at time 0 on the timeline.

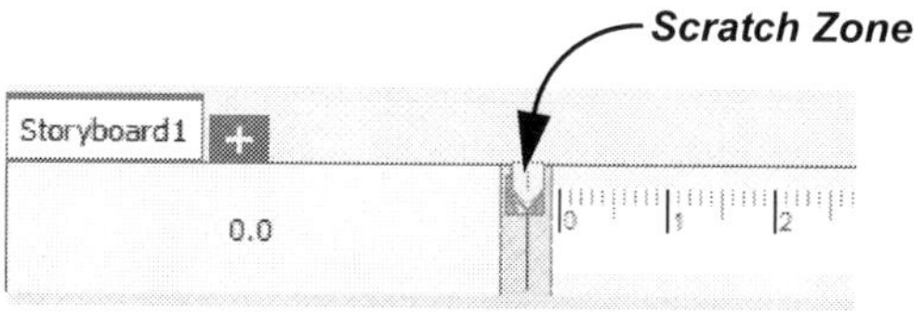

Figure 20–17

- To set the options, position the playhead of the timeliner in this area, and use the **Visibility**, **Opacity**, and **Capture Camera** options, as required.
- Modifications cannot be made to the actions in the *Scratch Zone*. Use the **Visibility**, **Opacity**, and **Capture Camera** options a second time to reset them.

Hint: Deleting all Actions for a Component

Individual Tweaks and Actions can be deleted directly on the timeline. To delete all actions associated with a component, right-click on the component name in the Storyboard panel and select **Delete Actions**.

- If the current storyboard was created using **Start from end of Previous**, the **Delete Actions** option will delete all current and inherited actions from the previous storyboard.

Playing a Storyboard

Once you have created an animation and have added actions, you can use the Timeline Controls to playback the entire storyboard. The Timeline Controls are located at the top of the Storyboard panel. The options in this panel are consistent with standard playback controls (rewind to beginning, play, pause, play in reverse, and fast forward to end).

Hint: Tweak and Action Selection

To quickly select all or multiple timeline entries for editing before or after a specific entry, right-click on the entry and select **Select>All Before** or **Select>All After**. When working with groups, right-click on one entry and select **Select>Group** to select all entries in the group.

20.3 Snapshot Views

Snapshot views store a combination of component display settings and positions in one view to communicate specific information in the model. The Snapshot view can be used to create image files for presentations or views in an Inventor drawing file. To create an exploded assembly view in a drawing you must create an exploded Snapshot view and reference it in a drawing.

The component display settings that can be assigned in a Snapshot view are similar to those used to create animations. They include:

- Component positions using tweaks
- Component visibility settings
- Component opacity settings
- Camera positions defined by the model's orientation
- View settings using the *View* tab.

A Snapshot view can be created using a previously created storyboard or they can be created independently.

Creating Snapshots from a Storyboard

How To: Create a Snapshot View from a Storyboard

1. Activate the scene to which the Snapshot view will be added.
    - To activate it, double click the scene name in the Model Browser.
2. In the Timeline, position the playhead at the point at which the Snapshot view is required.
3. In the Workshop panel, click (New Snapshot View).

To rename a Snapshot view, right-click on its thumbnail image and select ***Rename****. Enter a new descriptive name for the image and press <Enter>.*

A new view is added in the Snapshot Views browser. The component display settings that exist in the storyboard at the location of the playhead are used in the Snapshot view.

- The marker displays on the Snapshot view's thumbnail image, indicating that it is associated with the storyboard animation, as shown in Figure 20–18.
- The marker also displays on the Timeline, indicating that a Snapshot view was created, as shown in Figure 20–18. The symbol can be dragged to change the snapshot location on the timeline, if required.

- If the Snapshot view marker is moved on the timeline or changes are made to any of the actions at that time, the symbol displays on the view in the Snapshot Views browser, indicating that it is out of date. Select the symbol to update it.

Snapshot in the Snapshot Browser

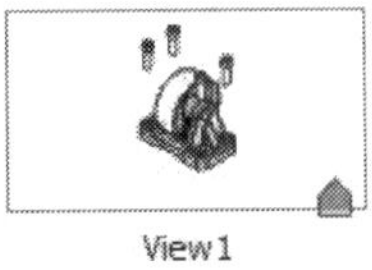

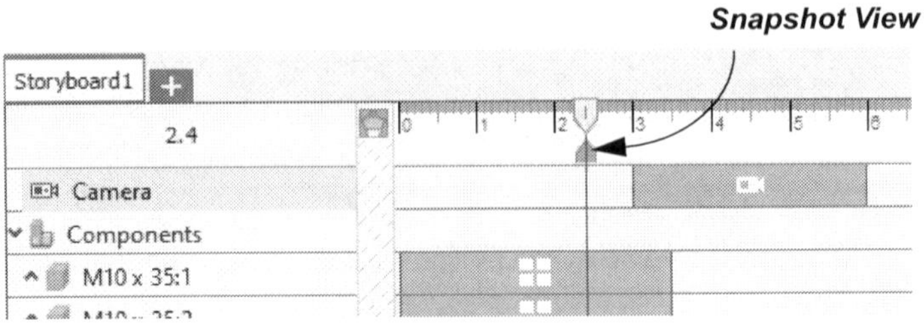

Figure 20–18

> **Hint: Snapshot Views at the Beginning of an Animation**
>
> Snapshot views that are created when the playhead is at the beginning of the animation timeline (0 seconds) will not create a dependent Snapshot view.

Creating Independent Snapshots

How To: Create an Independent Snapshot View

1. Activate the scene to which the Snapshot view will be added.
   - To activate it, double click the scene name in the Model Browser.
2. Position the Storyboard playhead in the *Scratch Zone*, as shown in Figure 20–19.
   - If an animation or actions exist in the Storyboard, position the playhead in the *Scratch Zone*.
   - If no animation or actions exist, independent Snapshot views will be created regardless of being in the *Scratch Zone*.

*To rename a Snapshot view, right-click on its thumbnail image and select **Rename**. Enter a new descriptive name for the image and press <Enter>.*

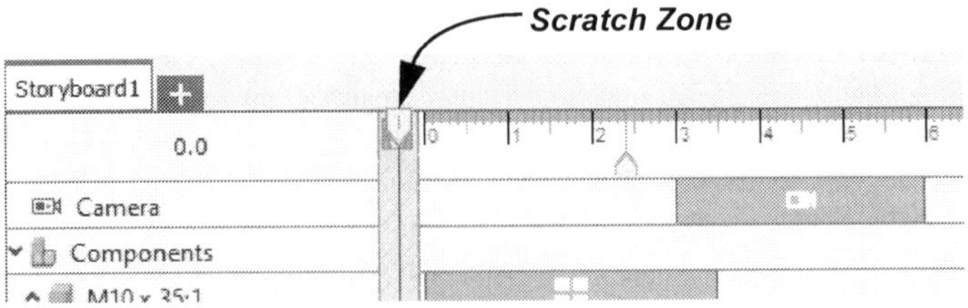

Figure 20–19

3. In the Workshop panel, click (New Snapshot View). The view is added to the Snapshot Views browser. The marker does not display on the view's thumbnail image as it does for dependent views.

Editing a Snapshot View

Snapshot views that are dependent on the Storyboard show the assembly at a specific time on the timeline. In the case of independent views, they will likely need to be customized once the view is created.

As you edit an existing view, you can click (New Snapshot View) in the Workshop to create an additional view.

How To: Edit an Independent Snapshot View

1. Activate the scene to which the Snapshot view exists.
2. In the Snapshot Views browser, right-click the view that is to be edited and select **Edit**. Alternatively, double-click the view to edit it. The *Edit View* tab becomes the active tab (shown in Figure 20–20) and the Storyboard panel is removed from the display.

Figure 20–20

3. Set the component's view display using any of the following tools:

   - Use the ViewCube and Navigation bar to set the model orientation. Click (Update Camera) to update the view.
   - Select components, right-click, and clear the **Visibility** option for components that are not required in the view.
   - Select component(s) and on the Component panel, click (Opacity) to assign an Opacity value to component(s) in the view.
   - In the *View* tab, assign view settings from the *View* tab to customize the view.
   - Use the (Tweak Components) command to move or rotate components in the Snapshot view. Use the mini-toolbar in the same way as is done for an animation to move and rotate components in the view.

4. Click (Finish Edit View) to complete the edit.

Hint: Making a Dependent Snapshot View Independent

The marker on a Snapshot view's thumbnail image indicates that it is associated (linked) with the storyboard animation. If you edit this type of view, you will be prompted that you cannot make changes to a view that is linked to the timeline (as shown in Figure 20–21). To permanently break the link, click **Break Link**.

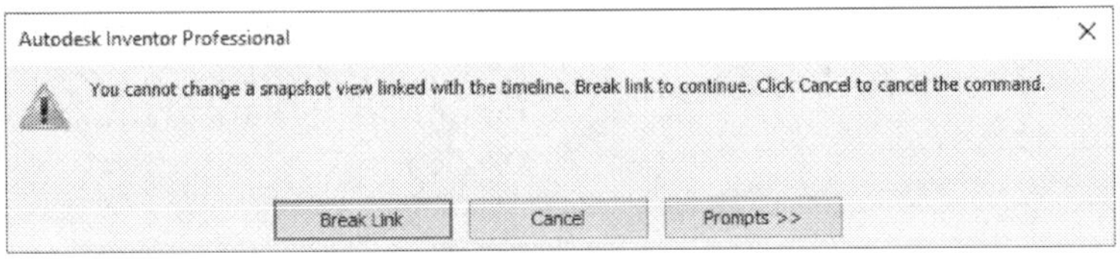

Figure 20–21

The marker is removed from the Snapshot view's thumbnail image. Only the addition of a tweak or the change of Opacity and Visibility for a component require you to break the link. Changes to the camera position/orientation are permitted without breaking the link.

Creating a Drawing View from a Snapshot View

Creating drawings will be discussed in more detail later in the guide.

Any of the Snapshot views listed in the Snapshot Views browser can be used to create a drawing view.

- The Snapshot view's name can be selected in the *Presentation* area of the Drawing View dialog box when an .IPN file is selected as the drawing model, as shown in Figure 20–22.

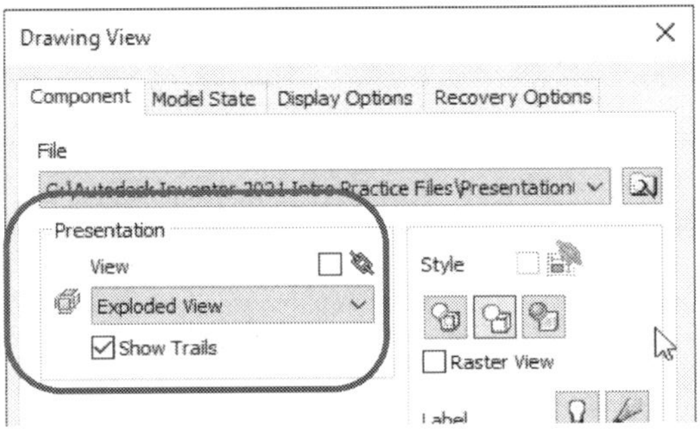

Figure 20–22

- A drawing view can also be created directly from the Presentation file using the following:
  - In the Snapshot Views browser, right-click on the thumbnail image and select **Create Drawing View**. The drawing view will be created using this Snapshot view.

- While editing a Snapshot view, in the *Edit View* tab>Drawing panel, click (Create Drawing View). The drawing view will be created using this Snapshot view.
- In the *Presentation* tab>Drawing panel, click (Create Drawing View). The drawing view will be created and defaults to using the first Snapshot view. You can select an alternate, if required.

Once the command is selected, you will be prompted to select a drawing template for the new drawing and then you will be immediately placed in the drawing. The Drawing View dialog box opens and you can begin to place the Base view and any additional Projected views, as shown in Figure 20–23.

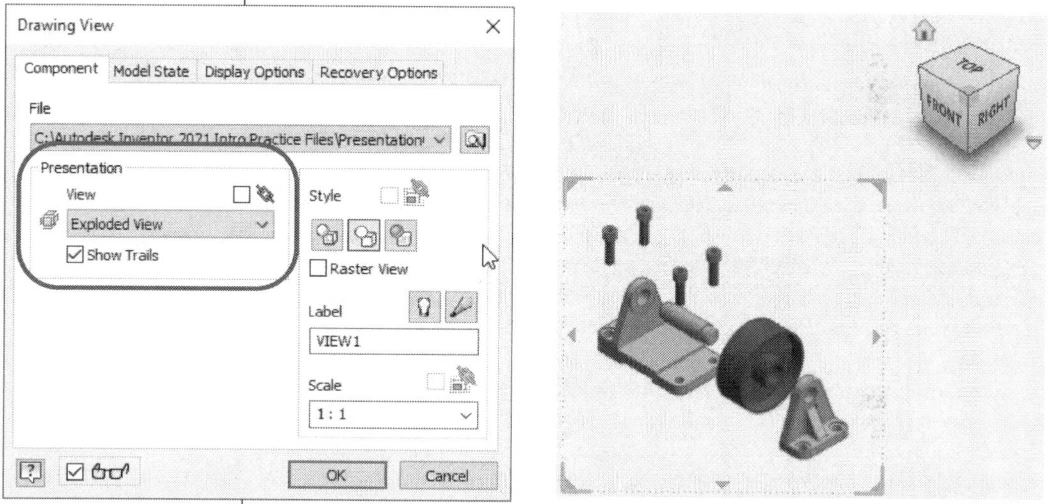

Figure 20–23

The *Presentation* area of the dialog box displays the name of the Snapshot view being used. Consider the following:

- Select an alternate Snapshot view in the drop-down list.
- Show or clear the trails in the view using **Show Trails**. Trails can only be controlled if they exist in the Snapshot view.
- Select to set the new view as associative. This ensures that if a change is made to the Snapshot view in the Presentation file, it will update the drawing view.

20.4 Publishing a Presentation File

Both Snapshot views and Storyboards can be published to various formats. Snapshot views can be published as raster images and Storyboards can be published as animations.

How To: Publish Snapshot Views

1. Activate the scene in which the Snapshot will be published.
2. Select the view(s) to publish in the Snapshot Views browser.
   - To publish multiple Snapshot views, press and hold <Ctrl> during selection.

A Snapshot view can be published while it is being edited by selecting (Raster) in the Edit View tab.

3. Open the Publish to Raster Images dialog box, as shown in Figure 20–24 to publish the snapshots.
   - In the *Presentation* tab>Publish panel, click (Raster).
   - Right-click a view in the Snapshot Views browser and select **Publish to Raster**.

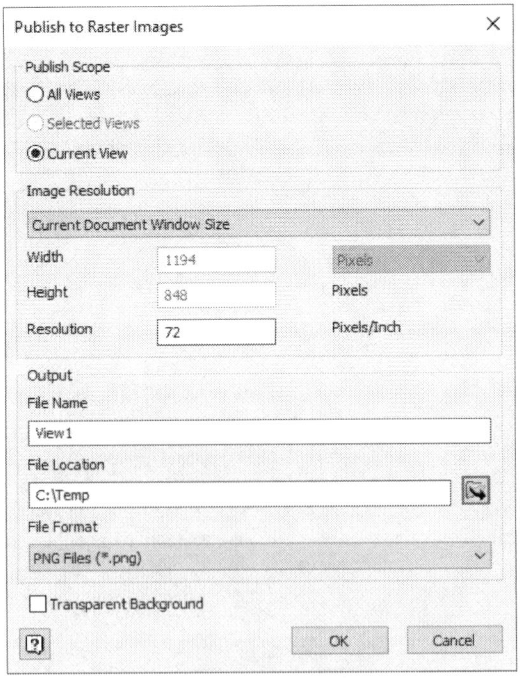

Figure 20–24

4. In the the *Publish Scope* area, define the scope of publishing.
   - Click **All Views** to publish all Snapshot views available in active scene.

- Use **Selected Views** to publish the views that were previously selected.

5. In the *Image Resolution* area, define the image size.
    - Use **Current Document Window Size** in the drop-down list to publish the view as it is currently displayed.
    - Select a predefined image size in the drop-down list.
    - Select **Custom** in the drop-down list and enter a custom *Width*, *Height*, and *Resolution* value by pixel or unit size.
    - Enter a *Resolution* value.
6. In the *Output* area, specify a folder to save the file. The Snapshot view name will be used as the published filename.
7. In the File Format drop-down list, select a publishing format.
8. Enable **Transparent Background**, if required.
9. Click **OK** to publish the image.

The supported image file formats include BMP, GIF, JPEG, PNG, or TIFF.

How To: Publish a Storyboard

1. Activate the scene in which the Storyboard will be published.
2. In the Storyboard panel, select the *Storyboard* tab that is to be published.
3. Open the Publish to Video dialog box, as shown in Figure 20–25 to publish the snapshots.
    - In the *Presentation* tab>Publish panel, click  (Video).
    - Right-click a *Storyboard* tab and select **Publish**.

*The **Video** option is only available if an animation exists in the Storyboard panel.*

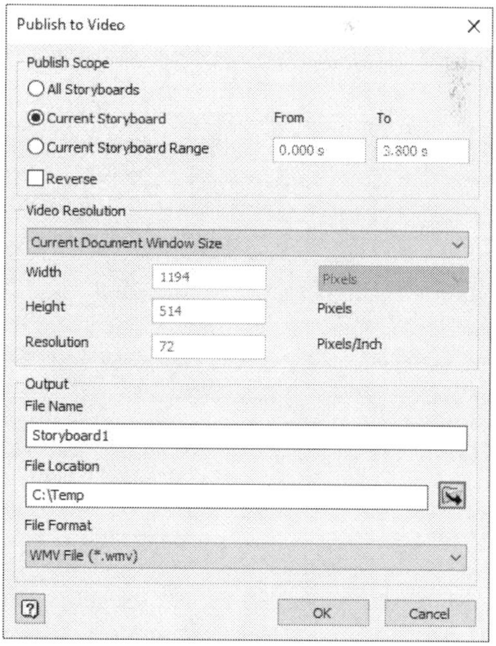

Figure 20–25

4. In the *Publish Scope* area, define the scope of publishing.
    - Use **All Storyboard** to publish all storyboards available in active scene.
    - Use **Current Storyboard** to publish the active storyboard.
    - Use **Current Storyboard Range** to publish a time range in the active storyboard. Enter values in the *From* and *To* fields.
    - Click **Reverse** to publish the video in a reverse order (end to start).
5. In the *Video Resolution* area, define the video size.
    - Use **Current Document Window Size** in the drop-down list to publish the video as it is currently displayed.
    - Select a predefined video size in the drop-down list.
    - Select **Custom** in the drop-down list and enter a custom *Width*, *Height*, and *Resolution* value by pixel or unit size.
6. In *Output* area, specify a name for the video and a folder to save the file.
7. In the File Format drop-down list, select a publishing format.
8. Click **OK** to publish the video.
9. For AVI formatted videos, select a video compressor and set compression quality, if available. Click **OK**.

The supported video file formats include WMV and AVI. A WMV video player must be installed on your computer to publish to WMV format.

Practice 20a Create an Animation

Practice Objectives

- Create a new presentation file using a standard template.
- Create an animation that explodes the components of an assembly using translational and rotational movements.
- Control the visual display and orientation of components in an animation.
- Play an animation and then publish it.

In this practice, you will create a presentation file using a wheel assembly. The assembly file that will be used is shown in Figure 20–26. Using the tools in the Presentation file, you will create an animation that explodes the components of the assembly to show how it is assembled.

*A video called **video2.wmv** has been provided in the Presentation folder of the practice files folder for you to review the animation that will be created in this practice.*

Figure 20–26

Task 1 - Create a presentation file.

*Alternatively, use the Quick Access toolbar, **File** menu, or the My Home tab to create a new file.*

1. In the *Get Started* tab>Launch panel, click  (New).
2. Select the *Metric* folder, select **Standard(mm).ipn** in the Create New File dialog box to create a new presentation file, and click **Create**.
   - You might need to scroll down in the list to locate this template.

*If a specific representation of the file is to be used, click **Options** and select the required Design View, Level of Detail, or Positional Representation to use.*

3. In the Insert dialog box, navigate to the *Presentation* folder and select **Wheel_Assembly.iam**. Click **Open**.
   - The presentation environment displays and the *Presentation* tab is the active tab.
   - By default, there is a single scene created using the wheel assembly and **Storyboard1** is active. No snapshots are initially created.

Task 2 - Define the initial model display for the animation.

The Scratch Zone is where you can set the initial visibility, opacity, and camera position for the model.

1. The playhead ( ) starts at time 0 seconds. Drag the playhead to the left into the *(Scratch Zone)* area of the panel, as shown in Figure 20–27.

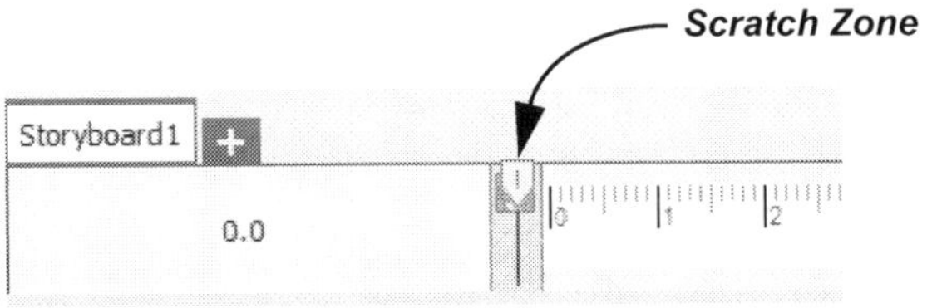

Figure 20–27

2. Rotate the model into a custom orientation using the ViewCube. Select the corner shown in Figure 20–28. This positions the model for the start of the animation.

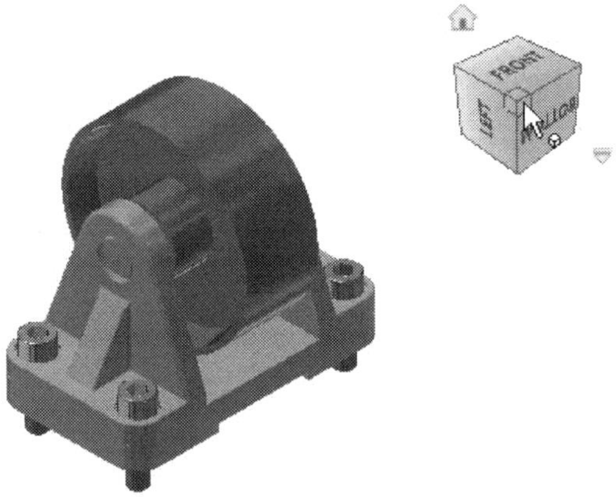

Figure 20–28

3. In the Camera panel, click (Capture Camera). This stores the orientation for the start position of the animation.

Task 3 - Create an exploded animation of the assembly.

1. Expand the **Scene1** node in the Model Browser and the **Wheel_Assembly.iam** node. All of the assembly component's names display. This provides a convenient way to select components.

2. To move components, in the *Presentation* tab>Component panel, click (Tweak Components). The Tweak Component mini-toolbar opens as shown in Figure 20–29.

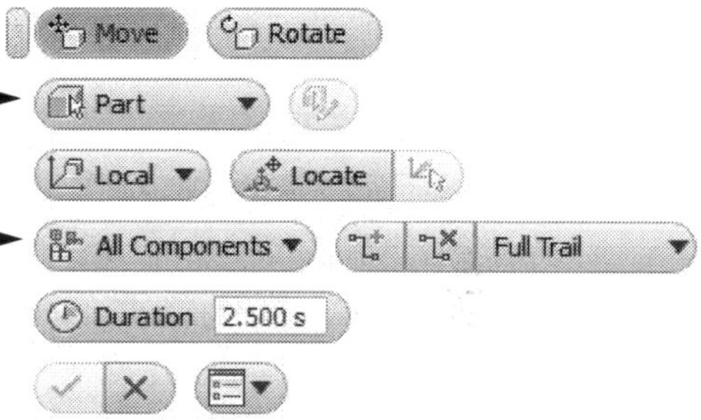

Figure 20–29

3. Ensure that **Part** is selected in the Model Type drop-down list.

*Alternatively, you can use the **Select Other** tool in the graphics window to select any hidden components to avoid rotating the model and changing its orientation in the animation.*

4. Press and hold <Ctrl> and select the four **M10 x 35** components in the Model Browser. All the components should be highlighted in the model and the tweak triad should be displayed.

5. Ensure that **Move** is selected in the top row of the mini-toolbar to move components in either the X, Y, or Z directions.

6. Expand the Trail Settings drop-down list in the mini-toolbar. The options in this field enables you to customize if trails are created. In this practice, they will be created and you will later learn how to quickly toggle them on and off. Ensure that **All Components** is selected.

7. The triad orientation displays the local coordinate system for the part. Expand the **Local** option and select **World** to change the orientation of the triad to be consistent with the assembly coordinate system.

8. Select the arrow that points in the Z direction relative to the assembly's origin, as shown in Figure 20–30.
   - If the model origin is not displayed, consider toggling it on in the Application Options>*Display* tab>**Show Origin 3D indicator**.

Depending on the order in which the components are selected, the triad may display in a different location or orientation.

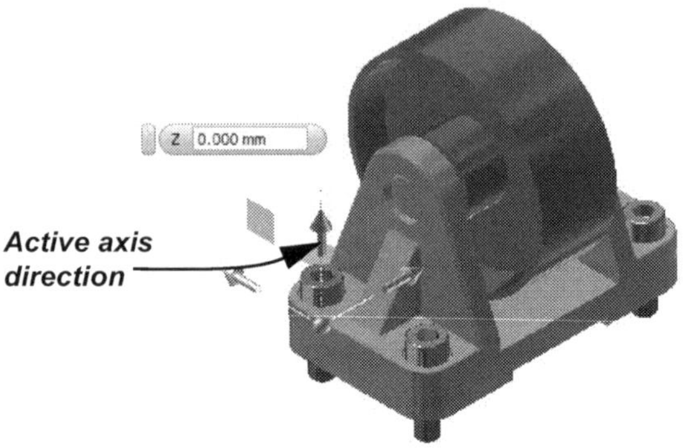

Figure 20–30

9. The active Z axis direction displays in gold. Drag the arrowhead upwards to move the four components. Enter **75** (or **-75**) in the *Z* entry field to move the components a specific distance.

10. Click  to complete the Tweak and close the mini-toolbar.

Tweak actions are set at 2.5 seconds by default. This can be modified in the Tweak mini-toolbar prior to closing it or it can be modified after it is created.

11. Note that the four components are listed in the Storyboard panel and the tweak actions are scheduled to last 2.5 seconds, as shown in Figure 20–31.

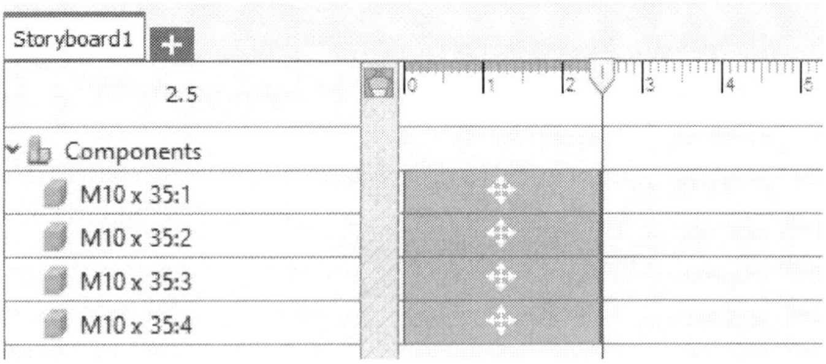

Figure 20–31

12. Hover the cursor over the Tweak action () for the first component in the list, right-click, and select **Edit Time**.

13. In the mini-toolbar, set the *Duration* value to **3.00**. Click .

14. The first component is now set to get into its exploded position slower than the others. Click in the playback controls to rewind the timeline to the beginning and click . Note the differences in the timing.

15. Hover the cursor over the Tweak action ( ) for the second component in the list and double-click to edit it. This is an alternative method to edit the timing.

16. Set the *Duration* value to **3.00**. Click .

17. Hold <Ctrl> and select the third and fourth component's Tweak actions ( ), hover the cursor over the right-hand edge of the action bar. Drag to the right to manually extend its duration. Ensure that it snaps to 3 seconds. The Storyboard panel should display as shown in Figure 20–32.

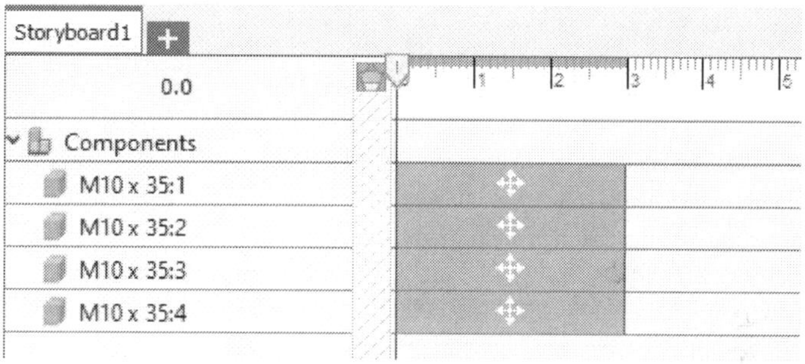

Figure 20–32

18. The fasteners have not been moved high enough. Right-click on any of the actions ( ) and select **Edit Tweak**.

19. In the *Distance* field, enter **140mm** as the new value. Click . Because they are a group, they all are edited together.

Task 4 - Add additional tweaks to components.

1. Click to move the playhead to the end of the current actions. This ensures that the next tweak is added immediately at the end of the last tweak.

2. In the Component panel, click  (Tweak Components). Using the following table, move and rotate the Bracket and Wheel components. The Storyboard timeline and component display should display as shown in Figure 20–33 after the two components are tweaked. Use the World coordinate system when tweaking. You might need to enter positive or negative tweak values to translate and rotate as shown.

Ensure that the playhead is at the correct position on the timeline when defining each tweak.

Component	Tweaks
Bracket:2	• Translate 175mm along the X-axis. • Define the tweak as 3.00 seconds.
Wheel	• Translate 110 mm along the X-axis. • Translate 120 mm along the Z axis. • Rotate 90 degrees in the XZ plane. • Modify each tweak to 3.00 seconds, if not already set.

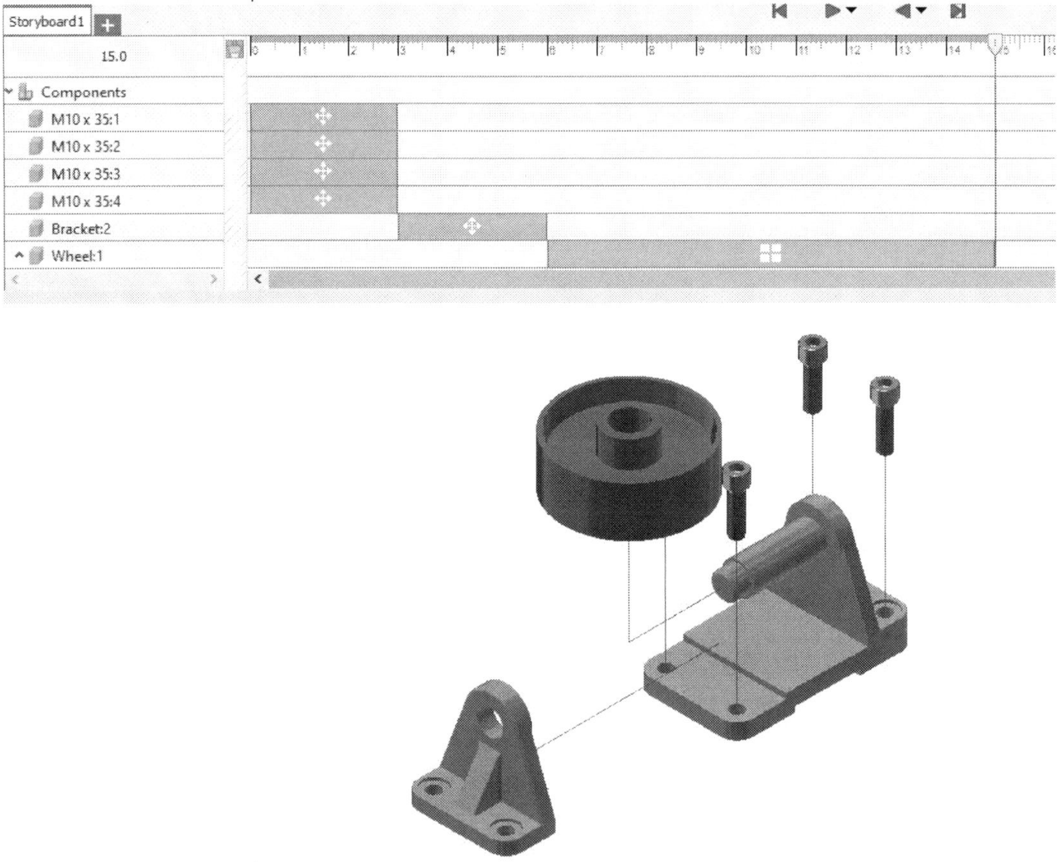

Figure 20–33

3. Play the animation from the beginning and note how the wheel is unassembled with three actions that occur consecutively. After playing, note that the model displays reassembled. This is only because the playhead returns to where it starts on the timeline. The animation will end fully disassembled at 15 seconds once published.

4. The three actions for the Wheel are grouped. In the Storyboard, expand the **Wheel** component in the component list to show the individual actions. To manipulate them, it must be expanded.

5. Manipulate the duration of the rotation action ( ) and relocate it on the timeline such that it occurs while the component is moving in the *Z* direction, similar to that shown in Figure 20–34.

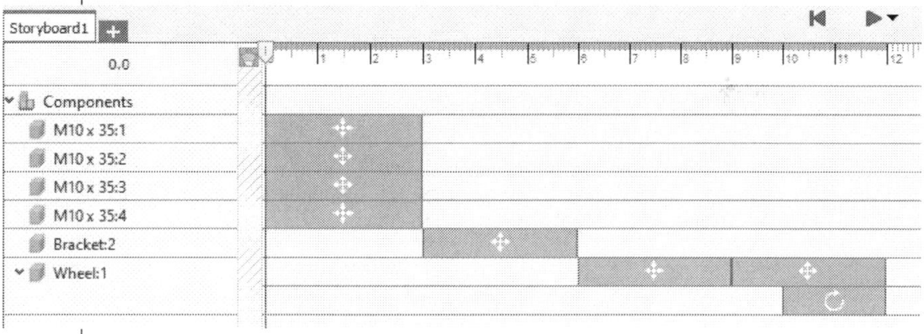

Figure 20–34

Ensure that the playhead is at the correct position on the timeline when defining each tweak.

6. Use the following table to apply tweaks to the remaining components. The components should display as shown in Figure 20–35 after the remaining three components are tweaked. Use the World coordinate system when tweaking the components. You might need to enter positive or negative tweak values to translate and rotate as shown.

Component	Tweaks
Axle	• Translate 110mm along the X-axis. • Define the tweak as 3.00 seconds.
Bracket:1	• Translate 110mm along the X-axis. • Define the tweak as 2.50 seconds.
Plate	• Translate 80 mm along the Z axis. • Define the tweak as 2.50 seconds.

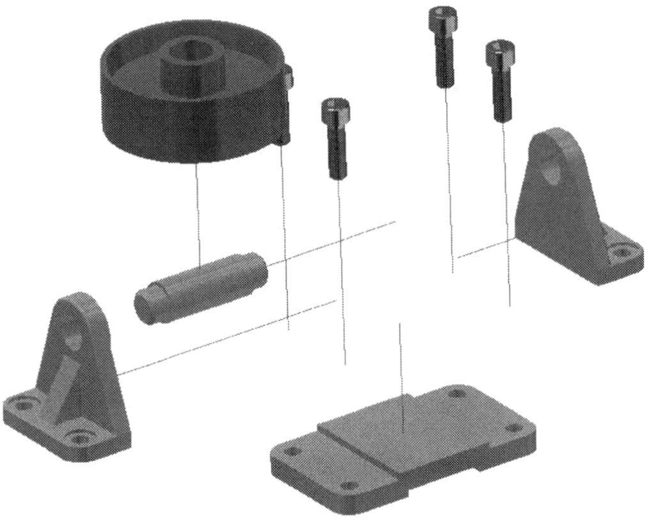

Figure 20–35

7. Manipulate the timeline such that the last two components assemble at the same time and run for 2.00 seconds.
8. Play the animation and verify that it functions as expected.
   - A video called **video1.wmv** has been provided in the practice files folder for you to compare with.
9. Save the presentation file using its default name into the *Presentation* folder.

If you were to expand the Tweaks folder, it lists all tweaks that were created and you can individually edit them or hide their trail lines.

Task 5 - Incorporate visual changes in the animation.

1. In the Model Browser, right-click on the *Tweaks* folder and select **Hide All Trails**, as shown in Figure 20–36. If **Hide All Trails** is not available, move your playhead past the start of the timeline and try again.

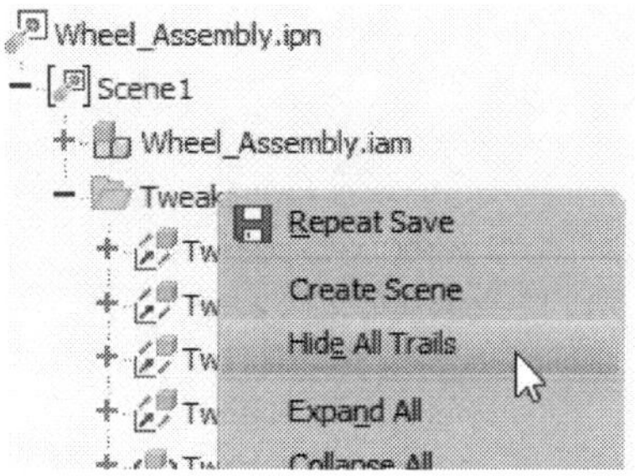

Figure 20–36

2. Return the playhead to the beginning of the timeline and play the animation. Note that the trail lines are all removed from the display.

3. Once the fasteners are exploded, they can fade from the display. Place the playhead at **3s** and select all four fasteners.

4. In the Component panel, click  (Opacity). When prompted that the scene is associated with a design view and that you must break or override the associativity, click **Break**. This makes the scene independent of the Master Design View that was imported into the scene.

5. On the mini-toolbar, drag the *Opacity* slider to **0**. Click .

6. Note how the new component opacity action is grouped with the other actions for these components. Expand the first component, as shown in Figure 20–37.

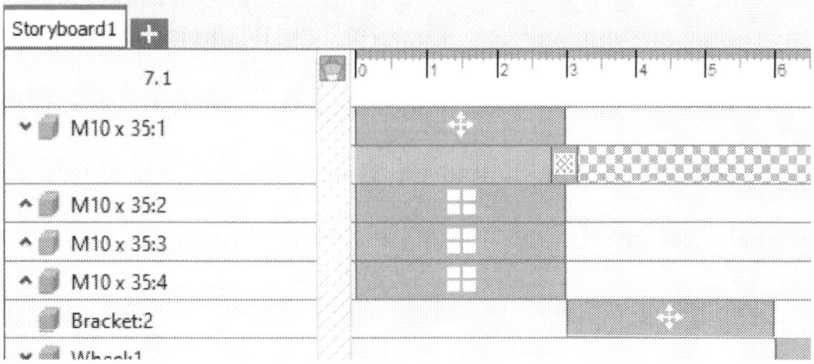

Figure 20–37

7. Right-click on the action for the first fastener and select **Edit Time**. By default, the action is created as an Instant action.

8. Select **Duration** in the drop-down list in the mini-toolbar.

9. Set the *Start* value to **2.50** and the *End* value to **3.50**.

   Click .

10. Play the animation and note the difference between the first fastener's visibility changes and the other fasteners.

As an alternative to using opacity, you could have also cleared the visibility of the components at a specific time. The Visibility action is only instantaneous.

11. Modify the other three fasteners such that they also fade out over a duration of 2.50 to 3.50 seconds.

12. Compress the **M10 x 35** component nodes in the Storyboard panel once your edits are complete.

Task 6 - Spin the model at the end of the animation.

1. Click to move the playhead to the end of the animation.

2. Reorient the model to the orientation shown on the ViewCube in Figure 20–38 and zoom in on the model.

Figure 20–38

3. In the Camera panel, click  (Capture Camera). A camera action is added to the top of the timeline.

4. Modify the length of the camera action by right-clicking on the  symbol and selecting **Edit Time**.

5. Modify the duration to start at 16 seconds and last until 19 seconds. Alternatively, you can drag the action and extend its action on the timeline.

6. Move the playhead to the beginning of the animation. The entire timeline should display similar to that shown in Figure 20–39.

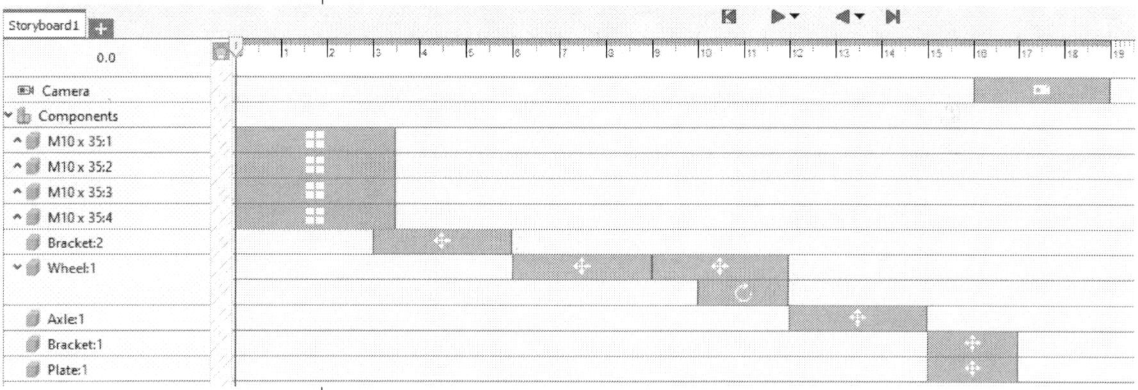

Figure 20–39

7. Play the animation to see how this new Camera action affects the animation.
   - A video called **video2.wmv** has been provided in the practice files folder for you to compare with.

Task 7 - Modify the View settings in the model.

1. Return the playhead into the *Scratch Zone* once again.

The settings that are defined in the View tab are temporary and are not saved with the Presentation file.

2. On the ribbon, select the *View* tab. Use the tools in the Appearance panel to set the following:
   - In the Shadows drop-down list, enable **Ambient Shadows**.
   - In the Visual Style drop-down list, select **Technical Illustration** or an alternate style. Note that threads do not display in a technical illustration.

3. Play the animation.

Task 8 - Publish the Storyboard.

1. In the *Presentation* tab>Publish panel, click  (Video). Alternatively, right-click on the *Storyboard1* tab and select **Publish to Video**.
2. In the Publish to Video dialog box, ensure that **Current Storyboard** is selected in the *Publish Scope* area.
3. In the *Video Resolution* area, maintain the **Current Document Window Size** option to publish the video as it is currently displayed.
4. In the *Output* area, set the video name to **my_wheel_assembly** and save it to the *Presentation* folder in the practice files folder.
5. In the File Format drop-down list, select **WMV File (*.wmv)**.
6. Click **OK** to publish the video.
7. Navigate to the *Presentation* folder in the practice files and play the video once it has published.
8. Save the presentation file and close the window.

Practice 20b Create Snapshots

Practice Objectives

- Create snapshots that are dependent on a storyboard animation.
- Create snapshots that are independent from a storyboard animation.
- Edit snapshots to manipulate component position and component display.
- Update snapshots that are dependent on a storyboard animation.

In this practice, you will create Snapshot views that are both dependent on an animation as well as independent of it. You will also learn how to edit both types of Snapshot views using the tools available in the Presentation environment. The independent exploded Snapshot view is shown in Figure 20–40.

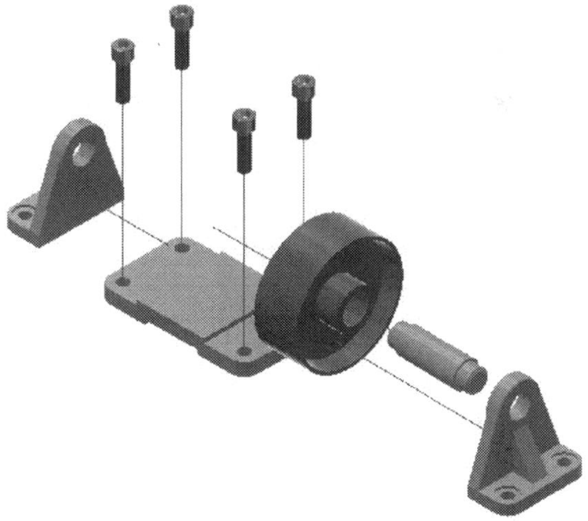

Figure 20–40

Task 1 - Create Snapshot Views that are dependent on a Storyboard animation.

In this task, you will create multiple Snapshot views all based on the storyboard animation that already exists in the presentation file.

1. Continue working with the Presentation file from the previous practice or open **Wheel_Assembly_Final.ipn** from the *Presentation* folder.

2. Note that there is currently one scene in the file (**Scene1**) and that this scene does not currently have any Snapshot views in the Snapshot Views browser.

3. In the timeline, move the playhead to the beginning of the animation (0 seconds). You can select or simply drag the playhead to the beginning of the animation.

4. In the Workshop panel, click (New Snapshot View).

5. **View1** is added to the Snapshot Views browser. Right-click on the **View1** thumbnail image and select **Rename**. Set the new name to **Fully Assembled**.

6. Move the playhead to approximately 2.5 seconds. This should show the fasteners exploded, but not yet set to an Opacity value of 0.

7. In the Workshop panel, click (New Snapshot View).

8. **View2** is added to the Snapshot Views browser. The marker displays on the Snapshot view's thumbnail image, indicating that it is associated with the storyboard animation. Snapshot views created at 0 seconds are not associative to the storyboard.

9. Select the view label for the **View2** thumbnail image. Set the new name to **Step1**. This is an alternative to using the **Rename** command.

Snapshot views can also be created by right-clicking on the playhead in the timeline.

10. Using the steps previously described, create the following snapshots. The Snapshots Views browser should display similar to that shown Figure 20–41.

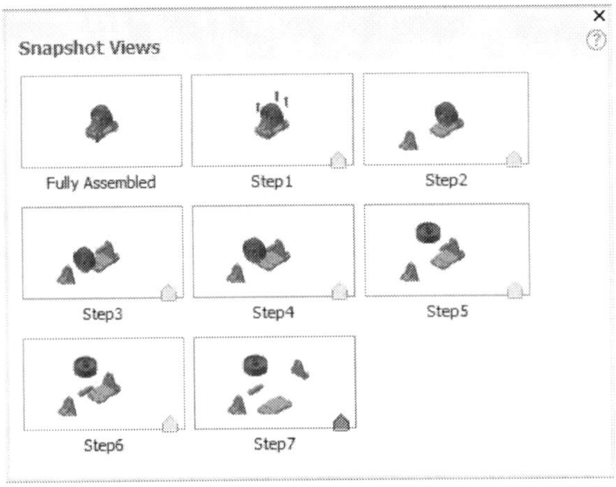

Figure 20–41

Time (seconds)	Snapshot View Name
6	Step2
9	Step3
10	Step4
12	Step5
15	Step6
16	Step7

11. Refer to the Snapshot Views browser and the Storyboard timeline and note the following:

    - The marker that displays on the last view (**Step7**) is blue and the outline of the view is also blue, indicating that the view is active.
    - The markers displays along the timeline, showing the locations where the snapshots were taken.

Task 2 - Modify a dependent snapshot view.

Between 15s and 16s, both the second **Bracket** and the **Plate** are moved apart. For static images, only the **Bracket** needs to be moved. The animation is to stay as it is; however, you will edit the Step 7 view to make the change.

1. Right-click on the **Step7** thumbnail image and select **Edit**. The *Edit View* tab is activated, as shown in Figure 20–42

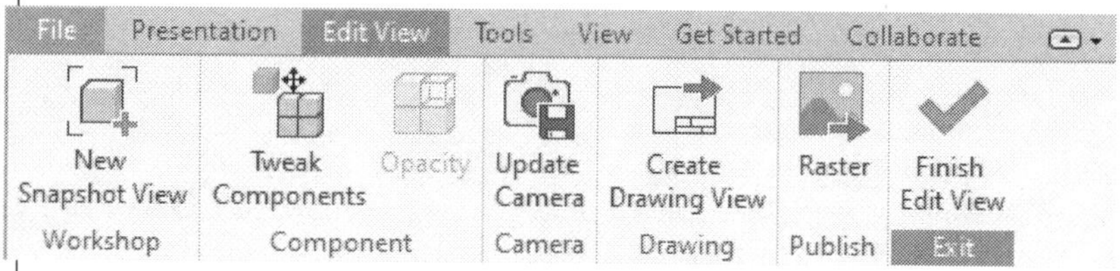

Figure 20–42

2. Select the **Plate** component in the graphics window. Right-click and select **Delete Tweak>Last**.
3. When prompted that you cannot make changes to a view that is linked to the timeline, click **Break Link** to permanently break the link. The **Plate** component returns to its original position. No other changes are required in this view.
4. In the Exit panel, click (Finish Edit View).
5. Note that the **Step7** view no longer has the marker. This indicates that it is now an independent view.

Task 3 - Modify actions on the timeline.

1. In the timeline, expand the four **M10 x 35** components.

2. Right-click on the symbol for the first component, right-click and select **Delete**, as shown in Figure 20–43. The first fastener is returned to the model display.

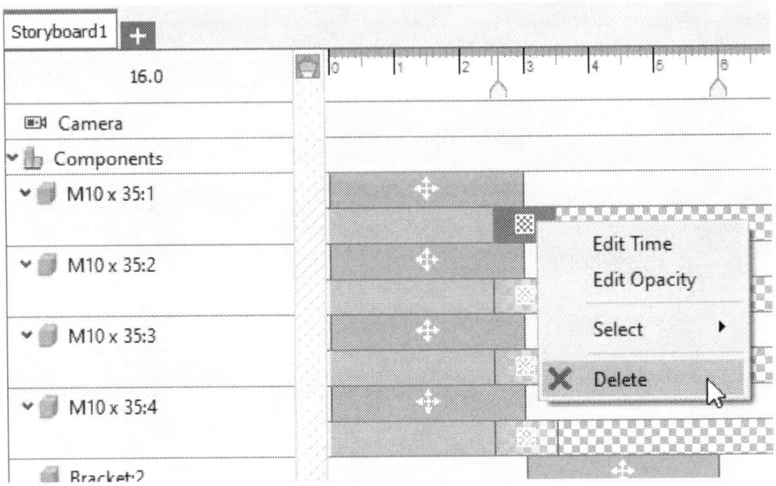

Figure 20–43

3. Delete the three other Opacity actions for the other fasteners. To delete the three fasteners at once, press and hold <Ctrl> to select them prior to selecting **Delete**. Five of the Snapshot views that are dependent on the timeline now show the symbol on their thumbnail image, as shown in Figure 20–44.

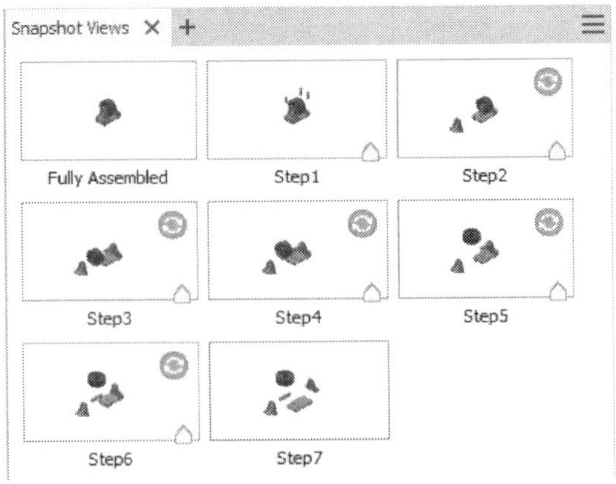

Figure 20–44

4. Select the symbol on each thumbnail image to update them to reflect the change in the animation.

Task 4 - Modify the orientation of a model in a Snapshot view.

1. Double-click on the **Step6** thumbnail image in the Snapshot Views browser to edit it.
2. Using the ViewCube, rotate the model into an alternate position so that you can see all of the fasteners. In the Camera panel, click (Update Camera). Note that the view changes in the thumbnail image and you were not prompted that the change would require you to break the link to the animation. Camera position changes do not affect the associativity with the animation.
3. In the Exit panel, click (Finish Edit View).

Task 5 - Create an independent view.

In this task, you will create a new Snapshot view that is independent of the timeline. You will then explode the assembly to create an alternate explode view that can be used in a drawing.

1. In the timeline, move the playhead to the beginning of the animation (0 seconds).
2. Create a new Snapshot view and rename it to **Exploded View**.
3. Edit the new Exploded View.

For more detail on tweaking components, refer to Practice 20a.

4. Rotate the model and use the (Tweak Components) command to explode the components similar to that shown in Figure 20–45.
   - When creating the exploded view, create it with visible trail lines.

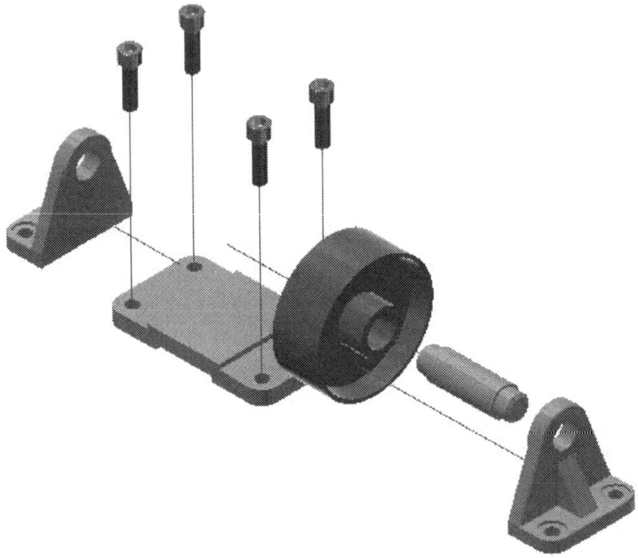

Figure 20–45

5. In the Camera panel, click (Update Camera).
6. Finish the edit to return to the *Presentation* tab.
7. Save the presentation file and close the window.

Hint: Creating a drawing view from a Snapshot view.

A Snapshot view can be created directly from a presentation file using the **Create Drawing View** option. Drawing views are discussed further in a later chapter.

Chapter Review Questions

1. Which of the following file formats is used to create an exploded assembly model in a Drawing view?
   a. .IAM
   b. .IPT
   c. .IPN
   d. .DWG
2. What is the purpose of a Presentation file? (Select all that apply.)
   a. To simplify the display of an assembly.
   b. To create an Exploded View of an assembly.
   c. To update an assembly more quickly.
   d. To create an animation of an assembly.
   e. To help document and visualize the assembly.
3. Which of the following statements are true regarding a Presentation file? (Select all that apply.)
   a. Once the Presentation template is selected for use, you are immediately prompted to open the model that will be used in **Scene1** of the presentation.
   b. A Snapshot view that is oriented in the model's Home view is automatically added to a new Presentation file.
   c. Multiple storyboards can be created in a presentation file to document an assembly.
   d. Storyboard animations can be used in a drawing view.
4. It is not possible to edit a Snapshot view that was created dependent on a specific time in an animation.
   a. True
   b. False
5. Which command enables you to save a specific view orientation at a set time in an animation?
   a. **New Storyboard**
   b. **New Snapshot View**
   c. **Tweak Components**
   d. **Capture Camera**

6. What is the purpose of adding a trail?
    a. To define a path for an animation.
    b. To move the position of a component.
    c. To change the color of a component.
    d. To help define the relationships between the components in terms of how they are assembled.
7. To create an animated assembly of a model's assembly process, you must create an animation that uses the _____ command.
    a. **New Storyboard**
    b. **Tweak Components**
    c. **Opacity**
    d. **Capture Camera**
8. Which of the following are valid methods to change the duration of an action in a storyboard animation? (Select all that apply.)
    a. Enter a *Duration* value in the mini-toolbar during Tweak creation.
    b. Use the **Edit Tweak** command and enter a new *Duration* value.
    c. Use the **Edit Time** command and enter a new *Duration* value.
    d. Drag the action's duration directly in the timeline.
9. **Move** and **Rotate** tweaks can be assigned to the same component at one time.
    a. True
    b. False
10. Which type of view setting can only be instantaneous when assigned to an animation?
    a. Opacity
    b. Visibility

Command Summary

Button	Command	Location
	**Capture Camera**	• **Ribbon:** *Presentation* tab>Camera panel • **Ribbon:** *Edit View* tab>Camera panel • **Context Menu**
	**Create Drawing View**	• **Ribbon:** *Presentation* tab>Drawing panel • **Ribbon:** *Edit View* tab>Drawing panel • **Snapshot Views browser**: right-click on a view • **Context Menu**
N/A	**Delete** (Tweak)	• **Timeline:** *right-click a tweak symbol* • **Model browser:** right-click on a Tweak • Graphics Window: right-click a component
N/A	**Edit Time**	• **Timeline:** *right-click a tweak symbol* • **Model browser:** right-click on a Tweak • Graphics Window: right-click a component
N/A	**Edit Tweak**	• **Timeline:** *right-click a tweak symbol* • **Model browser:** right-click on a Tweak
N/A	**Hide Trails /Hide Trail Segments**	• **Model browser:** right-click on a Tweak • Graphics Window: right-click a component
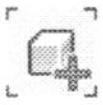	**New Snapshot View**	• **Ribbon:** *Presentation* tab>Workshop panel • **Ribbon:** *Edit View* tab>Workshop panel • **Context Menu** • Storyboard Panel (right-click on the playhead )
	**New Storyboard**	• **Ribbon:** *Presentation* tab>Workshop panel • **Context Menu** • Storyboard Panel (click )
	**Opacity**	• **Ribbon:** *Presentation* tab>Component panel with a component selected • **Ribbon:** *Edit View* tab>Component panel with a component selected • **Context Menu** with a component selected
	**Raster**	• **Ribbon:** *Presentation* tab>Publish panel • **Ribbon:** *Edit View* tab>Publish panel • **Context Menu**
	**Tweak Components**	• **Ribbon:** *Presentation* tab>Component panel • **Ribbon:** *Edit View* tab>Component panel • **Context Menu**

	**Video**	• **Ribbon:** *Presentation* tab>Publish panel • **Ribbon:** *Edit View* tab>Publish panel • **Context Menu** • **Storyboard Panel** (right-click on the tab)
N/A	**Visibility**	• **Context Menu** with a component selected • **Model browser** with a component selected

Assembly Tools

The Autodesk® Inventor® software provides a number of different tools in the assembly environment that enable you to more efficiently modify and analyze your assemblies. For example, there are tools that enable you to replace models and restructure them in the assembly, and other tools that enable you to simulate motion in an assembly. The knowledge and efficient use of these tools can help you to analyze and change a design as required.

Learning Objectives in This Chapter

- Replace single or multiple instances of components in an assembly.
- Duplicate components in an assembly using copy, mirror, and pattern tools.
- Restructure components from a lower level subassembly to a higher level in the assembly structure.
- Restructure components from a higher level in the assembly structure to a subassembly.
- Create an assembly folder to organize and simplify the display of the Model browser.
- Drive an assembly constraint to simulate a required range of motion for an assembly.
- Limit the range of motion between selected components by defining contact sets.
- Determine interference between components in an assembly.
- Resolve constraint conflicts that arise due to changes made in the assembly.

21.1 Replacing Components

The **Replace/Replace All** and **Save and Replace Component** commands enable you to replace components when design specifications for an assembly change, if you need to know whether new parts are going to fit with other assembly components, or to test alternate design scenarios.

Replace Components

You can replace a single instance of a part or all instances of a part at the same level of the assembly. To replace a part, expand (Replace) in the *Assemble* tab>expanded Component panel and select one of the following options:

*You can also right-click on the component in the Model browser or in the window and select **Component>Replace**.*

- **(Replace):** Replaces a single instance of a part. When the Place Component dialog box opens, browse to the part to replace the selected part in the assembly.
- **(Replace All):** Replaces all instances of a part at the same level of the assembly.

You can remove the constraints of the old part when the new part is placed, especially if the two parts are different shapes. Once relocated, constrain the new component as required.

Save and Replace Components

The **Save and Replace Component** command enables you to replace a selected component in an assembly with a copy of itself. The newly created copy maintains the same constraints as the original component.

How To: Replace a Component with a Saved Copy

1. Select the component to be replaced.
2. In the *Assemble* tab>Productivity panel, click (Save and Replace Component).
3. In the Create Part dialog box, give the newly copied component an appropriate name and click **Save**. The selected component is replaced with the copy.

21.2 Duplicating Components

Mirroring, copying, and patterning can all be used as an alternative to individually placing components in an assembly. Each of these commands are located on the *Assemble* tab in the Pattern panel, as shown in Figure 21–1. Each of these duplication techniques are further described below.

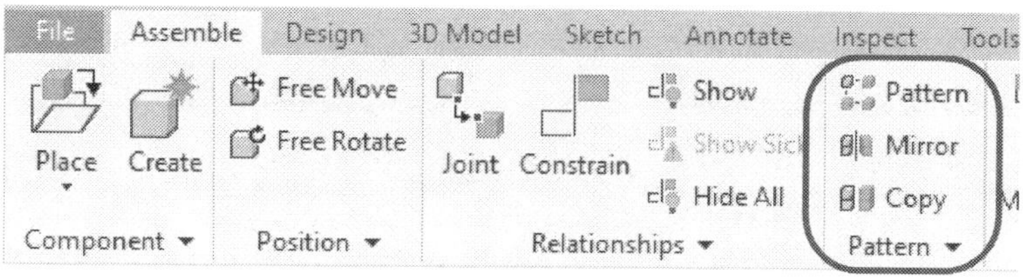

Figure 21–1

Mirror

The **Mirror** command enables you to duplicate a single or multiple components in an assembly based on a mirror plane. For example, the two assembled screws shown in Figure 21–2 were mirrored to place two additional screws in the assembly. The relationships that were established between multiple mirrored components are copied when mirrored. The mirrored instances are created as derived models. Any changes made to the source model(s) will reflect in the mirrored versions.

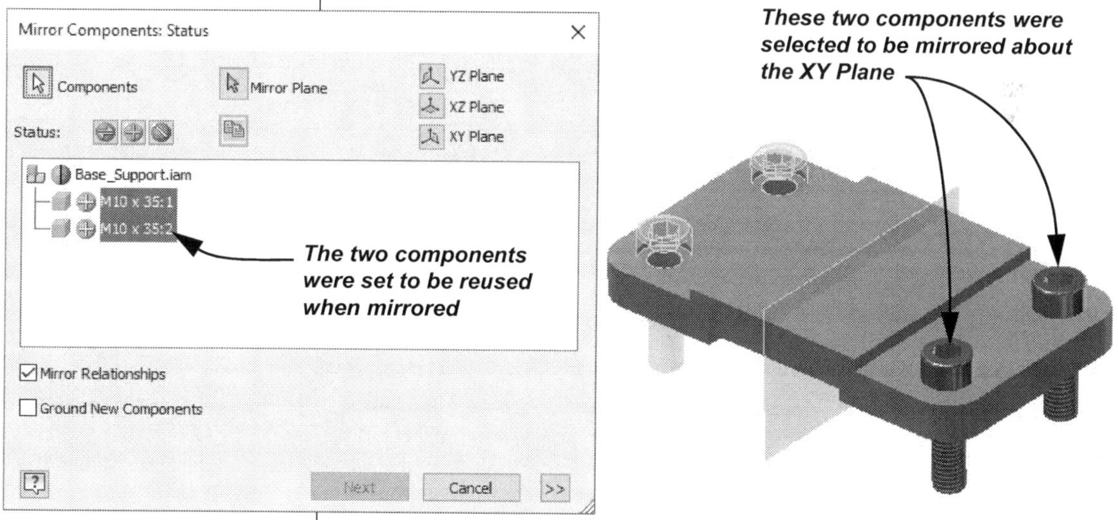

Figure 21–2

In the Mirror Components dialog box, you can select the components and manipulate their status as follows:

- **(Mirror Component):** Enables you to create a mirrored copy of the component. You will be prompted to define the new name for it.
- **(Reuse Component):** Enables you to reuse the original component for mirroring.
- **(Exclude Component):** Enables you to remove a component from the selection set.

Additional options in the Mirror dialog box enable you to:

- Select an origin plane button to use it as the mirror plane.
- Enable the **Mirror Relationships** option to maintain relationships between the components being copied, if they exist.
- Enable the **Ground New Components** option to locate the copied components in the assembly by grounding them.

Copy

The **Copy** command enables you to create a duplicate of an existing component(s) in an assembly. Similar to the **Mirror** command, you are required to select the components to be copied and set their status, using the options in the Copy Components dialog box shown in Figure 21–3.

Relationships between copied components are retained after a Copy operation.

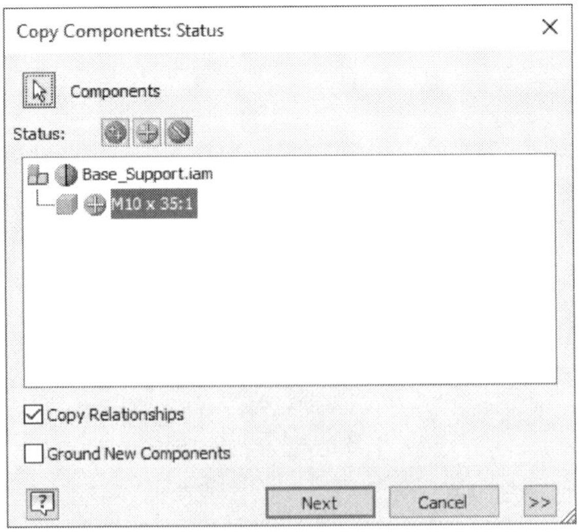

Figure 21–3

The status settings can include the following:

- **(Copy Component):** Enables you to create a duplicate version of the original component. The new instance can be opened and modified independently of the parent component.
- **(Reuse Component):** Enables you to reuse the original component for mirroring.
- **(Exclude Component):** Enables you to remove a component from the selection set.

Similar to the **Mirror** option, the **Copy Relationships** and **Ground New Components** options can be set to copy relationships between copied models or ground the copied instances.

Pattern

Components can be patterned in any one of three ways using the Pattern dialog box. Constraints used to place the original components are not copied to the patterned components. Each tab provides an alternative patterning technique.

- *(Associative)* tab: Enables you to pattern a selected component based on a feature pattern that already exists in an assembly component, as shown in Figure 21–4. Once the component being patterned is selected, you simply select the feature pattern that it should reference and the component is patterned.

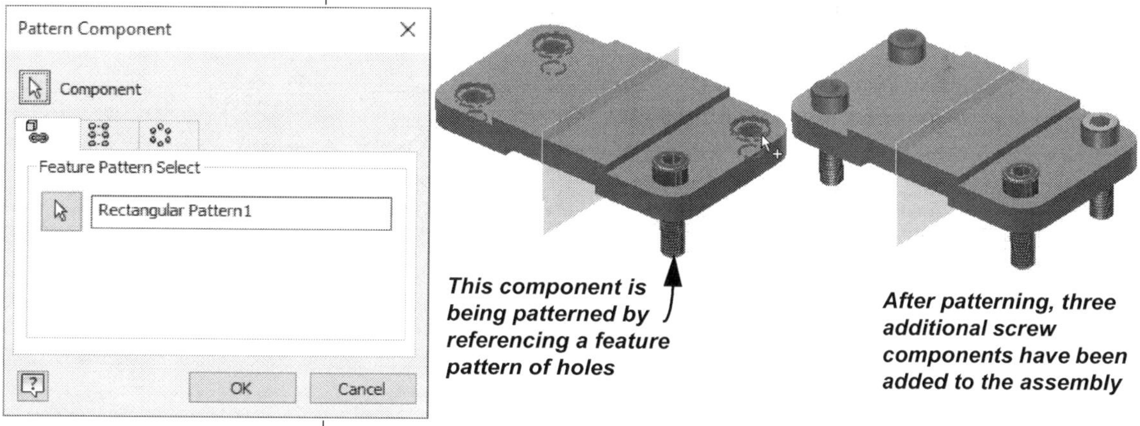

Figure 21–4

- *(Rectangular)* and *(Circular)* tabs: Enable you to pattern components similarly to rectangular and circular feature patterns. You can select direction references and enter the number of occurrences and pattern dimensions to create the pattern of components.

21.3 Restructuring Components

As you design an assembly, you might want to move parts in and out of subassemblies, or up and down in the Model browser hierarchy. You can use the Model browser to restructure assembly components, as shown in Figure 21–5, without changing the physical position of previously placed parts.

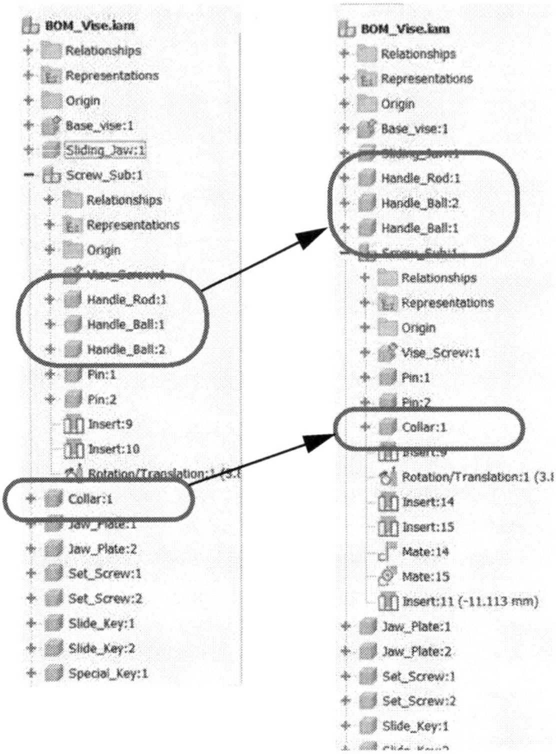

Figure 21–5

- To move an assembly component in the Model browser, drag and drop it in the Model browser.
- If a circle with a slash symbol (⃠) displays, you cannot place the component in that area.
- A component moved from a different assembly is placed at the bottom of the assembly tree by default.
- You can also restructure components using **Promote** and **Demote**.
- Component patterns cannot be restructured by dragging, but can be repositioned by promoting or demoting.

Promote

Use **Promote** to move components out of a subassembly and up one level in the Model browser. To accomplish this, select the component in the Model browser or in the graphics window, right-click, and select **Component> Promote**. The **Promote** option is not available if the selected component is a child of the top-level assembly.

Demote

If you need to restructure components into a subassembly that does not yet exist, select components in the Model browser or in the graphics window, right-click, and select **Component> Demote**. The Create In-Place Component dialog box opens as shown in Figure 21–6.

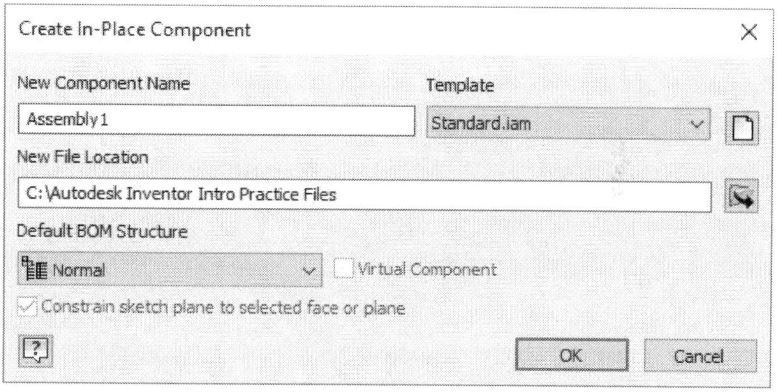

Figure 21–6

Enter a name for the subassembly in the *New Component Name* field. You can specify a new file location and template or use the defaults. Click **OK** to create the subassembly. The demoted parts are placed in the new subassembly.

The following rules apply when restructuring an assembly:

- Moving components in or out of subassemblies might impact assembly constraints. A warning dialog box opens indicating that assembly references might be lost during restructuring.
- Components are removed from existing design view representations and relocated to design view representations in the new assembly.
- The enabled, visibility, and color status of the moved component is preserved in the new assembly.

Assembly Folders

Assembly folders help organize assemblies by grouping components together and can be used to simplify the Model browser. Unlike subassemblies, folders do not create another physical component.

To create a folder, right-click on the component(s) that you want to add to the folder and select **Add to New Folder**, as shown in Figure 21–7. To rename the folder, click on the folder in the Model browser (do not double-click), then click on the folder again, and enter a new name.

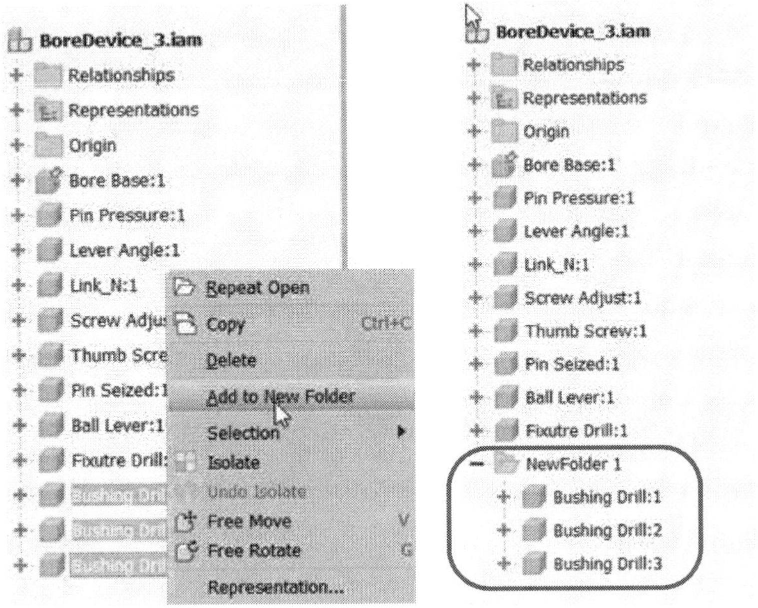

Figure 21–7

21.4 Driving Constraints

Assembly constraints are static. If parts in the assembly are intended to move, you might want to see the assembly in motion. One way to do this is to use a Drive constraint. This enables you to assign motion between constrained components by setting an offset or angle value in a constraint so that it changes incrementally.

How To: Create a Drive Constraint

1. Right-click on a constraint in the Model browser and select **Drive** to assign a Driving constraint. The Drive dialog box opens.
2. Define the parameters and options in the Drive dialog box.
   - Enter the *Start* and *End* values to drive the constraint. The values depend on the required extent for the offset or angle values that have been selected to drive the motion. You can also enter a time delay between steps by entering a value in the *Pause Delay* field.
   - Click >> to access additional options, as shown in Figure 21–8.

The constraint being driven and its current offset/angular value display at the top of the Drive dialog box.

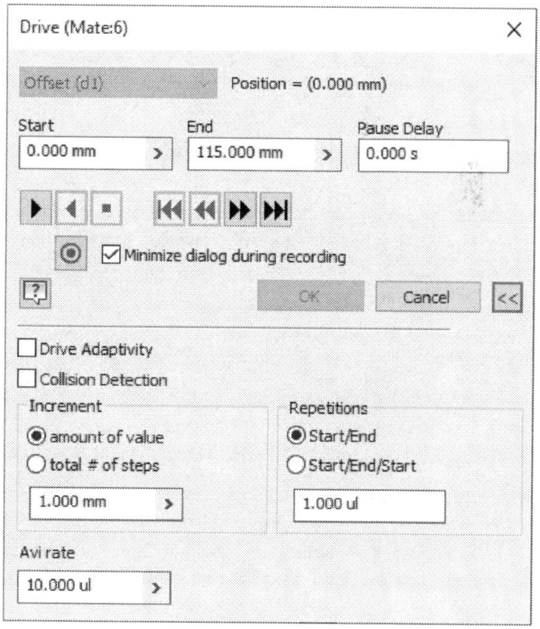

Figure 21–8

- The additional options are described as follows:

Option	Description
Drive Adaptivity	Enables you to adapt the components while maintaining the constraints.
Collision Detection	Moves the assembly until interference is detected.
Increment	Sets how to move the assembly. **Amount of value** sets the percentage of the total move to make in each step. For example, if set to 0.1, the total move is completed in ten steps. **Total # of steps** sets the number of steps to move the entire range.
Repetitions	Sets the number of times to complete the movement and how the movement proceeds. **Start/End** progresses from start to end and then begins again at start. **Start/End/Start** progresses from start to end and then returns from end to start.
Avi rate	Specifies the increment for frames in the animation file.

3. Select the standard control buttons in the Drive dialog box to play/drive the constraint.
4. Click to record the motion as an .AVI or .MWV file. To stop recording, click again.
    - Before starting, you are prompted for the filename and export properties of the recording.
    - The default export properties provide the optimal quality for both AVI and WMV formats. If changes are made to these properties, the new values apply for only the current session.

21.5 Contact Solver

The **Contact Solver** is used to limit the range of motion between components by stopping movement when they come into contact with each other, as shown in the example in Figure 21–9. This tool can be used to help analyze motion in an assembly.

In this example, there would be two degrees of transitional freedom and one degree of rotational freedom left when the puck is constrained.

You can use the Contact Solver to limit the motion of the puck so that it can move along the tray, but stops when it comes in contact with its edges

Figure 21–9

How To: Create a Contact Set

1. Constrain the assembly, as required. Leave the motion that is to be tested unconstrained.
2. In the Model browser, select the components to be analyzed, right-click and select **Contact Set**. The Model browser displays the **Contact Set** symbol next to the selected components, as shown in Figure 21–10.

These symbols indicate that the components are part of the Contact Set

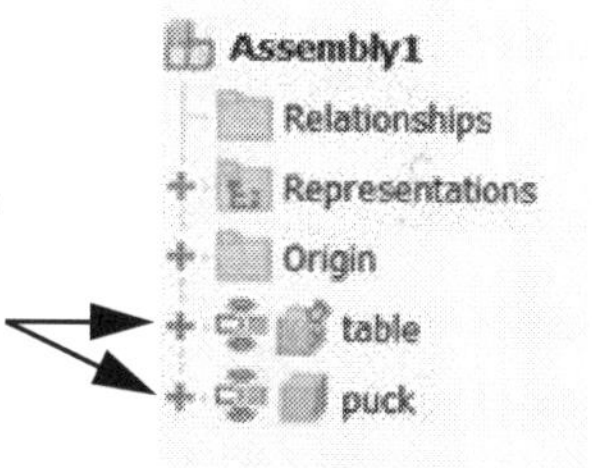

Figure 21–10

3. In the *Inspect* tab>Interference panel, click (Activate Contact Solver).
4. Move the components as required. The motion stops once a component comes in contact with one of the other components in the contact set.
5. To toggle off the Contact Solver, click (Activate Contact Solver) again.

You can control how the Contact Solver behaves in the *Interactive Contact* area in the Document Settings dialog box (*Tools* tab>Options panel, click (Document Settings), and select the *Modeling* tab). When (Activate Contact Solver) is active, contact is only detected between the components specified in the Contact Set (**Contact Set only**). When **All Components** is selected, you do not need to specify a Contact Set. Any contact between any components in the assembly stops the motion.

21.6 Interference

In an assembly, components can be assembled so that two parts occupy the same space at the same time. To identify if components overlap, you should analyze the model. For example, you can check for interference between the parts shown in Figure 21–11.

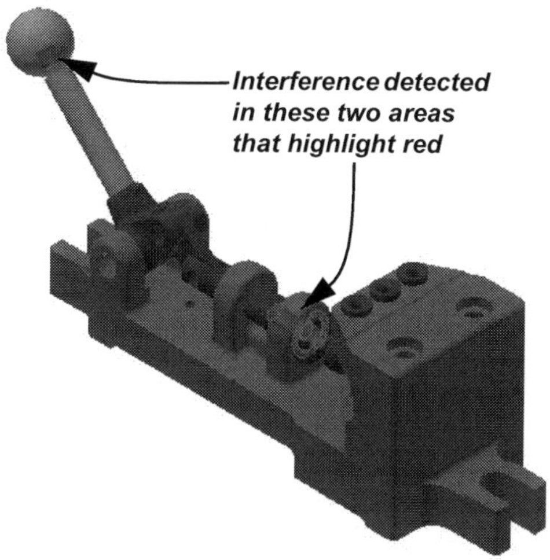

Figure 21–11

How To: Check for Interference

1. In the *Inspect* tab>Interference panel, click (Analyze Interference). The Interference Analysis dialog box opens, as shown in Figure 21–12.

Interference analysis can take a long time in large assemblies. As the analysis is proceeding, the percentage completed displays in a dialog box.

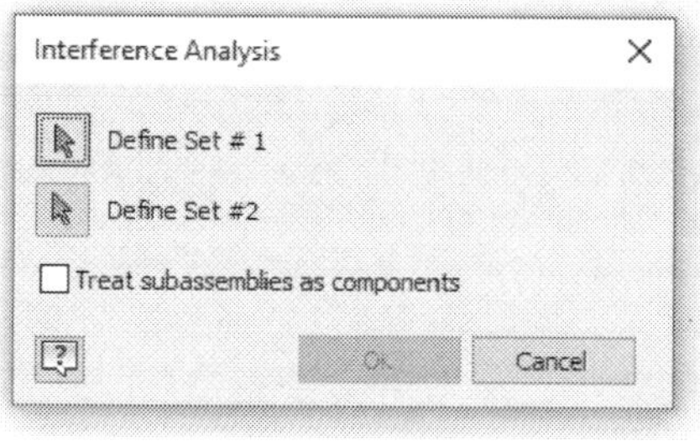

Figure 21–12

2. Click (Define Set # 1) and select the first set of components to include.
3. Click (Define Set # 2) and select the second set.

4. (Optional) Enable the **Treat subassemblies as components** option, if required, to analyze interference between all of the components in a subassembly. Clear this option to treat the subassembly as one component, ignoring any interferences between its components.
5. Click **OK**.

Alternatively, you can drag a selection box around multiple components when defining the first set and click **OK** to analyze multiple components at once.

If no interference is detected between the selected sets, a dialog box opens to notify you that no interference was found. If there is interference, the Interference Detected dialog box opens similar to that shown in Figure 21–13.

- The dialog box describes the number of interferences and the total interfering volume. The interference volume is also highlighted in the assembly window.
- Click **>>** to display the details of each interference, as shown in Figure 21–13.
    - Double-click or click (magnifier icon) in the first column of any of the interference listings to zoom to them in the model. Click **Reset** to return to a zoomed out view.
    - Use the options in the *Interference Type* area to filter which interferences are listed in the dialog box.

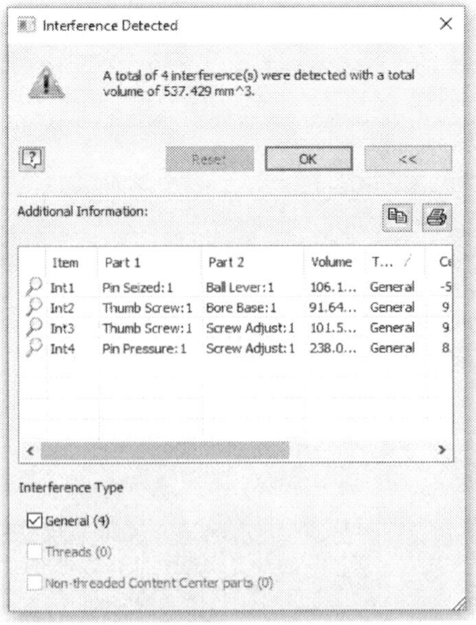

Figure 21–13

- Right-click on an interference and use the Ignore options (shown in Figure 21–14) to ignore specific interferences or interferences that are less than the volume that was calculated.

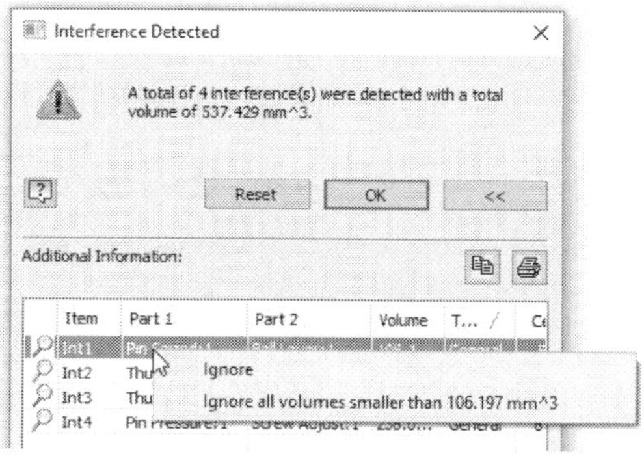

Figure 21–14

Modify the components or constraints to resolve the interference between parts in an assembly and rerun the analysis to verify it has been corrected.

21.7 Error Recovery

When working in an assembly, existing constraints can fail due to conflicts with other constraints or when changes are made to the model. When a constraint fails, a dialog box similar to that shown in Figure 21–15 opens indicating there is a problem. Expand the messages to read the information.

Assembly components are not affected when constraints conflict. Only their defined position in the model fails.

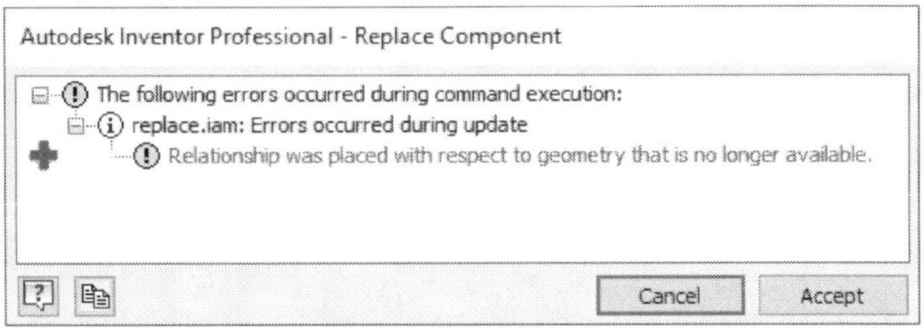

Figure 21–15

- To fix the error, click + to start recovering. The Design Doctor dialog box opens, as shown in Figure 21–16. Step through the recovery process by clicking **Next**. The components involved are highlighted in the graphics window. You do not have to immediately fix constraint errors. Click **Accept** in the Place/Edit Constraint dialog box to accept the error and proceed with your design.

The recovery process is similar to the process used to correct sketch and feature errors.

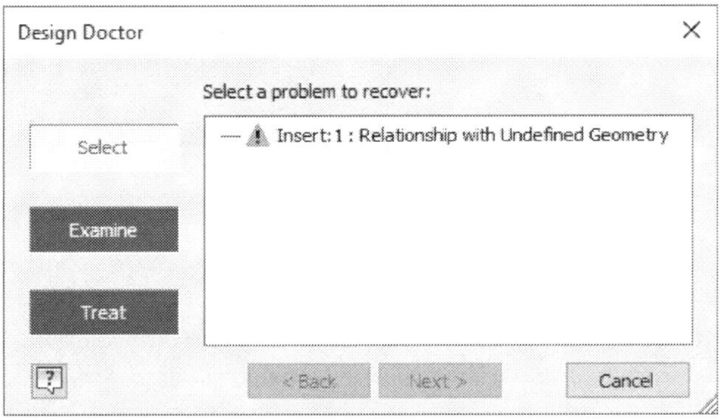

Figure 21–16

- Failed constraints are marked with ⚠ in the Model browser.
- To resolve constraint conflicts that were skipped when initially identified, right-click on the failed constraint (⚠) in the Model browser and select **Recover** to launch the Design Doctor and step you through the recovery process.

Practice 21a Using Assembly Tools

Practice Objectives

- Replace an existing component in an assembly.
- Determine interference between components in an assembly.
- Resolve interference issues between components.
- Demote a component from a top-level assembly into a newly created subassembly.
- Promote a component from a subassembly to the top-level of the assembly structure.

In this practice, you will use the assembly tools to check for interference between two assembly components. You will make changes to the assembly components, and restructure the assembly components in the Model browser. The completed assembly is shown in Figure 21–17.

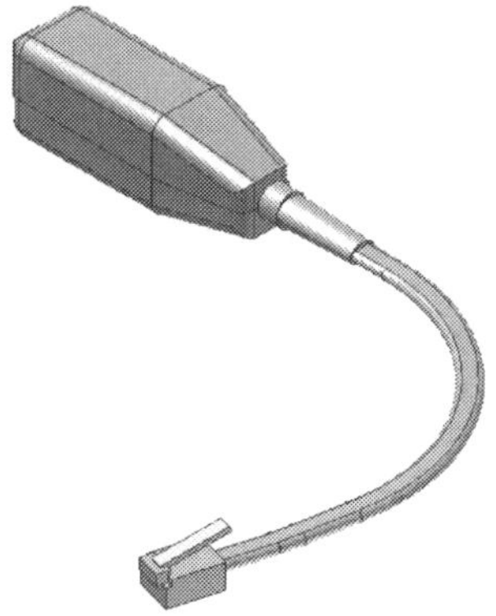

Figure 21–17

Task 1 - Open an assembly file.

1. Open **socket_final.iam**.
2. Expand the **Representations>View** nodes in the Model browser. Double-click on **Interference_view** to set it as the active Design View.

Task 2 - Replace a component.

1. Toggle off the display of the **encbase**, **wire final**, and **enctop** components. The assembly displays as shown in Figure 21–18.

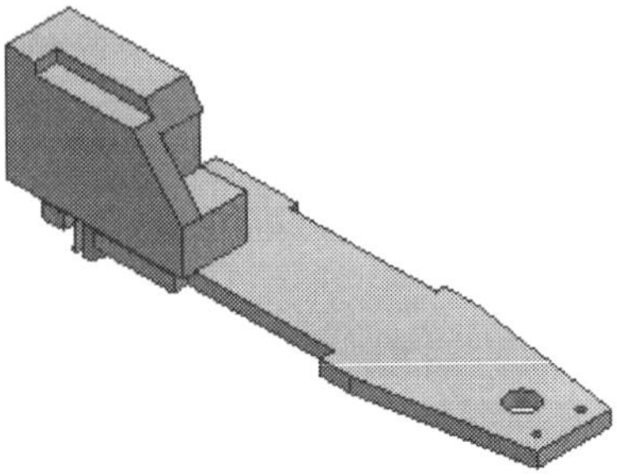

Figure 21–18

2. Right-click on **connect:1** in the Model browser and select **Component>Replace**.

When replacing components, the Possible Constraint Loss dialog box might open. This indicates that the existing constraints are unable to be applied and they must be re-established.

3. Select and open the **connect_mirror** part in the Open dialog box. In this situation, the constraint references are recognized in the new model, as shown in Figure 21–19.

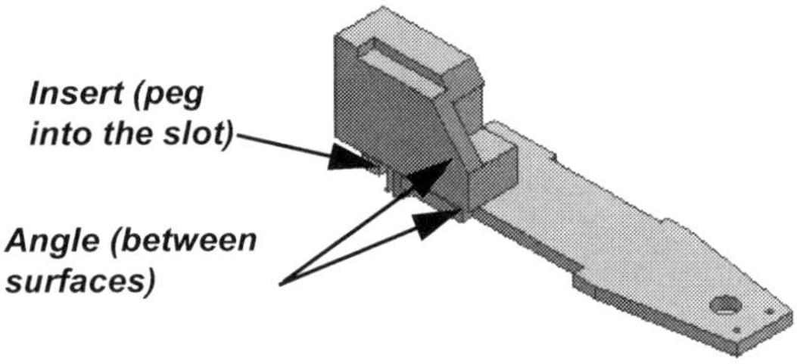

Figure 21–19

Task 3 - Conduct an interference analysis.

1. Toggle on the display of the **encbase** part and toggle off the display of the **connect_mirror** part.

2. Select the *Inspect* tab>Interference panel, click  (Analyze Interference). The Interference Analysis dialog box opens.

Interference analysis can take a long time in large assemblies. As the analysis is processing, the percentage completed displays in a dialog box.

3. With  (Define Set # 1) selected, select the **pcb** part.

4. Click  (Define Set # 2) and select the **encbase** part.

5. Click **OK**. The Interference Detected dialog box opens, as shown in Figure 21–20, describing the number of interferences and the total volume. The interference volume is highlighted in the assembly window, as shown in Figure 21–20.

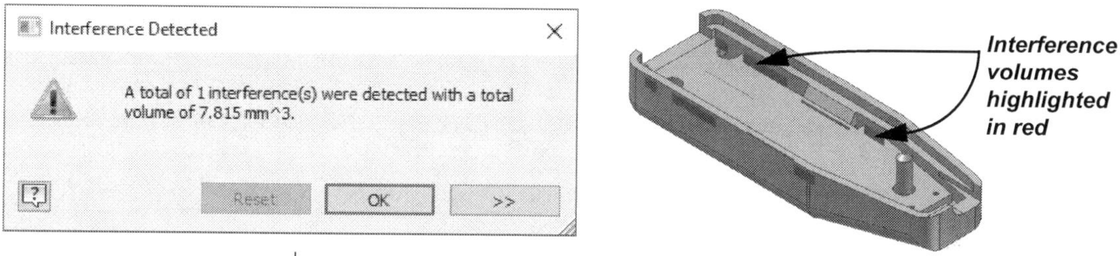

Figure 21–20

6. Click **OK** to close the Interference Detected dialog box.

Task 4 - Modify the pcb part.

1. Double-click on **pcb:1**. All assembly components are grayed out except **pcb:1**. This means **pcb:1** is the only active component in the assembly that can be modified.

2. Right-click on **Extrusion1** in the Model browser and select **Show Dimensions**. The model displays as shown in Figure 21–21.

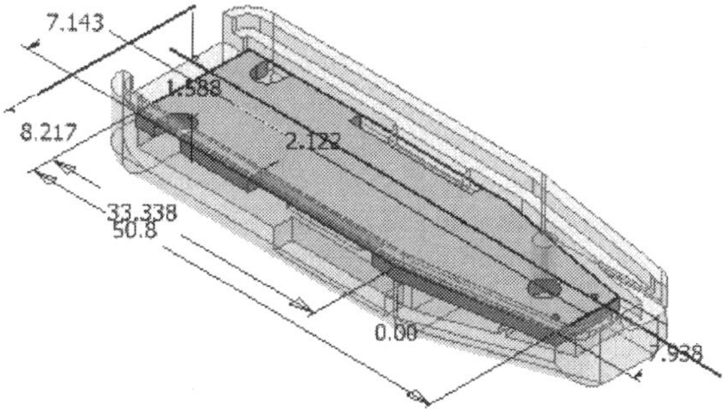

Figure 21–21

3. Modify the **7.143** dimension to **6.80**.

4. In the Quick Access Toolbar, click (Local Update) to update the **pcb** part.

5. Double-click on **socket_final.iam** in the Model browser to activate the assembly.

6. Run an interference check on the two assembly components. The interference has been reduced.

The components were originally built in imperial and the units were changed. When modifying the original imperial unit will display. Ensure that you enter the units of measure when entering the metric value.

7. Modify the **pcb** part to the following to completely remove the interference:
   - Modify the dimension of **Work Plane5** to **-6.8 mm**.
   - Modify the **50.8** dimension of **Extrusion1** to **50 mm**.

8. Update the model.

9. Activate the top-level assembly.

10. Run an interference check again on the **pcb** and **encbase** parts. No interferences were detected.

Task 5 - Restructure the assembly components.

In this task, you will create a subassembly and place the **connect_mirror** component in it.

1. Display all of the assembly components.

2. Right-click on **connect_mirror** in the Model browser and select **Component>Demote**. The Create In-Place Component dialog box opens as shown in Figure 21–22.

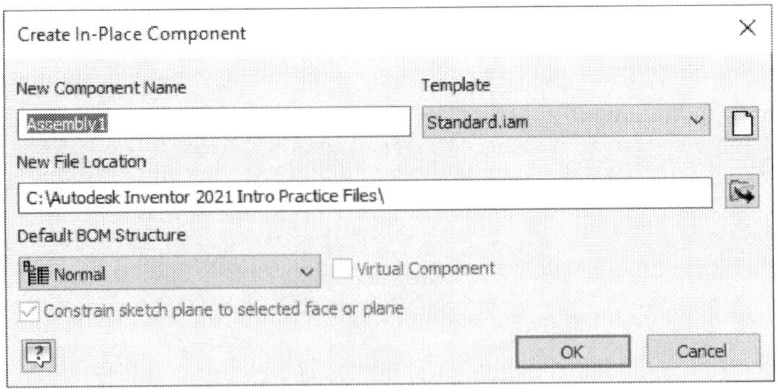

Figure 21–22

3. Enter **Mirror_Parts** in the *New Component Name* field.

4. Click **OK**. The subassembly **Mirror_Parts** displays in the Model browser with the demoted part in the subassembly list, as shown in Figure 21–23.

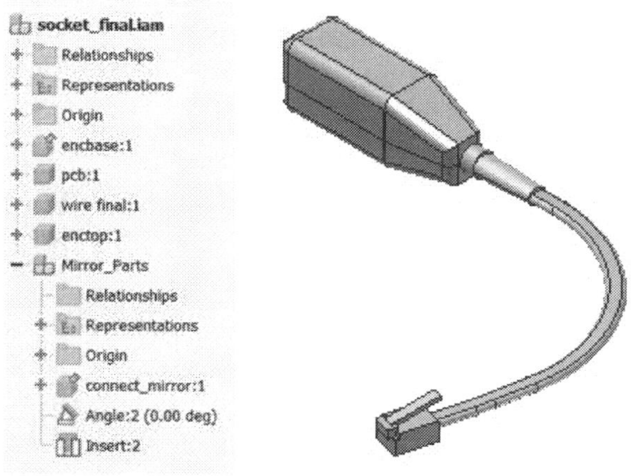

Figure 21–23

5. Save the assembly and subassembly.

Task 6 - Promote the assembly components.

Moving components in or out of subassemblies might impact patterns and assembly constraints. This means you might need to redefine assembly references that are lost due to restructuring.

In this task, you will move the component out of the **Mirror_Parts** subassembly and back into the **top-level** assembly.

1. Ensure that all of the assembly components are displayed.
2. Right-click on the **connect_mirror** component in the Model browser and select **Component>Promote**. A message dialog box opens warning you of the consequences of promoting the assembly components, as shown in Figure 21–24.

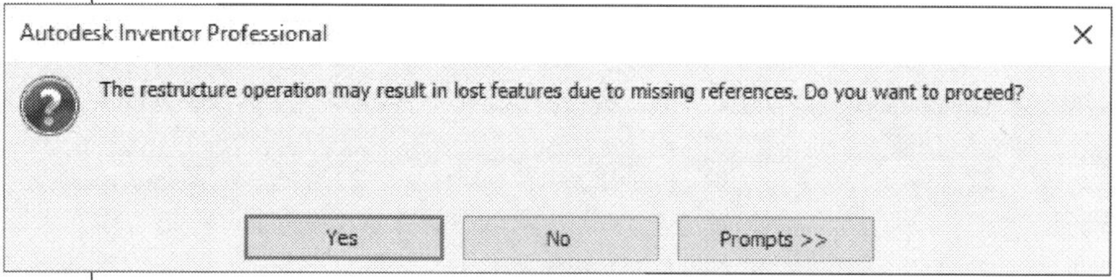

Figure 21–24

3. Click **Yes** to close the message dialog box. Note that once promoted, the subassembly still remains in the assembly.
4. Save and close the assembly.

Practice 21b Replacing Components

Practice Objectives

- Replace existing components in an assembly with alternate models.
- Redefine constraint references for those that are lost when components are replaced.

In this practice, you will replace similar components in an assembly, as shown in Figure 21–25.

Figure 21–25

Task 1 - Replace a single component instance.

1. Open **replace.iam**. There are four instances of a component named **round** in the assembly. They are constrained in the assembly using Insert constraints to the cylindrical pegs.

2. Expand the Component panel, click  (Replace), and select one of the components named **round** as the component to replace. Alternatively, you can right-click on the component in the Model browser or graphics window and select **Component>Replace**.

3. Right-click and select **Continue**.

4. Select **spacer.ipt** as the replacement component. Only the selected component is replaced, similar to that shown in Figure 21–26.

Figure 21–26

Task 2 - Replace multiple component instances.

1. In the expanded Component panel, click (Replace All), and select one of the remaining **round** components as the component to replace. Alternatively, you can right-click on one of the remaining components in the Model browser or graphics window and select **Component>Replace All**.
2. Right-click and select **Continue**.
3. Select **spacer.ipt** as the replacement component. This time, the remaining three components are all replaced at the same time, as shown in Figure 21–27.

Figure 21–27

4. Expand one of the **spacer** components in the Model browser and note that it has retained the Insert constraint that was used to originally place the **round** component.

Task 3 - Replace with a dissimilar component.

1. In the Component panel, click (Replace) and select one of the **spacer** components to replace. Alternatively, right-click the **spacer** in the Model browser or graphics window and select **Component>Replace**.

2. Right-click and select **Continue**.

3. Select **square.ipt** as the replacement component. Note that you are prompted about possible constraint loss, as shown in Figure 21–28.

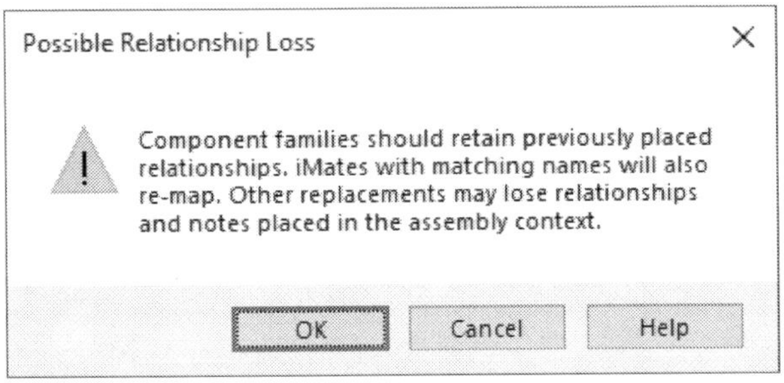

Figure 21–28

4. Click **OK** to continue. The **square** component can be placed, but it is not constrained or correctly located because its origin and shape are different from the part that was being replaced. The dialog box shown in Figure 21–29 opens, stating that an error occurred during command execution. Expand the error and note that a constraint reference (relationship) no longer exists because the geometry is no longer available.

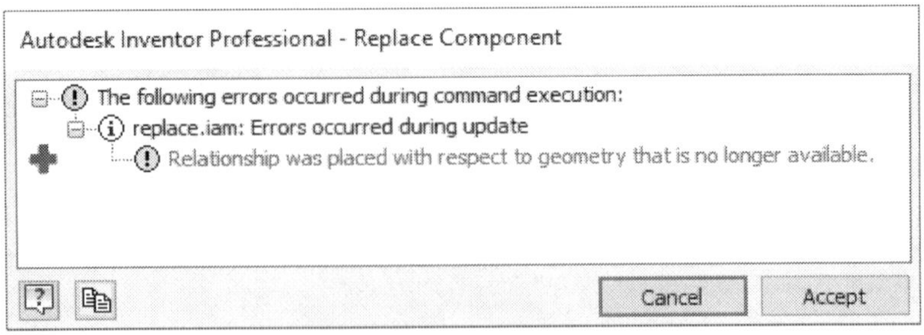

Figure 21–29

5. Click **Accept**. The Model browser displays as shown in Figure 21–30. The selected **round** component is replaced with the **square** component, and the Insert constraint is missing its references.

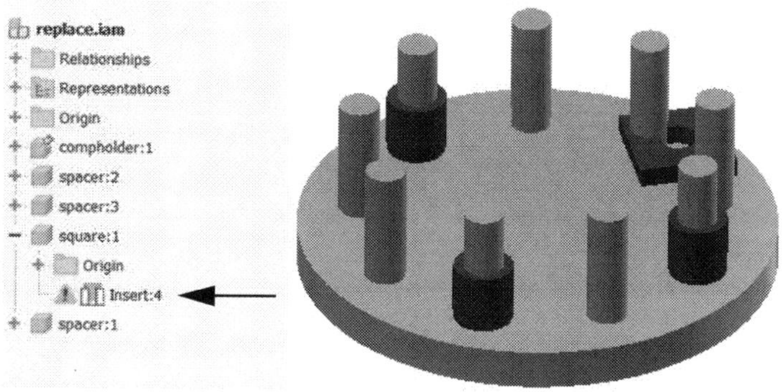

Figure 21–30

6. Select the failed **Insert** constraint in the **square** component in the Model browser, right-click, and select **Recover**. The Design Doctor dialog box opens as shown in Figure 21–31.

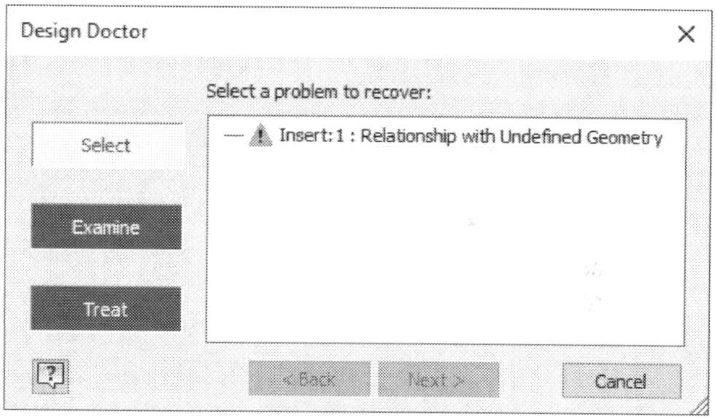

Figure 21–31

7. Select the error in the Design Doctor dialog box.

8. Click **Next** to toggle through the areas in the Design Doctor dialog box.

9. Select **Edit** in the Select a treatment window and click **Finish**. The Edit Constraint dialog box opens.

10. The reference on the **square** component has been lost. Reapply the lost reference for the Insert constraint.

11. Click **OK** to close the Edit Constraint dialog box.

12. Save and close the file.

Practice 21c Restructuring the Assembly

Practice Objective

- Restructure components of an assembly by demoting them into a newly created subassembly.

In this practice, you will use the restructuring functionality to restructure components in an assembly. The assembly is shown in Figure 21–32.

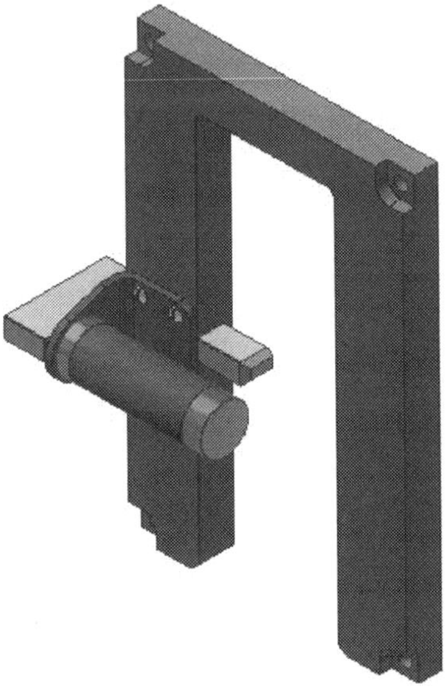

Figure 21–32

Task 1 - Open and review an assembly in the Model browser.

1. Open **indexassy.iam**.
2. In the Model browser, double-click on **cylinder.iam** to make the subassembly active. Note that there are four parts in that subassembly.
3. Double-click on **indexassy.iam** to make the top-level assembly active again.

Task 2 - Create a new component in the assembly.

1. In the Component panel, click (Create). In the *Template* area, select **Standard.iam**. In the *New Component Name* area, enter **Finger**. The dialog box should display as shown in Figure 21–33.

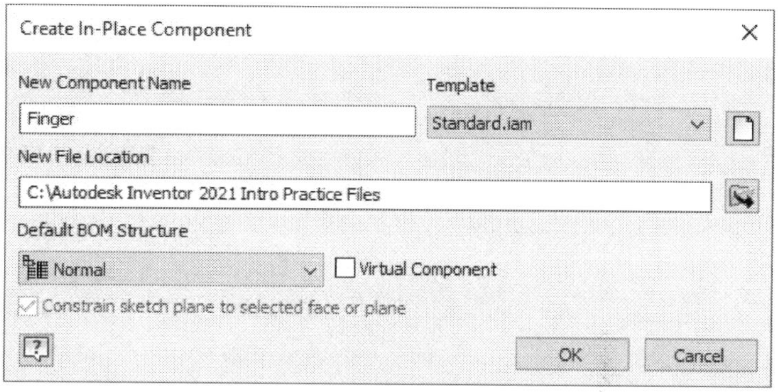

Figure 21–33

2. Click **OK**.

3. Select a point in space to create the sketch plane. A new subassembly is created. It is listed at the bottom of the Model browser and is active. Double-click on **indexassy.iam** to make the top-level assembly active again.

Task 3 - Restructure components into the Finger subassembly.

1. Expand the **cylinder** subassembly component in the Model browser. Using the drag and drop technique, restructure **cyl body** under the **finger** assembly. Click **Yes** in the warning dialog box.

2. Make the **cylinder** subassembly active, and note that the body of the cylinder (**cyl body**) is grayed out because it is not part of the active subassembly.

3. Double-click on **indexassy.iam** to make the top-level assembly active again.

4. Restructure the subassembly **cylinder** and the part **index finger** under the **Finger** subassembly.

5. Make **Finger** subassembly active, and note which parts are grayed. Double-click on **indexassy.iam** to make the top-level assembly active again.

6. Restructure **cyl body** under **cylinder** again.

7. Restructure **cyl mount** under **Finger**. The Model browser displays similar to that shown in Figure 21–34, depending on the order in which the files were dropped during restructuring.

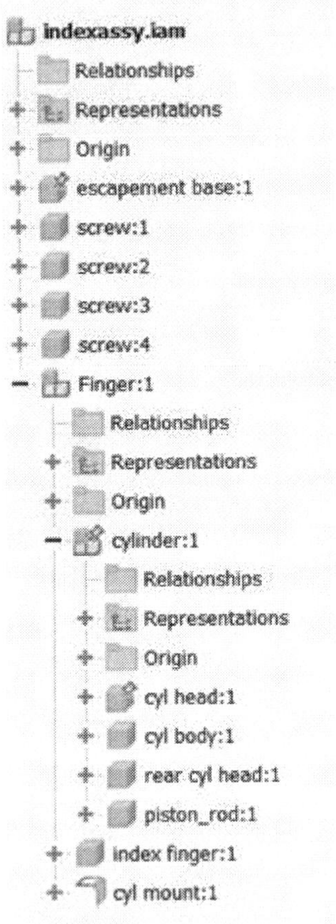

Figure 21–34

8. Save and close the file.

Practice 21d Controlling Assembly Motion

Practice Objective

- Simulate the range of motion for an assembly using the Drive and Contact Solver commands.

In this practice, you will use the **Drive** and **Contact Solver** commands to control the range of motion for an assembly. Each of these commands will be used independently as well as together.

Task 1 - Open an assembly and assign a Drive constraint to an existing constraint.

1. Open **Vise_final.iam**.

The design intent of the model requires that the **MovingJaw** can move between two parallel faces. To limit the motion of the **MovingJaw** component you will add a Drive constraint to the existing Mate constraint.

2. Expand the **MovingJaw** component in the Model browser, right-click on the **Mate:6(40.00mm)** constraint and select **Drive**, as shown in Figure 21–35.

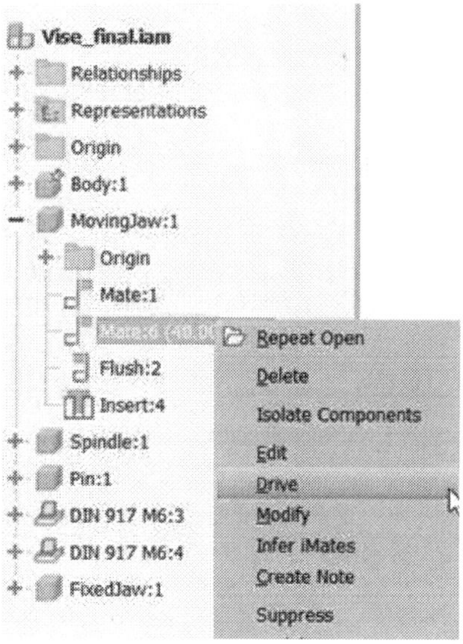

Figure 21–35

3. Enter **0.000 mm** in the *Start* field and **115 mm** in the *End* field.

4. Click [>>] in the Drive dialog box.
5. Enable **Collision Detection**, as shown in Figure 21–36.

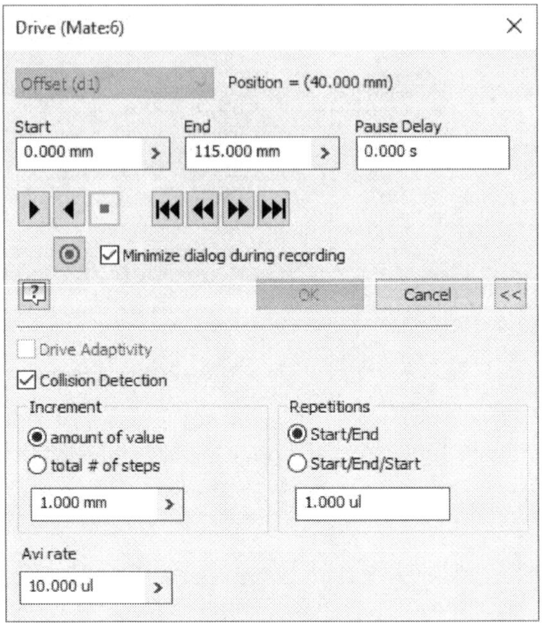

Figure 21–36

*Disabling **Collision Detection** enables the animation to play, regardless of collision. Doing so might help you identify where the collision occurs.*

6. Click [▶]. A dialog box opens indicating that a collision has been detected. Click **OK** and close the Drive dialog box.

   The **Drive** command cannot be used if interferences exist in the model.

7. Select the *Inspect* tab. In the Interference panel, click (Analyze Interference).
8. Click (Define Set # 1) and select the **Pin** component to include.
9. Click (Define Set # 2) and select two **DIN 917** components.
10. Click **OK** to run the interference analysis.

Interference analysis can take a long time in large assemblies. As the analysis is proceeding, the percentage completed displays in a dialog box.

11. There are two interferences found in the model (104.202mm).

12. To identify the interference, click [>>] to expand the dialog box. Select the **Threads** and **Matching Threads** options in the *Interference Type* area. The interference is highlighted in red, as shown in Figure 21–37.

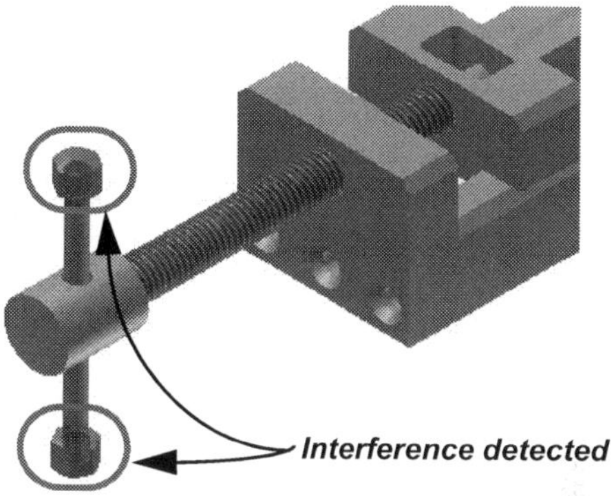

Figure 21–37

13. Click **OK** to close the Interference Detected dialog box.

The interference displays between threaded components because of the way threads were generated. In this situation, the interference can be ignored. To proceed with the **Drive** command you must suppress the components causing the interference.

*Ignoring interferences in the Interference Analysis dialog box does not ignore interferences experienced when the **Drive** option is used. Components must be suppressed to ignore them.*

14. Select the two **DIN 917** components in the Model browser, right-click and select **Suppress**. This temporarily suppresses the components to work with the **Drive** command.

15. Right-click on the **Mate:6(40.00mm)** constraint again and select **Drive**. Ensure that the *Start* and *End* values are still set and that **Collision Detection** is still enabled.

16. Click [▶] in the Drive dialog box to view the motion. Another collision is detected. Click **OK**.

Note that the **Body** and **Spindle** components are highlighted, indicating that they are the components that are in conflict. The **Spindle** is not long enough to permit the full range of motion.

17. Click [◀] to reverse the motion.

18. Disable the **Collision Detection** option in the Drive dialog box.

19. Click ▶ in the Drive dialog box to continue the motion. Visually you can see that there is also going to be a collision between **MovingJaw** and **FixedJaw**.

20. Click ◀ to reverse the motion.

The Start and End values that were provided did not take into account the thickness of the **MovingJaw** component. This is required because the offset surface that was used to create the constraint is not the face that will initially come in contact with the **Body** component. The actual end value should only be 95 mm.

21. Enter **95 mm** as the new *End* field and enable **Collision Detection**.

22. Click ▶ in the Drive dialog box to view the motion again. As expected the collision is identified between the **Body** and **Spindle** components. Click **OK**.

The appropriate next step in your design would be to modify the length of the **Spindle** component and retest for collision. You are going to leave the size of the **Spindle** model as it is for the next Task so that you can learn an alternate option for testing range of motion.

23. Click **OK** to close the Drive dialog box.

Task 2 - Use the Contact Solver.

In this task, you will use the Contact Solver as an alternate tool for simulating the required range of motion.

1. In the Model browser, double-click on **Mate:6** and enter **40 mm** to ensure that initially there is no collision in the model before getting started.

2. In the Model browser, right-click on the **Mate:6(40.00mm)** constraint and select **Suppress**. The Contact Solver cannot be used with constraints that prevent the required degree of freedom.

3. Select the *Inspect* tab, if not already active. In the Interference panel, click (Activate Contact Solver) if not already active.

If any interference exists between components in the Contact Set, you will not be able to drag the components.

4. Right-click on **Spindle** in the Model browser and select **Contact Set**. Return to the model and drag the spindle. No other components have been included in the contact set so you are able to drag through other components.

5. Right-click on **Body** in the Model browser and select **Contact Set**. Return to the model and drag the spindle. Note that this time as soon as the **Spindle** comes in contact with the **Body**, movement stops because a collision is detected. This was also the collision that was found using the **Drive** command.

6. Modify the length of the **Spindle**. Double-click on the **Splindle:1** component in the Model browser to activate it. Edit the sketch associated with the **Revolution1** feature. Change the overall length of the sketch from *140 mm* to **160 mm**, as shown in Figure 21–38.

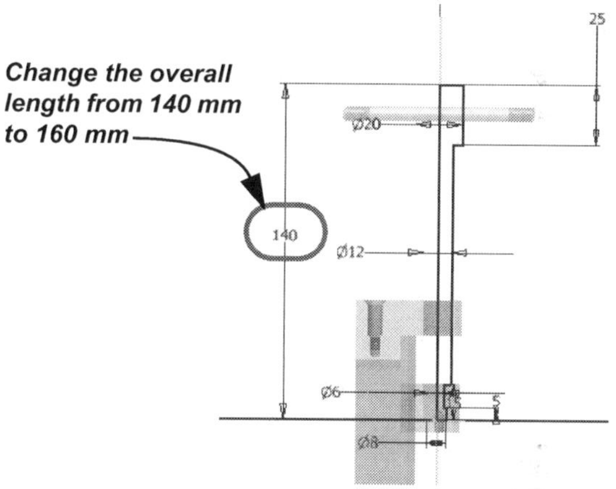

Figure 21–38

7. Finish the sketch and in the *3D Model* tab>Return panel, click  (Return) to return to the assembly.

8. Return to the model and drag the spindle. Note that once the **Spindle** and **Body** come in contact there is collision between **MovingJaw** and **FixedJaw**.

The number of components in a Contact Set can affect system performance. It is recommended that only the required components be added.

9. Right-click on **MovingJaw** in the Model browser and select **Contact Set**.

10. Right-click on **FixedJaw** in the Model browser and select **Contact Set**.

11. Return to the model and drag the spindle. The movement is now limited to all of the correct points of contact and there are no interferences for this range of motion.

Task 3 - Use the Contact Solver with the Drive command.

In this task you will learn how to use a combination of the **Contact Solver** and **Drive** commands to simulate motion.

1. Right-click on the **Mate:6(40.000mm)** constraint in the Model browser and clear the **Suppress** option.
2. Right-click on the **Mate:6(40.000mm)** constraint in the Model browser and select **Drive**. All of the contact sets should remain set.
3. Expand the dialog box and clear the **Collision Detection** option.
4. Enter **0.000 mm** in the *Start* field, **115.000 mm** in the *End* field, and click . Originally, when you entered 115 mm as the extent of the offset there was a collision. Note that the motion stops when the offset is 95.000 mm, as shown at the top of the dialog box. The Contact Solver can also be used to help determine where components will come into contact with each other when you are using the **Drive** command.
5. Close the Drive dialog box.
6. Resume the two suppressed components and save the assembly. When prompted to save the **Level of Detail Representation** changes, click **No**. The dialog box opens because of the suppression changes made to the two **DIN 917** components.

Chapter Review Questions

1. When replacing a part in the assembly, you can replace all instances of the part at the same level of the assembly.
   a. True
   b. False

2. What is the effect of Promoting a component (as shown in Figure 21–39) in an assembly?

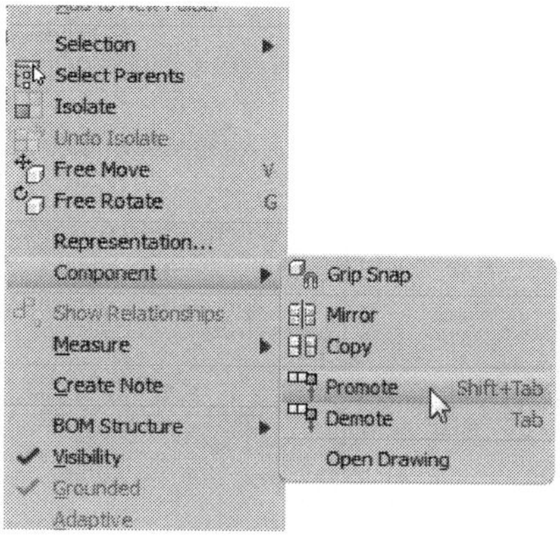

Figure 21–39

   a. It makes that component active for editing.
   b. It moves it from a subassembly into the next higher level assembly.
   c. It makes it a separate part file.
   d. It makes it the grounded component.

3. You can use the **Demote** option to move components into an existing subassembly.
   a. True
   b. False

4. Which of the following best describes the purpose of a Drive constraint?
   a. A Drive constraint is a dimension type that is created in a sketch of an assembly feature so that the value can be easily changed to update the assembly.
   b. A Drive constraint is the terminology used for the full set of constraints to fully locate a component in an assembly.
   c. A Drive constraint enables you to assign motion between the constrained components by setting the offset or angle value in a constraint so that it changes incrementally.
   d. A Drive constraint is a type of constraint that is assigned in the Place Constraint dialog box.
5. Which of the following components have been specified as members in a Contact Set, as shown in Figure 21–40? (Select all that apply.)

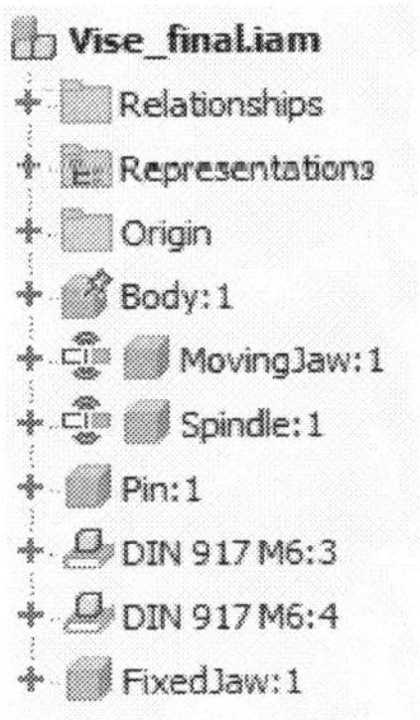

Figure 21–40

   a. Body
   b. Moving Jaw
   c. Spindle
   d. Pin
   e. DIN 917 M6:3
   f. DIN 917 M6:4
   g. Fixed Jaw
6. You cannot assemble components so that two parts occupy the same space at the same time.
   a. True
   b. False

7. Which of the following determines where two selected assembly components overlap?

   a. In the *Assemble* tab>Productivity panel, expand the commands and click .

   b. In the *Inspect* tab>Interference panel, click .

   c. *Inspect* tab>Measure panel, click .

   d. An interference analysis can only be done on the whole model, not individual components.

8. What information can you find in the Interference Detected dialog box? (Select all that apply.)

   a. Number of interferences

   b. Total Volume of interference

   c. Part names

   d. Subassembly names

9. Which of the following statements regarding the **Design Doctor** tool is true?

   a. It toggles the visibility of the component.

   b. It displays options to resolve a constraint issue.

   c. It enables a component so that it can be selected.

   d. It moves a component out of the subassembly.

Command Summary

Button	Command	Location
	**Activate Contact Solver**	• **Ribbon:** *Inspect* tab>Interference panel
	**Analyze Interference**	• **Ribbon:** *Inspect* tab>Interference panel
N/A	**Contact Set**	• **Context Menu:** In Model browser with multiple components selected
N/A	**Demote**	• **Context Menu:** In Model browser with a component selected>Component • **Context Menu:** In the graphics window with a component selected>Component
N/A	**Drive**	• **Context Menu:** (*select a constraint in the Model browser to access command*)
N/A	**Promote**	• **Context Menu:** In Model browser with a component selected>Component • **Context Menu:** In the graphics window with a component selected>Component
	**Replace (components)**	• **Ribbon:** *Assemble* tab>Component panel • **Context Menu:** In Model browser with a component selected>Component • **Context Menu:** In the graphics window with a component selected>Component
	**Replace All (components)**	• **Ribbon:** *Assemble* tab>Component panel • **Context Menu:** In Model browser with a component selected>Component • **Context Menu:** In the graphics window with a component selected>Component
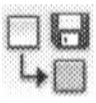	**Save and Replace Component**	• **Ribbon:** *Assemble* tab>Productivity panel

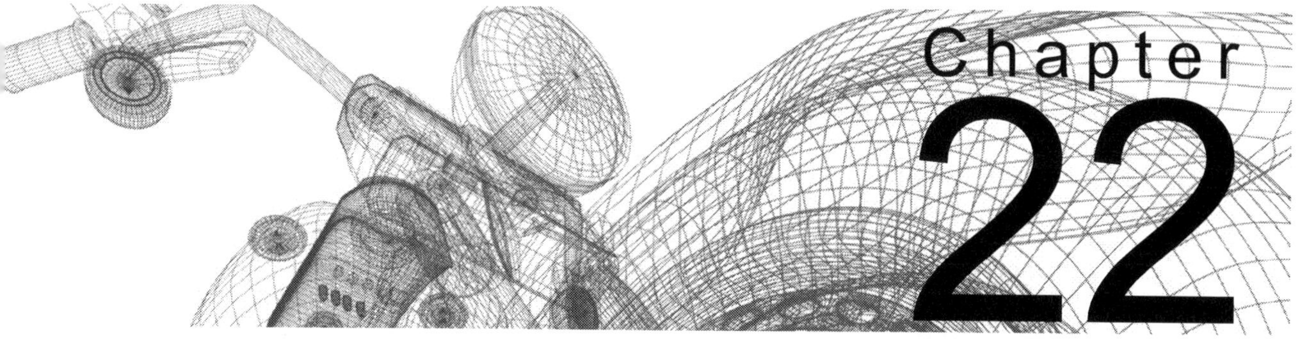

Chapter 22

Assembly Parts and Features

Understanding the process of creating parts and features in an assembly enables you to build parts in relation to other parts, helping you to build the required design intent into your assembly.

Learning Objectives in This Chapter

- Create a new component (part or assembly) in the context of an assembly model.
- Create assembly features in the context of an assembly model.

22.1 Assembly Parts

As an alternative to creating components (parts and assemblies) and assembling them, you can create components directly in the assembly. Creating parts in an assembly has the following advantages:

- You can use faces and edges from other assembly components to locate the first sketch in the model.
- You can use geometry (i.e., points, edges) from other assembly components to create entities in the sketch.
- If you use geometry from other components in the sketch, the part automatically references the other components and any changes made in them reflect in the new component.
- If you use geometry from other components, the part is already constrained in the assembly.

How To: Create a New Component in an Assembly

1. Select the *Assemble* tab>Component panel, and click  (Create). The Create In-Place Component dialog box opens as shown in Figure 22–1.

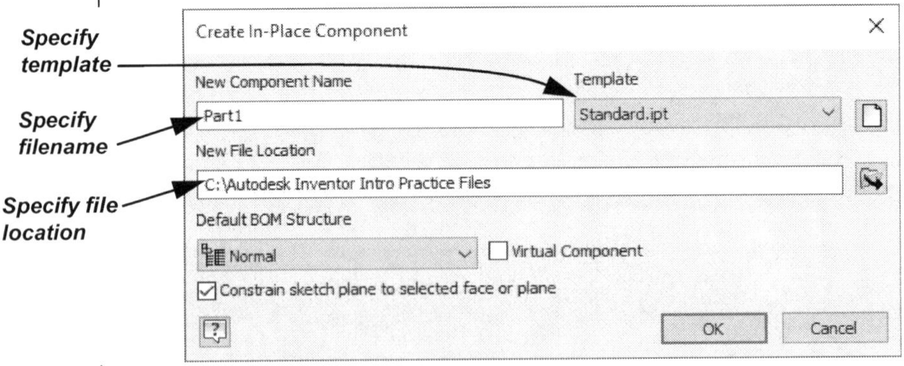

Figure 22–1

2. Complete the Create In-Place Component dialog box, as follows:
   - Enter the name of the new component in the *New Component Name* field.
   - Select the part or assembly template in the *Template* field that should be used for the new file.
   - Define the default bill of materials structure for the new component.

Using virtual components is a valid workflow. However, if using Vault consider creating blank .IPT files for virtual type components, such as paint and grease. Once created, you can place them in the assembly. Vault item numbers have a history of not working well with virtual parts.

- Select **Virtual Component** to create a new component that does not have a file (and therefore no geometry). Its information is stored in the assembly file.
- Select **Constrain sketch plane to selected face or plane** to automatically assign a Mate constraint between the selected part face and sketch plane when the component is created.

3. Click **OK** to create the new component.
4. Select a work plane or face on another component as the sketch plane for the new component. The sketch plane locates the first feature of the component in the assembly. The component is then added to the Model browser and it becomes the active component.

Hint: Creating Subassemblies in the Context of an Assembly

To create a subassembly, select an assembly template when creating the new file. You do not need to select a sketching plane, select anywhere on the display window to activate the subassembly. Avoid creating a subassembly in an assembly unless you are restructuring existing components to prevent any unwanted references.

5. Sketch the base feature for the new component using the standard sketching procedure. Consider incorporating any of following to build relationships between the new component and existing components in the assembly:
   - Project geometry and sketch entities referencing other assembly components to build relationships between components in the assembly.
   - Sketch new geometry and dimension it independently.
   - Sketch new geometry and dimension to the edges or faces of other components.
   - Use a combination of sketched and projected geometry.
   - Consider using the **Project Cut Edges** option to project the edges defined by the intersection of a sketch plane and existing solid geometry.

Hint: Controlling if Projected Geometry is Associative

To control whether projected geometry or sketched entities are associative with their parent, use **Cross part geometry projection** in the *Assembly* tab of the Application Options dialog box. As an alternative, you can also hold <Ctrl> while selecting entities to project so that they lose their associative reference to the selected entities.

6. To complete the sketch, click (Finish Sketch) in the Exit panel or right-click and select **Finish 2D Sketch**.
7. Use the sketch to create the first feature of the part (e.g, **Extrude**, **Revolve**, **Loft**, etc.). Create additional features on your part as required.
8. Once you have finished working on the part, click (Return) in the Return panel or right-click and select **Finish Edit** to activate the assembly.

*To open a created part or subassembly in a separate window, right-click on the file and select **Open**.*

If you create the new part using references to existing components in the assembly, you are establishing parent-child relationships between the components. When a relationship is established, the adaptive icon ( ) displays next to the part and any of its adaptive features, as shown in Figure 22–2. This icon indicates that references were established with other components when the part was created. Any changes to the source geometry reflect in the new part.

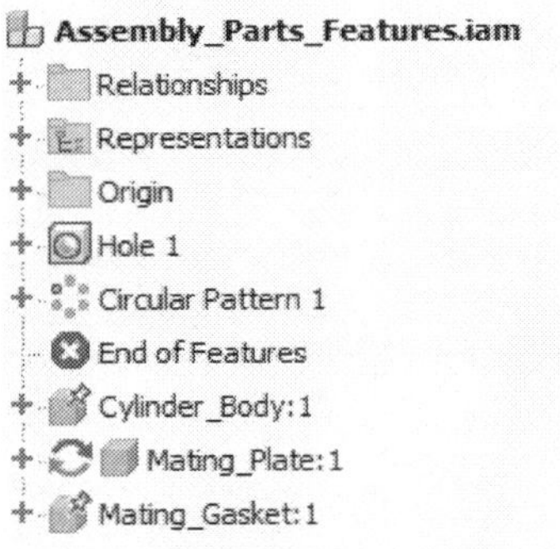

Figure 22–2

To remove adaptivity from a part, right-click on the feature and clear the **Adaptive** option, or right-click on the model name and clear the option. If adaptivity is cleared from the model name, all adaptivity is cleared. If cleared at the feature level, it enables other features to remain adaptive.

22.2 Assembly Features

You can create cuts (extruded, revolved, and swept features), holes, chamfers, fillets, and work features in an assembly using the *3D Model* tab. Assembly features have the following advantages:

The process of creating assembly features is the same as creating them in a part model.

- You can define a feature (e.g., hole or cut) to affect multiple components in an assembly.
- You can use geometry from other components for sketching.
- You can constrain assembly components to these features.

Assembly features are useful after you have placed and constrained components, and might need to add features to facilitate manufacturing of the assembly. For example, you might need to create cuts or holes in the assembly so that you can insert pins or screws.

Participant Parts

When you create assembly holes and cut features, you can control which part(s) they affect. Parts affected by assembly features are called participant parts and are identified in the feature's node, as shown in Figure 22–3

Components are added as participants rather than new features being added in each component.

Parts affected by (participating in) the hole feature display in the feature in the Model browser

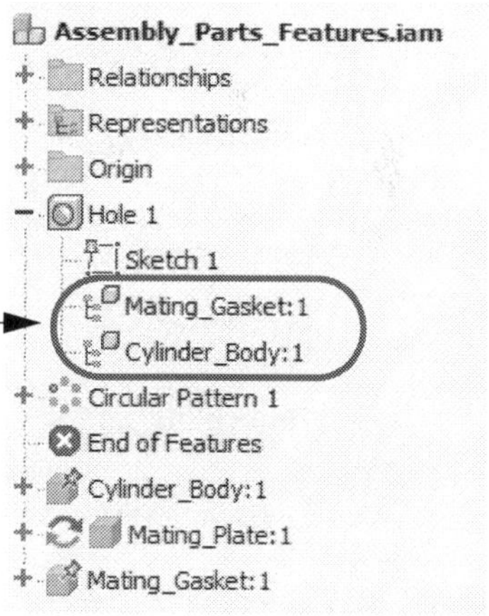

Figure 22–3

By default, components are added as participants. However you can add or remove participants:

- To add a participant component, right-click on the feature in the Model browser, select **Add Participant** (as shown on the left in Figure 22–4), and select new part(s).
- To remove a participant part, right-click on the participating part(s) in the Model browser and select **Remove Participant**, as shown on the right in Figure 22–4.

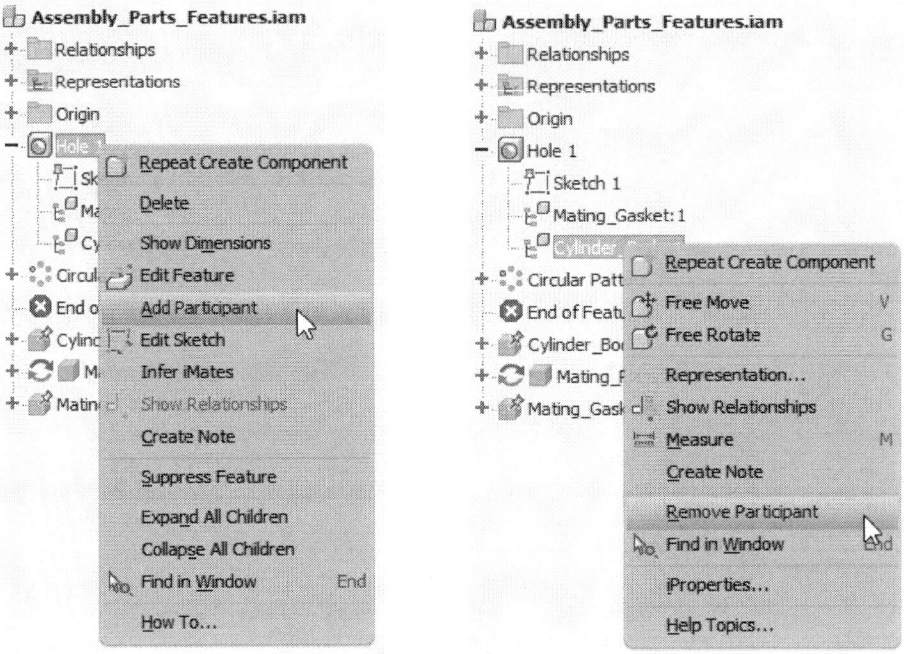

Figure 22–4

Practice 22a Creating Parts and Features in an Assembly

Practice Objectives

- Create a part in an assembly and add solid geometry to it by establishing adaptive references with other components.
- Create a part in an assembly and add solid geometry to it by using, but not establishing a permanent reference with other components.
- Create assembly hole features and ensure that the participant components are correctly assigned.

In this practice, you will work in the assembly environment to create two new components. In both components, you will use entities from another model to create solid geometry. In one of them, you will maintain the reference and in the other, you will not maintain the reference. Additionally, you will create assembly level holes and add/remove the participating parts. The final model created is shown in Figure 22–5.

Figure 22–5

Task 1 - Open an assembly file.

1. Open **Assembly_Parts_Features.iam**. The assembly displays with a single component already assembled.

Task 2 - Create new adaptive components in the assembly.

In this task, you will create a new adaptive component that references geometry from the **Cylinder_Body** component.

1. Select the *Assemble* tab>Component panel and click  (Create). The Create In-Place Component dialog box opens.

2. Enter **Mating_Plate** in the *New Component Name* field.

3. Browse and select the metric standard part template, **Standard(mm).ipt**. Click **OK**.

4. In the Create In-Place Component dialog box, verify that **Constrain sketch plane to selected face or plane** is selected and accept the defaults in the other fields, as shown in Figure 22–6.

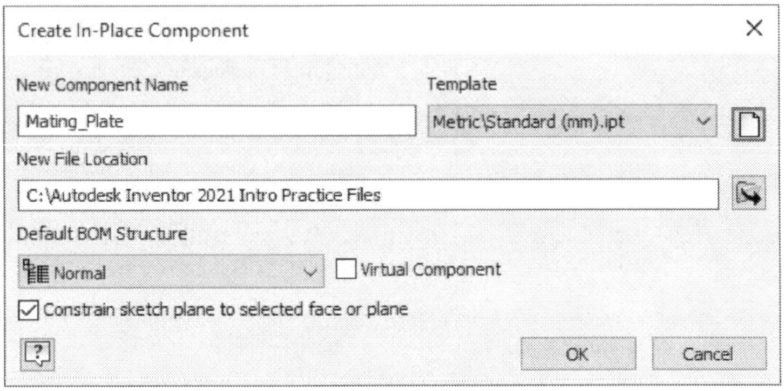

Figure 22–6

5. Click **OK** to create the part.

6. Select the face shown in Figure 22–7 as the sketch plane. All of the assembly components, except **Mating_Plate** are grayed out in the Model browser. This means that only **Mating_Plate** is active and you can add features to it.

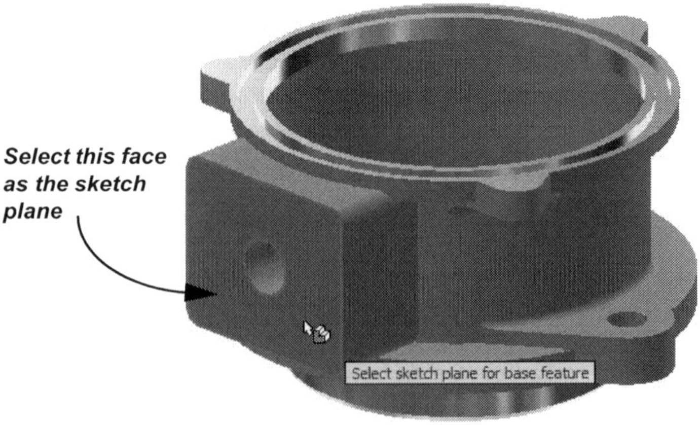

Figure 22–7

7. Select the *3D Model* tab>Sketch panel, click 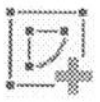 (Start 2D Sketch). Select the XY Plane in the new **Mating_Plate** component as the sketch plane.

8. In the sketch environment, project the edges of the face shown in Figure 22–8. Rotate the model into a 3D orientation to select the face. The projected edges display in yellow, indicating that they are referencing other geometry. In this case, they are referencing geometry in another model.

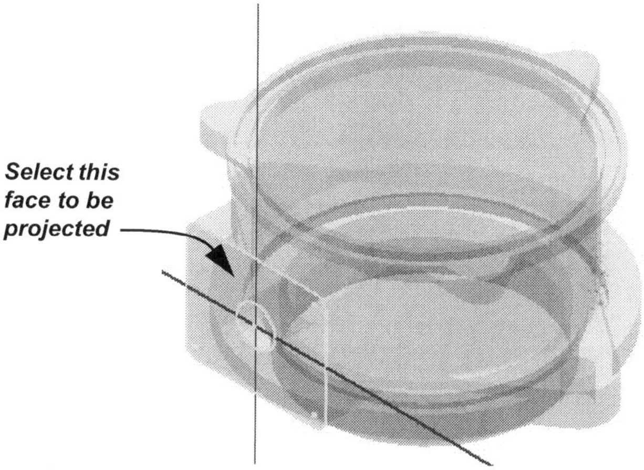

Figure 22–8

9. Sketch a circle and add a **2** dimension value to dimension it relative to the projected circle, as shown in Figure 22–9.

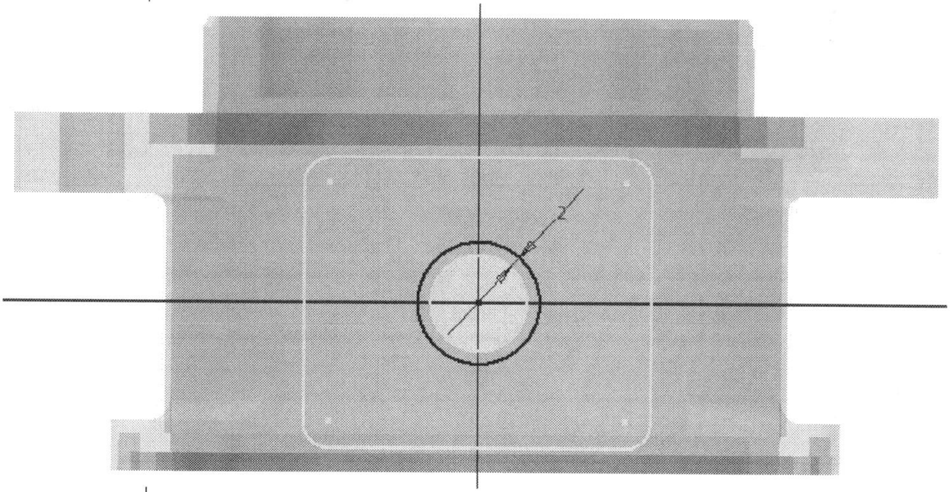

Figure 22–9

10. Finish the sketch. Do not return to the top-level assembly or you will have to reactivate **Mating_Plate**.

11. Extrude the sketch by **10 mm** (as shown in Figure 22–10) and complete the feature.

Figure 22–10

12. Double-click on the **Assembly_Parts_Features.iam** node at the top of the Model browser to activate it. The model displays as shown in Figure 22–11. Note that a Flush constraint has been created in the Model browser. This is because you selected **Constrain sketch plane to selected face or plane** when you created the new component. It automatically created the constraint between the selected part face and sketch plane.

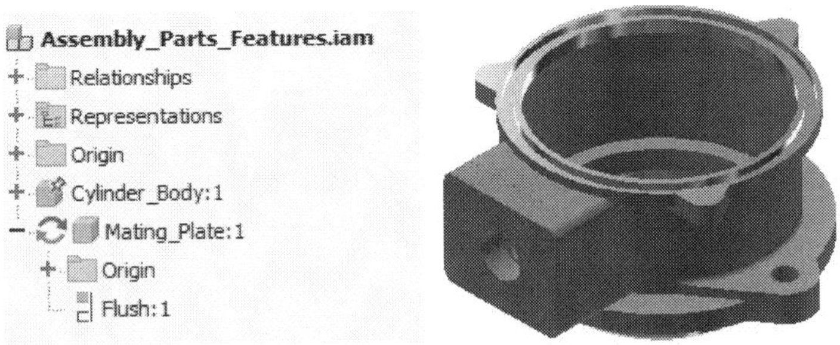

Figure 22–11

13. Note that the (Adaptive) icon displays next to the **Mating_Plate** part indicating that it is adaptive. In the Model browser's header, select **Modeling**. Note that the (Adaptive) icon displays next to the **Extrusion1** feature, indicating that it is an adaptive feature.

14. Double-click on the **Cylinder_Body** component in the Model browser to activate it.

15. Right-click on **Hole9** in the Model browser and select **Show Dimensions**. Set the new diameter for the hole to **20**.

16. Double-click on the **Assembly_Parts_Features.iam** node at the top of the Model browser to activate it. Note that the hole in the **Mating_Plate** component updates to reflect the change. Regardless of the hole size in the **Cylinder_Body** component the diameter in the **Mating_Plate** will be 2 mm larger.

Task 3 - Create a new non-adaptive component in the assembly.

In this task, you will create a new component that uses geometry but does not create a lasting reference to the **Cylinder_Body** component.

1. Select the *Assemble* tab>Component panel, click (Create). The Create In-Place Component dialog box opens.
2. Enter **Mating_Gasket** in the *New Component Name* field.
3. Browse and select the metric standard part template, **Standard(mm).ipt**.
4. Verify that **Constrain sketch plane to selected face or plane** is selected and accept the defaults in the other fields.
5. Click **OK** to create the part.

6. Select the face shown in Figure 22–12 as the sketch plane. A Flush constraint will be established automatically between the new component and this face on the **Cylinder_Body** component. All of the assembly components are grayed out in the Model browser, except **Mating_Gasket**. This means that only **Mating_Gasket** is active and you can add features to it.

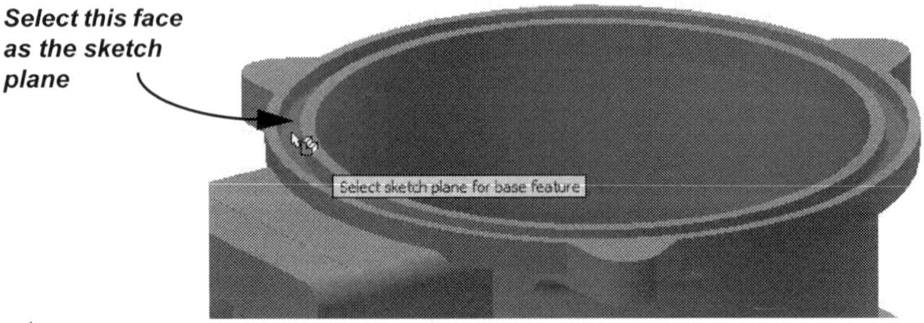

Figure 22–12

7. Select the *3D Model* tab>Sketch panel, click  (Start 2D Sketch). Select the XY Plane in the new **Mating_Gasket** component as the sketch plane.

8. In the sketch environment, hold <Ctrl> and project the two circular edges that lie on the selected sketch plane, as shown in Figure 22–13.
   - Remember to rotate the model into a 3D orientation to select the edges.
   - The new entities display fully constrained as indicated in the Status Bar and the Sketch icon in the Model browser. This is because fixed and reference constraints were automatically added.
   - By holding <Ctrl> as you are selecting the entities, you are projecting them without establishing a relationship. The projected entities should display in blue (not yellow).

At any point you can return to the sketch and delete the fixed and reference constraints that were automatically added and explicitly add a dimension scheme.

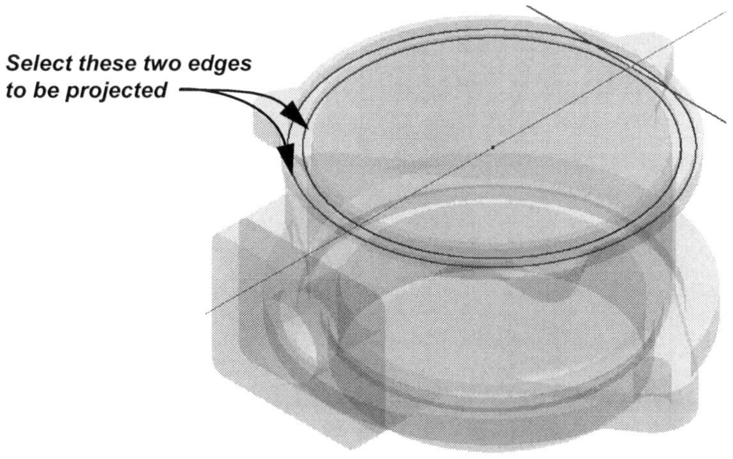

Figure 22–13

9. Finish the sketch. Do not return to the top-level assembly or you will have to reactivate **Mating_Gasket**.

10. Extrude the sketch using the **To** ( ) option and select the face as shown in Figure 22–14.

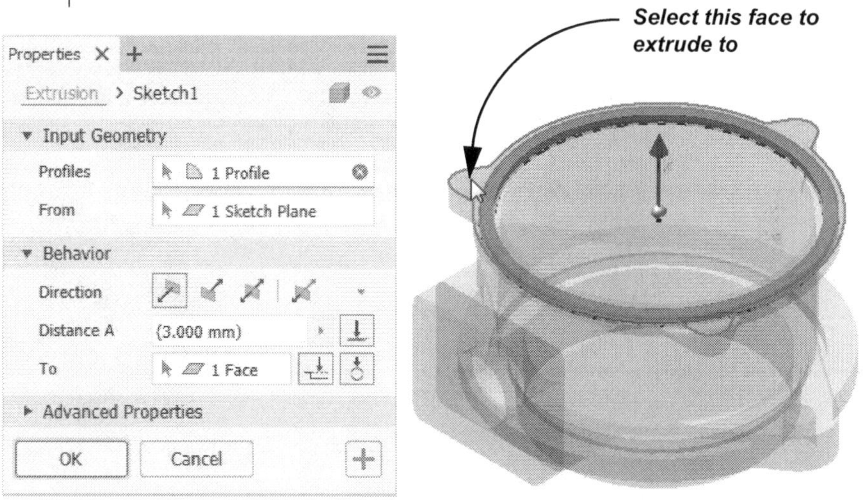

Figure 22–14

11. Complete the extrude feature. Note that a Work Plane has been added to the Model browser. This Work Plane indicates the extent of the extrusion but does not create a reference between the components.

12. Select the *3D Model* tab>Sketch panel, click (Start 2D Sketch). Select the top of the extrusion that you just created in the new **Mating_Gasket** component as the sketch plane.

13. In the sketch environment, hold <Ctrl> and select all of the edges around the outer edge of the **Cylinder_Body** component and the circular inner edge, as shown in Figure 22–15. Remember to rotate the model into a 3D orientation to select the edges. You will need to select these entities individually. The sketch is also fully constrained with fixed and reference constraints.

At any point you can return to the sketch and delete the fixed and reference constraints that were automatically added and explicitly add a dimension scheme.

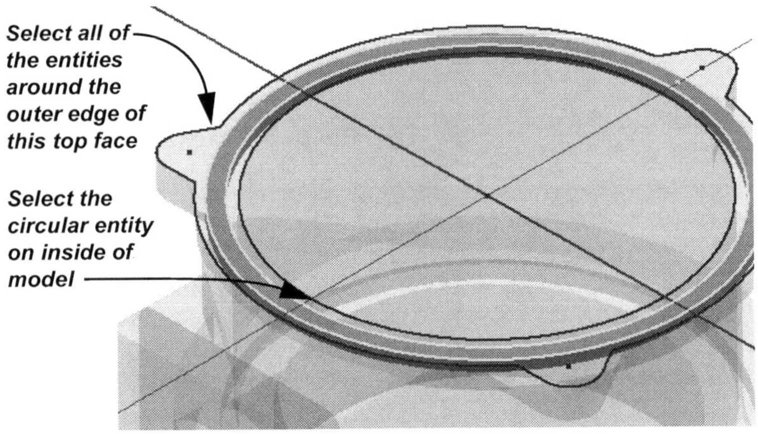

Figure 22–15

14. Finish the sketch. Do not return to the top-level assembly or you will have to reactivate **Mating_Gasket**.

15. Extrude the sketch by selecting the closed sections so that the preview displays as shown in Figure 22–16. Extrude the feature by **10 mm**.

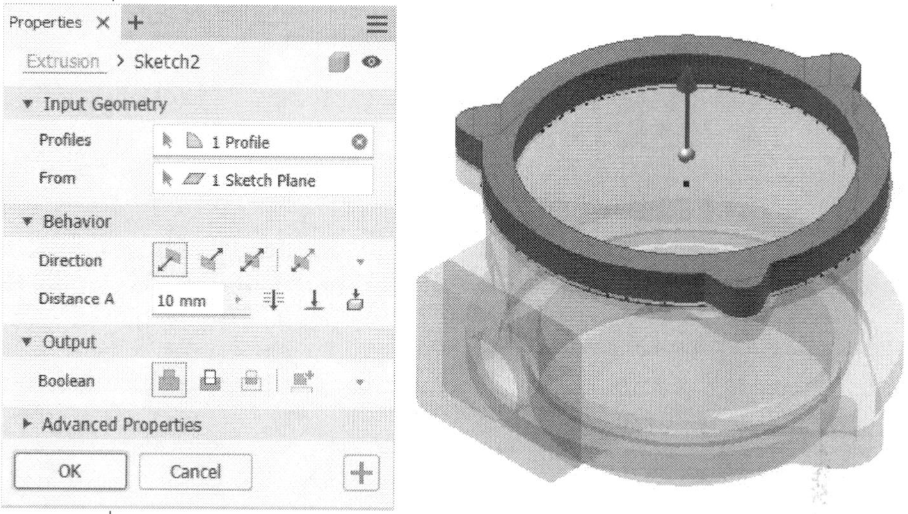

Figure 22–16

In this practice, the adaptivity was cleared to show you how this is done. In this scenario, adaptivity is important to maintain components that fit together.

16. Complete the extrude feature. Note that there is no adaptive icon ( ) displayed next to the **Mating_Gasket** part, indicating that it is not adaptive. This is because you used <Ctrl> when projecting the references from the **Cylinder_Body** component.

17. Double-click on the **Cylinder_Body** component in the Model browser to activate it.

18. Right-click on **Extrusion 5** in the Model browser and select **Show Dimensions**. Set the new diameter for the arc to **20**.

19. Double-click on the **Assembly_Parts_&_Features.iam** node at the top of the Model browser to activate it. Note that the geometry in the **Mating_Gasket** component does not update to reflect the change. This is because the component is not adaptive.

20. In the Quick Access Toolbar, click (Undo) twice to undo the change.

21. Return to the top-level assembly, if not already active.

Task 4 - (Optional) Fully constrain the non-adaptive model.

In this task, you will display the Degrees of Freedom that remain in the assembly and ground the **Mating_Gasket** component so that it is fully located.

1. In the *View* tab>Visibility panel, click (Degrees of Freedom) to display any degrees of freedom in the assembly. Note that the non-adaptive model, **Mating_Gasket** is missing constraints to fully locate it in the assembly.

2. Right-click the **Mating_Gasket** component in the Model browser and select **Grounded** to fully constrain the components in the assembly.

Task 5 - Create assembly holes.

In this task, you will create three assembly holes.

1. In the *3D Model* tab>Modify Assembly panel, click (Hole).

2. Select the face shown in Figure 22–17 as the placement plane for this hole. Select the edge shown in Figure 22–17 as the Concentric Reference.

3. Set the diameter to **7 mm** and select (Through All) as the *Termination* setting.

4. Complete the feature. The model displays as shown in Figure 22–17.

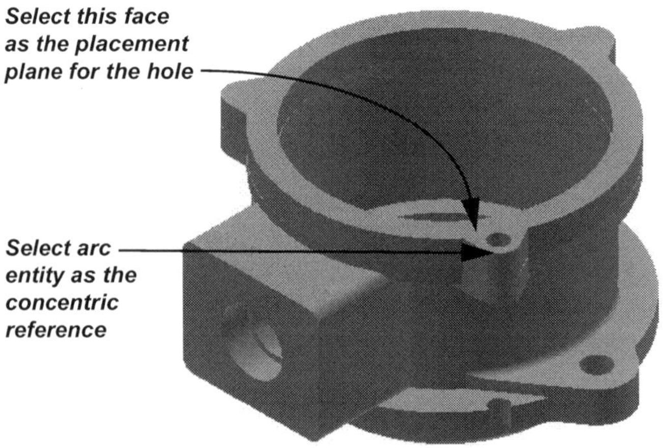

Figure 22–17

5. Note that the hole intersects the bottom of the model as well. In the Model browser, expand the **Hole 1** node, right-click on the **Cylinder_Body** component, and select **Remove Participant** to remove it entirely from cutting through the **Cylinder_Body**.

6. You want the hole to cut through the top portion of the component but not the bottom. In the Model browser, right-click on **Hole 1** and select **Add Participant**. Select **Cylinder_Body** in the graphics window to add it back as a participant in the hole feature.

7. Edit **Hole 1**. Change the *Termination* setting from (Through All) to (To) and select the face shown in Figure 22–18.

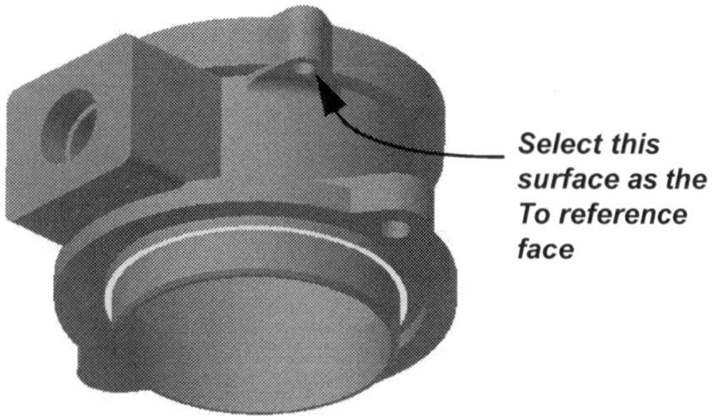

Figure 22–18

8. Create the remaining holes using a circular pattern. The model should display as shown in Figure 22–19.
   - Note: Ensure that you are using a feature pattern option on the *3D Model* tab.

Figure 22–19

9. Save the assembly and its components.

Chapter Review Questions

1. Which command sequence is used to create a new part model while in the context of an assembly model?
    a. *Get Started* tab>Launch panel, click .
    b. *3D Model* tab>Sketch panel, click .
    c. *Assemble* tab>Component panel, click .
    d. *Assemble* tab>Component panel, and click .
2. When creating a sketch for an assembly part, why is it advantageous to reference edges or faces on other components? (Select all that apply.)
    a. Creates a parent child relationship to help align components accurately with one another.
    b. If you use geometry from other components, the part is already constrained in the assembly.
    c. Changes made in the referenced component automatically reflect in the new component.
    d. Other than the ease of creating the sketch geometry, there is no significant benefit.
3. When creating a new part model, while in the context of an assembly model, you must use the same template as the last component that was placed into the assembly.
    a. True
    b. False
4. Which of the following types of files can be created in the context of an assembly? (Select all that apply.)
    a. Part (.IPT)
    b. Sheet Metal (.IPT)
    c. Presentation (.IPN)
    d. Assembly (.IAM)
    e. Weldment (.IAM)
    f. Drawing (.IDW)

5. What types of features can be added to an assembly? (Select all that apply.)
    a. Extrude
    b. Revolve
    c. Sweep
    d. Loft
    e. Hole
    f. Fillet
    g. Chamfer
    h. Shell
6. What command would you use after you placed a hole through three part models in an assembly and then wanted to remove that hole from one of the parts?
    a. **Extrude**
    b. **Add Participant**
    c. **Remove Participant**
    d. **Visibility**

Command Summary

Button	Command	Location
	**Create**	• **Ribbon:** *Assemble* tab>Component panel • **Context Menu**: In the graphics window

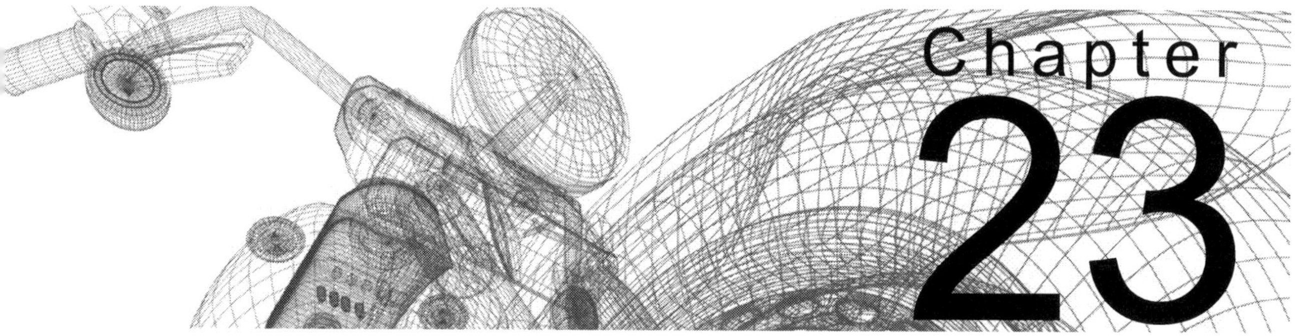

Assembly Bill of Materials

The Bill of Materials (BOM) functionality is used to communicate the parts that are used in an assembly. In addition, you are able to add parts to the BOM that do not have any physical geometry, but are critical to the model (e.g., grease).

Learning Objectives in This Chapter

- Create virtual components that represent non-geometrical parts that are required in the BOM.
- Generate an assembly BOM that lists the components of an assembly.
- Customize and edit the properties that display in the BOM.
- Export a BOM for use in the Engineer's Notebook, an external database, a text, or a .CSV file.
- Synchronize the assembly BOM and the Parts List that documents the BOM in a drawing.

23.1 Create Virtual Components

A virtual component is created to represent a non-geometrical part that is required in the bill of materials (e.g., paint, grease, etc.). They can also be used to represent parts you do not want to model, such as fasteners. Like real components, the properties of a virtual component can be fully defined.

Virtual components are not separate part files.

How To: Create a Virtual Component:

1. In the *Assemble* tab>Component panel, click  (Create) to open the Create In-Place Component dialog box.
2. To create a virtual component, select **Virtual Component** in the Create In-Place Component dialog box, as shown in Figure 23–1. The Template and New File Location areas become gray because information about a virtual component is stored with the assembly.

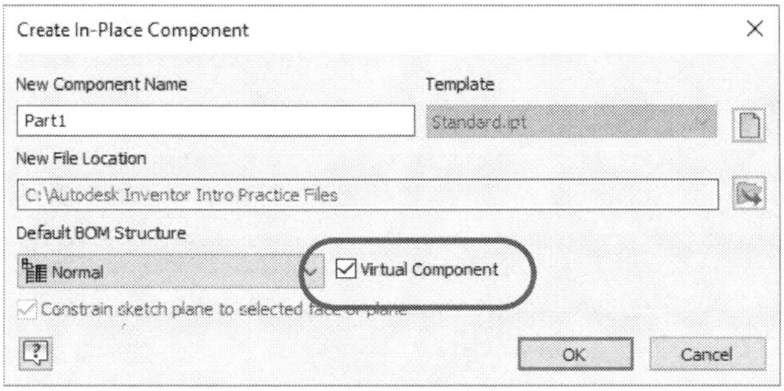

Figure 23–1

3. Enter a name for the virtual component in the *New Component Name* field, and click **OK**. The Model browser displays the virtual component, as shown in Figure 23–2.

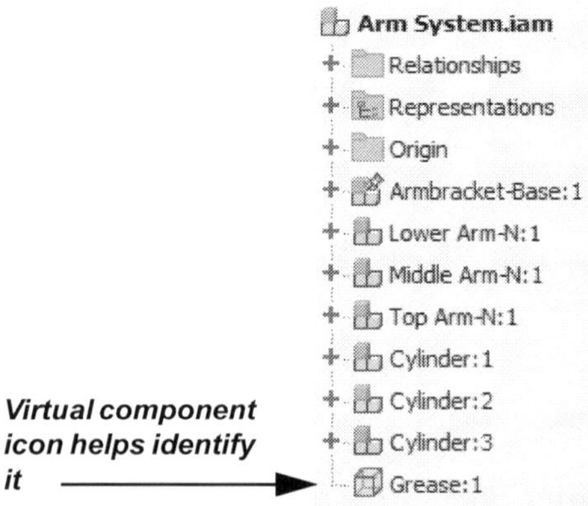

Figure 23–2

Material properties can be assigned to Virtual Components in the same manner as other components, either through the Properties dialog box or the BOM Editor.

Like real components, the properties of the virtual component can be defined.

- Using the iProperties dialog box (right-click on the component and select **iProperties**), you can set the default material for virtual components as well as manually enter a value for its mass in the *Physical* tab. Alternatively, you can assign a material by selecting the virtual component in the Model browser and selecting a material in the Materials drop-down list in the Quick Access Toolbar.
- The component name, BOM structure properties, and the base quantities can be defined by right-clicking on the virtual component and selecting **Component Settings**.

As an alternative to creating a virtual component in the Create Component dialog box, you can also click (Create Virtual Component) in the Bill of Materials dialog box to create a new virtual component. Using this alternative method, you are simply prompted for the component's name and you can define its BOM Structure directly in the dialog box. To make modifications to its base quantities, you must still define its Component Settings.

23.2 Create Bill of Materials

A Bill of Materials (BOM) is a list of all of the components in an assembly. The information used in a BOM is generated from iProperties and used to generate the Parts List in a drawing.

General Steps

Use the following steps to create a BOM:

1. Generate the BOM.
2. Add properties.
3. Modify the properties.
4. Organize the BOM.
5. Export the BOM.
6. Synchronize BOM and Parts List, if required.

Step 1 - Generate the BOM.

In the *Assemble* tab>Manage panel and click (Bill of Materials) to create a BOM. Three views can be displayed:

- Model Data
- Structured
- Parts Only

Model Data View

The *Model Data* tab displays BOM data similar to the Model browser, as shown in Figure 23–3. You can use the *Model Data* tab to modify the BOM Structure or component properties. This view is not used for display in a Parts List.

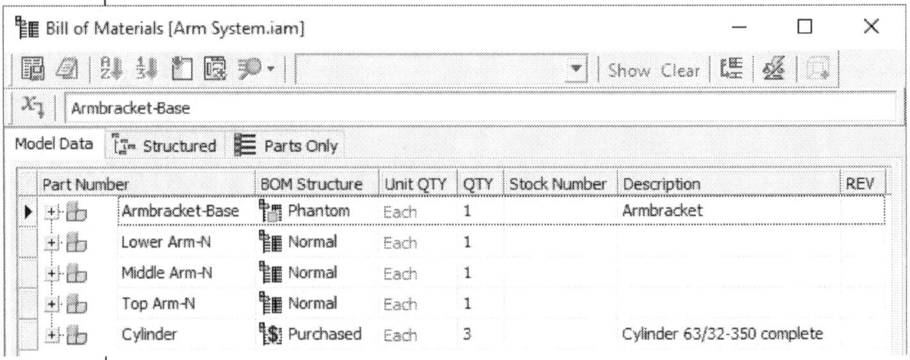

Figure 23–3

Structured View

In the *Structured* tab, components are listed based on the BOM Structure property, as shown in Figure 23–4. This enables you to manipulate how components display in the BOM, enabling you to hide part and subassemblies from display in a parts list.

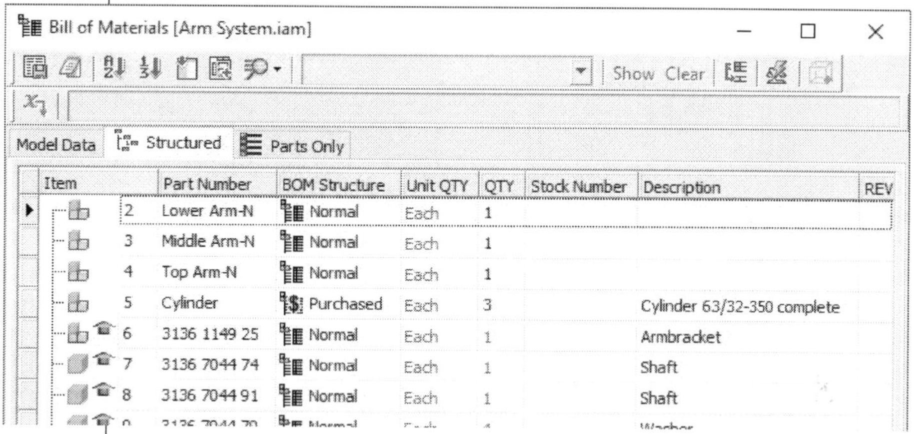

Item	Part Number	BOM Structure	Unit QTY	QTY	Stock Number	Description	REV
2	Lower Arm-N	Normal	Each	1			
3	Middle Arm-N	Normal	Each	1			
4	Top Arm-N	Normal	Each	1			
5	Cylinder	Purchased	Each	3		Cylinder 63/32-350 complete	
6	3136 1149 25	Normal	Each	1		Armbracket	
7	3136 7044 74	Normal	Each	1		Shaft	
8	3136 7044 91	Normal	Each	1		Shaft	

Figure 23–4

Parts Only View

The Parts Only view displays only parts or subassemblies whose BOM Structure property is set to **Normal**, **Purchased** or **Inseparable**, as shown in Figure 23–5. Subassembly components are promoted to the top level to create a flat view. This flat view provides a good summary of the parts used (including their quantities) to make the top-level assembly.

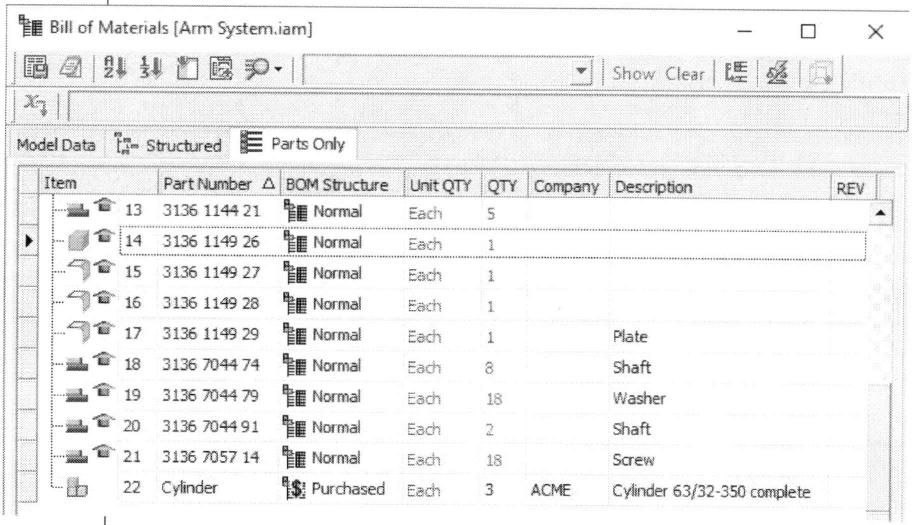

Item	Part Number	BOM Structure	Unit QTY	QTY	Company	Description	REV
13	3136 1144 21	Normal	Each	5			
14	3136 1149 26	Normal	Each	1			
15	3136 1149 27	Normal	Each	1			
16	3136 1149 28	Normal	Each	1			
17	3136 1149 29	Normal	Each	1		Plate	
18	3136 7044 74	Normal	Each	8		Shaft	
19	3136 7044 79	Normal	Each	18		Washer	
20	3136 7044 91	Normal	Each	2		Shaft	
21	3136 7057 14	Normal	Each	18		Screw	
22	Cylinder	Purchased	Each	3	ACME	Cylinder 63/32-350 complete	

Figure 23–5

By default, if a tab is disabled, right-click on the tab name and enable it. Figure 23–6 shows how the *Parts Only* tab is enabled.

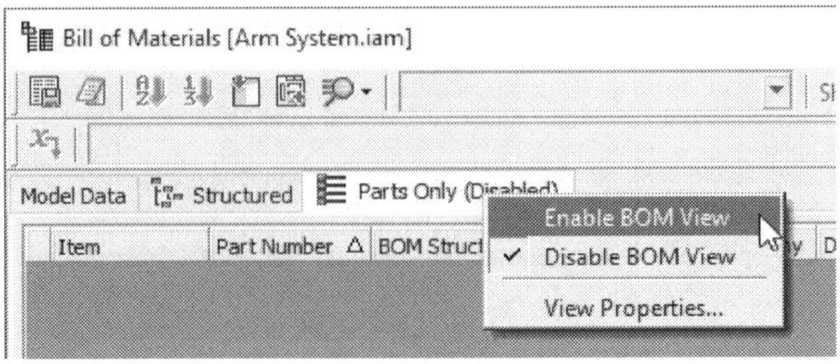

Figure 23–6

Step 2 - Add properties.

Any component iProperty can be displayed in the BOM. The *Part Number*, *BOM Structure*, *Quantity*, *Stock Number*, *Description*, and *Revision* columns display by default.

Customized column headings are unique for each of the tabs in the Bill of Materials dialog box.

- To add a system-defined component iProperty column, click  (Choose Columns) in the toolbar to open the Customization dialog box, as shown in Figure 23–7. To add a column to the table, select the property in the Customization dialog box and drag it into position in the column header bar in the BOM table. To remove a column, select the column title and drag it to the Customization dialog box.

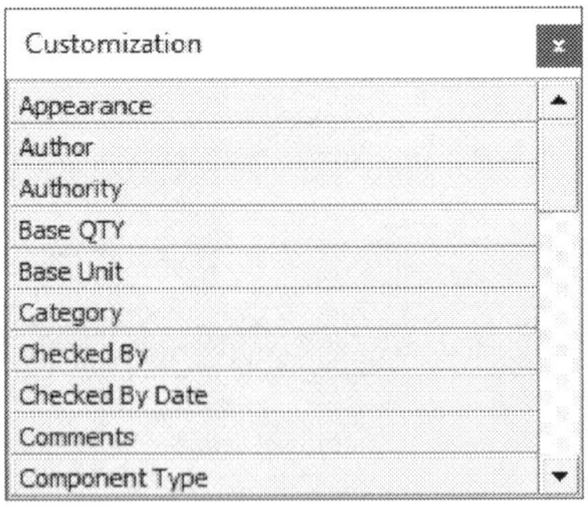

Figure 23–7

- To add Custom iProperties to the BOM table, use the following steps.

How To: Add a Custom iProperty to the Table

1. Click (Add Custom iProperty Columns) in the top toolbar.
2. Select the *<Click to add iProperty column>* field and enter the name of the property.
3. Define the data type (**Text**, **Date**, **Number**, or **Yes/No**) using the drop-down list.
4. Click **OK** to close the dialog box.
5. The custom iProperty column is added to the table. If the iProperty name already exists in the component its value automatically updates; otherwise, you can enter the values.

You can remove custom iProperty columns using the same drag and drop technique as when removing non-custom columns.

Step 3 - Modify the properties.

Component iProperties can be modified using the Properties dialog box or using the Bill of Materials dialog box. Changes made in one location update in the other. To change a property, select the appropriate cell and edit the value.

BOM Structure

The BOM Structure options can be used to provide a more accurate BOM. It is used to filter out components in the assembly that are used in its construction but are not actually part of the assembly design. The BOM Structure can be defined in the *Occurrence* tab in the iProperties dialog box or from inside the Bill of Materials dialog box, as shown in Figure 23–8.

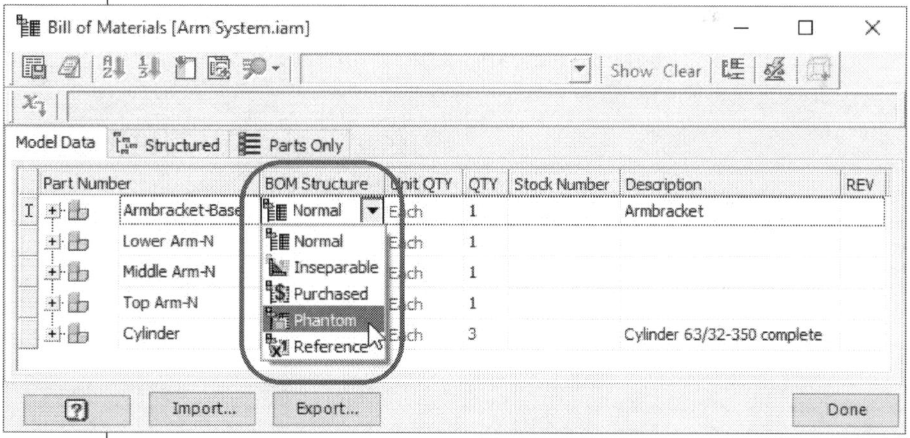

Figure 23–8

The five available BOM Structure options are **Normal**, **Phantom**, **Reference**, **Inseparable**, and **Purchased**.

Normal

A normal component is the default status for a component. Normal components are placed in the BOM based on their parent assembly. They are included in the quantity calculations and have no direct influence on their children's inclusion in the BOM.

Phantom

A phantom component is used to simplify the design. Although they exist in the model, they are not included in the BOM and are not included in the quantity calculations. Children of phantom components are listed in the BOM at the same level as their phantom parent. Phantom components are often used to ease placement of components.

Reference

A reference component is used in the construction of the assembly but is not part of the actual design, such as a skeleton model. Neither the Reference component nor its children are included in mass, volume, BOM, or quantity calculations. If a subassembly is referenced, the entire subassembly's physical properties are excluded. If a single component in the subassembly is referenced, it is the only one that is excluded.

Purchased

Purchased components are purchased instead of fabricated. In the *Structured* tab in the BOM, purchased components display like normal components. In the parts-only view, components with the **Purchased** status are listed as a single item, even if they are an assembly. Children of an assembly with a **Purchase** status are not displayed in the Parts-only view and are excluded in quantity calculations.

Inseparable

Inseparable components are assemblies that must be physically damaged to be taken apart. Inseparable components behave in the BOM like purchased components. However, if a child of an inseparable assembly's status is set to **Purchased**, it is listed in the parts-only BOM.

Quantity

Quantity in the BOM is based on three properties: item quantity, unit quantity, and total quantity.

- Item quantity is the number of instances of a component in the assembly.
- Unit quantity is a multiplier.
- Total quantity (QTY) is the item quantity multiplied by the unit quantity.

*To restore the calculated quantity, right-click on the quantity cell and select **Calculated Quantity**.*

For most components, unit quantity equals one and displays in the BOM table as **Each**. However, it can also equal a parameter (i.e., for lengths of wires). To override the quantity value in the BOM, select the *QTY* cell and enter a new value. The value displays in blue, indicating that it is a static quantity value.

Equivalent Components

If two or more components in an assembly have the same part number property, they are considered equivalent components. Equivalent components that are at the same level in the BOM are added together and placed on the same line. If the properties of these components do not match, the BOM reports the line as **varies**. To match the varied properties, select the *varies* cell and enter the required value. The value updates in all of the equivalent components.

Material

The material for each item can be modified from the BOM Editor by adding the *Material* column, selecting the *Material* cell for a specific item, and expanding the Material drop-down list. A list of materials displays, as shown in Figure 23–9. Changing the material using this method is equivalent to changing the material properties using the *Physical* tab in the Properties dialog box or activating the model in the Model browser and using the Appearance drop-down list in the Quick Access Toolbar.

Use <Shift> or <Ctrl> to select multiple items at the same time and then assign the same material to all of those selected.

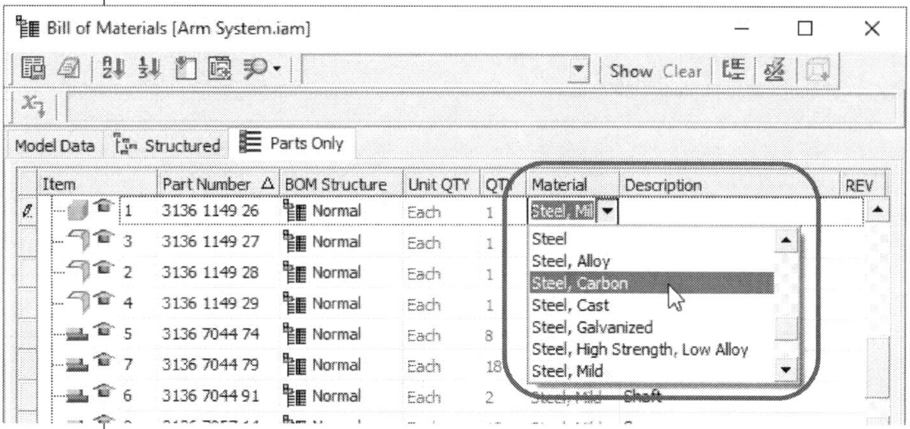

Figure 23–9

Step 4 - Organize the BOM.

Column and Row Organization

You can organize the columns and rows in a BOM table.

- The order of the table columns can be changed by selecting a column header and dragging it to a new location.
- Columns can be resized by selecting and dragging the divider between the column headings. Alternatively, you can right-click on a column heading and select **Best Fit** or **Best Fit (all columns)**. Columns are resized to fit the cell contents.
- Items in the BOM can be reordered by selecting the row and dragging it to a new location.
- Columns can be sorted by right-clicking on the column to be used to sort and selecting **Sort Ascending** or **Sort Descending**. Alternatively, click to combine multiple columns in the sort order or to set whether to sort numerically or by string.

Item Numbering

Once rows are reordered they are generally renumbered to match the customized view.

How To: Renumber

1. Click (Renumber Items) to open the Item Renumber dialog box, as shown in Figure 23–10.

The number of digits in an item number can be set in the View Properties.

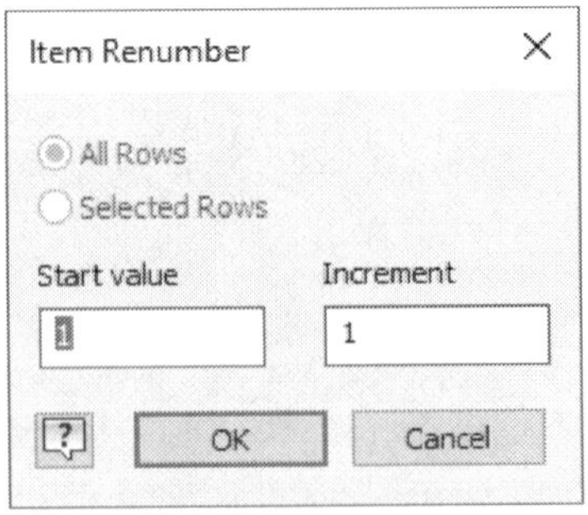

Figure 23–10

2. Enter a value that the first item should begin with in the *Start value* field.
3. Enter the value by which each consecutive item should increment in the *Increment* field.

4. Click **OK**.

> **Hint: Renumbering Individual Items**
>
> To only renumber specific items, select the items using <Ctrl> before clicking (Renumber Items).

View Properties

View properties set the options that affect item numbering. To display the view properties for the active tab, click (View Options) and select **View Properties**.

For the *Structured* tab, the Structured Properties dialog box opens as shown in Figure 23–11. Select the required options and click **OK** to change the properties.

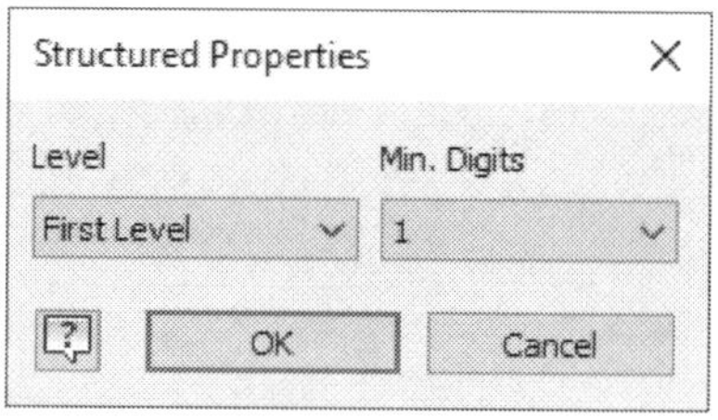

Figure 23–11

*To set minimum digits and display all subassembly models, set the Min. Digits field first, click **OK**, re-enter the View Properties dialog box, select **All Levels**, and click .*

- The *Level* drop-down list contains two options: **First Level** and **All Levels**. Use **First Level** to assign integers to direct children of the assembly and prevent the components of subassemblies from displaying in the BOM view. Selecting **All Levels** in the Level drop-down list includes all of the subassembly components in the BOM view. All subassembly components also have item numbers, as shown in Figure 23–12.

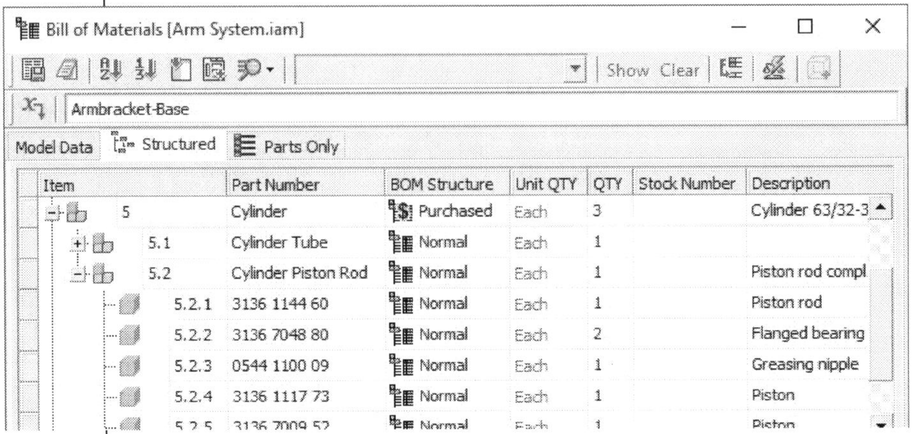

Figure 23–12

After changing the Min. Digits field and accepting the change, the item numbers do not update until you use (Renumber Items).

- The *Min. Digits* field is available to select the number of digits to include when **First Level** is selected. For example, a *Min. Digits* field to **0001** assigns the first item number at 0001 and the second at 0002.

- The *Delimiter* field enables you to select the separator symbol to use for subassembly components (comma, colon, etc.), when **All Levels** is selected.

For the *Parts Only* tab, the Parts Only Properties dialog box opens as shown in Figure 23–13. Select the required options and click **OK** to change the properties.

Figure 23–13

- The Numbering drop-down list contains two options: **Numeric** and **Alpha**. Use **Numeric** to assign a numerical index for item numbers and use **Alpha** to use a character-based index.
- The *Min. Digits* field is available to select the number of digits to include when **Numeric** is selected.
- The *Case* field enables you to set the case as upper or lower when **Alpha** is selected.

Part Number Merge Settings

The **Part Number Row Merge Settings** option enables you to control how different components with identical part numbers are handled. Click (Part Number Row Merge Settings) to open the Part Number Row Merge Settings dialog box, as shown in Figure 23–14.

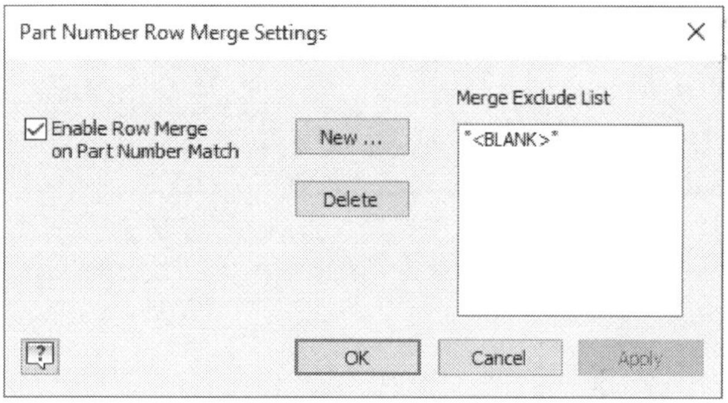

Figure 23–14

Exclusions can be copied from this list and pasted into another BOM list, by selecting the ones to be copied, right-clicking, and selecting ***Copy****. Right-click and select Paste to paste them.*

Activate **Enable Row Merge on Part Number Match** to merge components that are different but have the same part number. When activated, you can exclude specific numbers from being merged by clicking **New** and entering the part name. The part numbers that are excluded are listed in the Merge Exclude List.

Step 5 - Export the BOM.

A BOM can be exported to the Engineer's Notebook, which is stored in the assembly file, or to an external database, spreadsheet, text file, or .CSV file. When exporting you can export using the Structured or Parts Only views.

- To export to an external file, click (Export Bill of Materials).
- To export to the Engineer's Notebook, click (Engineer's Notebook).

Step 6 - Synchronize BOM and Parts List, if required.

Item numbers in a BOM and the Parts List are fully associative. A change to an item number in the Assembly BOM updates in the Parts List, as shown in Figure 23–15.

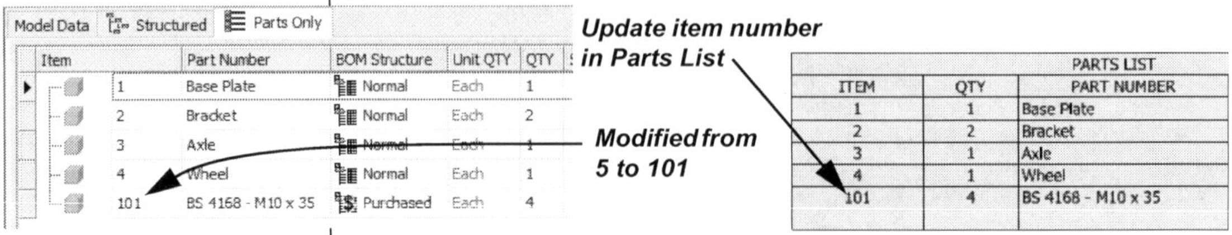

Figure 23–15

The color of static values in the Edit Parts List dialog box is blue.

- Use the **Static Value** option (shown in Figure 23–16) in the Parts List to set an override that prevents item numbers from updating if the Assembly BOM is changed.

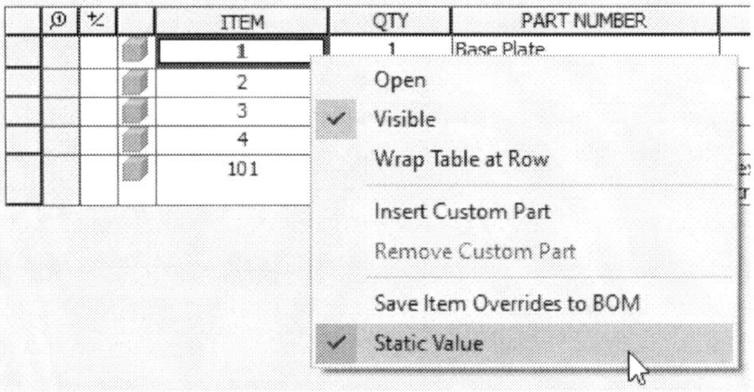

Figure 23–16

The color of locked item numbers in the Assembly BOM is gray.

- Use the **Lock Items** option (shown in Figure 23–17) in the Assembly BOM to lock an item number to prevent it from being modified in the Parts List and updating in the BOM.

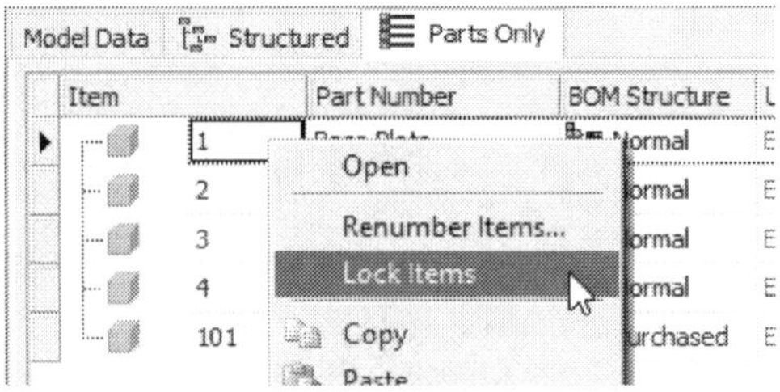

Figure 23–17

- To apply a static override from the Parts List to the BOM, in the Parts List, right-click on the item number, and select **Save Item Overrides to BOM**. If the item number is not locked, it updates and the Parts List item number is no longer static.

Practice 23a Bill of Materials

Practice Objectives

- Generate a Bill of Materials for an assembly file.
- Change the BOM Structure for purchased and phantom components in an assembly.
- Create a virtual component in an assembly to represent a purchased component.
- Customize the columns and components that are listed in the Bill of Materials.
- Output a Bill of Materials file as a unicode text file.

In this practice, you will create and customize a BOM for a mechanical arm system model. You will define a BOM structure to accurately display the list of parts for the model and output the BOM to a unicode text file.

Task 1 - Open an assembly file and generate a BOM.

1. Open **Arm System.iam** from the *BOM* folder.

2. In the *Assemble* tab>Manage panel, click 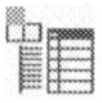 (Bill of Materials). The Bill of Materials dialog box opens as shown in Figure 23–18.

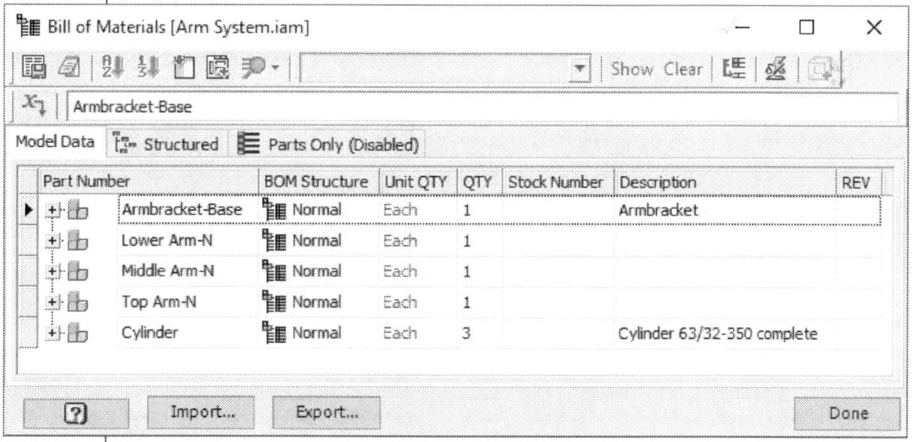

Figure 23–18

3. Review the BOM for the model. This assembly consists of several subassemblies.

Task 2 - View the Parts Only view.

By default, the Parts Only view is disabled. You must first enable the Parts Only view to display the parts list for the assembly.

1. Select the *Parts Only (Disabled)* tab.
2. Click (View Options) and select **Enable BOM View** in the drop-down list.
3. Review the list of parts in the *Parts Only* tab.

Task 3 - Change the BOM Structure.

The **Armbracket-Base** subassembly was only created to ease in its placement, it should not be listed in the BOM as an assembly. In addition, the **cylinder** assembly is going to be purchased and not manufactured.

1. Select the *Structured* tab and review the listed components.
2. Select the *Model Data* tab.
3. Double-click on the *BOM Structure* cell for the **Armbracket-Base** to edit the BOM structure.
4. Select **Phantom** in the BOM Structure drop-down list for the **Armbracket-Base**, as shown in Figure 23–19.

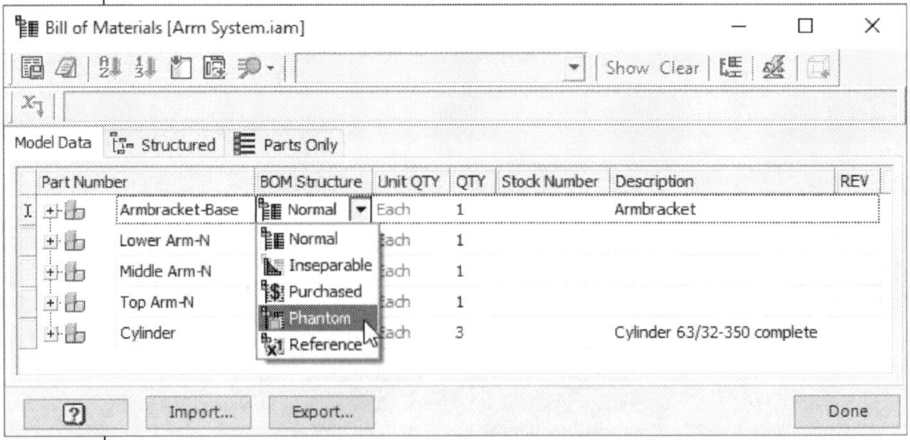

Figure 23–19

Changing the BOM Structure of the **Armbracket-base** component to **Phantom** means that all components in this assembly will be promoted to the top-level assembly, and the **Armbracket-base** subassembly will not display in the BOM.

5. Change to the *Structured* tab. Note that the components that have been promoted in the BOM have an upward arrow next to them, as shown in Figure 23–20.

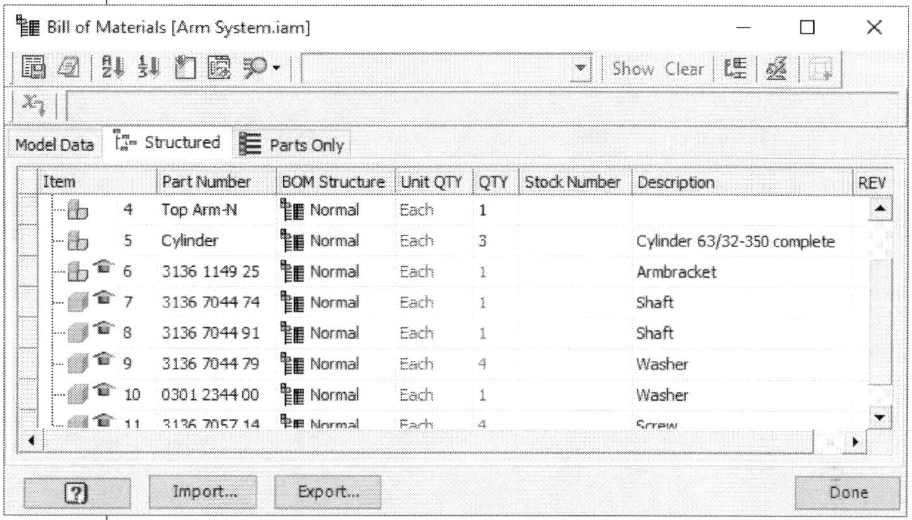

Figure 23–20

6. Select **Purchased** in the BOM Structure drop-down list for the **Cylinder**. In the structured view, the Purchased components do not change. However, in the Parts Only view, the individual parts of the **Cylinder** assembly no longer display; only the **Cylinder** assembly displays, as shown in Figure 23–21.

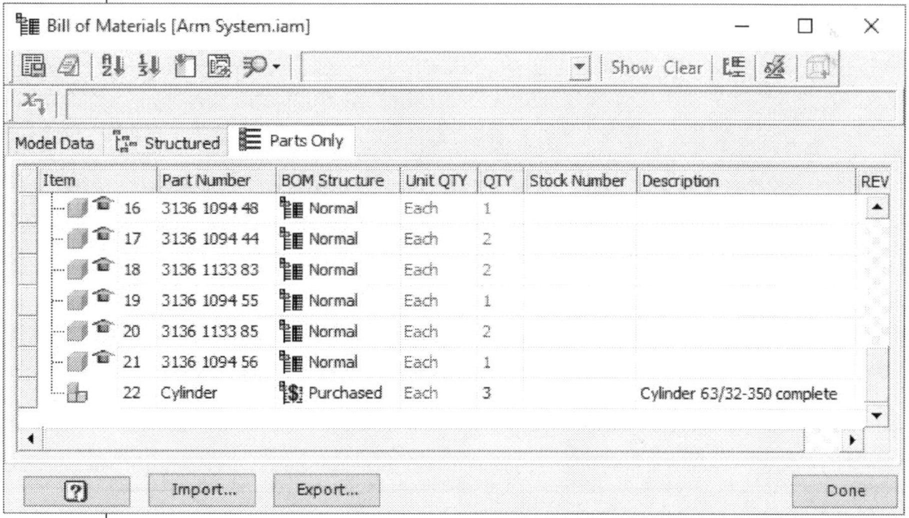

Figure 23–21

7. Click **Done** to close the dialog box.

Task 4 - Add a virtual component.

The assembly requires a certain amount of grease. This is not a physical component in the assembly but does need to be included in the BOM.

1. In the *Assemble* tab>Component panel, click (Create).
2. Create a new component called **Grease**, select **Virtual Component**, and select **Purchased** as the *Default BOM Structure*, as shown in Figure 23–22.

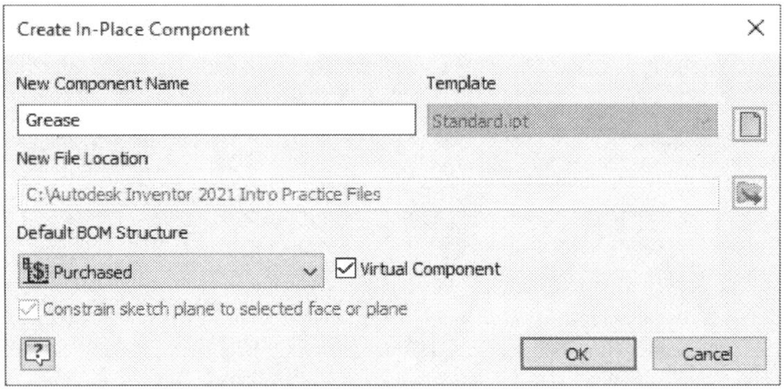

Figure 23–22

3. Click **OK**.

Task 5 - Define a Base Quantity for the virtual component.

The quantity of grease is measured in milliliters. This unit of measure must be defined using a user parameter.

1. Right-click on the **Grease** component in the Model browser and select **Component Settings**.
2. Click to open the Parameters dialog box.
3. Click **Add Numeric** in the Parameters dialog box.

4. Create a new parameter called **Base_Qty**, set the *units* to ***ml*** and the *equation* to ***1 ml***, as shown in Figure 23–23.

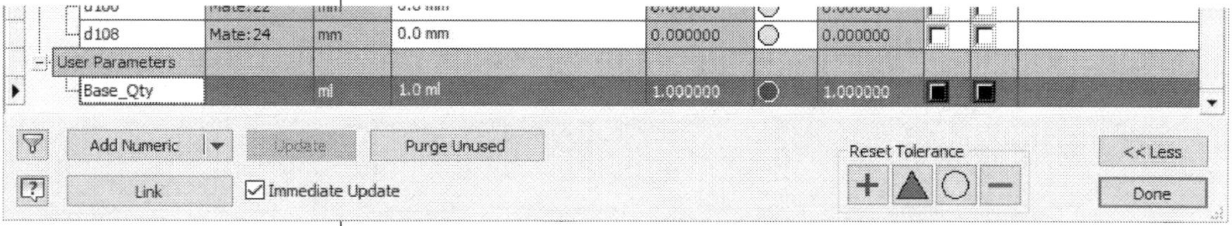

Figure 23–23

5. Click **Done** to close the Parameters dialog box.

6. In the Grease Component Settings dialog box, select **Base_Qty (1.0ml)** in the Base Quantity drop-down list, and click **OK** to close the drop-down list. The dialog box updates as shown in Figure 23–24.

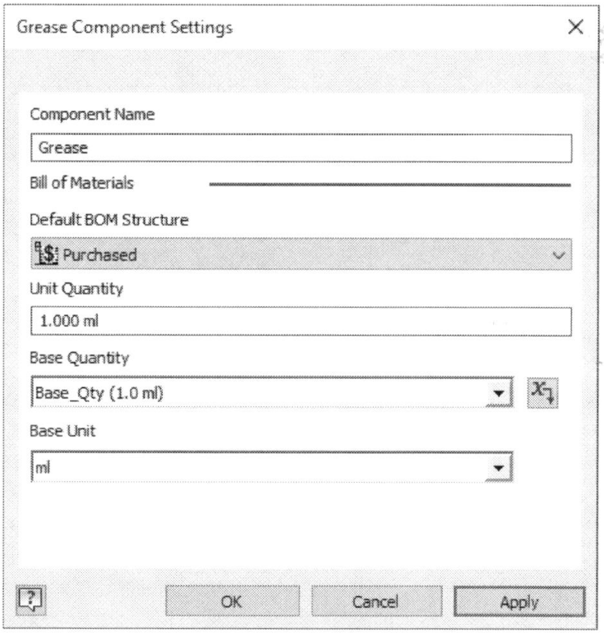

Figure 23–24

7. Click **OK** to close the Grease Component Settings dialog box.

8. In the *Assemble* tab>Manage panel, click (Bill of Materials).

9. Scroll down to display the new **Grease** component.

10. Set the *QTY* for the **Grease** component to **3 ml**, as shown in Figure 23–25.

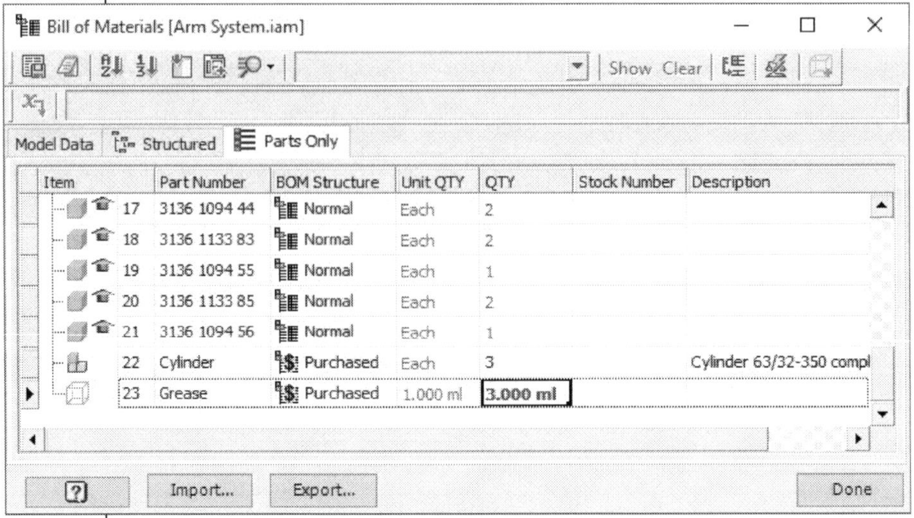

Figure 23–25

As an alternative to creating a virtual component in the Create Component dialog box, you can also click (Create Virtual Component) in the Bill of Materials dialog box to create a new virtual component. Using this alternative method, you are simply prompted for the component's name and you can define its BOM Structure directly in the dialog box. To make modifications to its Unit QTY, you must still define its Component Settings.

Task 6 - Customize the BOM.

Columns can be customized to display the required information. Columns can be added or removed. Components listed in the BOM can be sorted by any of the columns.

1. Select the *Parts Only* tab, if it is not already active.

2. Click (Choose Columns) to open the Customization dialog box.

3. Press and hold the left mouse button over the *Stock Number* column heading and drag the mouse into the customization box to remove the column from the table, as shown in Figure 23–26.

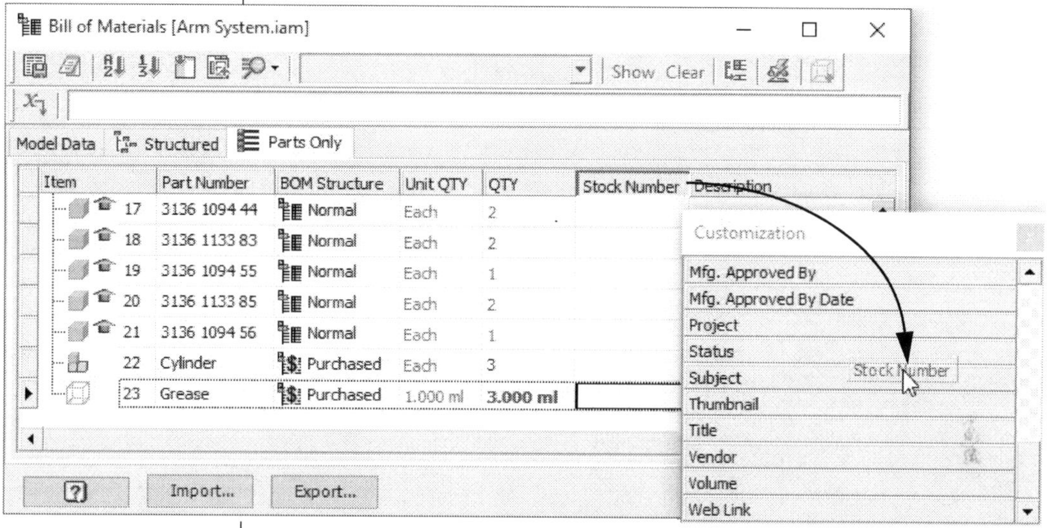

Figure 23–26

4. In the Customization box, press and hold the left mouse button on *Company* and drag and drop it over the headings in the table. Close the Customization dialog box.

5. Enter the company names for the purchased components, as shown in Figure 23–27.

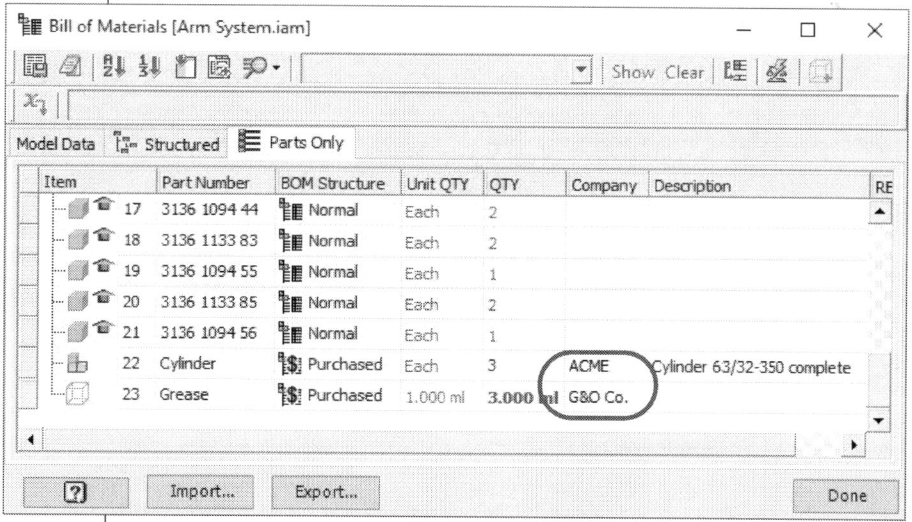

Figure 23–27

6. Select the *Part Number* heading cell to sort the BOM data by this column.

7. Click (Renumber Items). Maintain the defaults and click **OK**.

Task 7 - Output the BOM.

1. Click (Export Bill of Materials) to open the Export Bill of Materials dialog box.

2. Select **Parts Only** in the View to Export drop-down list. Click **OK** to export the BOM.

3. Select **Text (Tab delimited) (*.txt)** as the file format to which to export. Enter **Arm System BOM** as the name for the exported BOM and save the file.

4. Click **Done** to close the Bill of Materials dialog box.

5. Using the Windows Explorer, find the text file in the *BOM* folder and open it. The file displays as shown in Figure 23–28.

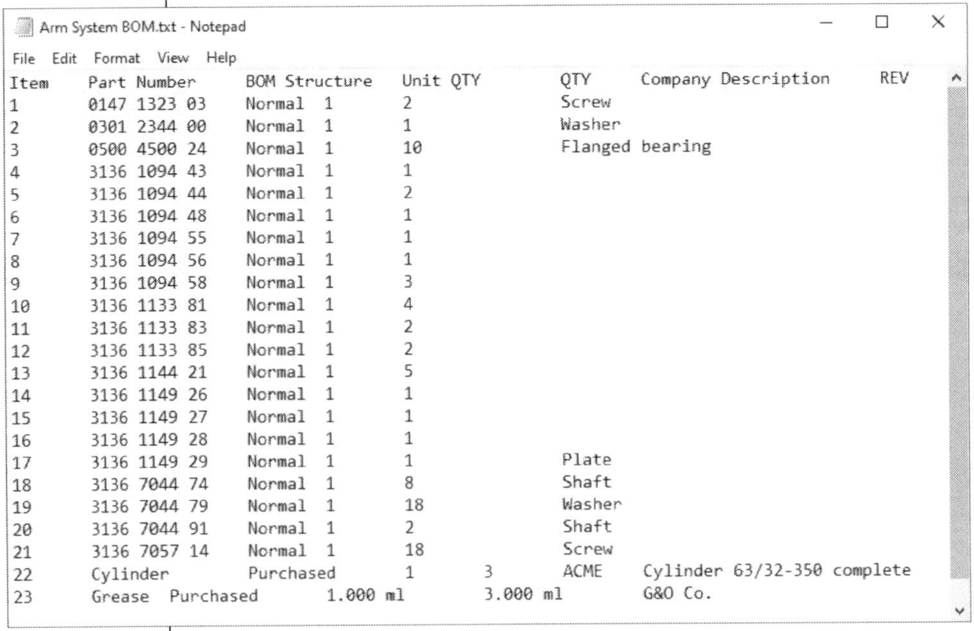

Item	Part Number	BOM Structure	Unit QTY	QTY	Company	Description	REV
1	0147 1323 03	Normal	1	2		Screw	
2	0301 2344 00	Normal	1	1		Washer	
3	0500 4500 24	Normal	1	10		Flanged bearing	
4	3136 1094 43	Normal	1	1			
5	3136 1094 44	Normal	1	2			
6	3136 1094 48	Normal	1	1			
7	3136 1094 55	Normal	1	1			
8	3136 1094 56	Normal	1	1			
9	3136 1094 58	Normal	1	3			
10	3136 1133 81	Normal	1	4			
11	3136 1133 83	Normal	1	2			
12	3136 1133 85	Normal	1	2			
13	3136 1144 21	Normal	1	5			
14	3136 1149 26	Normal	1	1			
15	3136 1149 27	Normal	1	1			
16	3136 1149 28	Normal	1	1			
17	3136 1149 29	Normal	1	1		Plate	
18	3136 7044 74	Normal	1	8		Shaft	
19	3136 7044 79	Normal	1	18		Washer	
20	3136 7044 91	Normal	1	2		Shaft	
21	3136 7057 14	Normal	1	18		Screw	
22	Cylinder	Purchased	1	3	ACME	Cylinder 63/32-350 complete	
23	Grease	Purchased	1.000 ml	3.000 ml	G&O Co.		

Figure 23–28

6. Save and close all of the open models.

Chapter Review Questions

1. Which of the following best describe the purpose of virtual components? (Select all that apply.)
   a. Virtual components are models that have been generated using the Frame Generator.
   b. Virtual components are created to represent non-geometrical parts required in the bill of materials.
   c. Virtual components can be used to represent parts you do not want to model, such as fasteners.
   d. Virtual components are models that have been placed from the Content Center.
2. The properties of a virtual component cannot be defined like a standard component is defined in a model.
   a. True
   b. False
3. Which command sequence is used to create a new virtual component while in the context of an assembly model? (Select all that apply.)
   a. *Get Started* tab>Launch panel, click .
   b. *Assemble* tab>Component panel, click .
   c. *Assemble* tab>Component panel, click .
   d. In the Bill of Material dialog box, click .
4. Fill in the Bill of Materials dialog box tab, *Model Data*, *Structured*, or *Parts Only*, with the best description of its purpose.
   a. The ______ tab displays only parts or subassemblies whose BOM Structure property has been set to **Normal**, **Purchased**, or **Inseparable**.
   b. The ______ tab displays BOM data in a tree view similar to the Model browser.
   c. The ______ tab displays components based on their BOM Structure property.

5. Which of the following views can be used to display data in the Parts List? (Select all that apply.)
   a. Model Data view
   b. Structured view
   c. Parts Only view
6. The numbering format (e.g., from 1, 2, 3, etc., to A, B, C, etc.) cannot be changed in the Bill of Materials and can only be changed when placed as a Parts List in a drawing.
   a. True
   b. False
7. Fill in the BOM Structure type, **Normal**, **Inseparable**, **Purchased**, **Phantom**, or **Reference**, with the best description of its purpose.
   a. A _______ component is an assembly that must be physically damaged to be taken apart.
   b. A _______ component is used to simplify the design. They are often used to ease in placement of components.
   c. A _______ component is used in the construction of the assembly but is not part of the actual design.
   d. A _______ component is used if the component is acquired instead of fabricated.
   e. A _______ component is the default status for a component.
8. Which of the following statements are true regarding synchronizing the Bill of Materials (BOM) and Parts List? (Select all that apply.)
   a. Item numbers in a BOM and the Parts List are fully associative. A change to an item number in the Assembly BOM through the BOM Editor results in an automatic update in the Parts List.
   b. Item numbers in a BOM are not fully associative with the balloons that are displayed in a drawing. Delete and recreate if the numbers have changed.
   c. Static overrides can be set for individual item numbers in the Parts List to prevent them from updating if changes are made in the Assembly BOM.

Command Summary

Button	Command	Location
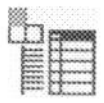	**Bill of Materials**	• **Ribbon:** *Assemble* tab>Manage panel • **Ribbon:** *Manage* tab>Manage panel
	**Create Component**	• **Ribbon:** *Assemble* tab>Component panel • **Context Menu:** In Model graphics window

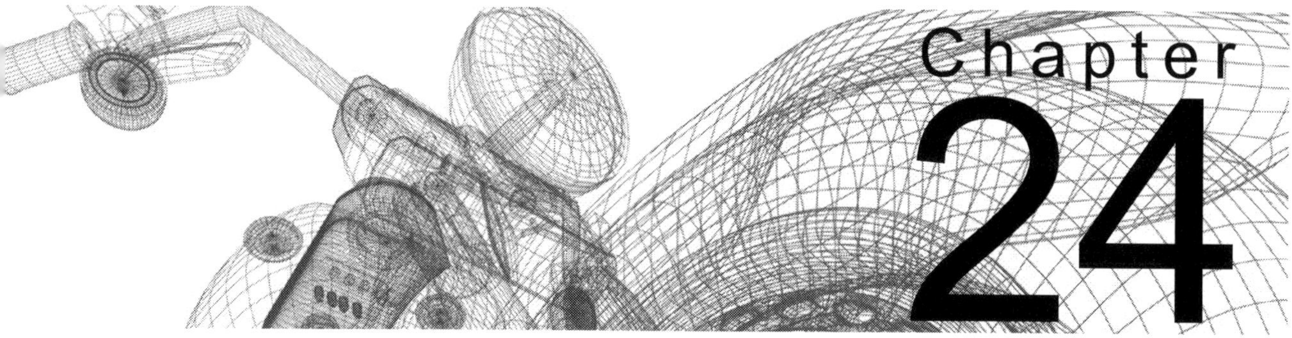

Chapter 24

Working with Projects

When working with assemblies in the Autodesk® Inventor® software, you need to access and manage multiple part, drawing, subassembly, and presentation files. If you work as part of a design team, managing access to the shared data becomes crucial. Project files enable you to organize and access these files.

Learning Objectives in This Chapter

- Activate a project file in an Autodesk Inventor session.
- Create new project files for use with your current working environment.
- Use the Resolve Link dialog box to locate, substitute, or ignore missing files.

24.1 Project Files

A Project file is used to organize and provide access to all files associated with a specific design project. You can create multiple project files as required to manage all of your work.

The project file (.IPJ) is a text file. It assigns a default project location for the files in the project and maintains all of the required links between files. Among other options, a project file also specifies who can access the files, and which libraries to access. When you open a model, the paths specified in the active project are searched to find all of the referenced files.

Project files are managed in the Project dialog box. Use one of the following methods to open the Project dialog box:

- **File** menu>**Manage**, and then select **Projects.**
- Click  (Projects) in the *Get Started* tab.
- Click **Projects** in the Open or Create New File dialog boxes.

All previously loaded project files are listed at the top of the The Projects dialog box. The active project is identified with a checkmark adjacent to its name. When you select a project, its details display in the Project Tree in the lower area of the dialog box, as shown in Figure 24–1.

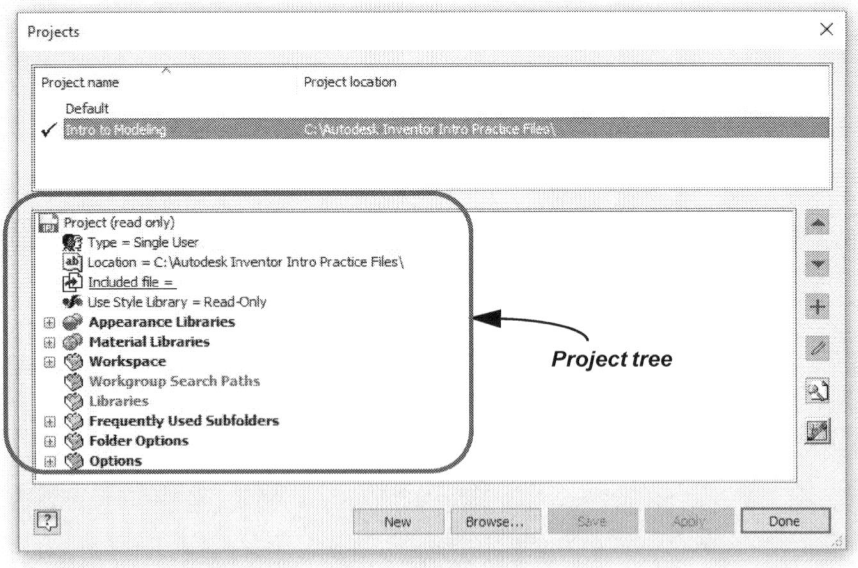

Figure 24–1

Activating a Project File

Any of the projects listed at the top of the Projects dialog box have been previously loaded and can be activated. To activate a project, ensure that all file(s) are closed and then use one of the following methods:

- Double-click on a project name at the top of the Projects dialog box.
- Select the name of the project at the top of the Projects dialog box and click **Apply**.
- Double-click on the project name in the *Project* area of the *My Home* tab.

Loading a Project File

To add an existing project file to the list of available projects, right-click and select **Browse**, or click **Browse** at the bottom of the dialog box and navigate to and select an existing .IPJ file. Once loaded, it becomes the currently active file.

Creating a New Project File

How To: Create a New Project File

1. Click **New** at the bottom of the Projects dialog box or right-click anywhere in the top area of the Projects dialog box and select **New**. The Inventor project wizard dialog box opens as shown in Figure 24–2.

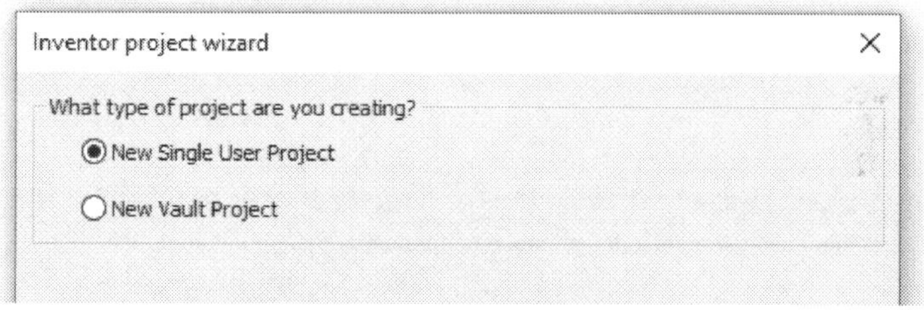

Figure 24–2

If Autodesk ®Vault® is not installed, only a Single User project type can be created.

- The **New Vault Project** type ensures files are stored in a vault and are never accessed directly. They can only be accessed through an Autodesk Vault installation. The vault maintains version history and other file attributes.
- The **New Single User Project** type stores all design files in a personal workspace or local paths that are only accessible to the user.

2. Click **Next**.

3. Enter the project name and home folder (workspace), as shown in Figure 24–3.

The Inventor project wizard might vary, depending on the type of project you are creating.

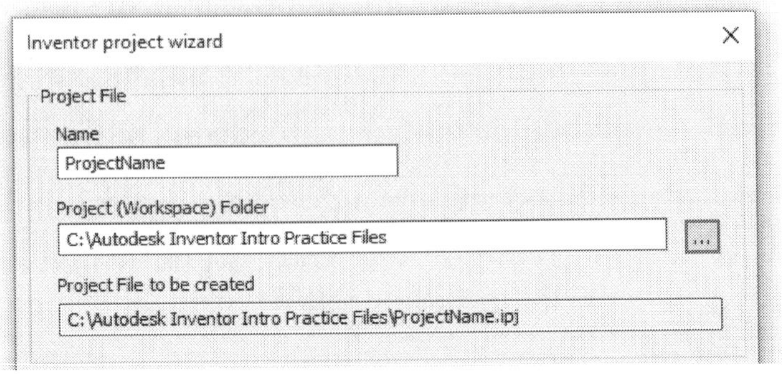

Figure 24–3

- The project file (.IPJ) is stored in this home folder. The project filename and path are automatically determined based on the name and folder specified.

4. Click **Next**.
5. Define the library paths using the Inventor project wizard window.
   - Library paths in existing projects are listed in the *All Projects* area on the left. Library paths that are added to the new file are listed in the *New Project* area on the right. Use the **Arrow** icons to add or remove libraries from the new project. The *Library Location* field displays the path for the selected library.
6. Click **Finish** to create the project and return to the Projects dialog box.
7. Modify the Project Tree options to customize the project file, as required.
8. Click **Done** to close the Projects dialog box. The new project becomes the active project.

The Project Tree options are described later this topic.

Project Tree Customization

The project tree enables you to customize specifics on the project using the categories shown in Figure 24–4.

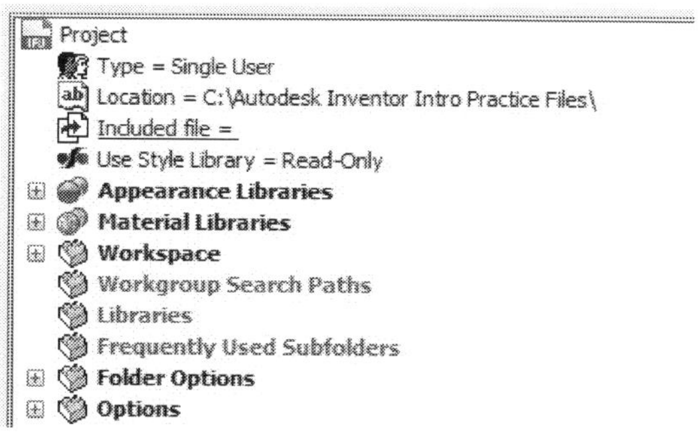

Figure 24–4

The categories that can be customized are as follows:

- The *Included File* setting enables you to add another project file so that path information in both projects can be combined. The included file typically defines the shared workgroup or library paths. To add a file, right-click on the node and select **Edit** or click  and browse to and select a file.
- The *Use Style Library* setting defines whether the style library is **Read-Only** or **Read-Write**, controlling whether a designer can make changes to the library. To set this option, right-click on its node and select the required permission setting.
- The *Appearance Libraries* and *Material Libraries* settings (shown in Figure 24–5) enable you to specify the default Appearance and Material Libraries that are initially opened. Additional libraries can be explicitly opened later. To set the default library, expand its node, right-click on the library and select **Active Library**. To load a new library, right-click on the parent node and select **Add Library** or click . The Inventor Material Library is set as default.

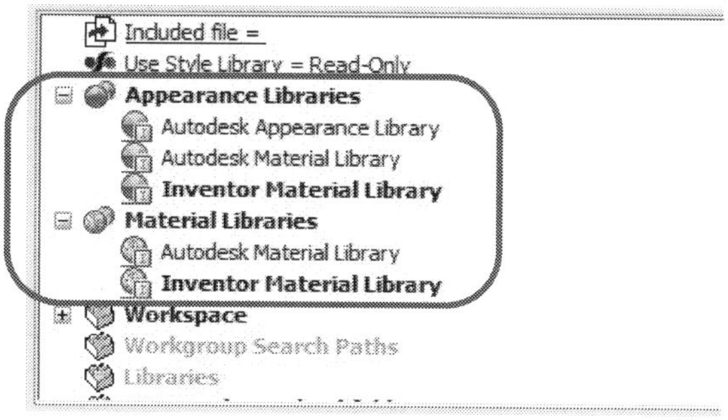

Figure 24–5

Only one Workspace can be set in a project file.

- The *Workspace*, *Workgroup Search Paths*, and *Libraries* categories specify locations for new files, files on a server/network drive, or the location of typically non-edited standard and custom parts, respectively. Additionally the *Frequently Used Subfolders* category can be used to add shortcuts to commonly used folders. To add libraries, right-click on the node and select **Add Path** or click +. Note the following when setting library paths:

Additional options for adding paths are available on the shortcut menu when selecting any of the path categories.

  - Library paths are searched first. Use the ▲ and ▼ arrows to reorder the paths.
  - Parts placed from a library have a special tag. When searching, the software reads the tag to obtain the path. If no tag exists, the library is not searched.
  - Libraries can be added to a new project from other projects.
  - Libraries should not be renamed, to maintain existing references.
  - Since standard parts are not intended to change, parts in libraries cannot be edited.
  - Any part created or placed in a library folder is considered a library part and cannot be edited in the project.
  - Click to configure the Content Center Libraries.
- The *Folder Options* category enables you to assign locations for design data, templates, and content center files that might be required when working in a project.
- Additional customization for a project can be made using the *Options* category in the project tree, as shown in Figure 24–6. These options enable you to control such things as the number of previous versions stored in the *OldVersions* folder, whether or not files in a project have unique names, identifies the project owner, etc.

For more information on the Options refer to the Help documentation.

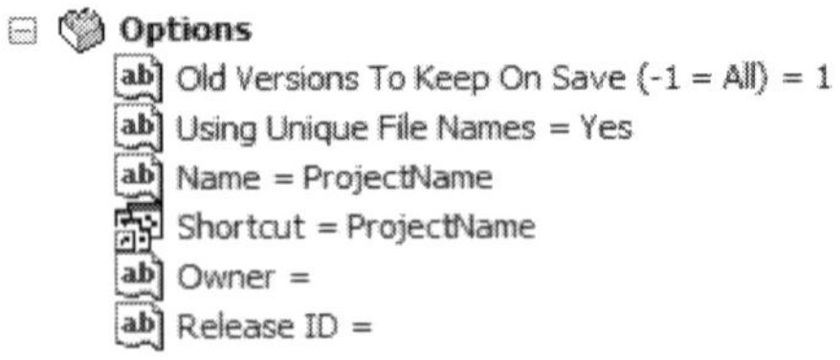

Figure 24–6

Search Sequence

When you open a file, the system searches through the project's Search Paths for referenced components in the following order: Library Paths (1), Workspace (2), Workgroup Search Paths (3), and the folder containing the file to be opened (4).

The search sequence flow chart is shown in Figure 24–7.

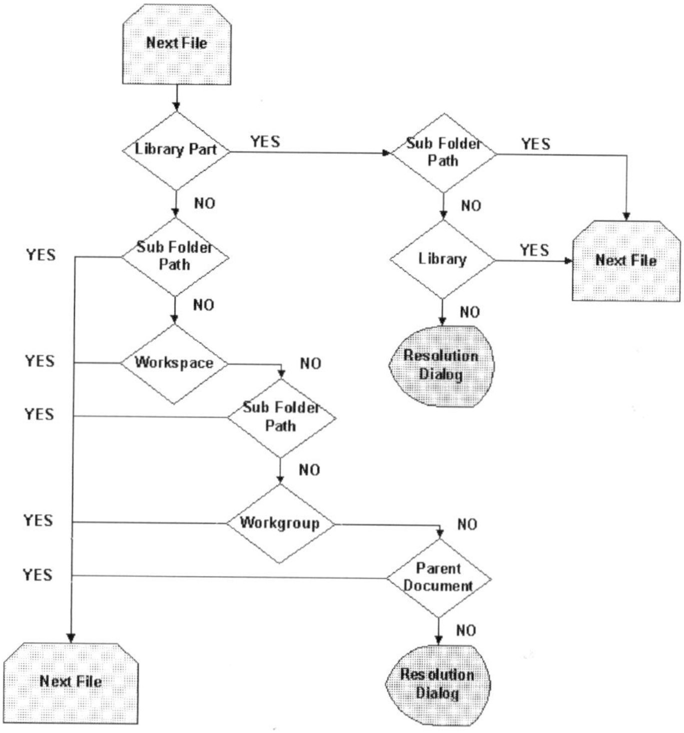

Figure 24–7

Note the following about the search sequence:

- When multiple paths are in a category, the order of listing determines the search order. Use the ▲ and ▼ arrows to reorder the paths.
- If files are found with the same name in multiple paths, the first file found is used.
- Paths can be added after a project has been started, but starting with the appropriate list helps avoid unresolved links.
- In general, the fewer search paths the better. For optimal performance, use a single workspace or workgroup location (plus libraries) per project, with relative paths (subfolders). This speeds file resolution and makes moving data easier.

Hint: Working with Subfolders

Note the following about subfolders:

- Do not define the subfolders of a project location as separate locations in the project. This causes file resolution problems that display red in the project's dialog box.
- When placing assembly components from a subfolder, the subfolder path (relative path) is saved as part of the assembly. When opening the assembly, the system combines the project's search location with this relative path to find components.
- Components moved into subfolders cannot be located because a relative subfolder path was not stored with the assembly. Use the Resolve Link dialog box to fix the failure.
- A flat directory structure (few subfolders) increases loading speed.

24.2 Resolving Links

If a referenced file cannot be found in the search paths of the active project, the Resolve Link dialog box opens as shown in Figure 24–8. Use this dialog box to find the referenced file, to substitute another file, or to ignore the missing file.

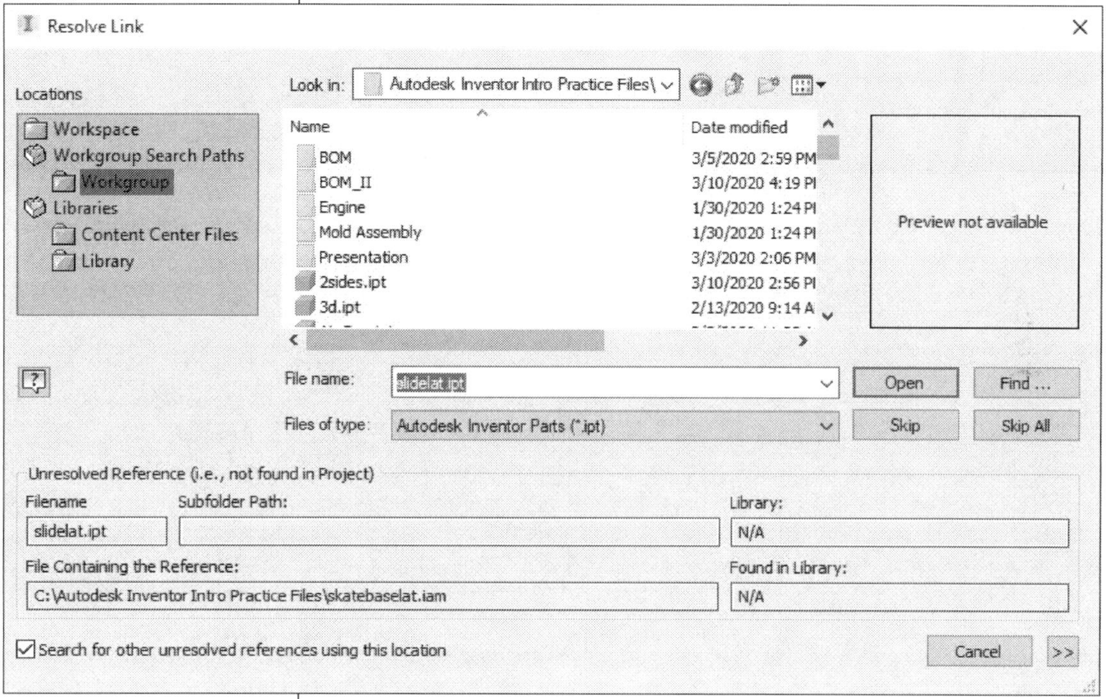

Figure 24–8

The Resolve Link dialog box displays the file location, folder, and file format. The operations on the right side of the dialog box are described as follows:

Open	Opens a selected file that will resolve the failure. You can also double-click on the name of the file to open it.
Find...	Opens the Find dialog box, which enables you to search for a file based on selected criteria. 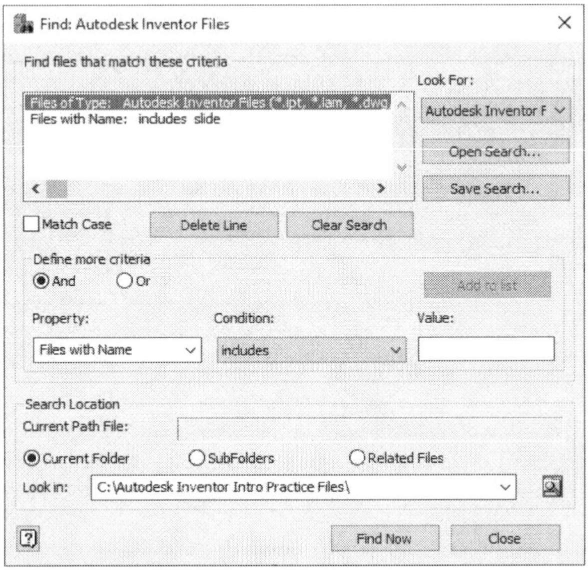
Skip	Skips the unresolved file and goes to the next file. The skipped file does not display in the assembly and any updates that depend on the unresolved component do not solve until the missing link is resolved. You can later replace the component in the assembly or resolve the link by right-clicking on the assembly name at the top of the Model browser and selecting **Resolve File**. 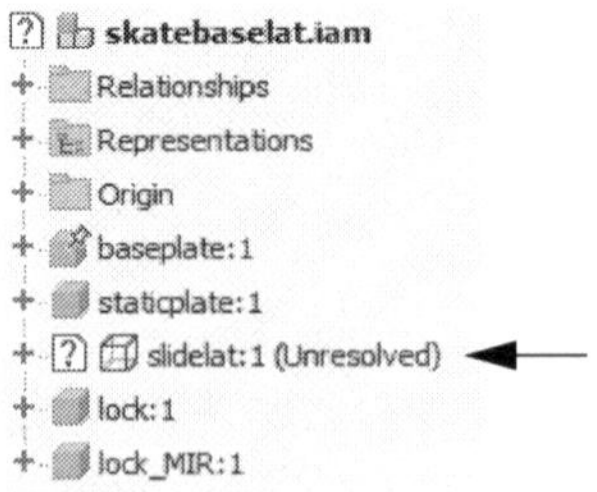 ***Model browser displays unresolved component and any dependent constraints with a question mark***
Skip All	Skips all unresolved files. All failed files display in the Model browser with a question mark icon and each should be individually resolved as described for individually skipped files.

The *Unresolved Reference* area in the Resolve Link dialog box displays information about the component that is not resolved (e.g., filename, path, etc.), as shown in Figure 24–9.

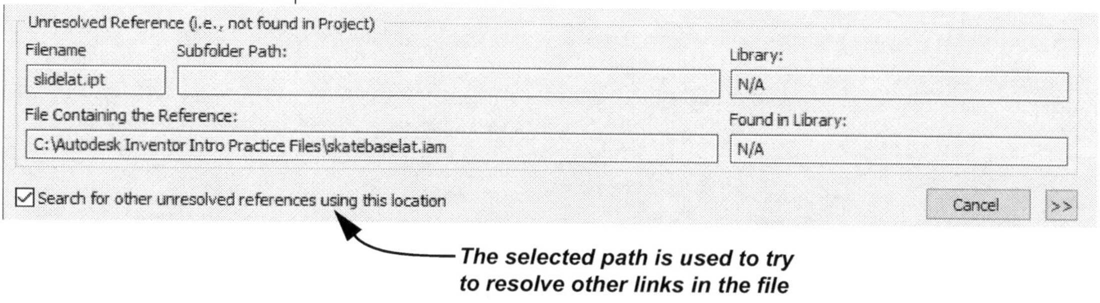

Figure 24–9

The file might be missing for the following reasons:

- The file no longer exists in the active project search paths.
- The file has been renamed outside context of its parent model.
- The file has been moved to another library or subfolder.
- There are network or server complications.

If the file that you select to resolve the link is in the project locations or their subfolders and you save the host file, the link is automatically resolved the next time you open the host file. If the file you select is not in the defined project location, you need to resolve the link each time you open the host file. To avoid this, the unresolved file(s) should be moved to one of the project search locations, or the project should be modified to include the file location.

Practice 24a Creating a Project File

Practice Objectives

- Create a new project that assigns and modifies various categories in the project file.
- Resolve a link for a missing assembly file in the project.

In this practice, you will create a new project file and resolve a link in the project.

Task 1 - Create a project file.

*Alternatively, in the **File** menu>**Manage**, select **Projects** to open the Projects dialog box.*

1. Ensure that all files are closed in the current session prior to starting this practice. Projects cannot be set with files open.
2. In the *Get Started* tab>Launch panel, click (Projects) or in the Open dialog box, click **Projects**. The Projects dialog box opens with the active project displayed with a checkmark to the left of its name.
3. Right-click in the top section of the dialog box and select **New** or click **New** at the bottom of the dialog box. The Inventor project wizard opens.
4. Select **New Single User Project** and click **Next**.
5. Enter **Your_Name** in the *Name* field.
6. Click next to the *Project (Workspace) Folder* field. In the Browse For Folder dialog box, browse to the directory in which your training files are located.
7. Click **OK** to close the Browse For Folder dialog box.
8. Click **Finish** to create the project. The **<Your_Name>** project displays in the Projects dialog box.

Task 2 - Assign workspace and libraries to the project file.

1. A checkmark displays next to the active project name. Double-click on **<Your_Name>** in the upper area of the dialog box to activate it, if not active. The lower area of the dialog box displays, as shown in Figure 24–10.

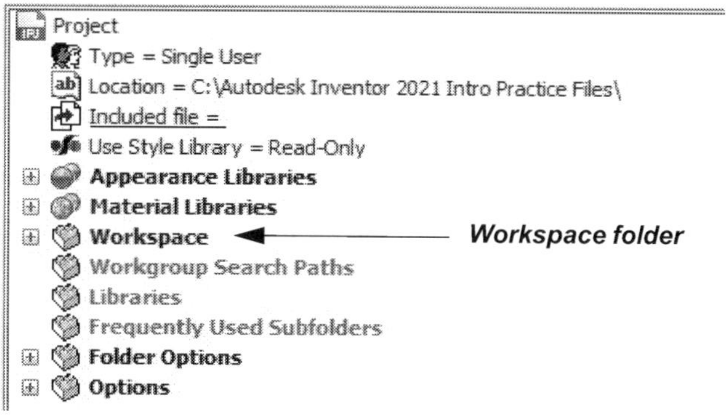

Figure 24–10

2. Expand the **Workspace** category in the project tree area.
3. Select the **Workspace** node, right-click, and select **Edit**.

The temp directory is only assigned for this practice. Normally, project files would use a well-defined folder structure.

4. Click and browse to the *C:\Temp* directory, or click **Make New Folder** to create the directory if it does not already exist.
5. Click **OK** to close the Browse For Folder dialog box.
6. Press <Enter> to apply the changes.
7. Select **Workgroup Search Paths** in the project tree area, right-click and select **Add Path**.
8. Click . Browse to your practice files directory. Delete the **Workgroup** node name in the path, if displayed.
9. Click **OK** to close the Browse For Folder dialog box.
10. Press <Enter> to apply the changes.
11. Select **Libraries** in the project tree area, right-click, and select **Add Path**.
12. Click . Navigate to and select the following folder:
    - *C:\Users\Public\Documents\Autodesk\Inventor 2021\Catalog*
13. Select the software's *Catalog* folder in the Browse For Folder dialog box.
14. Click **OK** in the Browse For Folder dialog box.

15. Press <Enter> to apply the changes. The project tree should display similar to that shown in Figure 24–11.

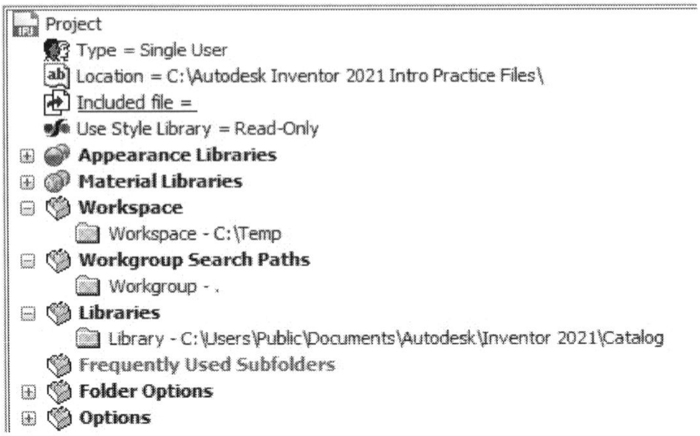

Figure 24–11

16. Expand the *Options* folder and select **Old Version To Keep On Save**.

17. Click  on the right side of the project tree. You can also select the option a second time to edit its value.

18. Enter **2** in the field that displays and press <Enter>. This option controls the number of previous versions of the file to keep after a save operation. The default is one.

19. Click **Save** at the bottom of the dialog box to save your changes to the project.

20. Click **Done** to close the Projects dialog box.

21. Open the *My Home* tab and scroll through the list of projects. Note that the **<Your_Name>** project that was just created is the active project. The *My Home* tab can be used to activate existing projects but cannot be used to create a new project.

Task 3 - Open an assembly and resolve the link.

1. Select **Open** in the **File** menu, *Get Started* tab, or Quick Access Toolbar.

2. Select **Workgroup** to switch to the *C:\Autodesk Inventor 2021 Intro Practice Files* path. The Open dialog box opens as shown in Figure 24–12.

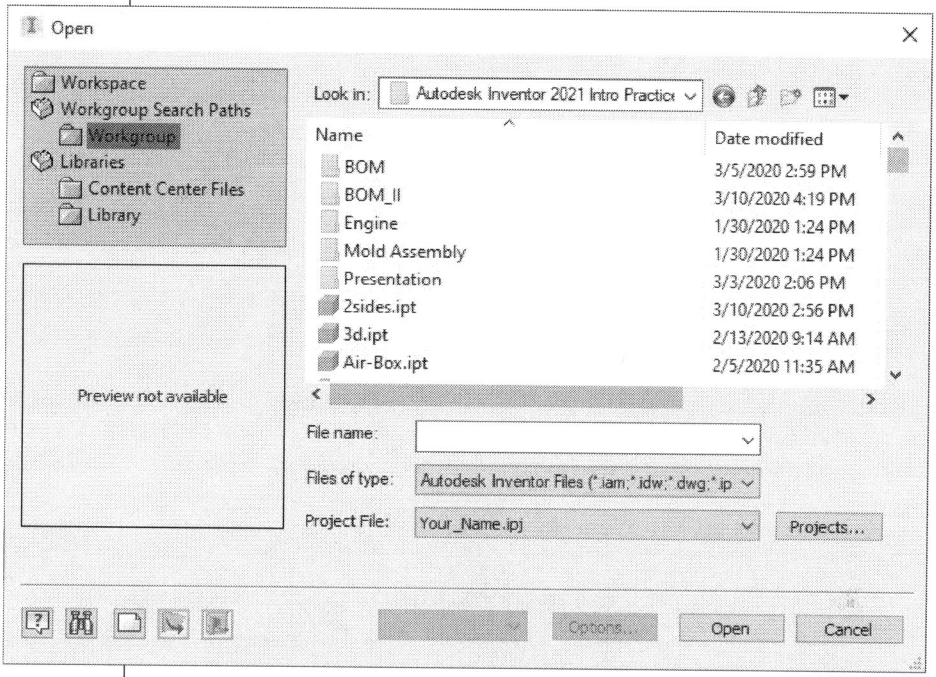

Figure 24–12

3. Select and open **skatebaselat.iam**. The Resolve Link dialog box opens and indicates that the **slidelat.ipt** part could not be found. For now, click **Skip** and continue opening the assembly.

4. A warning box displays explaining that you can work in assemblies with unresolved components. However, updates that depend on the unresolved component will not solve until components are resolved. Click **OK**.

5. The assembly displays in the graphics window. Note the missing part (**slidelat**) displays the icon, as shown in Figure 24–13, indicating that the part definition is missing.

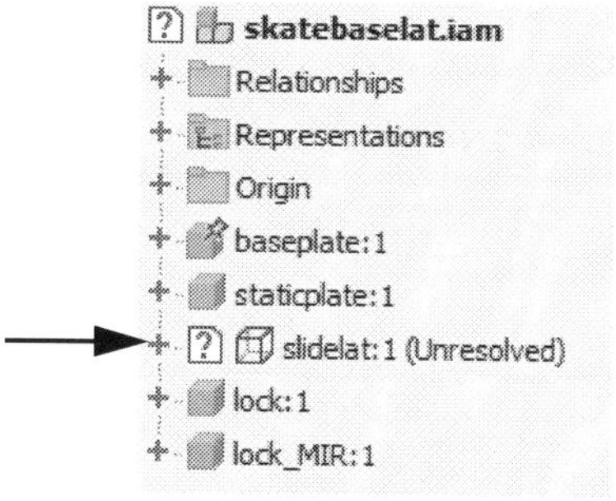

Figure 24–13

6. Right-click on **skatebaselat.iam** in the Model browser and select **Resolve File**.
7. The Resolve Link dialog box opens. Click **Find**. The Find dialog box opens.
8. Select **Files with Name** in the Property drop-down list. Select **includes** in the Condition drop-down list. Enter **slide** in the *Value* field. Click **Add to List**.
9. Set the *Look in* folder to your course directory if not already set. The Find dialog box opens as shown in Figure 24–14.

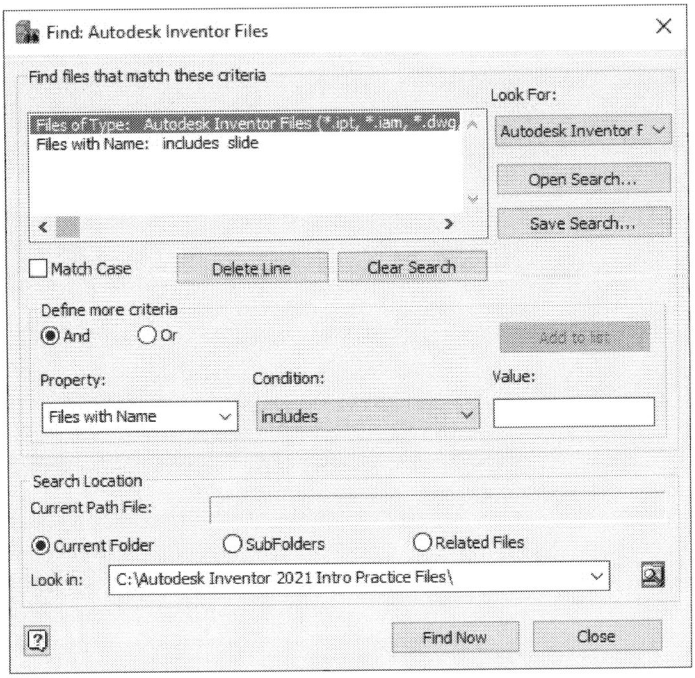

Figure 24–14

10. Click **Find Now** to perform the search. The Autodesk Inventor Files Found dialog box opens as shown in Figure 24–15, indicating that files were found.

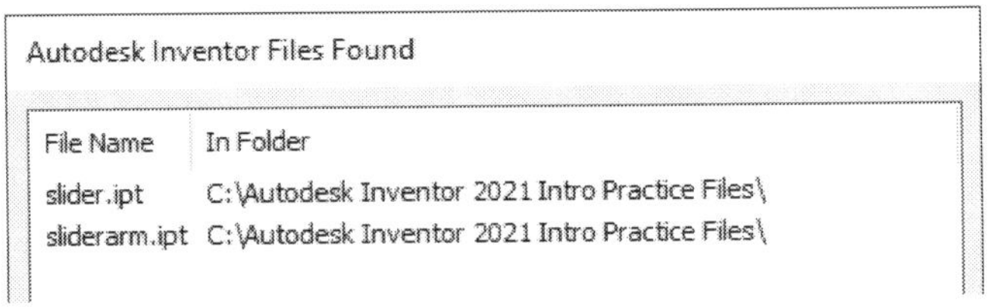

Figure 24–15

11. Select **slider.ipt** in the list and click **OK**.

12. Close the Find dialog box. The assembly displays in the graphics window, as shown in Figure 24–16. Note that the filename in the Model browser is now displayed correctly. The assembly has been reoriented for clarity.

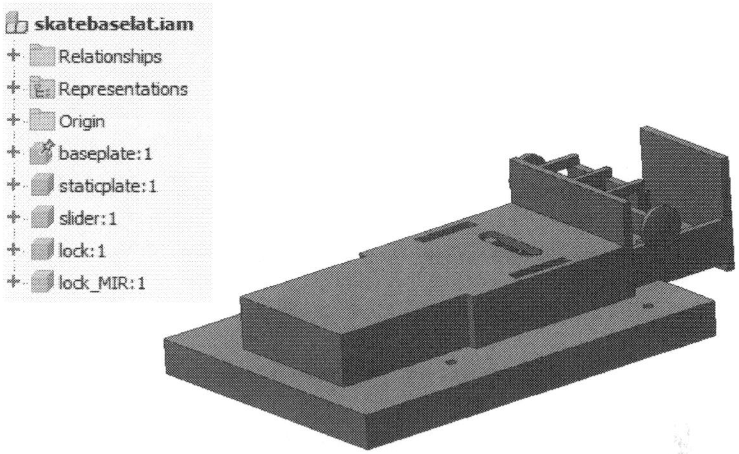

Figure 24–16

13. Save the assembly and close the window.

Chapter Review Questions

1. What is the primary purpose of Projects in the Autodesk Inventor software? (Select all that apply.)
   a. To set default templates for new files.
   b. To manage file locations and links between related files.
   c. To control default text styles, dimension format, etc.
   d. To define a search sequence for the projects folders.

2. You can change the active project while an Autodesk Inventor file is open.
   a. True
   b. False

3. Which file extension is used to store the information in a project file?
   a. .IPT
   b. .IPN
   c. .IPJ
   d. .IPK

4. Which command sequence is used to open the Projects dialog box? (Select all that apply.)
   a. *Get Started* tab>Launch panel, click .
   b. In the Create New File dialog box, select **Projects**.
   c. In the Open dialog box, select **Projects**.
   d. **File** menu>**Manage** and click .
   e. In the *Tools* tab>Options panel, click .

5. Which of the following can be customized in the Project tree to create an Autodesk Inventor Project file? (Select all that apply.)
   a. Project's directory location.
   b. Model names that reference the Project file.
   c. Library locations.
   d. Active Material library.
   e. Default Material setting.
   f. Template folder location.
   g. Number of versions to keep when saving.
   h. Content Center folder location.
6. All of the missing links must be resolved to open and edit an assembly.
   a. True
   b. False
7. When a component in an assembly is missing during retrieval, what actions can be done to resolve the failure? (Select all that apply.)
   a. Open an alternate file to replace the failed file.
   b. Skip the failed file.
   c. Delete the failed file.
   d. Find the failed file.

Command Summary

Button	Command	Location
	**Projects**	• **Ribbon:** *Get Started* tab>Launch panel • **Dialog Box:** Open • **Dialog Box:** New • **File Menu:** Manage

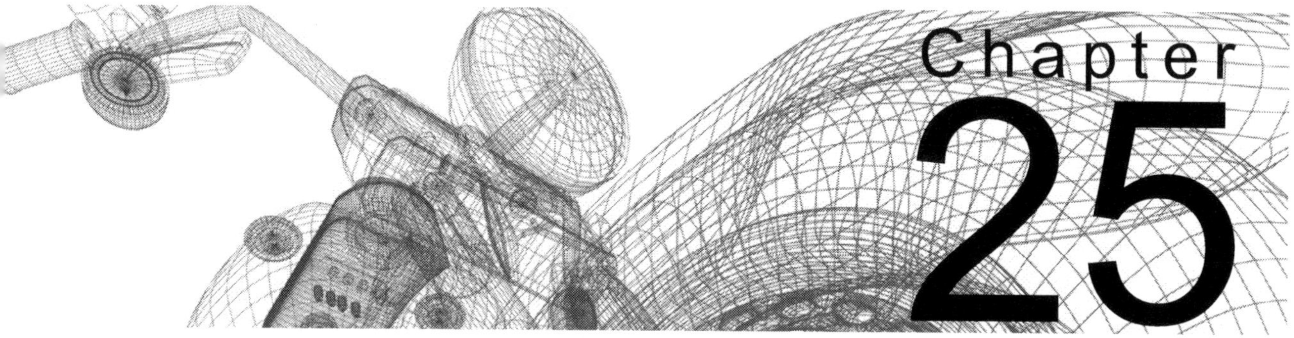

Drawing Basics

A drawing file is used to document the 3D geometry that is created in either part or assembly models in a 2D format. To begin creating a drawing, you must select and add drawing views that best communicate how the 3D geometry is to be created. Learning how to create and select the view types (e.g., base, projected, or section) enables you to efficiently create accurate drawings of your models.

Learning Objectives in This Chapter

- Create a new drawing based on a drawing template.
- Identify and add the available view types to a drawing file to appropriately document model geometry.
- Delete and Suppress drawing views.
- Edit existing drawing views to change the properties that were defined during view creation.
- Replace a current drawing model with an alternate model.

25.1 Creating a New Drawing

Once your part or assembly has been designed, the next step is to create a 2D drawing. The shape, dimensions, and orientation of the parts or assemblies have already been defined in Part or Assembly mode. A drawing file is where this information is taken to create the required views. The components are not actually contained in a drawing file. There is a link between the drawing file and the source model (e.g., part, assembly, or presentation file). If a change is made to the source model, all drawing views that reference it automatically update.

You can save an .IDW file as .DWG or save a .DWG as .IDW, if required.

The Autodesk® Inventor® software supports the .IDW and .DWG drawing file extensions. Files with an .IDW extension are native files and are typically used for documenting files. Files with a .DWG extension are typically used if the drawing is going be viewed by downstream users (shop personnel, managers, customers, etc.) using the AutoCAD® software.

*You can also open the New File dialog box by clicking (New) in the Quick Access Toolbar or in the **File** menu.*

The first step in creating a drawing is to start a new file based on a drawing template. This can be done using any of the following methods:

- Select the *My Home* tab in the graphics window and click (Drawing). The drawing template that is assigned as the default is automatically used to create the drawing. Use the (Configure Template) options in the *New* area to review and change the default template.
- In the *Get Started* tab>Launch panel, click (New). In the Create New File dialog box, select a .DWG or .IDW template from the *Drawing* area and click **Create**. If the selected template has any sheet formats assigned to it, they will be listed vertically along the right-hand side of the dialog box. Select a sheet format or simply leave the Use Template option selected at the top of the list to create the drawing with an empty sheet.
- Click **File** menu>**New**. In the expanded list, you can choose to create a drawing using the default template with sheet format, or click **New** to access the Create New File dialog box to select a template and subsequent sheet format.

.IDW files do not have the AutoCAD Blocks drawing resource. .DWG files are transferable with the AutoCAD software and are the preferred file format.

Once a new drawing is created the drawing environment displays with the following:

- The *Place Views* tab is active, by default, in a new drawing. It contains tools to create drawing views, sheets, and drafting views.
- The Model browser contains a *Drawing Resources* folder that contains sheet formats, borders, title blocks, sketched symbols, and AutoCAD blocks.

The five drawing resources are described as follows:

<table>
<tr><td>Sheet Formats</td><td>Displays the default formats in the selected drawing template file. These formats can contain title blocks, borders, and views.
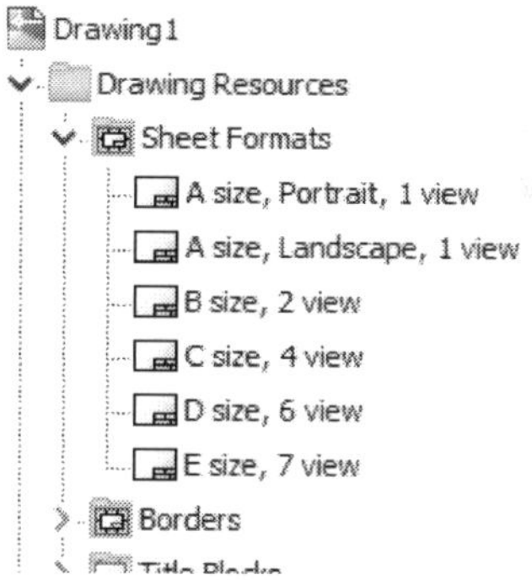
</td></tr>
<tr><td>Borders</td><td>Displays the default border and any user-defined borders.</td></tr>
<tr><td>Title Blocks</td><td>Displays the default and user-defined title blocks. It tabulates information about the drawing (e.g., drawing name).
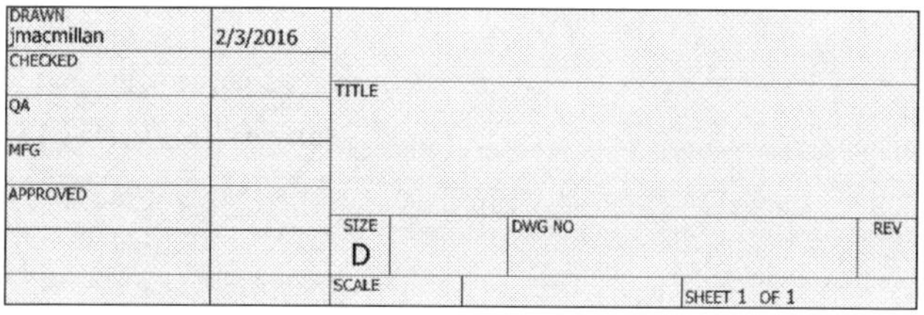
</td></tr>
<tr><td>Sketched Symbols</td><td>Displays 2D symbols that can be added to a drawing file.</td></tr>
<tr><td>AutoCAD Blocks</td><td>Only available for DWG files. Lists any blocks added to the DWG file in the AutoCAD software. AutoCAD blocks cannot be created in the Autodesk Inventor software, but can be inserted into the current sheet.</td></tr>
</table>

25.2 Base and Projected Views

The first view in a drawing is called the *base* view. It is used as the reference view when placing any additional views that are used to document the drawing model.

Base Views

How To: Create the Base View

1. In the Create panel, click (Base). The Drawing View dialog box opens as shown in Figure 25–1.

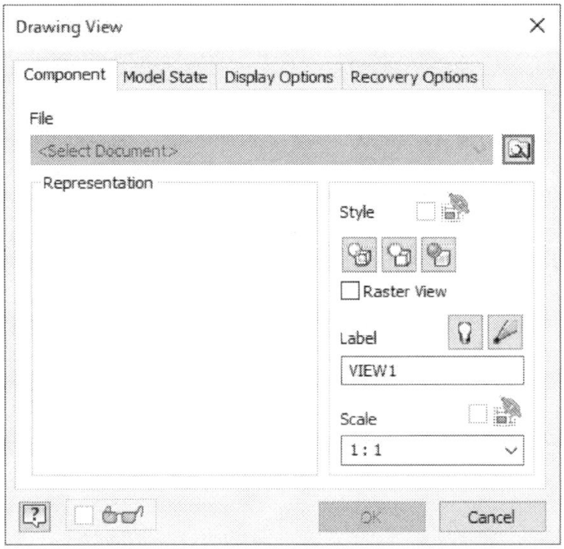

Figure 25–1

2. If a model was active when the drawing was created it is automatically set as the drawing model in the *File* area. If no model is listed in the *File* area, or if you want to change it, click browse ( ) and select a model to use in the drawing. Alternatively, you can use (Find) to locate a file to use in the drawing

> **Hint: Temporary Base View Position**
>
> As soon as a model is assigned in the Drawing View dialog box a base view is placed in a temporary position on the drawing sheet. You might be required to move the Drawing View dialog box so that it doesn't interfere with the drawing sheet.

specifies that the drawing updates if changes are made in the referenced model or assembly.

3. In the *Representation* area, select as required.
   - For part and assembly models, you can select a Design View, Position, or Level of Detail representations that should be used in the drawing view.
   - For a presentation file, you can select a snaphot view and whether to display the components trails.
4. Assign the visual display style for the new view. The style options are available in the *Style* area and enable you to set the view display as hidden line ( ) or no hidden line ( ). Additionally you can set the view as shaded by toggling the (Shaded) option.
5. Select **Raster View** to create the base view so that it remains a raster view once placed.

in the Scale and Styles area sets the scale and display style of a dependent view to be the same as its parent view.

6. Select (Toggle Label Visibility) in the *Label* area to display the view name and scale value below the drawing view, if required.
7. Set the scale of the view in the *Scale* area.
8. (Optional) Use the *Model State* and *Display Options* tabs to further customize the display of the view. Click in the Drawing View dialog box to obtain Help on these additional display options.
9. Hover the cursor over the temporary base view to display the manipulators for the drawing view. A temporary base view is shown in Figure 25–2.

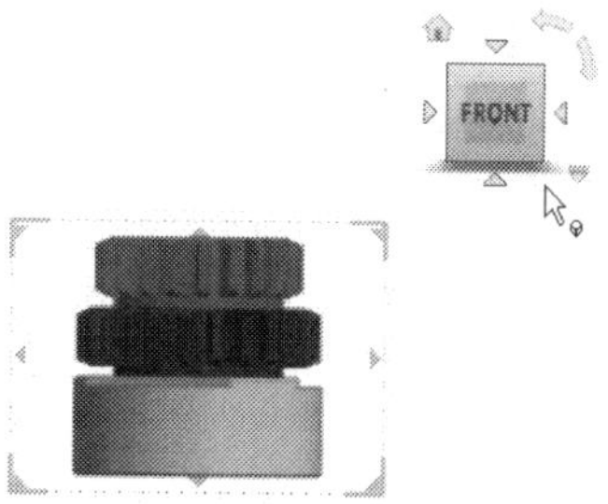

Figure 25–2

- Use the ViewCube to reorient the base view. The default view is Front. You can select alternate faces, edges, or corners on the ViewCube to reorient the model.
- Select on the ViewCube to reorient the model to its default isometric view.
- Select inside the view's frame and drag the view to reposition it on the sheet.

- Select the corner manipulator of the temporary view to scale the view.

The expanded ViewCube options also provides access to setting either Orthographic or Perspective views.

Hint: User-Defined Orientation Views

To create a user-defined orientation, click on the ViewCube and select **Custom View Orientation**. A custom view window opens, as shown in Figure 25–3. You can use this view window to zoom, pan, and rotate the component to create the view you want to display in the drawing. You can also change the view to a perspective view. The majority of the icons in this toolbar are the same as those used when modeling. Consider using the **Rotate at Angle** command to obtain more precise orientations.

Figure 25–3

Once the view orientation has been defined click (Finish Custom View) in the Exit panel.

Once you have placed a Base view you can continue placing projected views. This procedure is explained in the Projected Views section.

10. After locating the base view, right-click and select **OK (Enter)** or click **OK** in the Drawing View dialog box to finalize the base view.

An alternative to creating a new drawing and then adding model views you can also create a drawing directly from a model or presentation view.

- For a part or assembly model, right-click on the model name node in the Model browser and select **Create Drawing View**, as shown in Figure 25–4.

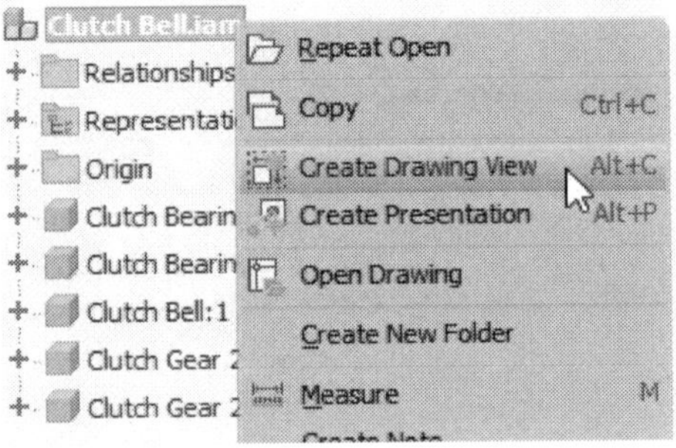

Figure 25–4

- For a presentation file, in the Snapshot Views browser, right-click on the thumbnail image and select **Create Drawing View**. Alternatively, click  (Create Drawing View) in the *Presentation* or *Edit View* tabs to create a new drawing using the active snapshot view.

Once the option is selected, you are prompted to select a drawing template and the temporary Base view is automatically placed in the drawing. An additional benefit of this method for creating a drawing is that the model orientation that is set in the model at the time of drawing creation is the default orientation used in the Base view.

Projected Views

A projected view is a view that is created by projecting from a parent view. The parent view must already exist. You can create eight possible views from one view: four orthographic and four isometric.

- The orthographic views are the top, bottom, and side views, as shown in Figure 25–5. These views align with the parent Base view and are dependent on that view.
- The isometric views are the diagonal views, as shown in Figure 25–5. These views are not dependent on the location of the parent Base view and can be relocated anywhere on the sheet.

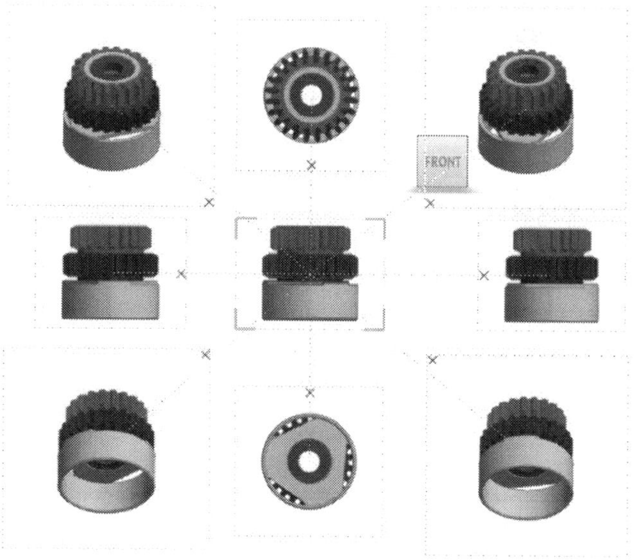

Figure 25–5

Once a base view is located, you can continue immediately with projected view placement without having to explicitly create Projected views. With the Drawing View dialog box still open during Base view creation, create Projected views using any of the following techniques:

- Drag off of the Base view in any of the eight directions shown in Figure 25–6. Select with the left mouse button to place the new Projected view.
- Select the arrows around the Base view outline to create Projected views, as shown in Figure 25–6.

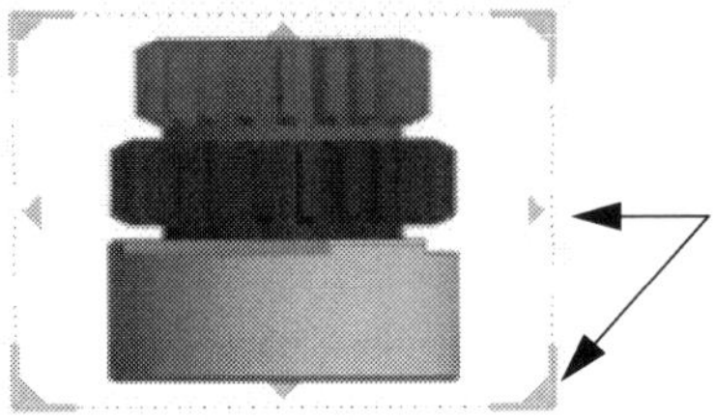

Figure 25–6

How To: Create a Projected View

*You can also right-click on the parent view and select **Create View> Projected View**.*

1. Click (Projected) in the Create panel.
2. Select the base view to be referenced. Alternatively, select the base view, right-click and select **Projected View**.
3. Move the cursor in the direction of the new view. Note the preview of the view.
4. Select the placement location of the view using the left mouse button. A rectangle is placed to mark the position of the view.
5. Continue moving the crosshairs to new locations and selecting points for each view you want to create. A rectangle is placed on the screen to indicate each additional view.
6. Right-click and select **Create** to generate the views.

Raster Views

Before a precise drawing view is generated it displays as a raster view until the view is finalized. Views can also be created so that they remain as raster views, or you can set an existing view to be a raster view.

- The purpose of a raster view is to help improve drawing view calculation times when working on complex drawing models. This is done by temporarily breaking the associativity with the drawing model.

- You can continue to annotate and work in a drawing with raster views present. Note that some features of the drawing are not available or work differently for raster views.
- Changes made to the model will not update in raster views unless the view is set as **Precise**.

A raster view can be easily identified in a drawing by its highlighted green corners of the view outline, as shown in Figure 25–7.

*Raster views can be disabled by clearing the **Enable background updates** option in the Drawing tab of the Application Options dialog box.*

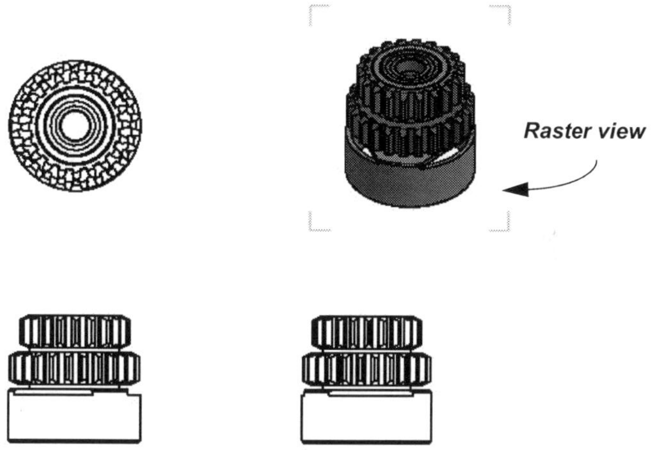

Figure 25–7

To create a new view as a raster view:

- Select **Raster View** in the Drawing View dialog box so that the new view is generated and maintained as a raster view.

There are multiple ways to convert views to raster views:

- Right-click on the drawing sheet and select **Make All Views Raster**.
- Hover over a view on the drawing sheet to activate its view outline, and then right-click and select **Make View Raster**.
- Right-click on a view name in the Model browser and select **Make View Raster**.

A raster view displays with a red line through it in the Model browser ( ) and with green corners in the graphics window. To make a raster view precise, use the same techniques listed above for converting existing views and select **Make View Precise** or **Make All Views Precise**.

25.3 Additional Drawing Views

Additional view types are available in the *Place Views* tab> Create panel, as shown in Figure 25–8.

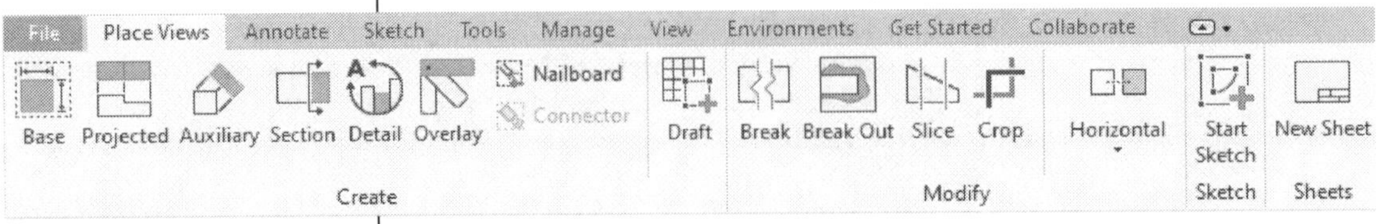

Figure 25–8

Auxiliary Views

Auxiliary views are similar to orthographic views. Orthographic views are created to the left, right, above, or below a parent view. Auxiliary views are created diagonally from the view based on a user-defined edge, as shown in Figure 25–9.

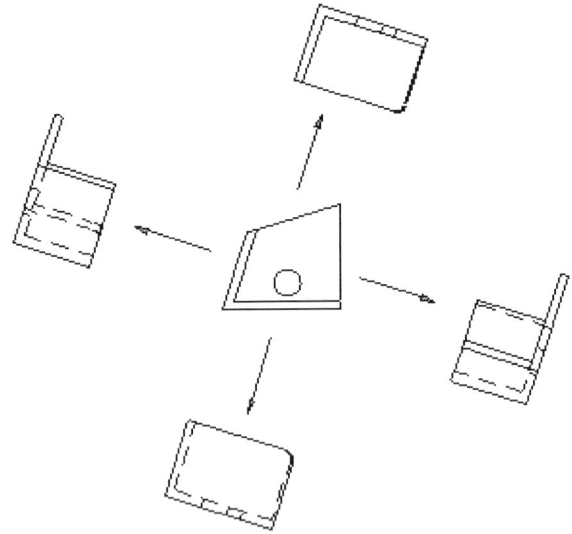

Figure 25–9

*You can also right-click on the parent view and select **Create View> Auxiliary View**.*

How To: Create an Auxiliary View

1. In the Create panel, click (Auxiliary).
2. Select the parent view that the auxiliary view is going to reference. The Auxiliary View dialog box opens as shown in Figure 25–10. Alternatively, select the parent view, right-click and select **Auxiliary View**.

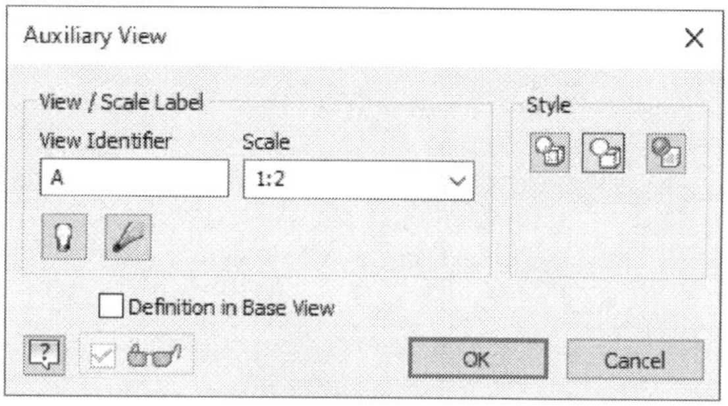

Figure 25–10

3. Set the options in the dialog box as required. The cursor displays as a cursor with a line symbol ( ).
4. Select a line in the reference view as the basis for the view.
5. Move the cursor and select the placement location of the view using the left mouse button.

Section Views

A section view displays the component with a cutaway, as shown in Figure 25–11. A projection view line, also known as a section line, is drawn on the parent view to locate the cut.

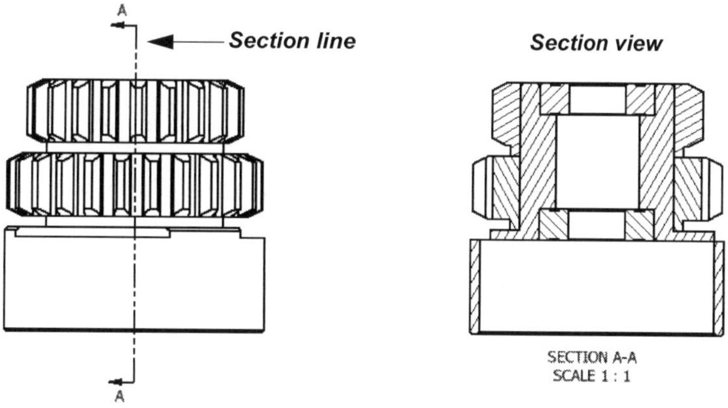

Figure 25–11

How To: Create a Section View

1. In the Create panel, click (Section).
2. Select the view that the section view is going to reference. Alternatively, select the base view, right-click and select **Section View**.
3. Select points on the reference view to draw the section line.
4. Right-click and select **Continue**. The Section View dialog box opens as shown in Figure 25–12.

Controls the depth of the section view

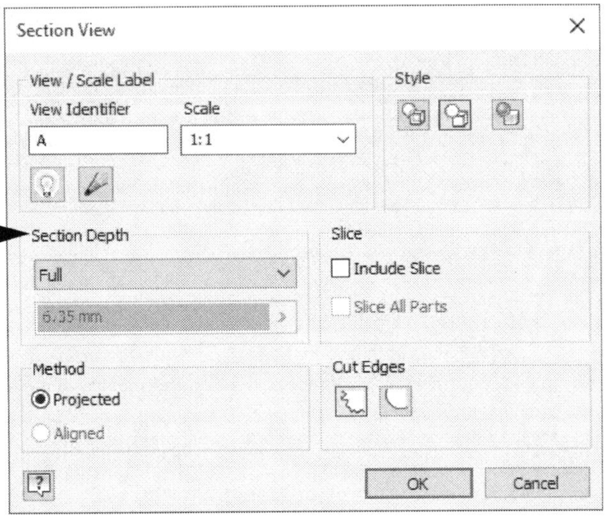

Figure 25–12

5. Set the options in the dialog box, as required.
6. Select the section depth (**Full** or **Distance**) of the view in the *Section Depth* area in the dialog box.
7. (Optional) Set whether to **Include Slice** and **Slice The Whole Part**.
8. Define the method of projecting the section view. **Projected** is the default if a single line entity represents the section line. If multiple section lines are sketched, you can select between **Projected** or **Aligned**.
9. Define how the break lines for partially sectioned components will display using the options in the *Cut Edges* area. The options enable you to select a smooth ( ) or jagged ( ) break. The default option is smooth.

10. Select the placement location of the view using the left mouse button. A section view is automatically aligned with the parent view by default. To break the alignment, press and hold <Ctrl> when dragging and left-click to locate the section view.

*To edit a sketched line, select it, right-click and select **Edit**. Any section view that is based on the sketch is updated with the changes.*

- A sketch that is associated with a view, can be used as the section line for a Section view. To use a sketch as the section line, the sketch must already exist and be associated with the parent view. Once created, right-click the sketch in the Model browser and select **Create Section View**. The Section View dialog box opens to define the view.
- To change the section properties, right-click on the view and select **Edit Section Properties**.
- To change the hatch patterns on section views, right-click on the pattern and select **Edit**. The default pattern is set in the Drafting Standards. Hatch patterns can also be assigned to material styles in the Style and Standard Editor.

Detailed Views

Detail views typically enlarge an area of a parent view to display the information more clearly, as shown in Figure 25–13.

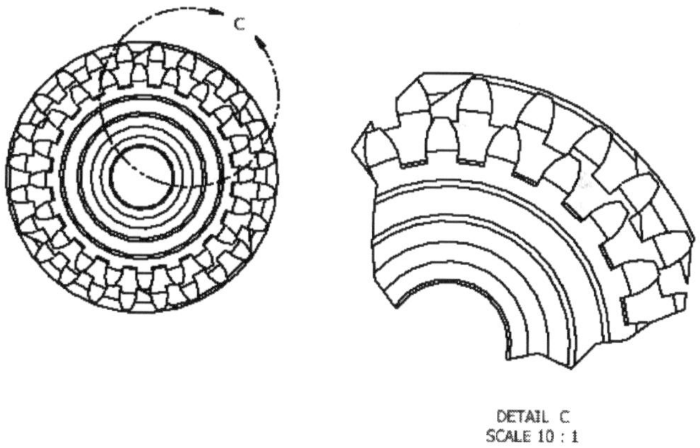

Figure 25–13

*You can also right-click on the parent view and select **Create View> Detail View**.*

How To: Create a Detail View

1. In the Create panel, click  (Detail).
2. Select the view that the detail view is going to reference. The Detail View dialog box opens as shown in Figure 25–14. Alternatively, select the base view, right-click and select **Detail View**.

In detail views, you can have a circular or rectangular fence shape. You also can have jagged or smooth cutout lines.

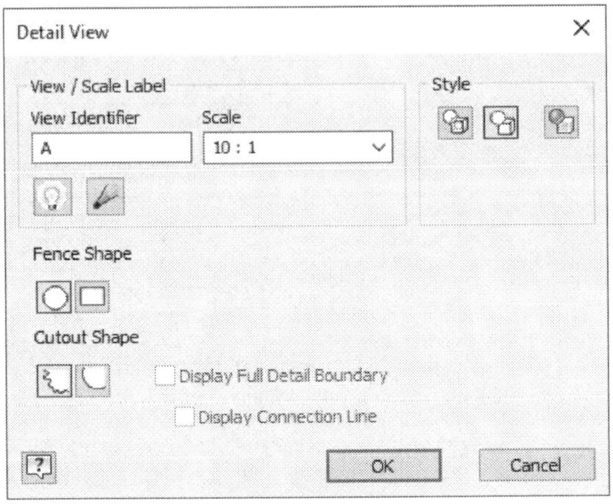

Figure 25–14

*To attach a detail view to its geometry, select the center green got on the detail view boundary, right-click and select **Attach**. This prevents the detail view boundary from shifting during model changes.*

3. Set the options in the dialog box, as required.
4. Select a point on the view from which the detail is taken to specify the center of the view.
5. Move the cursor away from the center point. A circle displays on the screen. Move the cursor to determine the size of the area that should be included in the detail view, and select a point.
6. Select the placement location of the view using the left mouse button.

Overlay Views

You can document assembly motion or component visibility using overlay views. These views use positional representations to display an assembly in multiple positions or visibilities in a single view, as shown in Figure 25–15. You must have at least two positional representations in the assembly to create overlay views.

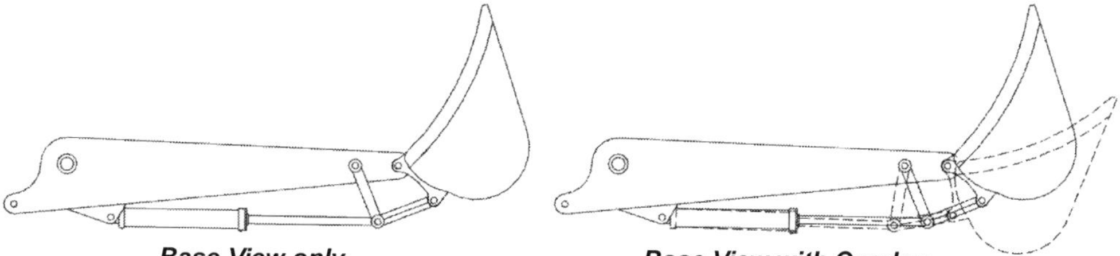

Base View only *Base View with Overlay*

Figure 25–15

The overlay view can be created for unbroken base, projected, and auxiliary views.

How To: Create an Overlay

You can also right-click on the parent view and select ***Create View> Overlay View****.*

1. Create a base view.
2. In the Create panel, click  (Overlay) and select the view. The Overlay View dialog box opens as shown in Figure 25–16.

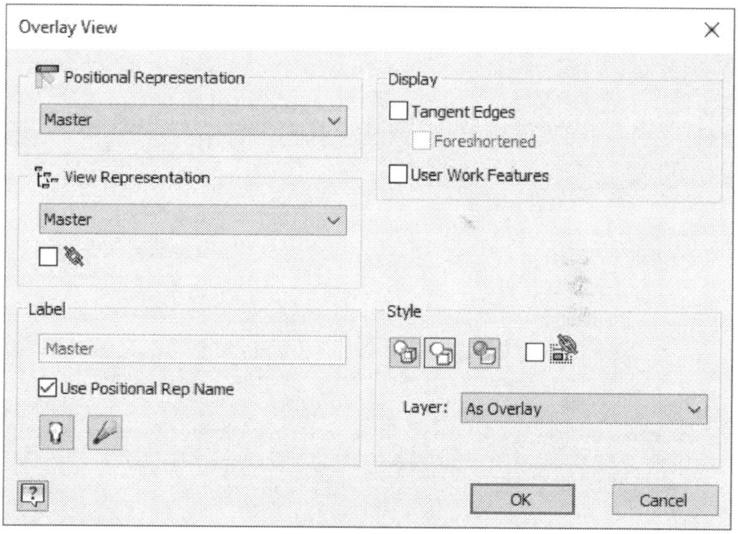

Figure 25–16

Positional Representations are discussed as advanced topics.

3. Select the positional representation to use.
4. Configure any other options, as required.
5. Click **OK**.

Draft Views

Draft views enable you to create independent sketches in a drawing that can provide additional information to the end user of the drawing, as shown in Figure 25–17. The draft view can contain information on the drawing model, be unique, or can also be used to add AutoCAD .DWG data into a drawing.

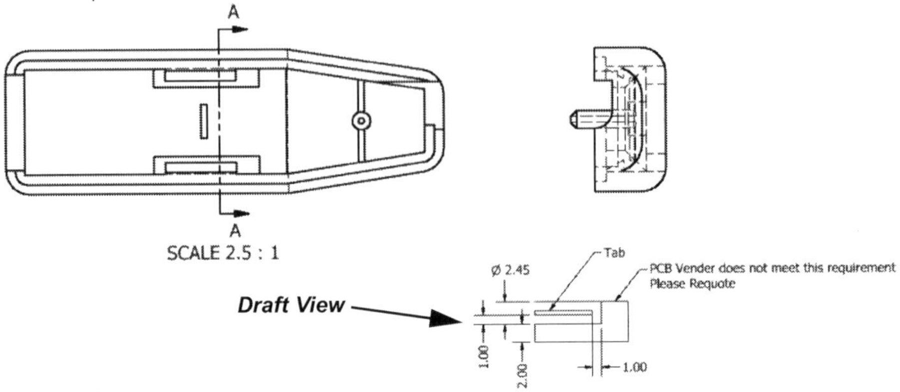

Figure 25–17

How To: Create a Draft View

1. In the Create panel, click (Draft). The Draft View dialog box opens as shown in Figure 25–18.

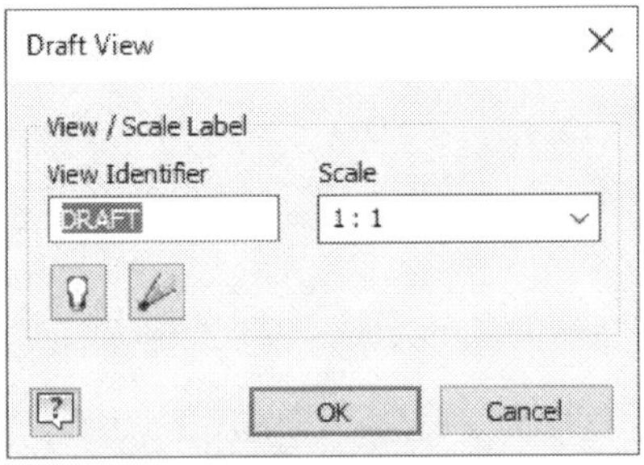

Figure 25–18

2. Set the options in the Draft View dialog box as required to define the view. Click **OK**. The *Sketch* tab becomes the active tab.
3. Use the standard sketching tools to create the entities that are to be represented in the Draft view. To import AutoCAD .DWG data, use **ACAD** in the Insert panel or copy and paste from an AutoCAD drawing file.
4. In the Exit panel, click (Finish Sketch) to complete the view.

Break Views

A break view displays portions of the drawing model with material removed. You can change any view to a break view, as shown in Figure 25–19.

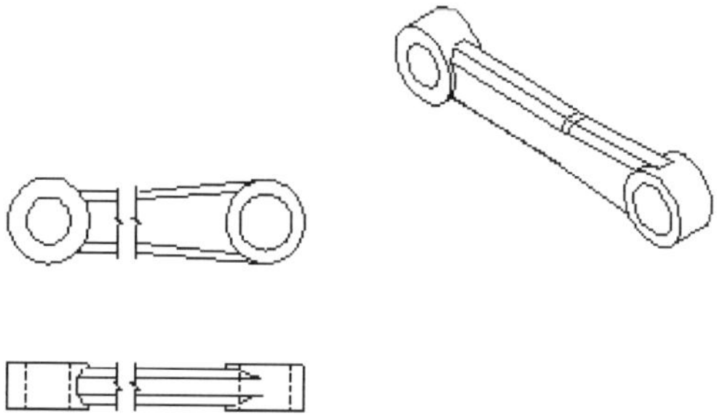

Figure 25–19

You can also right-click on the parent view and select ***Create View> Break****.*

How To: Create a Break View

1. In the Modify panel, click  (Break).
2. Select the view to be broken. The Break dialog box opens as shown in Figure 25–20.

You can control the location and size of the breaks and appearance of the break lines. A view can have multiple breaks.

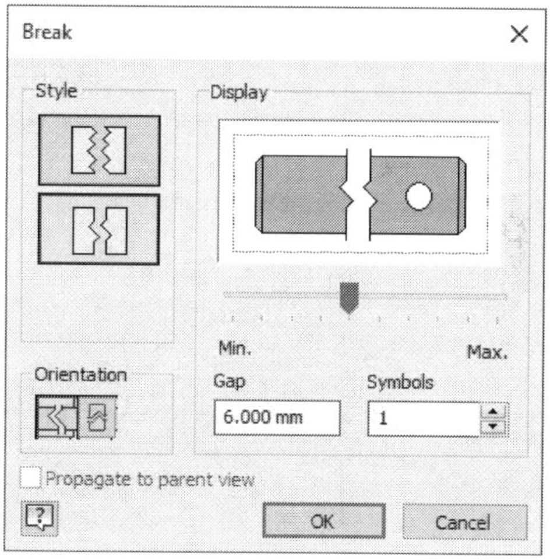

Figure 25–20

3. Set the options in the dialog box, as required.
4. Select a point on the view where you want the break to begin, and select a point on the view where you want the break to end. The Break view is automatically created.

Break Out Views

A break out view is created from an existing view.

A break out view is a view of the drawing model with a portion of the components removed. This type of view is used to expose areas hidden by assembly components. An example is shown in Figure 25–21.

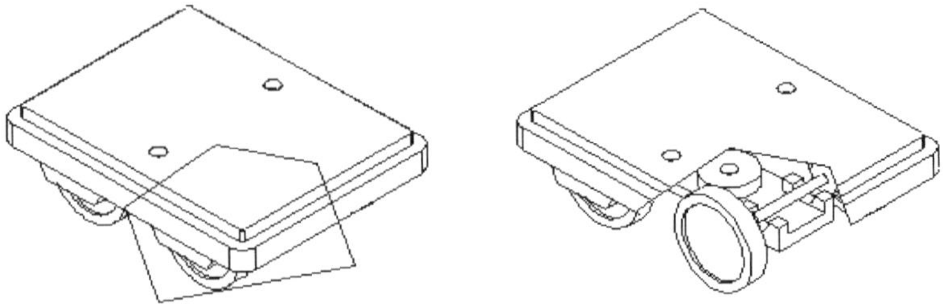

Figure 25–21

A break out view requires a sketch to define the break. The sketch must be associated with the drawing view and be a closed loop.

How To: Create a Break Out View

1. Create a view.
2. Select the view in the Model browser or window.
3. In the Sketch panel, click  (Start Sketch) to create a sketch associated with the view.
4. Sketch a closed profile to outline the break area. Exit the sketch. The sketch is listed for the view in the Model browser.
5. In the Modify panel, click  (Break Out) and select the view. The Break Out dialog box opens as shown in Figure 25–22.

*You can also right-click on the view and select **Create View>Break Out**.*

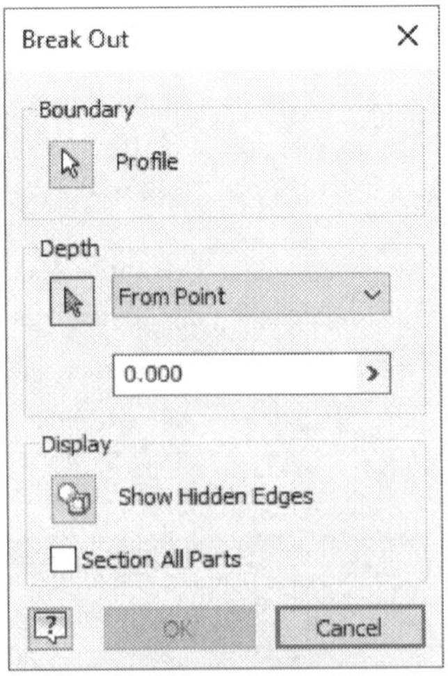

Figure 25–22

6. If multiple closed profile sketches are associated with the view, click (Profile) and select the required profile you sketched.
7. Select the depth type (**From Point**, **To Sketch**, **To Hole**, **Through Part**).
8. Click **OK**.

Slice Views

A Slice view enables you to display slices of the model with zero-depth sections. An open sketch is used to create the slices in the model.

How To: Create a Slice View

1. Create the required base and projected planar views and an isometric view. The isometric view is used as the target view that is going to be sliced. The base or projected planar views provide the view to sketch the slice lines.
2. Create an associated sketch on the base or projected view defining the slicing that is to be displayed in the target view. The sketch must be an open section to be defined as a slice line, must be unconsumed, and cannot be created in a Draft view.

*To create an associated sketch, select the view before selecting **Create Sketch**.*

3. In the Modify panel, click (Slice).
4. Select the target view to be sliced.
5. Select the associated sketch to define the slice view.
6. For an assembly drawing, enable **Slice All Parts** to slice all intersecting components. Otherwise, leave this option cleared.
7. Click **OK**.
8. (Optional) To manually select assembly components to display as sliced in the target view (i.e., participate), expand the assembly node for the target view, right-click on a component name, and select **Section Participation>Slice**.

The target view does not have to be an isometric view. However, multiple slices are not visible if it is a planar view.

The views at the top of Figure 25–23 show the target view and the associated sketch that was created on a planar part view. The views at the bottom of Figure 25–23 show the final slice view created on a 3D isometric view.

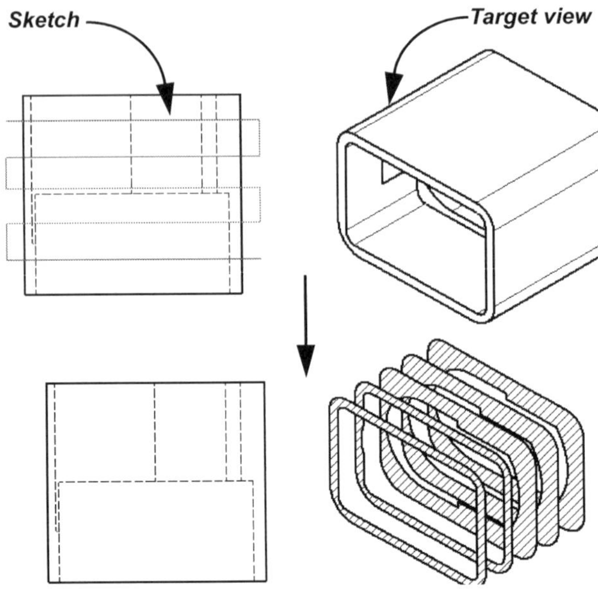

Figure 25–23

Crop Views

Existing drawing views can be cropped/clipped to help focus on important areas of a view, as shown in Figure 25–24.

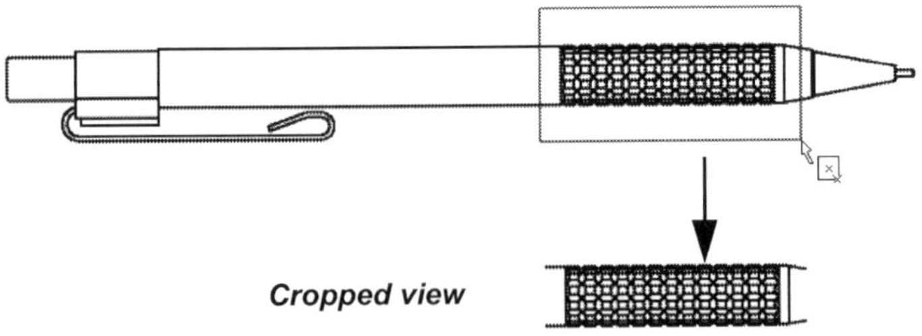

Figure 25–24

Cropping is permitted on most existing views. However, it is not available for broken or overlay views, or previously cropped views. Although you cannot create an additional crop on a previously cropped view, you can create a Broken view, Detail view, or Slice on a cropped view.

How To: Crop a View

1. Create a view.
2. Select the view in the Model browser or graphics window.
3. In the Modify panel, click (Crop) or right-click and select **Crop**.

*Alternatively, you can right-click and select **Circular** to change the boundary type instead of opening the Crop Settings dialog box.*

4. (Optional) By default, the cropped area is rectangular and crop cut lines display. To change the crop settings, right-click and select **Crop Settings** before sketching the area. Define the options using the Crop Settings dialog box, as in Figure 25–25.

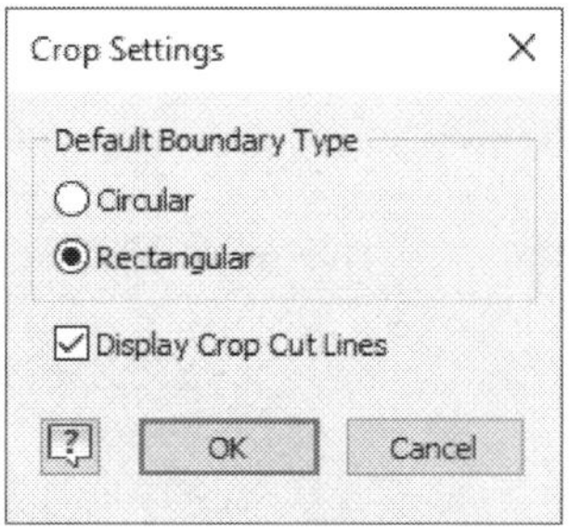

Figure 25–25

Alternatively, you can have a pre-existing sketch that is associated with a view, select it, and initiate the creation of a Crop view to use it as the cropping border.

5. Sketch a bounding box around the area of the selected view that is to be cropped. You can also select an existing sketch as the crop boundary.

> **Hint: Model Dimensions and Cropping**
>
> Model dimensions that have been added to a view that is being cropped remain displayed. Existing drawing dimensions also remain and reference points are added to the view. It is recommended that you crop views before annotating your drawing. Drawing dimensions can be added after cropping and can reference the cut lines of the crop boundary, if required.

25.4 Manipulating Views

Once views have been added to a drawing, changes might be required. Some common changes that can be made to drawing views include the following:

Delete Views

Views can be deleted from a drawing using any of the following methods:

- Right-click on the view in the graphics window or the view name in the Model browser and select **Delete**.
- Select the view and press <Delete>.

When deleting a parent view, a dialog box opens that enables you to select dependent views to be retained (click  in the dialog box to display a list if they exist), as shown in Figure 25–26. To prevent a dependent view from being deleted, click **Yes** in the Delete column for the view to toggle it to **No**. Any retained children remain associative with the source model.

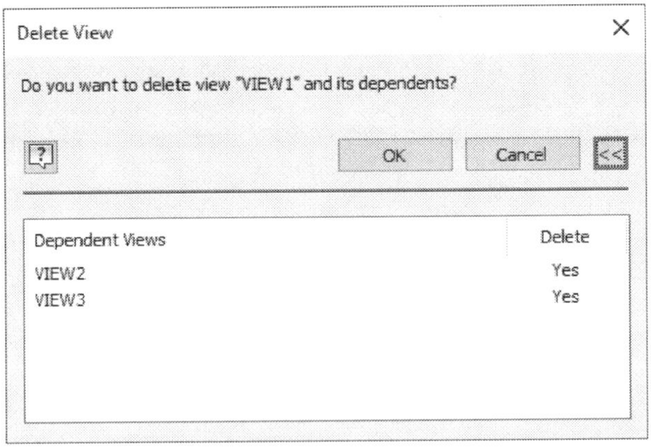

Figure 25–26

Suppress Views

Views can be suppressed in a drawing. When a view is suppressed, it is not visible on the drawing sheet and is grayed out in the Model browser. This is similar to suppressing features. To suppress a view, select it in the Model browser or on the drawing sheet, right-click, and select **Suppress**. Repeat the procedure in the Model browser to unsuppress a view.

Move Views

To move a view, select its border and drag it to the new location on the drawing. All dependent views move relative to their parents.

View Orientation

View orientation for a base view can be modified in the Drawing View dialog box. Select the view to reorient, right-click and select **Edit View**. Use the ViewCube to reorient the model. Click **OK** to update the view. Any dependent views also inherit the new orientation.

Transparent Components

In an assembly model drawing view you can set individual components to be transparent in a precise view (not raster). Setting as transparent keeps the component visible in the view but prevents it from hiding the geometry of other components in the same view. To make a component transparent, right-click on the part in the Model browser or in the graphics window and select **Transparent**.

View Alignment

Dependent views (projected views, auxiliary views, etc.) are aligned to parent views and update position if the parent view is moved. You can also explicitly remove or add view alignment as follows:

- To remove an alignment, in the Model browser or in the drawing sheet, right-click the dependent view and select **Alignment>Break** or click (Break Alignment) in the Modify panel. Once the view alignment is broken, a section or view line is added to the parent view to identify its origin. The dependent view remains dependent on the parent view although it is broken.
- To add an alignment, in the Model browser, right-click on the view and select **Alignment>Vertical / Horizontal / In Position**.
    - (Vertical), (Horizontal), and (In Position) can also be selected in the Modify panel.
    - The **Vertical/Horizontal** options line up the vertical/horizontal center line of the view with the center line of the other view. **In Position** maintains the position of the view horizontally and vertically, relative to the base view.

The available alignment options in the Modify panel are shown in Figure 25–27.

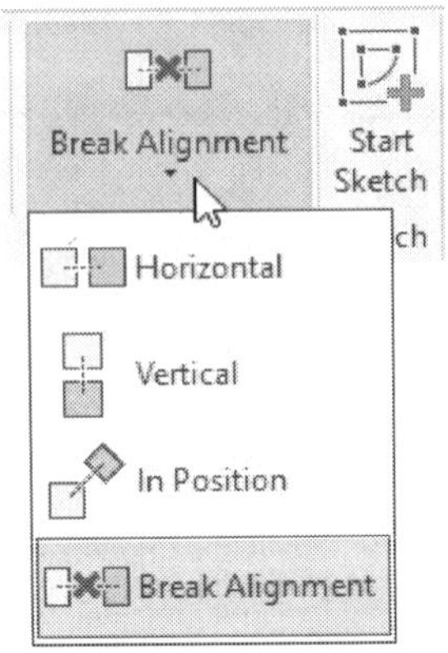

Figure 25–27

Change View Scale

To modify a view scale, right-click on the view and select **Edit View**. The Drawing View dialog box opens. Enter a new scale in the *Scale* field or drag the corners of the view outline and click **OK**. Changing this value affects the scale of all child views, except independently scaled views.

To independently change the view scale on a child view (i.e., Projected view), clear  (Scale from base) in the Drawing View dialog box to enter an independent scale value for the child view.

Editing View Labels

You can add extra lines of text in a view label and control the formatting. Hover the cursor over a label (an **A** displays near the cursor), right-click and select **Edit View Label**. The Format Text dialog box opens as shown in Figure 25–28.

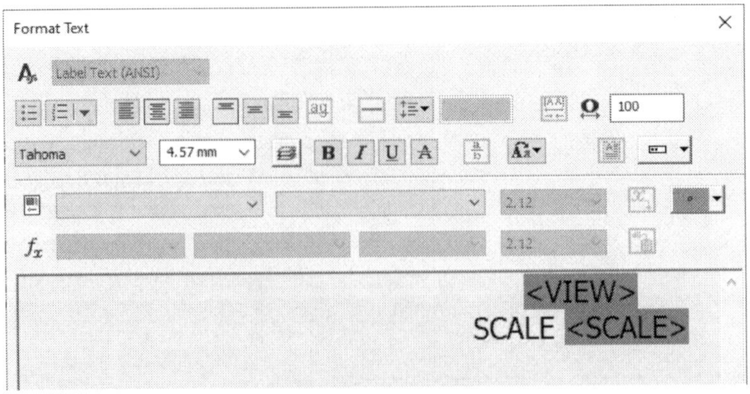

Figure 25–28

- The Label information is represented by brackets in the edit area. The top brackets represent the title, and the bottom brackets represent the scale. You cannot change the text inside the brackets, but you can add text before, between, or after them. You can also change the format of the text inside the brackets.

- The dialog box offers standard options for text formatting, such as font, height, justification, etc. To change the font or style of existing text, highlight the text to be changed in the edit box and apply the changes.

- Move a label by dragging it. It remains connected to the view even after it has been moved.

Replace Models

When a base drawing view is added to a drawing, you must select a drawing model to reference. Dependent views are created referencing this base view. Once a reference model is selected for use in the drawing, it is possible to replace it with another model. The replacing model is then reflected in all existing views.

How To: Replace an Existing Drawing Model

1. In the *Manage* tab>Modify panel, click (Replace Model Reference). The Replace Model Reference dialog box opens as shown in Figure 25–29.

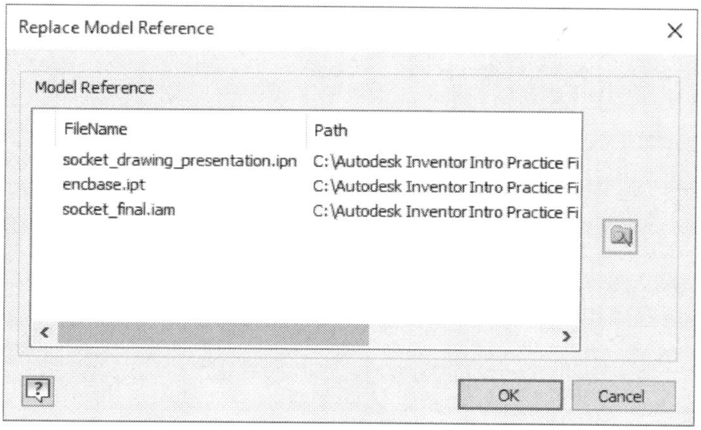

Figure 25–29

Replacement models must be the same file format as the original model. For example, you cannot replace a part file with an assembly file.

2. Select the drawing model to be replaced.
3. Click and browse and select a new model.
4. Click **Yes** and **OK** to confirm replacement.

View Properties

You can change the line weight, line type, or color of an object in a view. Select the item, right-click, and select **Properties** to open the Edge Properties dialog box, shown in Figure 25–30.

Consider using the Selection filter to select all of the lines of a part or assembly instead of simply selecting individual lines. Hint: To quickly display the list of filter options, press <Shift> and right-click.

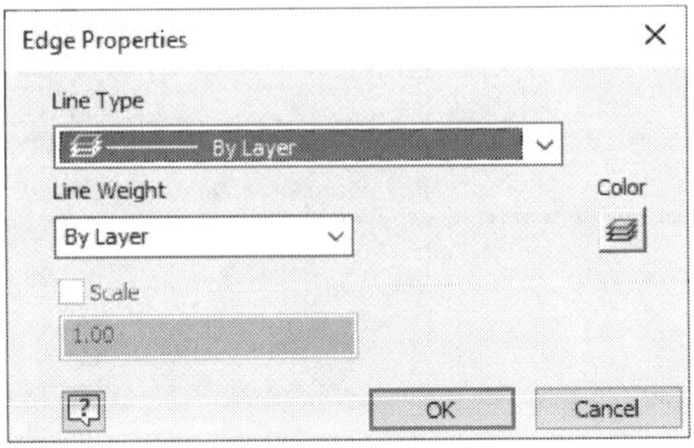

Figure 25–30

The **By Layer** setting for *Line Type* and *Line Weight* means that the property is determined by the layer on which the line is located. The settings for the layers can be modified in the Style and Standard Editor.

Editing Sheets

The default type of sheet that is added to a drawing is dependent on the sheet assigned for use with the selected template. To make changes to a sheet once a drawing has been created, right-click on the sheet name in the Model browser and select **Edit Sheet**. Using the Edit Sheet dialog box (shown in Figure 25–31), you can make changes to the sheet's size, name, orientation, and set exclude options for count and printing.

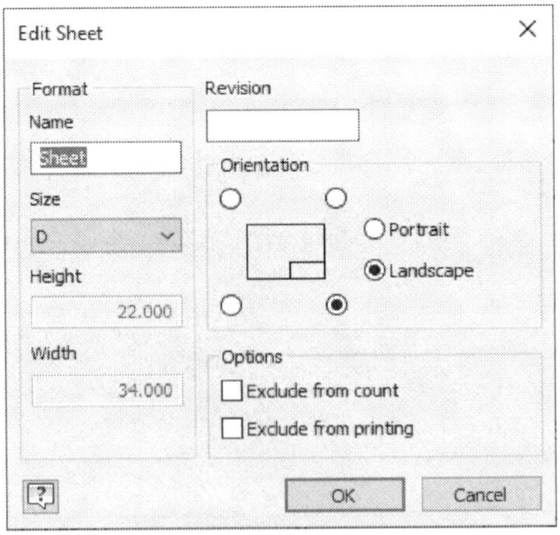

Figure 25–31

Practice 25a Create a Drawing I

Practice Objectives

- Create a new drawing based on a drawing template.
- Add Base, Projected, Section, Detail, and Break Out views to create a drawing.
- Edit a drawing view to change the location, display style, and scale.

In this practice, you will create the drawing shown in Figure 25–32. You will use the drawing commands to complete the drawing, add all the required views, and manipulate them as required.

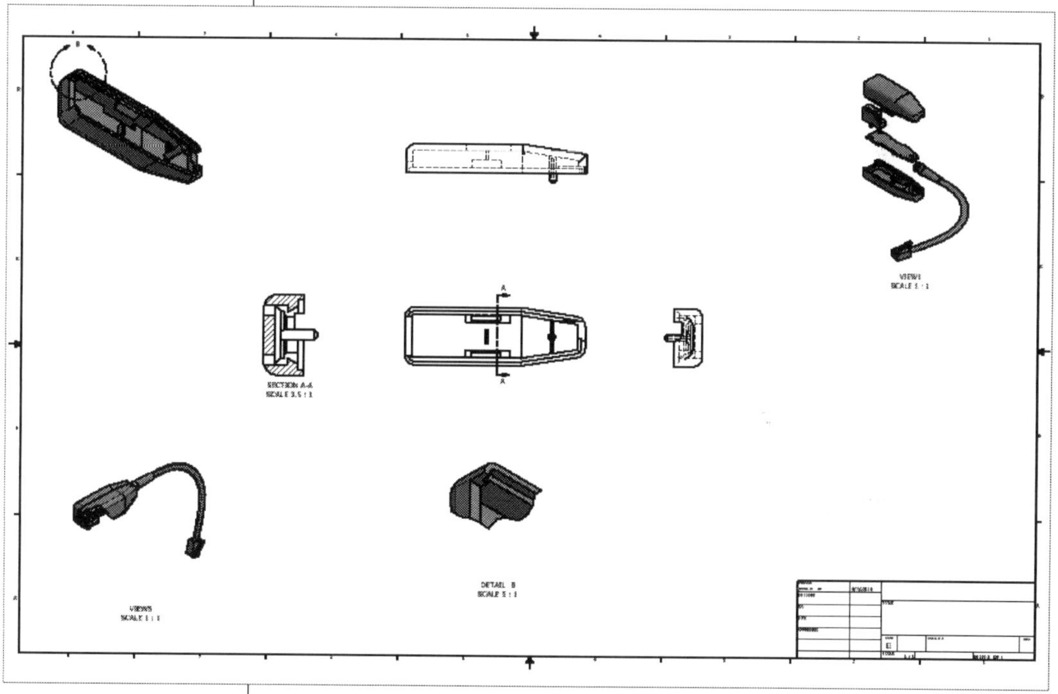

Figure 25–32

Task 1 - Create a drawing.

1. Start a new drawing using the **ANSI (mm).dwg** metric template. If you are unsure about the template that is assigned to the **Drawing** option on the *My Home* tab, use **New** in the ribbon.

Task 2 - Add a base view to the drawing.

1. In the Create panel, click (Base). The Drawing View dialog box opens.
2. Click and open **socket_drawing_presentation.ipn**.
3. If you cannot see the preview of the drawing view that is being placed, relocate the Drawing View dialog box.
4. Click on the ViewCube to orient the model to its default orientation, as shown in Figure 25–33. Note that in the *Presentation* area of the Drawing View dialog box the **Explosion1** view is selected by default. This is because this is the only snapshot view that exists in the presentation file.

Figure 25–33

5. Click (Toggle Label Visibility) in the *Label* area to toggle on label visibility.

6. Ensure that (Hidden Line Removed) and (Shaded) are set in the *Style* area to display the model as shaded with hidden lines removed.

7. Click and hold the cursor inside of the drawing view's frame and drag it to the top right corner of the drawing sheet.

8. Right-click and select **OK (Enter)** or click **OK** in the Drawing View dialog box.

Task 3 - Add another base view.

1. In the Create panel, click (Base). The Drawing View dialog box opens.

2. Click and select and open **encbase.ipt**.

3. By default, the ViewCube is set to the model's front view. Keep this orientation.

4. Click and hold the cursor inside of the drawing view's frame. Drag and drop it in the middle of the drawing sheet to place it, as shown in Figure 25–34.

5. Enter **2.5:1** in the *Scale* field and click (Toggle Label Visibility) in the *Label* area.

Alternatively, you can create projected views by clicking (Projected) in the Create panel, selecting the base reference view, and placing the new projected views.

6. Hover the cursor above the base view. A preview of the projected view displays at the crosshairs. Select a point to place the projected view.

7. Continue moving the crosshairs to the new location (bottom left corner of the base view). Select the location for the isometric view.

8. Right-click and select **OK (Enter)** to create the views that were placed.

9. If dimensions display, toggle them off by selecting the view in the Model browser, right-clicking, and selecting **Annotation Visibility>Model Dimensions**.

10. Move the new views as required so that the drawing displays as shown in Figure 25–34.

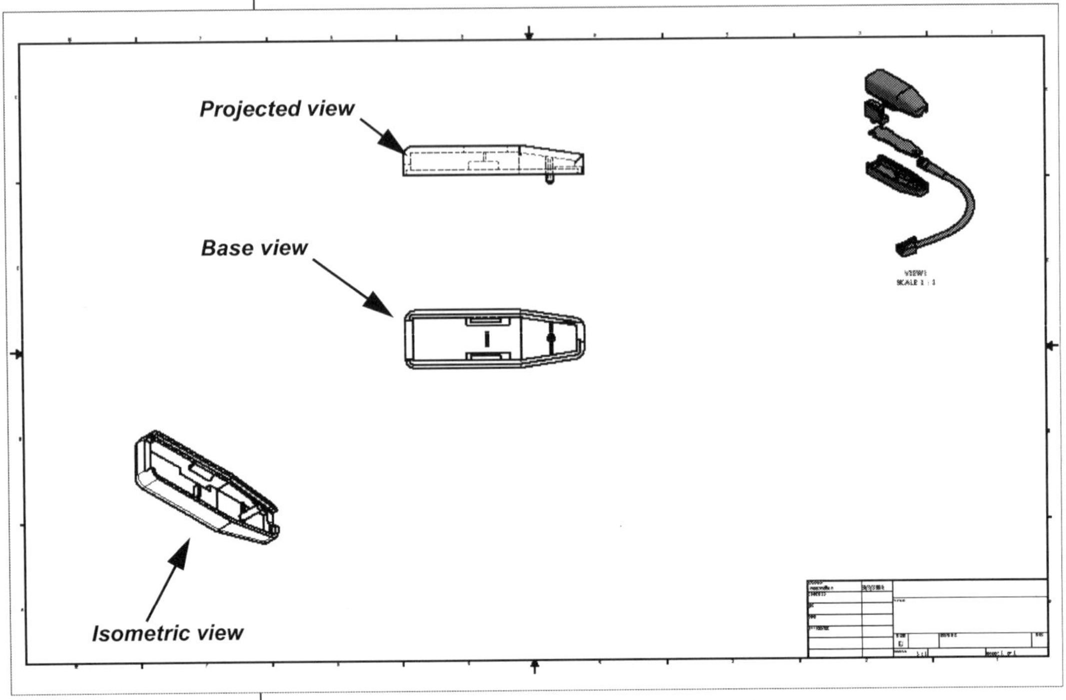

Figure 25–34

Task 4 - Edit the isometric view.

1. Right-click on the isometric view shown in Figure 25–34 (above) and select **Edit View**. The Drawing View dialog box opens.

2. Click  (Shaded) in the *Style* area to set the view to shaded and then click **OK**.

3. Move the isometric view to the location shown in Figure 25–35. To move the view, select it so that view's outline displays around it, select the outline, and drag it.

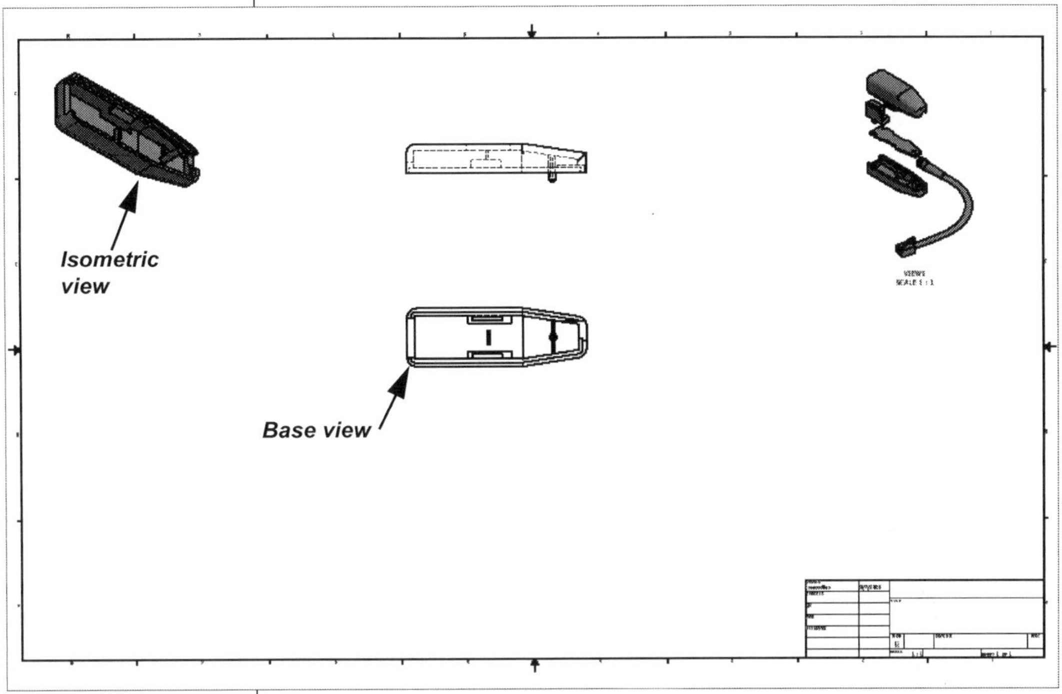

Figure 25–35

Task 5 - Add a section view.

Alternatively, you can create section views by clicking  *(Section) in the Create panel.*

1. Select the base view, right-click and select **Section View**.
2. Select points on the base view to draw the section line shown in Figure 25–36.

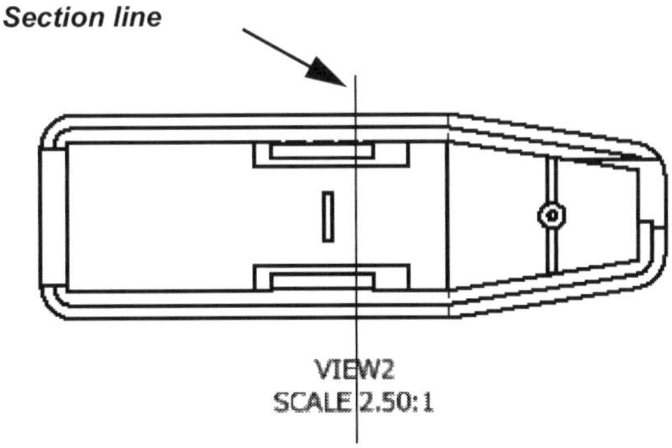

Figure 25–36

3. Right-click and select **Continue**. The Section View dialog box opens.

4. Enter **3.5:1** in the *Scale* field.

5. Ensure that is set to display the label.

6. Select the location shown in Figure 25–37 to place the section view.

*The default section depth option is **Full**.*

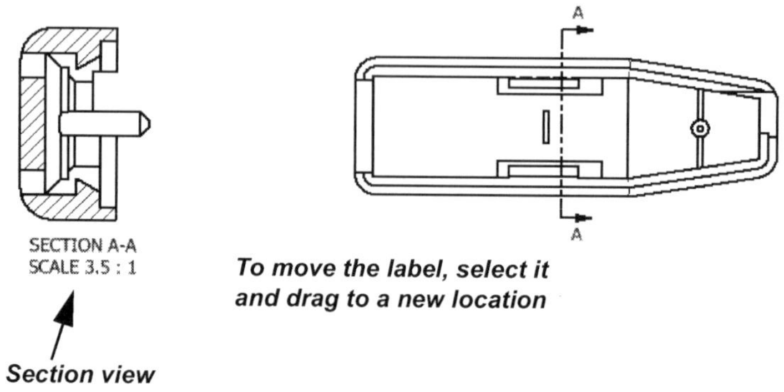

Figure 25–37

7. Hover the cursor over the section line, right-click and select **Edit**. The *Sketch* tab becomes the active tab.

8. In the Constrain panel, click (Dimension) and dimension the section line as shown in Figure 25–38.

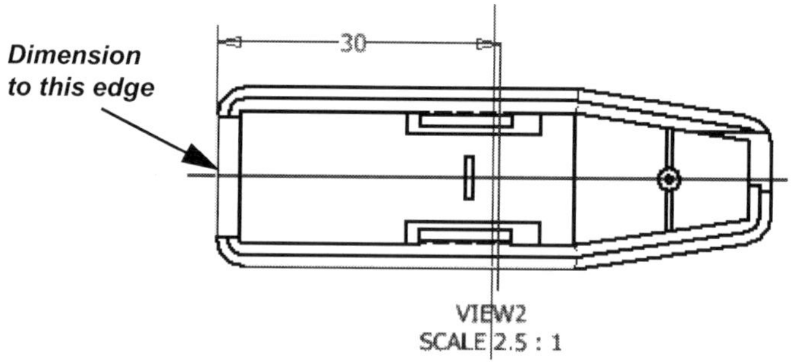

Figure 25–38

9. Finish the sketch. The section line is now parametrically placed and cannot be moved in error. To move the line, right-click and select **Edit** and change the dimension value.

Task 6 - Add a base view of another assembly.

1. In the Create panel, click (Base). The Drawing View dialog box opens.

2. Click [icon] and select and open **socket_final.iam**.
3. Select **Interference_view** in the View drop-down list, in the *Representation* area.
4. Select the corner of the ViewCube shown in Figure 25–39 to customize the view's orientation.

Figure 25–39

5. Click [icon] (Hidden Line Removed) and [icon] (Shaded) in the *Style* area, enter **1:1** in the *Scale* field, and select [icon] to display the label.
6. Place the view as shown in Figure 25–40.
7. Right-click and select **OK (Enter)**.

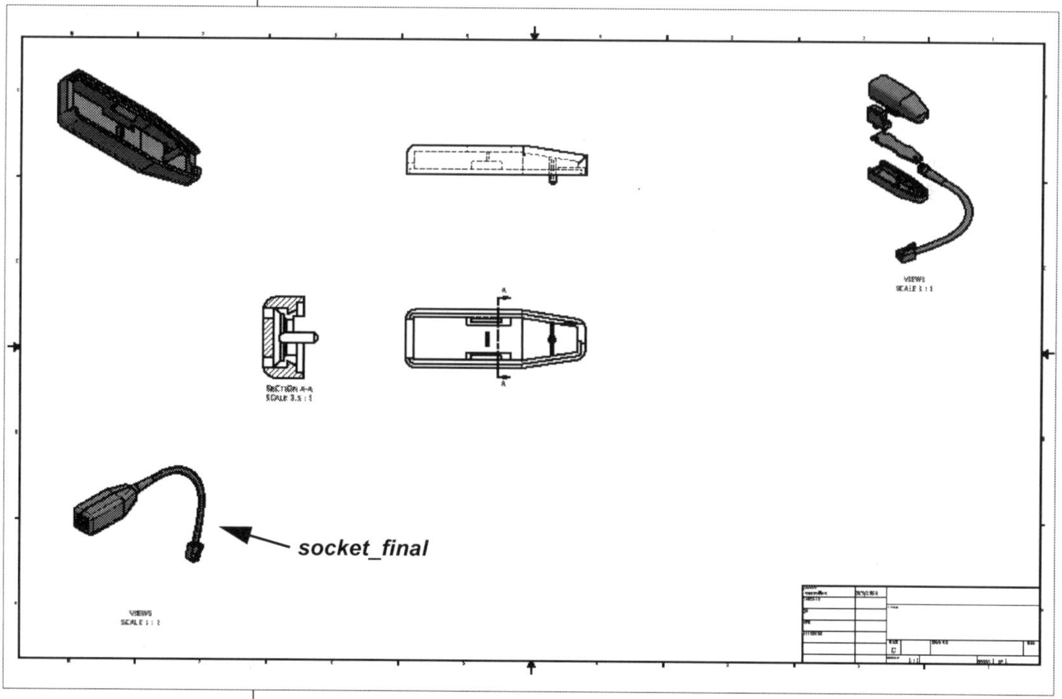

Figure 25–40

Task 7 - Add a detail view to the drawing.

1. In the Create panel, click  (Detail) and then select the isometric view in the top left corner of the window as the reference view. The Detail View dialog box opens.

2. Display the view as Hidden Line Removed () and Shaded (). Accept the remaining defaults in the Detail View dialog box and select the point shown in Figure 25–41 for the center of detail.

3. Drag the cursor away from the point and click to create a circle.

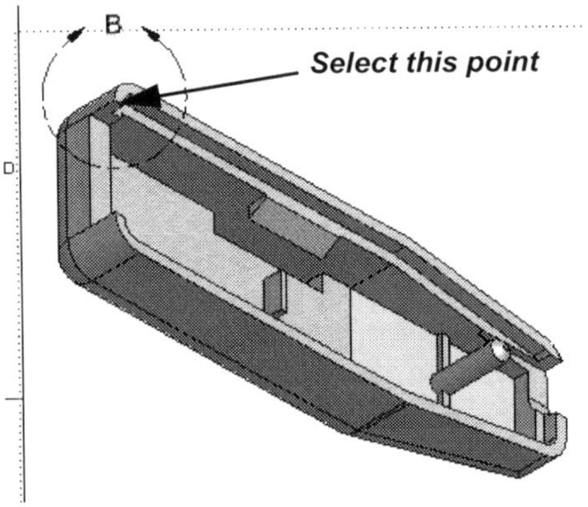

Figure 25–41

4. Place the detail view, as shown in Figure 25–42.

5. Select the detailed view boundary that was drawn for Detail B. Right-click on the green dot that displays at the center of the view boundary and select **Attach**. Select a vertex in the same area where the boundary was created. This attaches the detail view to the geometry of the view, regardless of any changes that are made to the view.

6. Add another projected view, as shown in Figure 25–42.

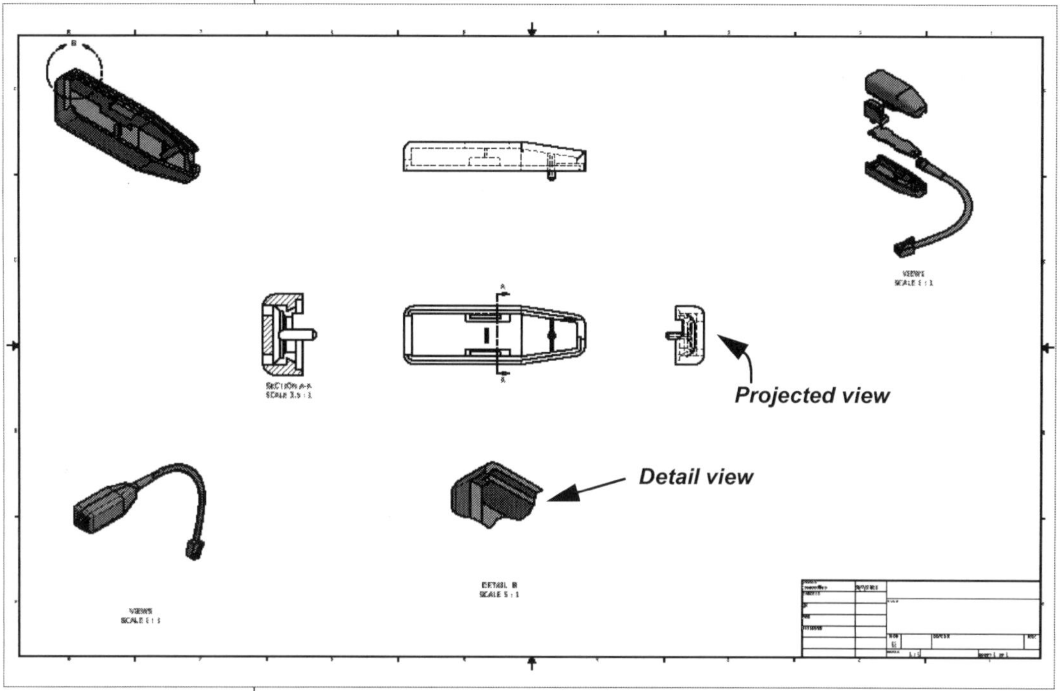

Figure 25–42

Task 8 - Add a break out view to the drawing.

1. A break out view requires a sketch that is associated with the drawing view to define the break. To create a sketch associated with the drawing view, select the bottom left view on the drawing sheet and in the Sketch panel, click  (Start Sketch).

2. Sketch the closed profile shown in Figure 25–43.

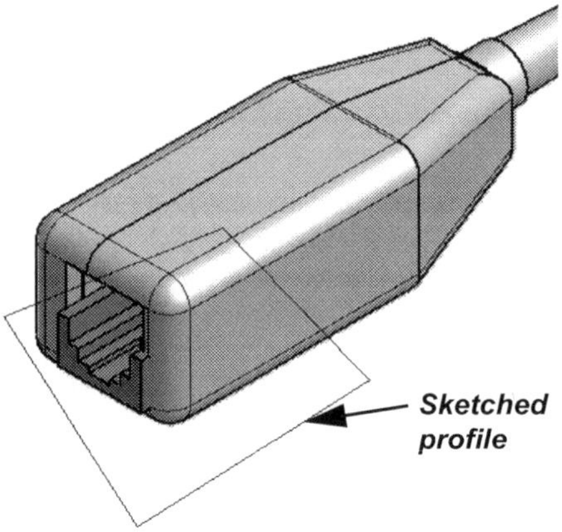

Figure 25–43

3. Finish the sketch. The sketch is now listed under the view name in the Model browser.

4. In the *Place Views* tab>Modify panel, click  (Break Out) and select the bottom left view. The Break Out View dialog box opens.

5. Select **Through Part** in the Depth drop-down list and select the **enctop** part shown on the left in Figure 25–44.

6. Click **OK** to cut away that part. The view displays as shown on the right in Figure 25–44.

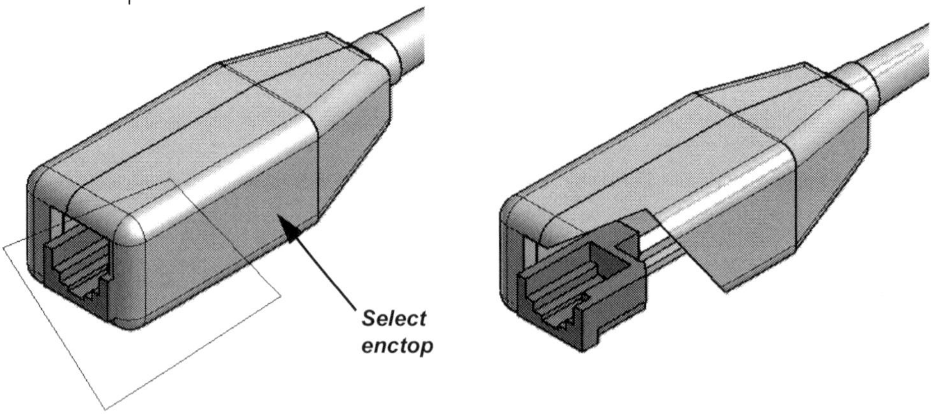

Figure 25–44

Task 9 - Convert all of the views to Raster Views.

1. Right-click in the graphics window, away from an existing view, and select **Make All Views Raster**. If prompted, click **OK** to update the components used by the drawing. All of the views display with green corners and their view icons in the Model browser are changed to include a slash (e.g., ). This indicates that the views do not update if changes are made.
2. Right-click on any of the views in the Model browser and select **Make View Precise**. This enables you to make any selected view in the drawing precise.
3. Right-click in the graphics window, away from an existing view, and select **Make All Views Precise**. All of the views are generated to reflect any changes to the model.
4. Save the drawing as **socket_drawing_presentation.dwg**. The drawing displays as shown in Figure 25–45.

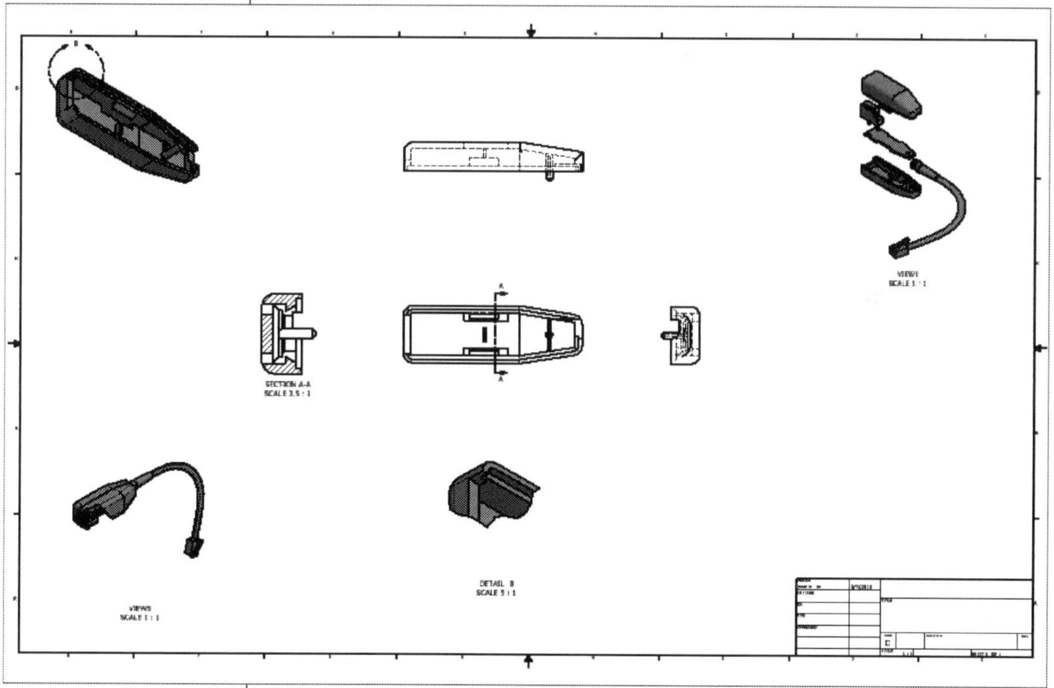

Figure 25–45

Practice 25b Create a Drawing II

Practice Objectives

- Create a new drawing based on a drawing template.
- Add Base, Projected, and Section views to create a drawing.
- Edit a drawing view to change its display style and scale.

In this practice, you will create a base view, projected views, and section views. You will also edit a view. The completed drawing is shown in Figure 25–46.

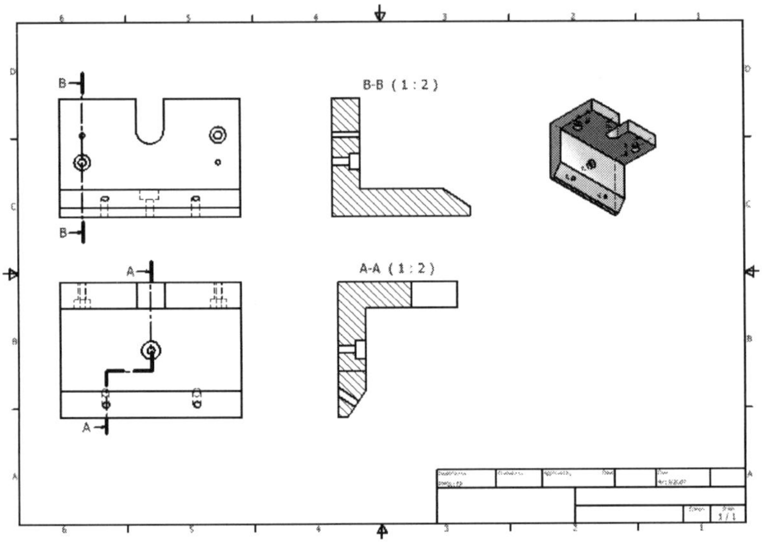

Figure 25–46

Task 1 - Create a drawing.

1. Start a new drawing file using the **ISO.dwg** Metric template.

Task 2 - Create base and projected views.

1. In the Create panel, click  (Base).
2. Click  and open **L_bracket.ipt**.
3. Set the *Scale* to **1:2** and the set the orientation of the view to **Top** using the ViewCube.

4. Move the view, as shown in Figure 25–47.

Alternatively, you can create projected views by clicking  *(Projected) in the Create panel, selecting the base reference view, and placing the new projected views.*

5. Hover the cursor above the base view. A preview of the projected view displays. Select a point to place the projected view.
6. Create a second projected view in the top right corner of the drawing, as shown in Figure 25–47.
7. Right-click and select **OK (Enter)** to create the views that were placed.
8. If dimensions display, toggle them off by selecting the view in the Model browser, right-clicking, and selecting **Annotation Visibility>Model Dimensions**. The drawing displays as shown in Figure 25–47. To toggle off the addition of model dimensions on view creation, select the *Tools* tab and click  (Application Options) in the Options panel. Select the *Drawing* tab and clear the **Retrieve all model dimensions on view placement** option.

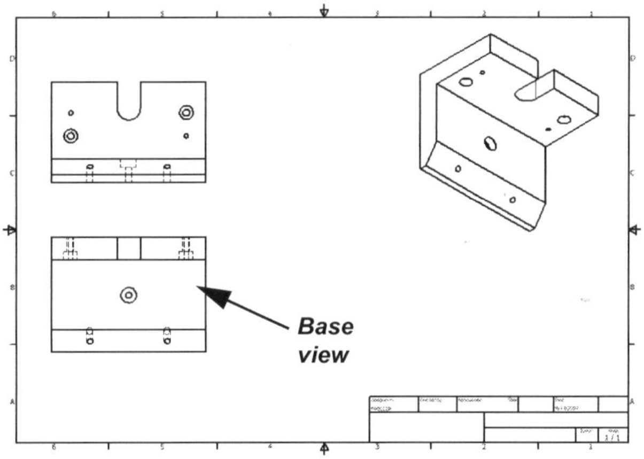

Figure 25–47

Task 3 - Edit the isometric view.

1. Right-click on the isometric view (VIEW3) in the Model browser and select **Edit View**.
2. In the Drawing View dialog box, set the *Scale* to **1:4**. In the *Style* area, click  and  to set the view as shaded with hidden lines displayed. Click **OK**.

Task 4 - Create section views.

1. In the Create panel, click (Section) and select **VIEW1** as the reference view.

2. Draw the section line shown in Figure 25–48. To align to the center of the holes, hover the cursor over a hole and move the cursor. Select the required point with the dashed line displayed.

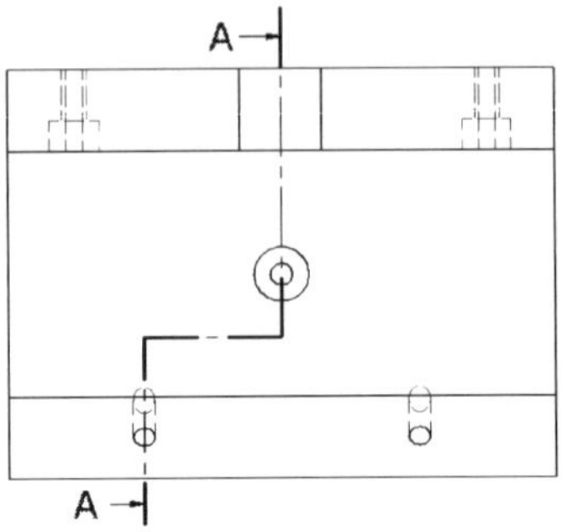

Figure 25–48

3. Right-click and select **Continue**.

4. Place the section view to the right of the reference view.

5. In the Create panel, click (Section) and select **VIEW2** as the reference view.

6. Draw the section line shown in Figure 25–49.

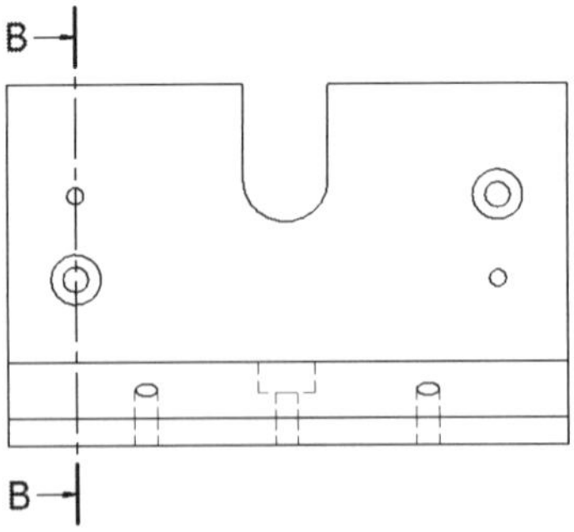

Figure 25–49

7. Right-click and select **Continue**.

8. Place the view to the right of the reference view.

9. The drawing displays as shown in Figure 25–50.

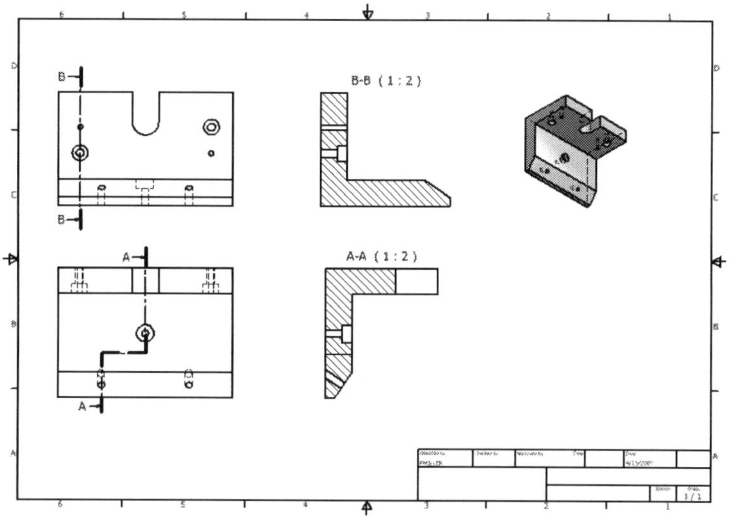

Figure 25–50

10. Save the file as **L_bracket.dwg**.

Practice 25c Create a Drawing III

Practice Objectives

- Create a new drawing based on a drawing template.
- Add Base, Projected, Section, and Detail views to create a drawing.

In this practice, you will create a drawing with a base view, projected views, a section view, and a detail view. The completed drawing is shown in Figure 25–51.

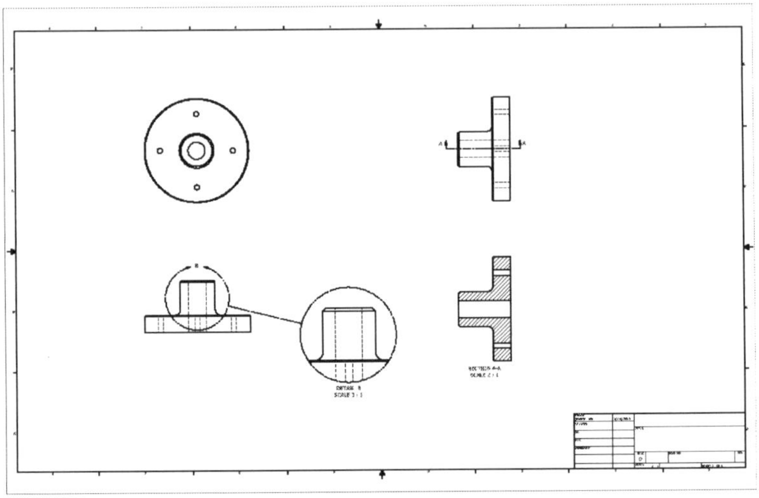

Figure 25–51

Task 1 - Create a drawing.

1. Start a new drawing file using the **ANSI (in).dwg** English template.

Task 1 - Create base and projected views.

1. Create a base view of **relation.ipt**. Move the view to the upper left corner of the drawing, as shown in Figure 25–52.
2. As an alternative to entering a scale value in the Drawing View dialog box, drag a corner of the view. Drag until the scale is 2:1.

*If dimensions display, toggle them off by selecting the view in the Model browser, right-clicking, and selecting **Annotation Visibility>Model Dimensions**. Alternatively, you can select the Tools tab and click*  *(Application Options) in the Options panel. Select the Drawing tab and clear the **Retrieve all model dimensions on view placement** option.*

3. Create the projected views shown in Figure 25–52.
4. Right-click in the graphics window and select **OK (Enter)**.

Figure 25–52

Task 2 - Create a section view.

1. Create the section view shown in Figure 25–53. Use extension lines to ensure that the section line cuts through the center of the part.

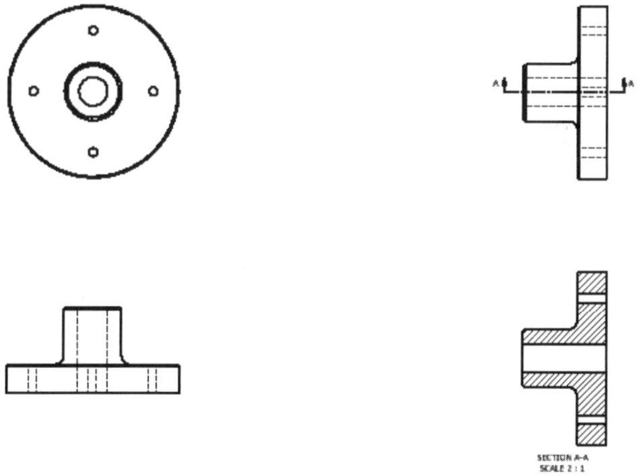

Figure 25–53

Task 3 - Create a detail view.

1. Create a detail view and select the bottom projected view as the reference view. Click  as the *Cutout Shape*. Select **Display Full Detail Boundary** and **Display Connection Line**. Set the *Scale* at 3:1, create the detail circle, and place the detail view as shown in Figure 25–54.

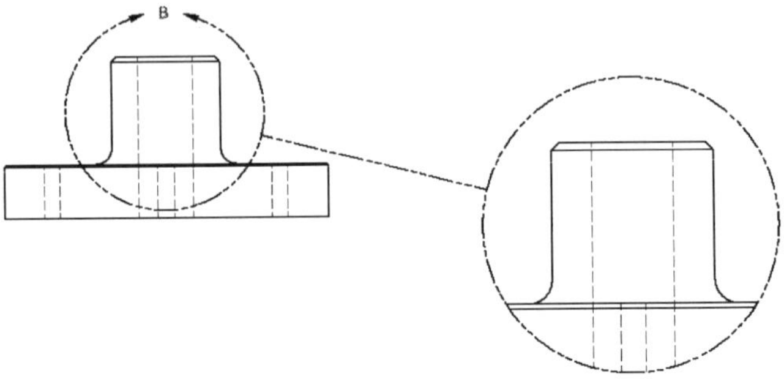

Figure 25–54

2. Save the file as **relation.dwg**.

Chapter Review Questions

1. Which of the following view types must be the first view in a drawing?
   a. Projection
   b. Base
   c. Auxiliary
   d. Detailed
2. If you have already placed a front view of a part in a drawing, which tool most easily creates a side view aligned with the front view, as shown in Figure 25–55?

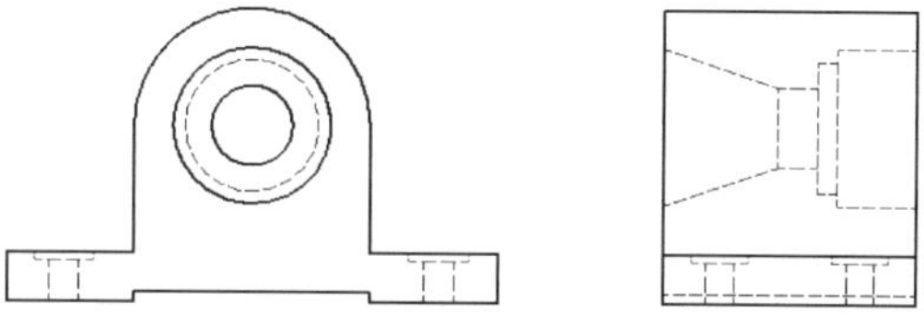

Figure 25–55

   a. Projected View
   b. Base View
   c. Draft View
   d. Aligned View
3. Which command can create the foreshortening effect in the views shown in Figure 25–56?

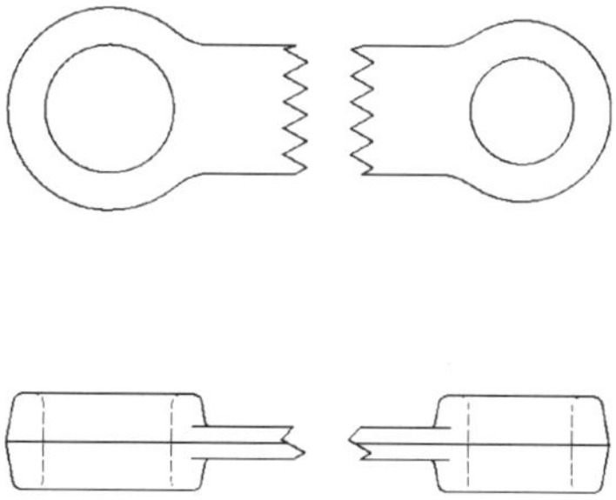

Figure 25–56

   a. Break View
   b. Crop View
   c. Auxiliary View
   d. Break Out View

4. Which view types enable you to create an independent 3D view? (Select all that apply.)
   a. Projection
   b. Base
   c. Auxiliary
   d. Detailed
5. You can break the alignment dependency between a parent and a child view.
   a. True
   b. False
6. If you change a part or assembly file, drawing views that show it update automatically by default.
   a. True
   b. False
7. When inserting a Base view into a drawing file, what is required to display a view name, similar to that shown in Figure 25–57?

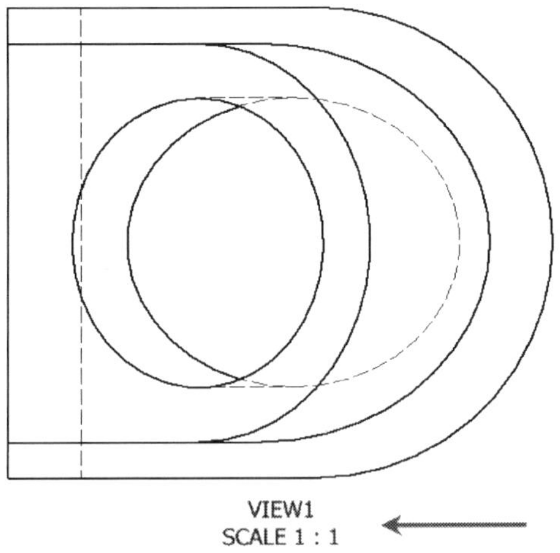

Figure 25–57

   a. Enable/Disable feature preview.
   b. Toggle the label **Visibility**.
   c. Ensure that you have edited the view label.
   d. Ensure that the **Scales** are on.

8. Which type of file is required to be created when you want to show an exploded view of an assembly in a drawing file, as shown in Figure 25–58?

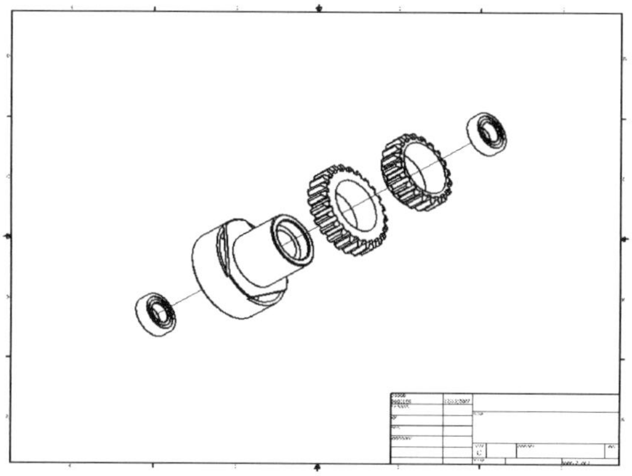

Figure 25–58

   a. Project
   b. Part
   c. Presentation
   d. Assembly

9. When you delete a view, as shown in Figure 25–59, what happens to the dependent views?

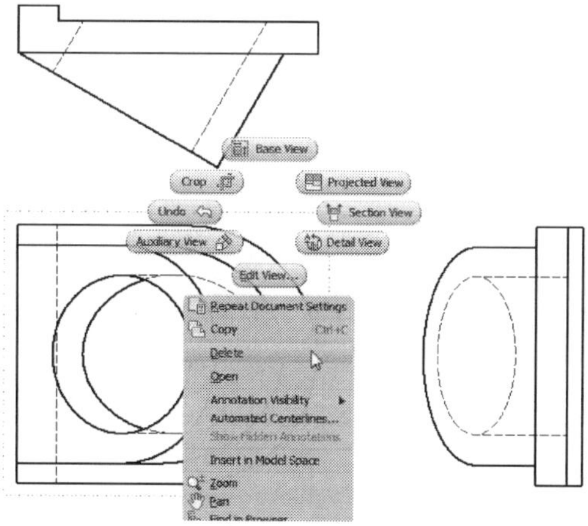

Figure 25–59

   a. They are automatically deleted.
   b. The dependent views are suppressed.
   c. You cannot delete a view that has dependent views.
   d. You are prompted to delete its dependent views.

10. A shaded Base view exists in a drawing. This base view is automatically displayed as shaded and it cannot be modified to remove the shaded display.
    a. True
    b. False
11. How can you move a base view and its dependent views?
    a. Move one of the dependent views and the base view moves with it.
    b. Move the base view and dependent views individually.
    c. Move the base view then realign the dependent views.
    d. Move the base view and the dependent views move with it.
12. Which of the following can be changed when you edit a view? (Select all that apply.)
    a. View Scale
    b. Line type
    c. View Label
    d. Hidden line visibility
13. You can change the scale of the projected views independent of the parent view scale.
    a. True
    b. False

Command Summary

Button	Command	Location
	**Auxiliary (view)**	• **Ribbon:** *Place Views* tab>Create panel • **Context Menu:** In the graphics window with a view selected • **Context Menu:** In Model browser with a view selected>Create View
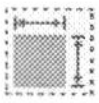	**Base (view)**	• **Ribbon:** *Place Views* tab>Create panel • **Context Menu:** In the graphics window with a view selected • **Context Menu:** In Model browser with a view selected>Create View
	**Break (view)**	• **Ribbon:** *Place Views* tab>Modify panel • **Context Menu:** In Model browser with a view selected> Create View
	**Break Alignment**	• **Ribbon:** *Place Views* tab>Modify panel • **Context Menu:** In Model browser with a view selected>Alignment
	**Break Out (view)**	• **Ribbon:** *Place Views* tab>Modify panel • **Context Menu:** In Model browser with a view selected>Create View
	**Crop (view)**	• **Ribbon:** *Place Views* tab>Modify panel • **Context Menu:** In the graphics window with a view selected • **Context Menu:** In Model browser with a view selected>Create View
N/A	**Delete (view)**	• **Context Menu:** In the graphics window with a view selected • **Context Menu:** In Model browser with a view selected • (*select view in the graphics window and press <Delete>*)
	**Detail (view)**	• **Ribbon:** *Place Views* tab>Create panel • **Context Menu:** In the graphics window with a view selected • **Context Menu:** In Model browser with a view selected>Create View
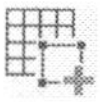	**Draft (view)**	• **Ribbon:** *Place Views* tab>Create panel
N/A	**Edit Sheet**	• **Context Menu:** In Model browser with a sheet selected
N/A	**Edit View**	• **Context Menu:** In the graphics window with a view selected • **Context Menu:** In Model browser with a view selected

N/A	**Edit View Label**	• **Context Menu:** In graphics window with a view label selected • Double-click on the view label
	**Horizontal (alignment)**	• **Ribbon:** *Place Views* tab>Modify panel • **Context Menu:** In Model browser with a view selected>Alignment
	**In Position (alignment)**	• **Ribbon:** *Place Views* tab>Modify panel • **Context Menu:** In Model browser with a view selected>Alignment
N/A	**Make All Views Raster / Make All Views Precise**	• **Context Menu:** In the graphics window
N/A	**Make View Raster / Make View Precise**	• **Context Menu:** In the graphics window with a view selected • **Context Menu:** In Model browser with a view selected
	**Overlay (view)**	• **Ribbon:** *Place Views* tab>Create panel • **Context Menu:** In Model browser with a view selected>Create View
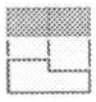	**Projected (view)**	• **Ribbon:** *Place Views* tab>Create panel • **Context Menu:** In the graphics window with a view selected • **Context Menu:** In Model browser with a view selected>Create View
N/A	**Properties**	• **Context Menu:** In Model browser with a sheet selected
	**Replace Model Reference**	• **Ribbon:** *Manage* tab>Modify panel
	**Section (view)**	• **Ribbon:** *Place Views* tab>Create panel • **Context Menu:** In the graphics window with a view selected • **Context Menu:** In Model browser with a view selected>Create View
	**Slice (view)**	• **Ribbon:** *Place Views* tab>Modify panel • **Context Menu:** In Model browser with a view selected>Create View
N/A	**Suppress (view)**	• **Context Menu:** In the graphics window with a view selected • **Context Menu:** In Model browser with a view selected
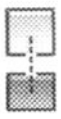	**Vertical (alignment)**	• **Ribbon:** *Place Views* tab>Modify panel • **Context Menu:** In Model browser with a view selected>Alignment

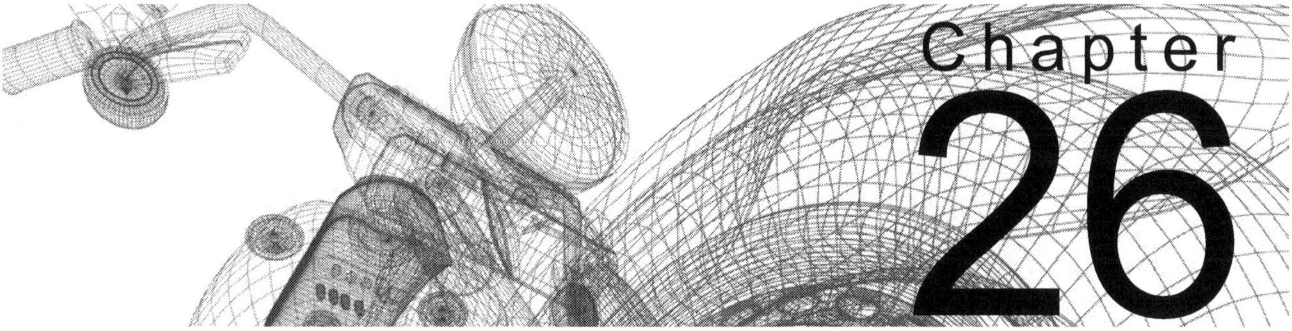

Chapter 26

Detailing Drawings

Adding details to your drawings enables you to communicate additional information to other designers working on a project. You can also apply styles and standards to control the appearance of your model.

Learning Objectives in This Chapter

- Show model dimensions and create dimensions to detail a drawing view.
- Edit the values, locations, and styles of dimensions in a drawing view.
- Work with multiple sheet drawings to manipulate their sheet display, sheet numbers, and the views on each sheet.
- Add a parts list to a drawing and edit it to customize values and column display.
- Create and edit balloons that identify the components in a drawing's parts list.
- Review and edit the style options to customize the display of annotations in a drawing.
- Assign and edit hatch patterns.

26.1 Dimensions

When you create a view, you have the option to display dimensions that are used to create the 3D model. These dimensions are called model dimensions. You can also add drawing dimensions directly in the drawing.

Model Dimensions

There are two ways to add model dimensions in a drawing. You can display all available model dimensions in a new view while creating the view, or display selected dimensions on existing views.

To display model dimensions in a new view, when creating the view, in the Drawing View dialog box, in the *Recovery Options* tab, select **All Model Dimensions**, as shown in Figure 26–1.

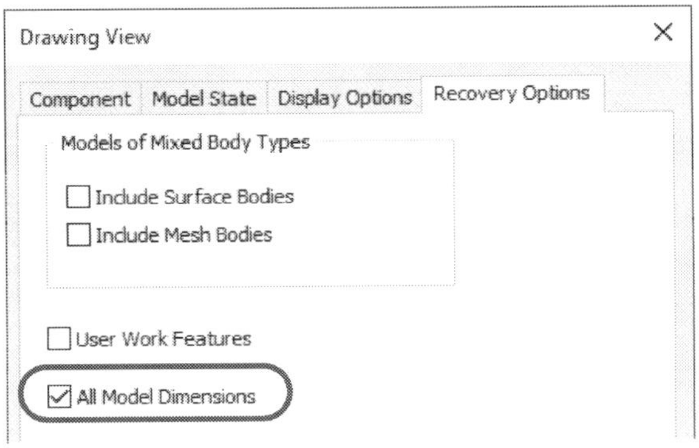

Figure 26–1

A view created using this option is shown in Figure 26–2.

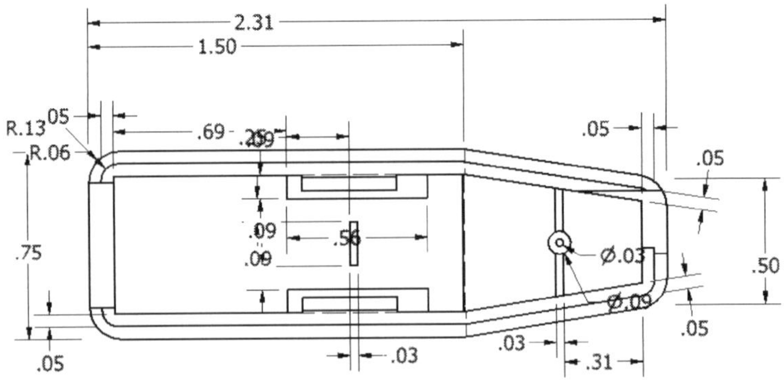

Figure 26–2

- Model dimensions can only be displayed in one view at a time.

How To: Display Model Dimensions

1. Activate **Retrieve Model Annotations** using one of the following methods:
   - Select the *Annotate* tab>Retrieve panel and click 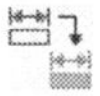 (Retrieve Model Annotations).
   - Use the shortcut menu on the drawing sheet and click **Retrieve Model Annotations**.

   The Retrieve Model Annotation dialog box opens as shown in Figure 26–3. Orthographic and Isometric appear in the title of the dialog box depending on the view selected.

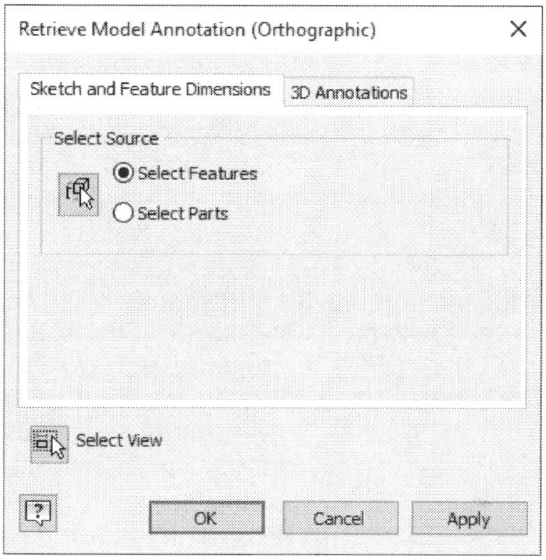

Figure 26–3

2. On the *Sketch and Feature Dimensions* tab, ensure that  (Select View) is active and select the view to which you want to retrieve the dimensions. All dimensions are previewed in that view.
3. Select dimensions to keep them in the view. You can select using any of the following techniques:
   - Select individual dimensions to keep them.
   - Drag a boundary box to keep multiple dimensions.
4. To retrieve dimensions on specific parts or features, select **Select Features** or **Select Parts** in the the *Select Source* area, and then select the parts or features. The dimensions on the selected items become available.
5. Click **OK** to add the dimensions to the drawing view.

Figure 26–4 shows a model with feature dimensions added to the view.

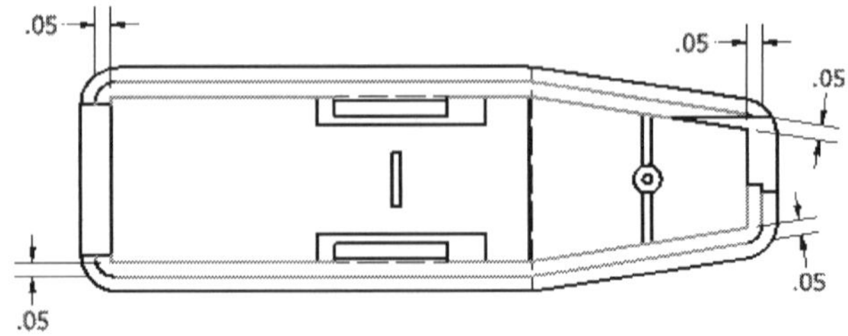

Figure 26–4

Edit Model Dimensions

*To prevent edits to model dimensions, clear the **Enable part modification from in drawings** option in the Drawing tab in the Application Options dialog box.*

To edit a model dimension in a drawing file, select the dimension, right-click, and select **Edit Model Dimension**. You must update the model once a model dimension is changed. **Edit Model Dimension** is not available for drawing dimensions.

- In general, if a change is major or affects multiple features, you should make the change in the part file.

Drawing Dimensions

In addition to model dimensions, you can also create dimensions directly on a drawing. Drawing dimensions are dependent on the part geometry and their value cannot be changed. However, if the part size changes, the drawing dimension updates automatically. Drawing dimensions can be placed on any view type (e.g., Base, Projected, or Isometric).

*The **Dimension** option in the drawing environment provides additional dimensioning flexibility than in the Sketch environment. For example, when a radius is selected for a drawing dimension, you can right-click and assign **Angle**, **Chord Length**, and **Arc Length** dimensions. These options are not available when dimensioning a sketch.*

To add dimensions to your drawing, select the *Annotate* tab and use any of the Dimension creation types (General Dimension, Baseline, Ordinate, and Chain) shown in Figure 26–5. The General dimension type is also located on the marking menu.

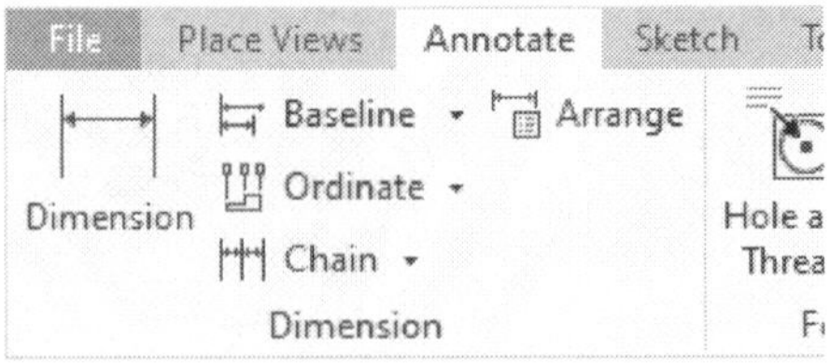

Figure 26–5

> **Hint: Measurements in a Drawing**
>
> As of Inventor 2021, the Measure command can now be used in the Drawing environment to measure entities in the same way as they are measured in part and assembly models. These measurements are temporary and do not create dimensions.

General Dimensions

A general dimension ( ) adds dimensions the same way model dimensions are added in the part file. The type of dimension placed (linear, diameter, angular, etc.) depends on the entity or entities selected.

- When a general dimension is placed, the Edit Dimension dialog box opens by default, enabling you to immediately modify the dimension.
  - You can modify the position of the text in relation to the text box, the display of the dimension value, add and edit text and symbols to go with the dimension, modify the tolerance format, or modify inspection dimensions.
  - To disable this dialog box from opening when a dimension is placed, clear the **Edit dimension when created** option and click **OK**.
- In addition to the standard entities and vertices that can be selected as references for dimensions, a virtual intersection of two lines can also be used. Select a line, right-click, and select **Intersection**. Then select a second line for the second dimension reference before placing the dimension as you would normally.
- When placing a Radial dimension, you can move it in 15-degree increments by holding <Ctrl> while dragging.
- When placing a general linear or diameter dimension, you can right-click and select from a list of types to customize the dimension type being placed or its orientation, as shown in Figure 26–6. Before locating the dimension, right-click and select a type in the Dimension Type list.

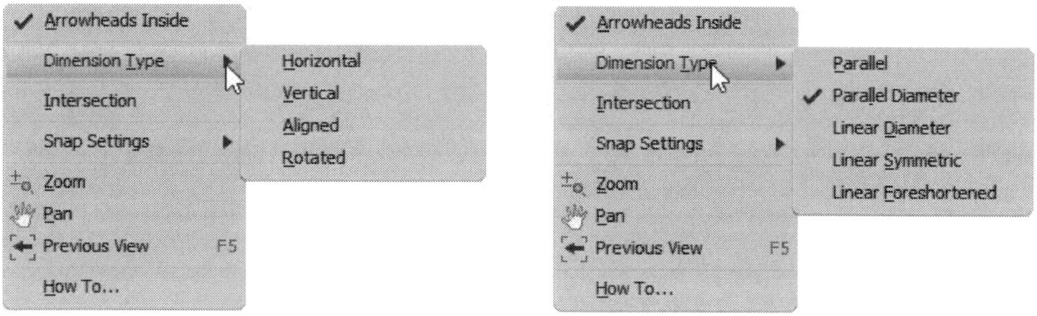

Figure 26–6

Foreshortened General Dimensions

Foreshortened dimensions are used for linear, angular, and arc length dimension types for referencing objects (e.g., work geometry) that are outside a drawing view. A foreshortened dimension displays even if the visibility of the referenced object is cleared in the view. Figure 26–7 shows two foreshortened dimensions. On the left, the arrow to the 2nd reference is shown and on the right, it is not shown.

2nd Arrowhead dimension shown

2nd Arrowhead dimension hidden

Figure 26–7

How To: Create a Foreshortened General Dimension

*To select the second reference you must ensure that it is included in the view. In the case of work geometry, locate the geometry in the view, right-click and select **Include**.*

1. In the Dimension panel, click (General Dimension).
2. Select the entities to be dimensioned. The first entity selected should be the reference that is going to remain or is visible in the drawing view. Select the included reference geometry as the second reference.
3. Before locating the dimension, right-click, expand Dimension type and select from the available foreshortened options. (i.e., **Linear Foreshortened**, **Angular Foreshortened**, or **Arc Length Foreshortened**).
4. (Optional) To clear the display of the second arrowhead, right-click on the dimension and select **Hide 2nd Arrowhead**.

Select the placement location for the foreshortened dimension.

Hint: Adding Text to Foreshortened Dimensions

Additional text can be added to a dimension value to further explain the intent of the dimension, as shown in Figure 26–8. To add text, double-click on the dimension value and enter text in the Edit Dimension dialog box. Ensure that the text is added before or after the **<<>>** symbols. These symbols represent the dimension value.

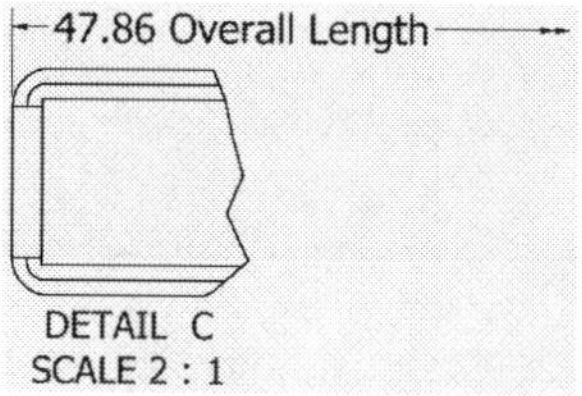

Figure 26–8

Isometric General Dimensions

You can place general dimensions on a view that is placed in an Isometric orientation, as shown in Figure 26–9. Press <Spacebar> while placing dimensions to toggle between alternate dimension orientations, if available.

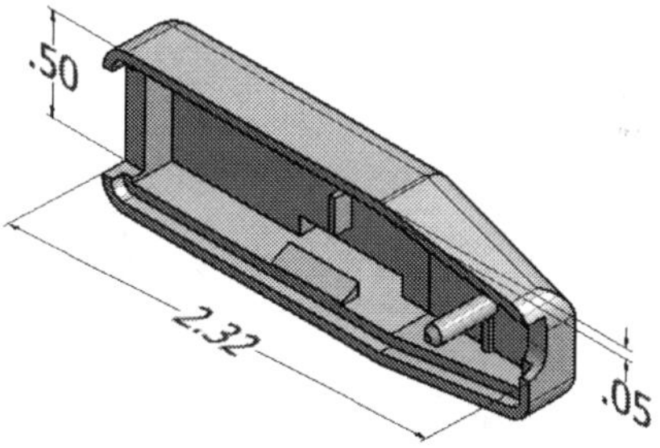

Figure 26–9

Baseline Dimensions

A Baseline dimension enables you to create dimensions that share a common extension line. Baseline dimensions are shown in Figure 26–10.

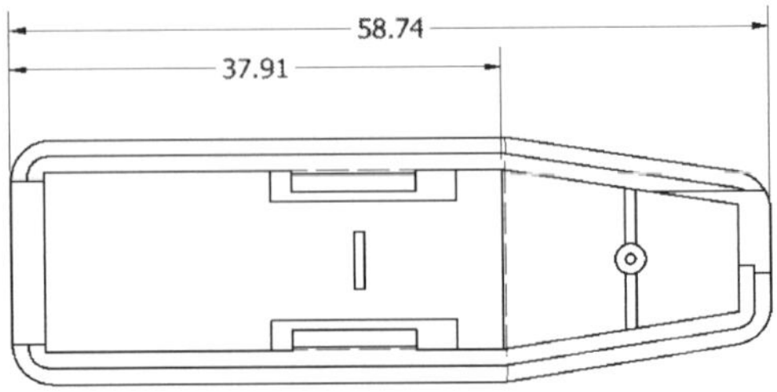

Figure 26–10

How To: Create a Baseline Dimension

To create a set of baseline dimensions that act as one unit, consider using (Baseline Set).

1. In the Dimension panel, click (Baseline).
2. Select the entities to be dimensioned. The first entity selected is used as the default origin from which all other dimensions are dimensioned. You can also drag a window to select multiple edges for dimensioning.
3. Right-click in the graphics window and select **Continue**.
4. Move the cursor and left-click to place the dimensions.
5. If required, you can change the origin point by right-clicking the dimension extension line you want to assign as the new origin, and selecting **Make Origin**.
6. Select additional entities to add more baseline dimensions.
7. Once you have finished selecting additional references, right-click in the graphics window and select **Create**. The baseline dimensions are created.

Ordinate Dimensions

An ordinate dimension enables you to create individual ordinate reference dimensions. Ordinate dimensions are shown in Figure 26–11.

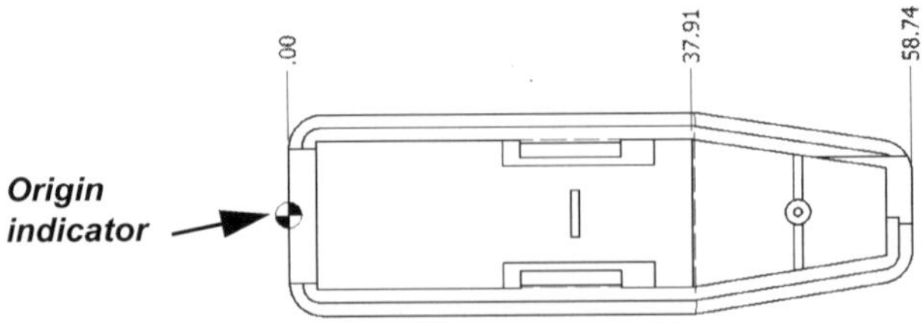

Figure 26–11

To create a set of ordinate dimensions that act as one unit, consider using (Ordinate Set).

How To: Create Ordinate Dimensions

1. In the Dimension panel, click (Ordinate).
2. Select the view to dimension.
3. Select a point for the origin indicator. The origin indicator is the location from which the ordinate dimensions are referenced.
4. Select the entities to which you want to dimension. You can also drag a window to select multiple edges to dimension.
5. Right-click in the graphics window and select **Continue**.
6. Move the cursor and left-click to place the dimensions.
7. Select additional entities to add more baseline dimensions, if required.
8. Once you are finished selecting additional references, right-click in the graphics window and select **OK**. The ordinate dimensions are created.

Chain Dimensions

A chain dimension enables you to create multiple dimensions that are chained to one another, as shown in Figure 26–12.

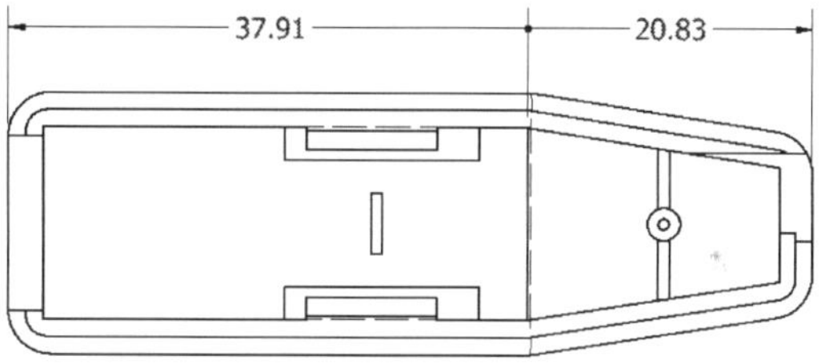

Figure 26–12

To create a set of chain dimensions that act as one unit, consider using (Chain Set).

How To: Create a Chain Dimension

1. In the Dimension panel, click (Chain).
2. Select the entities to be dimensioned. The first entity selected is used as the default origin from which all other dimensions are dimensioned. You can also drag a window to select multiple edges for dimensioning.
3. Right-click in the graphics window and select **Continue**.
4. Move the cursor and click to place the dimensions.
5. Select additional entities to add more chain dimensions, if required.
6. Once you have finished selecting additional references, right-click in the graphics window and select **Create**. The chain dimensions are created.

Editing Drawing Dimensions

Some common editing options are available in the shortcut menu that can be used when editing drawing dimensions. They vary depending on which dimension is selected. The list of options are described as follows:

Delete	Deletes the dimension from the drawing.
Move Dimension	Enables you to select another view, and have the dimension switch to that view. If no valid reference points exist in the selected view, a message displays indicating this, and the operation is canceled.
Arrange Dimensions	Enables you to arrange groups of selected dimensions so that they lie along one axis or multiple axes. The dimensions can be selected in one or multiple views. This command is also available in the *Annotate* tab in the Dimension panel.
Copy Properties	Enables you to copy dimension properties, including style, layer, text, precision, and tolerance between dimensions.
Hide Extension Line	Enables you to clear the display of an extension line in the drawing. Right-click on the extension line that is to be removed to select the option. Right-click on the dimension and click **Show all Extension Lines** to return them to the display.
Edit Arrowheads	Enables you to change the display style of either the first or second arrowhead associated with the dimension.
Options	The options available vary depending on the type of dimension selected. For example, for General dimensions you can customize the arrow heads and leaders.
Precision	Sets the precision for the dimension.
Edit	Opens the Edit Dimension dialog box, in which you can modify the position of the text in relation to the text box, the display of the dimension value, add and edit text and symbols to go with the dimension, modify the tolerance format, and modify inspection dimensions.
Text	Opens the Format Text dialog box.

Edit Dimension Dialog Box

*Unlike a general dimension, the Edit Dimension dialog box does not display when a Baseline, Ordinate, or Chain dimension is placed. To open it, right-click on the dimension value and select **Edit**.*

When editing a model or drawing dimensions using the **Edit** option, the Edit Dimension dialog box is available, as shown in Figure 26–13.

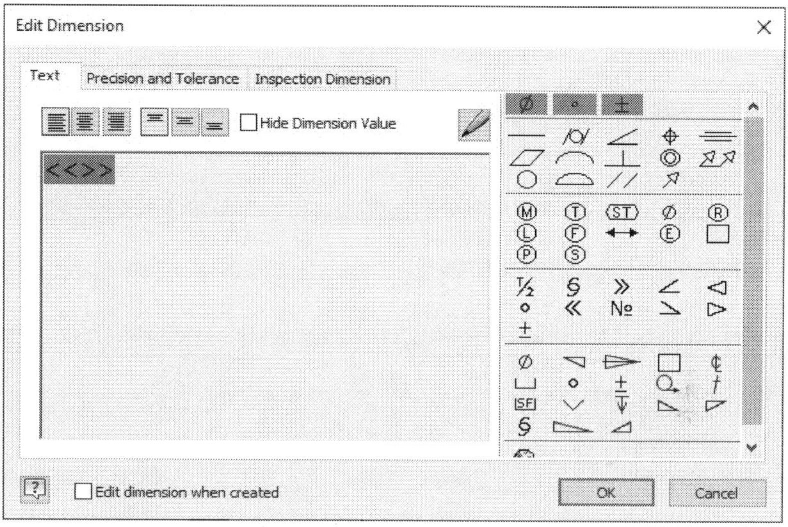

Figure 26–13

Settings specified in the Precision and Tolerance tab for a selected dimension overrides any settings made to the active dimension style.

- The *Text* tab enables you add text before and after the dimension value (**<<>>**), change its position or justification, and specify text properties ( ). Additionally, symbols can be embedded by selecting them and adding them to the text line.
- The *Precision and Tolerance* tab enables you to override dimension values, set a tolerance method, and define the precision setting for the dimension.
- The *Inspection Dimension* tab enables you to set the selected dimension as an inspection dimension, and customize how it displays.

Hint: Dimension Selection and Filters

To select dimensions for editing, you can do any one of the following:

- Select individual dimensions in the drawing.
- Hold <Ctrl> to add multiple dimensions to the selection set.
- Drag a selection box around the required dimensions.
- Use any of the four selection filter options in the drop-down list in the Quick Access Toolbar, as shown in Figure 26–14.

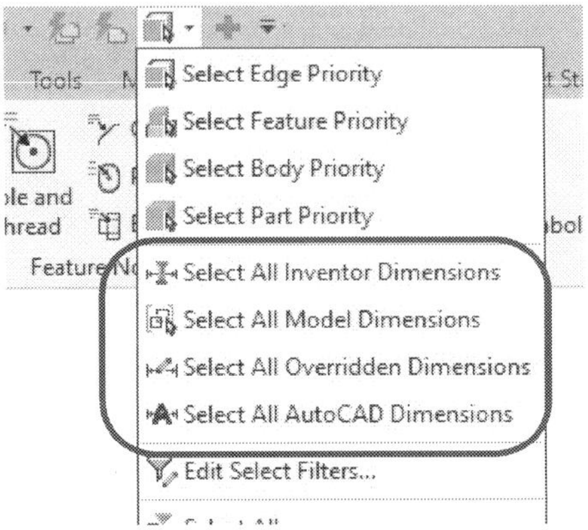

Figure 26–14

Dimension Styles

You can control the appearance of dimensions by applying or changing dimension styles. The software comes installed with a number of predefined styles for each of the major drafting standards such as ANSI, ISO, JIS, etc. The styles available in a new drawing are determined by the active standard in the template that was used to create the drawing file.

- To set the style for a dimension before you place it, start the dimension command, and select the dimension style in the Format panel, as shown in Figure 26–15.

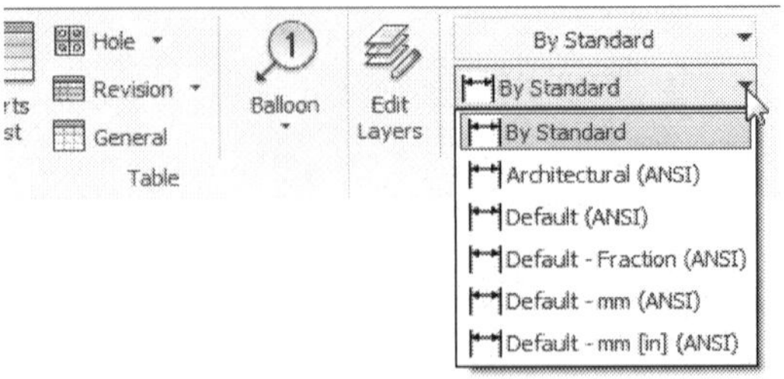

Figure 26–15

To retain the last used dimension style so that it is automatically used as the style for future dimensions, set the ***Default Object Style*** *option to* ***Last Used*** *in the Drawing tab in the Application Options dialog box.*

- To change the style of an existing dimension, select the dimension first and then select the style in the drop-down list.

A dimension style controls the attributes of dimensions, such as units, precision, text size, font, default orientations, etc. You can create your own dimension styles or change existing dimension styles.

- To display dimension styles, select the *Manage* tab and in the Styles and Standards panel, click (Styles Editor). In the Style and Standard Editor dialog box, expand the *Dimension* area to view the list of styles.
- To edit a dimension style, select it and use the options and tabs in the right-hand pane (shown in Figure 26–16) to make modifications.

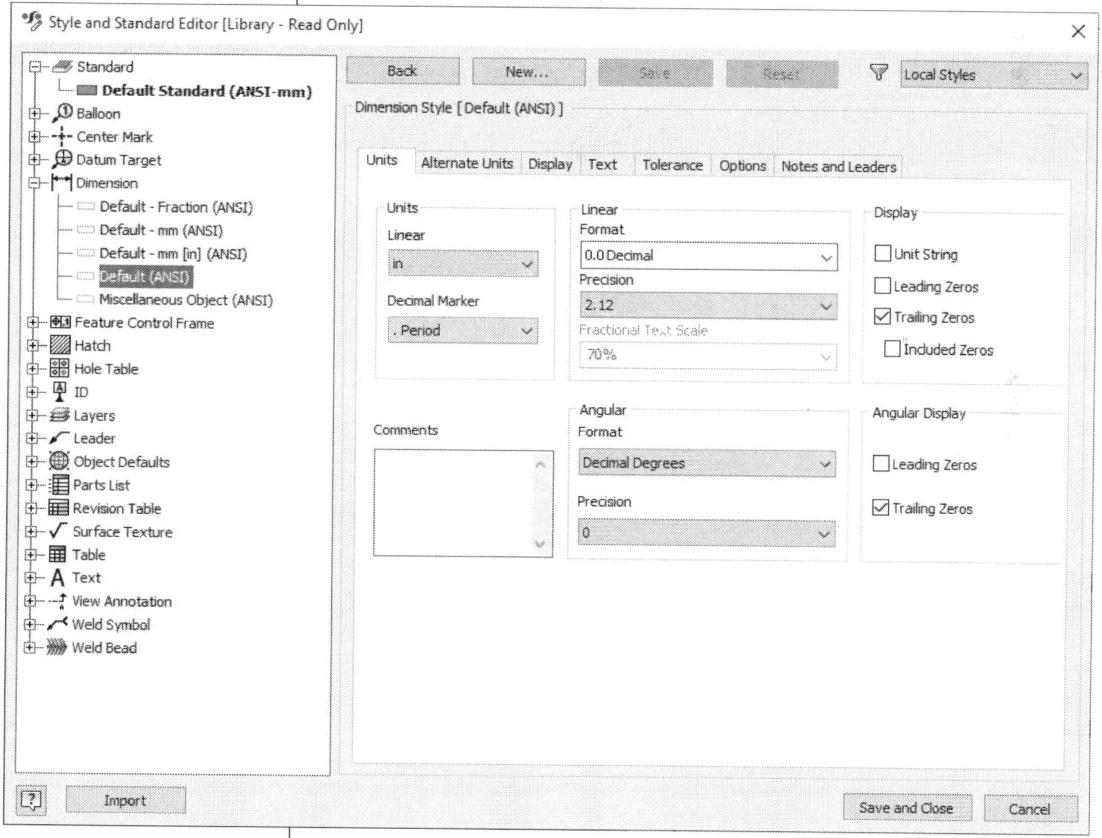

Figure 26–16

26.2 Drawing Sheets

All drawings can contain an unlimited number of sheets and each sheet can contain a variety of views, annotations, tables, etc. Once multiple sheets have been added to a drawing you can use the Model browser to navigate between them, delete them, or move views between them.

Use any of the following procedures to work with drawing sheets:

- To add a new sheet to a drawing, right-click in the graphics window and select **New Sheet**. Alternately, in the *Place Views* tab, in the Sheets panel, click (New Sheet). You can also right-click on the drawing name in the Model browser and select **New Sheet**.
- To switch between sheets in a drawing, double-click on the sheet name in the Model browser. The Model browser shown in Figure 26–17 shows that **Sheet:2** is the active sheet.

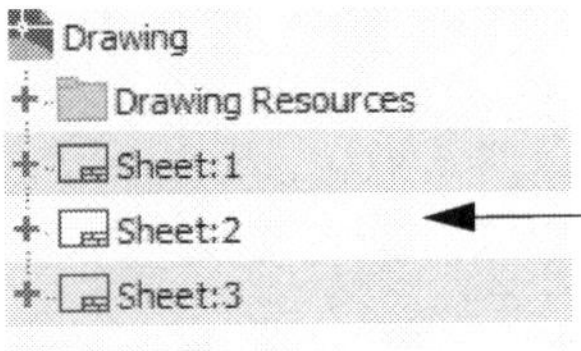

Once a sheet is active, all of the other sheets are grayed out to indicate that they are not active

Figure 26–17

- Views can be duplicated on a sheet by selecting it, and using the right-click **Copy** and **Paste** commands.
- Views can be copied between sheets by selecting them in the source view, right-clicking and selecting **Copy**. Activate the new sheet, right-click and select **Paste**.
- To move a view between sheets, select it in the Model browser and drag it to the new sheet.

- To delete a sheet, right-click on the sheet name in the Model browser and select **Delete Sheet**. The Delete Sheet dialog box opens. Click **OK** to delete the selected sheet. Click >> to expand the dialog box to refine which sheets to delete, as shown in Figure 26–18.

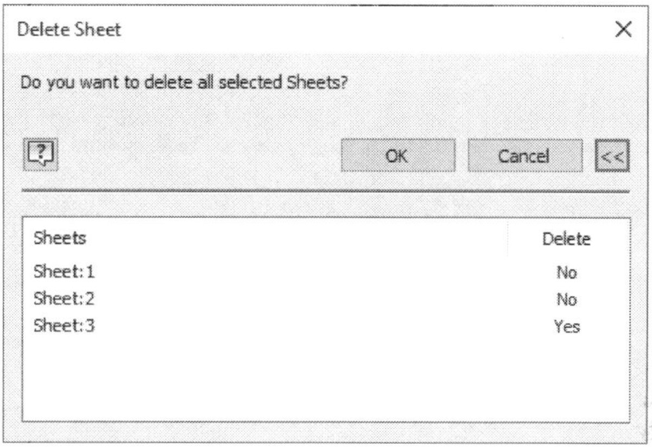

Figure 26–18

How To: Change Sheet Color

1. Select the *Tools* tab>Options panel and click (Document Settings).
2. In the Document Settings dialog box select the *Sheet* tab.
3. In the *Colors* area, select the color swatch for the **Sheet** and select a new color.
4. Click **OK** in the Color palette and close the Document Settings dialog box.

Hint: Drawing Sheet Formats

Once the layout of a drawing sheet has been defined (views, tables, parts list, etc.), it can be saved as a sheet format in the existing drawing by right-clicking on the sheet name in the Model browser and selecting **Create Sheet Format**. Once saved, it is listed in the **Sheet Formats** node in the **Drawing Resources**. This format can be used in the future to create additional sheets in the drawing by right-clicking its name in the **Drawing Resources** node and clicking **New Sheet**.

To include any custom sheet formats in a drawing template, you must edit the template or create a new template with the new sheet format included.

26.3 Parts List

A parts list is a list of the components in an assembly, as shown in Figure 26–19. You can add a parts list to a drawing file.

Parts List			
ITEM	QTY	PART NUMBER	DESCRIPTION
1	1	Base_Vise	
2	1	Sliding_Jaw	
3	1	Collar	
4	2	Jaw_Plate	
5	2	Set_Screw	
6	2	Slide_Key	
7	1	Special_Key	
8	4	ANSI B18.6.3 - 1/4-20 x 3/4	Countersunk Flat Head Screw
9	1	Screw_Sub	

Figure 26–19

Creating the Parts List

How To: Create a Parts List

You can add multiple parts lists to a single drawing.

1. Select the *Annotate* tab>Table panel, and click 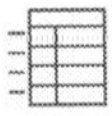 (Parts List). The Parts List dialog box opens as shown in Figure 26–20.

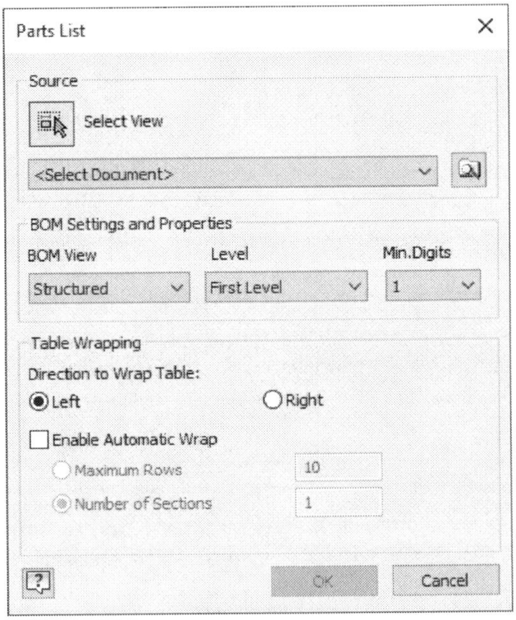

Figure 26–20

*The **Parts Only** BOM View option provides a row in the BOM for each component in the assembly, regardless of whether or not it is in a subassembly. Subassembly components are not provided with a row in this view. The **Structured** BOM View option provides a row in the BOM for the top-level components (**First Level**) or the top-level and all sub-levels (**All Levels**).*

2. To identify the assembly from which to generate the Parts List, click (Select View) and select a view in the drawing.
   - To add the parts list without creating a drawing view, in the *Source* area browse to and select an assembly to reference.

3. Define the remaining options in the Parts List dialog box. The options in the Parts List dialog box are described as follows:

BOM View	Enables you to determine what is shown in the bill of materials, such as whether or not subassemblies are included. 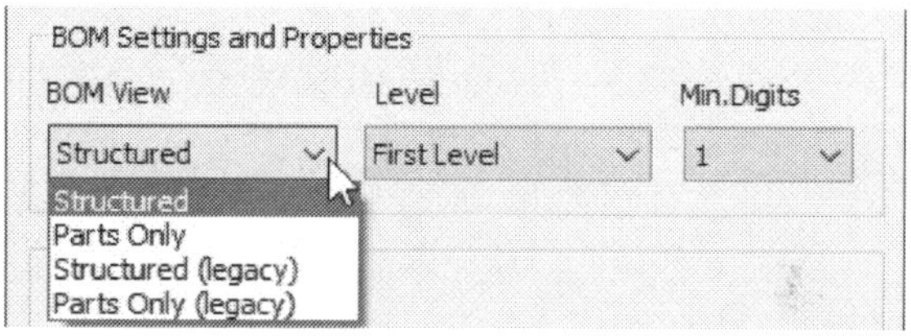
Level	This option (in Structured) controls whether first level children or all children are listed in the parts list.
Min. Digits	This option (in Structured and Parts Only) controls the minimum number of digits in the item number.
Numbering	This option (in Parts Only) selects from numeric or alphanumeric schemes.
Delimiter	This option (in Structured (Legacy)) is a character that marks the beginning or end of data.
Inheritance	This option (in Structured (Legacy)) enables parts at subassembly levels to update with changes made to the item or to the value of the parent assembly. (For example, if the assembly item value changes from 1 to A, the subassembly parts change from 1.1, 1.2, to A.1, A.2).
Table Wrapping	This option enables you to wrap the parts list rows, and control the direction to wrap.

4. Once all of the options have been selected, click **OK** and select a point to place the parts list in the drawing.

Editing the Parts List

To edit the parts list, select the list, right-click and select **Edit Parts List**. The Parts List dialog box opens as shown in Figure 26–21.

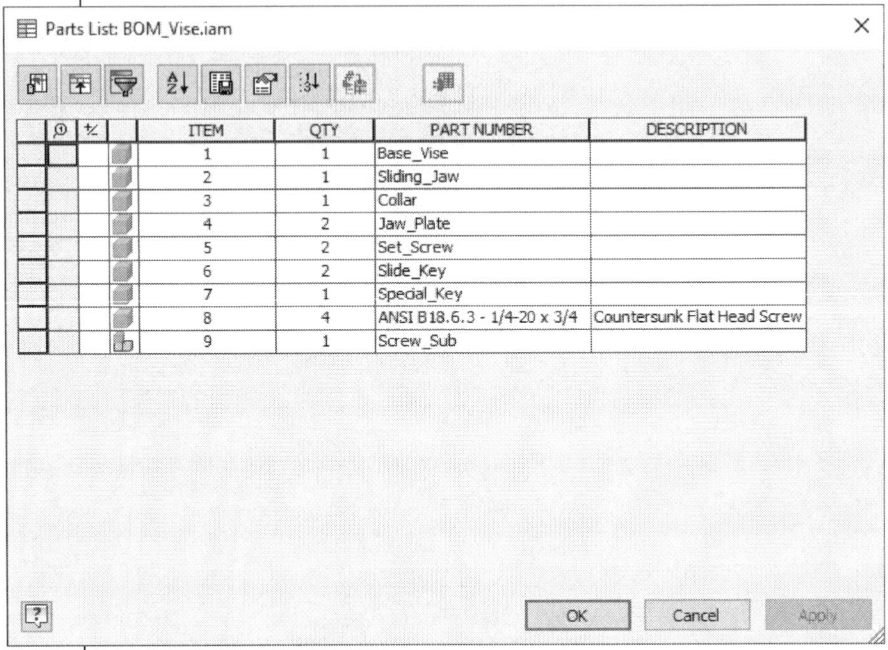

Figure 26–21

*A file can be opened directly from the Parts List dialog box or the table, by right-clicking the model name and selecting **Open**.*

The tools at the top of the Parts List dialog box enables you to customize the parts list. The available customizations include:

- To change the columns displayed in the Parts list, click (Column Chooser) and use the Parts List Column Chooser dialog box to add and remove columns from the list.
- To group rows, click (Group Settings) and use the Group Settings dialog box to assign the keys that define groupings. You can define up to three keys to specify groupings.
- To filter items from display in the parts list, click (Filter Settings). Use the Filter Settings dialog box to define the filter items. You can assign one or more filters.

*By default, a sort must be re-executed if parts are added or removed from the list. To automatically sort when a change in parts is made, select **Auto Sort on Update**.*

- To specify a sort order, click (Sort). The Sort Parts List dialog box enables you to specify the column name that is going to be used for initial sorting. Additionally, you can specify a second or third column by which to sort as well. Expand the dialog box to set whether the sort is done numerically or by string.
- To export the Parts List, click (Export) and select the file format to export to. Available types include .XLS, .TXT, .CSV, etc.
- To customize the layout of the Parts List table, click (Table Layout) to open the Parts List Table Layout to set how the parts list text will display and will wrap.
- If the assembly contains iParts or iAssemblies, click to select the members to include in the parts list.

Hint: Displaying Subassembly Components

To show all components of a subassembly in the parts list, verify that the assembly BOM's *View Property* is set to **All Levels** (right-click on the *Structured* tab heading in the BOM and select **View Properties**). This enables you to click the + sign in the drawing's Parts List to list the sub-components.

Additional customization of the Parts List can be done with direct manipulation of the rows and columns in the list.

Items displayed in red cannot be edited.

- To make changes to editable items in the list (e.g., item numbers or descriptions) click in the cell and enter a new value. Edited cells display in blue.
  - To return an override to the BOM value, right-click on the cell and select **Static Value**.
  - To save item numbers changes to the assembly BOM, click .

A custom part can be used to represent a part that is referenced in the assembly but not modeled. It can also be used as a placeholder for a removed part.

- To create an additional row to represent a part, right-click and select **Insert Custom Part**.
- To make a row invisible, select the row, right-click and clear the **Visible** option. Invisible rows are shaded gray in the dialog box, and are not displayed in the drawing.
- Columns can be dragged to adjust their width. Headings automatically wrap and can be resized to fit the largest word.

- To force a column break in the list, select a row in the Parts List dialog box, right-click and select **Wrap Table at Row**. An unwrapped and wrapped table is shown in Figure 26–22.

Unwrapped table

PARTS LIST		
ITEM	QTY	PART NUMBER
1	1	Base_Vise
2	1	Sliding_Jaw
3	1	Collar
4	2	Jaw_Plate
5	2	Set_Screw
6	2	Slide_Key
7	1	Special_Key
8	4	ANSI B18.6.3 - 1/4-20 x 3/4
9	1	Screw_Sub

Break row

Wrapped table

PARTS LIST		
ITEM	QTY	PART NUMBER
6	2	Slide_Key
7	1	Special_Key
8	4	ANSI B18.6.3 - 1/4-20 x 3/4
9	1	Screw_Sub

PARTS LIST		
ITEM	QTY	PART NUMBER
1	1	Base_Vise
2	1	Sliding_Jaw
3	1	Collar
4	2	Jaw_Plate
5	2	Set_Screw

Figure 26–22

- To split a table into multiple individual tables, right-click on a row in the Parts List table (not on a row in the Parts List dialog box that is used for editing) and select **Table>Split Table**. To unsplit a table, select anywhere in the table and select **Table>Un-split Table**. An original Parts List table and split table are shown in Figure 26–23.
    - A table can be split multiple times.
    - Split tables can be moved freely on the sheet or dragged between sheets in the Model browser.
    - Once split, the **Parts List** node in the Model browser is subdivided to represent the parent table and split tables.

Original Parts List Table

PARTS LIST		
ITEM	QTY	PART NUMBER
1	1	Base_Vise
2	1	Sliding_Jaw
3	1	Collar
4	2	Jaw_Plate
5	2	Set_Screw
6	2	Slide_Key
7	1	Special_Key
8	4	ANSI B18.6.3 - 1/4-20 x 3/4
9	1	Screw_Sub

Split row

Split tables

PARTS LIST		
ITEM	QTY	PART NUMBER
1	1	Base_Vise
2	1	Sliding_Jaw
3	1	Collar
4	2	Jaw_Plate

PARTS LIST		
ITEM	QTY	PART NUMBER
5	2	Set_Screw
6	2	Slide_Key
7	1	Special_Key
8	4	ANSI B18.6.3 - 1/4-20 x 3/4
9	1	Screw_Sub

Figure 26–23

- To format individual columns, right-click on the column and select the required option, as shown in Figure 26–24. The **Format Column** option enables you to change the column heading, justification, units formatting, and substitute values from another column. The **Column Width** option enables you to enter an exact width for the column.

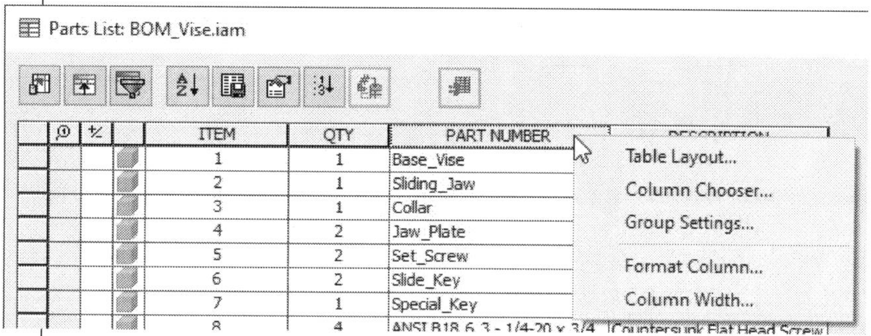

Figure 26–24

Hint: Parts Lists for Design Views

For Parts List tables, you can control how the parts list is filtered if you are creating a parts list for a design view. To enable the Autodesk Inventor software to take into account the design view settings, you must edit the parts list table and in the Filter settings ( ), enable the **Limit QTY to visible components only** option, as shown in Figure 26–25.

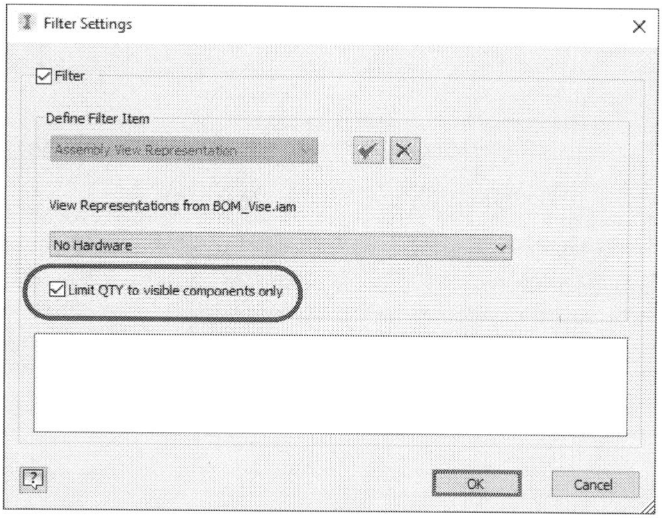

Figure 26–25

26.4 Balloons

Balloons are used to identify the components in the Parts List with their associated geometry in a drawing view. This is done using item numbers. You can place balloons either individually on parts or globally on all parts in a view, as shown in Figure 26–26.

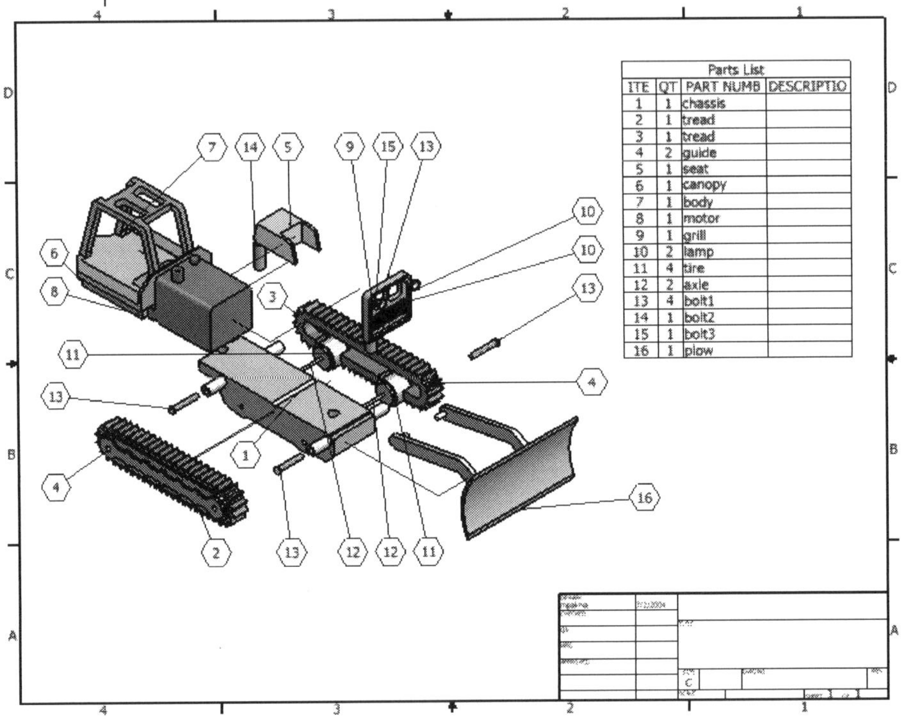

Figure 26–26

Placing Balloons Individually

To enable 15-degree snapping when placing the balloon, hold <Ctrl> while dragging.

How To: Place Individual Balloons

1. Select the *Annotate* tab>Table panel, click (Balloon).
2. Select the part.
3. Click to select vertices for the leader. Drag to position the leader.
4. Right-click after the final location for the balloon has been set, and select **Continue** to add a balloon for another part.
5. Right-click and select **Cancel [Esc]** to finish creating the balloons.

Placing Balloons Globally

How To: Globally Place Balloons

1. Select the *Annotate* tab>Table panel, expand **Balloon** and click  (Auto Balloon). The Auto Balloon dialog box opens as shown in Figure 26–27.

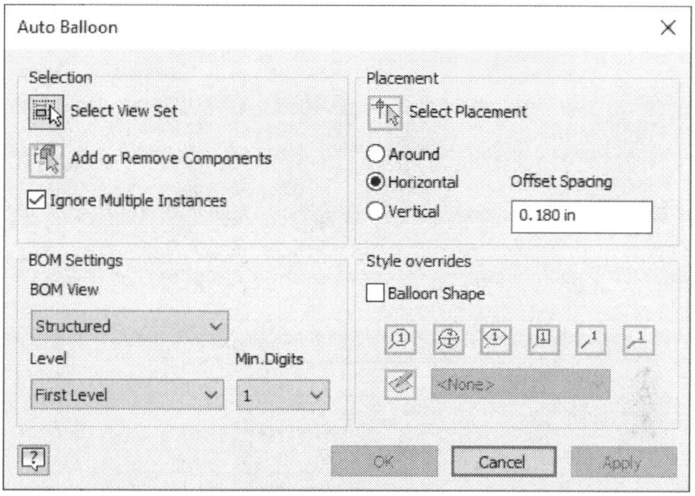

Figure 26–27

2. Select the drawing view.
3. Select the parts to which to add balloons.
4. Click  to place balloons and select the **Around**, **Horizontal**, or **Vertical** option to place balloons around, in a horizontal row, or in a vertical column of the view, respectively.
5. Enter a value in the *Offset Spacing* field to fix the spacing between balloons.
6. If required, select **Balloon Shape** to override the balloon default shape.
7. Click in the drawing to place the balloons.
8. Click **OK** to place the balloons and complete the operation.

Balloons are associated with the view to which they are attached. If you move the view, the balloons also move.

Manipulating Balloons

Once a balloon has been placed, you can manipulate it in the following ways:

- Move balloons and the ends of the balloon segments by dragging them.

- Align multiple balloons by selecting them by holding <Ctrl> or window selecting, right-clicking, and selecting an **Align** option in the context menu. The alignment options can be horizontally or vertically with one another, horizontally or vertically with an offset, or aligned based on a reference edge.

- Create additional segments by right-clicking on the balloon and selecting **Add Vertex/Leader**. Select the location on the existing leader to place the new vertex and then drag it.

- Add another balloon and label to an existing balloon by right-clicking on the balloon and selecting **Attach Balloon**. An example is shown in Figure 26–28. To sort the attached balloons from smallest to largest or from A to Z, right-click on the stack and select **Sort Balloons**.

- To delete a balloon, right-click on the balloon and select **Delete**. Alternatively, select the balloon and press <Delete>.

- To delete a balloon from a multi-item balloon, right-click on the balloon that you want to remove and select **Remove Balloon**.

- To change a balloon arrowhead, right-click on the balloon and select **Edit Arrowhead**. Change the arrowhead in the Change Arrowhead dialog box, as shown in Figure 26–28.

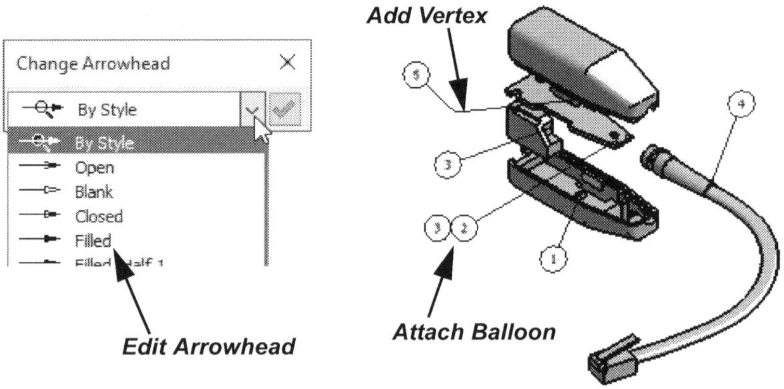

Figure 26–28

Balloon styles can be specified in the Style and Standard Editor dialog box.

- To edit a balloon, right-click on the balloon and select **Edit Balloon**. The Edit Balloon dialog box opens. Use this dialog box to change the balloon type, the symbol used (standard or custom), and the value of the balloon. Alternatively, you can double-click on the balloon or on its leader to edit the balloon.

26.5 Styles and Standards

The Style and Standard Editor controls the appearance of part edges, center-lines, dimension components, layers, part lists, balloons, and other annotations in a drawing. The software is installed with a default standard, and several other drafting standards are included (e.g., ANSI, ISO, and JIS). You can also create your own standards, as required.

To share a style library, copy the styles to a common network location and map the Design Data in the project file. You can also set the Application Options to identify the network location in which the style library is stored.

- A central library is used to store information pertaining to styles and standards. A file can reference one or more styles from this library. If a change is made to a style in the library, it is reflected in all files that reference that style.

Hint: Central Library Location

The central library is located in the following location: *C:\Users\Public\Public Documents\Autodesk\Inventor 20XX\Design Data*.

- Unique styles and standards can be created and stored with the drawing file. These can include new styles or modifications to existing library styles.

To open the Style and Standard Editor, select the *Manage* tab> Styles and Standards panel and click (Styles Editor). The Style and Standard Editor dialog box opens as shown in Figure 26–29.

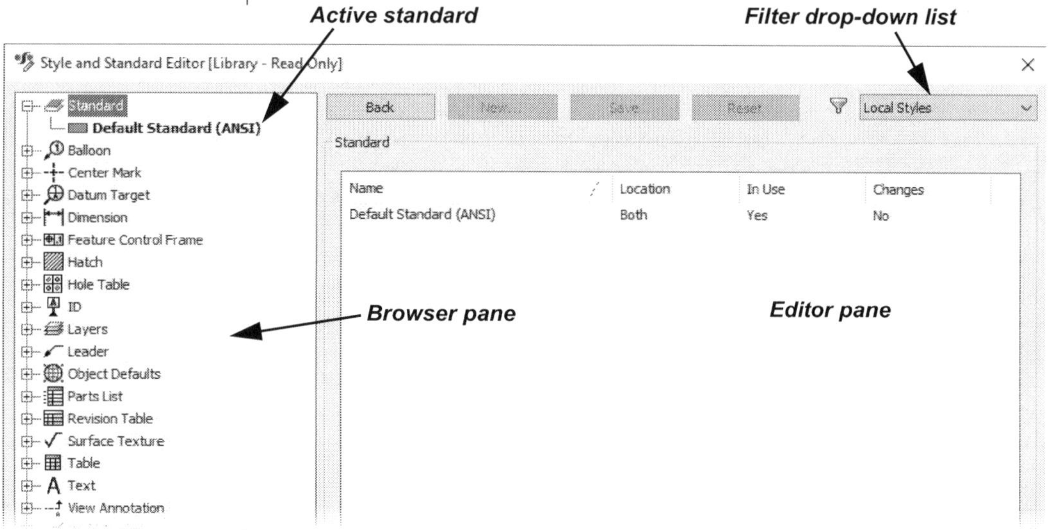

Figure 26–29

Hint: Displaying All Styles

By default, only styles and standards used in the active document are listed, as indicated by the **Local Styles** option in the Filter drop-down list. To display all of the available styles and standards, select **All Styles** in the Filter drop-down list.

Standards

Standards are comprised of all of the styles assigned for the various annotation types (e.g., Dimensions, Balloons, Hatching, Parts List, etc.). They also control the appearance of such drawing items as part edges, line weights, and projection type (first angle or third angle). The active standard is identified in bold in the dialog box. Select the standard to review the settings in the right-hand pane, as shown in Figure 26–30.

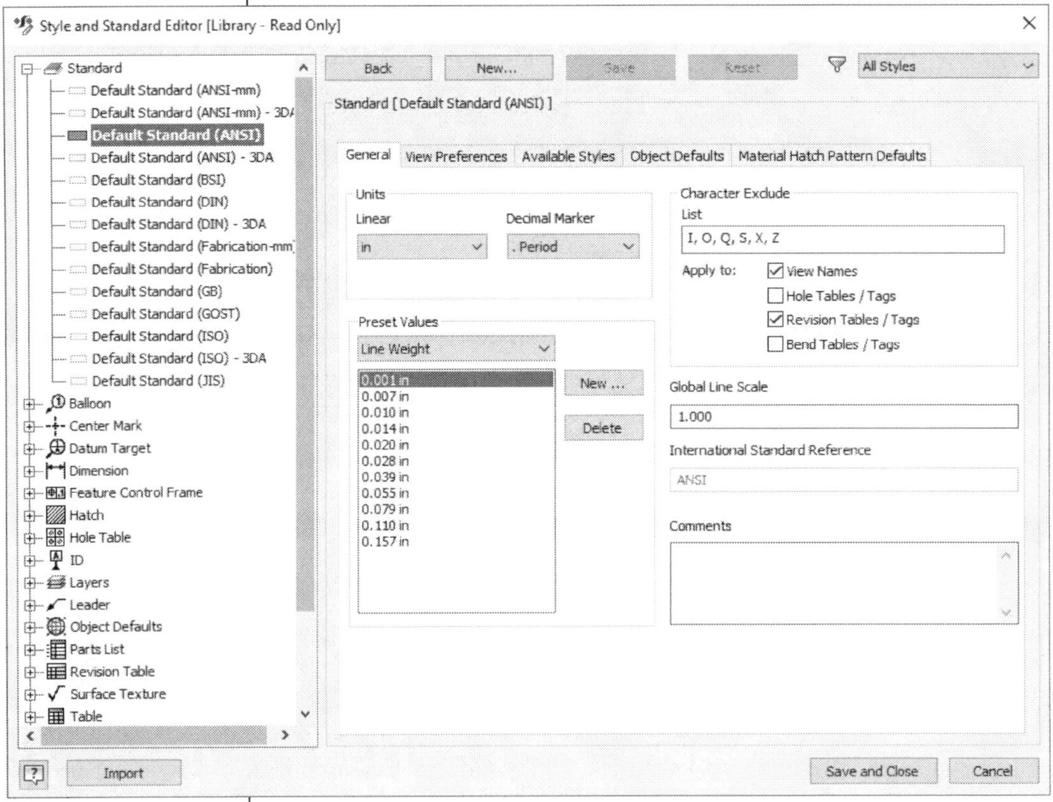

Figure 26–30

If multiple standards are used, consider creating a different template for each standard you use.

The active standard for a new drawing is based on the template file that is selected to create the drawing file. However, you can double-click on a different standard to activate it. The tabs that are available for the selected standard enable you to customize drawing annotation. The following two tabs specifically enable you to set further styles for annotation categories and objects:

- The *Available Styles* tab for a Standard controls the style being used for each of the drawing annotation categories.
- The *Object Defaults* tab controls the default layer and style for specific drawing objects.

Styles

Multiple styles can exist in each of the style type categories. To display a category's available styles, select it in the browser pane. For example, Figure 26–31 shows the styles available for the Dimension style type category.

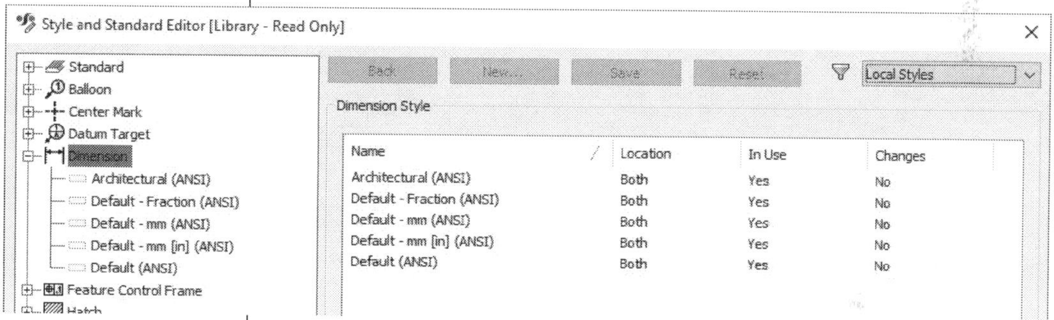

Figure 26–31

- The *Name* column lists the names of the available styles.
- The Location indicates whether the style is located in the **Library**, **Local** to the file, or **Both**.
- The *In Use* column indicates whether the style is used in the active standard.
- The *Changes* column indicates whether the changes that have been made are in the **Library**, the **Local** file or **Both**, or if **No** changes have been made.

To edit a style, select it in the browser pane and edit the options as required. For example, Figure 26–32 shows the options that can be edited to modify the Default (ANSI) Dimension style type.

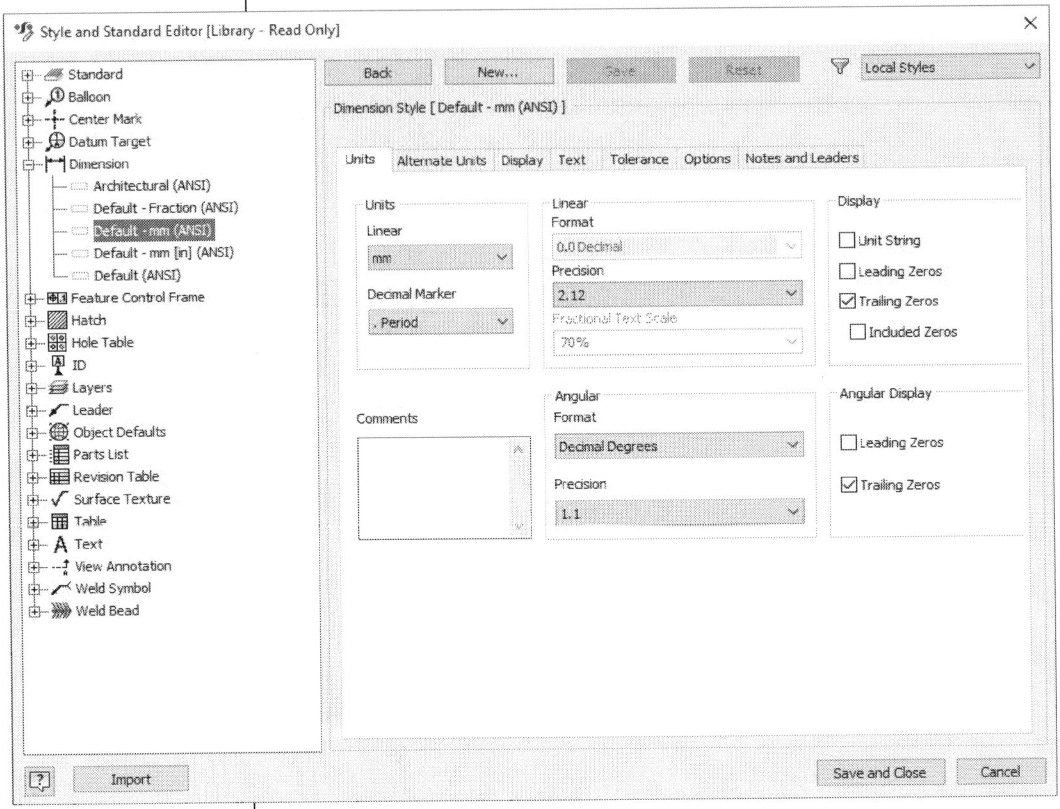

Figure 26–32

- When changes are made and saved for a style, they are saved to the active file.
- To save the changes to the style library, right-click on the style and select **Save to Style Library**. You need to have the correct permissions to save to the style library (controlled in the project file).
- To replace local changes by overwriting with the settings from the original style library, right-click on the style and select **Update Style**.
- To create a new style, select a style and click **New** in the browser pane. The selected style becomes the basis for the new style.

26.6 Hatching

The default hatch pattern is set in the Hatch style type category in the Style and Standard Editor, as shown in Figure 26–33.

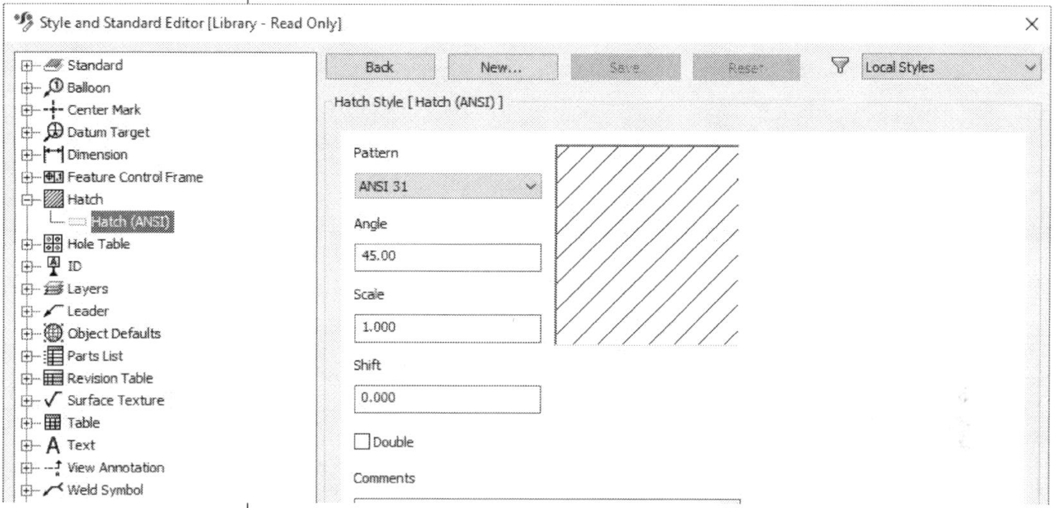

Figure 26–33

Note the following about hatching:

- Hatch patterns can be assigned from the internal style library or from an external *.PAT file. To load or assign additional patterns, select **Other** in the Pattern drop-down list to open the Select Hatch Pattern dialog box, as shown in Figure 26–34.

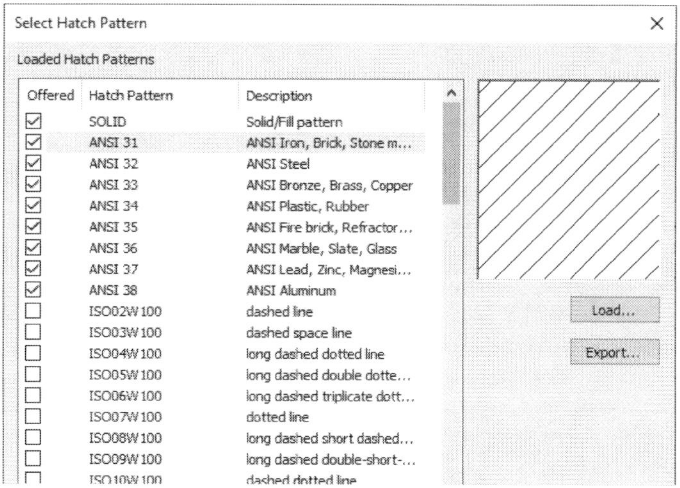

Figure 26–34

- Hatch patterns can be individually assigned to material types. In the default drawing standard, select the *Material Hatch Pattern Defaults* tab and assign the hatching for each material, as shown in Figure 26–35.

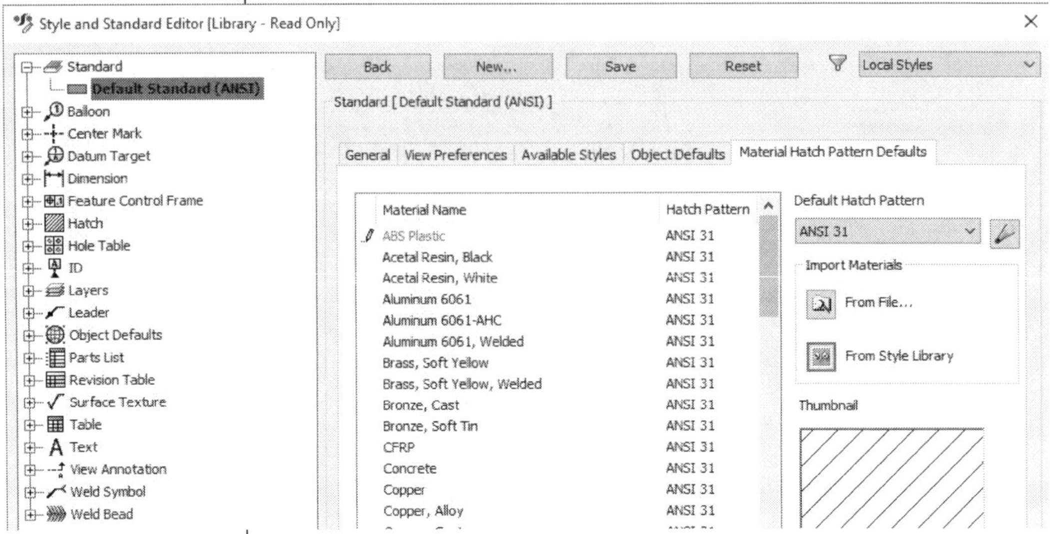

Figure 26–35

- Changes to the Hatch style are reflected in all existing hatched objects that use it. Any hatch overrides done directly on a hatched section in the drawing are independent of the Hatch style. Hatch overrides remain unchanged if the Hatch style is changed.

- Hatch patterns (or fill) can be assigned to a closed sketched section in a drawing by clicking  (Hatch/Fill Region) and selecting a closed area in the sketch. The default Hatch style that is used for sketches is specified for the **Sketch Hatch** object in the **Object Defaults** item.

- To ensure that hatching is clipped around overlapping text, ensure that **Cross Hatch Clipping** is enabled in the *Drawing* tab in the Document Settings. To change the clipped border size, select the text and drag.

- For section views, you can edit the hatching by right-clicking on the hatching in the view and selecting **Edit**. This opens the Edit Hatch Pattern dialog box, where you can change the pattern type, angle, scale, shift, line weight, and color.

Practice 26a

Detailing a Drawing I

Practice Objectives

- Change the sheet color of the active drawing.
- Retrieve and create the dimensions in the drawing.
- Add a new drawing sheet in a drawing.
- Move a drawing view between drawing sheets.
- Create a parts list table in a drawing.
- Add balloons to a drawing view to identify the components listed in a parts list table.

In this practice, you will open an existing drawing, modify it, and add the dimensions shown in Figure 26–36.

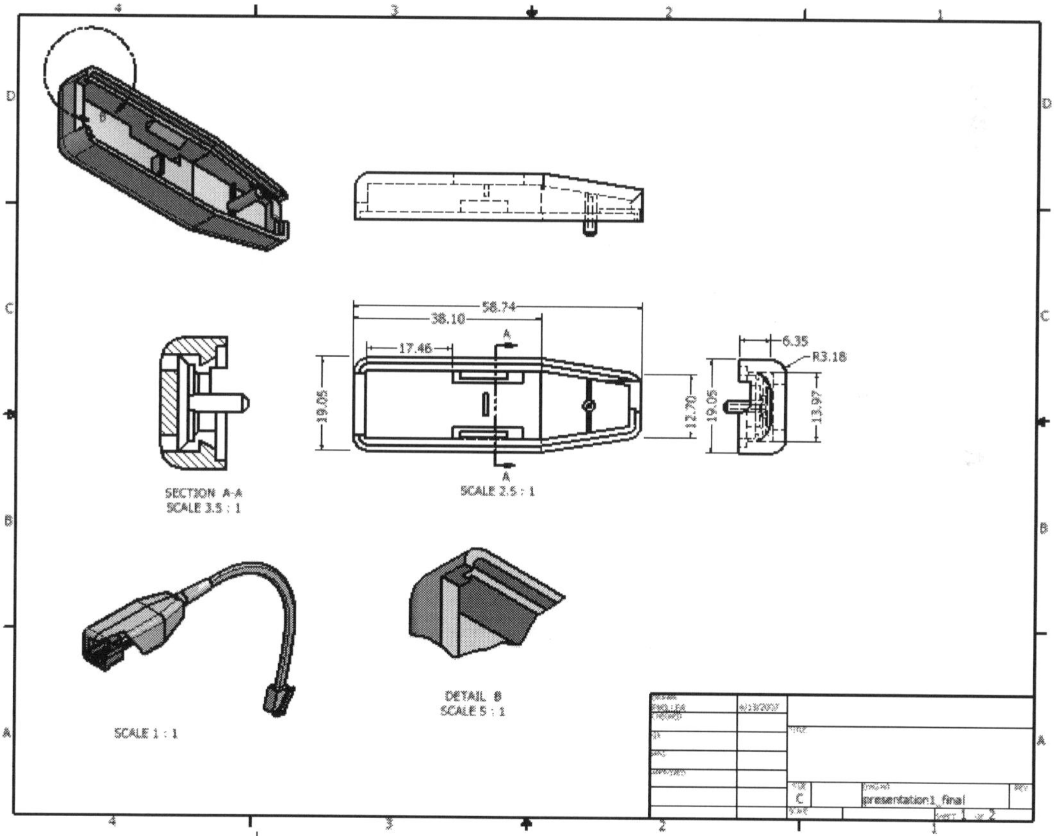

Figure 26–36

On a second drawing sheet, you will move a view from a previous sheet, create a parts list for the model, and add balloons to the drawing view, as shown in Figure 26–37.

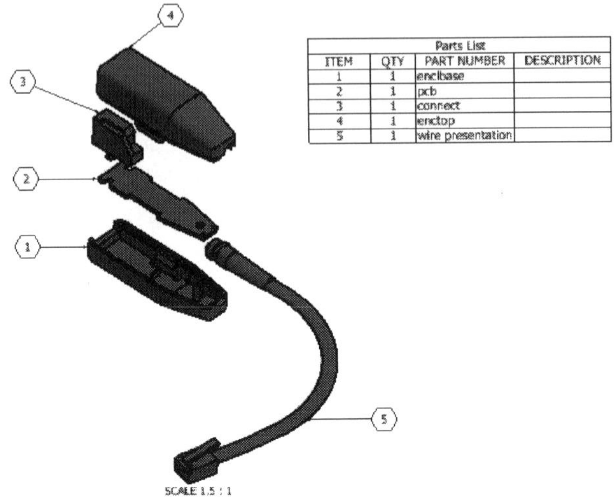

Parts List			
ITEM	QTY	PART NUMBER	DESCRIPTION
1	1	enclbase	
2	1	pcb	
3	1	connect	
4	1	enctop	
5	1	wire presentation	

Figure 26–37

Task 1 - Open a drawing file and modify the sheet color.

To display an assembly in an exploded state, the assembly must be inserted into a presentation file, an exploded snapshot view created, and the presentation file then inserted into a drawing so that the snapshot can be used.

1. Open **presentation1_final.dwg**. The drawing displays as shown in Figure 26–38.

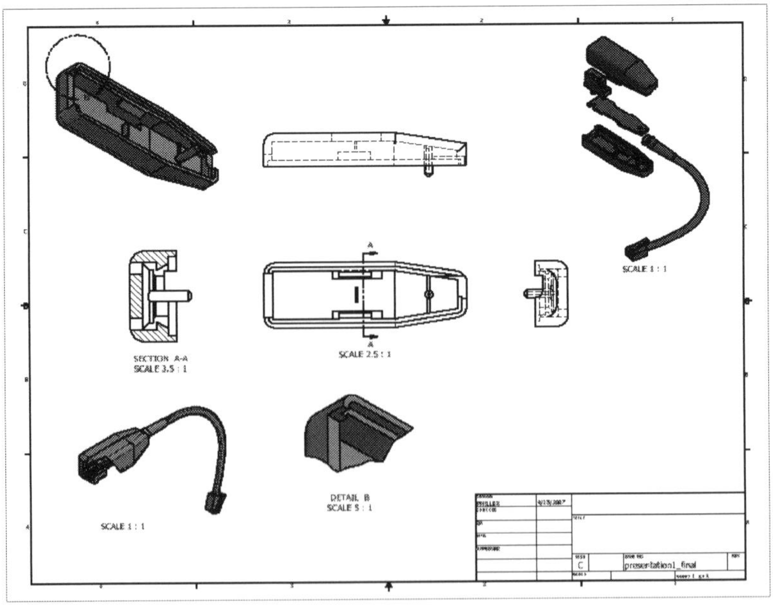

Figure 26–38

2. Select the *Tools* tab>Options panel and click (Document Settings). The Document Settings dialog box opens for the current drawing.

3. Select the *Sheet* tab.

4. Select the colored box in front of **Sheet** in the *Colors* area. Select the white cell in the *Basic colors* area.

5. Click **OK** in the Color dialog box and close the Document Settings dialog boxes. Note that the sheet color is now white.

Task 2 - Retrieve model dimensions.

Alternately, you can retrieve dimensions by selecting the Annotate tab>Dimension panel, and clicking (Retrieve).

1. Right-click in the graphics window and select **Retrieve Model Annotations**. The Retrieve Model Annotation dialog box opens.

2. Ensure that the *Sketch and Feature Dimensions* tab is active.

3. Select the base view in the center of the drawing as the view to retrieve dimensions into. All dimensions are displayed.

4. Ensure that the **Select Features** option is active in the *Select Source* area and select the dimensions to keep, as shown in Figure 26–39.

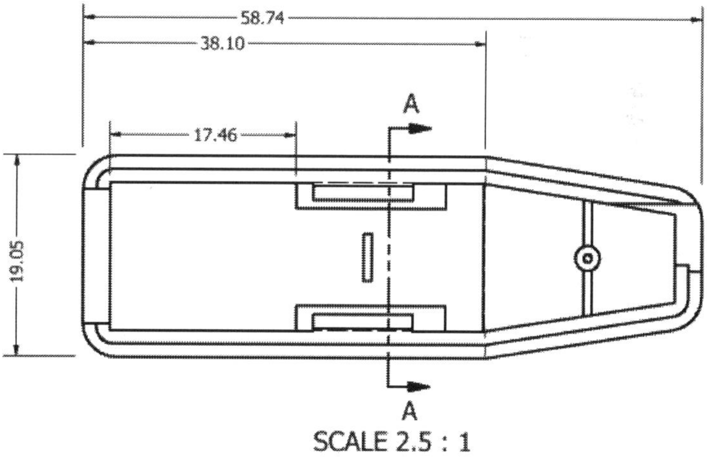

Figure 26–39

5. Click **OK** to apply and close the dialog box.

Task 3 - Add drawing dimensions.

The value of a drawing dimension cannot be changed in the drawing view. If the part changes, the drawing dimensions update automatically.

You can use drawing dimensions to add dimensions to your drawing that are not model dimensions. Drawing dimensions can be placed as you would place model dimensions in a part file, but the dimensions are dependent on the part geometry, and you cannot change their value.

1. Select the *Annotate* tab.

2. In the Dimension panel, click  (Dimension).

3. Add the 12.7 dimension shown in Figure 26–40 to the middle base view. This dimension references points that are at the virtual intersections of lines in a drawing view. To place the dimension, select the top slanted edge first, right-click, select **Intersection**, and select a vertical line (not a point) on the right edge. The first reference point for the dimension is now assigned. Select the bottom slanted edge, right-click, select **Intersection**. Select the right vertical edge again to define the second reference point. Use the left mouse button to place the dimension.

4. The Edit Dimension dialog box opens, enabling you to immediately edit the dimension value. Click **OK** to close the dialog box without making changes to the dimension.

    (Dimension) remains active.

*To disable this dialog box from displaying when a dimension is placed, clear the **Edit dimension when created** option. To open this dialog box to edit dimensions, select a dimension value and it becomes available. You can enable the option again if you want the Edit Dimension dialog box to open by default on dimension placement.*

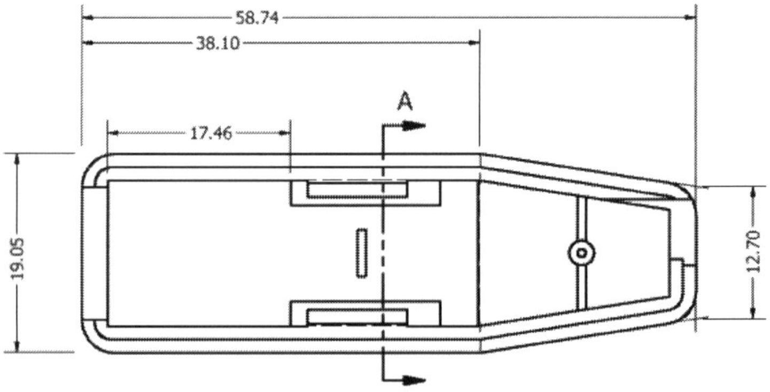

Figure 26–40

5. Add the 6.35 dimension shown in Figure 26–41 to the middle right view. To create this dimension, select and dimension the horizontal linear edge. Selecting the end points of the entity is also possible. However, it is sometimes difficult to ensure that you are selecting the correct end point. Zooming into a view can help ensure that the correct end points are selected.

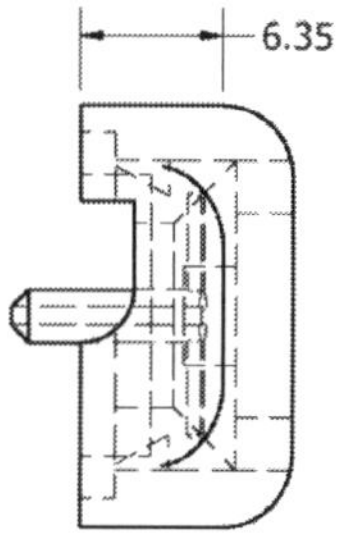

Figure 26–41

6. Click **OK** to close the dialog box without making changes to the dimension.

When placing or moving dimensions, a dimension displays as dashed lines when it is at the standard spacing set in the dimension style.

7. Add the remaining three dimensions, as shown in Figure 26–42. If your dimensions display differently to those shown, you might have selected points as references instead of edges.

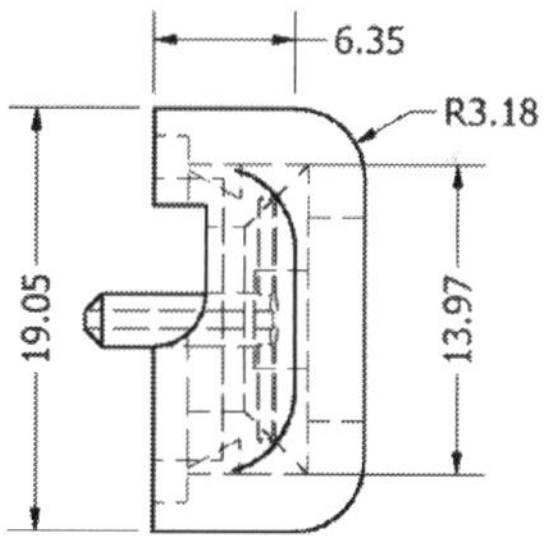

Figure 26–42

Task 4 - Create ordinate dimensions.

*You can right-click on the dimension and select **Delete**, or select the dimension and press <Delete>.*

1. Press <Esc> to ensure that the **Dimension** option is disabled.
2. Delete the **38.10** dimension.
3. Delete the **58.74** dimension.
4. In the Dimension panel, click (Ordinate).
5. Select the base view.

6. Select the location for the origin, as shown in Figure 26–43.

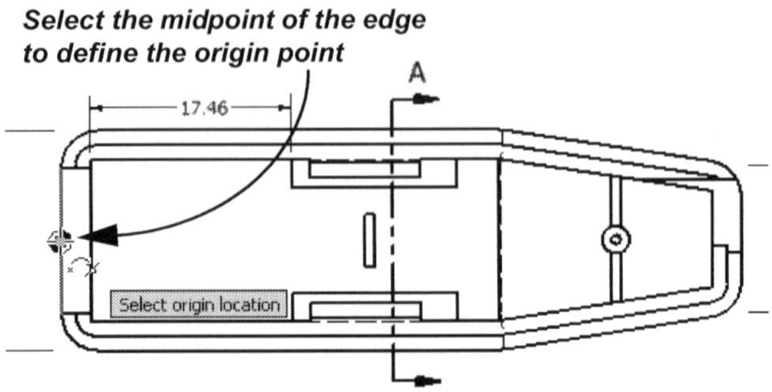

Figure 26–43

7. Select the three edges shown in Figure 26–44 for the dimension references.

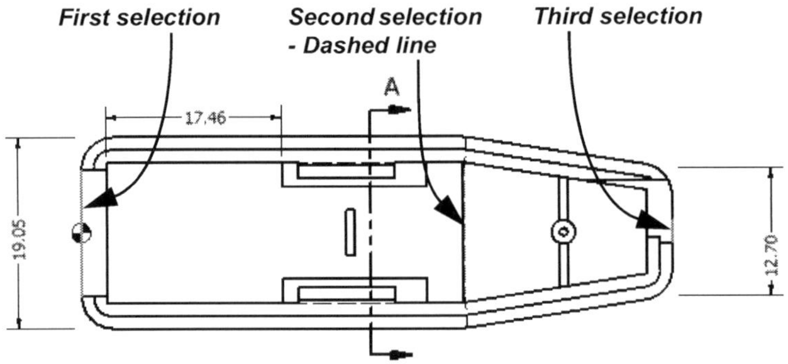

Figure 26–44

8. Right-click and select **Continue**.

Depending on where you place the cursor, both horizontal and vertical ordinate dimensions are previewed.

9. Click a location above the view to place the dimensions.

10. Right-click and select **OK**. The ordinate dimensions display as shown in Figure 26–45.

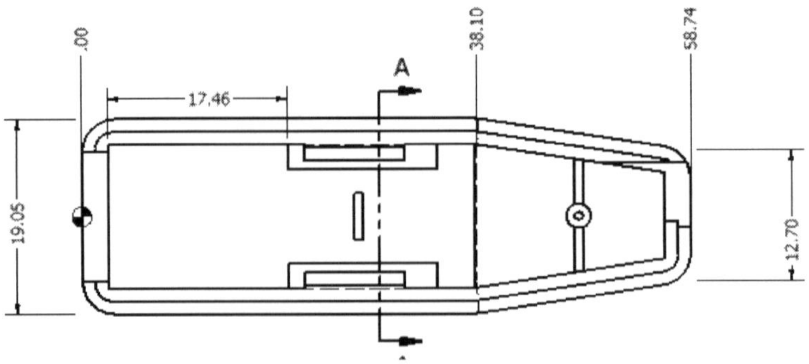

Figure 26–45

Task 5 - Create baseline dimensions.

1. Click [icon] twice to remove the ordinate dimensions and the origin indicator.

2. In the Dimension panel, click [icon] (Baseline).

3. Select the entities in order, as shown in Figure 26–46. The first entity you select will be the origin from which other entities will reference.

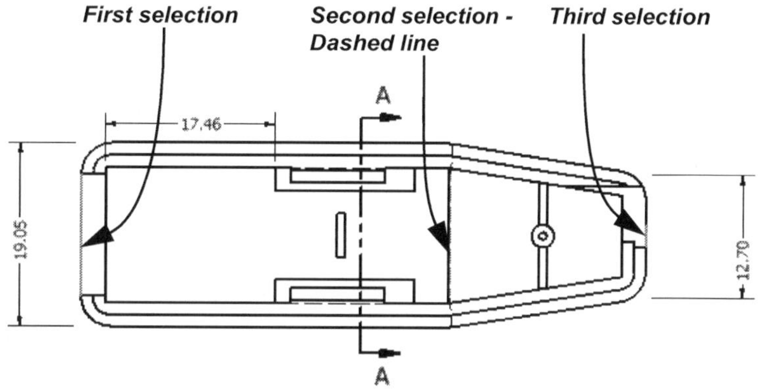

Figure 26–46

4. Right-click and select **Continue**.

5. Select a location above the view to place the dimensions.

6. Right-click and select **Create**. The baseline dimensions display as shown in Figure 26–47.

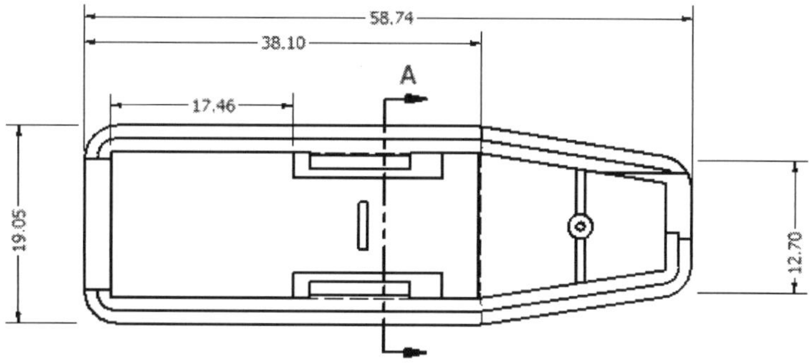

Figure 26–47

Task 6 - Create chain dimensions.

1. Click to remove the baseline dimensions.
2. In the Dimension panel, click (Chain).
3. Select the entities in the order shown in Figure 26–48. The first entity you select will be the origin from which other entities will reference.

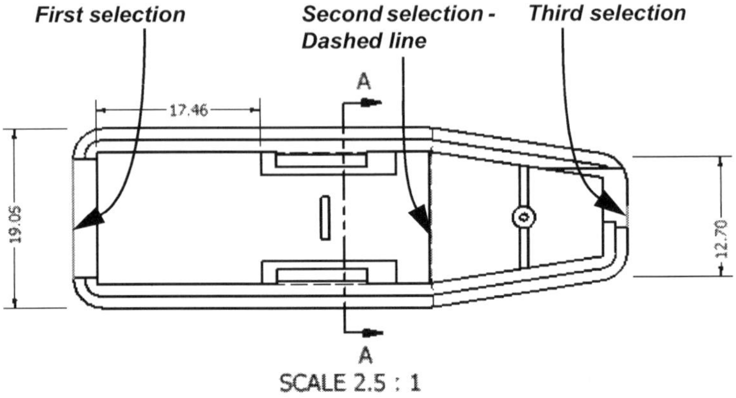

Figure 26–48

4. Right-click and select **Continue**.
5. Select a location above the view to place the dimensions.
6. Right-click and select **Create**. The chain dimensions display as shown in Figure 26–49.

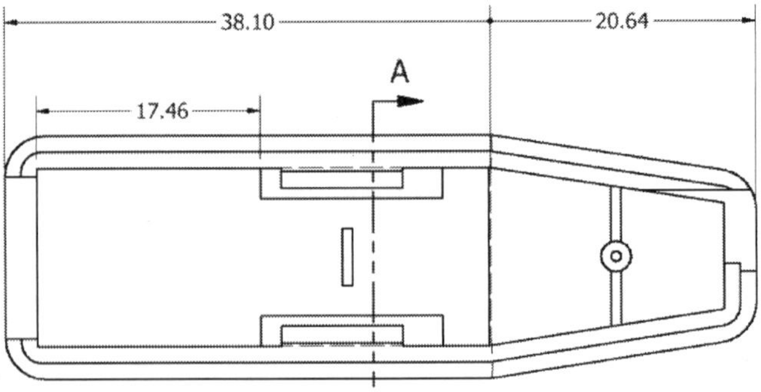

Figure 26–49

Task 7 - Create a new drawing sheet.

In this task, you will create a new drawing sheet and move the exploded view (**VIEW7:socket_drawing_presentation.ipn**) to the new sheet and add a parts list and balloons to the drawing.

Alternatively, you can add a sheet by selecting the Place Views tab> Sheets panel and clicking  *(New Sheet).*

1. Right-click anywhere in the window and select **New Sheet**. A new drawing sheet (Sheet:2) displays and becomes active. All elements of Sheet:1 are grayed out in the Model browser, as shown in Figure 26–50.

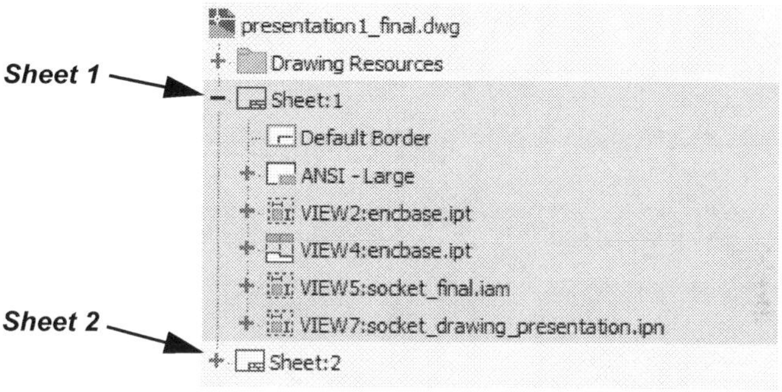

Figure 26–50

2. Double-click on Sheet:1 in the Model browser to activate it

3. Select **VIEW7:socket_drawing_presentation.ipn** in the Model browser, hold the left mouse button, and drag the view to **Sheet:2** in the Model browser. The view moves to **Sheet:2**. The Model browser displays as shown in Figure 26–51.

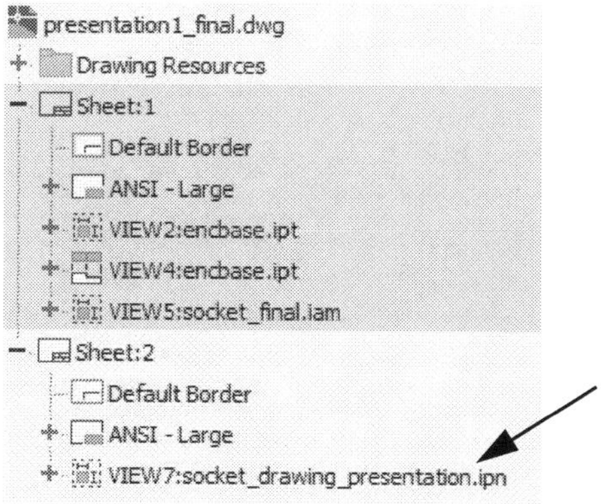

Figure 26–51

4. Once the view is moved, **Sheet:2** becomes the active sheet. Move the view to the center of the sheet.

5. Double-click to edit the view. Change the view scale to **1.5: 1** by editing the view.

Task 8 - Create a parts list.

1. Select the *Annotate* tab, if it is not already active. In the Table panel, click (Parts List) to create a parts list for the model.

2. Click (Select View) if not selected, and select the drawing view in **Sheet:2**.

3. Maintain all of the default settings in the Parts List dialog box. Click **OK** and place the list, as shown in Figure 26–52. Update the view, if prompted.

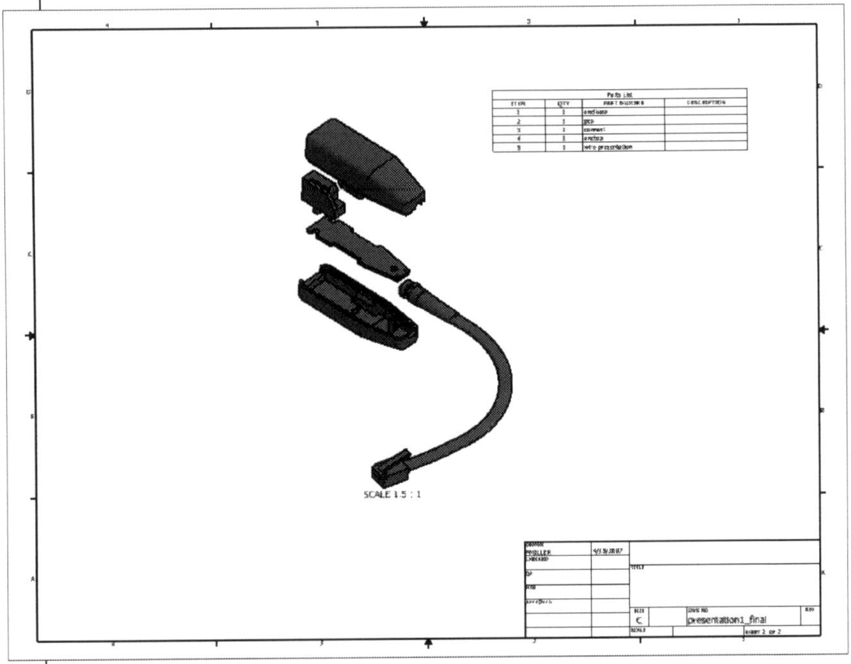

Figure 26–52

4. Select the parts list, right-click, and select **Edit Parts List Style**. The Style and Standard Editor dialog box opens. Note the style and standard options.

5. Click to the right side of the Title drop-down list.

6. Set the *Text Height* to **5.00 mm**.

7. Click **Save and Close** to close the dialog box and save the changes. The Style and Standard Editor dialog box has many options to customize the parts list display.

Task 9 - Add balloons.

1. In the Table panel, expand **Balloon** and click (Auto Balloon). The Auto Balloon dialog box opens.
2. Select the drawing view in **Sheet:2**.
3. Select all of the parts in the view.
4. Select **Around** in the *Placement* area in the dialog box so that balloons are placed around the view.
5. Click (Select Placement) in the *Placement* area, and select the location on the view to place balloons.
6. Select **Balloon Shape** to override the balloon default shape and click in the *Style overrides* area in the dialog box.
7. Click **OK** to complete the operation.
8. Move the balloons similar to that shown in Figure 26–53.
   - To move the balloons, select a balloon and drag it to a new location.
   - To move the leader, select the balloon and drag the end of the leader to a new location.

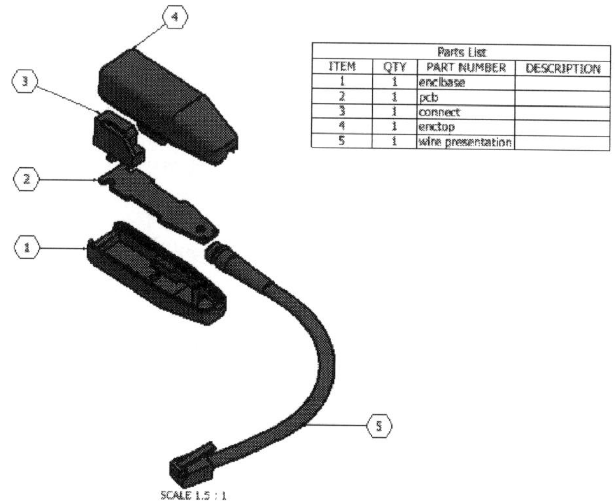

Parts List			
ITEM	QTY	PART NUMBER	DESCRIPTION
1	1	enclbase	
2	1	pcb	
3	1	connect	
4	1	enctop	
5	1	wire presentation	

Figure 26–53

9. Save the drawing and save all of the files that require saving.
10. Close the window.

Practice 26b Detailing a Drawing II

Practice Objectives

- Create a parts list and customize the information displayed in the columns.
- Map material styles to hatch patterns such that the hatching pattern varies for different materials.
- Modify the cut inheritance for a projected view.
- Duplicate a parts list between sheets.
- Add dimension to an isometric assembly view.

In this practice, you will map hatch patterns to material styles and create a section view using those styles. Next, you will modify the cut inheritance properties of a view, copy and paste a Parts List from one sheet to another, and create dimensions on an isometric view.

Task 1 - Open a drawing file.

1. Open **Clutch Bell.dwg**. The drawing displays as shown in Figure 26–54.

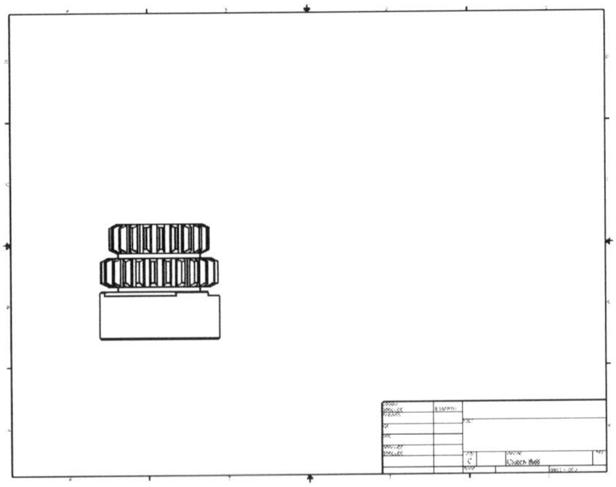

Figure 26–54

Task 2 - Create a parts list.

1. Select the *Annotate* tab>Table panel and click  (Parts List).
2. Select the view of **Clutch Bell.iam** and click **OK**.

3. Place the parts list as shown in Figure 26–55.

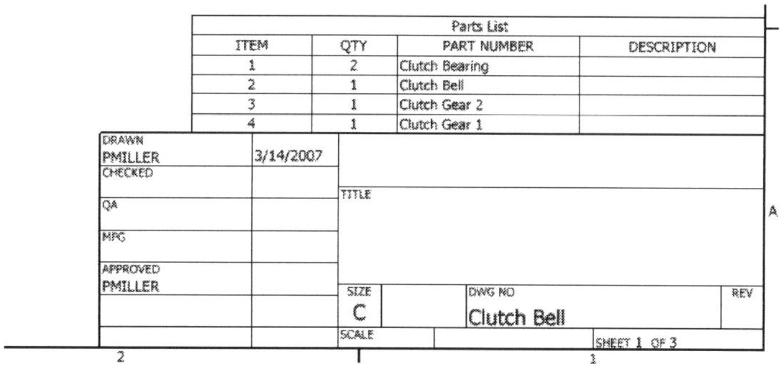

Figure 26–55

Task 3 - Add a material column to the parts list.

1. Right-click on the parts list and select **Edit Parts List**. The Parts List dialog box opens.
2. Click 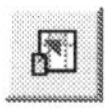 (Column Chooser). The Parts List Column Chooser dialog box opens.
3. Select **DESCRIPTION** on the right side and click **Remove**.
4. Select **MATERIAL** on the left side and click **Add**. The Parts List Column Chooser dialog box updates as shown in Figure 26–56. Click **OK**.

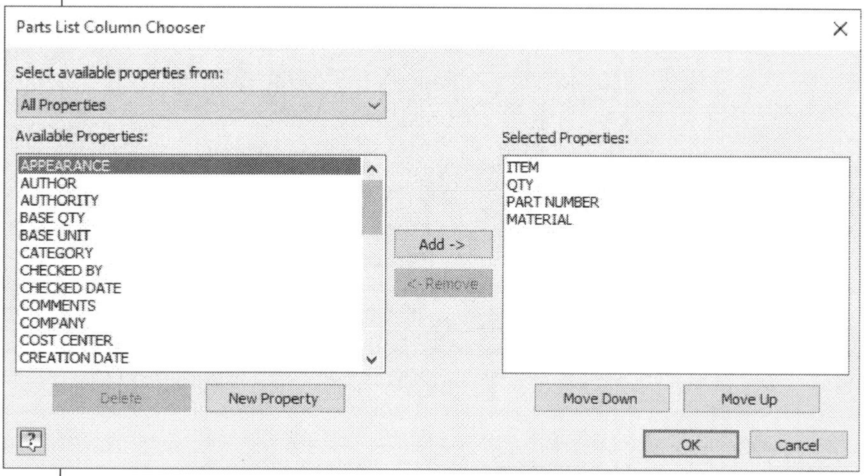

Figure 26–56

5. Click **OK** in the Parts List dialog box. The parts list now displays the material for each part as shown in Figure 26–57.

Parts List			
ITEM	QTY	PART NUMBER	MATERIAL
1	2	Clutch Bearing	Bronze, Cast
2	1	Clutch Bell	Steel
3	1	Clutch Gear 2	Generic
4	1	Clutch Gear 1	Copper, Cast

Figure 26–57

Task 4 - Map material styles to hatch patterns.

1. Note that each part in the parts list is assigned a material. Zoom all to display the entire drawing.
2. Select the *Manage* tab. In the Styles and Standards panel, click (Styles Editor).
3. In the Style and Standard Editor, expand **Standard** if it is not already expanded. Select **Default Standard (ANSI)**.
4. Select the *Material Hatch Pattern Defaults* tab. Note that it is empty. You need to map the material styles to hatch patterns.
5. Click (From Style Library) in the *Import Materials* area. This imports all of the material styles from the style library. You will only map the materials used in the assembly.
6. Select **Bronze, Cast** in the *Material Name* column. Select **ANSI 31**, next to *Bronze, Cast* and select **ANSI 32** in the drop-down list.
7. Change **ANSI 31** for *Copper, Cast* to **ANSI 33** in the drop-down list.
8. Change **ANSI 31** for *Steel* to **ANSI 34** in the drop-down list.
9. Click **Save and Close** to save the changes to the standard and close the Style and Standard Editor. This only saves the changes for the active .DWG file.

Task 5 - Create a section view and customize its inheritance.

1. Select the *Place Views* tab and create a section view through the middle of the assembly, as shown in Figure 26–58. Note that each part receives a different hatch pattern as assigned in the standard.

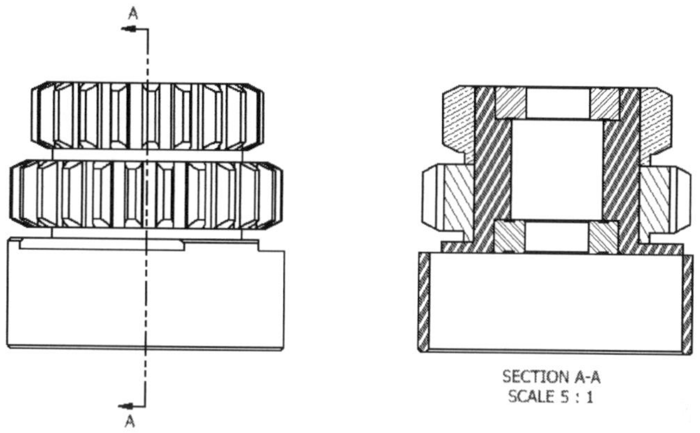

Figure 26–58

2. Create the isometric view projected from the section view, as shown in Figure 26–59.

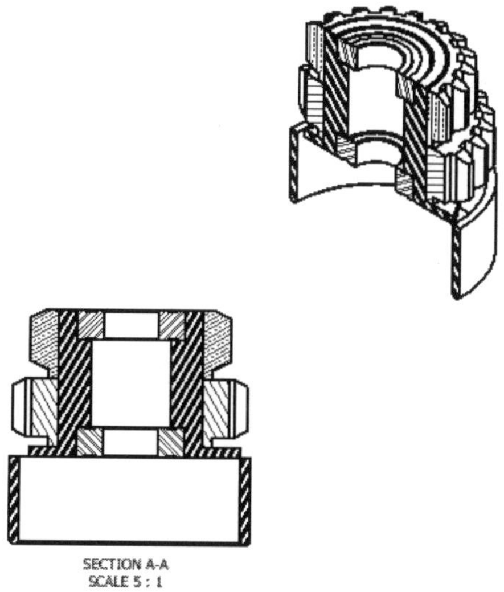

Figure 26–59

3. Right-click on the isometric view and select **Edit View**.
4. In the Drawing View dialog box, select the *Display Options* tab.

5. Clear the **Section** option in the *Cut Inheritance* area.
6. Click **OK**. Note that the cut is removed from the isometric view.
7. Right-click on the isometric view and select ***Edit View***.
8. In the Drawing View dialog box, select the *Display Options* tab.
9. Select **Section** to add the cut back to the isometric view.
10. Click **OK**. Note that the cut is added to the isometric view and hatching should be displayed. If hatching is not displayed, edit the view again and on the *Display Options* tab select **Hatching**.
11. In the Model browser, right-click on the section view and select **Suppress** to suppress the section view. Note that the isometric view remains.

Task 6 - Copy and paste the parts list to a new drawing sheet.

1. Right-click on the parts list and select **Copy**.
2. Double-click on **Sheet2:2** in the Model browser to activate **Sheet2**.
3. Right-click on a blank area of the sheet and select **Paste**. The parts list is copied onto **Sheet2**.

Task 7 - Dimension the isometric view.

1. Create an isometric view projected from the base view on **Sheet2**, as shown in Figure 26–60.

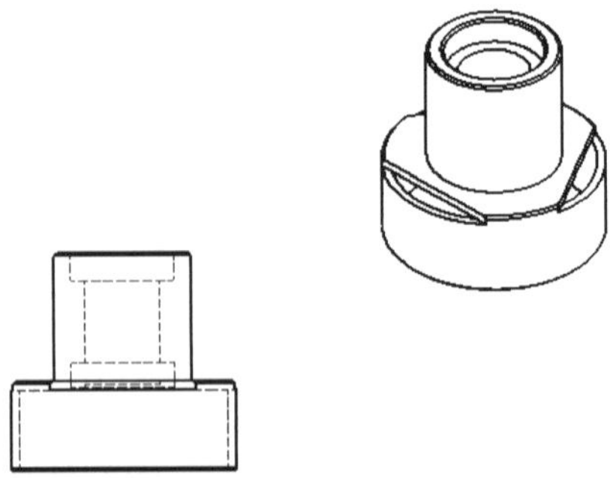

Figure 26–60

2. Select the *Annotate* tab>Dimension panel, click (Dimension), and add the dimensions shown in Figure 26–61. You can press <Spacebar> while placing dimensions to toggle the dimension orientation if different dimension placements are available.

To create the .10 dimension, select the circular edge, then select the linear edge, and finally select the snap point on the circular edge prior to placing the dimension.

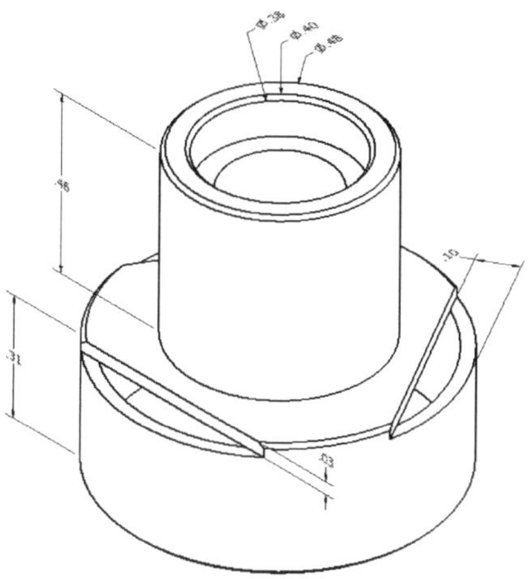

Figure 26–61

3. Right-click on the isometric view and select **Edit View**.
4. In the Drawing View dialog box, change the view display to **Hidden Line** () and **Shaded** ().
5. Click **OK**.
6. Delete the model dimensions.
7. Right-click in the graphics window and select **Retrieve Model Annotations**. The Retrieve Model Annotation dialog box opens. The options in the marking menu are context sensitive. If the **Retrieve Model Annotations** option is not available in the marking menu, verify that the view is not active or hold <Ctrl> if a view is active.

Alternatively, you can retrieve dimensions by selecting the Annotate tab>Dimension panel and clicking (Retrieve).

8. Select the isometric view. All of the model dimensions for the base view display.
9. Select all of the dimensions by drawing a bounding box around the view.

Depending on how the dimensions are placed, it might be more efficient to create the dimensions you require for an isometric view.

10. Click **OK** to apply and close the dialog box. The isometric view displays as shown in Figure 26–62. The dimensions can be moved as required to clean up the view.

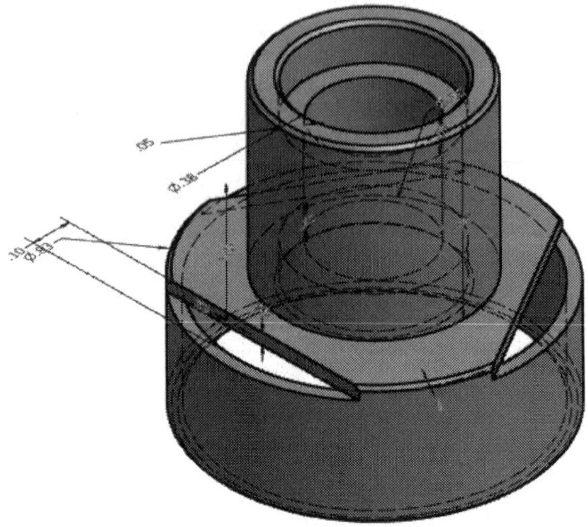

Figure 26–62

11. Save and close the drawing.

Practice 26c (Optional) Create a Drawing

Practice Objectives

- Create a new drawing using a default template.
- Create drawing views of a part model.
- Add dimensions to a drawing view.

Create a new drawing file named **Project_I**, using the **ANSI (in).dwg** template. Create drawing views of the part file **valvebody.ipt** and add dimensions. The completed drawing displays as shown in Figure 26–63. Save the drawing file.

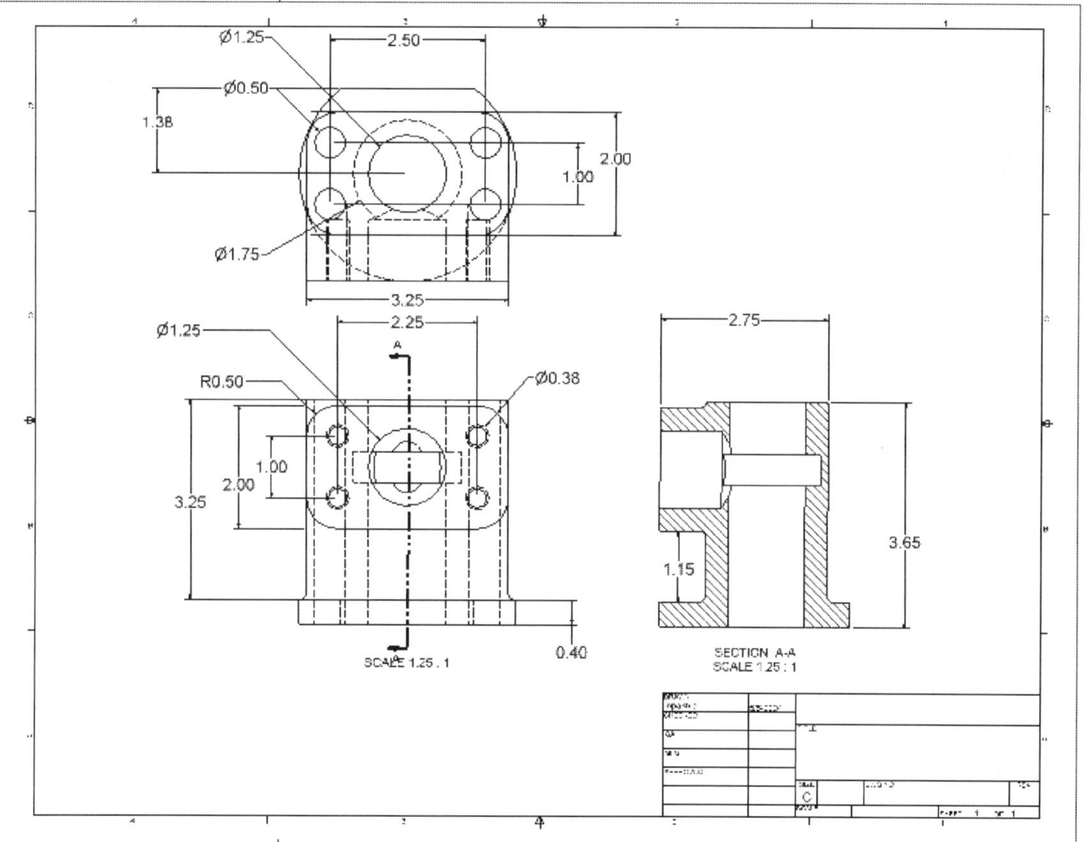

Figure 26–63

- To change the text height for the dimensions in the views, open the Style and Standard dialog box and in the Text category edit the Note Text (ANSI) standard that is being used for the dimension size.

Chapter Review Questions

1. Which describes the difference between Model dimensions and Drawing dimensions?
   a. Model dimensions can be edited to change the part, while Drawing dimensions are descriptive only and cannot be edited directly.
   b. There is no difference, except whether you are viewing the dimensions in the model or in the drawing.
   c. Model dimensions only display in part files, while Drawing dimensions display in drawing views.
   d. Model dimensions cannot be deleted, but Drawing dimensions can be deleted.
2. How would you display model dimensions in an existing view where they are not showing?
   a. Use General Dimension.
   b. Right-click on the view and select **Retrieve Model Annotations**.
   c. Update the view.
3. You can display the same model dimension in multiple views at the same time.
   a. True
   b. False
4. Which of the following best describes the **Ordinate Set** command, as shown in Figure 26–64?

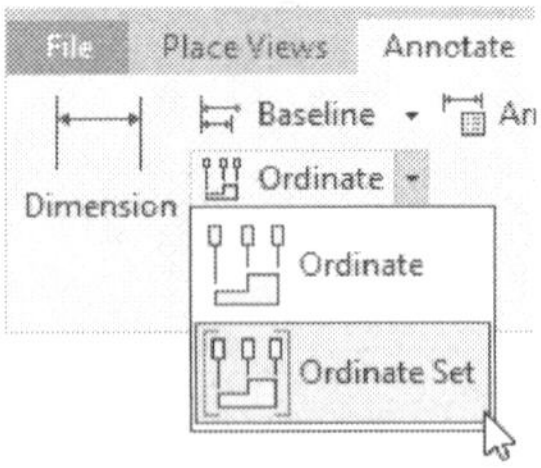

Figure 26–64

   a. It sets the 0,0 point to be used with Ordinate Dimensions.
   b. It creates a group of dimensions that act as one unit.
   c. It sets the format to be used for Ordinate Dimensions.
   d. It creates the dimensions automatically without picking points.

5. How would you change a single dimension to a different dimension style, as shown in Figure 26–65?

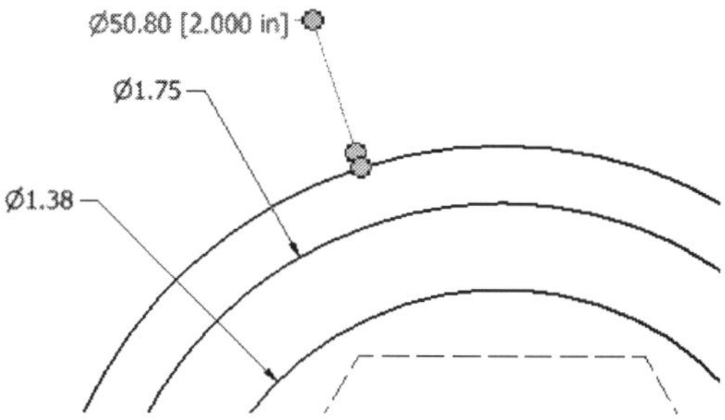

Figure 26–65

   a. Edit the text to change the dimension.
   b. Delete the dimension and reapply using a different style.
   c. Select the dimension and choose a different style from the toolbar list.

6. How many sheets can you add to a drawing?
   a. Two
   b. Odd number
   c. Even number
   d. No limit

7. Only a single sheet can be deleted at one time.
   a. True
   b. False

8. When creating a parts list, how do you set the assembly that is used as the source?
   a. You set the source file in the Styles and Standards.
   b. The first view created in the drawing is used as the source.
   c. You set the source file in the Document Settings.
   d. You select a view in the drawing or browse to a file.

9. When creating a parts list, you can display only top-level components.
   a. True
   b. False

10. Which of the following statements is true regarding balloons in a drawing view?
    a. Balloons identifying item numbers in a Parts List must be individually placed on each component in the assembly view.
    b. When using **Auto Balloon**, you can use the **Around**, **Horizontal**, or **Vertical** sub-options to align balloons around the view.
    c. Offset spacing enables you to position balloons at a fixed distance from the model.
    d. The shape of all balloons driven by the Parts List is circular.

11. What controls the appearance of drawing annotations, such as centerlines, default text style, or parts lists?
    a. Document Settings
    b. Styles Editor
    c. Sheet Formats
    d. Application Options

12. What is the process to edit the hatching for a component in a section view, as shown in Figure 26–66?

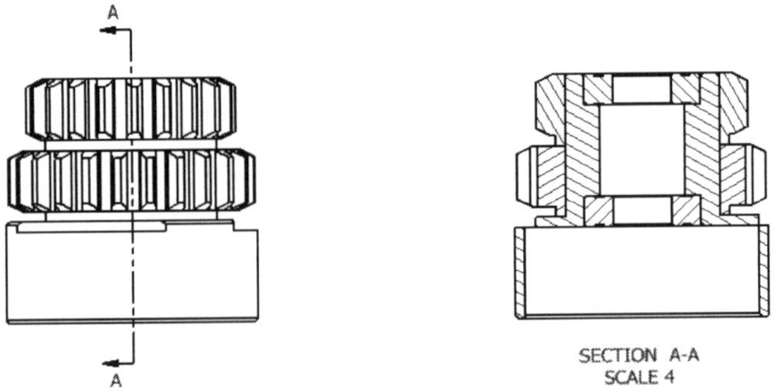

Figure 26–66

    a. In the *Tools* tab, select **Document Settings** and select the *Drawing* tab.
    b. Right-click on the hatch and select **Edit** to open the Edit Hatch Pattern dialog box.
    c. In the *Tools* tab, select **Application Options**, and select the *Drawing* tab.
    d. Delete the section view and create a new one.

Command Summary

Button	Command	Location
	Auto Balloon	• **Ribbon:** *Annotate* tab>Table panel> expand Balloon
	Balloon	• **Ribbon:** *Annotate* tab>Table panel • **Context Menu:** In the graphics window
	Baseline (drawing dimension)	• **Ribbon:** *Annotate* tab>Dimension panel
	Baseline Set (drawing dimension)	• **Ribbon:** *Annotate* tab>Dimension panel
	Chain (drawing dimension)	• **Ribbon:** *Annotate* tab>Dimension panel
	Chain Set (drawing dimension)	• **Ribbon:** *Annotate* tab>Dimension panel
	Dimension (drawing dimension)	• **Ribbon:** *Annotate* tab>Dimension panel • **Context Menu:** In the graphics window
N/A	**Edit Model Dimension**	• **Context Menu:** In the graphics window with a dimension selected
	New Sheet	• **Ribbon:** *Place Views* tab>Sheets panel • **Context Menu:** In the graphics window • **Context Menu:** In Model browser with the drawing name selected
	Ordinate (drawing dimension)	• **Ribbon:** *Annotate* tab>Dimension panel
	Ordinate Set (drawing dimension)	• **Ribbon:** *Annotate* tab>Dimension panel
	Parts List	• **Ribbon:** *Annotate* tab>Table panel
	Retrieve Model Annotations	• **Ribbon:** *Annotate* tab>Retrieve panel • **Context Menu:** In the graphics window with a view selected • **Context Menu:** In Model browser with a view selected
	Styles Editor	• **Ribbon:** *Annotate* tab>Styles and Standards panel

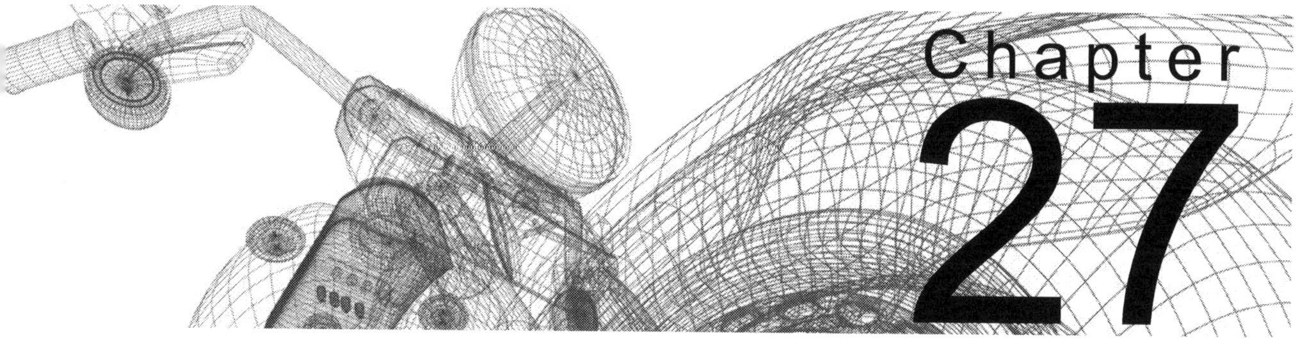

Chapter 27

Drawing Annotations

Drawings communicate design information. In most cases, drawings, dimensions, and parts lists are not enough and drawing annotations are required to identify additional information.

Learning Objectives in This Chapter

- Add leader and non-leader text to a drawing to communicate information about the drawing.
- Add various symbol types to a drawing to identify important drawing information.
- Create and edit a hole or thread note in a drawing view.
- Create and edit a chamfer note in a drawing view.
- Add center marks, centered patterns, center lines, and bisector lines to drawing views.
- Create hole tables based on selected features, feature types, and views.
- Add and edit revision tables and tags in a drawing to track model changes.

27.1 Text

Text is used to communicate information that cannot be communicated through views or dimensions. You can create text with or without a leader.

How To: Create Text with a Leader

Any leader or dimension lines that intersect with a text box are clipped.

*To create note text immediately after placing the first segment, right-click during note creation and select **Single-Segment Leader**. With this option enabled you are not required to right-click and select **Continue**. The Format Text dialog box will immediately open to create the note. Once enabled it remains active until it is disabled.*

1. Select the *Annotate* tab>Text panel and click (Leader Text).
2. Select a location to point the leader. Select another location to create the line. Each click creates an *elbow* in the leader line.
3. Select a location to place the text, right-click, and select **Continue**. The Format Text dialog box opens, as shown in Figure 27–1.

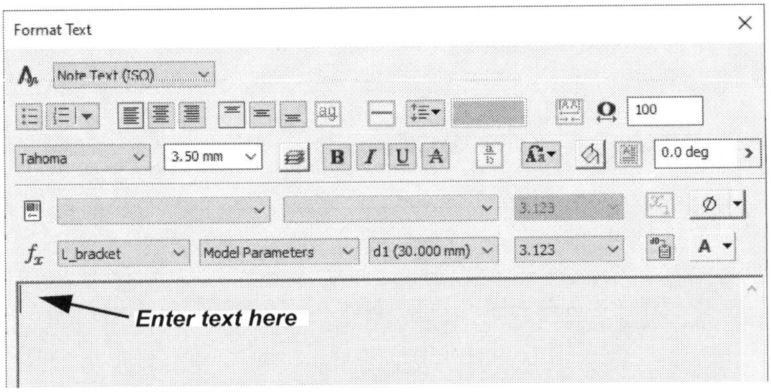

Figure 27–1

4. Enter the required text and modify the text options, as required:
   - Use the editing tools available in the dialog box to customize the look of the text.
   - To add a symbol, place the cursor and select a symbol from the drop-down list.
   - Text is previewed on the drawing sheet as you are entering information in the Format Text dialog box.
5. Click **OK** to complete the text.

To create text without a leader, click (Text) in the Text panel and select a location on the drawing. As with text created with a leader, the Format Text dialog box opens, in which you can enter the text.

Modifying Text

You can modify the following text properties:

- Edit existing text by double-clicking on it in the drawing. Use the Format Text dialog box to modify the text and formatting.
- Move text that has leaders by selecting the text, pressing and holding the left mouse button on any of the green dots, and dragging the mouse to the required location. To move text without leaders, the dots display around the text.
- To rotate text without a leader, select the text and drag the blue dot associated with the text.
- For text without a leader, you can adjust the size of the text box by dragging the green dots in the required direction.
- To align multiple text boxes with leaders or without leaders, select them, right-click, and select **Align**. Define how to align the selected text boxes using the options in the Align Text dialog box, as shown in Figure 27–2.

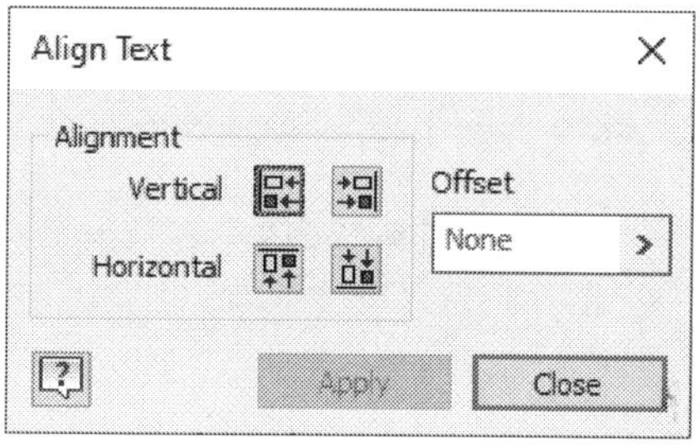

Figure 27–2

Adding Model or User Parameters as Text

For drawings with a single reference model, only one component is going to be listed. For assembly drawings, you can select from any of the components in the assembly.

Using options in the Format Text dialog box, you can include the values of existing parameters in the text.

How To: Add Parameter Values in Text

1. Begin the creation of text in your drawing to open the Format Text dialog box.
2. In the Component drop-down list, select the component containing the parameter value.
3. In the Source drop-down list, select whether the parameter to be added is a model or user parameter. If no user parameters exist a warning box opens.
4. In the Parameter drop-down list, select the parameter that is to be added. The list of parameters displayed is dependent on the source for the defined component. The User-Defined parameter can be a Numeric, Text, or T/F parameter.
5. In the Precision drop-down list, define the precision format for numerical parameters.

   The Component, Source, Parameter, and Precision drop-down lists are shown in Figure 27–3.

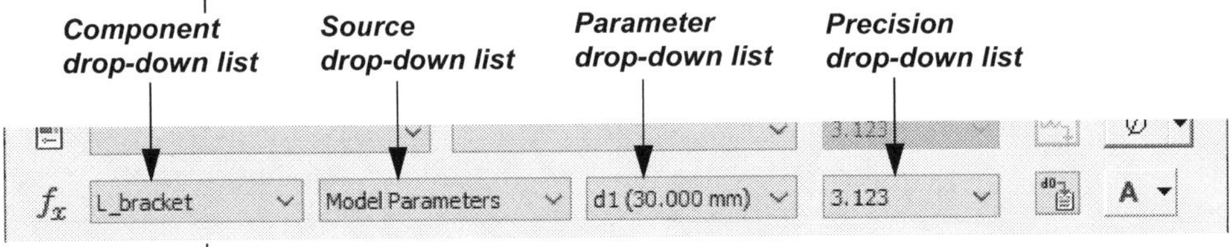

Figure 27–3

6. Click (Add Parameter) to include the selected parameter in the text area at the bottom of the Format Text dialog box. Parameter values are highlighted in gray and cannot be edited, but you can add text around the value or delete it.
7. Click **OK** to complete the text and add it to the drawing.

Adding Properties as Text

Using options in the Format Text dialog box, you can include the values of an existing model, a drawing, or custom properties in text.

How To: Add Property Values in Text

1. Begin the creation of text in your drawing to open the Format Text dialog box.
2. In the Type drop-down list, select the type of property from which you require the value. The available options include model, drawing, sheet, physical model, and sheet metal properties.
3. In the Property drop-down list, select a property. The list of properties displayed are dependent on the type of property selected.
4. In the Precision drop-down list, select a setting to define the precision format for numerical properties in the text.

   The Type, Property, and Precision drop-down lists are shown in Figure 27–4.

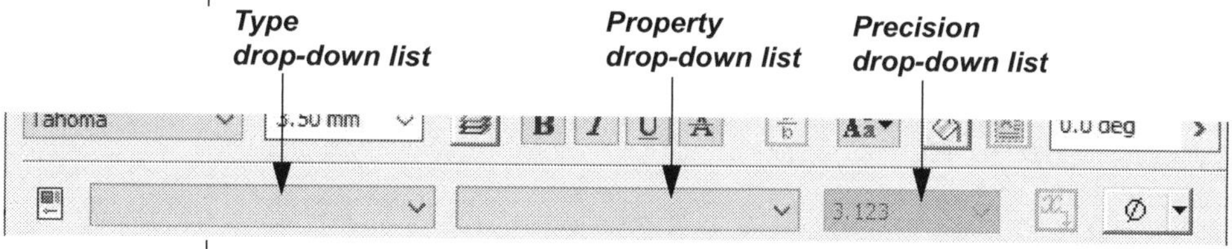

Figure 27–4

5. Click  (Add Text Parameter) to include the selected property in the text area at the bottom of the Format Text dialog box. Property values are highlighted in gray and are surrounded by angled brackets. They cannot be edited, but you can add text around the value or delete it.
6. Click **OK** to complete the text and add it to the drawing.

27.2 Symbols

Symbols enable you to identify critical surfaces, explain how they relate to one another, and set inspection criteria.

How To: Create Symbols

1. In the *Annotate* tab>Symbols panel, select one of the symbol types, as shown in Figure 27–5. You can use the scroll buttons to display all of the symbol types.

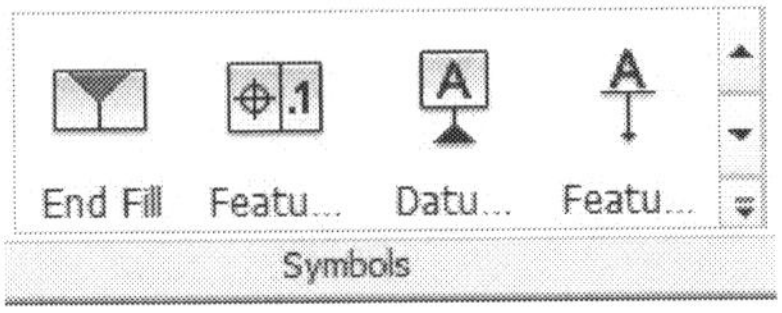

Figure 27–5

2. Select an entity (e.g., an edge) to which the symbol references.
3. To add the symbol with a leader, continue making selections with the left mouse button after the entity has been selected to define the leader location.
4. Right-click, and select **Continue.** The dialog box associated with the symbol opens. Depending on the type of symbol being created, different dialog boxes open. Figure 27–6 shows the Surface Texture, Feature Control Frame, and Datum Target dialog boxes.

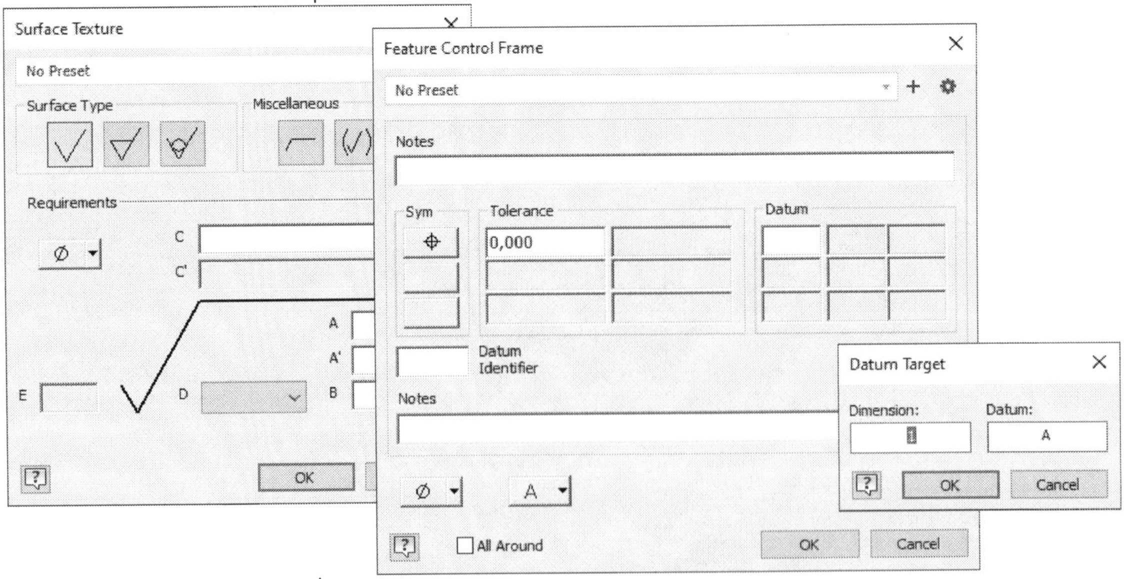

Figure 27–6

5. Regardless of the type of symbol, define the required symbol parameters in their respective dialog boxes.
6. Click **OK** in the dialog box to complete the symbol. The symbol displays based on the selected references.
7. (Optional) Continue to add symbols of the same type.
8. Right-click and select **Cancel [ESC]** or press <Esc> to cancel the operation.

Hint: Custom Symbols

Custom symbols can be created and shared in a read/write library for quick access by an entire team. Creating custom symbols is discussed in the *Autodesk® Inventor® 2021: Advanced Part Modeling* guide.

27.3 Hole and Thread Notes

You can add hole notes in a drawing view to holes, extruded cuts (other than mid-plane extrusions), iFeatures, patterned holes, center marks, or sheet metal flat patterns

Thread notes can be added in a drawing view to features that were created with a thread feature. Changes made to the hole or thread in the model update in the hole drawing note.

Creating a Hole or Thread Note

How To: Create a Hole or Thread Note

The default settings for how Hole Notes display are set in the Styles Editor.

1. In the *Annotate* tab>Feature Notes panel, click  (Hole and Thread).
2. Select the required hole or thread in the drawing view.
3. Position the note with the cursor and click the left mouse button to place it. To enable 15-degree snapping when placing the note, hold <Ctrl> while dragging.
4. Complete the creation of the note by right-clicking and selecting **OK**.

Adding Text to a Hole Note

How To: Add Text or Symbols to an Existing Hole/Thread Note

1. Right-click on the hole/thread note and select **Text**. The Format Text dialog box opens.
2. Enter text before and after the <<>> symbols, as required. The symbols are place holders for the hole/thread note. You cannot enter additional data between the symbols.
3. To add a symbol to the note, expand the Ø flyout to display the symbol palette. Place the cursor at the required location and select a symbol in the drop-down list.
4. To change text properties, highlight the text to change, and select the required properties.
5. Click **OK** to update the Hole note.

Editing a Hole Note

How To: Modify a Hole Note

1. Right-click on a hole note and select **Edit Hole Note** or double-click on the note. The Edit Hole Note dialog box opens as shown in Figure 27–7.

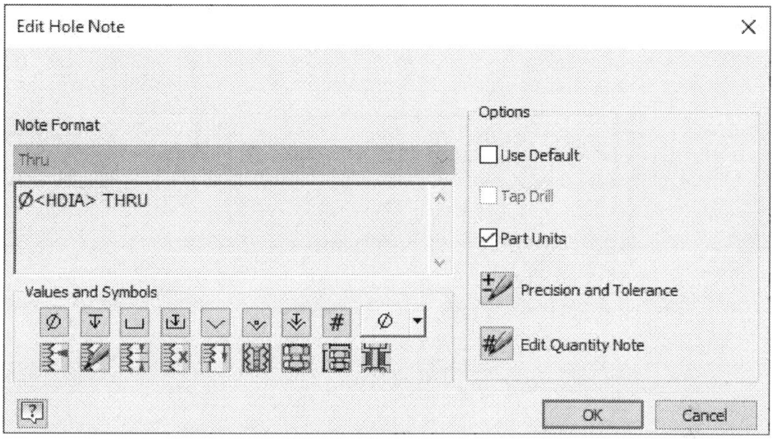

Figure 27–7

2. Clear the **Use Default** option, if required, to enable editing. The option in the Note Format drop-down list cannot be modified, but the hole note itself can be modified using the options, icons, and changing the text.
3. Click **OK** to update the hole note.

Hole Quantity in Notes

In a hole note, you can add the quantity of holes of the same type, as shown in Figure 27–8.

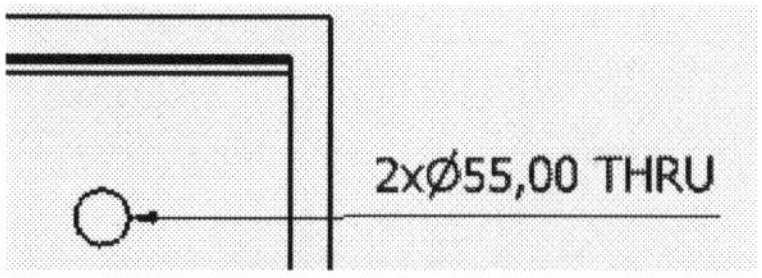

Figure 27–8

Holes are considered the same type if the following criteria apply:

- The hole type is the same (i.e. drilled, counterbore, or countersink).
- The same depth option and value is used.
- The holes are the same size.
- The hole axis is normal to the view.

Add the quantity note by editing the hole note and using # in the required location in the note, as shown in Figure 27–9.

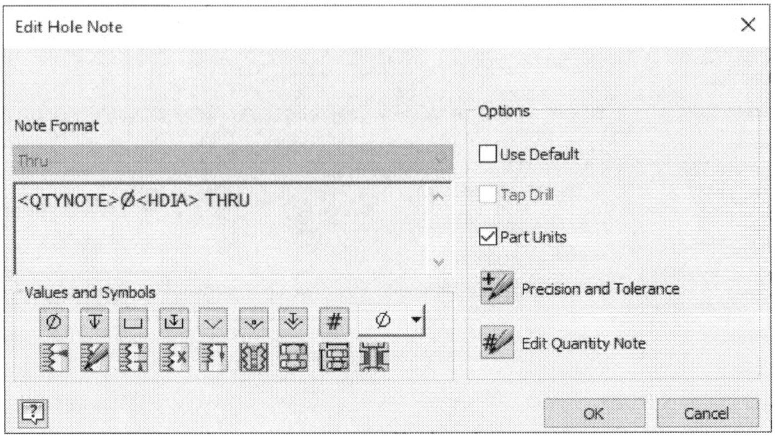

Figure 27–9

To edit the quantity note display, click (Edit Quantity Note) in the *Options* area in the Edit Hole Note dialog box. The available options are shown in Figure 27–10.

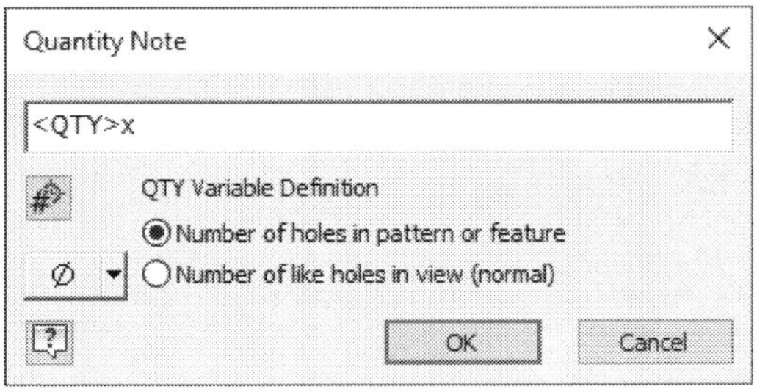

Figure 27–10

Hiding Hole or Thread Note Values

You can hide hole and thread note values. However, any text or symbols added to a hole or thread note remain visible on the drawing.

To hide hole and thread note values, right-click on the thread note and select **Hide Value**. The note value is hidden and any custom text is shown as <Text>. Toggle the option again to display the value.

27.4 Chamfer Notes

Creating Chamfer Notes

You can add chamfer notes in a drawing view to a linear model edge or sketch line. Note that the reference edge used in a chamfer calculation must be a linear model edge, or a sketch line that has common end points or intersects with the chamfer.

How To: Create a Chamfer Note

The default settings for how chamfer notes display are set in the Styles Editor.

1. In the *Annotate* tab>Feature Notes panel, click  (Chamfer).
2. Select the required linear model edge or sketch line in the view.
3. Select a reference line in the drawing view to calculate the dimension.
4. Position the note with the cursor and click the left mouse button to place it.
5. Complete the creation of the note by right-clicking and selecting **OK**.

Editing Chamfer Notes

How To: Modify a Chamfer Note

1. Right-click on a chamfer note and select **Edit Chamfer Note**. The Edit Chamfer Note dialog box opens as shown in Figure 27–11.

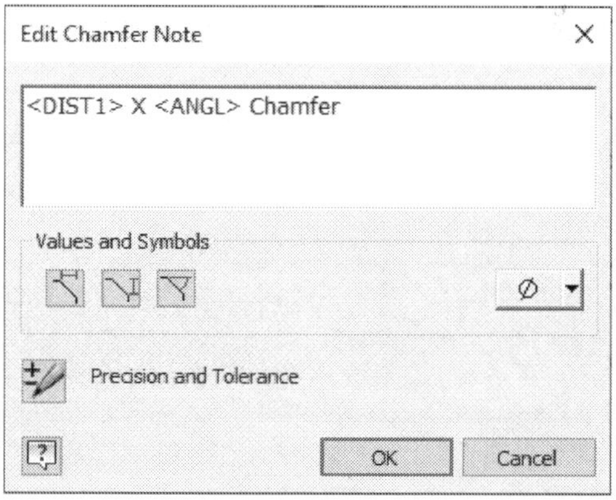

Figure 27–11

2. Enter the required text or edit/remove existing text.

3. You can also add parameters by selecting the required options in the *Values and Symbols* area. Three different parameters are available:

   - **(Distance 1):** Horizontal distance between selected edge and reference line.
   - **(Distance 2):** Vertical distance between selected edge and reference line.
   - **(Angle):** Angle between selected edge and reference line.

4. To add a symbol to the note, expand Ø to display the symbol palette. Place the cursor in the required location and select a symbol in the drop-down list.
5. Click (Precision and Tolerance) to modify settings.
6. Click **OK** to close the dialog box and complete the change.

27.5 Center Marks and Center Lines

Center Marks

How To: Create the Center Mark

1. In the *Annotate* tab>Symbols panel, click  (Center Mark).
2. Select a feature to which to add the center mark.
3. Complete the creation of the center marks by right-clicking and selecting **OK**.

Figure 27–12 shows an example of center mark.

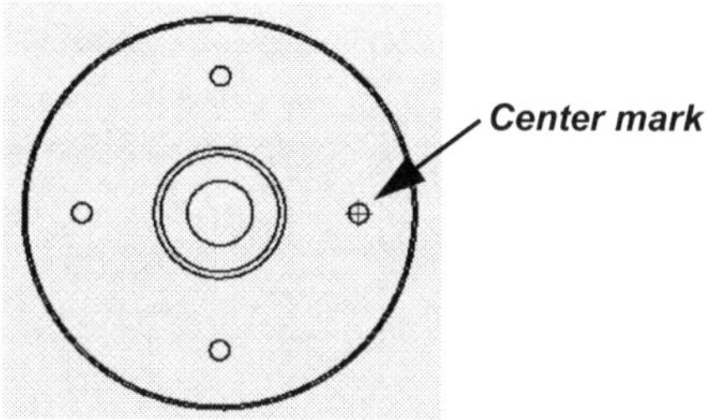

Figure 27–12

Center Line

How To: Create the Center Line

1. In the *Annotate* tab>Symbols panel, click  (Centerline).
2. Select a feature in the drawing view to start a center line.
3. Keep selecting features until all of the required features have been added. Once selected, a center line is connected between the features.
4. Complete the creation of the center lines by right-clicking and selecting **Create**.

Figure 27–13 shows an example of center line.

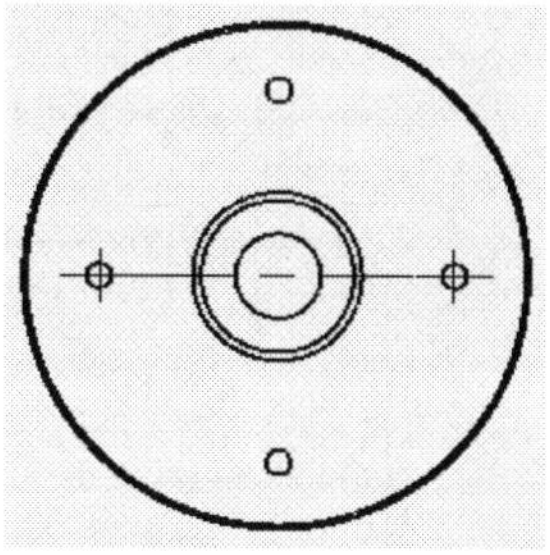

Figure 27–13

To select multiple views, press and hold <Ctrl> or <Shift> while selecting views.

As an alternative to individually selecting features to add center lines and center marks, click (Automated Centerline) in the Symbols panel and select a view. The Automated Centerlines dialog box enables you to determine which types of features to apply center lines and center marks to in a view, as well as to define thresholds for radius and arc angle values. Alternatively, you can also access the Automated Centerlines option by right-clicking on a view and selecting **Automated Centerlines**.

Center Line Bisector

How To: Create the Center Line Bisector

1. In the *Annotate* tab>Symbols panel, click (Centerline Bisector).
2. Select two lines to add the center line bisector between them.
3. Complete the creation of the center lines by right-clicking and selecting **Cancel [ESC]**.

   Figure 27–14 shows an example of center line bisector.

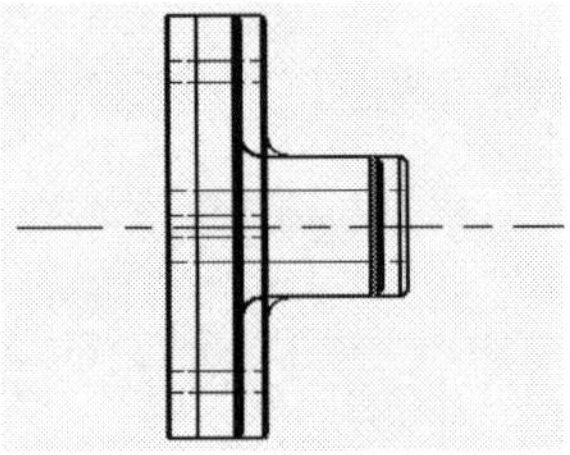

Figure 27–14

Centered Pattern

How To: Create the Centered Pattern

1. In the *Annotate* tab>Symbols panel, click (Centered Pattern).
2. Select a circular feature to locate the center of the pattern.
3. Select all of the required circular features.
4. Complete the creation of the center lines by right-clicking and selecting **Create**.

   Figure 27–15 shows an example of centered pattern.

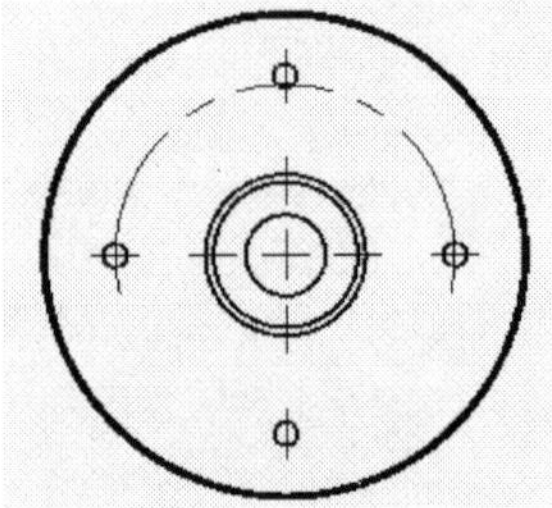

Figure 27–15

27.6 Hole Tables

Using hole tables in a drawing is an effective method of providing information on the holes in a model. A hole table can be created to contain information for all holes, selected holes only, or extruded cuts (except for mid-plane extrusions) in a selected drawing view.

How To: Create a Hole Table

1. In the *Annotate* tab>Table panel, select one of three hole table creation methods shown in Figure 27–16. The hole selection method defines how the holes are identified for inclusion in the table.

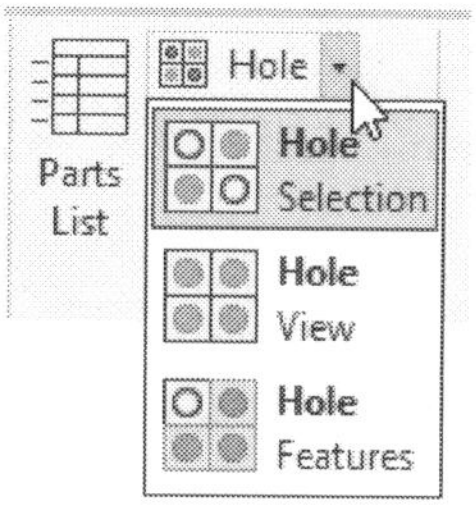

Figure 27–16

Method	Description
(Hole Selection)	Each hole included in the hole table is selected individually.
(Hole View)	All holes of any type in a selected view are included in the hole table.
(Hole Features)	All identical holes of a selected type are automatically included.

2. Select the drawing view that includes the holes, which are required in the table.

The origin used for a hole table is also used for ordinate dimensions and vice-versa.

3. Define a location to use as the origin for the hole table by selecting a point on the view from which all hole locations are measured.
   - The origin indicator displays with . Only one origin can exist per view.
   - To hide the origin indicator, right-click on it and select **Hide Origin Indicator**.
   - To move the origin indicator relative to its current location, right-click on it and select **Edit**. Enter dimension values for the X- or Y-direction (relative to the original location).

4. If you selected either **Hole Selection** or **Hole Features**, select the holes required for the hole table.
   - If you used the **Hole View** selection method, you can skip this step because all of the holes in the selected view are automatically added to the hole table.
5. Once you have finished selecting the holes, right-click anywhere in the drawing and select **Create**.
6. Place the hole table by clicking to place it. The hole table displays similar to that shown in Figure 27–17.

Hole Table			
HOLE	XDIM	YDIM	DESCRIPTION
A1	150,00	400,00	Ø50,00 -5,00 DEEP
B1	590,00	300,00	Ø70,00 -5,00 DEEP
B2	690,00	300,00	Ø70,00 -5,00 DEEP

Figure 27–17

Hint: Splitting Hole Tables

To split a hole table into multiple individual tables, right-click on a row in the table and select **Table>Split Table**. A table can be split multiple times to create individual tables. Once split, the **Hole Table** node in the Model browser is subdivided to represent the parent table and split tables. Select a portion of the table and freely move it on the sheet or use the Model browser to select a portion of the split table and drag it to another sheet.

To unsplit a table, select anywhere in the table and select **Table>Un-split Table**. All portions of the table (even those on other sheets) are returned to the parent table.

Hole tags (e.g., A1 and B1) are assigned to each hole in the hole table and each hole is automatically labeled with the hole tag in the drawing view. Holes of the same type contain the same letter. For example, holes B1 and B2 are of the same type.

Editing Hole Tables or Tags

*The **Edit Hole Table Style** option enables you to open the Style and Standards Editor to create a style to be used when creating all your company tables.*

Consider the following when editing a hole table or tag:

- To edit the text format for an individual hole tag, right-click on the hole tag and select **Edit Tag**.
- To hide a hole tag in the drawing view, right-click on the hole tag and select **Hide Tag**
- The hole table can be modified by right-clicking on the hole table and selecting **Edit Hole Table**. You can use the options in the *Formatting* and *Options* tabs as required to customize the look of the table.
- You can make additional modifications to the hole table and its contents using the shortcut menu, as shown in Figure 27–18.

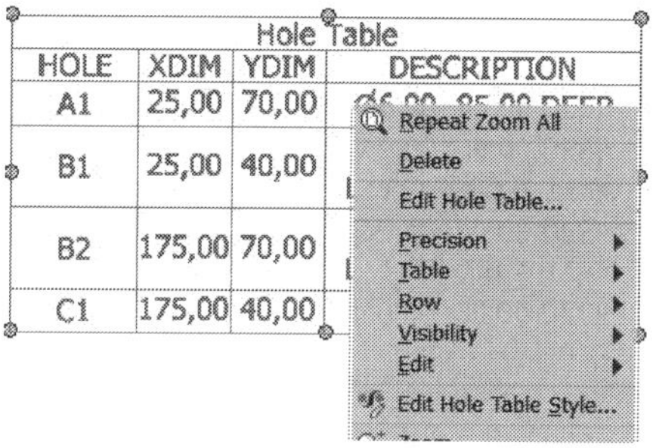

Figure 27–18

27.7 Revision Tables and Tags

Revision tables and tags help track and distinguish the various changes in the model between revisions.

How To: Create a Revision Table

1. Select the *Annotate* tab>Table panel and click (Revision).
2. Define the options in the Revision Table dialog box:
   - Use the *Table Scope* area to define whether the table is for the entire drawing or for the active sheet.
   - Use the *Revision Index* area to define if indexing is done alphabetically or numerically.
   - Use the **Update Property on Revision Number Edit** option to ensure that the active row is connected with the revision number property in drawing iProperties.
3. Click **OK** to close the Revision Table dialog box.
4. Move the cursor and click to place the table. A table displays similar to that shown in Figure 27–19.

REVISION HISTORY				
ZONE	REV	DESCRIPTION	DATE	APPROVED
	1		3/9/2020	

Figure 27–19

Editing the Revision Table Format

To edit the revision table, select the revision table so that it is highlighted, right-click and select **Edit**. The Revision Table: Drawing Scope dialog box opens as shown in Figure 27–20.

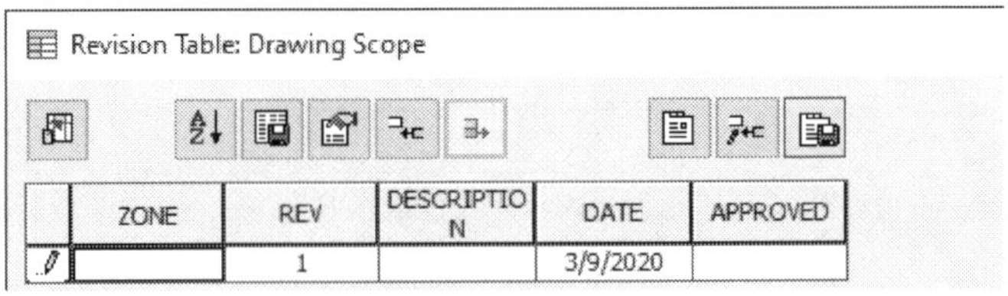

Figure 27–20

How To: Edit the Revision Table

1. Click  to open the Revision Table Layout dialog box. The options in this dialog box enable you to customize the look of the table. The options include the following:
   - Changing the Title row title.
   - Locating the title row heading at the top or bottom of the table, or not including it at all.
   - Controlling the list of table entries in ascending or descending order.
   - Controlling the format of the text in the table.
   - Controlling the table wrapping for the table.
2. Click  to add and move columns in the table, as required. Revision tables can include any iProperties.
3. Right-click on the revision table and select **Rotate** to rotate the table in 90-degree increments. You can rotate **clock-wise** (**CW**) or **counter clock-wise** (**CCW**).
4. Right-click on the revision table and select **Add Revision Row** to add a revision to the table. The new row automatically increments the revision number.
5. Click  in the Revision Table dialog box to add a blank row to the table.
6. Place the cursor between two rows or columns and drag to adjust the height and width. When editing the layout of the table you can also customize the Heading Gap and Row Gap for the cells in the table.
7. Double-click the field to modify. The Revision Table dialog box opens to enable you to edit the text.

Hint: Revision Table Styles and Standards

The default table that is added to a drawing is controlled by the default Style and Standard entry. You can edit this standard by selecting the revision table so that it is highlighted, right-clicking and selecting **Edit Revision Table Style**. The customization options are the same as the Revision Table Layout dialog box, and are stored as a style that can be used for future tables.

Revision Tags

*To change the symbol shape or change the formal, right-click and select **Edit Revision Tag** or double-click on the tag to open the Edit Revision Tag dialog box.*

Revision tags enable you to identify the revision directly on the drawing.

How To: Add Revision Tags

1. In the Table panel, expand Revision and click  (Revision Tag).
2. Select the entity or location to which the revision tag refers.
3. Click to place the revision tag or select again to place an elbow on the tag. Once placed, right-click and select **Continue**. You can continue to place tags or right-click and select **Cancel [ESC]**.
4. To set the revision level of a placed tag, right-click, select **Tag** and select the revision level.

Practice 27a

Adding Text and Symbols

Practice Objectives

- Add text to a drawing file to provide additional information.
- Create surface texture, datum identifier, and feature control frame symbols to views in a drawing.

In this practice, you will create the note and symbols shown in Figure 27–21.

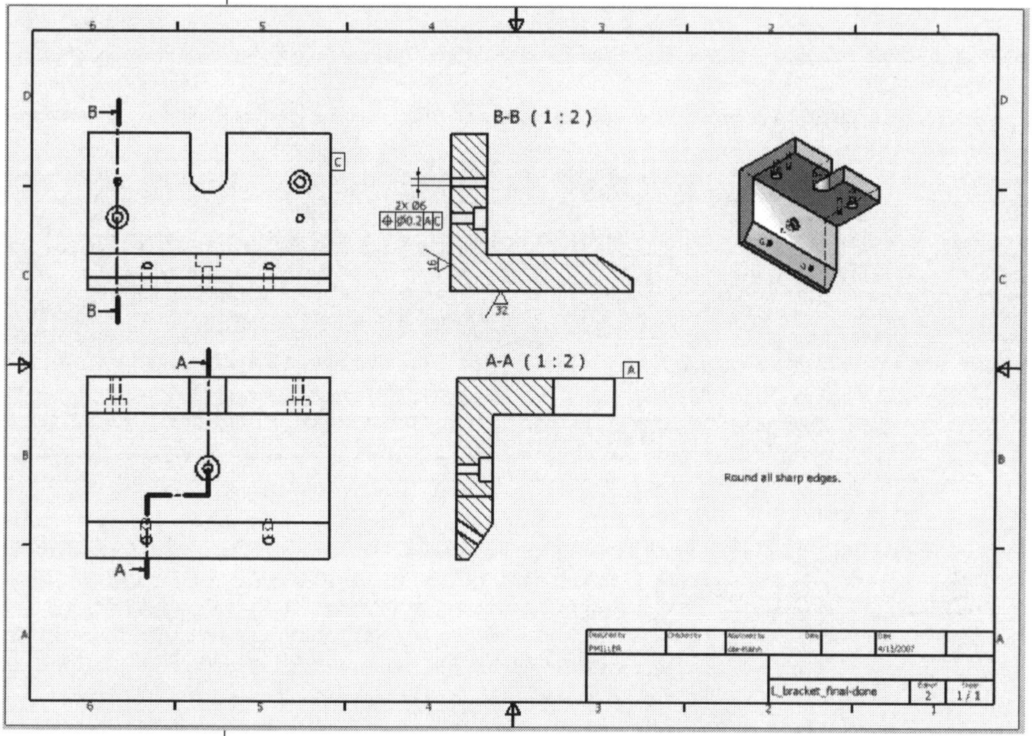

Figure 27–21

Task 1 - Open a drawing file.

1. Open the **L_bracket.dwg** that you created previously. If you did not complete it, open **L_bracket_final.dwg** instead. The drawing displays as shown in Figure 27–22.

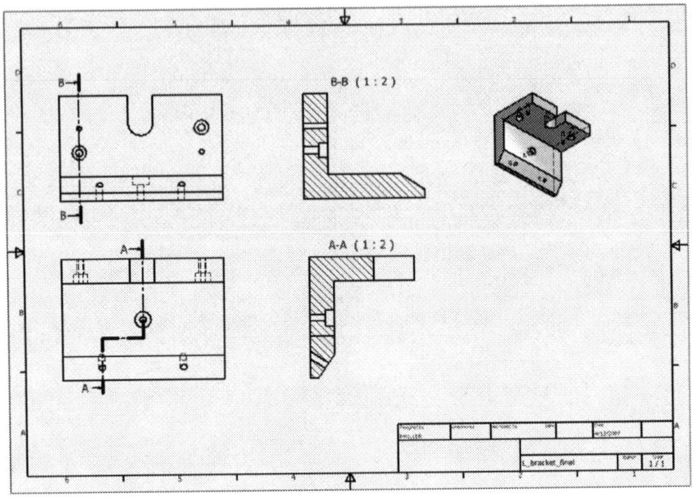

Figure 27–22

Task 2 - Add text.

1. Select the *Annotate* tab>Text panel and click **A** (Text).
2. Select in the open area on the right side of the drawing to place the text. The Format Text dialog box opens.
3. Enter **Round all sharp edges** in the *Text* field and click **OK**. The text displays as shown in Figure 27–23.

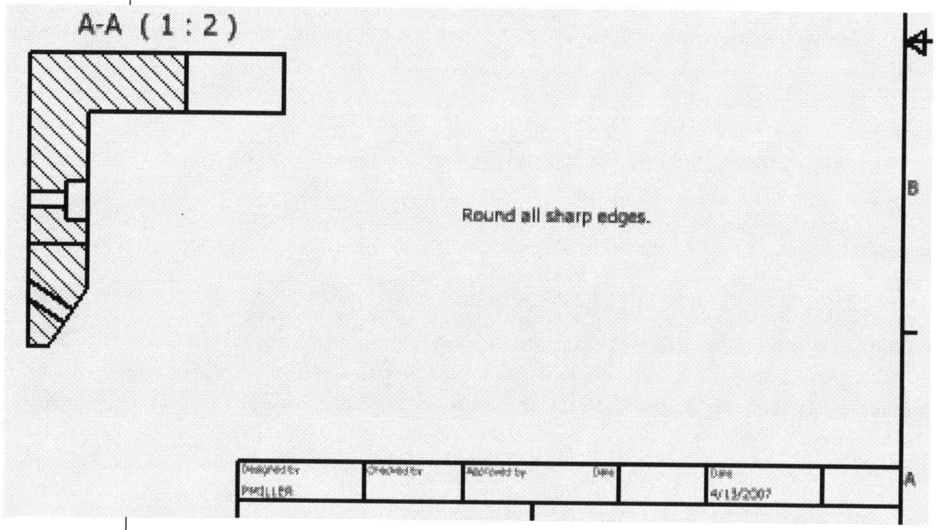

Figure 27–23

4. Select and move the text, if required.

Task 3 - Add surface texture symbols.

1. In the Symbols panel, click √ (Surface).
2. Select the edge in section B, as shown in Figure 27–24.

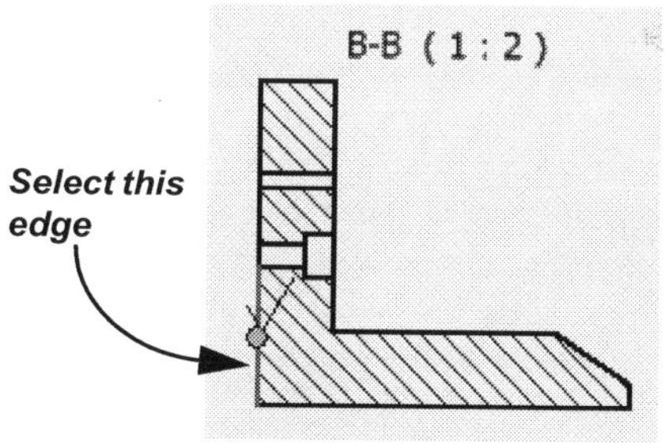

Figure 27–24

3. Right-click and select **Continue**. The Surface Texture dialog box opens as shown in Figure 27–25.

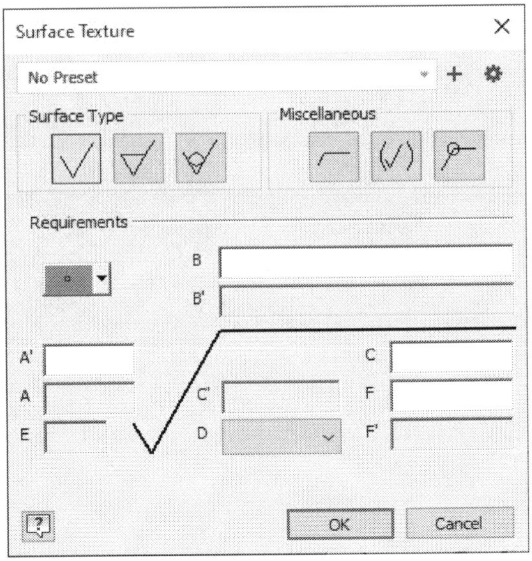

Figure 27–25

4. Click  in the *Surface Type* area.

If the surface texture symbol is not oriented correctly, select it and drag the green dot to the required location. It will toggle through the available placement options as you drag. Release when the preview is as required.

5. Enter **16** in the *A'* field and click **OK**. The surface texture symbol displays as shown in Figure 27–26.

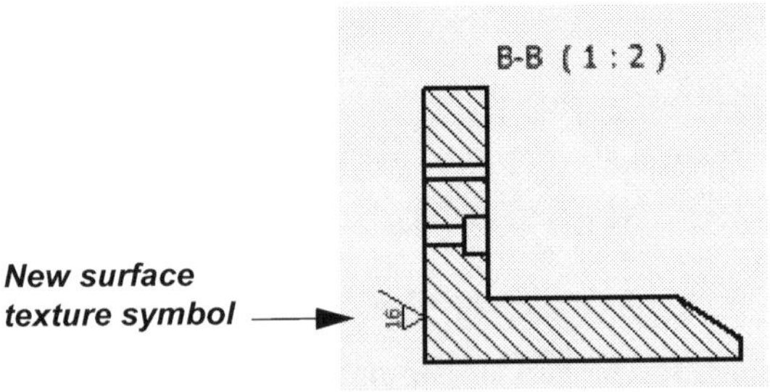

Figure 27–26

6. Create a second surface texture symbol, as shown in Figure 27–27.

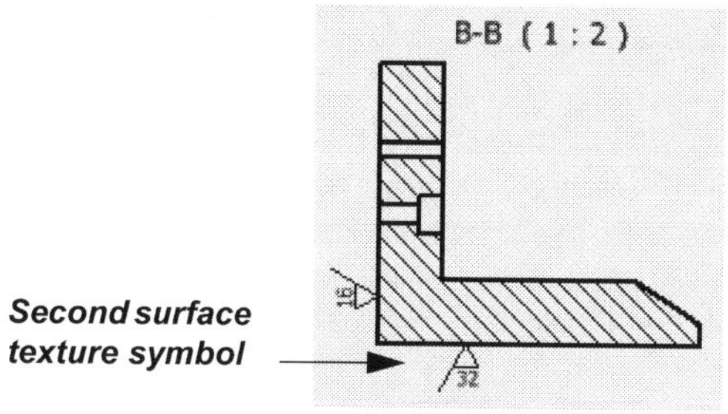

Figure 27–27

7. Press <Esc> to end the command.

Task 4 - Add datum identifier symbols.

1. Scroll down in the Symbols panel and click (Datum Identifier Symbol).
2. Select the edge in section A, as shown in Figure 27–28.

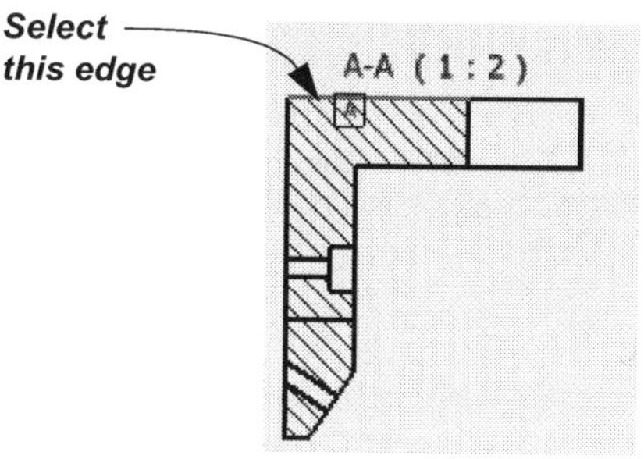

Figure 27–28

3. Right-click and select **Continue**. The Format Text dialog box opens. The letter **A** is entered automatically. Accept this default.
4. Click **OK**. The datum identifier is added, as shown in Figure 27–29.

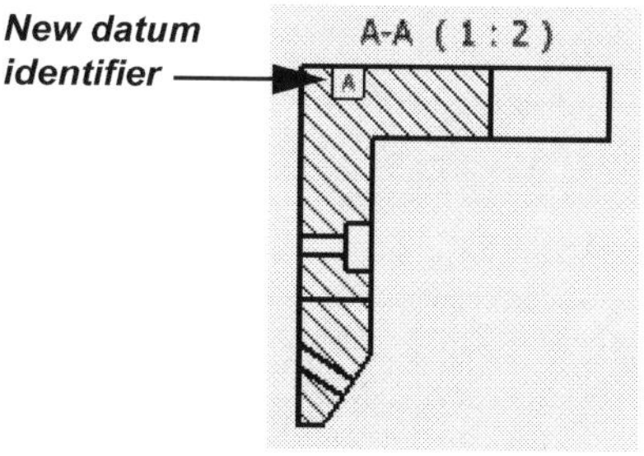

Figure 27–29

5. Right-click and select **Cancel [Esc]** to finish creating additional datum identifiers.

6. Move the datum identifier by selecting it. A green-colored dot will display, indicating that the symbol has been selected.

7. Move the cursor to the green circle and drag the symbol to the position shown in Figure 27–30.

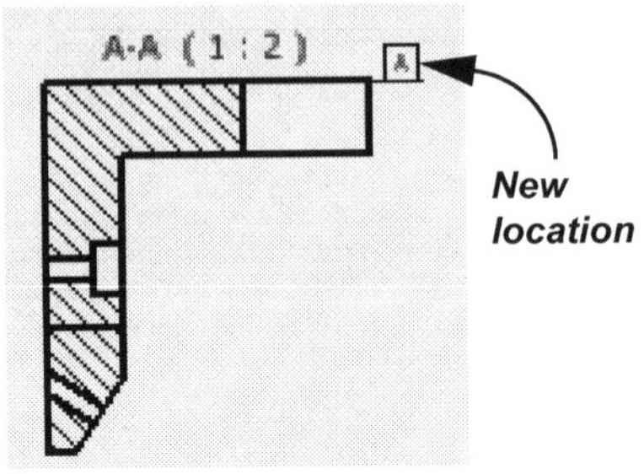

Figure 27–30

8. Create a second datum identifier, as shown in Figure 27–31.

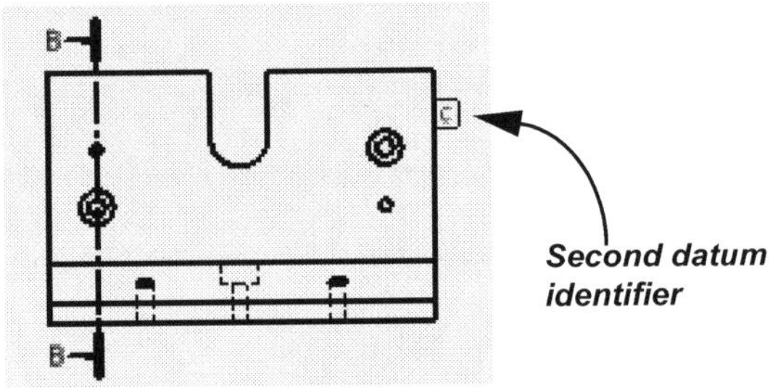

Figure 27–31

Task 5 - Add a feature control frame.

1. Start the creation of a General Dimension and select the dimension style **Default-Method 2b** in the Style drop-down list, as shown in Figure 27–32.

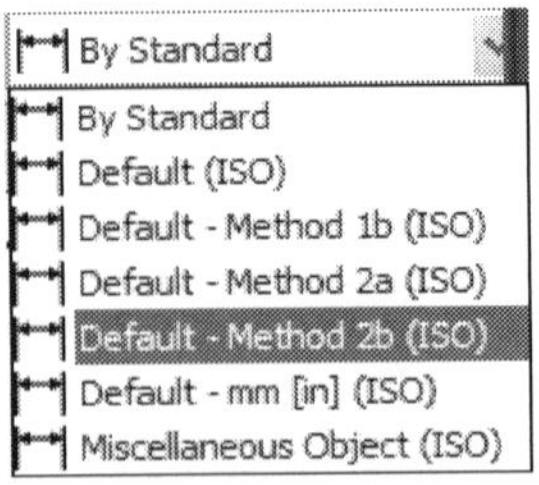

Figure 27–32

2. Add the dimension shown in Figure 27–33.

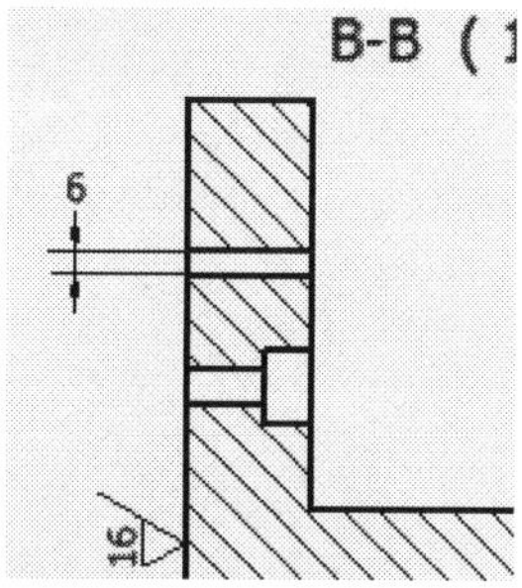

Figure 27–33

3. Edit the dimension to indicate two holes as shown in Figure 27–34. You must edit the text for the dimension (before the **<<>>** symbols) and also add the diameter symbol, if it does not automatically appear.

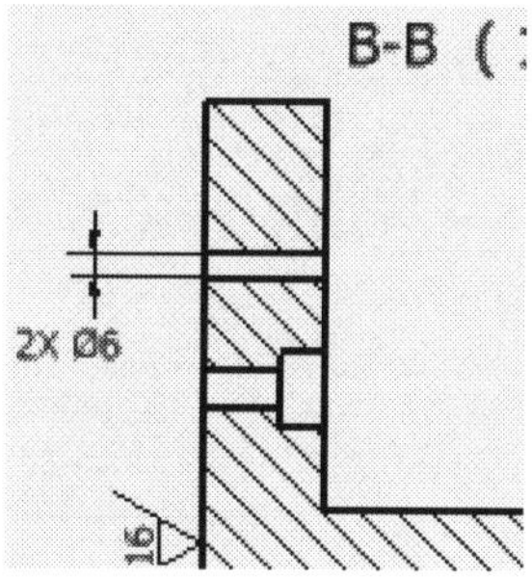

Figure 27–34

4. Scroll down in the Symbols panel, and click (Feature Control Frame).

5. Select the dimension in section B, as shown in Figure 27–35.

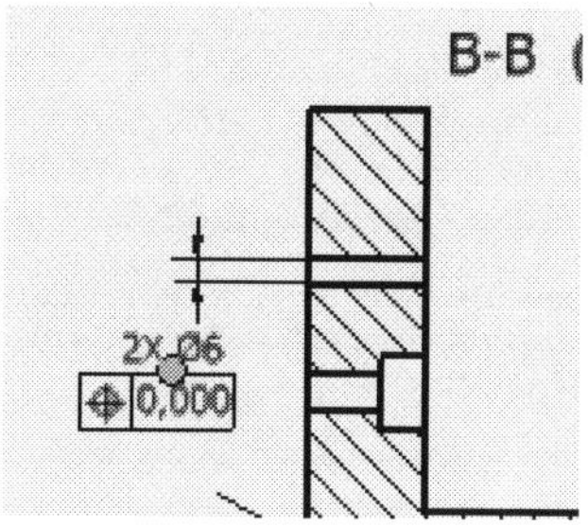

Figure 27–35

6. Right-click and select **Continue**. The Feature Control Frame dialog box opens.

7. Place the cursor at the beginning of the *Tolerance* field.

8. Click 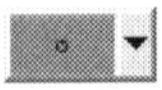 to expand the symbols list and select  to insert the diameter symbol. Fill in the rest of the dialog box with the values shown in Figure 27–36.

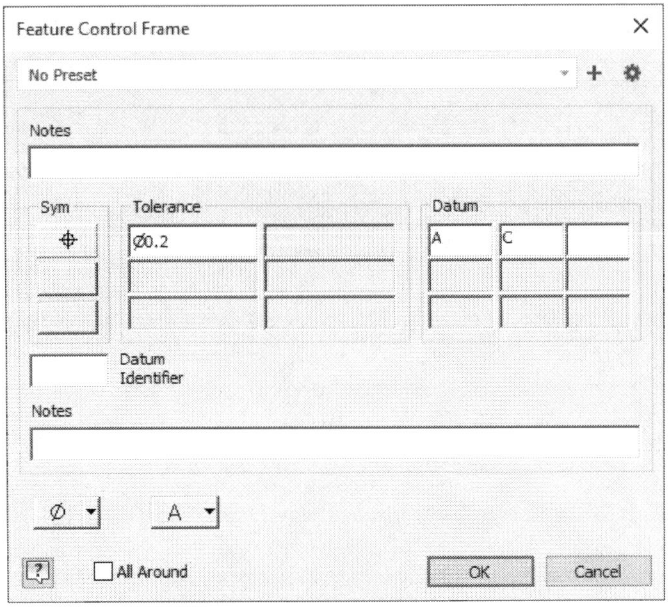

Figure 27–36

9. Click **OK**.

10. Right-click and select **Cancel [ESC]**.

11. Move the dimension and symbol as required. The feature control frame should display similar to that shown in Figure 27–37.

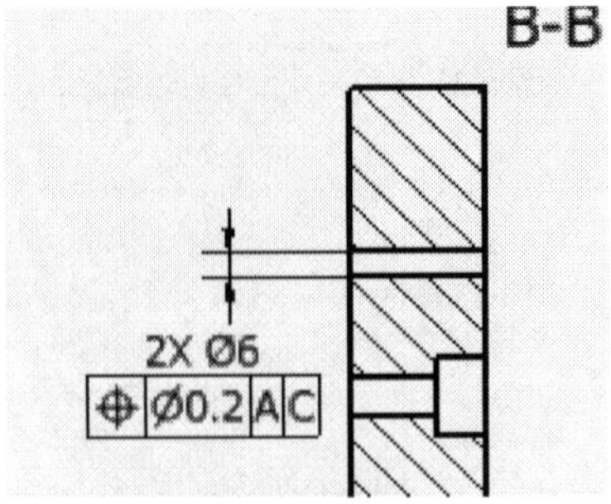

Figure 27–37

12. Save and close the drawing.

Practice 27b

Notes, Center Marks, and Center Lines

Practice Objectives

- Add and edit a hole note in a drawing file.
- Add a chamfer note to a drawing view.
- Create a centerline bisector and centered pattern on views in a drawing.

In this practice, you will create different types of notes, center marks, and center lines. The completed drawing is shown in Figure 27–38.

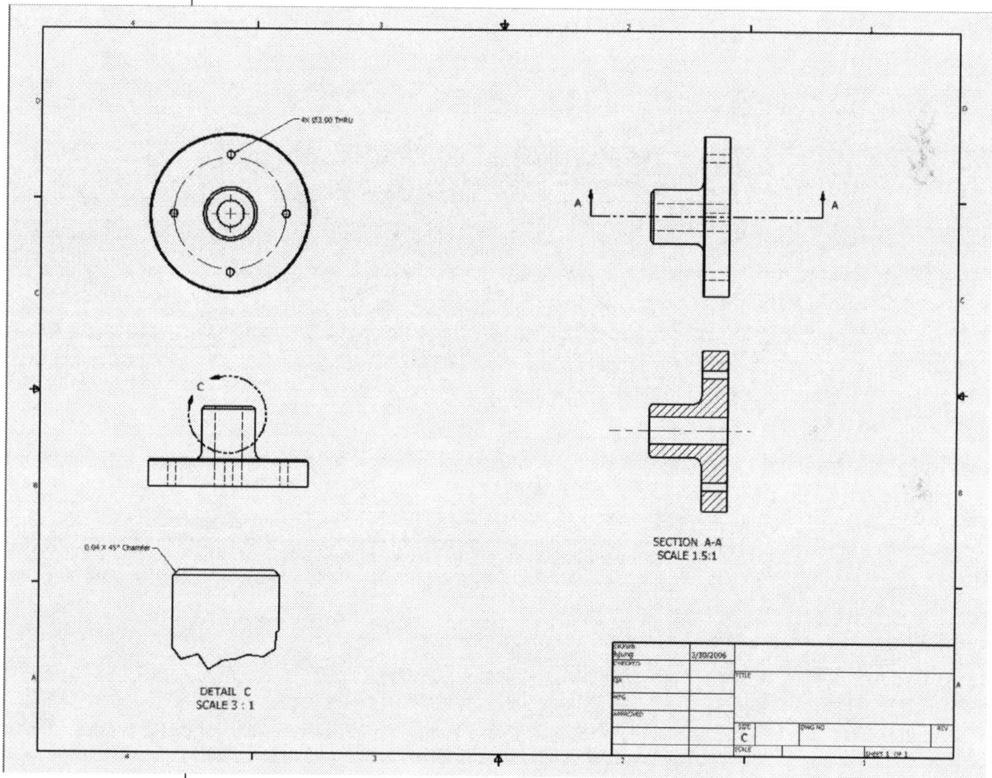

Figure 27–38

Task 1 - Open a drawing file.

1. Open the **relation.dwg** that you created previously. The drawing displays as shown in Figure 27–39. If you did not complete it, open **relation_final.dwg** instead.

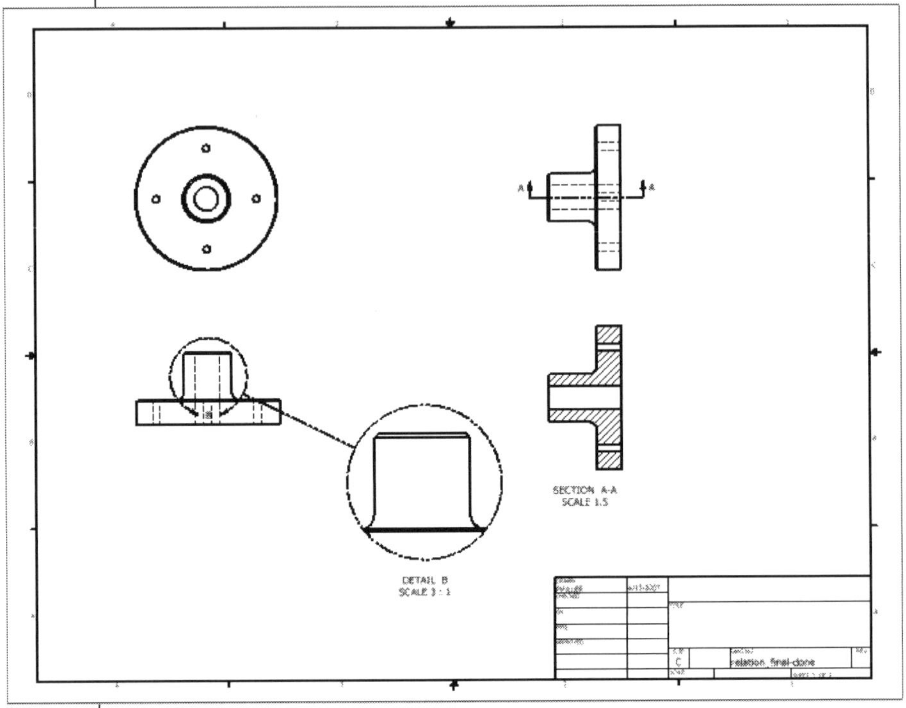

Figure 27–39

Task 2 - Add a hole note.

1. Select the *Annotate* tab>Feature Notes panel and click (Hole and Thread).
2. Select the hole in the drawing view shown in Figure 27–40.

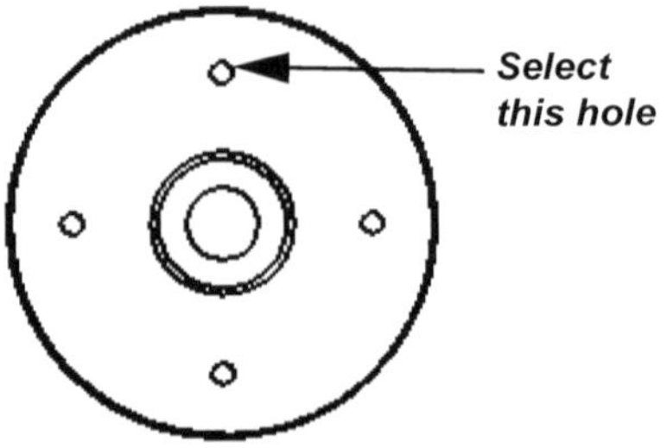

Figure 27–40

3. Position the note with the cursor and click the left mouse button to place it.

4. Complete the creation of the note by right-clicking and selecting **OK**. The hole note is added to the drawing, as shown in Figure 27–41.

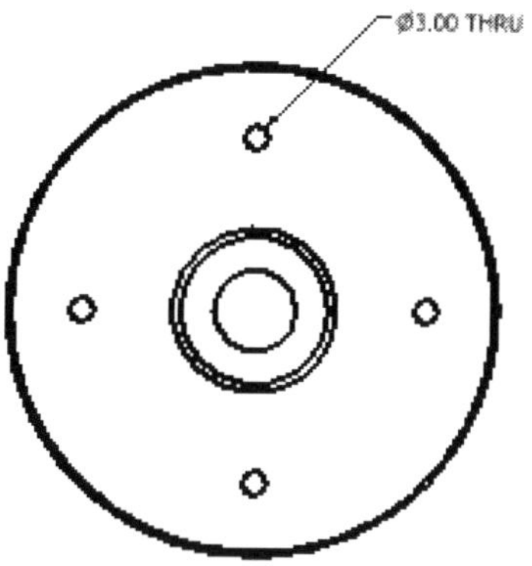

Figure 27–41

Task 3 - Edit the hole note.

1. Right-click on the hole note and select **Edit Hole Note**. The Edit Hole Note dialog box opens.

2. Place the cursor at the beginning of the hole note.

3. Add the quantity note to the hole note by clicking # in the *Values and Symbols* area. It displays as shown in Figure 27–42.

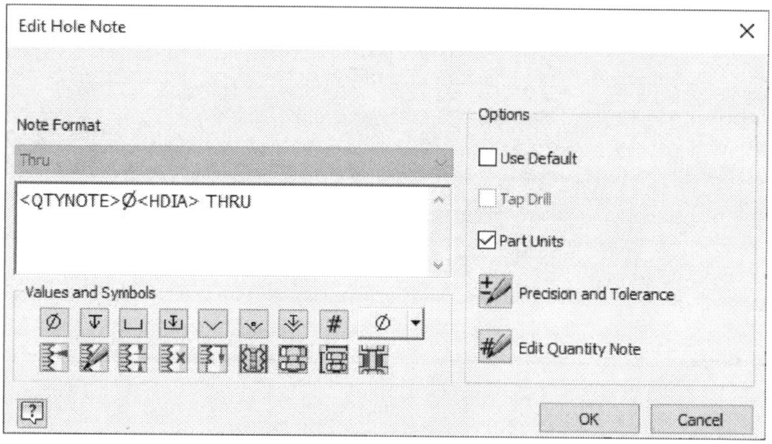

Figure 27–42

4. Click **OK**. The revised note displays as shown in Figure 27–43.

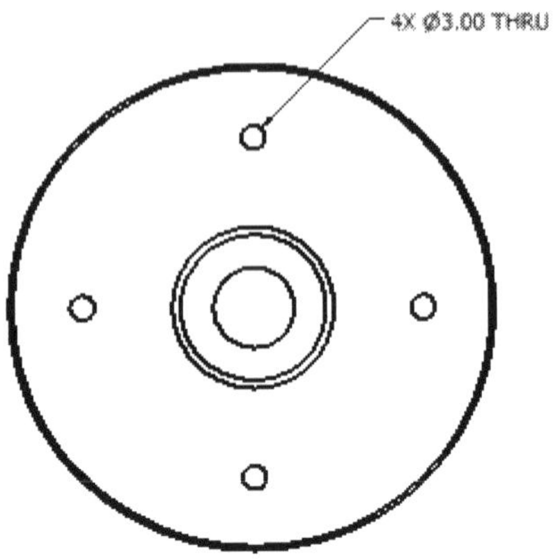

Figure 27–43

Task 4 - Add a chamfer note.

1. In the Feature Notes panel, click  (Chamfer).
2. Select the two edges of the detailed view, as shown in Figure 27–44. Review the prompts in the status bar to verify the order of selection.

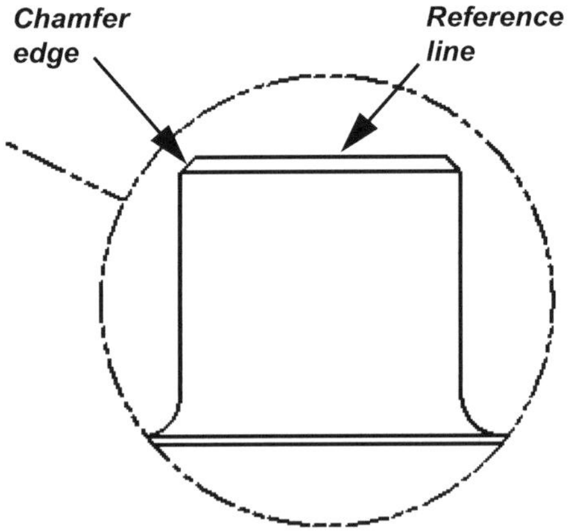

Figure 27–44

3. Position the note with the cursor and click the left mouse button to place it, as shown in Figure 27–45.

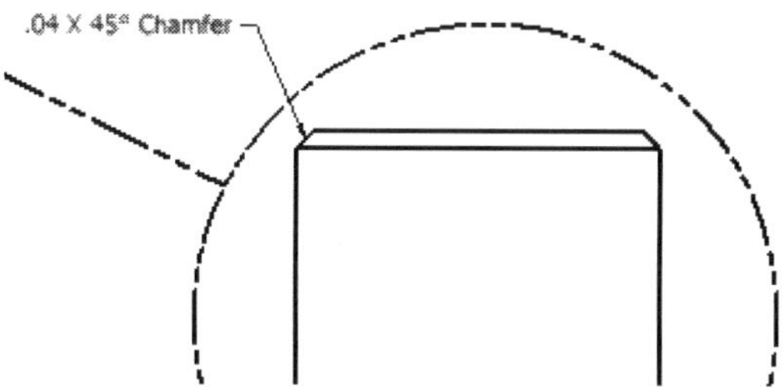

Figure 27–45

4. Complete the creation of the note by right-clicking and selecting **OK**.

Task 5 - Add a center line bisector.

1. In the Symbols panel, click  (Centerline Bisector).
2. Select the two lines shown on the left in Figure 27–46 to add a center line bisector to the section view.
3. Complete the creation of the centerline bisector by right-clicking and selecting **Cancel [ESC]**. The centerline bisector is added to the drawing view, as shown on the right in Figure 27–46.

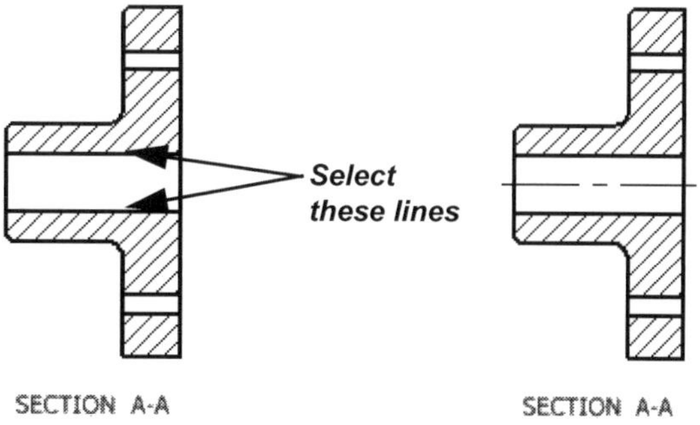

Figure 27–46

Task 6 - Add a centered pattern.

1. In the Symbols panel, click  (Centered Pattern).
2. Select the circular edge of the center circle to locate the center of the pattern, as shown in Figure 27–47. Any of the circular edges at the center of the circle can be selected.

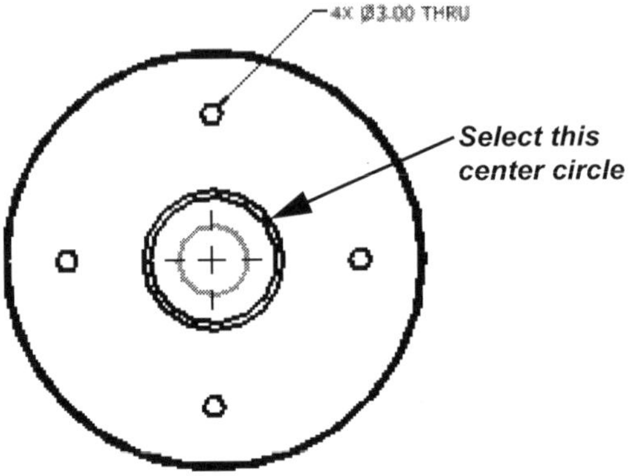

Figure 27–47

Alternatively, you can select the holes in a counter-clockwise order.

3. Select the four hole features shown on the left in Figure 27–48 in the order specified. You must select the first hole a second time.
4. Complete the creation by right-clicking and selecting **Create**. The centered pattern is now added to the drawing view, as shown on the right in Figure 27–48.

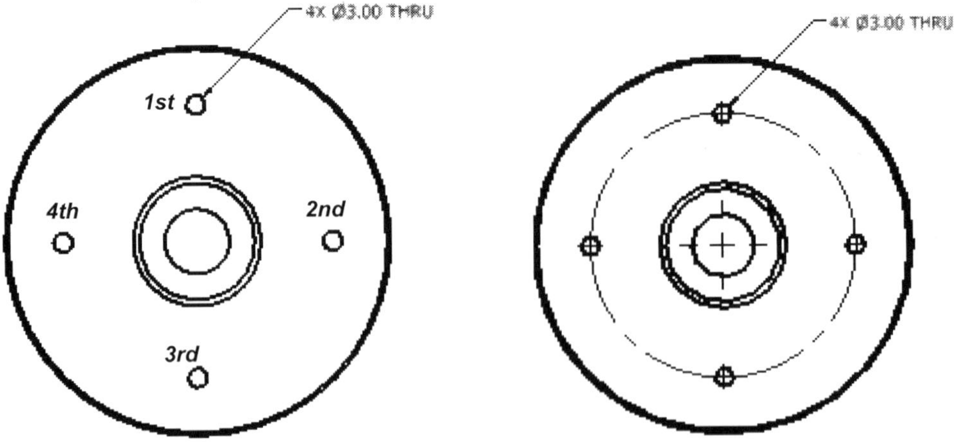

Figure 27–48

5. Save and close the drawing.

Practice 27c Adding a Revision Table and Tags

Practice Objectives

- Add a revision table to a drawing file.
- Add revision tags to dimensions in a drawing file to indicate modifications made to the file.
- Edit the number of rows and properties of the Revision table to create a required table.

In this practice, you will create a revision table and revision tags. The completed drawing is shown in Figure 27–49.

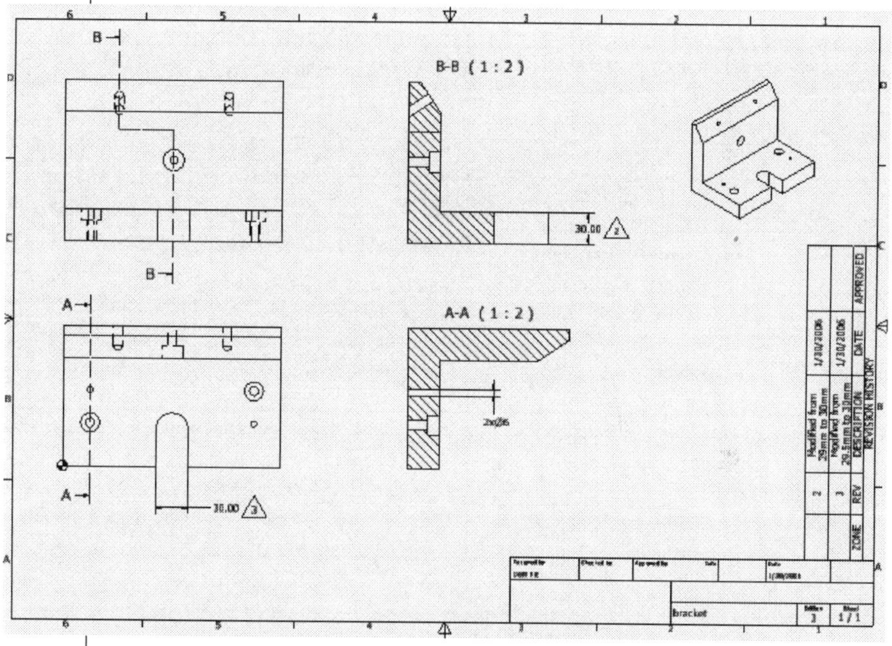

Figure 27–49

Task 1 - Add a revision table.

The Revision Table dialog box provides you with options to create the table for the entire drawing or for the active sheet.

1. Open **bracket_Rev Table.dwg**.
2. Select the *Annotate* tab>Table panel and click (Revision).
3. Accept the default values in the Revision Table dialog box and click **OK**. A border displays that moves with the cursor.

4. Move the cursor to the bottom right side of the drawing, just above the title block. The revision table snaps to the title block and border. Click to place the revision table, as shown in Figure 27–50.

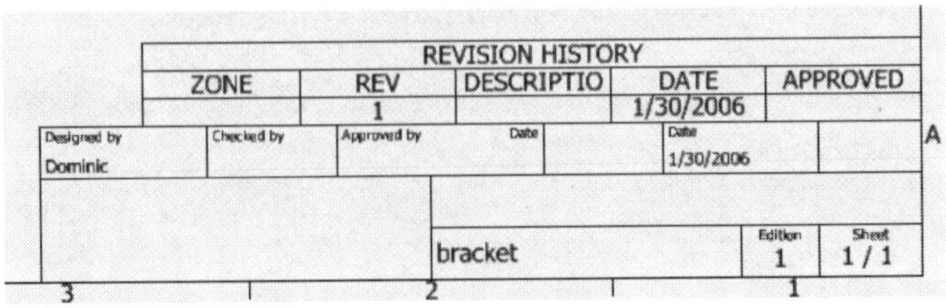

Figure 27–50

The Style and Standard Editor dialog box enables you to customize the style for tables and tags in a drawing.

5. Right-click on the *Revision History* title and select **Edit Revision Table Style**. The Style and Standard Editor dialog box opens. You can customize text styles, line format, gap for rows, position of the title, and whether the title displays. You can also use the *Revision Tags* tab to customize tags.

6. Select the Heading drop-down list and click  to place the title of the revision table at the bottom. Click **Save and Close**. The revision table displays as shown in Figure 27–51.

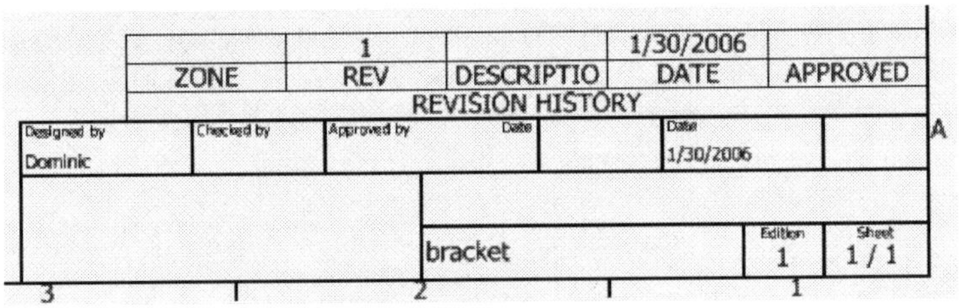

Figure 27–51

7. Add a new row by right-clicking on any of the text in the table and selecting **Add Revision Row**. The Revision Table: Drawing Scope dialog box opens. Verify that the new row has been added and click **OK**. A revision row is added, as shown in Figure 27–52.

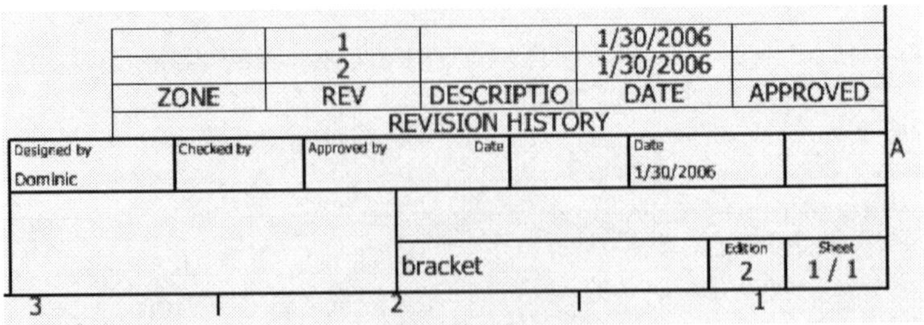

Figure 27–52

8. Delete the row that was just created in the table by selecting a value in the first row, such as 1, right-clicking and selecting **Delete Row**. The row is removed. You cannot delete the default row in the table.

9. Adjust the columns to provide more space for the *DESCRIPTION* column. First drag the entire table away from the title block and border. Then drag the table by selecting on any text in the table and dragging the table.

10. Increase the width of the *DESCRIPTION* column by placing the cursor on the line between the *DESCRIPTION* and *DATE* columns and dragging the cursor to the right.

11. Decrease the width of the *REV* and *ZONE* columns.

12. Move the table back so that it snaps to the title block and border, as shown in Figure 27–53.

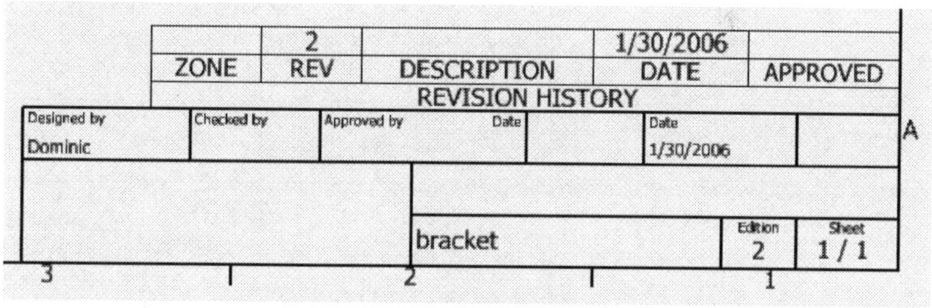

Figure 27–53

Task 2 - Add a revision tag.

1. In the Table panel, expand Revision and click  (Revision Tag).

2. Select the area next to the 30.00 dimension value in section B, right-click and select **Continue**. The revision tag is placed.

3. Press <Esc> to cancel creating another revision tag.

4. Move the revision tag as shown in Figure 27–54.

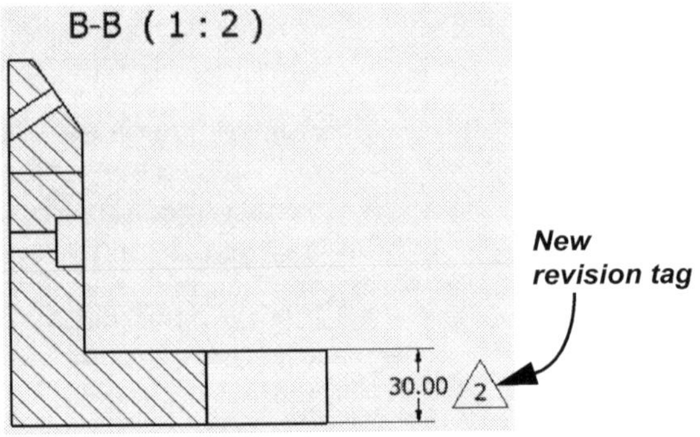

Figure 27–54

5. Right-click on the table and select **Edit**. The Revision Table: Drawing Scope dialog box opens.

6. Enter the text **Modified from 29mm to 30mm** in the *DESCRIPTION* column.

7. Click **OK**. The table displays as shown in Figure 27–55.

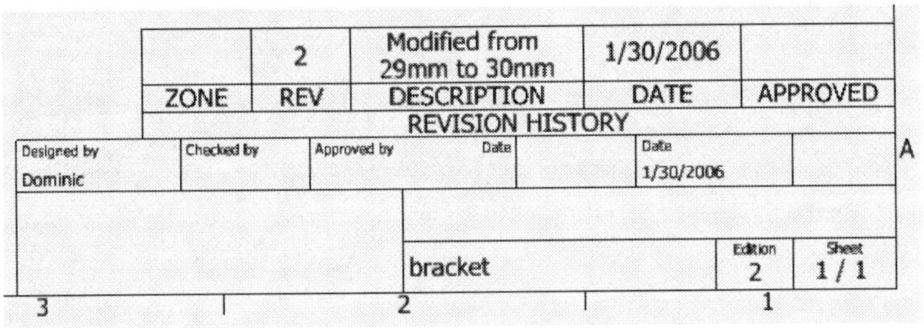

Figure 27–55

Task 3 - Add a row to the revision table.

1. Select any text in the revision table, right-click and select **Add Revision Row**. The Revision Table: Drawing Scope dialog box opens.

2. A new revision row is added with an incremental revision value. Modify the *DESCRIPTION* column in this new row of the table to **Modified from 29.5mm to 30mm** and close the dialog box.

The revision tag number is incremented when a new revision row is added in the revision table.

3. Add the revision tag to the 30.00 mm dimension located in the other view, as shown Figure 27–56.

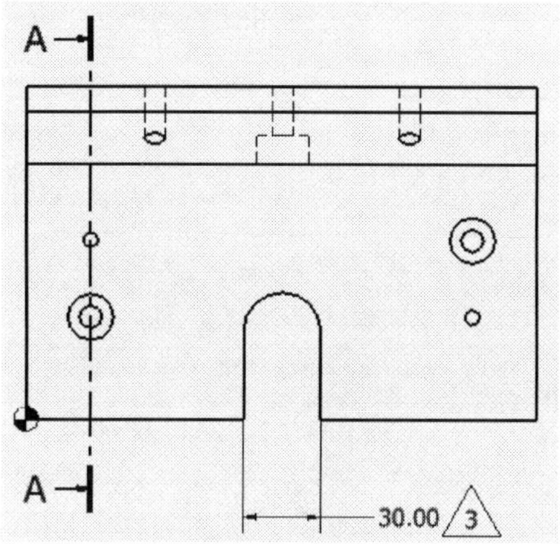

Figure 27–56

4. Right-click on the table, select **Rotate>Rotate 90 CCW**, and position the table along the right edge, as shown in Figure 27–57.

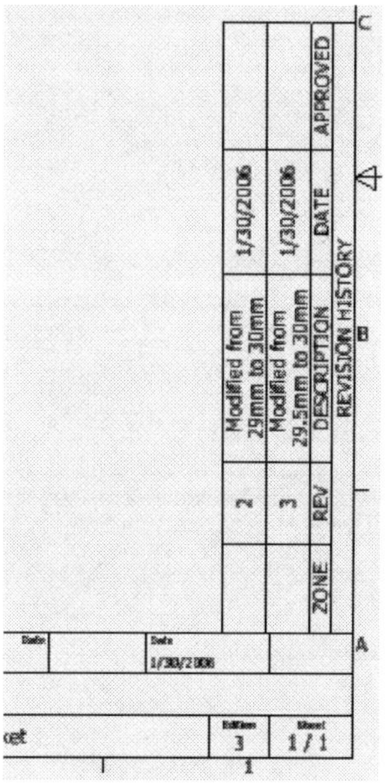

Figure 27–57

5. Save and close the drawing.

Practice 27d Adding Hole Tables

Practice Objective

- Create hole tables based on selected features, feature types, and views.

In this practice, you will create three hole tables using three different methods. The completed drawing is shown in Figure 27–58.

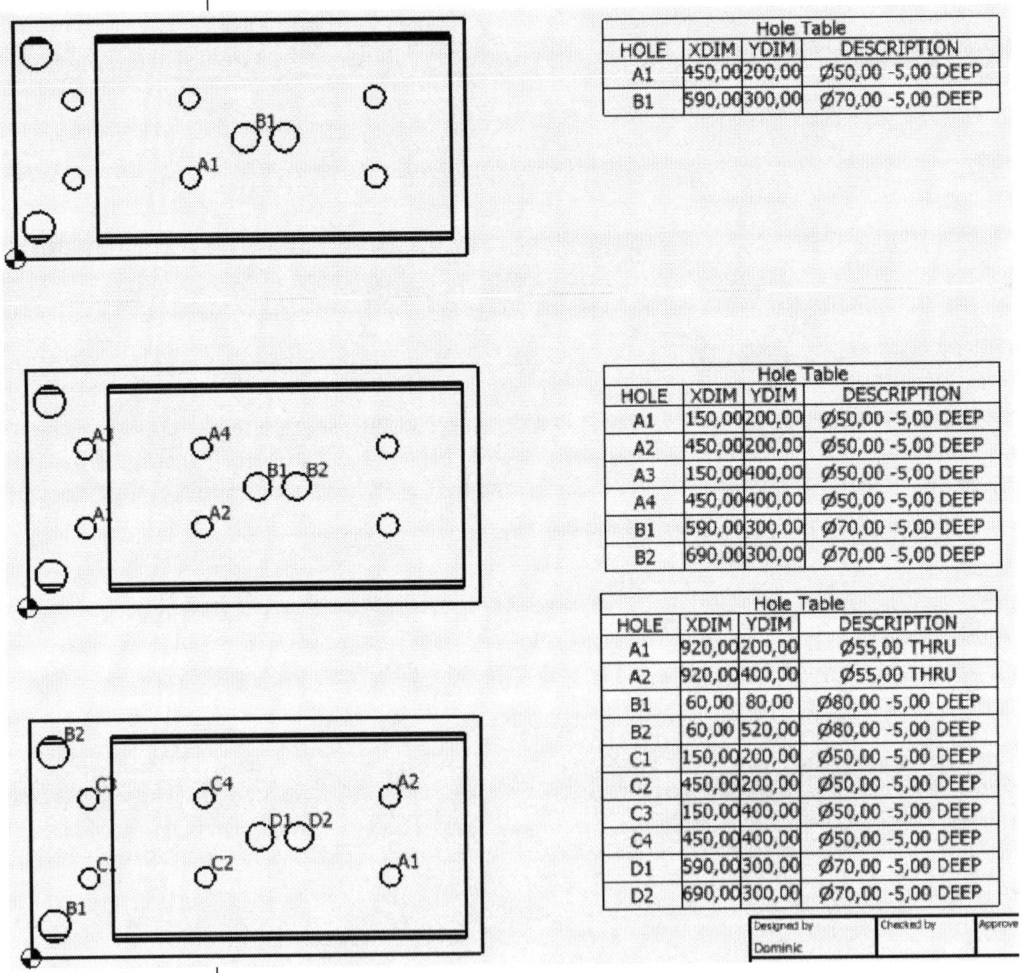

Figure 27–58

Task 1 - Add a hole table by selecting each hole.

1. Open **hole_chart.dwg**. There are three identical views.
2. Select the *Annotate* tab>Table panel and expand **Hole**, as shown in Figure 27–59. The expanded list displays three hole options. Each option displays in the same way; you can identify the option by its icon or by hovering the cursor over the command and reviewing its tooltip.

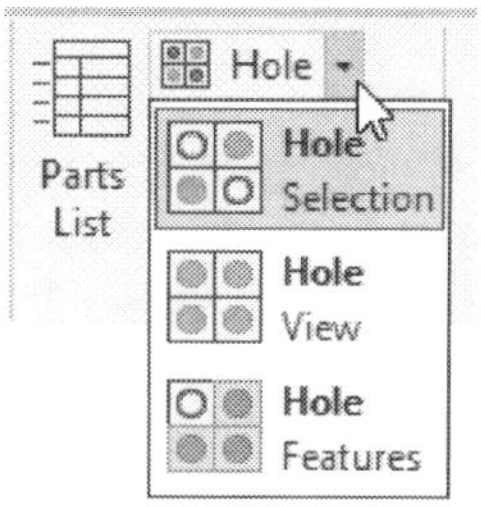

Figure 27–59

3. In the expanded Hole list, click  (Hole Selection).
4. Select the view at the top of the drawing sheet.
5. Select the bottom left corner of the part as the origin for the hole table. All coordinates will use this as their 0,0 reference.
6. Select the two holes shown in Figure 27–60.

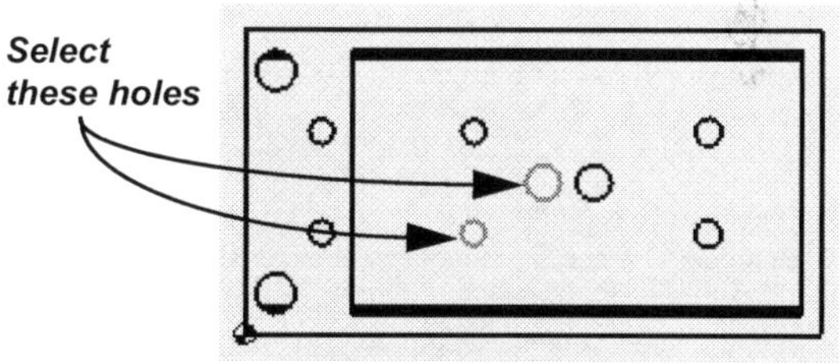

Figure 27–60

7. Right-click and select **Create**. A box opens that now follows the cursor.

8. Place the hole table in the top right area of the drawing by selecting the left mouse button. The hole table displays and is automatically populated with the hole information for the two holes that were selected, as shown in Figure 27–61.

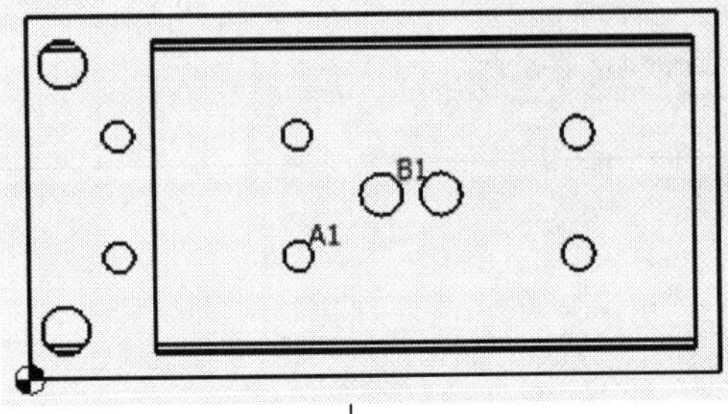

Hole Table			
HOLE	XDIM	YDIM	DESCRIPTION
A1	450,00	200,00	Ø50,00 -5,00 DEEP
B1	590,00	300,00	Ø70,00 -5,00 DEEP

Figure 27–61

Task 2 - Add a hole table by selecting feature types.

1. In the expanded Hole list, click (Hole Features).
2. Select the middle view on the drawing sheet.
3. Select the bottom left corner of the part as the origin.
4. Select the two holes shown in Figure 27–62.

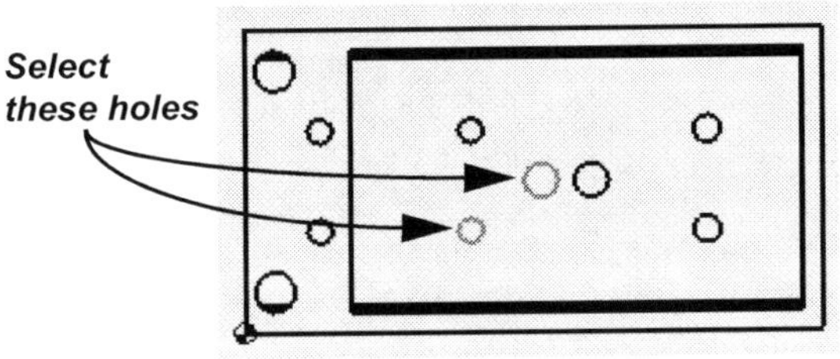

Figure 27–62

5. Right-click and select **Create**.

6. Place the hole table in the middle right area of the drawing. The hole table displays and is automatically populated with the information for the two holes and any hole that is similar to those selected, as shown in Figure 27–63.

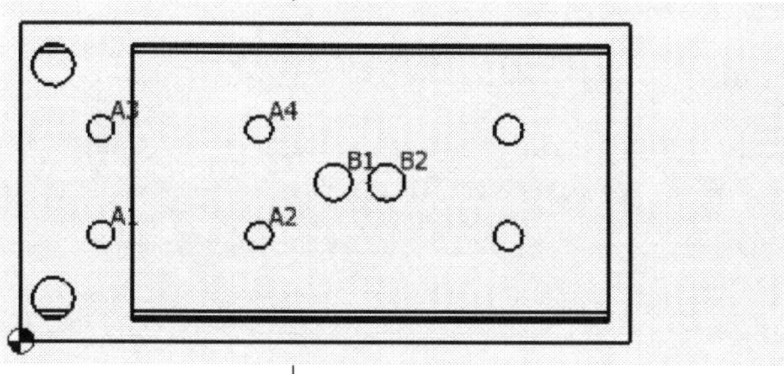

Hole Table			
HOLE	XDIM	YDIM	DESCRIPTION
A1	150,00	200,00	Ø50,00 -5,00 DEEP
A2	450,00	200,00	Ø50,00 -5,00 DEEP
A3	150,00	400,00	Ø50,00 -5,00 DEEP
A4	450,00	400,00	Ø50,00 -5,00 DEEP
B1	590,00	300,00	Ø70,00 -5,00 DEEP
B2	690,00	300,00	Ø70,00 -5,00 DEEP

Figure 27–63

Task 3 - Add a hole table by selecting a view.

1. In the expanded Hole list, click (Hole View).
2. Select the bottom view of the drawing sheet.
3. Select the bottom left corner of the part as the origin.
4. Place the hole table in the bottom right area of the drawing. The hole table displays and is automatically populated with all of the hole information for the selected view, as shown in Figure 27–64.

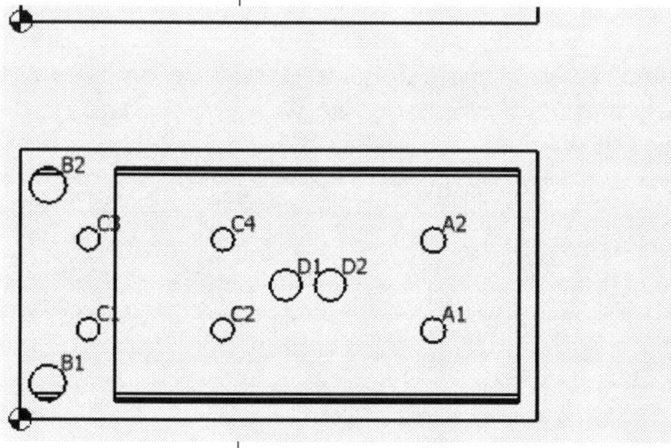

Hole Table			
HOLE	XDIM	YDIM	DESCRIPTION
A1	920,00	200,00	Ø55,00 THRU
A2	920,00	400,00	Ø55,00 THRU
B1	60,00	80,00	Ø80,00 -5,00 DEEP
B2	60,00	520,00	Ø80,00 -5,00 DEEP
C1	150,00	200,00	Ø50,00 -5,00 DEEP
C2	450,00	200,00	Ø50,00 -5,00 DEEP
C3	150,00	400,00	Ø50,00 -5,00 DEEP
C4	450,00	400,00	Ø50,00 -5,00 DEEP
D1	590,00	300,00	Ø70,00 -5,00 DEEP
D2	690,00	300,00	Ø70,00 -5,00 DEEP

Designed by Dominic | Checked by | Appro

Figure 27–64

5. Save and close the drawing.

Chapter Review Questions

1. You can only create text with a leader.
   a. True
   b. False
2. Which of the following are valid symbols that can be created in a drawing? (Select all that apply.)
   a. 
   b. 
   c. 
   d. 
3. To which of the following features can you add a hole note in a drawing view? (Select all that apply.)
   a. Holes
   b. Extruded circular cuts
   c. Extruded circular solids
   d. Chamfer
   e. Center marks
   f. Flat patterns
4. Which chamfer note option displays the horizontal distance between a selected edge and a reference line?
   a.  (Distance 1)
   b.  (Angle)
   c.  (Distance 2)

5. Which command is used to automatically place center marks on all holes in a view, as shown in Figure 27–65?

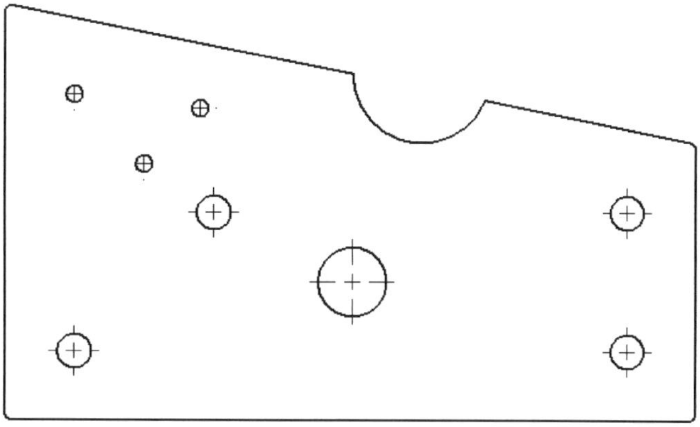

Figure 27–65

   a. **Centerline** tool.
   b. **Center Mark** tool.
   c. Right-click on the view and select **Automated Centerlines.**
   d. Select **All Model Dimensions** in Drawing View dialog box.

6. Fill in the Hole Table type, **Selection**, **View**, or **Features**, with the best description of how it can be used to create a table.
   a. Using the _______ type, all identical holes of all selected types are automatically included.
   b. Using the _______ type, all holes included in the hole table are selected individually.
   c. Using the _______ type, all holes of any type in a selected view are included in the hole table.

7. Which of the following drawing annotation types is used to help track and distinguish the various changes in the model between revisions?
   a. Parts list
   b. Revision table
   c. Hole table created using **Hole View**
   d. Balloons

Command Summary

Button	Command	Location
	**Center Mark**	• **Ribbon:** *Annotate* tab>Symbols panel • **Context Menu**: In the graphics window
	**Centered Pattern**	• **Ribbon:** *Annotate* tab>Symbols panel
	**Centerline**	• **Ribbon:** *Annotate* tab>Symbols panel
	**Centerline Bisector**	• **Ribbon:** *Annotate* tab>Symbols panel
	**Chamfer (note)**	• **Ribbon:** *Annotate* tab>Feature Notes panel
	**Hole and Thread (note)**	• **Ribbon:** *Annotate* tab>Feature Notes panel • **Context Menu**: In the graphics window
	**Hole Features (table)**	• **Ribbon:** *Annotate* tab>Table panel
	**Hole Selection (table)**	• **Ribbon:** *Annotate* tab>Table panel
	**Hole View (table)**	• **Ribbon:** *Annotate* tab>Table panel
	**Leader Text**	• **Ribbon:** *Annotate* tab>Text panel • **Context Menu**: In the graphics window
	**Revision (table)**	• **Ribbon:** *Annotate* tab>Table panel
	**Revision Tag**	• **Ribbon:** *Annotate* tab>Table panel
	**Text**	• **Ribbon:** *Annotate* tab>Text panel
N/A	**Various Symbol Types**	• **Ribbon:** *Annotate* tab>Symbols panel

Customizing Autodesk Inventor

Customizing the software enables you to change the system's default appearance and options to tailor to specific needs or preferences. You can customize settings to affect the entire company or changes can be user-specific.

Learning Objectives in This Chapter

- Use the Application Options to globally customize the modeling environment.
- Use the Document Settings to customize the active part, assembly, or drawing file.
- Edit iProperty information for parts, assemblies, and drawing files.
- Change the part units in your model.
- Add a User Commands panel, with commands, to any of the tabs on the ribbon.
- Assign command aliases using keyboard keys for commonly used commands.
- Customize the marking menu that displays when accessing commands in the shortcut menu.

28.1 Application Options

*You can also click **Options** on the **File** menu to open the Applications Options dialog box.*

The Application Options dialog box contains settings that control the software's behavior and configuration. Select the *Tools* tab> Options panel and click (Application Options) to open the Application Options dialog box. Alternatively,

General Tab

The *General* tab sets operation behaviors, such as startup, tooltips, selection, etc., as shown in Figure 28–1.

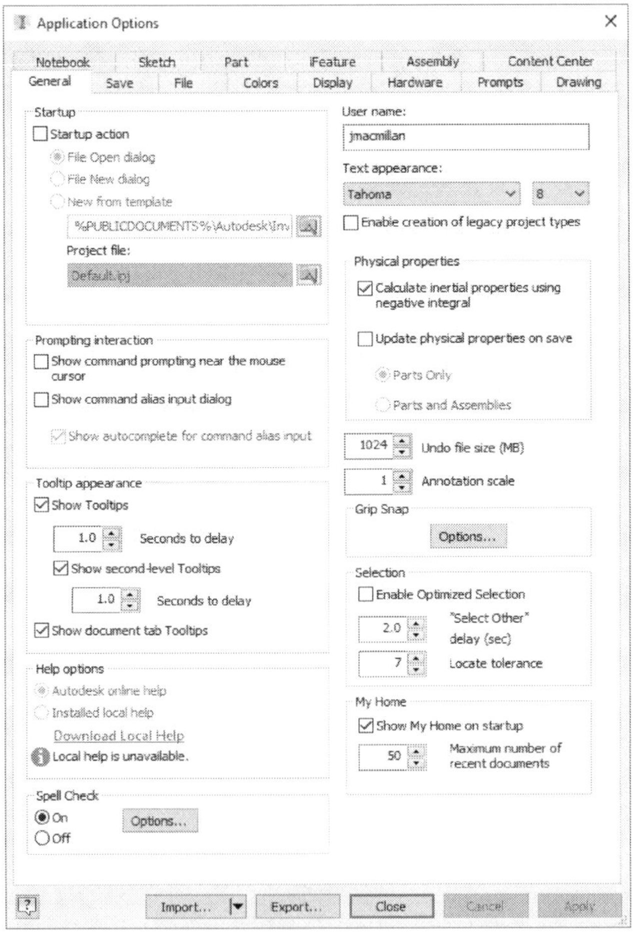

Figure 28–1

File Tab

The *File* tab controls the default locations of the files used by the software. To change a file location, click next to the appropriate field. It also controls the default options and settings to accelerate file opening times for assemblies.

Colors Tab

The *Colors* tab controls the colors used in the graphics window and the presence of reflections and textures, assigns a color scheme for objects in the graphics window or drawing files, or assigns a background color (color, gradient, or .BMP). The *Colors* tab also enables you to control the color theme of the software (command frame and icons).

Display Tab

The *Display* tab controls the appearance of active and inactive components and a model's display quality. In addition, it controls the **3D Navigation** tools.

Drawing Tab

The *Drawing* tab (shown in Figure 28–2) sets options for the behavior of drawings.

*The **Enable part modification from in drawings** enables you to allow model dimension changes at the drawing level, or not.*

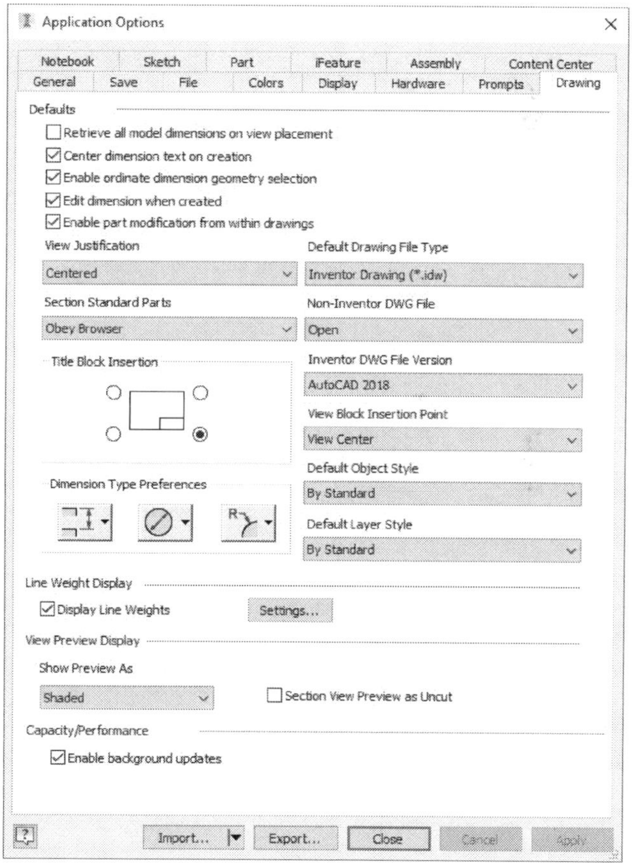

Figure 28–2

Prompts Tab

The *Prompts* tab enables you to select the prompts that display while working. To do so, select a prompt and right-click in their *Response* or *Prompt* columns.

Sketch Tab

The *Sketch* tab (shown in Figure 28–3) controls the sketch settings.

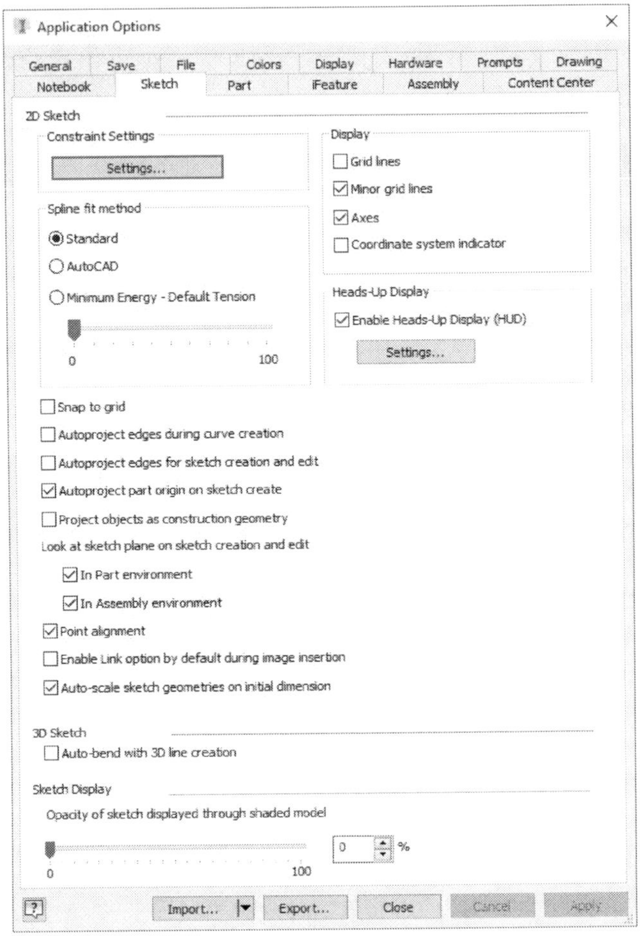

Figure 28–3

Part Tab

The *Part* tab (shown in Figure 28–4) controls the defaults for creating new parts, along with some constraint settings.

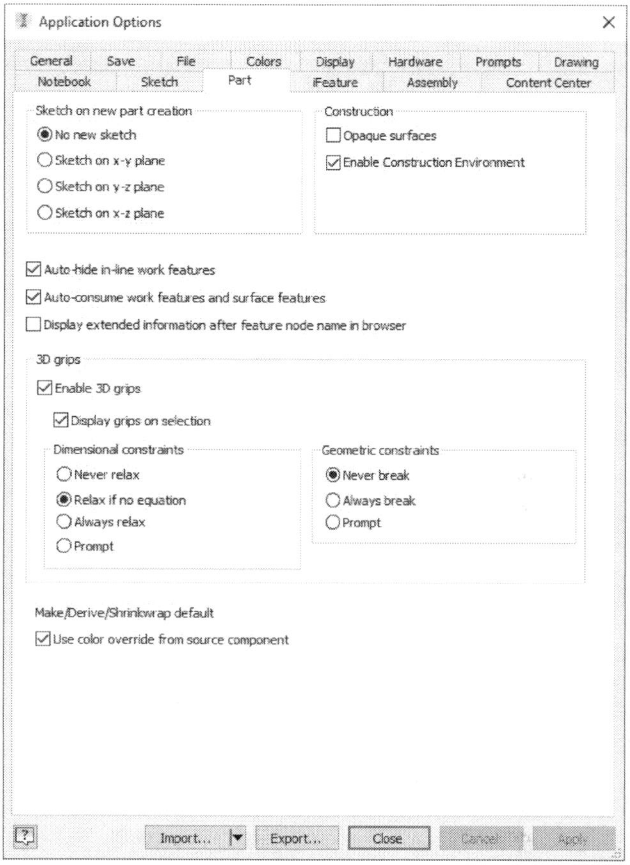

Figure 28–4

Assembly Tab

The *Assembly* tab (shown in Figure 28–5) controls the defaults for working with assemblies.

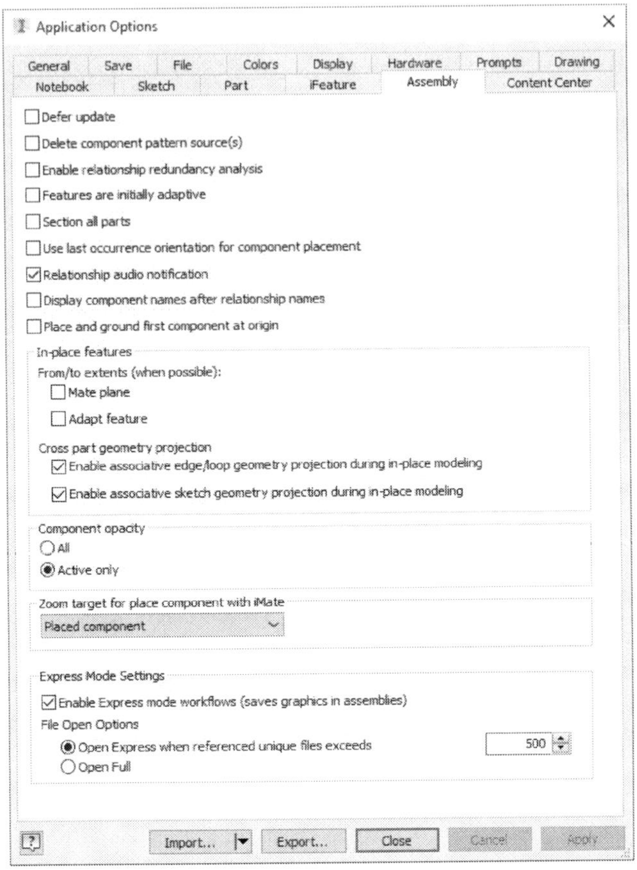

Figure 28–5

28.2 Document Settings

The options that are available in the Document Settings dialog box depend on the file format that is active.

To control the current file settings (e.g., grid or units) you use the Document Settings. Setting made here only apply to the current file. Select the *Tools* tab>Options panel, and click (Document Settings) to open the Document Settings dialog box.

Standard Tab

The *Standard* tab enables you to set the following:

- Material and lighting style in a model.
- Lighting style, material for virtual components, and active standard for annotations in an assembly.
- Active standard for annotations in a drawing.

Units Tab

The Units tab is not available in Drawing. In Assembly, the Units tab is the same as in a Part.

The *Units* tab (shown in Figure 28–6) displays the default unit system, precision values, and display settings for model dimensions and parameters.

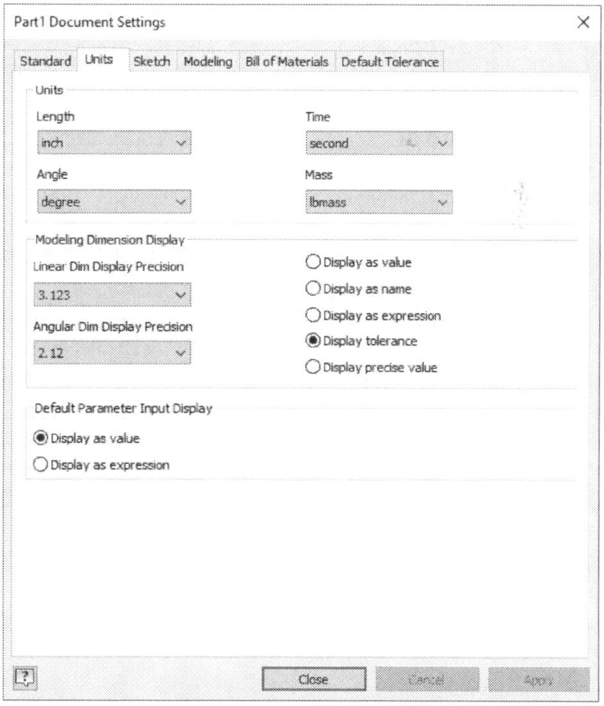

Figure 28–6

Sketch Tab

In Drawing, the Sketch tab only contains Snap Spacing and Grid Display. In Assembly, the Sketch tab has the same options as a Part, except for 3D Sketch options.

To set the sketch grid settings, select the *Sketch* tab, as shown in Figure 28–7. You can also set the radius for corner bends placed on 3D lines as you sketch them, as well as line weight display.

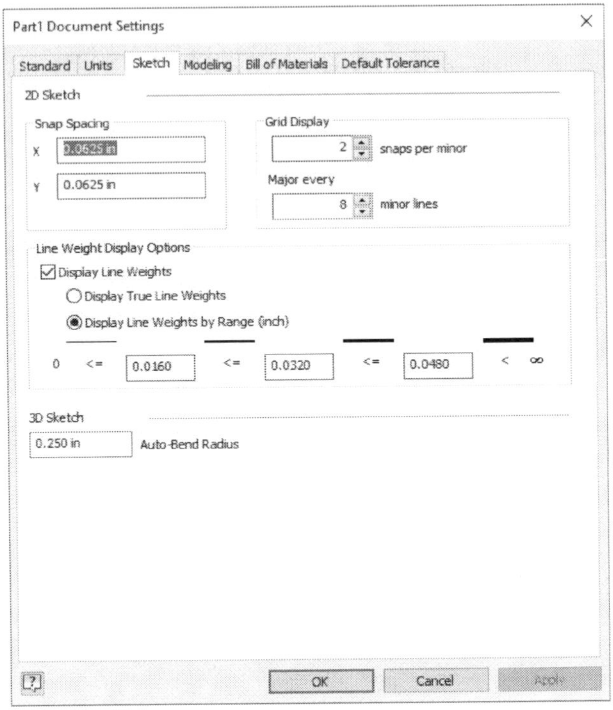

Figure 28–7

Modeling Tab

The Modeling tab is not available in Drawing. In Assembly, the Modeling tab contains some additional options for Interactive Contact.

The *Modeling* tab (shown in Figure 28–8) controls the adaptivity, addition, or removal of the following: file history, 3D snap spacing when you sketch in 3D in an active part, sectioning through a part, and tapped hole diameter. In addition, you can define naming prefixes.

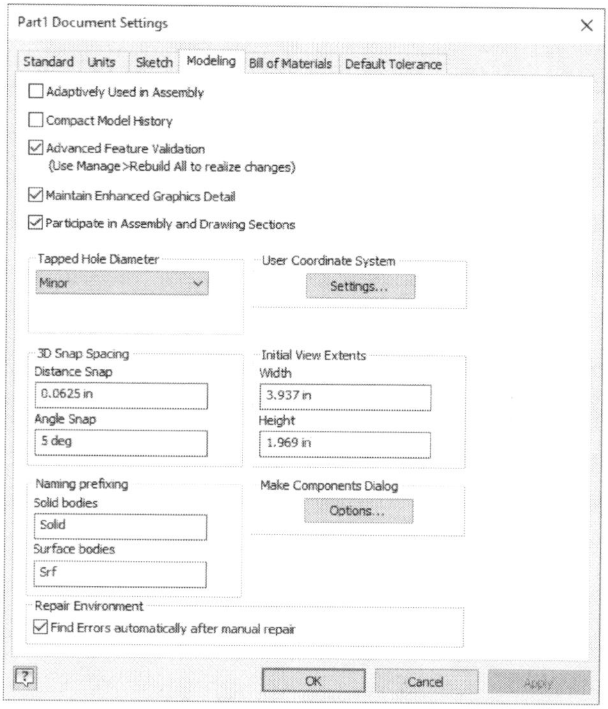

Figure 28–8

Bill of Materials Tab

The Bill of Materials tab is not available in Drawing. In Assembly, the Bill of Materials tab is the same as a Part.

The *Bill of Materials* tab (shown in Figure 28–9) controls the bill of materials settings, such as BOM structure and unit quantity.

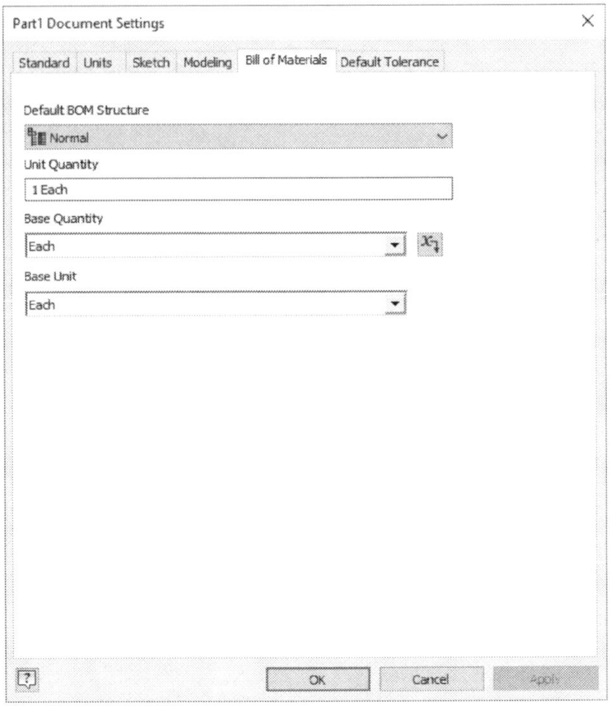

Figure 28–9

Default Tolerance Tab

The *Default Tolerance* tab controls the linear and angular part dimension tolerances and precision levels. The Default Tolerance tab is not available in Drawing or Assembly.

Drawing Tab

The Drawing tab is only available in a drawing.

The *Drawing* tab (shown in Figure 28–10) controls settings such as deferring updates to drawings, dimension updates, cross hatch clipping, automated centerlines, and shaded view settings.

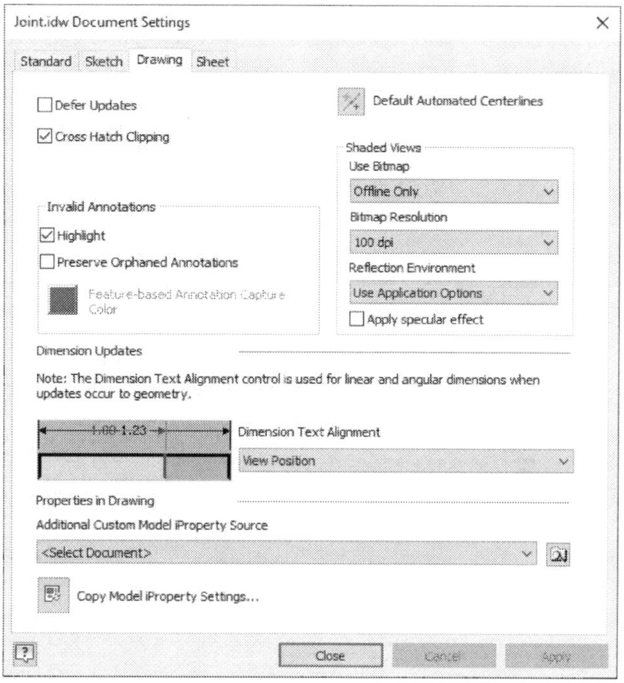

Figure 28–10

Sheet Tab

The *Sheet* tab controls colors in a drawing. The Sheet tab is only available in a Drawing.

28.3 File Properties

*Alternatively, in the **File** menu, select **iProperties** to open the iProperties dialog box.*

You can store non-graphical information in a file using the iProperties dialog box. To open the iProperties dialog box, right-click on the filename at the top of the Model browser and select **iProperties**. The iProperties dialog box for the current file opens, similar to that shown in Figure 28–11. Information from the iProperties dialog box is automatically entered in the drawing title block of your model.

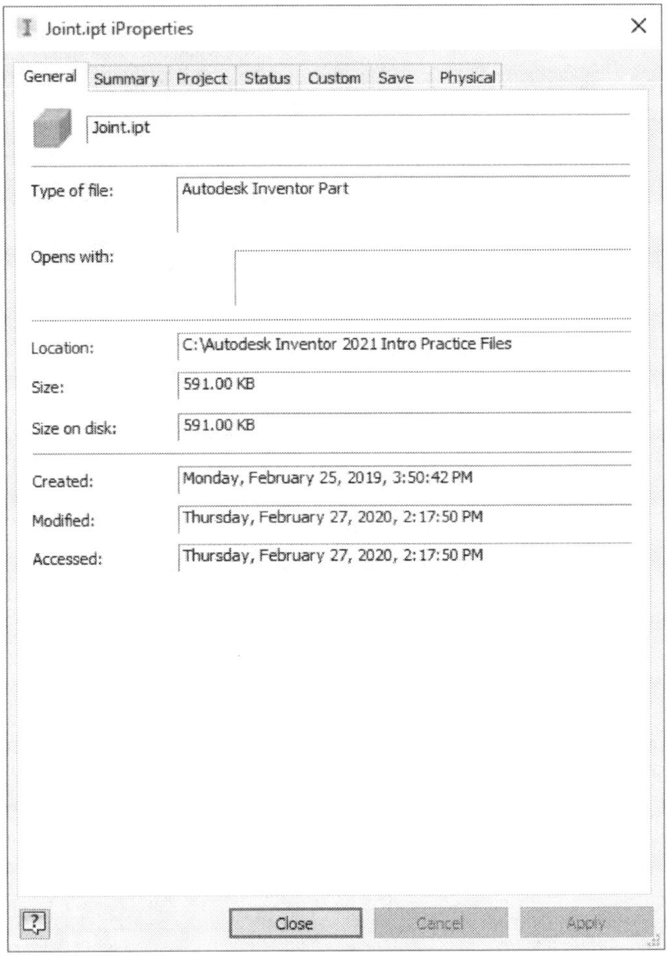

Figure 28–11

The tabs on the Properties dialog box are described as follows:

Tabs	Description
General tab	Displays basic file information, such as file format, location, and size. This information is read-only.
Summary tab	Enables you to enter information in several categories. The information can be used in a title block, or for sorting and searching for files. • In the *Author* field, the username for the user logged onto the computer is automatically entered when the file is created. You can change the name by typing over it. • The **Save Preview Picture** option at the bottom of the dialog box is grayed out and is no longer used.
Project tab	Enables you to enter information for tracking the design. • **Location:** Entered automatically when you assign the filename. It contains the path where the file is located. • **File Subtype:** Entered automatically and describes the type of file, such as **Modeling**, **Assembly**, or **Drawing**. • If you do not enter a *Part Number*, the name of the file is automatically entered in that field. • The *Designer* field populates with the username for the user logged onto the computer when the file is created. You can change the name by typing over it. • The *Creation Date* field populates with the date on which the file was created. You can change the date by selecting the calendar on the right and selecting a new date.
Status tab	Enables you to track the status of the file.
Custom tab	Enables you to define your own properties. The properties display in the lower area of the dialog box. • You can set the type to **Text**, **Date**, **Number**, or **Yes/No**. • Custom properties can be used to search/sort files and create reports.
Save tab	Enables you to create a thumbnail image of the file that displays in the File Open dialog box and to determine which image is used.
Physical tab	Enables you to display the physical properties of the part or assembly. It is not available in presentation or drawing files. In a part file, you can change the material of the part to change the properties.

Some information in the iProperties dialog box can also be accessed from outside of the Autodesk Inventor software. Right-click on the name of the file in Windows Explorer and select **iProperties** to open the Properties dialog box for that file.

28.4 Changing Part Units

To change the part units of a model, you need to convert the existing units to the new system of units. Select the *Tools* tab> Options panel, click (Document Settings), and select the *Units* tab. The Document Settings dialog box displays as shown in Figure 28–12.

Figure 28–12

Select new units in the *Units* area and select the required **Modeling Dimension Display** options. Click **Apply** to apply the new units and click **OK** to close the dialog box.

*The **Display As** options determine how you want to display dimensions and parameters in your model.*

Note that this controls the display units. The system remembers the original value of a dimension. If you switch from inch to millimeter, all dimensions display in millimeters. If you edit a dimension that was input in inches, the original value displays in the Edit dimension dialog box.

28.5 Command Customization

How you access commands can be customized to help you work more efficiently.

Ribbon

A User Commands panel can be added to any of the tabs on the ribbon. This enables you to add specific commands to the ribbon for easy access. To create a User Commands panel, use the Customize dialog box. This is accessed on the *Tools* tab>Options panel by clicking (Customize). You can customize the panels on the *Ribbon* tab (shown in Figure 28–13).

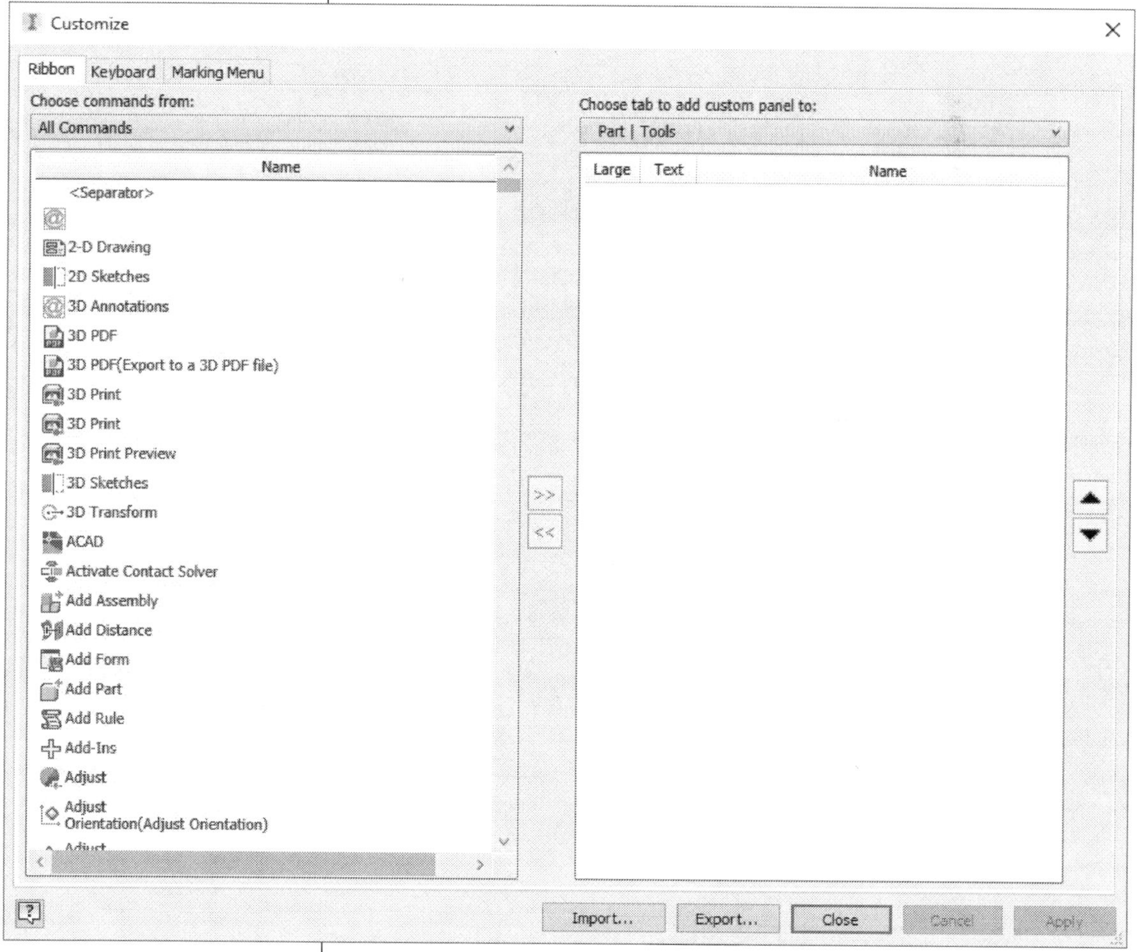

Figure 28–13

To add a User Commands panel, in the *Choose tab to add custom panel to*: drop-down list, select the tab to which you want to add the panel. In the left column, select the command to be added and click [>>] to add the command. The command that was added to the *Zero Document | Get Started* tab is shown at the top in Figure 28–14. The resulting panel on the *Get Started* tab is shown at the bottom in Figure 28–14. Multiple commands can be added to each User Commands panel.

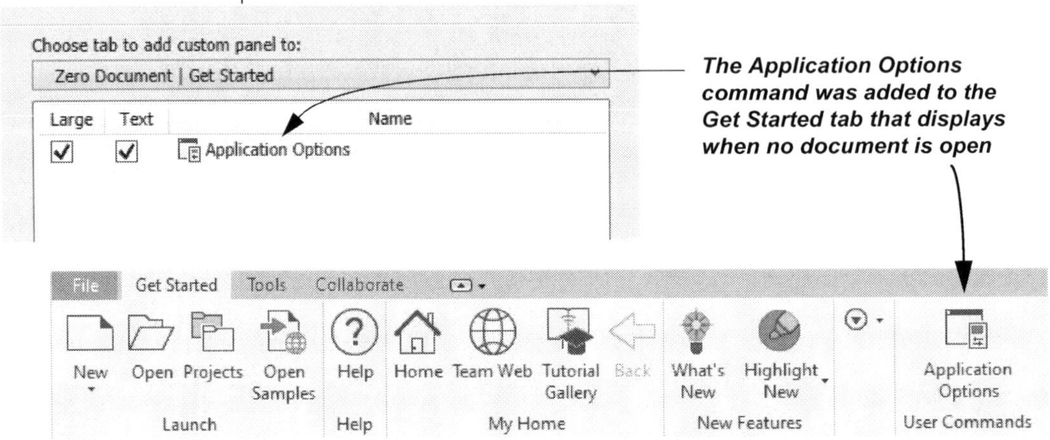

Figure 28–14

Keyboard

You can expand the functionality of keyboard shortcuts by assigning command aliases in the Customize dialog box. This is accessed on the *Tools* tab>Options panel, by clicking (Customize) and selecting the *Keyboard* tab. The Customize dialog box is shown in Figure 28–15.

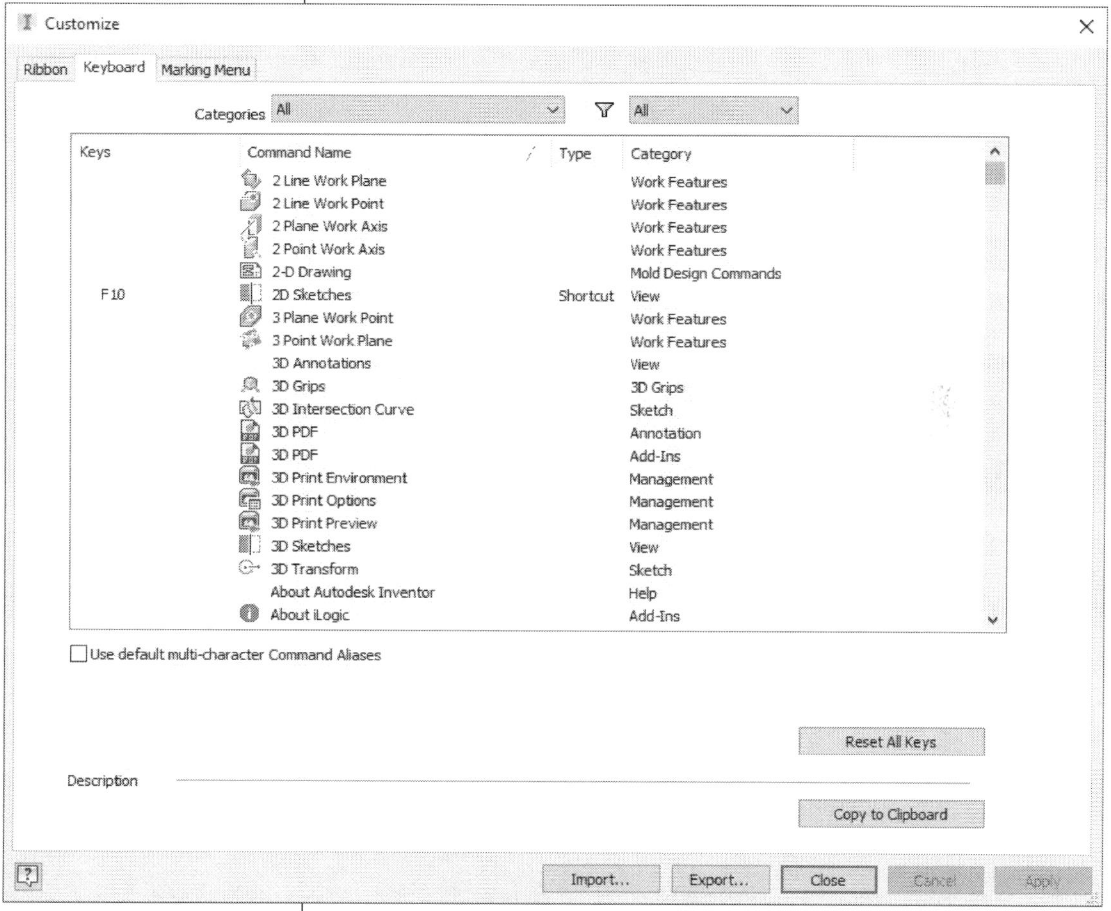

Figure 28–15

There are many predefined aliases and keyboard shortcuts that can be loaded using ***Import****. You can also create your own and save them using* ***Export****.*

Command aliases are alphanumeric key sequences, where shortcuts are keys or key combinations. Both quickly start commands versus selecting options. The following keyboard sequences can be used:

- A single or sequence of keys with letters (A-Z) and numbers (0-9).
- A punctuation key (e.g., ` - = [ ] \ ; ' , . /).
- A miscellaneous keyboard key (i.e., Home, End, or Page Up).

- A combination of <Shift> and numeric (0-9), punctuation, or the miscellaneous keyboard keys mentioned above.
- Any combination of <Shift>, <Ctrl>, and <Alt> with alphanumeric characters. It is not recommended that you use <Alt> without a modifier.

Once assigned, you might have multiple commands starting with the same alpha character. In that case, a list of options displays in the Status Bar and you can use the up and down keyboard arrows to scroll through them.

Prompting Interaction

Command prompts can be controlled using the *Prompting interaction* area in the *General* tab, in the Application Options (*Tools* tab>Options panel, click  (Application Options)). The Prompting interaction options include:

- When **Show command prompting near the mouse cursor** is on, command prompts display as tooltips at the cursor.
- When **Show command alias input dialog** is on, the Command Alias Input dialog box opens next to the cursor when you start typing the first character of a command, as shown in Figure 28–16.

Figure 28–16

*The **Show autocomplete for alias command input** option has no effect if **Show command alias input dialog** is not enabled.*

- When **Show autocomplete for alias command alias input** is on, the Autocomplete List dialog box opens for ambiguous or incomplete commands. For example, if you have **Center** as the alias for **Point**, **Center Point** and **CIRCLE** as the alias for **Center Point Circle**, autocomplete displays a drop-down list for both commands when you enter **C**, as shown in Figure 28–17.

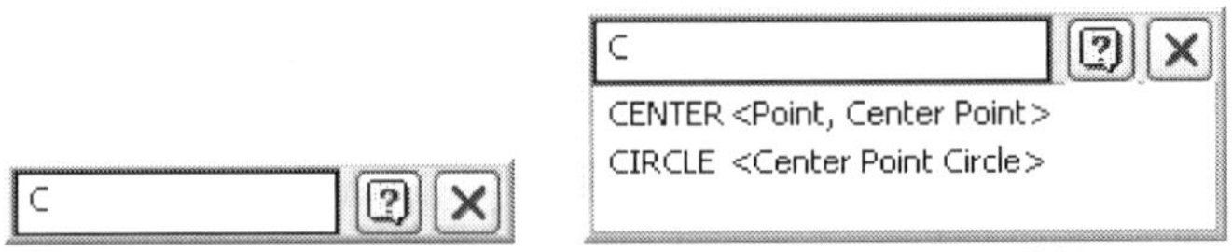

Autocomplete OFF ***Autocomplete ON***

Figure 28–17

Marking Menu

The marking menu can be customized for each environment (e.g., Part, Assembly, Drawing). To customize the marking menu, you use the Customize dialog box (*Tools* tab>Options panel, click (Customize), and select the *Marking Menu* tab), as shown in Figure 28–18.

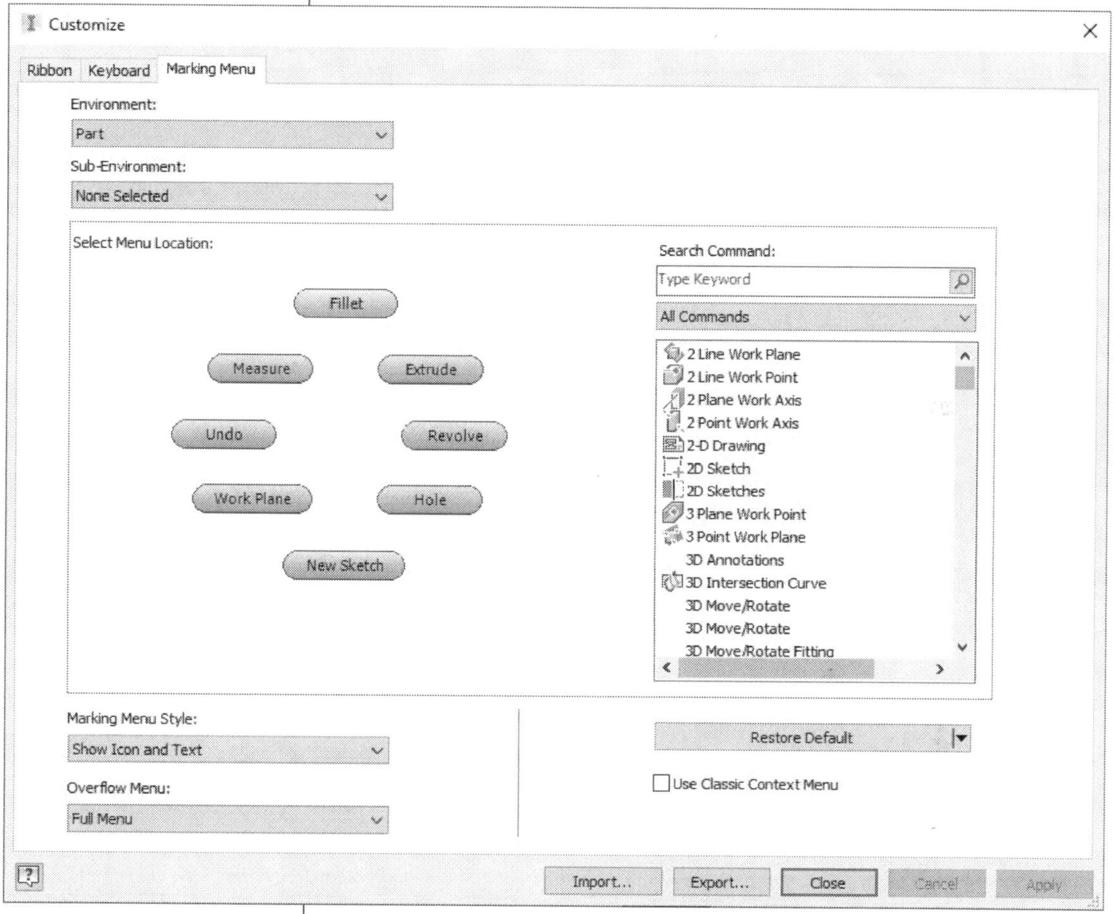

Figure 28–18

How To: Customize the Marking Menu

1. Select the required environment and sub-environment from their respective drop-down lists. If no sub-environment is required, select **None Selected** in the Sub-Environment drop-down list or you can select **Add Ctrl + Right Click Menu** to add a custom shortcut menu.
2. In the *Select Menu Location* area, use the previewed marking menu to select any of its slots. For example, to replace the Fillet slot with an alternate command, select it.

*To restore all of the marking menu commands to their defaults, select **Restore Default**.*

*Select **Use Classic Context Menu** to disable the marking menu.*

3. In the right pane, select the command to add in the selected marking menu slot.
4. Continue to select slots and commands, as required, to customize the menu.
5. In the Marking Menu Style drop-down list, select an option to determine how the command will be displayed in the marking menu. The options enable you to show the icon of the command along with a text descriptor, show an icon only, or show text only.
6. In the Overflow Menu drop-down list, select an option to determine whether a detailed list of overflow commands (**Full Menu**) or if a shortened list (**Short Menu**) displays. You also have the option to toggle off the overflow menu (**Radial Menu Only**).
7. Click **Apply** to apply the changes and **OK** to close the Customize dialog box.

Practice 28a

Customizing File Properties

Practice Objectives

- Set an application option so that dimensions are brought into a drawing when views are placed.
- Set drawing properties using the iProperties dialog box to ensure that the drawing titleblock updates as required.
- Change the drawing's title block and border.

In this practice, you will customize the properties of a file. You will also change the title block and drawing border used on a drawing sheet.

Task 1 - Open a part file and set the drawing options.

1. Open **2sides.ipt**.
2. Select the *Tools* tab>Options panel and click  (Application Options). The Application Options dialog box opens.
3. Select the *Drawing* tab and ensure that **Retrieve all model dimensions on view placements** is selected.
4. Click **Apply** and click **Close** to close the dialog box.

Task 2 - Create a new drawing file.

1. Create a new drawing file using the **2sides.ipt** model. Use the **ANSI (mm).dwg** template and create the drawing views shown in Figure 28–19. Note that the dimensions for the base view are automatically displayed when the view is placed. You might need to move them so that they display as shown in Figure 28–19.

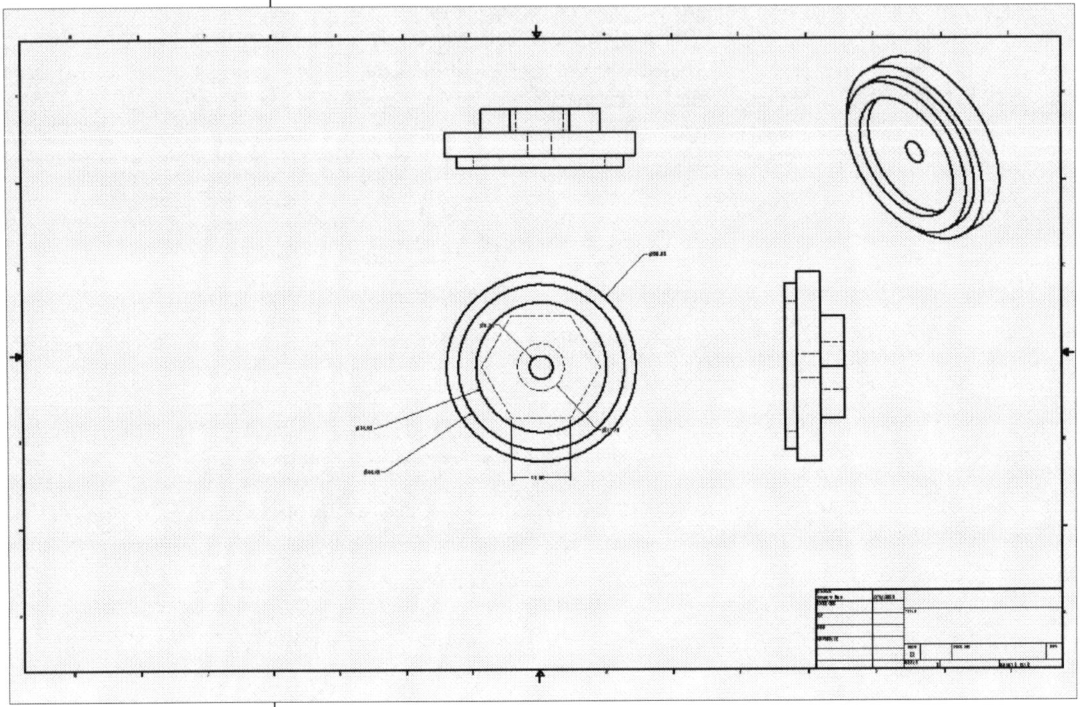

Figure 28–19

Task 3 - Set the drawing properties.

*Alternatively, you can expand the **File** menu and select **iProperties** to open the Properties dialog box.*

1. Zoom to examine the information in the drawing title block.
2. Right-click on **2sides** at the top of the Model browser and select **iProperties**. The iProperties dialog box opens.
3. Select the *Summary* tab and set the following information in the respective fields.
   - *Title*: **Disk Drawing**
   - *Author*: **Your Name**
   - *Manager*: **Your Manager**
   - *Company*: **Your Company**

4. Select the *Project* tab and set the following information:
   - *Part Number*: **365-584**
   - *Revision Number*: **1**
   - *Designer*: **Your Name**
   - *Engineer*: **Your Engineer**

5. The *Creation Date* field must display today's date. If not, click to open a calender. Select today's date as the creation date.

6. Click **Apply** to update the iProperties.

7. Select the *Status* tab and set the following information.
   - *Design State:* **Released**
   - *Checked By:* **Engineer**
   - *Eng. Approved By:* **Chief Engineer**
   - *Mfg. Approved By:* **Manager**
   - Select the boxes next to the dates and verify that the date is correct.

8. Select the *Custom* tab. Set the *Name* to **Date Completed**, set the *Type* to **Date**, and place a check in the box next to today's date in the *Value* field.

9. Click **Add** to add that property to the list. The information is listed in the lower half of the dialog box, similar to that shown in Figure 28–20.

Name	Value	Type
Date Co...	2/21/2017	Date

Figure 28–20

10. Click **Apply** to apply the changes and click **Close** to close the dialog box. The drawing title block displays as shown in Figure 28–21.

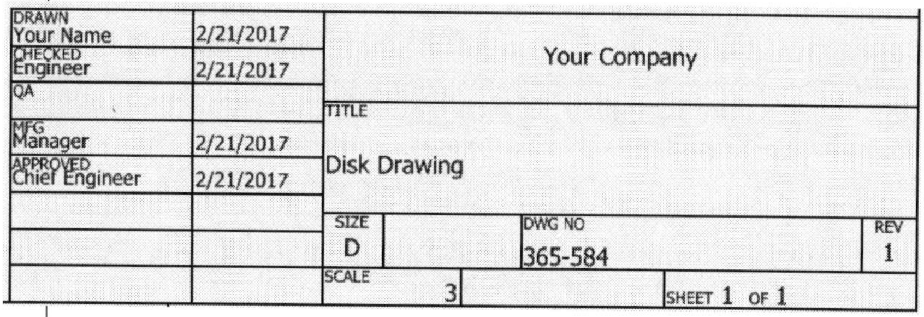

Figure 28–21

Task 4 - Change the title block and drawing border.

Replace the existing title block and border in the drawing.

1. Click  (Zoom All) in the Navigation Bar to refit the drawing to the full screen.
2. In the Model browser, expand **Sheet:1**, if required. Right-click on **ANSI-Large** and select **Delete**. The title block disappears.
3. In the Model browser, expand **Drawing Resources** and expand **Title Blocks**. Right-click on **ANSI A** and select **Insert**. A smaller title block containing the same Properties information is inserted in the lower right corner.
4. Zoom to examine the border. Note that each edge is divided into areas and that each area is labeled with numbers across the top and bottom, and letters on both sides.
5. Right-click on **Default Border** under **Sheet:1** in the Model browser and select **Delete**. The border disappears.
6. Expand **Drawing Resources** and expand **Borders** in the Model browser. Right-click on **Default Border** and select **Insert Drawing Border**. The Default Drawing Border Parameters dialog box opens, as shown in Figure 28–22.

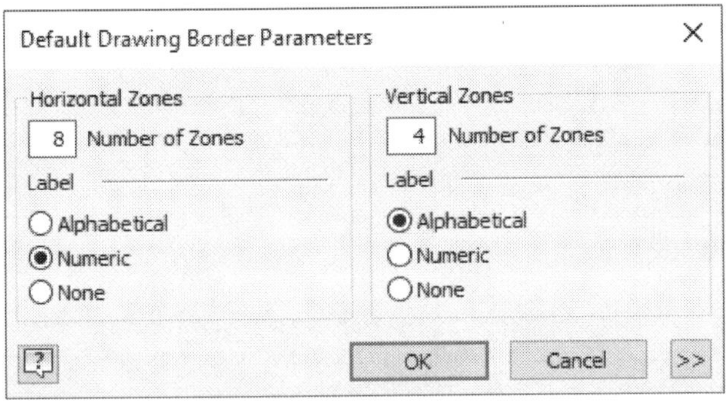

Figure 28–22

7. Set *Horizontal Zones* to **6** and label them alphabetically.
8. Set *Vertical Zones* to **4** and label them numerically.
9. Click **OK** to place the border. Note that the new border is now divided as you specified.
10. Save the drawing file and enter **DWGProperties** as the name.
11. Close all of the windows.

Chapter Review Questions

1. Which of the following statements is true about the Application Options or Document Settings dialog boxes?
   a. The options set in the Document Settings dialog box only apply to the current file.
   b. The color scheme for the software is applied only to the current file using the Document Settings dialog box.
   c. The Document Settings dialog box is only accessible when working in a drawing file.
   d. Any Application Option settings are maintained for the entire session that the Autodesk Inventor software is open. The option must be reset in any future sessions, even if using the same model file.
2. Which of the following describe how to access the iProperties dialog box? (Select all that apply.)
   a. **File** menu**>iProperties**
   b. Right-click on the filename in the Model browser and select **iProperties**.
   c. Right-click on the feature name in the Model browser and select **Properties**.
   d. Using the Select Bodies selection priority, right-click on the model in the graphics window and select **Properties**.

3. Which tabs in the iProperties dialog box (shown in Figure 28–23) are used to add non-geometrical information to the model? (Select all that apply.)

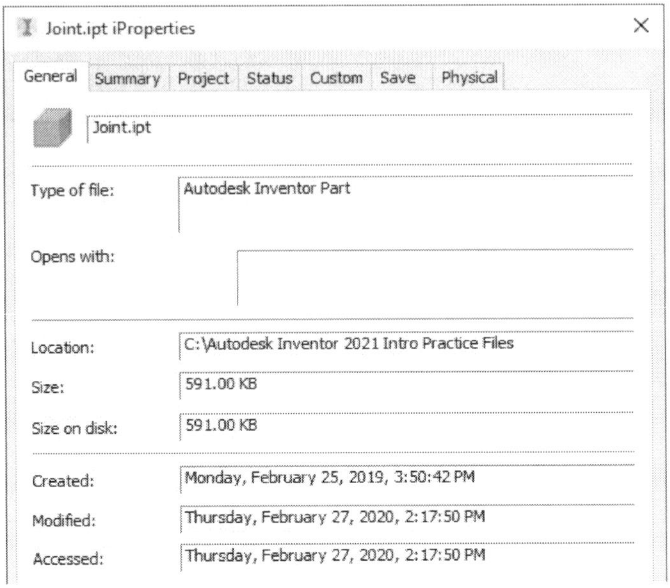

Figure 28–23

a. *Summary*
b. *Project*
c. *Status*
d. *Custom*
e. *Save*
f. *Physical*

4. Which of the following best describes how to change the part units?
   a. *Tools* tab>Options panel, select **Document Settings** and use the options in the *Units* tab.
   b. *Tools* tab>Options panel, select **Application Options** and use the options in the *Display* tab.
   c. *Tools* tab>Measure panel, select **Distance** and set the units in the Measure dialog box.
   d. Model units cannot be changed once the template has been selected. You must recreate the geometry.

5. Which Interface components can be customized to control the commands that are displayed? (Select all that apply.)
    a. Ribbon tabs
    b. Ribbon panels
    c. Marking menu

Command Summary

Button	Command	Location
	**Application Options**	• **Ribbon:** *Tools* tab>Options panel • **File** menu>Options
	**Customize**	• **Ribbon:** *Tools* tab>Options panel
	**Document Settings**	• **Ribbon:** *Tools* tab>Options panel
N/A	**iProperties**	• **File** menu • **Context Menu**: In Model browser with model name selected • **Windows Explorer**: right-click on the model name and select **iProperties**

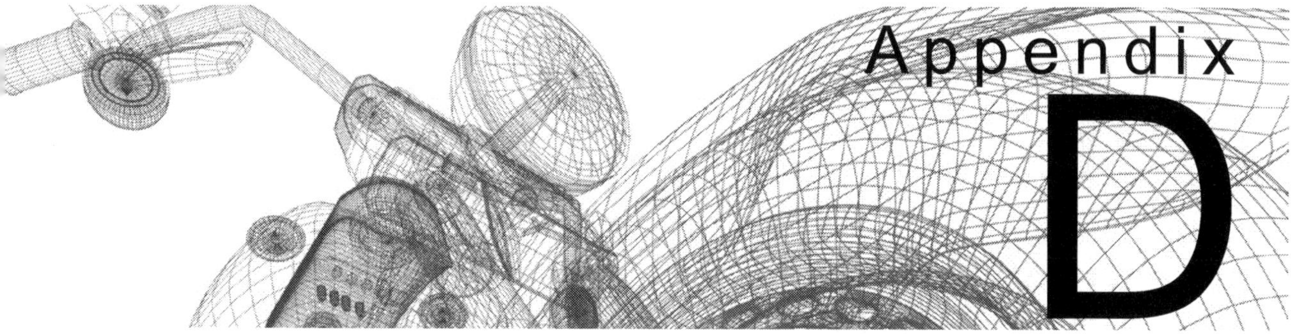

Appendix D

Effective Modeling Final Review

Before creating any model (part or assembly), you should consider its design intent. Planning ahead helps you select the most appropriate options to maximize design flexibility.

Learning Objectives in This Appendix

- Understand the key modeling questions that should be considered before creating a new model.
- Understand the techniques that help you build parametric, feature-based solid models so that their behavior is flexible and predictable.
- Investigate model hierarchy, equations, and size to better understand how a model was designed.

D.1 Design Considerations

A designer strives to create models with the following criteria:

- Communicates design intent.
- Can be manufactured to meet design goals.
- Is flexible to future design changes with minimal effort.
- Can be used to generate design documentation (drawings).

Considering *what if* scenarios that might be introduced into the model in the future helps to create a robust model that requires minimal effort when the time comes for modifications.

Part Design Considerations

Consider the following questions:

- What is the best selection for the base feature?
- Which feature relationships are required and which should be avoided?
- Which dimensions are required to drive the design?
- Which dimensions on the part might change?
- How should the part react to dimension changes?
- Which dimensions are required in the drawing?
- Should equations be added to capture design intent?
- What feature order best captures the design intent?

Assembly Design Considerations

Consider the following questions:

- What is the best selection for the base component?
- Which assembly constraints capture the design intent?
- Which feature relationships are required and which should be avoided?
- Should subassembly components be incorporated?
- Should assembly equations be added?
- What component order best captures the design intent?

D.2 Modeling Tips and Techniques

The key to building robust, parametric, feature-based solid models is to construct them so that their behavior is flexible and predictable. The result of constructing them this way is known as the *design intent*.

Capturing Design Intent

Design intent can be captured in a variety of ways. When creating models, pay special attention to the features used, how they are created (pick and place or sketched), and the dimensioning scheme. The feature relationships established during feature creation and the explicit relations set after feature creation are also important for incorporating design intent.

Many companies have their own design requirements or *best practice* recommendations. The following sub-sections discuss some common recommendations:

Features

Features add or remove material from the model. Consider the following when adding features to a model:

- Select a stable base feature that does not require many changes. It is used as a parent for additional features.
- Use feature forms (extrude, sweep, etc.), feature types (pick and place or sketched), feature attributes, and equations to capture design intent.
- Select references that correctly reflect the design intent. Any reference that is selected while creating a new feature, establishes a dependency between the new feature and the reference. This is true when defining the sketching plane, sketching references, and dimensioning references.
- Use the sketching tools that best capture the design intent.
- Use depth options (**Distance**, **To Next**, **To**, **Between**, **All**, or **Distance from Face**) to capture the design intent.
- Create features in the order that best captures the design intent.
- Change feature names to easily identify them in the Model browser.

Dimensioning Scheme

This method of capturing design intent is used to determine the feature's dimensioning scheme. A part with a hole is shown in Figure D–1. When the base feature increases in length, the design intent of the hole determines how it behaves. If the hole is dimensioned to the end of the base feature, the hole moves when the length of the base feature increases, but remains 3.00 from the end. If the hole is dimensioned to the face, it remains 6.00 from that face.

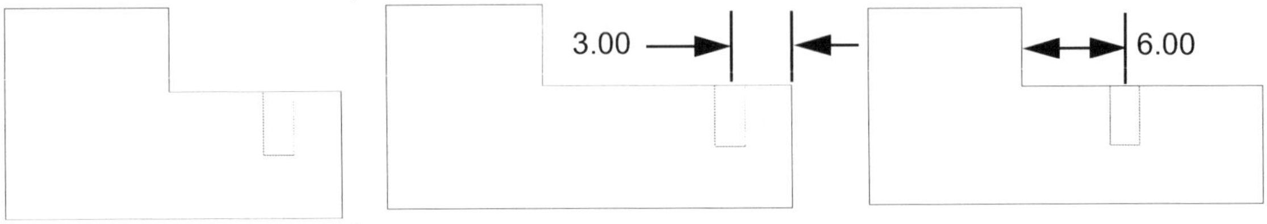

Figure D–1

Depth Options

This method of capturing design intent is to determine the type of depth required for your feature. A part with a hole is shown in Figure D–2. The design intent is for the hole to pass through the entire model. When the depth of the base feature changes from 5.00 to 6.00, the resulting geometry displays differently, depending on the depth option set for the hole. If the hole is given a blind depth value of 5.00, it no longer passes though the entire part. Therefore, the hole depth must also be changed to maintain the design intent. A better solution is to set the depth option for the hole to **Through All**. As a result, the hole always passes through the part, regardless of the height of the base feature.

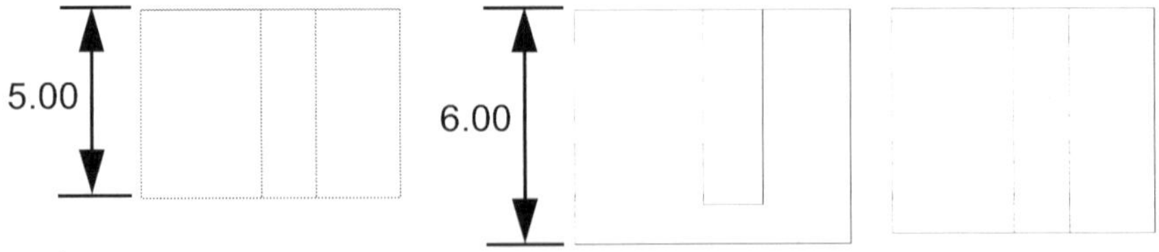

Figure D–2

Symmetrical Geometry

This method of capturing design intent is to create symmetrical geometry. The design intent for the part shown in Figure D–3 is to have the extruded cut remain at the center of the part. Constraining the cut from either end of the base feature does not capture the design intent. Constructing the base feature and cut relative to the center of the part is preferable, or you can use relations.

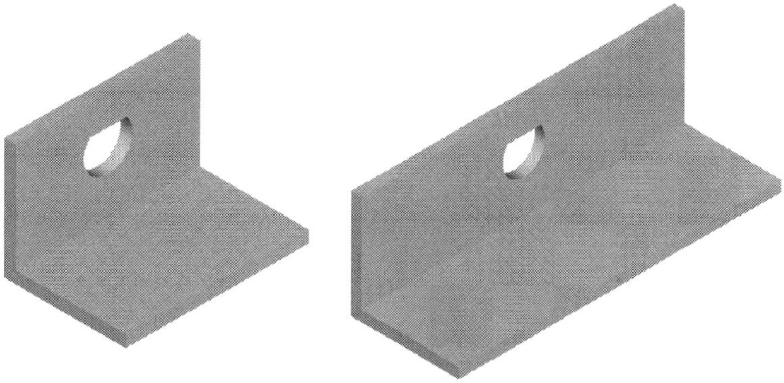

Figure D–3

Face Drafts and Fillets

Review company standards when considering whether to add face drafts. Some companies prefer not to add face drafts, while other companies insist on it. Some considerations include the following:

- Does adding face drafts increase model accuracy or is it going to adversely affect drawing creation?
- If face drafts are not added to the model, how are you going to communicate this requirement to the manufacturer?
- Does the model need to undergo interference or analysis testing? If so, consider adding the face draft to ensure accurate results.

Fillets generally represent the finishing stages of the design. Similar to face drafts, always consider company standards when deciding whether to add fillets. Some considerations include the following:

- Is the model going to be used for FEA analysis? If so, fillets are sometimes removed before the analysis and are therefore not required.

- The manufacturing department might remove fillets that are created at the end of the process (depending on the type of fillets that make up the model). In this situation, you might want to add all of the fillets and only suppress the ones that you do not need for generating the NC toolpaths.
- Variable and G2 fillets are difficult to manufacture. Consider the necessity of this feature as you are creating your model.

Always consider the order in which features are manufactured. The order of fillet and face draft creation can affect the resulting geometry and should be added as late as possible in the feature order. For example, face draft geometry should be added to the model before fillets. Also consider the order in which fillets are added to the model and how the order affects the geometry and each other.

You can suppress the display of the face drafts and fillets. They remain suppressed until you un-suppress them. In the Model browser, suppressed features are grayed out.

D.3 Model Investigation

It is not practical to assume that you are always going to create new models. In many cases, you are required to continue someone else's design or make modifications to a previously completed model. In these cases, always investigate the model to understand the existing design and feature relationships.

Model Browser

The Model browser displays all of the features in the model. By reviewing the Model browser, you can understand the hierarchy of the model and understand which feature can reference others.

To select features directly in the Graphics Window, ensure that ***Select Features*** *is the active option in the selection filter list.*

To provide a better overview of the relationships between features, you can right-click on a feature name in the Model browser and select **Relationships**. The Relationships dialog box displays, similar to that shown in Figure D–4. This dialog box can quickly reveal the relationships between features and enable you to make changes, if required.

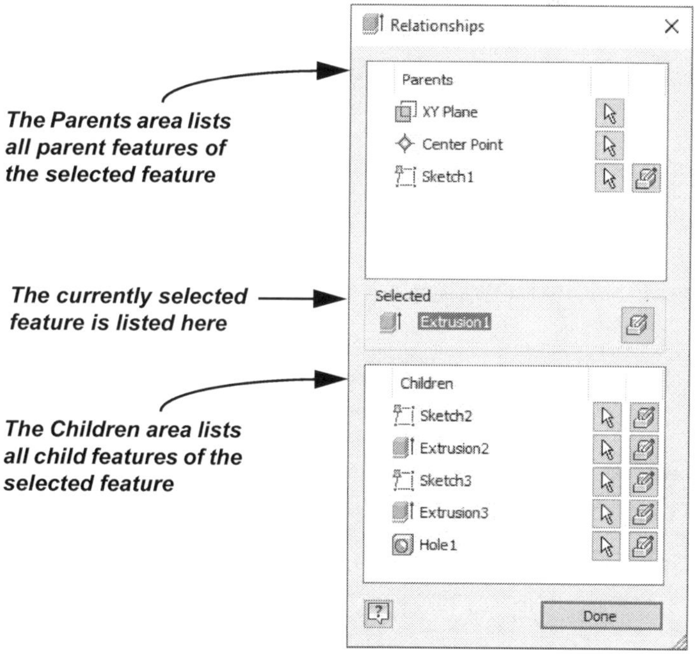

Figure D–4

- **(Make Selected):** Enables you to set any of the parent or child features as the new selected item.
- **(Edit Feature):** Enables you to access the Edit Feature dialog box for any of the parent or child features.

Equations

Equations are used in models to control the design intent. In doing so, they establish feature relationships. To investigate existing equations in a model, select the *Manage* tab> Parameters panel and click (Parameters) or click in the Quick Access Toolbar. Any existing equations display in the *Equation* column in the Parameters dialog box.

> **Hint: Displaying Equations in a Model**
>
> To display equations when dimensions are shown, right-click and select **Dimension Display**>**Expression**. To display sketch dimensions as an expression, click in the Status Bar and select **Expression**.

Measuring Options

The measurement tools enable you to measure distances, angles, loops, and areas without creating dimensions. To use the measurement tools, select the *Inspect* tab. The measurement tools display as shown in Figure D–5 for part and assembly files. The measurement tools are also available on the *Tools* tab.

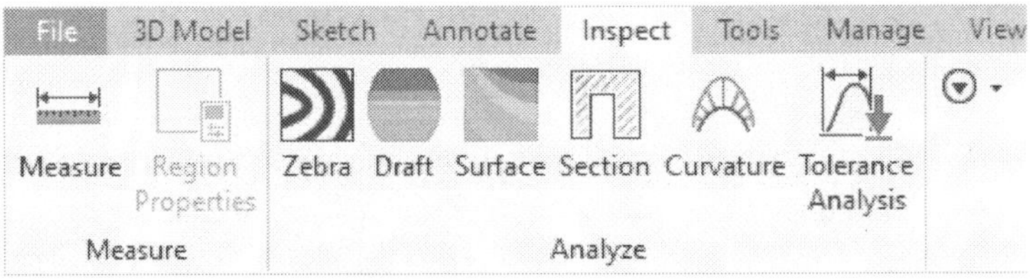

Inspect tab for a Part file

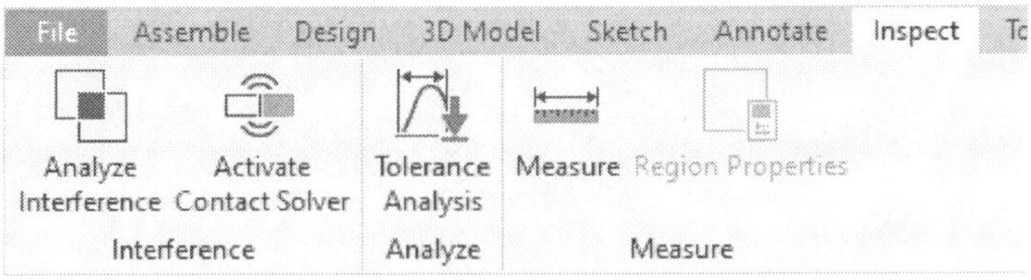

Inspect tab for an Assembly file

Figure D–5

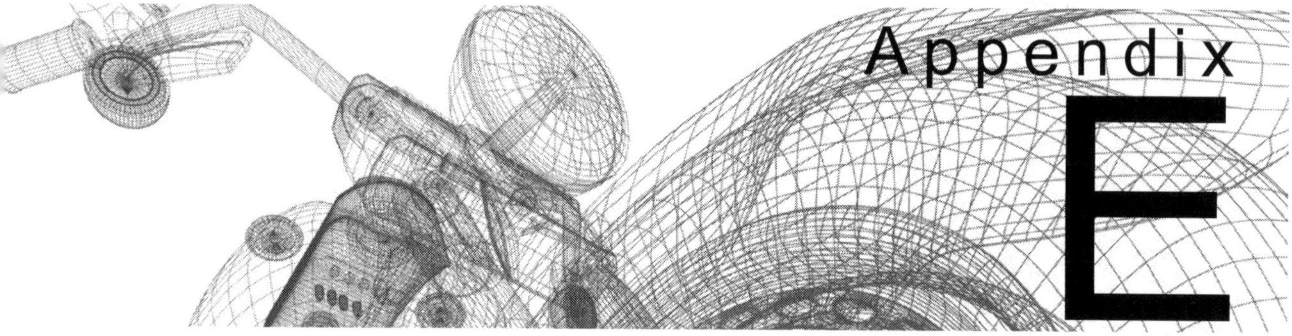

Appendix E

Additional Practices II

This appendix provides additional practices that can be used to review some of the functionality that was previously covered.

Practice E1

Assembling with Joints

Practice Objectives

- Use the **Joint** command to fully connect components in an assembly.
- Apply limits to a joint to define a specified range of motion.
- Drag components to verify the movement in the assembly.
- Copy and paste components to efficiently duplicate components in an assembly.

In this practice, you will create a new assembly and assemble the components as shown in Figure E–1. To assemble the components you will use the **Joint** command, which will connect components relative to one another so that the assembly can easily be tested for movement.

Figure E–1

Task 1 - Create a new assembly and assemble the first component.

1. Create a new assembly file using the **Standard(in).iam** template file.

2. In the Component panel, click  (Place).

3. Navigate to the *Engine* folder in the practice files folder. Select **RBlock.ipt** in the Place Component dialog box and click **Open**. The component is added to the assembly.

4. If the component displays in a 2D orientation, return the model to its default Home View using the ViewCube.

5. Right-click on the model and select **Rotate X 90**. Right-click and select **Rotate X 90** again to rotate the component a total of 180 degrees about the X-axis.

6. Right-click on the model and select **Place Grounded at Origin** to ground the component. The model displays as shown in Figure E–2.

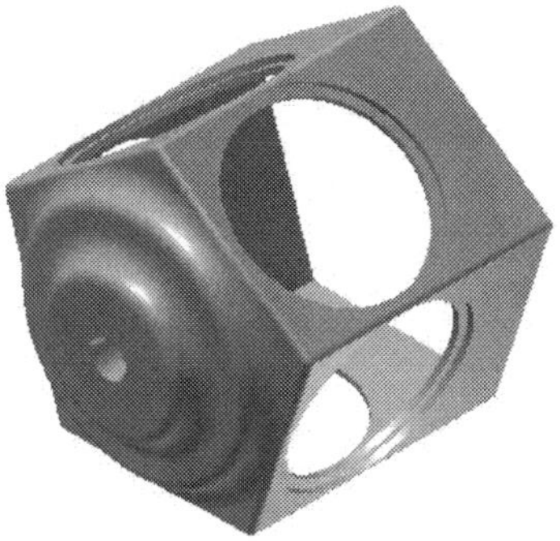

Figure E–2

7. Right-click and select **OK** to assemble a single instance of the component into the assembly.

8. Review the Model browser and note the pushpin ( ) symbol next to the **RBlock**, as shown in Figure E–3. Hover the cursor over the **RBlock.ipt** component in the graphics window. The cursor symbol indicates that it is grounded.

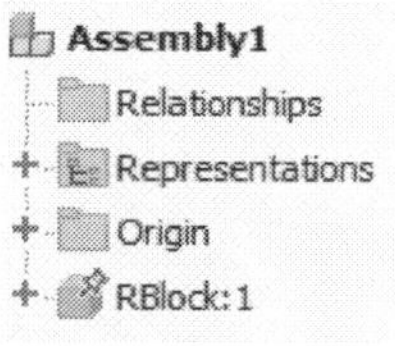

Figure E–3

Task 2 - Assemble the RCylinder component.

1. In the Component panel, click (Place).

2. Select **Rcylinder.ipt** in the Place Component dialog box and click **Open**. The component is added to the assembly.

3. Right-click on the model and select **Rotate X 90**. Right-click and select **Rotate X 90** again to rotate the component into a more convenient orientation for constraining.

4. Use the left mouse button to place the component next to the **RBlock** component, as shown in Figure E–4. Right-click and select **OK** to assemble a single instance

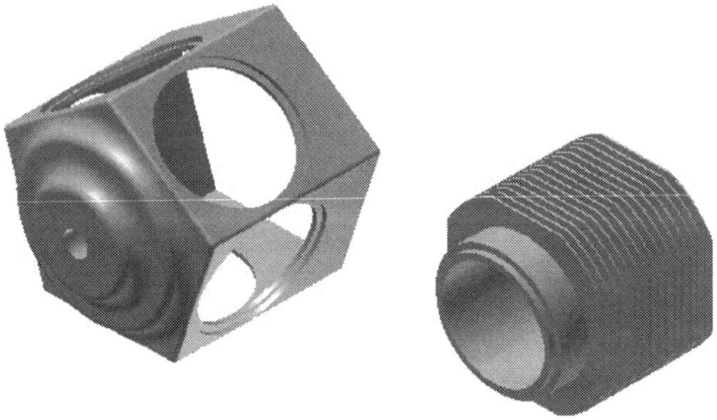

Figure E–4

5. In the *Assemble* tab>Relationships panel, click (Joint). The Place Joint dialog box and mini-toolbar open.

Once the Place Joint dialog box is toggled off, it must be enabled again to open it.

6. In the mini-toolbar, click to toggle off the display of the Place Joint dialog box. You will use the mini-toolbar to constrain components. All of the commands are also available in the Place Joint dialog box.

7. In the Type drop-down list in the mini-toolbar, select **Rigid**. Note that the *Connect* fields remain active and the *Align* fields are not selectable. This indicates that to use the Rigid joint only two references are required to remove all of the degrees of freedom from the component.

8. On the **Rcylinder** component (first reference), hover the cursor over the edge shown in Figure E–5. It will display in red with a green dot at the center of the edge. Use the left mouse button to select the reference.

9. On the **RBlock** component (second reference), hover over the edge shown in Figure E–5. It will display in red with a green dot at the center of the edge. Use the left mouse button to select the reference.

*Figure E–5 shows the reference on **Rcylinder** already selected and the reference on **RBlock** highlighted. The images displaying the reference selection in this practice will be shown in this way for the remainder of the practice.*

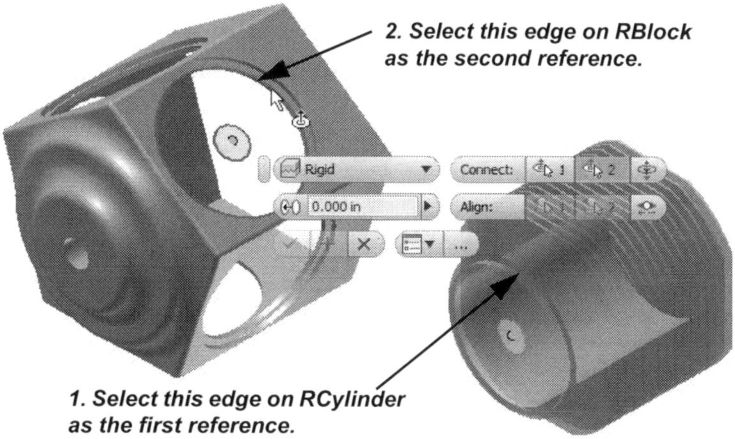

Figure E–5

The **Rcylinder** component (reference 1) moves into position and displays animated movement indicating its allowable degrees of freedom. In this case it is a rigid constraint and because no movement is permitted, the animated movement is very small.

Note that you did not have to activate any of the fields in the mini-toolbar. The first reference field is immediately active and the second is activated once the first reference has been selected. Selecting the reference fields in the *Connect* field is only required when redefining a reference.

10. The components assemble in the wrong orientation. In the *Connect* area in the mini-toolbar, click  (Flip Component) to flip the component.

11. Click  in the mini-toolbar to complete the joint. The assembly displays as shown in Figure E–6.

Figure E–6

12. Expand the **Relationships** node and note that the Rigid joint has been added. A **Rigid** node is also listed in the node for the two components.

Task 3 - Assemble the Crankshaft and Master Rod components in the assembly.

1. In the Component panel, click (Place).
2. Press and hold <Ctrl> and select **Crankshaft.ipt** and **Master Rod1.ipt** in the Place Component dialog box. Click **Open**. The components are added to the assembly.
3. Right-click and select **Rotate X 90** twice to rotate the two components into a more convenient orientation.
4. Use the left mouse button to place the components next to the existing components. Right-click and select **OK** to assemble a single instance of both components.
5. Press and hold <Ctrl>, select **RBlock** and **Rcylinder** in the Model browser, right-click and select **Visibility** to clear them from the display. Clearing the components from the display enables you to focus on the required components and prevents you from selecting inappropriate references when constraining.
6. Hold the left mouse button on the **Master Rod1** component and move it as shown in Figure E–7. Move the **Crankshaft** component in a similar way, if required.

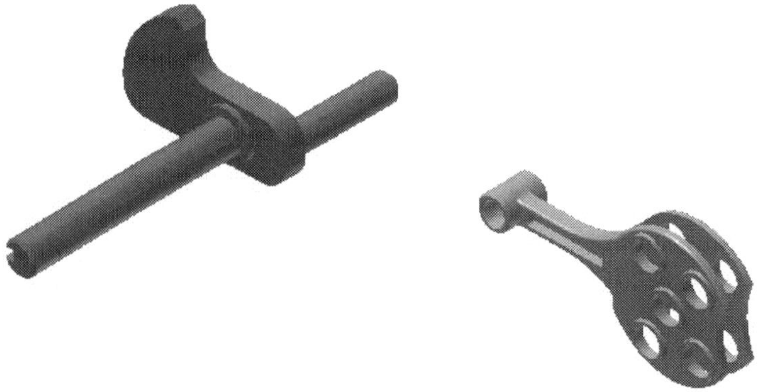

Figure E–7

7. In the *Assemble* tab>Relationships panel, click (Joint).
8. In the Type drop-down list in the mini-toolbar, select **Rotational**.

9. On the **Master Rod1** component (first reference), hover the cursor over the edge shown in Figure E–8. It will display in red with a green dot at the center of the edge. Use the left mouse button to select the reference.

10. On the **Crankshaft** component (second reference), hover the cursor over the center of the cylindrical surface. The surface highlights in red with a green dot at the center of the cylinder. Continue hovering over different locations on the surface until the model displays as shown in Figure E–8. Use the left mouse button to select the reference.

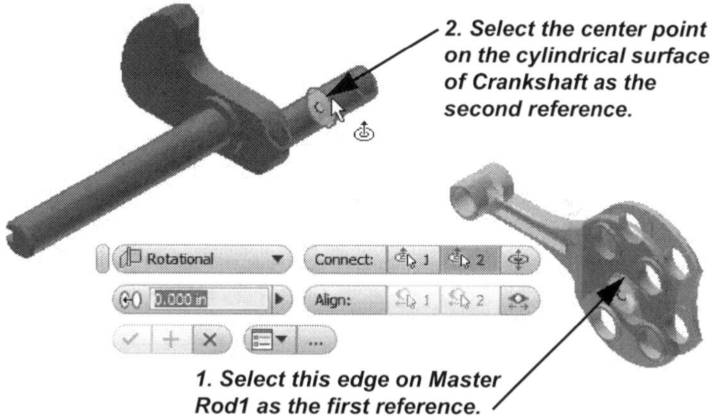

Figure E–8

11. Enter an *Offset* value of **-1.1 in**.

12. Click ✓ in the mini-toolbar to complete the joint. The components display as shown in Figure E–9.

Figure E–9

13. Expand the **Relationships** and **Components** nodes and note that the Rotational joint has been added.

14. Select the **Master Rod1** component and try to drag it to determine its rotational degree of freedom. Both components move together because neither of them are grounded.

15. By temporarily grounding the **Crankshaft** component you can test the joint movement. Select the **Crankshaft** component in the graphics window or in the Model browser, right-click and select **Grounded** to ground the component.

16. Select the **Master Rod1** component and drag it to determine its rotational degree of freedom. Rotate the component as shown in Figure E–10.

Figure E–10

Task 4 - Assemble the Piston Head Pin and Piston Head components in the assembly.

1. Place an instance of the **Piston head pin.ipt** and **Piston head.ipt** components in the assembly.

2. Rotate, move, and place the components in a similar orientation to that shown in Figure E–11.

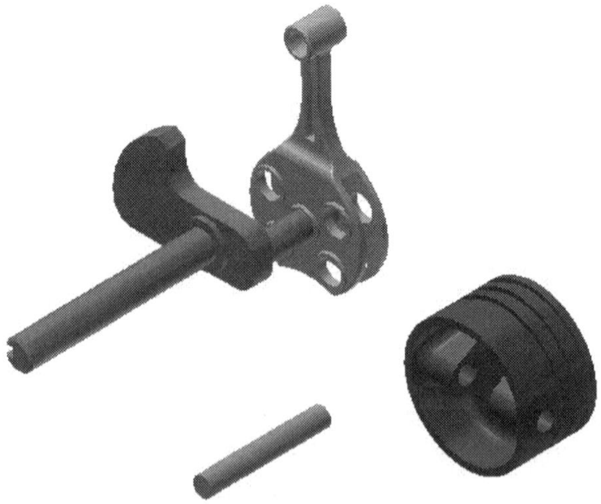

Figure E–11

3. In the *Assemble* tab>Relationships panel, click (Joint).
4. In the Type drop-down list in the mini-toolbar, select **Rigid**.
5. On the **Piston head pin** component (first reference), hover the cursor over the midpoint shown in Figure E–12. It will display in red with a green dot at the center of the edge. Use the left mouse button to select the reference.
6. On the **Piston head** component (second reference), hover the cursor over the edge shown in Figure E–12. Note that this point is not being recognized. Right-click in the graphics window and select **Between Two Faces**. Select the two planar faces in the middle of the component to enable the midpoint to be used as a placement reference. It will display in red with a green dot at the center of the edge. Use the left mouse button to select the reference.

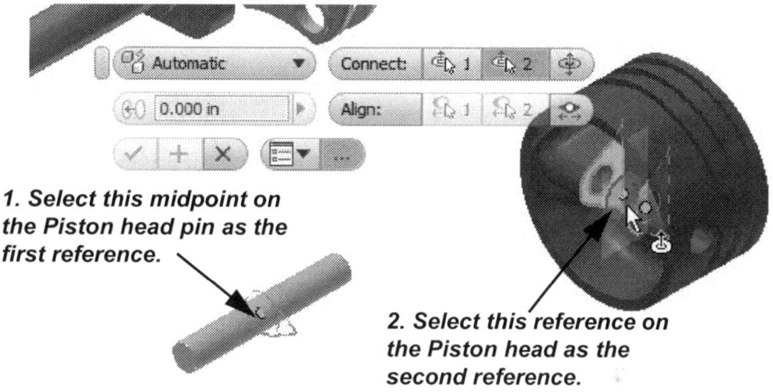

Figure E–12

7. Click in the mini-toolbar to complete the joint. The components display as shown in Figure E–13.

Figure E–13

8. In the *Assemble* tab>Relationships panel, click  (Joint).

9. In the Type drop-down list in the mini-toolbar, select **Rotational**.

10. On the **Piston head pin** component (first reference), hover the cursor over its cylindrical surface. When the green dot displays at the center of the surface at its midpoint (as shown in Figure E–14), click the left mouse button.

11. On the **Master Rod1** component (second reference), hover the cylinder over its cylindrical surface. When the green dot displays at the center of the surface at its midpoint (as shown in Figure E–14), click the left mouse button.

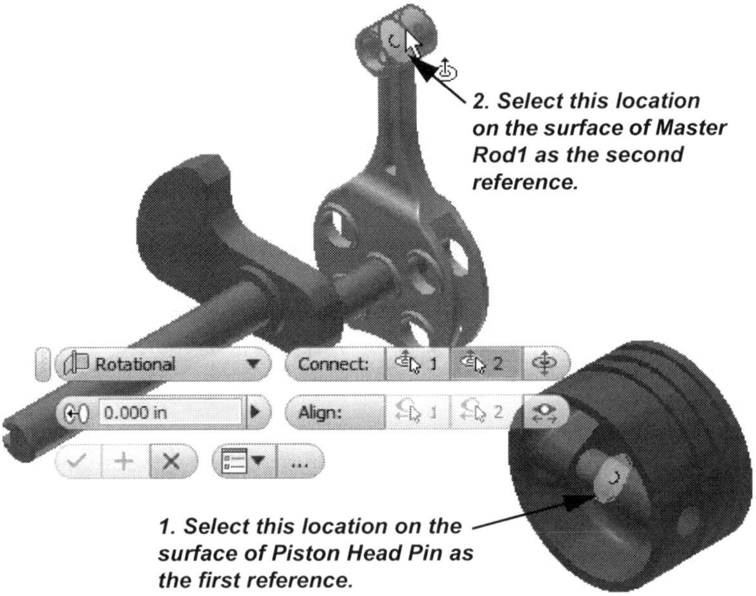

Figure E–14

Note how the preview for the Rotational joint only moves the **Piston head pin** component. The preview does not take into account any secondary constraints. Once completed, the relationship between the **Piston head** and **Piston head pin** will be maintained.

12. Click  in the mini-toolbar to complete the joint. Note how both the **Piston head pin** and **Piston head** move into position.

13. Select the **Piston head** component and drag it to verify its rotational degree of freedom. The components should display similar to those shown in Figure E–15.

Figure E–15

14. Select the **RBlock** and **Rcylinder** components in the Model browser, right-click, and select **Visibility**.

15. Select the **Crankshaft** component in the Model browser or the graphics window, right-click and clear the **Grounded** option so that additional joints can be added to join the components to the housing. The components display as shown in Figure E–16. With the **Crankshaft** ungrounded it can be constrained with respect to the other components.

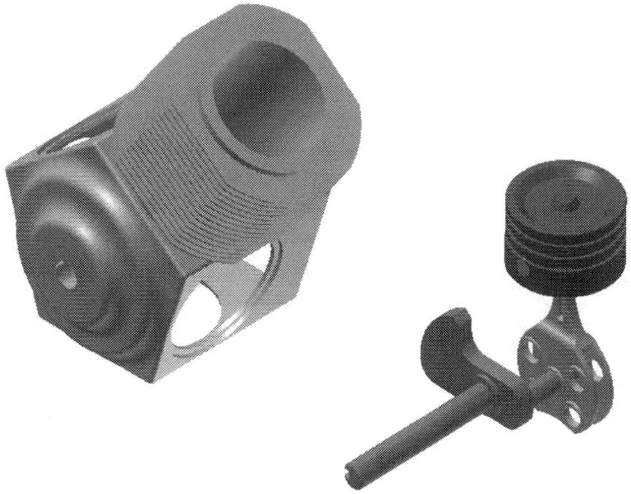

Figure E–16

Task 5 - Constrain the piston components in the housing.

1. In the *Assemble* tab>Relationships panel, click (Joint).
2. In the Type drop-down list in the mini-toolbar, select **Cylindrical**.
3. On the **Piston head** component (first reference), hover the cursor over the edge as shown in Figure E–17. It will display in red with a green dot at the center of the edge. Use the left mouse button to select the reference.
4. On the **Rcylinder** component (second reference), hover the cursor over the edge shown in Figure E–17. It will display in red with a green dot at the center of the edge. Use the left mouse button to select the reference.

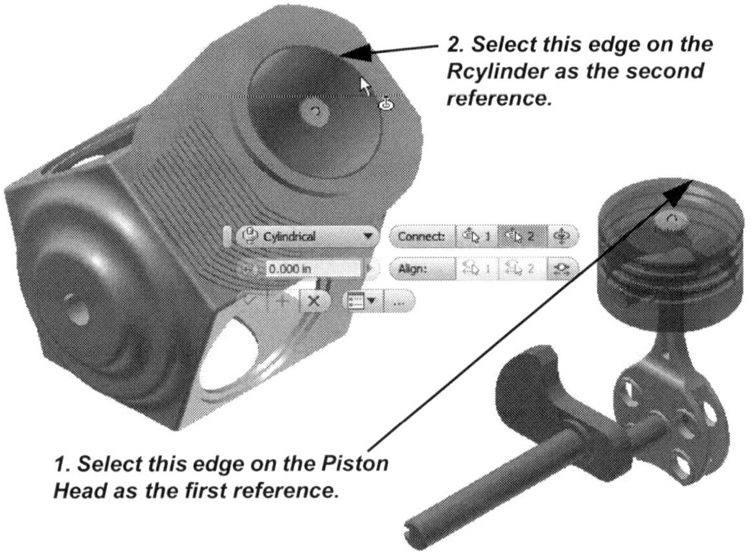

Figure E–17

5. Click in the mini-toolbar to complete the joint. The assembly displays as shown in Figure E–18.

Figure E–18

6. Select the **Piston head** component and drag it to verify its cylindrical degree of freedom.

7. In the *Assemble* tab>Relationships panel, click (Joint).

8. In the Type drop-down list in the mini-toolbar, select **Cylindrical**.

9. On the **Crankshaft** component (first reference), hover the cursor over the edge shown in Figure E–19. It will display in red with a green dot at the center of the edge. Use the left mouse button to select the reference.

10. On the **RBlock** component (second reference), hover the cursor over the edge shown in Figure E–19. It will display in red with a green dot at the center of the edge. Use the left mouse button to select the reference.

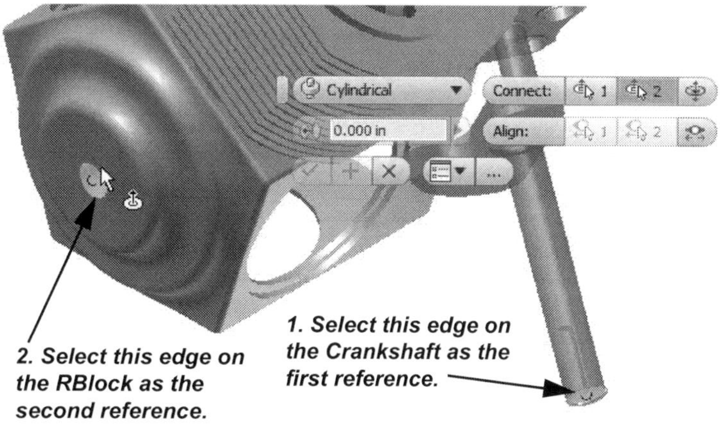

Figure E–19

11. Click  in the mini-toolbar to complete the joint. The assembly displays as shown in Figure E–20. Note how both cylindrical joints are used together to correctly position the components.

Figure E–20

12. Rotate the assembly (similar to that shown in Figure E–21), until the **Master Rod1** component displays. Select it and drag it to verify that the assembly movement permits the rotation of the crankshaft while the **Piston head** component maintains its alignment in the **Rcylinder** component.

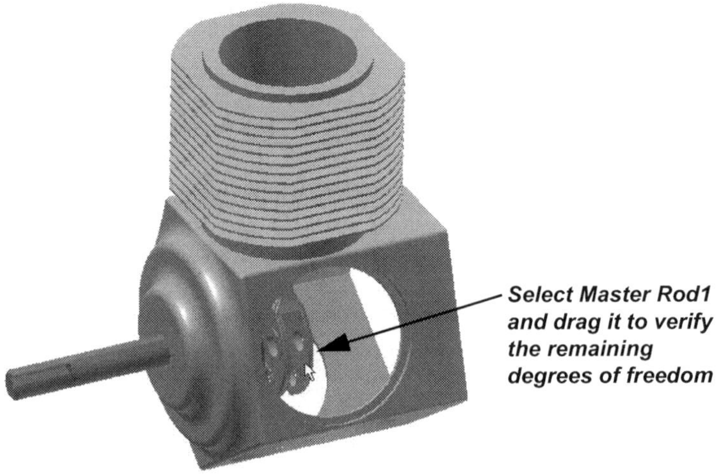

Figure E–21

Task 6 - Assemble two of the components for the propeller.

1. Place an instance of the **Hub.ipt** and **Shuttle.ipt** components into the assembly.
2. Rotate, move, and place the components in a similar orientation to that shown in Figure E–22.

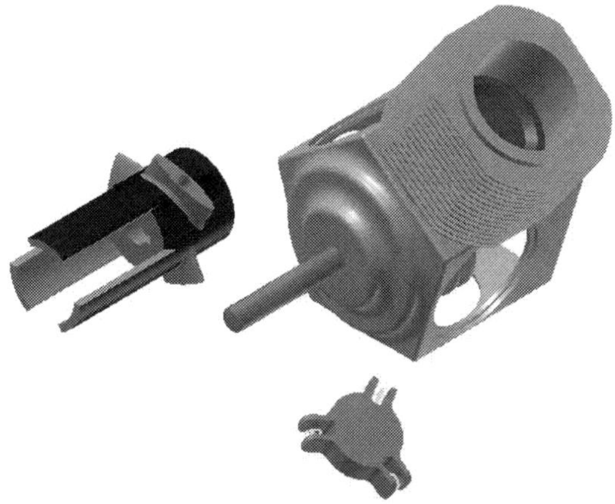

Figure E–22

3. Initiate the creation of a **Rigid** joint connection.
4. On the **Hub** component (first reference), hover the cursor over the face shown in Figure E–23. It will display in red with a green dot at the center of the edge. Use the left mouse button to select the reference.
5. On the **Crankshaft** component (second reference), hover the cursor over the face shown in Figure E–23. It will display in red with a green dot at the center of the edge. Use the left mouse button to select the reference.

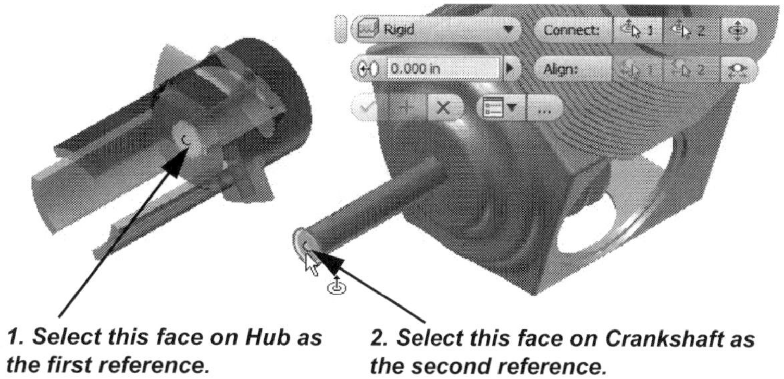

Figure E–23

6. Complete the joint. The components display as shown in Figure E–24.

Figure E–24

7. Drag the **Hub** and note how it moves the shaft and the piston components.

8. Initiate the creation of a **Cylindrical** joint connection.

9. On the **Shuttle** component (first reference), hover the cursor over the face shown in Figure E–25. It will display in red with a green dot at the center of the edge. Use the left mouse button to select the reference.

10. On the **Hub** component (second reference), hover the cursor over the face shown in Figure E–25. It will display in red with a green dot at the center of the edge. Use the left mouse button to select the reference.

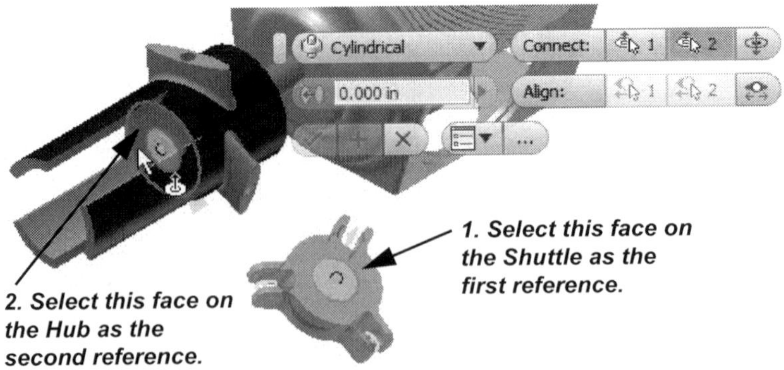

Figure E–25

11. Complete the joint. The components display as shown in Figure E–26.

Figure E–26

12. Drag the **Hub** and the **Shuttle** and note how they move. Note that the **Shuttle** component can still rotate and can clash with the **Hub** component.

13. In the *Assemble* tab>Relationships panel, click  (Constrain). Constraints can be used to remove any unwanted degrees of freedom that result from a joint connection. In this case you will remove the rotational degree of freedom in the **Shuttle** component.

14. Click  (Angle) as the constraint type in the Place Constraint dialog box. Click  (Directed Angle) in the *Solution* area.

15. Expand the **Hub** component in the Model browser and select **Work Plane1**.

16. Expand the **Shuttle** component and its **Origin** node in the Model browser and select the **YZ Plane**.

17. Enter **180** as the *Angle* value to rotate the **Shuttle**, as required.

18. Click **OK** to complete the constraint definition. Drag the Shuttle and note that only one translational degree of freedom remains.

19. The **Shuttle** has a limit to its range of motion in the **Hub**. Right-click on the **Cylindrical** connection in the **Shuttle** node of the Model browser. Select **Edit**.

20. Click  on the mini-toolbar to open the Edit Joint dialog box.

Limits can only be set in the dialog box, these controls are not available in the mini-toolbar.

21. Select the *Limits* tab.

22. In the *Linear* area, select **Start** and enter **1.9 in**. Select **End** and enter **4.3**, as shown in Figure E–27. This sets a limit on the range of movement from the surface that was selected as the reference on the **Hub** component. Depending on your reference selection you might need to enter negative values.

The Current value in the Edit Joint dialog box might vary. It reports the current position of the component.

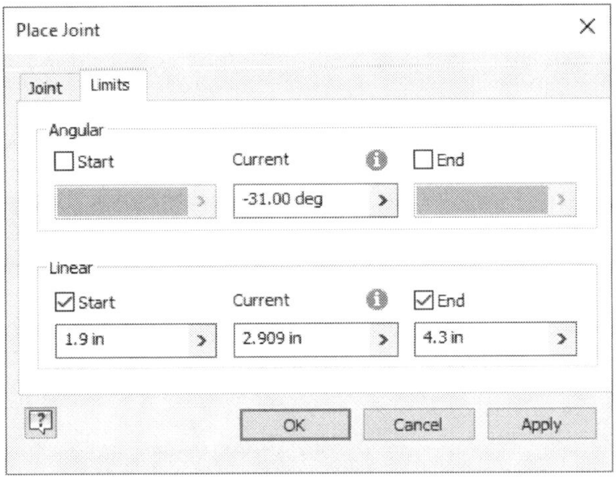

Figure E–27

23. Complete the edit and drag the **Hub** and the **Shuttle** and note how they move. Note that the **Shuttle** component can no longer rotate and has a defined limit to its translational movement.

Task 7 - Assemble the final components for the propeller.

1. Place an instance of the **Pro_blade.ipt** and **Prop_Conrod.ipt** components into the assembly.

2. Rotate, move, and place the components in a similar orientation to that shown in Figure E–28.

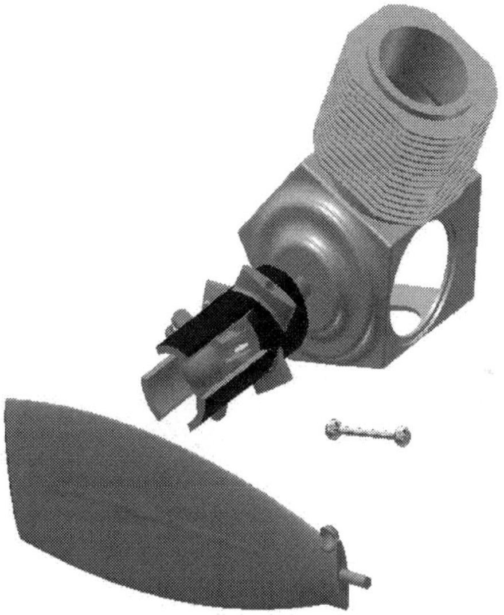

Figure E–28

The Place Joint dialog was previously opened and remains displayed until closed. Close the Place Joint dialog box.

3. Add a **Rotational** joint and select the references shown in Figure E–29 to join the **Pro_blade** and **Hub** components. Flip the component as required if they are not oriented correctly.

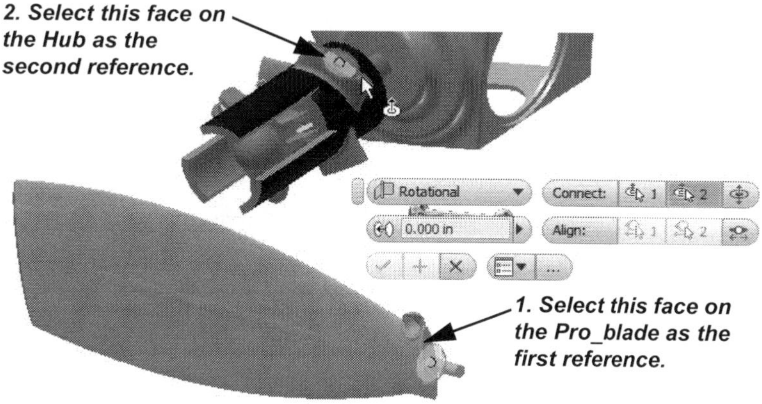

Figure E–29

4. Complete the joint connection.

5. Add a **Ball** joint and select the references shown in Figure E–30 to join the **Pro_blade** and **Prop_Conrod** components. When selecting the reference for a Ball joint, the reference should highlight at the center of the circular feature that is being used as the reference.

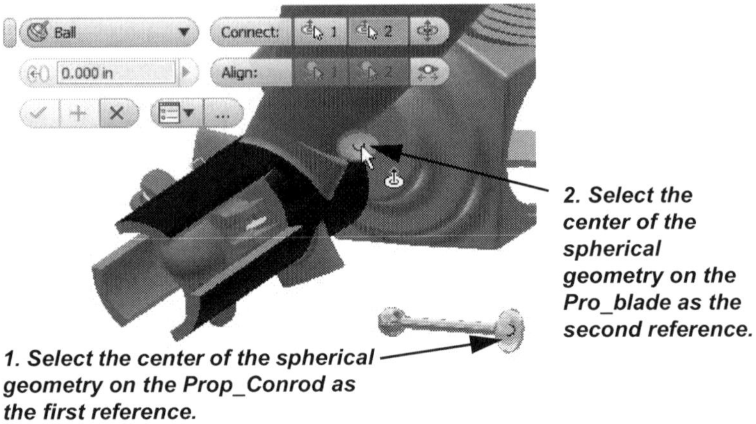

Figure E–30

6. Drag the **Prop_Conrod** to a more convenient location so that there is no interference between the two components. Note that all the other components will also move. You can temporarily ground components to reorient the components, if required.

7. Add another **Ball** joint and select the references shown in Figure E–31 to join the **Shuttle** and **Prop_Conrod** components. The reference that is to be selected on the Shuttle is the center of a sketch that was created to define the center of the joint.

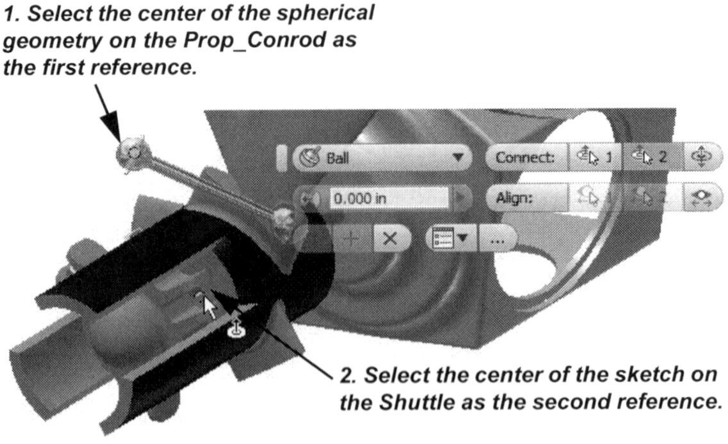

Figure E–31

8. Drag the **Shuttle** and note how the movement is now a little more limited based on the connections that have been defined.

9. Select the **Pro_blade** and the **Prop_Conrod** components in the Model browser, right-click and select **Copy**.

10. Press <Esc> to clear the selection, right-click on the graphics window and select **Paste**. The two components are pasted into the assembly.

11. Right-click and select **Paste** again to copy another set of the components into the assembly.

12. Expand the Model browser nodes associated with the copied **Pro_blade** and **Prop_Conrod** components. Note that the joint connections that placed the components relative to one another are maintained.

13. Add the required additional joint connections to constrain the components as shown in Figure E–32.

Figure E–32

14. Drag the components in the assembly to verify movement.

15. Save the assembly as **Radial Engine.iam**.

*A completed model called **Radial Engine Final.iam** has been provided in the practice files folder for your review.*

Task 8 - (Optional) Assemble the remaining housings and piston components.

1. Place and use joint connections to complete the Radial Engine assembly, as shown in Figure E–33.

Figure E–33

Hints:

- The rod used to connect the **Piston head.ipt** to the **Master Rod1.ipt** components is called **Connector Arm.ipt** and is available in the practice files folder.
- You can use the **Copy** and **Paste** functionality to duplicate components that are used multiple times (e.g., **Rcylinder**, **Piston head**, and **Piston head pin**). Doing so copies any joints that already exist between the copied components so that they do not have to be established again.
- When constraining the **Connector Arm** component to the **Master Rod1** component, consider temporarily grounding the **Master Rod1** component to prevent movement. This helps to ensure that the components are not flipped into positions that cannot be easily undone when a connection is made.

2. Save the assembly and close the files.

*A completed model called **Radial Engine Final2.iam** has been provided in the practice files folder for your review.*

Practice E2

Turntable Assembly

Practice Objectives

- Create a new assembly file using a standard template.
- Assemble parts with one another to create a required assembly.
- Use the **Drive** command to simulate the required range of motion for an assembly.
- Use the **Contact Solver** command to simulate the required range of motion for an assembly.
- Combine the use of the **Drive** and **Contact Solver** commands to simulate the required range of motion for an assembly.

In this practice, you will use the **Drive** and **Contact Solver** commands to control the range of motion for a turntable assembly.

Task 1 - Create a new assembly and add components.

1. Create a new assembly file using the **Standard(in).iam** template file.

2. Add **SRbase** to the assembly. Since this is the first component in the assembly, rotate it, as required, and use the **Place Grounded at Origin** command to ground it. Once placed, the component should be oriented as shown in Figure E–34 when in its default Home view.

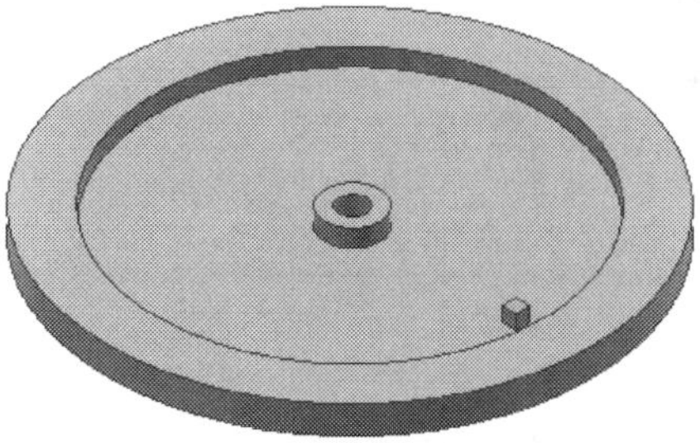

Figure E–34

Task 2 - Constrain the SRturntable component.

1. Add **SRturntable** to the assembly. Note the tab in the **SRbase** component and the slot in the **SRturnable** component. The tab and slot features were included to limit the motion of the assembly.

2. Add an Insert constraint between the two components, as shown in Figure E–35.

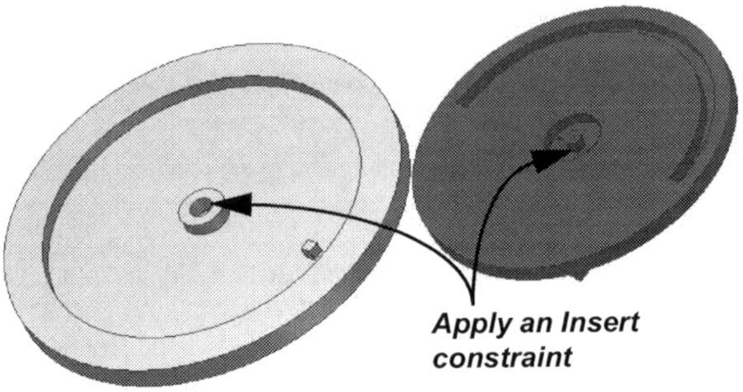

Figure E–35

3. Change the view display to **Wireframe**.

4. Rotate the **SRturntable** component. Note that it can turn 360 degrees, but this is not the design intent. The range of motion should be limited by the tab and the slot, as shown in Figure E–36.

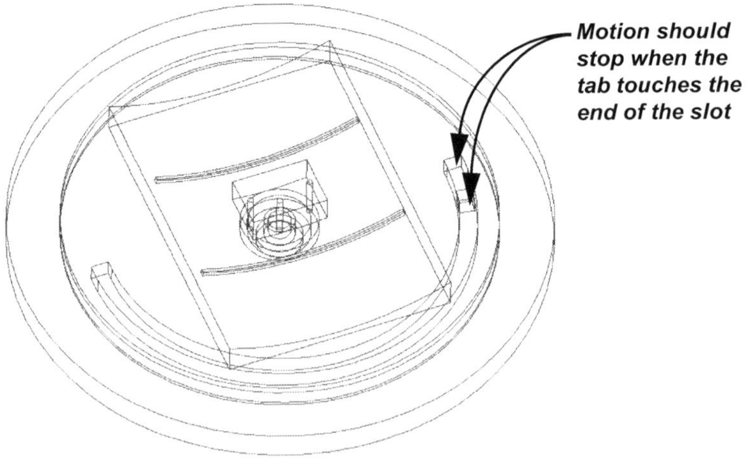

Figure E–36

Task 3 - Drive a constraint.

To limit the motion of the **SRturntable** component, you will add an Angle constraint. You will then use the **Drive** command to drive the Angle constraint 180 degrees and observe the motion. In the next task, you will suppress the Angle constraint and use the **Contact Solver** command to limit the range of motion.

Select the XZ planes in the Model browser.

1. Create a 0 degree Angle constraint between the XZ planes in the **SRbase** and the **SRturntable** components.
2. Expand the **SRbase** node in the Model browser to display the constraints.
3. Right-click on the Angle constraint and select **Drive**.
4. Enter **0.00 deg** in the *Start* field and **180 deg** in the *End* field. Depending on the constraint references, you might need to enter **-180 deg** in the *End* field instead.
5. Click  in the Drive dialog box to view the motion. Click  to reverse the motion.
6. Click  in the Drive dialog box.
7. Enable **Collision Detection** and change the *End* value to **200 deg** (or **-200 deg**), as shown in Figure E–37.

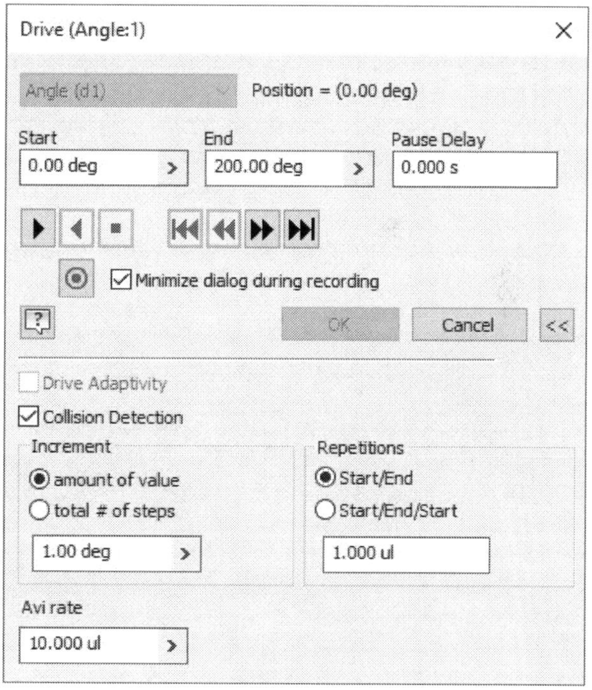

Figure E–37

8. Click . A dialog box opens indicating that collision is detected. If components do not collide, verify the Insert constraint references.

9. Click **OK**.

10. Click **Cancel** to close the Drive dialog box.

Task 4 - Use the Contact Solver.

In this task, you will use the Contact Solver to simulate the range of motion required.

1. In the Model browser, right-click on the Angle constraint and select **Suppress**.

2. Select the *Inspect* tab>Interference panel and click (Activate Contact Solver).

3. While holding <Ctrl>, select the **SRbase** and the **SRturntable** components in the Model browser, right-click and select **Contact Set**.

If any interference exists between components in the Contact Set, you will not be able to drag the components.

4. Rotate the **SRturnable** component. Note that the rotation stops once it is in contact with the **SRbase** component.

Task 5 - Use the Contact Solver with the Driven Constraint command.

1. Right-click on the **Angle** constraint in the Model browser and clear the **Suppress** option.

2. Right-click on the **Angle** constraint in the Model browser and select **Drive**.

3. Expand the dialog box and clear the **Collision Detection** option.

4. Enter **0.00 deg** in the *Start* field and **200 deg** (or **-200 deg**) in the *End* field, and click .

   Note that the motion stops when the angle is 180 degrees. The **Contact Solver** can also be used to help determine where components will come into contact with each other when you are using the **Drive** command.

5. Suppress the Angle constraint again if you want to continue displaying the range of motion using the Contact Solver.

6. Save the assembly as **SRassembly**.

Task 6 - (Optional) Complete the assembly.

To add components at the same time, use <Shift> to select components. If using this technique to populate the first and all subsequent components, ensure that the correct component is grounded.

1. Assemble **SRrocker**, **SRlocator**, **SRwasher**, and three instances of **SRscrew** to the assembly.

Apply constraints to the remaining components and display the degrees of freedom to verify that they are fully constrained. Each screw and washer should have one rotational degree of freedom when you finish. The assembly displays as shown in Figure E–38.

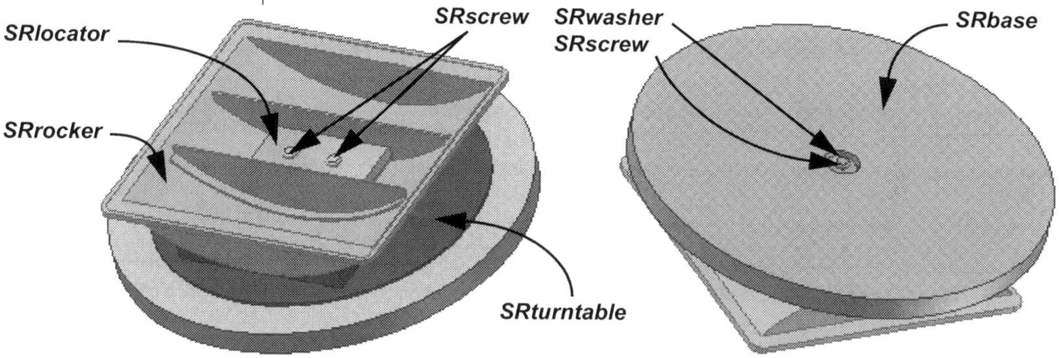

Figure E–38

2. Constrain the **SRturntable** and **SRrocker**:
   - Apply a Mate constraint between Work Axis1 of **SRrocker** and Work Axis2 of **SRturntable**. These axes represent the center lines of the round portions of each of these components.
   - Apply a Mate constraint between Work Plane3 of **SRrocker** and Work Plane2 of **SRturntable**. This locates the components along the axis. However, the SRrocker can still rotate.
   - Add **SRrocker** to the contact set to find the range of motion.
3. Use Insert constraints to constrain the two holes in **SRlocator** and **SRturntable**.
4. Use an Insert constraint between **SRscrew:1** and **SRlocator**. Repeat the process for **SRscrew:2**.
5. Apply an Insert constraint between **SRbase** and **SRwasher**.

6. Apply an Insert constraint between **SRscrew:3** and **SRwasher**.

7. Save the assembly. A completed model, **SRassembly_final.iam**, has been provided. Enable **Activate Contact Solver** in the *Inspect* tab to use the Contact Solver.

Practice E3

Assembly Parts and Features

Practice Objectives

- Create an assembly hole feature and ensure that the participant components are correctly assigned.
- Create a new part model in the context of the assembly and add solid geometry to the part by referencing other assembly components.

In this practice, you will work with the assembly shown on the left in Figure E–39 and create four assembly holes, as shown on the right. You will then create new parts that fit inside these holes while remaining in the Assembly environment.

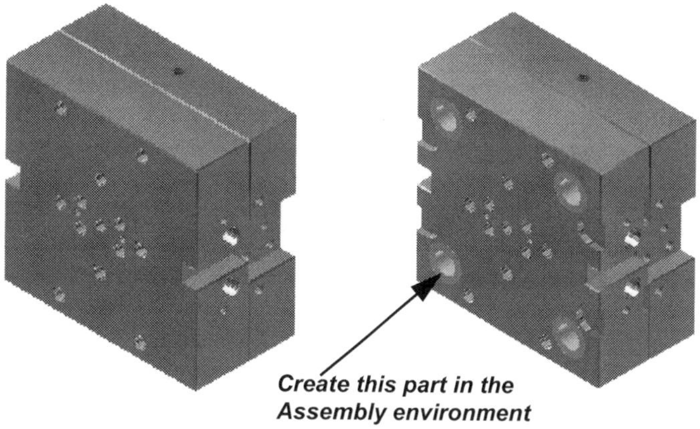

Figure E–39

Task 1 - Create the assembly holes.

In this task, you will create four **From Sketch** assembly holes. Creating the holes using this option enables you to create all of the holes at once.

*To clear a component from the display, select it, right-click, and clear the **Visibility** option. Alternatively, you can select the components that you want to keep, right-click and select **Isolate**.*

1. Open **Final Mold Assy.iam** from the *Mold Assembly* folder.
2. Toggle off the display of all of the assembly components, except the **topplate2 Assy** and the **Middleplate Assy** subassemblies.

3. In the *3D Model* tab>Sketch panel, click (Start 2D Sketch) and place the sketch for the holes on the large face shown in Figure E–40.

4. Sketch a point on the face, and then dimension and pattern it, as shown in Figure E–40. Modify the dimensions as shown, if required.

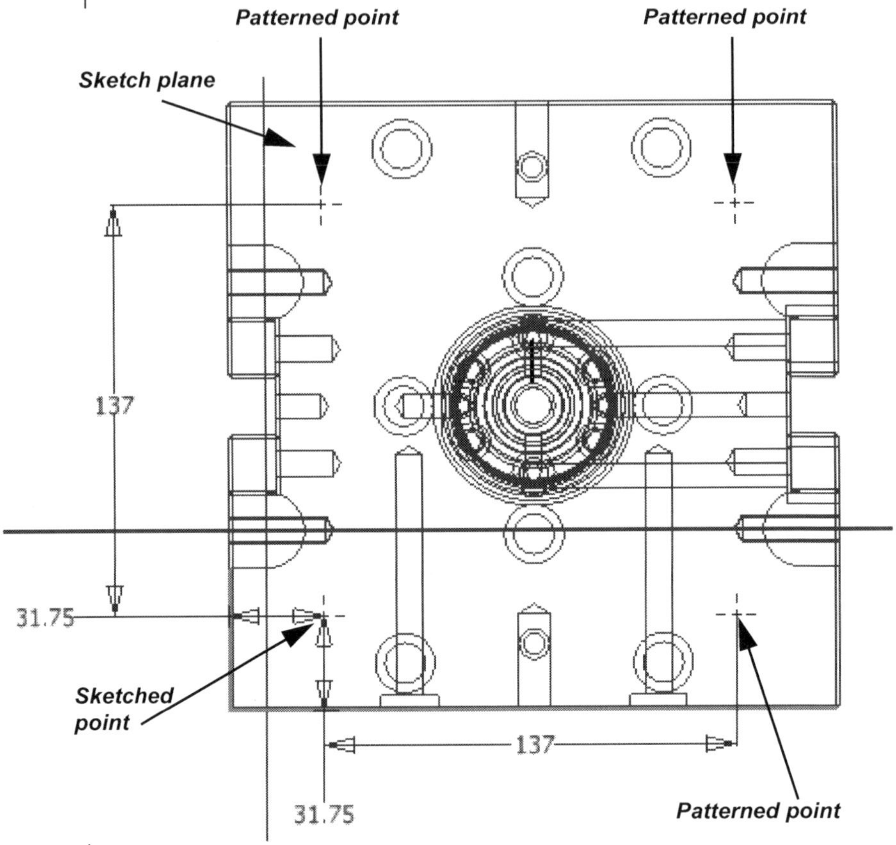

Figure E–40

5. Finish the sketch.

6. In the *3D Model* tab>Modify Assembly panel, click (Hole). Create four counterbore assembly holes as shown in Figure E–41. The holes are by default added to the sketched points from the sketch.

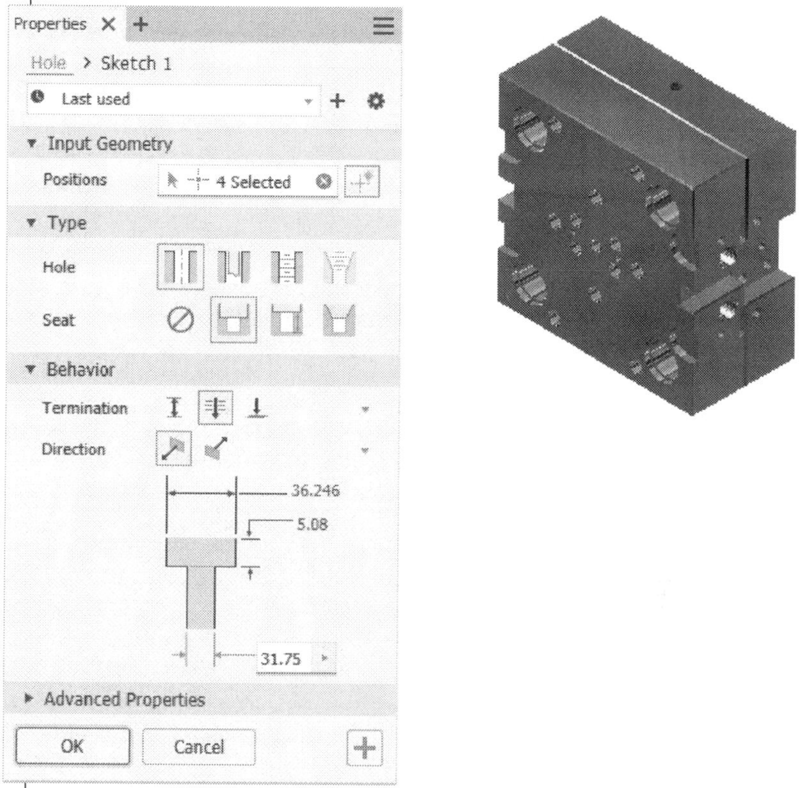

Figure E–41

7. Expand **Hole 1** in the Model browser to display the two participants in the **Hole 1** feature, as shown in Figure E–42. This means that the hole is cutting through both of these components. These components were selected by default. You can manually add or remove components, if required.

To add a participant component so that it is intersected by the hole, right-click on the hole in the Model browser, select ***Add Participant****, and select a component.*

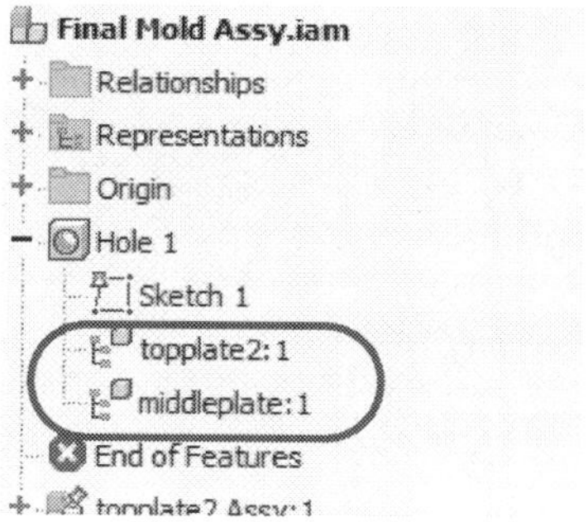

Figure E–42

Task 2 - Create an assembly part.

1. Select the *Assemble* tab>Component panel, click  (Create). The Create In-Place Component dialog box opens.
2. Enter **bush_part** in the *New Component Name* field.
3. Browse to and select the metric standard part template, **Standard(mm).ipt**.
4. Clear the Constrain sketch plane to selected face or plane option and accept the defaults in other fields.
5. Click **OK** to create the part.
6. Select the counterbore face of one of the holes shown in Figure E–43 as the sketch plane. All of the assembly components are grayed out in the Model browser, except **bush_part**. This means that only **bush_part** is active and you can add features to it.

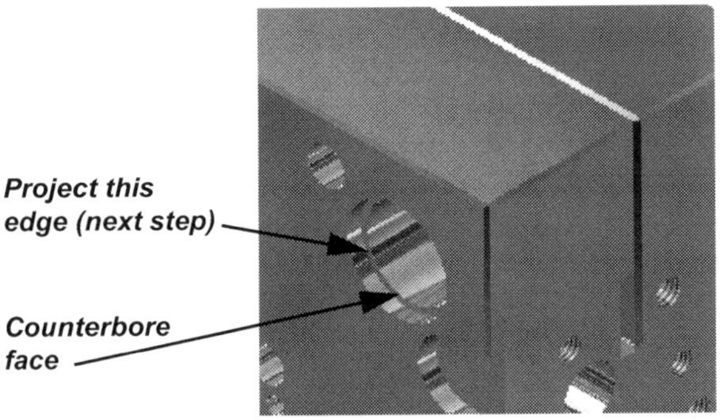

Figure E–43

7. In the *3D Model* tab>Sketch panel, click  (Start 2D Sketch). Select the XY Plane in the new **bush_part** component as the sketch plane.

8. In the sketch environment, project the edge of the 31.75 mm diameter circle shown in Figure E–43, and sketch the concentric circle, as shown in Figure E–44.

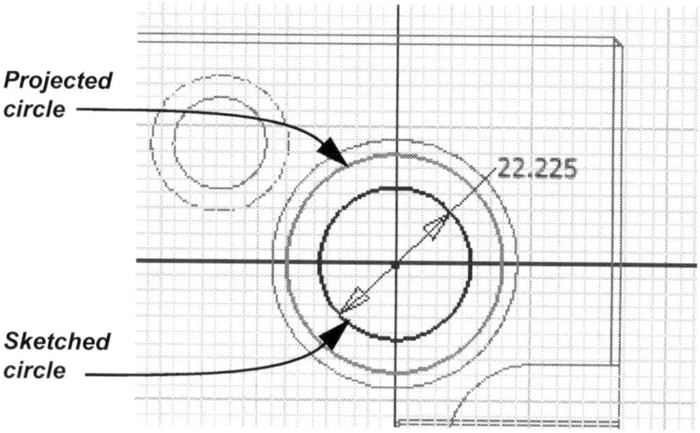

Figure E–44

9. Finish the sketch. Do not return to the **top-level** assembly or you will have to reactivate **bush_part**.

10. Extrude the sketch **47.625 mm** inside of the hole, as shown in Figure E–45.

Figure E–45

To disable the automatic assigning of adaptivity during reference selection, consider pressing and holding <Ctrl> (e.g., when selecting a face to extrude).

11. Create another extruded feature for **bush_part**. Select the front face of the protrusion that you just created as the sketch plane. This reduces the number of references to other parts in the assembly. Project the geometry as required to obtain the sketch shown in Figure E–46. (**Hint:** You will need to work in the part.) Extend the extrusion to the top face of the **topplate2 Assy** subassembly. The completed **bush_part** is shown in Figure E–46.

    Note the adaptive icons in front of **bush_part** and its features and sketches. The adaptive icon indicates that the feature contains references to other components in the assembly and requires these references to generate its geometry.

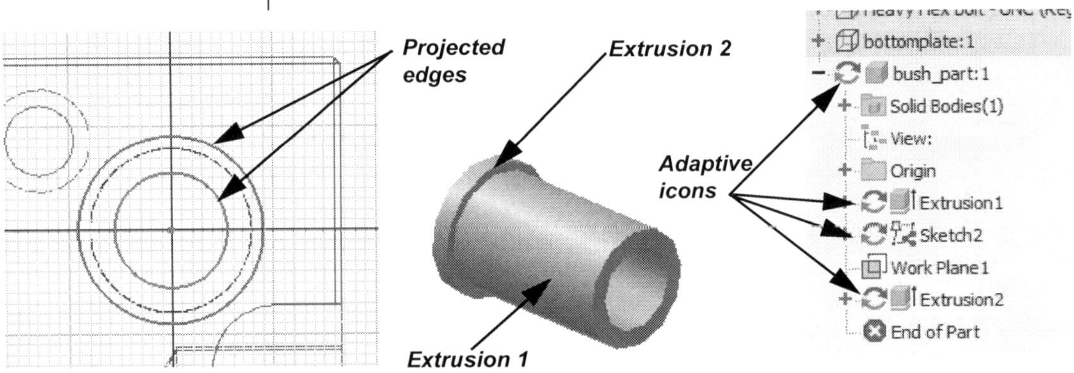

Figure E–46

12. Activate the top-level assembly and open **bush_part** in its own window.

13. Display the dimensions for **Extrusion1**. The only dimensions that can be modified are its depth (currently 47.625) and the inside diameter (currently 22.25), as shown in Figure E–47. These are not dimensions that are driven by other references in the assembly and that is why you can still modify them. The outside diameters on the two extrusions are examples of dimensions that are being driven by references in other components of the assembly, as the design intent for the model requires.

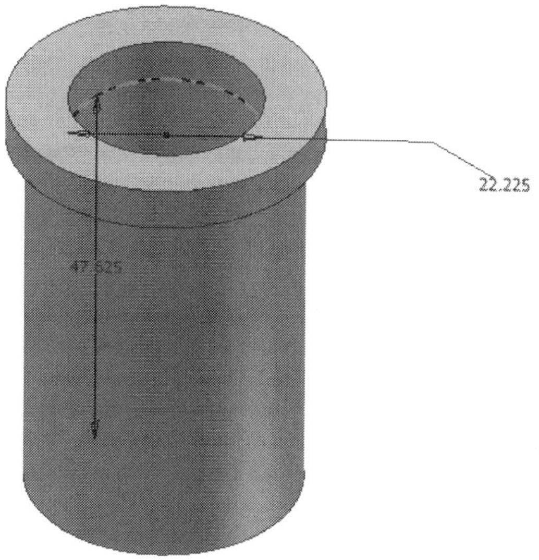

Figure E–47

14. Save **bush_part** and close the window.
15. Save the assembly and close the window.

Practice E4 Drawing Creation I

Practice Objectives

- Create a new drawing file using a standard drawing template.
- Add required views to a drawing file.

In this practice, you will create a new drawing file named **Project_II**, based on the **Standard.dwg** template. You will also add views of the part file **bevelwasher.ipt** (as shown in Figure E–48), using base views, projected views, auxiliary views, and section views.

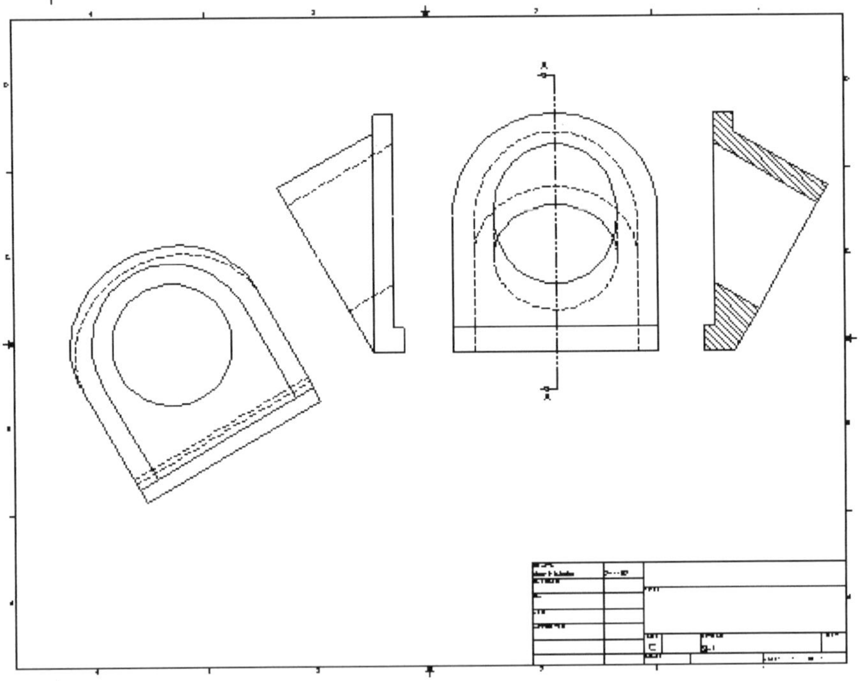

Figure E–48

Practice E5 Drawing Creation II

Practice Objectives

- Create a new drawing file using a standard drawing template.
- Add required views to a drawing file.
- Create a new presentation file using a standard presentation template.
- Add manual tweaks and trail line to the presentation file to display the components as exploded.

1. Create a new drawing file named **Project _II**, based on the **Standard.dwg** template. Add views of the following four parts, as shown in Figure E–49:
   - **latchbase.ipt**
   - **handle.ipt**
   - **tongue.ipt**
   - **latchpin.ipt**

   Show projected views (top and side) for the parts. Include labels and scale as appropriate. Save the drawing file.

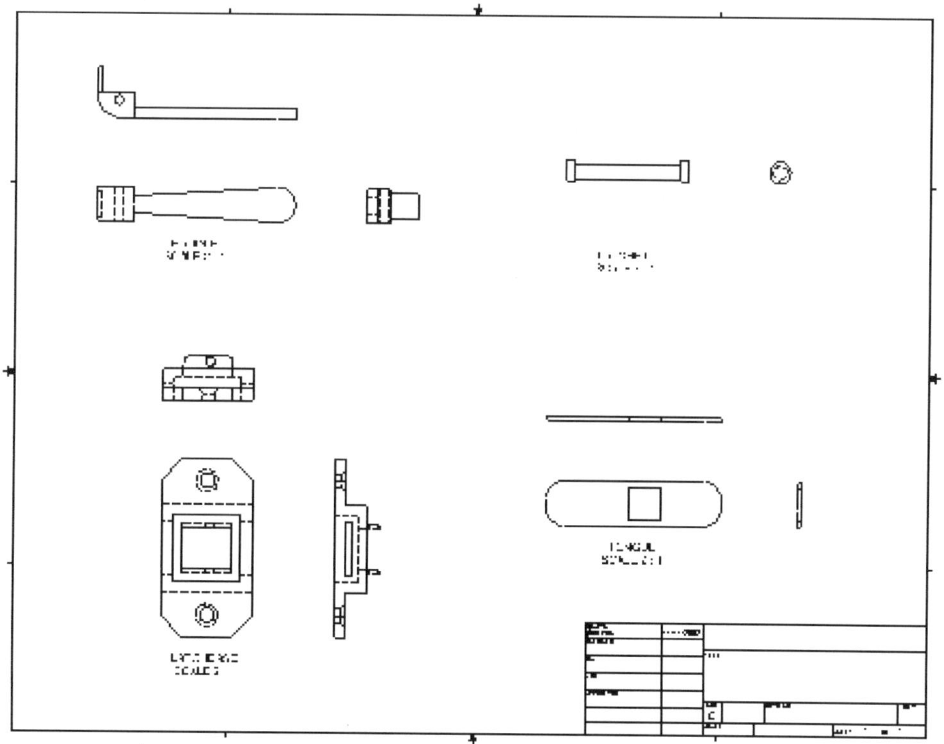

Figure E–49

2. Create a new assembly file named **Latch** using the **Standard.iam** template. Assemble and constrain the following components, similar to that shown in Figure E–50.
   - **latchbase.ipt**
   - **handle.ipt**
   - **tongue.ipt**
   - **latchpin.ipt**
3. Create a new presentation file named **Latch Presentation**, using the **Standard.ipn** template. In the presentation, create a view of the assembly **Latch.iam** to display the components exploded, as shown in Figure E–50. Save the file.

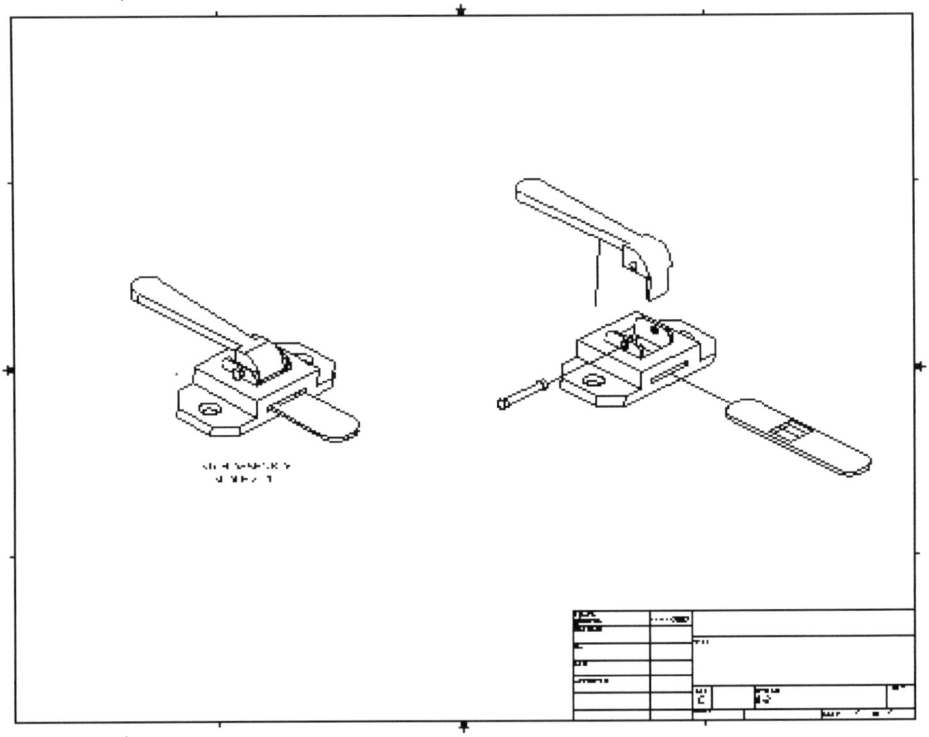

Figure E–50

Practice E6 Drawing Creation III

Practice Objectives

- Generate a Bill of Materials and change the BOM structure for assembly components.
- Create virtual components to represent purchased components in the assembly.
- Create a parameter to represent the base quantity of virtual components.

In this practice, you will create virtual components and generate a BOM using general instructions. The final drawing is shown in Figure E–51.

PARTS LIST			
ITEM	PART NUMBER	QTY	DESCRIPTION
1	Base_Vise	1	
2	Sliding_Jaw	1	
3	Collar	1	
4	Jaw_Plate	2	
5	Set_Screw	2	
6	Slide_Key	2	
7	Special_Key	1	
8	ANSI B18.6.3 - 1/4-20 x 3/4	4	Countersunk Flat Head Screw
10	Vise_Screw	1	
11	Handle_Rod	1	
12	Handle_Ball	2	
13	Pin	2	
14	Paint	150.000 ml	
15	Machine Oil	20.000 ml	

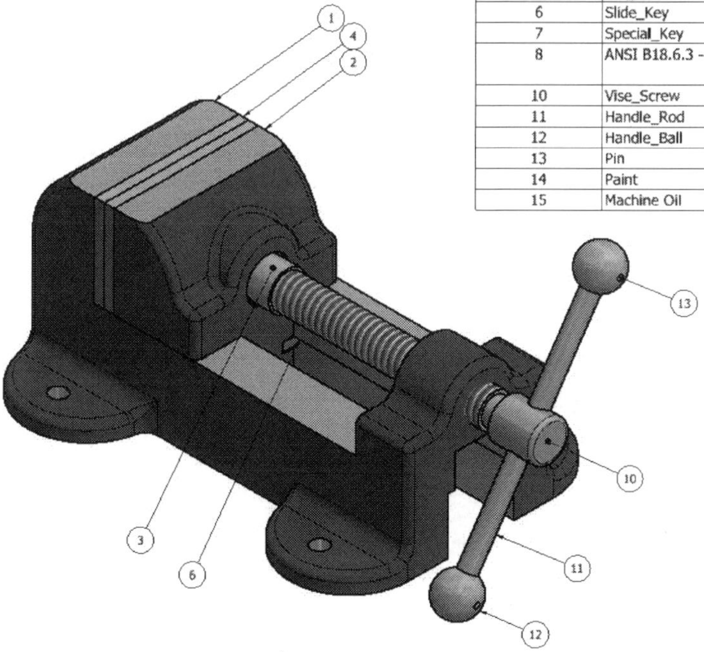

Figure E–51

Task 1 - Generate the BOM.

1. Open **BOM_Vise.iam** from the *BOM_II* folder.
2. In the *Assemble* tab>Manage panel, click (Bill of Materials) to open the Bill of Materials dialog box, as shown in Figure E–52.

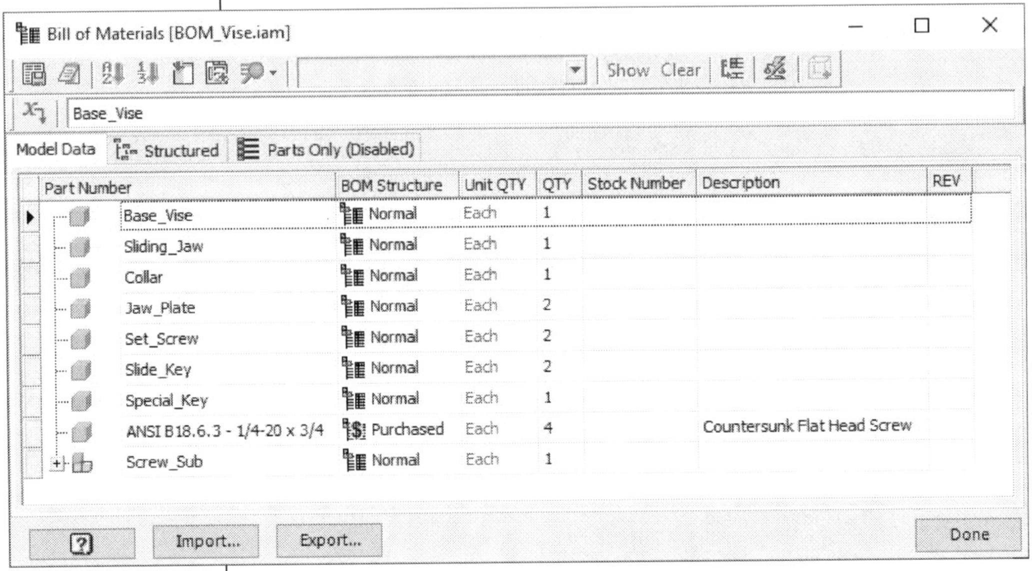

Figure E–52

3. Set the *BOM Structure* property of the **Set_Screw** to **Purchased**.
4. Set **Screw_Sub** subassembly to **Phantom**.
5. Click **Done** to close the Bill of Materials dialog box.
6. Create a virtual component called **Paint** and set its *BOM Structure* property to **Purchased**.
7. Right-click on **Paint** in the Model browser and select **iProperties**.
8. In the *Project* tab, ensure that the *Part Number* is set to **Paint** and close the dialog box.
9. Create a parameter called **Base_Qty** and set the *units* to **ml**. You will need to enter the value as **1.0ml**, once the units have been set.
10. Right-click on **Paint** in the Model browser and select **Component Settings**.

11. Set the *Base Quantity* to the **Base_Qty** parameter, as shown in Figure E–53, and click **OK** to close the dialog box.

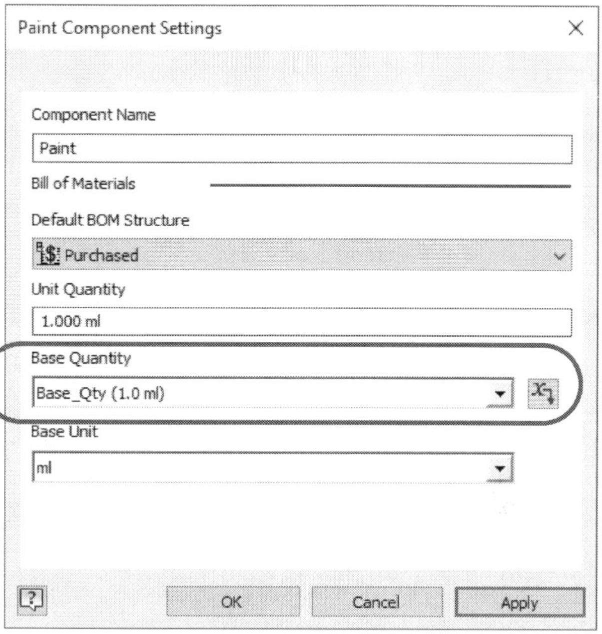

Figure E–53

12. Create another virtual component called **Machine Oil**. Set the *BOM Structure* property to **Purchased** and change the base quantity to **Base_Qty** in the component settings, as you did for the **Paint** component. Ensure that **Machine Oil** is set as the *Part Number* for the component in its iProperties dialog box.

13. Return to the Bill of Materials dialog box and change the quantities of the **Paint** and **Machine Oil** components to **150ml** and **20ml** respectively.

14. Save the assembly and close the file.

15. If time permits, create a new drawing of the assembly and create a structured parts list with balloons.

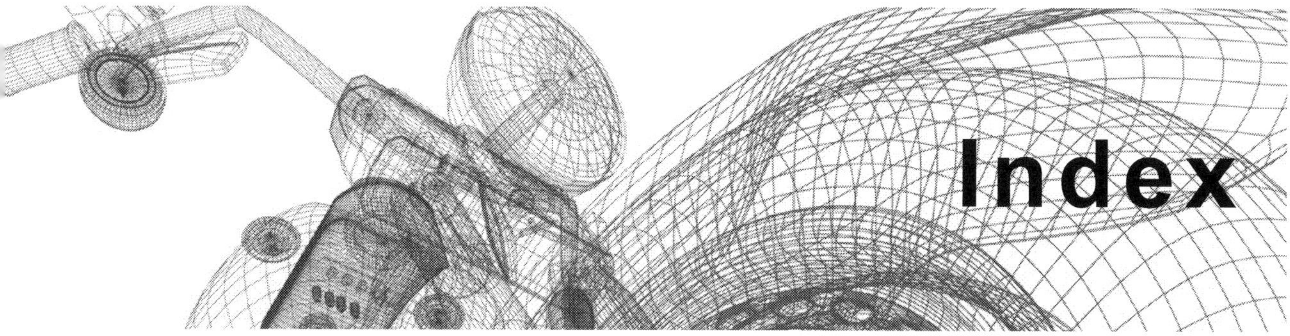

Index

#

2020.1 Enhancements
  Hole Placement (Allow Center Point Creation) **6-23**
  Virtual Component Creation **23-3**
2021 Enhancements
  Assigning Sheet format with Drawing Creation **25-2**
  Automated Centerline Ribbon Command **27-14**
  Measurements in a Drawing **26-4**
  Split Interface **9-12**

A

Annotation
  Center Line **27-13**
  Center Line Bisector **27-14**
  Center Mark **27-13**
  Centered Pattern **27-14**
  Chamfer Note **27-11**
  Hole Table **27-15**
  Hole/Thread Note **27-8**
  Symbols **27-6**
  Tables **27-18**
  Tags **27-20**
  Text **27-2**
Application Options **4-10**, **28-2**
Arc **3-3**
Assemble
  Assembly Browser **16-21**
  Autodrop **16-20**
  Bill of Materials **23-4**
  Components **16-2**, **17-2**
    Copy **21-4**
    Enable **18-6**
    Interference **21-13**
    Isolate **18-7**
    Mirror **21-3**
    Move **18-2**
    Pattern **21-5**
    Replace **21-2**
    Restructure **21-6**
    Rotate **18-3**
    Transparent **18-8**
    Visible **18-6**
  Constraint
    Angle **16-7**
    Drive Constraint **21-9**
    Insert **16-8**
    Mate **16-6**
    References **16-9**
    Suppress **18-5**
    Symmetry **16-8**
    Tangent **16-7**
    UCS **16-9**
  Contact Solver **21-11**
  Content Center **16-19**
  Create Part **22-2**
  Explode **20-2**
  Failure **21-16**
  Joint **17-2**
    Automatic **17-3**
    Ball **17-4**, **17-10**
    Cylindrical **17-4**, **17-9**
    Editing **17-13**
    Limits **17-11**
    Planar **17-4**
    References **17-4**
    Rigid **17-4**, **17-8**
    Rotational **17-4**, **17-8**
    Slider **17-4**, **17-9**
  Methods **16-2**, **16-16**, **17-2**
  Presentations **20-2**
  Resolve Link **24-9**
  Save Files **16-23**
  Section View **18-8**
  Selection Options **18-14**
  Storyboards **20-19**
  Update **18-4**
  Virtual Component **22-3**, **23-2**
Assembly Modeling **1-7**
Associative Design **1-7**
AutoCAD
  Insert Data **5-10**
Automatic Dimensions **2-14**

Auxiliary Views **25-10**
Axis **2-5**, **7-7**

B

Ball Joint **17-10**
Balloons **26-22**
Base View **25-4**
Baseline Dimension **26-8**
Bill of Materials **23-4**
  BOM Structure Types **23-7**
  Parts List **23-14**
Box **B-2**
Break Link **5-9**
Break Out View **25-18**
Bridge Curve **3-3**
Broken View **25-17**

C

Camera View **18-13**
Center Mark **27-13**
Centerline **27-13**
Centerline Bisector **27-14**
Chain Dimensions **26-9**
Chamfer
  Feature **6-2**
  Notes **27-11**
  Sketch **3-6**
Circle **2-10**, **3-3**
Color **19-12**
Constraints
  Assembly
    Angle **16-7**
    Drive **21-9**
    Insert **16-8**
    Mate **16-6**
    Suppress **18-5**
    Symmetry **16-8**
    Tangent **16-7**
    UCS **16-9**
  Inferred Constraint Reference **2-16**
  Joint **17-2**
  Show **2-16**, **3-12**
  Sketch **2-16**, **3-12**
    Coincident **3-15**
    Collinear **3-14**
    Concentric **3-15**
    Constraint Settings **3-19**
    Delete **3-22**
    Equal **3-16**
    Fix **3-17**
    Horizontal and Vertical **3-16**
    Inference **3-20**
    Over Constrained **3-18**
    Parallel and Perpendicular **3-13**
    Reference **3-18**
    Relax Mode **3-22**
    Smooth (G2) **3-14**
    Symmetric **3-18**
    Tangent **3-13**
  Suppress **18-5**
Construction Entities **3-8**
Contact Solver **21-11**
Content Center **16-19**
Copy **4-5**, **21-4**
  Entities **4-2**
Create Part **22-2**
Crop View **25-20**
Cut **5-3**
Cylinder **B-2**
Cylindrical Joint **17-9**

D

Degrees of Freedom **3-12**, **16-5**
Delete
  Constraints **3-22**
  Dimensions **2-14**
  Parameter **8-11**
  Patterns **14-19**
Demote **21-7**
Depth **2-20**
Design Doctor **11-6**
Design Views **10-8**, **18-10**
Detail Views **25-13**
Dimensions **A-7**
  Delete **2-14**
  Display **8-2**
  Drawing
    Baseline **26-8**
    Chain **26-9**
    Edit **26-4**, **26-10**
    Foreshortened **26-6**
    General **26-5**
    Isometric **26-7**
    Model **26-2**
    Ordinate **26-8**
    Styles **26-12**
  Dynamic **2-12**
  Modify **2-14**
  Show **2-23**
  Sketch **2-12**, **3-24**
    Angular **3-25**
    Arc Length **3-26**
    Automatic **2-14**
    Center Dimensions **3-24**
    Diameter **3-24**
    Driven **2-15**
    Linear **2-13**
    Linear Diameter **2-13**
    Over Dimensioned Entities **3-27**
    Radius **3-24**
    Revolved **3-26**
    Tangent **3-25**

Direction **2-20**
Document Settings **4-11, 28-7**
Draft
- Face **9-2**
- Fixed Edge **9-3**
- Fixed Plane **9-4**
- Parting Line **9-4**
- View **25-16**

Drawing **1-7**
- Annotation
  - Center Mark **27-13**
  - Centered Pattern **27-14**
  - Centerline **27-13**
  - Centerline Bisector **27-14**
  - Chamfer Note **27-11**
  - Hole Table **27-15**
  - Hole/Thread Note **27-8**
  - Symbols **27-6**
  - Tables **27-18**
  - Tags **27-20**
  - Text **27-2**
- Hatching **26-29**
- Parts List **26-16**
- Sheets **26-14**
- Styles and Standard Editor **26-25**
- Symbols **27-6**
- Transparent Component **25-23**
- View Orientation **25-5, 25-6, 25-23**

Drawing Resources Folder **25-3**
Driven Dimensions **2-15**
DWG **1-3, 5-11**
Dynamic Dimensioning **5-12**
Dynamic Input **2-12, 5-12**

E
Edit
- Feature **2-25**
- Redefine **2-25**
- Sketch
  - Entities **2-24, A-5**
  - Plane **2-25**

Ellipse **3-3**
Enabling Components **18-6**
Environments **1-2**
Equation Curve **3-2**
Equations **8-2, 15-9**
Explode **20-2**
Extend **3-10**
Extrude **2-18, 5-2**

F
Failure
- Assembly **21-16**
- Design Doctor **11-6**
- Feature **11-4**
- Resolve Link **24-9**
- Sketch **11-2**
- Sketch Doctor **11-4**

Feature Based Modeling **1-4**
Features
- Assembly Features **22-5**
- Creation **2-6**
- Delete **15-10**
- Insert **10-3**
- Participant Parts **22-5**
- Relationships **15-1**
- Rename **2-23**
- Reorder **10-2**
- Suppress **10-4**

File Types **1-2**
Fillets
- Constant **6-7**
- Face **6-18**
- Full Round **6-20**
- Sketch Entity **3-6**
- Variable **6-14**

Folders **21-8**
Foreshortened Dimensions **26-6**
Full Navigation Wheel **1-26**
Functions **8-7**

G
General Dimension **2-12**
Graphics Window **1-14**
Grid Lines **2-9**

H
Hatching **25-13, 26-29**
Help **1-20**
Hole Notes **27-8**
Hole Table **27-15**
Holes
- Create **6-22**
- Threads **6-34**

I
Insert ACAD File **5-10**
Insert Features **10-3**
Interface **1-8, 1-12**
- Customization **28-15**
- Marking Menu **28-19**
- Model Browser **15-8**
- Ribbon **28-15**

Interference **21-13**
Intersect **5-3**
iProperties **19-10, 28-12**
Isolating Components **18-7**
Isometric Dimensions **26-7**

J

Join **5-3**
Joint **17-2**
  Ball **17-4, 17-10**
  Cylindrical **17-4, 17-9**
  Planar **17-4, 17-10**
  Rigid **17-4, 17-8**
  Rotational **17-4, 17-8**
  Slider **17-4, 17-9**

L

Line **2-10, 3-5**
Line Close **2-10**
Loft **2-18**
  Center Line Loft **13-2**
  Conditions **13-6**
  Rail Loft **13-2**
  Transitions **13-11**
Look At **1-25**

M

Marking Menu **1-17, 28-19**
Measure
  Add to Accumulate **19-7**
  Angle **19-5**
  Between Components **19-4**
  Context Sensitive **19-8**
  Distance **19-3**
  Region Properties **19-9**
  Restart **19-7**
  Using Values **19-8**
Minimum Solution **5-4**
Mini-Toolbar **1-19**
Mirror **3-11, 21-3**
  Components **21-3**
  Features **14-17**
  Parts **14-17**
  Sketch Entities **3-11**
Model Browser **1-16, 16-21**
  Representations **18-10**
Model Dimensions **26-2**
Model Display **1-27**
Move
  Components **18-2**
  Entities **4-2**
Move EOP Marker **10-3**
Move EOP to End **10-3**
My Home **1-8**

N

Navigation Wheel **1-26**
New
  Base Feature **2-6**
  File **2-3, 2-4**
  New Sketch **2-6**
  New Solid **5-3**

O

Offset **5-7**
Operators **8-6**
Optimize for Single Selection **12-4**
Ordinate Dimension **26-8**
Orientation **1-22**
  Drawing Views **25-6, 25-23**
Origin Features
  Axes **2-5, 7-7**
  Planes **2-5, 7-2**
  Points **2-5, 7-10**
  Visibility **2-5**
Overlay Views **25-14**

P

Pan **1-22**
Panels **1-13**
Parameters
  Delete **8-11**
  Dialog Box **8-8**
  Filtering **8-11**
  Immediate Update **8-12**
  Key **8-11**
  Make Multi-Value **8-10**
  Model Parameters **8-8**
  Numeric **8-9**
  Purge Unused **8-11**
  Text **8-9**
  True/False **8-9**
  User Parameters **8-9**
Parametric **1-6**
Participant Parts **22-5**
Parts List **23-14, 26-16**
Paste **4-5**
Patterns
  Circular Feature **14-9**
  Components **21-5**
  Delete **14-19**
  Edit **14-19**
  Rectangular Feature **14-2**
  Sketch
    Circular **4-8**
    Rectangular **4-6**
  Sketched Driven Features **14-14**
  Suppress **14-19**
Planar Joint **17-10**
Planes **2-5, 7-2**
Point Snaps **3-8**
Points **2-5, 7-10**
Polygon **3-4**
Precise Input **5-12**
Presentations **20-2**
  Publish **20-24**
Primitives **B-2**

Project
  Cut Edges **5-8**
  DWG Geometry **5-11**
  Geometry **2-9**, **5-2**, **5-8**
Project Files **1-10**, **24-2**
Projected View **25-7**
Promote **21-7**
Properties **10-5**

Q

Quick Access Toolbar **1-15**

R

Raster Views **25-8**
Rectangle **2-10**, **3-3**
Redefine **2-25**, **15-10**
Refit **1-25**
Relationships **15-8**
Relax Mode **3-22**
Rename **2-23**
Reorder Features **10-2**
Replace
  Components **21-2**
  Drawing Models **25-25**
Resolve Link **24-9**
Restructure **21-6**
Retrieve Model Dimensions **26-3**
Revision Table **27-18**
Revision Tags **27-20**
Revolve **2-11**, **2-18**, **5-2**
Rib **9-19**
Ribbon **1-13**
Rigid Joint **17-8**
Rotate **1-23**
  Components **18-3**
  Entities **4-2**
Rotational Joint **17-8**

S

Scale
  Drawing View **25-24**
  Entities **4-2**
Section Views **10-6**, **18-8**, **25-11**
  End Section **10-6**
  Half **10-6**
  Quarter **10-6**
  Three Quarter **10-6**
Selection
  Hidden Features **1-31**
  Options **18-14**
  Sketched Entities **1-28**
Share Sketch **5-9**
Sheets **26-14**
  Editing **25-26**
Shell **9-15**
Show All Constraints **3-12**
Show Dimensions **2-23**
Show Input **2-25**
Similar **13-3**
Sketch
  Constraints *(see Constraints)*
  Creation **2-9**
  Dimensions *(see Dimensions)*
  Edit **2-24**
  Entities
    Arc **3-3**
    Bridge Curve **3-3**
    Chamfers **3-6**
    Circle **2-10**, **3-3**
    Construction **3-8**
    Copy **4-2**
    Copy and Paste **4-5**
    Degrees of Freedom **3-12**
    Ellipse **3-3**
    Equation Curve **3-2**
    Extend **3-10**
    Fillets **3-6**
    Line **2-10**, **3-5**
    Line Close **2-10**
    Mirror **3-11**
    Move **4-2**
    Offset **5-7**
    Over Dimensioned **3-27**
    Polygon **3-4**
    Rectangle **2-10**, **3-3**
    Relax Mode **3-22**
    Rotate **4-2**
    Scale **4-2**
    Slot **2-11**, **3-4**
    Spline **3-2**
    Split **4-5**
    Stretch **4-2**
    Tangent Arc **3-5**
    Tangent Line **3-5**
    Trim **3-10**
  Grid and Axis **2-9**
  Patterns **4-6**, **4-8**
  Point Snaps **3-8**
  Preferences **4-10**, **4-11**
  Revolved Sections **2-11**
  Share Sketch **5-9**
  Show Sketch Plane **2-25**
  Visibility **2-24**
Sketch Doctor **11-4**
Sketch Plane **2-7**
Slice Graphics **5-2**
Slice Views **25-19**
Slider Joint **17-9**
Slot **2-11**, **3-4**
Sphere **B-2**
Spline **3-2**
Split
  Entities **4-5**

Status Bar **1-17**
Storyboards **20-5**
Stretch Entities **4-2**
Style and Standard Editor **26-25**
Suppress
  Constraints **18-5**
  Views **25-22**
Suppress Features **10-4**
Sweep **2-18, 12-2**
Symbols **27-6**

T

Table
  Revision Table **27-18**
Tabs **1-13**
Tags **27-20**
Taper **5-6**
Templates **2-2, 16-2, 25-2**
Text **27-2**
Threads **6-34**
Torus **B-2**
Transparency **25-23**
Transparent Components **18-8**
Trim **3-10**

U

Units **8-7, 28-7, 28-14**
Update Assembly **18-4**

V

ViewCube **1-25, 25-5**
Views
  Alignment **25-23**
  Auxiliary **25-10**
  Balloons **26-22**
  Base **25-4**
  Break **25-17**
  Break Out **25-18**
  Crop **25-20**
  Delete **25-22**
  Design Views **10-8, 18-10**
  Detailed **25-13**
  Draft **25-16**
  Labels **25-24**
  Move **25-23**
  Orientation **25-6, 25-23**
  Overlay **25-14**
  Projected **25-7**
  Properties **25-26**
  Raster Views **25-8**
  Replace Models **25-25**
  Scale **25-24**
  Section **25-11**
  Sheets **25-26, 26-14**
  Slice **25-19**
  Suppress **25-22**
  Transparent Components **25-23**
Virtual Component **22-3, 23-2**
Visibility **2-24**
  Components **18-6**
  Sketch **2-24**
Visual Style **1-27**

W

Work Features
  Axis **7-7**
  Planes **7-2**
  Points **7-10**

Z

Zoom **1-24**

Made in United States
Orlando, FL
05 November 2026

90295298R10304